GUIDE FOR THE CLASSIFICATION FOR OVERSEAS TR

General Information:

The Combined Nomenclature (CN) which classifies goods at 8-digit le
integrated classification for both Duty purposes and for import and expo
1988. Because of the introduction of a new system of intra-EC trade statistics (INTRASTAT),
January 1993, the Intrastat Classification Nomenclature (ICN) has been compiled. It also provides
details of 8-digit classifications and is issued to all businesses required to submit supplementary
declarations.

For extra-EC trade the Integrated Tariff of the United Kingdom must be used for the purpose of
completing the Single Administrative Document (the SAD) for both imported and exported goods. It
contains information concerning the entry of imported or exported goods, including their descriptions
and appropriate 8-digit code numbers, the units of quantity to be shown and the SAD.

Copies of the Tariff may be obtained from The Stationery Office Bookshop at 49 High Holborn, London
WC1V 6HB; 71-73 Lothian Road, Edinburgh EH3 9AZ; 9-21 Princess Street, Manchester M60 8AS;
Southey House, Wine Street, Bristol BS1 2BQ; 258 Broad Street, Birmingham, B1 2HE; 80 Chichester
Street, Belfast BT1 4JY; or through booksellers. Copies of the ICN can be obtained by telephoning
0272 408118 (24 hour recorded message) or completing the order form at the end of the Customs &
Excise Public Notice 60 which is a general guide to INTRASTAT and is available, free of charge, from
all VAT offices.

About the Guide:

This Guide is intended primarily for users of the statistics of overseas trade. It sets out the descriptions
at 8-digit level of the code numbers under which goods are classified. The classification of these
statistics follows the United Nation's Standard International Trade Classification (Revision 3) (SITC
(R3)) which was also introduced for use on 1 January 1988. The SITC (R3) provides headings
corresponding directly to those of the Harmonised System, which forms the basis of the CN referred to
above; however, the order in which articles are grouped differs between the two classifications.

A list of recognised designations of countries follows these notes.

Trade under certain headings is not included in the statistics; bank notes after issue into circulation,
being legal tender in any country (490700 30), issued stock, share and bond certificates and similar
documents of title (490700 91), revenue stamps imported for affixation to tobacco or spirited goods and
subsequent re-exportation thereof (970400 00) and printed advertising material which is not the subject
of a commercial transaction (490900 10, 490900 90, 491110 90).

Since publication of the 1988 Guide, commodity codes relating to defence equipment have been
transferred from Section 8 to Section 9.

With the introduction of new classifications - the CN and SITC (R3) - there was a discontinuity in the
comparison of trade statistics between 1987 and 1988. To help users over this problem, a companion
volume, The Guide to the Classification of Overseas Trade Statistics - Correlation Tables, was
produced for the 1988 Guide. This gives correlations between the SITC (R2) and SITC (R3). However,
to assist users, the correlation between the harmonised system (first 6 digits of the combined
nomenclature) and the SITC (R3) is included before the index at the back of this publication. Copies of
the Correlation Tables are separately available from The Stationery Office.

Publication of Statistics:

Summarised statistics of overseas trade are published monthly and annually for extra-EC trade and
quarterly and annually for intra-EC trade in the relevant "Overseas Trade Statistics of the United
Kingdom" volumes. These publications employ abbreviations and, in certain tables, 8-digit code
numbers in place of the full commodity descriptions.

With a few exceptions further detail in respect of the individual descriptions in this Guide and monthly
data at 8-digit level may be obtained from any of the marketing agents appointed by HM Customs and
Excise Tariff and Statistical Office. Details of the marketing agents are given overleaf.

CLASSIFICATION OF PRODUCTS

The nature of some of the changes to the Combined Nomenclature (CN) in 1996 (primarily arising from the need to accomodate changes to the Harmonised System to be introduced in 1996) has led to the loss of some of the information needed to allow a complete correlation to be made between the Combined Nomenclature and the Standard International Trade Classification (SITC) Revision 3. This affects, in particular,the allocationof CN codes for chapter 72 -Iron and Steel. As such, users of the trade data are advised to check the detailed CN coverage of the particular SITC headings they are using, as some discontinuities may be introduced to SITC based series due to this problem.

MARKETING AGENTS APPOINTED BY HM CUSTOMS AND EXCISE STATISTICAL OFFICE

For :

(a)   Monthly Trade Statistics at
        Tariff/Trade or Commodity Code Number or
        Standard International Trade Classification levels.

(b)   Identity of Importers by Commodity.

	Name and Address	Telephone	Fax
*	Abacus Data Services (UK) Ltd Challenge House 616 Mitcham Road CROYDON Surrey CR9 3AU	0181-683 6444	0181-683 6445
+	Business and Trade Statistics Ltd Lancaster House More Lane ESHER Surrey KT10 8AP	01372 463121	01372 469847
*	Knight-Ridder Information Ltd Haymarket House 1 Oxendon Street LONDON SW1Y 4EE	0171-930 7646	0171-930 2581
	Forvus Forvus House 53 Clapham Common South Side London SW4 9BX	0171-498 2602	0171-498 1939
+	MDS Transmodal (Overseas Trade Data) 5/6 Hunters Walk Canal Street CHESTER CH1 4EB	01244 348391/2	01244 348471

---

*   Trade Statistics from 1987
+   Trade Statistics from 1979

Code **EUROPEAN COMMUNITY (EC)**

AT	Austria (excluding Jungholz and Mittelberg)
BE	Belgium and Luxembourg
DK	Denmark (excluding Faroe Islands)
FI	Finland (including Aland Islands)
FR	France (including Monaco but excluding French Overseas
DE	Germany (including the former German Democratic Republic, Jungholz, Mittelberg and Heligoland but excluding Büsingen)
GR	Greece (including Mount Athos)
GS	Guernsey**
IE	Irish Republic
IT	Italy (excluding Livigno, Campione d'Italia, San Marino, the Italian Waters of Lake Lugano and the Vatican)
JS	Jersey**
GB	Man, Isle of (excluding ACP 80 transhipments to IoM Freeport only)
IM	Man, Isle of (ACP 80 transhipments to IoM Freeport only)
NL	Netherlands
PT	Portugal (including Azores and Madeira)
ES	Spain (including Balearic Islands: excluding Canary Islands, Ceuta and Melilla)
SE	Sweden
GB	United Kingdom (Great Britain, Northern Ireland and Isle of Man - excluding ACP 80 transhipments to IoM Freeport)

Code **WESTERN EUROPE EXCLUDING EC (W EUROPE EX EC)**

AD	Andorra
	Continental Shelf (NW European) -
FO	Faroe Islands
GI	Gibraltar
IS	Iceland
LI	Liechtenstein
MT	Malta (including Gozo and Comino)
NO	Norway (including Jan Mayen Island)
SM	San Marino
SJ	Svalbard Archipelago
CH	Switzerland (including Büsingen and Campione)
TR	Turkey
VA	Vatican City

Code **EASTERN EUROPE**

AL	Albania
AM	Armenia
AZ	Azerbaijan
BY	Belarus
BA	Bosnia & Herzegovina
BG	Bulgaria
HR	Croatia
CZ	Czech Republic
EE	Estonia
HU	Hungary
KZ	Kazakhstan
KG	Kyrgyzstan

Code **EASTERN EUROPE**-cont

LV	Latvia
LT	Lithuania
MK	Macedonia (Former Yugoslav Republic of)
MD	Moldova*
PL	Poland
RO	Romania
RU	Russia*
SX	Serbia & Montenegro
SK	Slovakia
SI	Slovenia
TJ	Tajikistan
TM	Turkmenistan
UA	Ukraine
UZ	Uzbekistan

Code **NORTH AMERICA (NORTH AMERICA)**

CA	Canada
GL	Greenland
MX	Mexico

PR	Puerto Rico
PM	St Pierre and Miquelon
US	United States of America

Code **LATIN AMERICA AND THE CARIBBEAN (OTHER AMERICA)**

AI	Anguilla
AG	Antigua and Barbuda
AR	Argentina
AA	Aruba
BS	Bahamas
BB	Barbados
BZ	Belize ,
BM	Bermuda
BO	Bolivia
BR	Brazil
VG	British Virgin Islands
KY	Cayman Islands
CL	Chile
CO	Colombia
CR	Costa Rica
CU	Cuba
QQ	Curacao (including Bonaire, Saba, St Eustatius and St Maarten (south)
DM	Dominica
DO	Dominican Republic
EC	Ecuador (including Galapagos Islands)
SV	El Salvador
FK	Falkland Islands
GF	French Guiana
GD	Grenada
GP	Guadeloupe (including St Barthelemy, St Martin (North), Iles des Saintes, Desirade and Marie-Galante)
GT	Guatemala
GY	Guyana
HT	Haiti
HN	Honduras
JM	Jamaica
MQ	Martinique
MS	Montserrat
NI	Nicaragua
PA	Panama (including the former Canal Zone)
PY	Paraguay
PG	Papua New Guinea
PH	Philippines
PE	Peru
KN	St Christopher and Nevis, Federation of (St Christopher may also be referred to as St Kitts)
LC	St Lucia
VC	St Vincent
SR	Surinam
TT	Trinidad and Tobago
TC	Turks and Caicos Islands
UY	Uruguay
VE	Venezuela
VI	Virgin Islands of the United States

Code **MIDDLE EAST AND NORTH AFRICA (ME & N AFRICA)**

DH	Abu Dhabi
DZ	Algeria
BH	Bahrain
IC	Canary Islands
XI	Ceuta & Melilla*
CY	Cyprus
DU	Dubai
EG	Egypt
GJ	Gaza and Jericho
IR	Iran
IQ	Iraq
IL	Israel
JO	Jordan
KW	Kuwait
LB	Lebanon
LY	Libya
MA	Morocco
OM	Oman
QA	Qatar
SA	Saudi Arabia

HA	Sharjah, Ras al Khaimah, Ajman, Umm al Qaiwain, Fujairah
SD	Sudan
SY	Syria
TN	Tunisia
YE	Yemen

Code **SUB-SAHARAN AFRICA**

AO	Angola (including Cabinda)
BJ	Benin
BW	Botswana
IO	British Indian Ocean Territory
BK	Burkina
BI	Burundi
CM	Cameroon
CV	Cape Verde
CF	Central African Republic
TD	Chad
KM	Comoros (Great Comoro, Anjouan and Moheli)
CG	Congo
DJ	Djibouti
GQ	Equatorial Guinea†
ER	Eritrea
ET	Ethiopia
GA	Gabon
GM	Gambia
GH	Ghana
GN	Guinea

Code **SUB-SAHARAN AFRICA**-*cont*

GW	Guinea-Bissau
CI	Ivory Coast
KE	Kenya
LS	Lesotho
LR	Liberia
MG	Madagascar (Malagasy Republic)
MW	Malawi
ML	Mali
MR	Mauritania
MU	Mauritius
ME	Mayotte (Grande Terre and Pamanzi)
MZ	Mozambique
NA	Namibia
NE	Niger
NG	Nigeria
RE	Reunion
RW	Rwanda
ST	Sao Tome and Principe
SN	Senegal
SC	Seychelles
SL	Sierra Leone
SO	Somalia
ZA	South Africa
SH	St Helena (including Ascension, Gough and Tristan da Cunha Islands)
SZ	Swaziland (Ngwame)
TZ	Tanzania (Tanganyika, Zanzibar, Pemba)
TG	Togo
UG	Uganda
ZR	Zaire
ZM	Zambia
ZW	Zimbabwe

Code **OTHER ASIA AND OCEANIA (ASIA & OCEANIA)**

AF	Afghanistan
AU	Australia
XE	Australian Oceania (Cocos (Keeling) Islands, Christmas Island □, Heard and McDonald Islands, Norfolk Island)
BD	Bangladesh
BT	Bhutan
BN	Brunei
BU	Burma
KH	Cambodia (formerly Kampuchea)
CN	China
CK	Cook Islands
FJ	Fiji
PF	French Polynesia
HK	Hong Kong
IN	India

ID	Indonesia
JP	Japan
KI	Kiribati
KR	Korea, South
KP	Korea, North
LA	Laos
MO	Macao
MY	Malaysia (Peninsular Malaysia, Labuan, Sabah, Sarawak)
MV	Maldives
MH	Marshall Islands
FM	Micronesia, Federated States of (including Chuuk, Kosrae, Pohnpei and Yap)
MN	Mongolia
NR	Nauru
NP	Nepal
NC	New Caledonia and Dependencies
NZ	New Zealand
NU	Niue and Tokelau Islands
MP	Northern Mariana Islands
PK	Pakistan
PW	Palau
PN	**Pitcairn**
	Antartic and Adjacent Regions-
XA	Australian Antarctic Territory
BQ	British Antarctic Territory
XF	French Antarctic Territory
FQ	French Southern Territory
XR	New Zealand Antarctic Territory (Ross Dependency)
AC	Polar Regions, including; South Georgia and South Sandwich Islands
SG	Singapore
SB	Solomon Islands
LK	Sri Lanka
TW	Taiwan
TH	Thailand
TO	Tonga
TV	Tuvalu
PU	United States Oceania - American Samoa, Guam, Palau, Puerto Rico, Baker Island, Howland Island, Jarvis Island, Johnston Atoll, Kingman Reef, Midway Islands, Navassa Island, Palmyra Atoll, Wake Island
VU	Vanuatu
VN	Vietnam
WF	Wallis and Futuna Islands
WS	Western Samoa

Code **EEA (Previously EFTA) (EEA/EFTA)**

IS	Iceland
LI	Liechtenstein
NO	Norway
SJ	Svalbard Archipelago
CH	Switzerland (former EFTA member)

Code **OECD (OECD)**

AU	Australia
AT	Austria
BE	Belgium and Luxembourg
CA	Canada
IC	Canary Islands
XI	Ceuta and Melilla*
DK	Denmark
FO	Faroe Islands
DE	Germany
FI	Finland
FR	France
GR	Greece
GL	Greenland
IS	Iceland
IE	Irish Republic
IT	Italy
JP	Japan
NL	Netherlands
NZ	New Zealand
NO	Norway
PT	Portugal
ES	Spain
SE	Sweden
CH	Switzerland
TR	Turkey

US   United States of America

Code   THE OIL EXPORTING COUNTRIES (OIL EXPORTERS)

DH   Abu Dhabi
DZ   Algeria
BH   Bahrain
BN   Brunei
DU   Dubai
EC   Ecuador
GA   Gabon
ID   Indonesia
IR   Iran
IQ   Iraq
KW   Kuwait
LY   Libya
NG   Nigeria
OM   Oman
QA   Qatar
SA   Saudi Arabia
HA   Sharjah; etc
TT   Trinidad and Tobago
VE   Venezuela

Code   NEWLY INDUSTRIAL ASIA (NEWLY INDUST ASIA)

HK   Hong Kong
KR   Korea, South
MY   Malaysia
SG   Singapore
TW   Taiwan
TH   Thailand

Code   THE COMMONWEALTH (COMMONWEALTH)

AI   Anguilla
AG   Antigua and Barbuda
AU   Australia
XE   Australian Oceania
BS   Bahamas
BD   Bangladesh
BB   Barbados
BZ   Belize
BM   Bermuda
BW   Botswana
IO   British Indian Ocean Territory
VG   British Virgin islands
BN   Brunei
CA   Canada
KY   Cayman Islands
CK   Cook Islands
CY   Cyprus
DM   Dominica
FK   Falkland Islands
FJ   Fiji
GM   Gambia
GH   Ghana
GI   Gibraltar
GD   Grenada
GY   Guyana
HK   Hong Kong
IN   India
JM   Jamaica
KE   Kenya
KI   Kiribati
LS   Lesotho
MW   Malawi
MY   Malaysia
MV   Maldives
MT   Malta

Code   THE COMMONWEALTH (COMMONWEALTH)-*cont*

MU   Mauritius
MS   Montserrat
NR   Nauru
NZ   New Zealand
NG   Nigeria
NU   Niue and Tokelau Islands

PG   Papua New Guinea
PK   Pakistan
PN   Pitcairn
SC   Seychelles
SL   Sierra Leone
SG   Singapore
SB   Solomon Islands
LK   Sri Lanka
KN   St Christopher and Nevis
SH   St Helana
LC   St Lucia
VC   St Vincent
SZ   Swaziland
TZ   Tanzania
TO   Tonga
TT   Trinidad and Tobago
TC   Turks and Caicos Islands
TV   Tuvalu
UG   Uganda
WS   Western Samoa
ZM   Zambia
ZW   Zimbabwe

* Including Penon de Velez de la Gomera, Penon de Alhucemas and Chafarinus Islands

† Equatorial Guinea comprises Río Muni and the islands of Bioco (formerly Fernando Po), Annobón, Mandyi (formerly Corisco), Elobey Grande, Elobey Chico, and associated islets

**The codes indicated are to be used for trade between mainland Great Britain and the Channel Islands only

☐ Christmas Island (Indian Ocean)

CLASSIFICATION BY DIVISIONS OF THE ARTICLES CONTAINED IN THE GUIDE TO THE CLASSIFICATION FOR OVERSEAS TRADE STATISTICS - 1996

00.- Live animals other than animals of division 03
01.- Meat and meat preparations
02.- Dairy products and birds' eggs
03.- Fish (not marine mammals), crustaceans, molluscs and aquatic invertebrates and preparations thereof
04.- Cereals and cereal preparations
05.- Vegetables and fruit
06.- Sugars, sugar preparations and honey
07.- Coffee, tea, cocoa, spices and manufactures thereof
08.- Feeding stuff for animals (not including unmilled cereals)
09.- Miscellaneous edible products and preparations
11.- Beverages
12.- Tobacco and tobacco manufactures
21.- Hides, skins and furskins, raw
22.- Oil seeds and oleaginous fruits
23.- Crude rubber (including synthetic and reclaimed)
24.- Cork and wood
25.- Pulp and waste paper
26.- Textile fibres (other than wool tops) and their wastes (not manufactured into yarn or fabric)
27.- Crude fertilizers, other than those of division 56, and crude minerals (excluding coal, petroleum and precious stones)
28.- Metalliferous ores and metal scrap
29.- Crude animal and vegetable materials nes
32.- Coal, coke and briquettes
33.- Petroleum, petroleum products and related materials
34.- Gas, natural and manufactured
35.- Electric current
41.- Animal oils and fats
42.- Fixed vegetable fats and oils, crude refined or fractionated
43.- Animal and vegetable fats and oils, processed; waxes of animal or vegtable origin; inedible mixtures or preparations of animal
     or vegetable fats oils nes
51.- Organic chemicals
52.- Inorganic chemicals
53.- Dyeing, tanning and colouring materials
54.- Medical and pharmaceutical products
55.- Essential oils and resinoids and perfume materials; toilet, polishing and cleansing preparations
56.- Fertilizers (other than those of group 272)
57.- Plastics in primary forms
58.- Plastics in non-primary forms
59.- Chemical materials and products nes
61.- Leather, leather manufactures nes and dressed furskins
62.- Rubber manufactures nes
63.- Cork and wood manufactures (excluding furniture)
64.- Paper, paperboard and articles of paper pulp, of paper or of paperboard
65.- Textile yarn, fabrics, made-up articles nes and related products
66.- Non-metallic mineral manufactures nes
67.- Iron and steel
68.- Non-ferrous metals
69.- Manufactures of metal nes
71.- Power generating machinery and equipment
72.- Machinery specialised for particular industries
73.- Metal working machinery
74.- General industrial machinery and equipment nes and machine parts nes
75.- Office machines and automatic data processing machines
76.- Telecommunications and sound recording and reproducing apparatus and equipment
77.- Electrical machinery, apparatus and appliances nes and electrical parts thereof (including non-electrical counterparts nes of electrical household
     type equipment)
78.-Road vehicles (including air-cushion vehicles)
79.- Other transport equipment
81.- Prefabricated buildings; sanitary plumbing, heating and lighting fixtures and fittings nes
82.- Furniture and parts thereof; bedding, mattresses, mattress supports, cushions and similar stuffed furnishings
83.- Travel goods, handbags and similar containers
84.- Articles of apparel and clothing accessories
85.- Footwear
87.- Professional, scientific and controlling instruments and apparatus nes
88.- Photographic apparatus and equipment and supplies and optical goods nes; watches and clocks
89.- Miscellaneous manufactured articles nes
91.- Postal packages not classified according to kind
93.- Special transactions and commodities not classified according to kind
96.- Coin (other than gold coin) not being legal tender
97.- Gold, non-monetary (excluding gold, ores and concentrates)
98.- Defence equipment
I .- Gold, monetary
II .- Gold coin and current coin

S.I.T.C. (R3)	Commodity Code No	Trade description

SECTION: 0

DIVISION 00 — LIVE ANIMALS OTHER THAN ANIMALS OF DIVISION 03

Bovine animals, live

001.11   **Pure bred breeding animals**
- 010210 10 0   Heifers (female bovines that have never calved)
- 010210 30 0   Cows
- 010210 90 0   Other

001.19   **Other than pure bred breeding animals**
- Domestic species
- 010290 05 0   Of a weight not exceeding 80
- Of a weight exceeding 80 kg but not exceeding 160 kg
- 010290 21 0   For slaughter
- 010290 29 0   Other
- Of a weight exceeding 160 kg but not exceeding 300 kg
- 010290 41 0   For slaughter
- 010290 49 0   Other
- Of a weight exceeding 300 kg
- Heifers (female bovines that have never calved)
- 010290 51 0   For slaughter
- 010290 59 0   Other
- Cows :
- 010290 61 0   For slaughter
- 010290 69 0   Other
- Other :
- 010290 71 0   For slaughter
- 010290 79 0   Other
- 010290 90 0   Other

001.21   **Sheep, live**
- 010410 10 0   Pure-bred breeding animals
- Other
- 010410 30 0   Lambs (up to a year old)
- 010410 80 0   Other

001.22   **Goats, live**
- 010420 10 0   Pure-bred breeding animals
- 010420 90 0   Other

Swine, live

001.31   010310 00 0   **Pure bred breeding animals**

001.39   **Other than pure bred breeding animals**
- Weighing less than 50 kg
- 010391 10 0   Domestic species
- 010391 90 0   Other
- Weighing 50 kg or more
- Domestic species
- 010392 11 0   Sows having farrowed at least once, of a weight of not less than 160 kg
- 010392 19 0   Other
- 010392 90 0   Other

Poultry, live (i.e., fowls of the species gallus domesticus, ducks, geese, turkeys and guinea fowls)

001.41   **Weighing not more than 185 g**
- Fowls of the species *Gallus domesticus*
- Grandparent and parent female chick
- 010511 11 0   Laying stocks
- 010511 19 0   Other
- Other
- 010511 91 0   Laying stocks
- 010511 99 0   Other
- *010512 00 0   Turkeys
- Other
- *010519 20 0   Geese
- 010519 90 0   Ducks and guinea fowl

S.I.T.C. (R3)	Commodity Code No	Trade description
001.49		**Weighing more than 185 g**
	*010592 00 0	Fowls of the species *Gallus domesticus* weighing not more than 2000 g
	*010593 00 0	Fowls of the species *Gallus domesticus* weighing more than 2000 g
		Other
	010599 10 0	Ducks
	010599 20 0	Geese
	010599 30 0	Turkeys
	010599 50 0	Guinea fowls
		Horses, asses, mules and hinnies, live
001.51		**Horses**
	010111 00 0	Pure-bred breeding animals
		Other
	010119 10 0	For slaughter
	010119 90 0	Other
001.52		**Asses, mules and hinnies**
	010120 10 0	Asses
	010120 90 0	Mules and hinnies
001.90		**Live animals, n.e.s.**
	010600 10 0	Domestic rabbits
	010600 20 0	Pigeons
	010600 90 0	Other

DIVISION 01

MEAT AND MEAT PREPARATIONS

MEAT OF BOVINE ANIMALS, FRESH, CHILLED OR FROZEN

Meat of bovine animals, fresh or chilled

S.I.T.C. (R3)	Commodity Code No	Trade description
011.11		**....with bone in**
	020110 00 0	Carcasses and half-carcasses
		Other cuts with bone in
	020120 20 0	"Compensated" quarters
	020120 30 0	Unseparated or separated forequarters
	020120 50 0	Unseparated or separated hindquarters
	020120 90 0	Other
011.12	020130 00 0	**....boneless**

Meat of bovine animals, frozen

S.I.T.C. (R3)	Commodity Code No	Trade description
011.21		**....with bone in**
	020210 00 0	Carcasses and half-carcasses
		Other cuts with bone in
	020220 10 0	"Compensated" quarters
	020220 30 0	Unseparated or separated forequarters
	020220 50 0	Unseparated or separated hindquarters
	020220 90 0	Other
011.22		**....boneless**
	020230 10 0	Forequarters, whole or cut into a maximum of five pieces, each quarter being in a single block; "compensated" quarters in two blocks, one of which contains the forequarter, whole or cut into a maximum of five pieces, and the other, the hindquarter, excluding the tenderloin, in one piece
	020230 50 0	Crop, chuck and blade and brisket cuts
	*020230 90 0	Other

OTHER MEAT AND EDIBLE MEAT OFFAL, FRESH, CHILLED OR FROZEN (EXCEPT MEAT AND MEAT OFFAL UNFIT OR UNSUITABLE FOR HUMAN CONSUMPTION)

Meat of sheep or goats, fresh, chilled or frozen

S.I.T.C. (R3)	Commodity Code No	Trade description
012.11		**Meat of sheep, fresh or chilled**
	020410 00 0	Carcasses and half-carcasses of lamb, fresh or chilled
		Other meat of sheep, fresh or chilled
	020421 00 0	Carcasses and half-carcasses
		Other cuts with bone in
	020422 10 0	Short forequarters
	020422 30 0	Chines and/or best ends
	020422 50 0	Legs
	020422 90 0	Other
	020423 00 0	Boneless

S.I.T.C. (R3)	Commodity Code No	Trade description
012.12		**Meat of sheep, frozen**
	020430 00 0	Carcasses and half-carcasses of lamb, frozen
		Other meat of sheep, frozen
	020441 00 0	Carcasses and half-carcasses
		Other cuts with bone in
	020442 10 0	Short forequarters
	020442 30 0	Chines and/or best ends
	020442 50 0	Legs
	020442 90 0	Other
		Boneless
	020443 10 0	Of Lamb
	020443 90 0	Other
012.13		**Meat of goats, fresh, chilled or frozen**
		Fresh or chilled
	020450 11 0	Carcasses and half-carcasses
	020450 13 0	Short forequarters
	020450 15 0	Chines and/or best ends
	020450 19 0	Legs
		Other
	020450 31 0	Cuts with bone in
	020450 39 0	Boneless cuts
		Frozen
	020450 51 0	Carcasses and half-carcasses
	020450 53 0	Short forequarters
	020450 55 0	Chines and/or best ends
	020450 59 0	Legs
		Other
	020450 71 0	Cuts with bone in
	020450 79 0	Boneless cuts
		Meat of swine, fresh, chilled or frozen
012.21		**Meat of swine, fresh or chilled**
		Carcasses and half-carcasses
	020311 10 0	Of domestic swine
	020311 90 0	Other
		Hams, shoulders and cuts thereof, with bone in
		Of domestic swine
	020312 11 0	Hams and cuts thereof
	020312 19 0	Shoulders and cuts thereof
	020312 90 0	Other
		Other
		Of domestic swine
	020319 11 0	Fore-ends and cuts thereof
	020319 13 0	Loins and cuts thereof, with bone in
	020319 15 0	Bellies (streaky) and cuts thereof
		Other
	020319 55 0	Boneless
	020319 59 0	Other
	020319 90 0	Other
012.22		**Meat of swine, frozen**
		Carcasses and half-carcasses
	020321 10 0	Of domestic swine
	020321 90 0	Other
		Hams, shoulders and cuts thereof, with bone in
		Of domestic swine
	020322 11 0	Hams and cuts thereof
	020322 19 0	Shoulders and cuts thereof
	020322 90 0	Other
		Other
		Of domestic swine
	020329 11 0	Fore-ends and cuts thereof
	020329 13 0	Loins and cuts thereof, with bone in
	020329 15 0	Bellies (streaky) and cuts thereof
		Other
	020329 55 0	Boneless
	020329 59 0	Other
	020329 90 0	Other
		Meat and edible offal of the poultry of heading 001.4, fresh, chilled or frozen
012.31		**Of fowls of the species *Gallus domesticus***
		Not cut in pieces, fresh or chilled
	*020711 10 0	Plucked and gutted, with heads and feet, known as "83 % chickens"
	*020711 30 0	Plucked and drawn, without heads and feet but with necks, hearts, livers and gizzards, known as "70 % chickens"

S.I.T.C. (R3)	Commodity Code No	Trade description
cont 012.31	*020711 90 0	Plucked and drawn, without heads and feet and without necks, hearts, livers and gizzards, known as "65% chickens", or otherwise presented
		Turkeys
		Not cut in pieces, fresh or chilled
	*020724 10 0	Plucked and drawn, without heads and feet but with necks, hearts, livers and gizzards, known as "80 % turkeys"
	*020724 90 0	Plucked and drawn, without heads and feet and without necks, hearts, livers and gizzards, known as "73 % turkeys", or otherwise presented
		Of ducks, geese or guinea fowls:
		Not cut in pieces, fresh or chilled:
		Of ducks
	*020732 11 0	Plucked, bled, gutted or not drawn, with heads and feet, known as "85 % ducks"
	*020732 15 0	Plucked and drawn, without heads and feet but with necks, hearts, livers and gizzards, known as "70 % ducks"
	*020732 19 0	Plucked and drawn, without heads and feet and without necks, hearts, livers and gizzards, known as "63 % ducks", or otherwise presented
		Of geese
	*020732 51 0	Plucked, bled, not drawn, with heads and feet, known as "82 % geese"
	*020732 59 0	Plucked and drawn, without heads and feet, with or without hearts and gizzards, known as "75 % geese", or otherwise presented
	*020732 90 0	Of guinea fowls
012.32		Of fowls of the species *Gallus domesticus*
		Not cut in pieces, frozen
	*020712 10 0	Plucked and drawn, without heads and feet but with necks, hearts, livers and gizzards, known as "70 % chickens"
	*020712 90 0	Plucked and drawn, without heads and feet and without necks, hearts, livers and gizzards, known as "65 % chickens", or otherwise presented
		Of turkeys
		Not cut in pieces, frozen
	*020725 10 0	Plucked and drawn, without heads and feet but with necks, hearts, livers and gizzards, known as "80 % turkeys"
	*020725 90 0	Plucked and drawn, without heads and feet and without necks, hearts, livers and gizzards, known as "73 % turkeys", or otherwise presented
		Of ducks, geese and guinea fowls
		Not cut in pieces, frozen
		Of ducks
	*020733 11 0	Plucked and drawn, without heads and feet but with necks, hearts, livers and gizzards, known as "70 % ducks"
	*020733 19 0	Plucked and drawn, without heads and feet and without necks, hearts, livers and gizzards, known as "63 % ducks", or otherwise presented
		Of geese
	*020733 51 0	Plucked, bled, not drawn, with heads and feet, known as "82 % geese"
	*020733 59 0	Plucked and drawn, without heads and feet, with or without hearts and gizzards, known as "75 % geese",or otherwise presented
	*020733 90 0	Of guinea fowls
012.33		Fatty livers of geese or ducks, fresh or chilled
	*020734 10 0	Of geese
	*020734 90 0	Of ducks
012.34		Of fowls of the species *Gallus domesticus*
		Cuts and other offal, fresh or chilled
		Cuts
	*020713 10 0	Boneless
		With bone in
	*020713 20 0	Halves or quarters
	*020713 30 0	Whole wings, with or without tips
	*020713 40 0	Backs, necks, backs with necks attached, rumps and wing tips
	*020713 50 0	Breasts and cuts thereof
	*020713 60 0	Legs and cuts thereof
	*020713 70 0	Other
	*020713 99 0	Offal, other than livers
		Of turkeys
		Cuts and other offal, fresh or chilled
		Cuts
	*020726 10 0	Boneless
		With bone in
	*020726 20 0	Halves or quarters
	*020726 30 0	Whole wings, with or without tips
	*020726 40 0	Backs, necks, backs with necks attached, rumps and wing tips
	*020726 50 0	Breasts and cuts thereof
		Legs and cuts thereof
	*020726 60 0	Drumsticks and cuts of drumsticks
	*020726 70 0	Other
	*020726 80 0	Other
	*020726 99 0	Offal, other than livers

S.I.T.C. (R3)	Commodity Code No	Trade description
cont 012.34		Of ducks, geese and guinea fowls
		Fresh or chilled:
		Cuts
		Boneless
	*020735 11 0	Of geese
	*020735 15 0	Of ducks and guinea fowls
		With bone in
		Halves or quarters
	*020735 21 0	Of ducks
	*020735 23 0	Of geese
	*020735 25 0	Of guinea fowls
	*020735 31 0	Whole wings, with or without tips
	*020735 41 0	Backs, necks, backs with necks attached, rumps and wing tips
		Breasts and cuts thereof
	*020735 51 0	Of geese
	*020735 53 0	Of ducks and guinea fowls
		Legs and cuts thereof
	*020735 61 0	Of geese
	*020735 63 0	Of ducks and guinea fowls
	*020735 71 0	Goose or duck paletots
	*020735 79 0	Other
	*020735 99 0	Offal, other than livers
		Poultry livers, other than fatty livers of geese or ducks
	*020713 91 0	Of the species *Gallus domesticus*
	*020726 91 0	Of turkeys
	*020735 91 0	Of ducks, geese or guinea fowls
012.35		Of fowls of the species *Gallus domesticus*
		Cuts and offal (other than liver), frozen
		Cuts
	*020714 10 0	Boneless
		With bone in
	*020714 20 0	Halves or quarters
	*020714 30 0	Whole wings, with or without tips
	*020714 40 0	Backs, necks, backs with necks attached, rumps and wing tips
	*020714 50 0	Breasts and cuts thereof
	*020714 60 0	Legs and cuts thereof
	*020714 70 0	Other
	*020714 99 0	Offal, other than livers
		Of turkeys
		Cuts and offal (other than liver), frozen
		Cuts
	*020727 10 0	Boneless
		With bone in
	*020727 20 0	Halves or quarters
	*020727 30 0	Whole wings, with or without tips
	*020727 40 0	Backs, necks, backs with necks attached, rumps and wing tips
	*020727 50 0	Breasts and cuts thereof
		Legs and cuts thereof
	*020727 60 0	Drumsticks and cuts thereof
	*020727 70 0	Other
	*020727 80 0	Other
	*020727 99 0	Offal, other than livers
		Of ducks, geese or guinea fowls
		Cuts and offal (other than liver), frozen
		Cuts
		Boneless
	*020736 11 0	Of geese
	*020736 15 0	Of ducks and guinea fowls
		With bone in
		Halves or quarters
	*020736 21 0	Of ducks
	*020736 23 0	Of geese
	*020736 25 0	Of guinea fowls
	*020736 31 0	Whole wings, with or without tips
	*020736 41 0	Backs, necks, backs with necks attached, rumps and wing tips
		Breasts and cuts thereof
	*020736 51 0	Of geese
	*020736 53 0	Of ducks and guinea fowls
		Legs and cuts thereof
	*020736 61 0	Of geese
	*020736 63 0	Of ducks and guinea fowls
	*020736 71 0	Goose or duck paletots
	*020736 81 0	Other
	*020736 90 0	Offal, other than livers
012.36		Livers, frozen
	*020714 91 0	Of the species *Gallus Domesticus*

S.I.T.C. (R3)	Commodity Code No	Trade description
cont 012.36	*020727 91 0	Of turkeys
	*020736 81 0	Fatty livers of geese
	*020736 85 0	Fatty livers of ducks
	*020736 89 0	Other
012.40		Meat of horses, asses, mules or hinnies, fresh, chilled or frozen
		Of horses
	020500 11 0	Fresh or chilled
	020500 19 0	Frozen
	020500 90 0	Of asses, mules or hinnies
		Edible offal of bovine animals, swine, sheep, goats, horses, asses, mules or hinnies, fresh, chilled or frozen
012.51		... of bovine animals, fresh or chilled
	020610 10 0	For the manufacture of pharmaceutical products
		Other
	020610 91 0	Livers
	020610 95 0	Thick skirt and thin skirt
	020610 99 0	Other
012.52		... Of bovine animals, frozen
	020621 00 0	Tongues
		Livers
	020622 10 0	For the manufacture of pharmaceutical products
	020622 90 0	Other
		Other
	020629 10 0	For the manufacture of pharmaceutical products
		Other
	020629 91 0	Thick skirt and thin skirt
	020629 99 0	Other
012.53		... of swine, fresh or chilled
	020630 10 0	For the manufacture of pharmaceutical products
		Other
		Of domestic swine
	020630 21 0	Livers
	020630 31 0	Other
	020630 90 0	Other
012.54		... of swine, frozen
		Livers
	020641 10 0	For the manufacture of pharmaceutical products
		Other
	020641 91 0	Of domestic swine
	020641 99 0	Other
		Other
	020649 10 0	For the manufacture of pharmaceutical products
		Other
	020649 91 0	Of domestic swine
	020649 99 0	Other
012.55		... of sheep, goats, horses, asses, mules or hinnies, fresh or chilled
	020680 10 0	For the manufacture of pharmaceutical products
		Other
	020680 91 0	Of horses, asses, mules and hinnies
	020680 99 0	Of sheep and goats
012.56		... of sheep, goats, horses, asses, mules or hinnies, frozen
	020690 10 0	For the manufacture of pharmaceutical products
		Other
	020690 91 0	Of horses, asses, mules and hinnies
	020690 99 0	Of sheep and goats
		Meat and edible meat offal, fresh, chilled or frozen, n.e.s.
012.91		Meat and edible meat offal of rabbits or hares
		Of domestic rabbits
	020810 11 0	Fresh or chilled
	020810 19 0	Frozen
	020810 90 0	Other
012.92	020820 00 0	Frogs' legs
012.93	030760 00 0	Snails (other than sea snails)
012.99		Other meat and edible meat offal, fresh, chilled or frozen
	020890 10 0	Of domestic pigeons
		Of game, other than of rabbits or hares

S.I.T.C. (R3)	Commodity Code No	Trade description
cont 012.99	020890 20 0	Of quails
	020890 40 0	Other
	020890 50 0	Whale and seal meat
	*020890 60 0	Of reindeer
	*020890 80 0	Other

MEAT AND EDIBLE MEAT OFFAL, SALTED, IN BRINE, DRIED OR SMOKED; EDIBLE FLOURS AND MEALS OF MEAT OR MEAT OFFAL

Bacon, ham and other dried, salted or smoked meat of swine

016.11		**Hams, shoulders and cuts thereof, with bone in**
		Of domestic swine
		Salted or in brine
	021011 11 0	Hams and cuts thereof
	021011 19 0	Shoulders and cuts thereof
		Dried or smoked
	021011 31 0	Hams and cuts thereof
	021011 39 0	Shoulders and cuts thereof
	021011 90 0	Other
016.12		**Bellies (streaky) and cuts thereof**
		Of domestic swine
	021012 11 0	Salted or in brine
	021012 19 0	Dried or smoked
	021012 90 0	Other
016.19		**Other**
		Of domestic swine
		Salted or in brine
	021019 10 0	Bacon sides or spencers
	021019 20 0	Three-quarter sides or middles
	021019 30 0	Fore-ends and parts thereof
	021019 40 0	Loins and cuts thereof with bone in
		Other
	021019 51 0	Boneless
	021019 59 0	Other
		Dried or smoked
	021019 60 0	Fore-ends and parts thereof
	021019 70 0	Loins and cuts thereof
		Other
	021019 81 0	Boneless
	021019 89 0	Other
	021019 90 0	Other

Meat and edible meat offal, other than meat of swine, salted, in brine, dried or smoked; edible flours and meals of meat or meat offal

016.81		**Meat of bovine animals**
	021020 10 0	With bone in
	021020 90 0	Boneless
016.89		**Other, including edible flours and meals of meat or meat offal**
		Meat
	021090 10 0	Horsemeat, salted, in brine or dried
		Of sheep and goats
	021090 11 0	With bone in
	021090 19 0	Boneless
	*021090 21 0	Of reindeer
	*021090 29 0	Other
		Offal
		Of domestic swine
	021090 31 0	Livers
	021090 39 0	Other
		Of bovine animals
	021090 41 0	Thick skirt and thin skirt
	021090 49 0	Other
	021090 60 0	Of sheep and goats
		Other
		Poultry liver
	021090 71 0	Fatty livers of geese or ducks, salted or in brine
	021090 79 0	Other
	021090 80 0	Other
	021090 90 0	Edible flours and meals of meat or meat offal

S.I.T.C. (R3)	Commodity Code No	Trade description
		MEAT AND EDIBLE MEAT OFFAL, PREPARED OR PRESERVED, N.E.S.
017.10		**Extracts and juices of meat, fish or crustaceans, molluscs or other aquatic invertebrates**
	160300 10 0	In immediate packings of a net capacity of 1 kg or less
	160300 30 0	In immediate packings of a net capacity of more than 1 kg but less than 20 kg
	160300 90 0	Other
017.20		**Sausages and similar products, of meat, meat offal or blood; food preparations based on these products**
	160100 10 0	Of liver
		Other
	160100 91 0	Sausages, dry or for spreading, uncooked
	160100 99 0	Other
017.30		**Liver of any animal, prepared or preserved, n.e.s.**
		Goose or duck liver
	160220 11 0	Containing 75 % or more by weight of fatty livers
	160220 19 0	Other
	160220 90 0	Other
017.40		**Meat and offal (other than liver) of poultry of heading 001.4, prepared or preserved, n.e.s.**
		Of turkeys
		Containing 57 % or more by weight of meat or offal
	160231 11 0	Containing exclusively uncooked turkey meat
	160231 19 0	Other
	160231 30 0	Containing 25 % or more but less than 57 % by weight of meat or offal
	160231 90 0	Other
		Of fowls of the species Gallus domesticus
		Containing 57 % or more by weight of poultry meat or offal
	*160232 11 0	Uncooked
	*160232 19 0	Other
	*160232 30 0	Containing 25 % or more but less than 57 % by weight of poultry meat or offal
	*160232 90 0	Other
		Other
		Containing 57 % or more by weight of poultry meat or offal
	*160239 21 0	Uncooked
	*160239 29 0	Other
	*160239 40 0	Containing 25 % or more but less than 57 % by weight of poultry meat or offal
	*160239 80 0	Other
017.50		**Meat and offal (other than liver), of swine, prepared or preserved, n.e.s.**
		Hams and cuts thereof
	160241 10 0	Of domestic swine
	160241 90 0	Other
		Shoulders and cuts thereof
	160242 10 0	Of domestic swine
	160242 90 0	Other
		Other, including mixtures
		Of domestic swine
		Containing by weight 80 % or more of meat or meat offal, of any kind, including fats of any kind or origin
	160249 11 0	Loins (excluding collars) and parts thereof, including mixtures of loins or hams
	160249 13 0	Collars and parts thereof, including mixtures of collars and shoulders
	160249 15 0	Other mixtures containing hams (legs), shoulders, loins or collars, and parts thereof
	160249 19 0	Other
	160249 30 0	Containing by weight 40 % or more but less than 80 % of meat or meat offal, of any kind, including fats of any kind or origin
	160249 50 0	Containing by weight less than 40 % of meat or meat offal, of any kind, including fats of any kind or origin
	160249 90 0	Other
017.60		**Meat and offal (other than liver), of bovine animals, prepared or preserved, n.e.s.**
	160250 10 0	Uncooked; mixtures of cooked meat or offal and uncooked meat or offal
		Other
		In airtight containers
	160250 31 0	Corned beef
	160250 39 0	Other
	160250 80 0	Other
017.90		**Other prepared or preserved meat or meat offal (incl. preparations of blood of any animal)**
	160290 10 0	Preparations of blood of any animal
		Other
	160290 31 0	Of game or rabbit
	*160290 41 0	Of reindeer
		Other
	160290 51 0	Containing meat or meat offal of domestic swine
		Other
		Containing bovine meat or offal
	160290 61 0	Uncooked; mixtures of cooked meat or offal and uncooked meat or offal
	160290 69 0	Other

S.I.T.C. (R3)	Commodity Code No	Trade description
cont 017.90		Other
		Of sheep or goats
		Uncooked; mixtures of cooked meat or offal and uncooked meat or offal:
	160290 72 0	Of sheep
	160290 74 0	Of goats
		Other
	160290 76 0	Of sheep
	160290 78 0	Of goats
	*160290 98 0	Other

DIVISION 02

DAIRY PRODUCTS AND BIRDS' EGGS

MILK AND CREAM AND MILK PRODUCTS OTHER THAN BUTTER OR CHEESE

Milk (including skimmed milk) and cream, not concentrated or sweetened

S.I.T.C. (R3)	Commodity Code No	Trade description
022.11		**Milk of a fat content, by weight, not exceeding 1%**
	040110 10 0	In immediate packings of a net content not exceeding two litres
	040110 90 0	Other
022.12		**Milk and cream, of a fat content, by weight, exceeding 1% but not exceeding 6%**
		Not exceeding 3 %
	040120 11 0	In immediate packings of a net content not exceeding two litres
	040120 19 0	Other
		Exceeding 3 %
	040120 91 0	In immediate packings of a net content not exceeding two litres
	040120 99 0	Other
022.13		**Cream of a fat content, by weight, exceeding 6%**
		Not exceeding 21 %
	040130 11 0	In immediate packings of a net content not exceeding two litres
	040130 19 0	Other
		Exceeding 21 % but not exceeding 45 %
	040130 31 0	In immediate packings of a net content not exceeding two litres
	040130 39 0	Other
		Exceeding 45 %
	040130 91 0	In immediate packings of a net content not exceeding two litres
	040130 99 0	Other

Milk and cream, concentrated or sweetened

S.I.T.C. (R3)	Commodity Code No	Trade description
022.21		**Milk, in solid form, of a fat content, by weight, not exceeding 1.5%**
		Not containing added sugar or other sweetening matter
	040210 11 0	In immediate packings of a net content not exceeding 2.5 kg
	040210 19 0	Other
		Other
	040210 91 0	In immediate packings of a net content not exceeding 2.5 kg
	040210 99 0	Other
022.22		**Milk and cream, in solid form, of a fat content, by weight, exceeding 1.5%**
		Not containing added sugar or other sweetening matter
		Of a fat content, by weight, not exceeding 27 %
		In immediate packings of a net content not exceeding 2.5 kg
	040221 11 0	Whole milk powder
		Other
	040221 17 0	Of a fat content, by weight, not exceeding 11 %
	040221 19 0	Of a fat content, by weight, exceeding 11 % but not exceeding 27 %
		Of a fat content, by weight, exceeding 27 %
	040221 91 0	In immediate packings of a net content not exceeding 2.5 kg
	040221 99 0	Other
		Other
		Of a fat content, by weight, not exceeding 27 %
	040229 11 0	Special milk for infants in hermetically sealed containers of a net content not exceeding 500 g of a fat content, by weight, exceeding 10 %
		Other
	040229 15 0	In immediate packings of a net content not exceeding 2.5 kg
	040229 19 0	Other
		Of a fat content, by weight, exceeding 27 %
	040229 91 0	In immediate packings of a net content not exceeding 2.5 kg
	040229 99 0	Other
022.23		**Milk and cream, not in solid form, not containing added sugar or other sweetening matter**
		Not containing added sugar or other sweetening matter
		Of a fat content, by weight, not exceeding 8 %
	040291 11 0	In immediate packings of a net content not exceeding 2.5 kg
	040291 19 0	Other

S.I.T.C. (R3)	Commodity Code No	Trade description
cont 022.23		Of a fat content, by weight, exceeding 8 % but not exceeding 10 %
	040291 31 0	In immediate packings of a net content not exceeding 2.5 kg
	040291 39 0	Other
		Of a fat content, by weight, exceeding 10 % but not exceeding 45 %
	040291 51 0	In immediate packings of a net content not exceeding 2.5 kg
	040291 59 0	Other
		Of a fat content, by weight, exceeding 45 %
	040291 91 0	In immediate packings of a net content not exceeding 2.5 kg
	040291 99 0	Other
022.24		**Milk and cream, not in solid form, containing added sugar or other sweetening matter**
		Of a fat content, by weight, not exceeding 9.5 %
	040299 11 0	In immediate packings of a net content not exceeding 2.5 kg
	040299 19 0	Other
		Of a fat content, by weight, exceeding 9.5 % but not exceeding 45 %
	040299 31 0	In immediate packings of a net content not exceeding 2.5 kg
	040299 39 0	Other
		Of a fat content, by weight, exceeding 45 %
	040299 91 0	In immediate packings of a net content not exceeding 2.5 kg
	040299 99 0	Other
		Yoghurt; buttermilk, curdled, fermented or acidified milk and cream; ice cream
022.31		**Yoghurt, whether or not concentrated or containing added sugar or other sweetening matter or flavoured or containing added fruit, nuts or cocoa**
		Not flavoured nor containing added fruit or cocoa
		Not containing added sugar or other sweetening matter, of a fat content, by weight
	*040310 11 0	Not exceeding 3 %
	*040310 13 0	Exceeding 3 % but not exceeding 6 %
	*040310 19 0	Exceeding 6 %
		Other of a fat content, by weight
	*040310 31 0	Not exceeding 3 %
	*040310 33 0	Exceeding 3 % but not exceeding 6 %
	*040310 39 0	Exceeding 6 %
		Flavoured or containing added fruit or cocoa
		In powder, granules or other solid forms, of a milkfat content by weight
	040310 51 0	Not exceeding 1.5 %
	040310 53 0	Exceeding 1.5 % but not exceeding 27 %
	040310 59 0	Exceeding 27 %
		Other, of a milkfat content, by weight
	040310 91 0	Not exceeding 3 %
	040310 93 0	Exceeding 3 % but not exceeding 6 %
	040310 99 0	Exceeding 6 %
022.32		**Buttermilk, curdled milk and cream, kephir and other fermented or acidified milk or cream, whether or not concentrated or containing added sugar or other sweetening matter or flavoured or containing added fruit, nuts or cocoa**
		Not flavoured nor containing added fruit or cocoa
		In powder, granules or other solid forms
		Not containing added sugar or other sweetening matter, of fat content, by weight
	040390 11 0	Not exceeding 1.5 %
	040390 13 0	Exceeding 1.5 % but not exceeding 27 %
	040390 19 0	Exceeding 27 %
		Other, of a fat content, by weight
	040390 31 0	Not exceeding 1.5 %
	040390 33 0	Exceeding 1.5 % but not exceeding 27 %
	040390 39 0	Exceeding 27 %
		Other
		Not containing added sugar or other sweetening matter, of a fat content, by weight
	040390 51 0	Not exceeding 3 %
	040390 53 0	Exceeding 3 % but not exceeding 6 %
	040390 59 0	Exceeding 6 %
		Other, of a fat content, by weight
	040390 61 0	Not exceeding 3 %
	040390 63 0	Exceeding 3 % but not exceeding 6 %
	040390 69 0	Exceeding 6 %
		Flavoured or containing added fruit or cocoa
		In powder, granules or other solid forms, of a milkfat content by weight
	040390 71 0	Not exceeding 1.5 %
	040390 73 0	Exceeding 1.5 % but not exceeding 27 %
	040390 79 0	Exceeding 27 %
		Other, of a milkfat content, by weight
	040390 91 0	Not exceeding 3 %
	040390 93 0	Exceeding 3 % but not exceeding 6 %
	040390 99 0	Exceeding 6 %
022.33		**Ice cream and other edible ice whether or not containing cocoa**
	210500 10 0	Containing no milk fats or containing less than 3 % by weight of such fats
		Containing by weight of milk fats
	210500 91 0	3 % or more but less than 7 %

S.I.T.C. (R3)	Commodity Code No	Trade description

cont
022.33   210500 99 0   7 % or more

Whey; products consisting of natural milk constituents, n.e.s.

022.41   **Whey and modified whey, whether or not concentrated or containing added sugar or other sweetening matter**

    In powder, granules or other solid form
        Not containing added sugar or other sweetening matter, of a protein content (nitrogen content x 6.38), by weight
            Not exceeding 15 % and of a fat content, by weight

	040410 02 0	Not exceeding 1.5 %
	040410 04 0	Exceeding 1.5 % but not exceeding 27 %
	040410 06 0	Exceeding 27 %

            Exceeding 15 % and of a fat content, by weight

	040410 12 0	Not exceeding 1.5 %
	040410 14 0	Exceeding 1.5 % but not exceeding 27 %
	040410 16 0	Exceeding 27 %

        Other, of protein content (nitrogen content x 6.38), by weight
            Not exceeding 15 % and of a fat content, by weight

	040410 26 0	Not exceeding 1.5 %
	040410 28 0	Exceeding 1.5 % but not exceeding 27 %
	040410 32 0	Exceeding 27 %

            Exceeding 15 % and of a fat content, by weight

	040410 34 0	Not exceeding 1.5 %
	040410 36 0	Exceeding 1.5 % but not exceeding 27 %
	040410 38 0	Exceeding 27 %

    Other
        Not containing added sugar or other sweetening matter, of a protein content (nitrogen content x 6.38), by weight
            Not exceeding 15 % and of a fat content, by weight

	040410 48 0	Not exceeding 1.5 %
	040410 52 0	Exceeding 1.5 % but not exceeding 27 %
	040410 54 0	Exceeding 27 %

            Exceeding 15 % and of a fat content, by weight

	040410 56 0	Not exceeding 1.5 %
	040410 58 0	Exceeding 1.5 % but not exceeding 27 %
	040410 62 0	Exceeding 27 %

        Other, of a protein content (nitrogen content x 6.38), by weight
            Not exceeding 15 % and of a fat content, by weight

	040410 72 0	Not exceeding 1.5 %
	040410 74 0	Exceeding 1.5 % but not exceeding 27 %
	040410 76 0	Exceeding 27 %

            Exceeding 15 % and of a fat content, by weight

	040410 78 0	Not exceeding 1.5 %
	040410 82 0	Exceeding 1.5 % but not exceeding 27 %
	040410 84 0	Exceeding 27 %

022.49   **Products consisting of natural milk constituents, n.e.s.**

    Not containing added sugar or other sweetening matter, of a fat content, by weight

	*040490 21 0	Not exceeding 1.5 %
	*040490 23 0	Exceeding 1.5 % but not exceeding 27 %
	*040490 29 0	Exceeding 27 %

    Other, of a protein content, of a fat content, by weight   .

	*040490 81 0	Not exceeding 1.5 %
	*040490 83 0	Exceeding 1.5 % but not exceeding 27 %
	*040490 89 0	Exceeding 27 %

BUTTER AND OTHER FATS AND OILS DERIVED FROM MILK

023.0   **Butter and other fats and oils derived from milk**

    Of a fat content, by weight, not exceeding 85 %
        Natural butter

	*040510 11 0	In immediate packings of a net content not exceeding 1 kg
	*040510 19 0	Other
	*040510 30 0	Recombined butter
	*040510 50 0	Whey butter
	*040510 90 0	Other

    Dairy Spreads

	*040520 10 0	Of a fat content, by weight, of 39% or more but less than 60%
	*040520 30 0	Of a fat content, by weight, of 60% or more but less than 75%
	*040520 90 0	Of a fat content, by weight, of more than 75% but less than 80%

    Other

	*040590 10 0	Of a fat content, by weight, of 99.3% or more and of a water content, by weight, not exceeding 0.5%
	*040590 90 0	Other

S.I.T.C. (R3)	Commodity Code No	Trade description
		CHEESE AND CURD
024.10		**Grated or powdered cheese, of all kinds**
	040620 10 0	Glarus herb cheese (known as Schabziger) made from skimmed milk and mixed with finely ground herbs
	040620 90 0	Other
024.20		**Processed cheese, not grated or powdered**
	040630 10 0	In the manufacture of which no cheeses other than Emmentaler, Gruyère and Appenzell have been used and which may contain, as an addition, Glarus herb cheese (known as Schabziger); put up for retail sale, of a fat content by weight in the dry matter, not exceeding 56 %
		Other
		Of a fat content, by weight, not exceeding 36 % and of a fat content, by weight, in the dry matter
	040630 31 0	Not exceeding 48 %
	040630 39 0	Exceeding 48 %
	040630 90 0	Of a fat content, by weight, exceeding 36 %
		Blue-veined cheese
024.30	040640 10 0	Roquefort
	040640 50 0	Gorgonzola
	040640 90 0	Other
		Other cheese; curd
024.91		**Fresh (unripened or uncured) cheese, including whey cheese, and curd**
	040610 20 0	Of a fat content, by weight, not exceeding 40 %
	040610 80 0	Other
024.99		**Other**
	040690 01 0	For processing
		Other
		Emmentaler, Gruyère, Sbrinz, Bergkäse and Appenzell
		Of a fat content of 45% or more by weight in the dry matter, matured for three months or more
	040690 02 0	Whole cheeses with a free-at-frontier value, per 100 kg net weight exceeding 401.85 ECU but not exceeding 430.62 ECU
	040690 03 0	Whole cheeses with a free-at-frontier value, per 100 kg net weight exceeding 430.62 ECU
	040690 04 0	Pieces packed in vacuum or inert gas, with rind on at least one side, of a net weight of 1 kg or more but less than 5 kg and with a free-at-frontier value exceeding 430.62 ECU but not exceeding 459.39 ECU per 100 kg net weight
	040690 05 0	Pieces packed in vacuum or inert gas, with rind on at least one side, of a net weight of 1 kg or more and with a free-at-frontier value exceeding 459.39 ECU per 100 kg net weight
	040690 06 0	Pieces without rind, of a net weight of less than 450 g and with a free-at-frontier value exceeding 499.67 ECU per 100 kg net weight, packed in vacuum or inert gas, in packings bearing the description of the cheese, the fat content, the packer responsible and the country of manufacture
		Other
	040690 07 0	Emmentaler
	040690 08 0	Gruyère, Sbrinz
	040690 09 0	Bergkäse, Appenzell
		Other
	040690 12 0	Emmentaler
	040690 14 0	Gruyère, Sbrinz
	040690 16 0	Bergkäse, Appenzell
	040690 18 0	Fromage fribourgeois, Vacherin Mont d'Or and Tête de Moine
	040690 19 0	Glarus herb cheese (known as Schabziger) made from skimmed milk and mixed with finely ground herbs
	040690 21 0	Cheddar
	040690 23 0	Edam
	040690 25 0	Tilsit
	040690 27 0	Butterkäse
	040690 29 0	Kashkaval
		Feta
	040690 31 0	Of sheep's milk or buffalo milk in containers containing brine, or in sheep or goatskin bottles
	040690 33 0	Other
	040690 35 0	Kefalo-Tyri
	040690 37 0	Finlandia
	040690 39 0	Jarlsberg
		Other
	040690 50 0	Cheese of sheep's milk or buffalo milk in containers containing brine, or in sheep or goatskin bottles
		Other
		Of a fat content, by weight, not exceeding 40 % and a water content calculated, by weight, of the non-fatty matter
		Not exceeding 47 %
	040690 61 0	Grana Padano, Parmigiano Reggiano
	040690 63 0	Fiore Sardo, Pecorino
	040690 69 0	Other
		Exceeding 47 % but not exceeding 72 %
	040690 73 0	Provolone
	040690 75 0	Asiago, Caciocavallo, Montasio, Ragusano

S.I.T.C. (R3)	Commodity Code No	Trade description
cont 024.99	040690 76 0	Danbo, Fontal, Fontina, Fynbo, Havarti, Maribo, Samsø
	040690 78 0	Gouda
	040690 79 0	Esrom, Italico, Kernhem, Saint-Nectaire, Saint-Paulin, Taleggio
	040690 81 0	Cantal, Cheshire, Wensleydale, Lancashire, Double Gloucester, Blarney, Colby, Monterey
	040690 82 0	Camembert
	040690 84 0	Brie
	040690 85 0	Kefalograviera, Kasseri
		Other cheese, of a water content calculated, by weight, in the non-fatty matter
	040690 86 0	Exceeding 47 % but not exceeding 52 %
	040690 87 0	Exceeding 52 % but not exceeding 62 %
	040690 88 0	Exceeding 62 % but not exceeding 72 %
	040690 93 0	Exceeding 72 %
	040690 99 0	Other

EGGS, BIRDS', AND EGG YOLKS, FRESH, DRIED OR OTHERWISE PRESERVED, SWEETENED OR NOT; EGG ALBUMIN

025.10		Birds' eggs, in shell, fresh, preserved or cooked
		Of poultry
		For hatching
	040700 11 0	Of turkeys or geese
	040700 19 0	Other
	040700 30 0	Other
	040700 90 0	Other

Birds' eggs, not in shell, and egg yolks

025.21		....dried
		Egg yolks
	040811 20 0	Unfit for human consumption
	040811 80 0	Other
		Other
	040891 20 0	Unfit for human consumption
	040891 80 0	Other
025.22		....other than dried
		Egg yolks
	040819 20 0	Unfit for human consumption
		Other
	040819 81 0	Liquid
	040819 89 0	Other, including frozen
		Other
	040899 20 0	Unfit for human consumption
	040899 80 0	Other
025.30		Egg albumin
		Dried:
	*350211 10 0	Unfit, or to be rendered unfit, for human consumption
	*350211 90 0	Other
		Other
	*350219 10 0	Unfit, or to be rendered unfit, for human consumption
	*350219 90 0	Other

DIVISION 03

FISH (NOT MARINE MAMMALS), CRUSTACEANS, MOLLUSCS AND AQUATIC INVERTEBRATES AND PREPARATIONS THEREOF

FISH, FRESH (LIVE OR DEAD), CHILLED OR FROZEN

Fish, fresh (live or dead) or chilled (excluding fillets and minced fish)

034.11		Fish, live
		Ornamental fish
	030110 10 0	Freshwater fish
	030110 90 0	Saltwater fish
		Other live fish
	*030191 90 0	Trout (*Salmo trutta, Oncorhynchus mykiss, Oncorhynchus clarki, Oncorhynchus aguabonita, Oncorhynchus gilae*)
	030192 00 0	Eels (*Anguilla spp.*)
	030193 00 0	Carp
		Other
		Freshwater fish
	*030191 10 0	Of the species *Oncorhynchus apache* and *Oncorhynchus chrysagaster*
	030199 11 0	Pacific salmon (*Oncorhynchus nerka, Oncorhynchus gorbushcha, Oncorhynchus keta, Oncorhynchus tschawytscha, Oncorhynchus kisutch, Oncorhynchus masou and Oncorhynchus rhodurus*), Atlantic salmon (*Salmo salar*) and Danube salmon (*Hucho hucho*)
	*030199 19 0	Other

S.I.T.C. (R3)	Commodity Code No	Trade description
cont 034.11	030199 90 0	Saltwater fish
034.12		**Salmonidae, fresh or chilled (excluding livers and roes)**
	*030111 10 0	Of the species *Oncorhynchus apache* and *Oncorhynchus chrysagaster*
	*030211 90 0	Trout (*Salmo trutta, Oncorhynchus mykiss, Oncorhynchus clarki, Oncorhynchus aguabonita, Oncorhynchus gilae*)
	*030212 00 0	Pacific salmon (*Oncorhynchus nerka, Oncorhynchus gorbushcha. Oncorhynchus keta. Oncorhynchus tschawytscha. Oncorhynchus kisutch, Oncorhynchus masou and Oncorhynchus rhodurus*), Atlantic salmon (*Salmo salar*) and Danube salmon (*Hucho hucho*)
	*030119 00 0	Other
034.13		**Flat fish, fresh or chilled (excluding livers and roes)**
		Halibut (*Reinhardtius hippoglossoides, Hippoglossus hippoglossus, Hippoglossus stenolepis*)
	030221 10 0	Lesser or Greenland halibut (*Reinhardtius hippoglossoides*)
	030221 30 0	Atlantic halibut (*Hippoglossus hippoglossus*)
	030221 90 0	Pacific halibut (*Hippoglossus stenolepis*)
	030222 00 0	Plaice (*Pleuronectes platessa*)
	030223 00 0	Sole(*Solea spp.*)
		Other
	030229 10 0	Megrim (*Lepidorhombus spp.*)
	030229 90 0	Other
034.14		**Tunas, skipjack or stripe-bellied bonito, fresh or chilled, excluding livers and roes**
		Albacore or longfinned tunas (*Thunnus alalunga*)
	030231 10 0	For the industrial manufacture of products falling within heading No. 037.1
	030231 90 0	Other
		Yellowfin tunas (*Thunnus albacares*)
	030232 10 0	For the industrial manufacture of products falling within heading No. 037.1
	030232 90 0	Other
		Skipjack or stripe-bellied bonito
	030233 10 0	For the industrial manufacture of products falling within heading No. 037.1
	030233 90 0	Other
		Other
		For the industrial manufacture of products falling within heading No. 037.1
	030239 11 0	Bluefin tunas (*Thunnus thynnus*)
	030239 19 0	Other
		Other
	030239 91 0	Bluefin tunas (*Thunnus thynnus*)
	030239 99 0	Other
034.15		**Herrings, sardines, sardinella, brislings or sprats, fresh or chilled (excluding livers and roes)**
		Herrings (*Clupea harengus, Clupea pallasii*), excluding livers and roes
	*030240 05 0	From 1 January to 14 February
	030240 10 0	From 15 February to 15 June
	*030240 98 0	From 16 June to 31 December
		Other fish, excluding livers and roes
	030261 10 0	Sardines of the species *Sardina pilchardus*
	030261 30 0	Sardines of the genus *Sardinops*; sardinella (*Sardinella spp.*)
		Brisling or sprats (*Sprattus sprattus*)
	*030261 90 0	From 1 January to 14 February
	030261 91 0	From 15 February to 15 June
	*030261 98 0	From 16 June to 31 December
034.16		**Cod, fresh or chilled (excluding livers and roes)**
	030250 10 0	Of the species *Gadus morhua*
	030250 90 0	Other
034.17		**Mackerel, (scombrids), fresh or chilled**
	*030264 05 0	From 1 January to 14 February
	030264 10 0	From 15 February to 15 June
	*030264 98 0	From 16 June to 31 December
034.18		**Other fish, fresh or chilled (excluding livers and roes)**
	030262 00 0	Haddock (*Melanogrammus aeglefinus*)
	030263 00 0	Coalfish (*Pollachius virens*)
		Dogfish and other sharks
	030265 20 0	Dogfish of the species *Squalus acanthias*
	030265 50 0	Dogfish of the species *Scyliorhinus spp*
	030265 90 0	Other
	030266 00 0	Eels (*Anguilla spp.*)
		Other
		Freshwater fish
	030269 11 0	Carp
	030269 19 0	Other
		Saltwater fish
		Fish of the genus *Euthynnus*, other than the skipjack or stripe-bellied bonitos (*Euthynnus (Katsuwonus) pelamis*) mentioned in subheadings 030233 10 and 030233 90
	030269 21 0	For the industrial manufacture of products falling within heading No. 037.1

S.I.T.C. (R3)	Commodity Code No	Trade description
cont 034.18	030269 25 0	Other
		Redfish (*Sebastes spp.*)
	030269 31 0	Of the species *Sebastes marinus*
	030269 33 0	Other
	030269 35 0	Fish of the species *Boreogadus saida*
	030269 41 0	Whiting (*Merlangus merlangus*)
	030269 45 0	Ling (*Molva spp.*)
	030269 51 0	Alaska pollack (*Theragra chalcogramma*) and pollack (*Pollachius pollachius*)
	030269 55 0	Anchovies (*Engraulis spp.*)
	030269 61 0	Sea bream (*Dentex dentex* and *Pagellus spp.*)
	030269 65 0	Hake (*Merluccius spp., Urophycis spp.*)
	030269 75 0	Ray's bream (*Brama spp.*)
	030269 81 0	Monkfish (*Lophius spp.*)
	030269 85 0	Blue whiting (*Micromesistius poutassou* or *Gadus poutassou*)
	030269 86 0	Southern blue whiting (*Micromesistius australis*)
	030269 87 0	Swordfish (*Xiphias gladius*)
	030269 91 0	Horse mackerel (*scad*) (*Caranx trachurus, Trachurus trachurus*)
	030269 92 0	Pink cusk-eel (*Genypterus blacodes*)
	030269 93 0	Fish of the species Kathetostoma giganteum
	*030269 94 0	Sea bass (*Dicentrarchus labrox*)
	*030269 95 0	Gilt-headed seabreams *(Sparus aurata)*
	*030269 99 0	Other
034.19	030270 00 0	**Livers and roes, fresh or chilled**
		Fish, frozen (excluding fillets and minced fish)
034.21		**Salmonidae, frozen (excluding livers and roes)**
	*030310 00 0	Pacific salmon (*Oncorhynchus nerka, Oncorhynchus gorbushcha, Oncorhynchus keta, Oncorhynchus tschawytscha. Oncorhynchus kisutch, Oncorhynchus masou* and *Oncorhynchus rhodurus*), excluding livers and roes
		Other salmonidae. excluding livers and roes
	*030321 10 0	Trout of the species *Oncorhynchus apache* and *Oncorhynchus chrysogaster*
	*030321 90 0	Trout (*Salmo trutta. Oncorhynchus mykiss. Oncorhynchus clarki, Oncorhynchus aguabonita. Oncorhynchus gilae*):
	*030322 00 0	Atlantic salmon (*Salmo salar*) and Danube salmon (*Hucho hucho*)
	*030329 00 0	Other
034.22		**Flat fish, frozen (excluding livers and roes)**
		Halibut (*Reinhardtius hippoglossoides, Hippoglossus hippoglossus, Hippoglossus stenolepis*)
	030331 10 0	Lesser or Greenland halibut (*Reinhardtius hippoglossoides*)
	030331 30 0	Atlantic halibut (*Hippoglossus hippoglossus*)
	030331 90 0	Pacific halibut (*Hippoglossus stenolepis*)
	030332 00 0	Plaice (*Pleuronectes platessa*)
	030333 00 0	Sole (*Solea spp.*)
		Other
	030339 10 0	Flounder (*Platichthys flesus*)
	030339 20 0	Megrim (*Lepidorhombus spp.*
	030339 30 0	Fish of the genus Rhombosolea
	030339 80 0	Other
034.23		**Tunas, skipjack or stripe-bellied bonito, frozen (excluding livers and roes)**
		Albacore or longfinned tunas (*Thunnus alalunga*)
		For the industrial manufacture of products falling within heading No. 037.1
	030341 11 0	Whole
	030341 13 0	Gilled and gutted
	030341 19 0	Other (for example "heads off")
	030341 90 0	Other
		Yellowfin tunas (*Thunnus albacares*)
		For the industrial manufacture of products falling within heading No. 037.1
		Whole
	030342 12 0	Weighing not more than 10 kg each
	030342 18 0	Other
		Gilled and gutted
	030342 32 0	Weighing not more than 10 kg each
	030342 38 0	Other
		Other (for example "heads off")
	030342 52 0	Weighing not more than 10 kg each
	030342 58 0	Other
	030342 90 0	Other
		Skipjack or stripe-bellied bonito
		For the industrial manufacture of products falling within heading No. 037.1
	030343 11 0	Whole
	030343 13 0	Gilled and gutted
	030343 19 0	Other (for example "heads off")
	030343 90 0	Other
		Other
		For the industrial manufacture of products falling within heading No. 037.1
		Bluefin tunas (*Thunnus thynnus*)

S.I.T.C. (R3)	Commodity Code No	Trade description
cont		
034.23	030349 21 0	Whole
	030349 23 0	Gilled and gutted
	030349 29 0	Other (for example "heads off")
		Other
	030349 41 0	Whole
	030349 43 0	Gilled and gutted
	030349 49 0	Other (for example "heads off")
	030349 90 0	Other
034.24		**Herrings, sardines, sardinella, brislings or sprats, frozen (excluding livers and roes)**
		Herrings (*Clupea harengus, Clupea pallasii*), excluding livers and roes
	*030350 05 0	From 1 January to 14 February
	030350 10 0	From 15 February to 15 June
	*030350 98 0	From 16 June to 31 December
		Other fish, excluding livers and roes
	030371 10 0	Sardines of the species *Sardina pilchardus*
	030371 30 0	Sardines of the genus *Sardinops*; sardinella (*Sardinella spp.*)
		Brisling or sprats (*Sprattus sprattus*)
	*030371 90 0	From 1 January to 14 February
	030371 91 0	From 15 February to 15 June
	*030371 98 0	From 16 June to 31 December
034.25		**Cod, frozen (excluding livers and roes)**
	030360 11 0	Of the species *Gadus morhua*
	030360 19 0	Of the species *Gadus ogac*
	030360 90 0	Of the species *Gadus macrocephalus*
034.26		**Mackerel, (scombrids), frozen (excluding livers and roes)**
		Of the species *Scomber scombrus* and *Scomber japonicus*
	*030374 10 0	From 1 January to 14 February
	030374 11 0	From 15 February to 15 June
	*030374 20 0	From 16 June to 31 December
	030374 90 0	Of the species *Scomber australasicus*
034.27		**Hake, frozen (excluding livers and roes)**
	030378 10 0	Hake of the genus *Merluccius*
	030378 90 0	Hake of the genus *Urophycis*
034.28		**Other fish, frozen (excluding livers and roes)**
	030372 00 0	Haddock (*Melanogrammus aeglefinus*)
	030373 00 0	Coalfish (*Pollachius virens*)
		Dogfish and other sharks
	030375 20 0	Dogfish of the species *Squalus acanthias*
	030375 50 0	Dogfish of the species *Scyliorhinus spp*
	030375 90 0	Other
	030376 00 0	Eels (*Anguilla spp.*)
	030377 00 0	Sea bass (*Dicentrarchus labrax, Dicentrarchus punctatus*)
		Other
		Freshwater fish
	030379 11 0	Carp
	030379 19 0	Other
		Saltwater fish
		Fish of the genus *Euthynnus*, other than the skipjack or stripe-bellied bonitos (*Euthynnus (Katsuwonus) pelamis*) mentioned in subheadings 030343 11 to 030343 90
		For the industrial manufacture of products falling within heading No. 037.1
	030379 21 0	Whole
	030379 23 0	Gilled and gutted
	030379 29 0	Other (for example "heads off")
	030379 31 0	Other
		Redfish (*Sebastes spp.*)
	030379 35 0	Of the species *Sebastes marinus*
	030379 37 0	Other
	030379 41 0	Fish of the species *Boreogadus saida*
	030379 45 0	Whiting (*Merlangus merlangus*)
	030379 51 0	Ling (*Molva spp.*)
	030379 55 0	Alaska pollack (*Theragra chalcogramma*) and pollack (*Pollachius pollachius*)
		Fish of the species *Orcynopsis unicolor*
	*030379 60 0	From 1 January to 14 February
	030379 61 0	From 15 February to 15 June
	*030379 62 0	From 16 June to 31 December
	030379 65 0	Anchovies (*Engraulis spp.*)
	030379 71 0	Sea bream (*Dentex dentex* and *Pagellus spp.*)
	030379 75 0	Ray's bream (*Brama spp.*)
	030379 81 0	Monkfish (*Lophius spp.*)
	030379 83 0	Blue whiting (*Micromesistius poutassou* or *Gadus poutassou*)
	030379 85 0	Southern blue whiting (*Micromesistius australis*)
	030379 87 0	Swordfish (*Xiphias Gladius*)
	030379 91 0	Horse mackerel (*scad*) (*Caranx trachurus, Trachurus trachurus*)
	030379 92 0	Blue grenadier (*Macruronus novaezealandiae*)

S.I.T.C. (R3)	Commodity Code No	Trade description
cont 034.28	030379 93 0	Pink cusk-eel (*Genypterus blacodes*)
	030379 94 0	Fish of the species Pelotreis flavilatus and Peltorhamphus novaezealandiae
	030379 95 0	Fish of the species Kathetostoma giganteum
	030379 96 0	Other
034.29	030380 00 0	Livers and roes, frozen
034.40		Fish fillets, frozen
		Of freshwater fish
	030420 11 0	Of trout (*Salmo trutta, Salmo gairdneri, Salmo clarki, Salmo aguabonita, Salmo gilae*)
	030420 13 0	Of Pacific salmon (*Oncorhynchus spp.*), Atlantic salmon (*Salmo salar*) and Danube salmon (*Hucho hucho*)
	030420 19 0	Of other freshwater fish
		Of cod (*Gadus morhua, Gadus macrocephalus, Gadus ogac*) and of fish of the species *Boreogadus saida*
	030420 21 0	Of cod of the species *Gadus macrocephalus*
	*030420 29 0	Other
	*030420 31 0	Of coalfish (*Pollachius virens*)
	*030420 33 0	Of haddock (*Melanogrammus aeglefinus*)
		Of redfish (*Sebastes spp.*)
	030420 35 0	Of the species *Sabastes marinus*
	030420 37 0	Other
	030420 41 0	Of whiting (*Merlangus merlangus*)
	030420 43 0	Of ling (*Molva spp.*)
	030420 45 0	Of tuna (of genus *Thunnus*) and of fish of the genus *Euthynnus*
		Of mackerel (*Scomber scombrus, Scomber australasicus, Scomber japonicus*) and of fish of the species *Orcynopsis unicolor*
	030420 51 0	Of mackerel of the species *Scomber australasicus*
	030420 53 0	Other
		Of hake (*Merluccius spp., Urophycis spp.*)
	030420 57 0	Of hake of the genus *Merluccius*
	030420 59 0	Of hake of the genus *Urophycis*
		Of dogfish and other sharks
	030420 61 0	Of dogfish (*Squalus acanthias* and *Scyliorhinus spp.*)
	030420 69 0	Of other sharks
	030420 71 0	Of plaice (*Pleuronectes platessa*)
	030420 73 0	Of flounder (*Platichthys fleusus*)
	030420 75 0	Of herring (*Clupea harengus, Clupea pallasii*)
	030420 79 0	Of megrim (*Lepidorhombus spp.*)
	030420 81 0	Of Ray's bream (*Brama spp.*)
	030420 83 0	Of monkfish (*Lophius spp.*)
	030420 85 0	Of Alaska pollack (*Theragra chalcogramma*)
	030420 87 0	Of Swordfish (*Xiphias Gladius*)
	030420 91 0	Of blue grenadier (*Macruronus novaezealandiae*)
	030420 96 0	Other

Fish fillets, fresh or chilled, and other fish meat (whether or not minced), fresh, chilled or frozen

S.I.T.C. (R3)	Commodity Code No	Trade description
034.51		Fish fillets and other fish meat, fresh or chilled
		Of freshwater fish
	030410 11 0	Of trout (*Salmo trutta, Salmo gairdneri, Salmo clarki, Salmo aguabonita, Salmo gilae*)
	030410 13 0	Of Pacific salmon (*Oncorhynchus spp.*), Atlantic salmon (*Salmo salar*) and Danube salmon (*Hucho hucho*)
	030410 19 0	Of other freshwater fish
		Other
	030410 31 0	Of cod (*Gadus morhua, Gadus ogac, Gadus macrocephalus*) and of fish of the species *Boreogadus saida*
	030410 33 0	Of coalfish (*Pollachius virens*)
	030410 35 0	Of redfish (*Sebastes spp.*)
	030410 38 0	Other
		Other fish meat (whether or not minced)
	030410 91 0	Of freshwater fish
		Other
		Flaps of herring
	*030410 94 0	From 1 January to 14 February
	*030410 95 0	From 15 February to 15 June
	*030410 96 0	From 16 June to 31 December
	030410 98 0	Other
034.55		Fish meat (other than fillets), frozen
	030490 05 0	Surimi
		Other
	030490 10 0	Of freshwater fish
		Other
		Of herring (*Clupea harengus, Clupea pallasii*)
	*030490 20 0	From 1 January to 14 February
	030490 21 0	From 15 February to 15 June
	*030490 27 0	From 16 June to 31 December

S.I.T.C. (R3)	Commodity Code No	Trade description
cont 034.55	030490 31 0	Of redfish (*Sebastes spp.*)
		Of cod (*Gadus morhua, Gadus ogac, Gadus macrocephalus*) and of fish of the species *Boreogadus saida*
	030490 35 0	Of cod of the species *Gadus macrocephalus*
	030490 38 0	Of cod of the species *Gadus morhua*
	030490 39 0	Other
	030490 41 0	Of coalfish (*Pollachius virens*)
	030490 45 0	Of haddock (*Melanogrammus aeglefinus*)
		Of hake (*Merluccius spp., Urophycis spp.*)
	030490 47 0	Of hake of the genus *Merluccius*
	030490 49 0	Of hake of the genus *Urophycis*
	030490 51 0	Of megrim (*Lepidorhombus spp.*)
	030490 55 0	Of Ray's bream (*Brama spp.*)
	030490 57 0	Of monkfish (*Lophius spp.*)
	030490 59 0	Of blue whiting (*Micromesistius poutassou* or *Gadus poutassou*)
	030490 61 0	Of Alaska pollack (*Theragra chalcogramma*)
	030490 65 0	Of Swordfish (*Xipias gladius*)
	030490 97 0	Other

FISH, DRIED, SALTED OR IN BRINE; SMOKED FISH (WHETHER OR NOT COOKED BEFORE OR DURING THE SMOKING PROCESS); FLOURS, MEALS AND PELLETS OF FISH, FIT FOR HUMAN CONSUMPTION

Fish, dried, salted or in brine, but not smoked

S.I.T.C. (R3)	Commodity Code No	Trade description
035.11		Cod (gadus morhua,gadus ogac, gadus macrocephalus, not in fillets), dried, whether or not salted
	030551 10 0	Dried, unsalted
	030551 90 0	Dried, salted
035.12		Fillets, dried, salted or in brine
		Of cod (*Gadus morhua, Gadus ogac, Gadus macrocephalus*) and of fish of the species *Boreogadus saida*
	030530 11 0	Of cod of the species *Gadus macrocephalus*
	030530 19 0	Other
	030530 30 0	Of pacific salmon (*Oncorhynchus spp.*), of Atlantic salmon (*Salmo salar*), and Danube salmon (*Hucho hucho*), salted or in brine
	030530 50 0	Of lesser or Greenland halibut (*Reinhardtius hippoglossoides*), salted or in brine
	030530 90 0	Other
035.13		Fish, dried, whether or not salted, n.e.s.
		Fish of the species *Boreogadus saida*
	030559 11 0	Dried, unsalted
	030559 19 0	Dried, salted
	030559 30 0	Herrings (*Clupea harengus, Clupea pallasii*)
	030559 50 0	Anchovies (*Engraulis spp.*)
	030559 60 0	Lesser or Greenland halibut (*Reinhardtius hippoglossoides*) Pacific halibut (*Hippoglossus stenolepis*)
	030559 70 0	Atlantic halibut (*Hippoglossus hippoglossus*)
	030559 90 0	Other

Fish salted but not dried or smoked and fish in brine

S.I.T.C. (R3)	Commodity Code No	Trade description
035.21	030562 00 0	Cod (gadus morhua, gadus ogac, gadus macrocephalus)
035.22	030563 00 0	Anchovies
035.29		Other fish
	030561 00 0	Herrings (*Clupea harengus, Clupea pallasii*)
		Other
	030569 10 0	Fish of the species *Boreogadus saida*
	030569 20 0	Lesser or Greenland halibut (*Reinhardtius hippoglossoides*) Pacific halibut (*Hippoglossus stenolepis*)
	030569 30 0	Atlantic halibut (*Hippoglossus hippoglossus*)
	030569 50 0	Pacific salmon (*Oncorhynchus spp.*), Atlantic salmon (*Salmo salar*) and Danube salmon (*Hucho hucho*)
	030569 90 0	Other
035.30		Fish (including fillets), smoked, whether or not cooked before or during the smoking process
	030541 00 0	Pacific salmon (*Oncorhynchus spp.*), Atlantic salmon (*Salmo salar*) and Danube salmon (*Hucho hucho*)
	030542 00 0	Herrings (*Clupea harengus, Clupea pallasii*)
		Other
	030549 10 0	Lesser or Greenland halibut (*Reinhardtius hippoglossoides*)
	030549 20 0	Atlantic halibut (*Hippoglossus hippoglossus*)
	030549 30 0	Mackerel (*Scomber scombrus, Scomber australasicus, Scomber japonicus*)
	*030549 45 0	Trout (*Salmo trutta, Oncorhynchus mykiss, Oncorhynchus clarki, Oncorhynchus aguabonita, Oncorhynchus gilae, Oncorhynchus apache and Oncorhynchus chrysogaster*)
	030549 50 0	Eels (*Anguilla spp.*)
	*030549 80 0	Other

S.I.T.C. (R3)	Commodity Code No	Trade description
035.40	030520 00 0	Fish liver and roes, dried, smoked, salted or in brine
035.50	030510 00 0	Flours, meals and pellets of fish, fit for human consumption

CRUSTACEANS, MOLLUSCS AND AQUATIC INVERTEBRATES, WHETHER IN SHELL OR NOT, FRESH (LIVE OR DEAD), CHILLED, FROZEN, DRIED, SALTED OR IN BRINE; CRUSTACEANS, IN SHELL, COOKED BY STEAMING OR BOILING IN WATER, WHETHER OR NOT CHILLED, FROZEN, DRIED, SALTED OR IN BRINE; FLOURS, MEALS AND PELLETS OF CRUSTACEANS OR OF AQUATIC INVERTEBRATES, FIT FOR HUMAN CONSUMPTION

Crustaceans, frozen

036.11		Shrimps and prawns, frozen
	030613 10 0	Of the *Pandalidae* family
	030613 30 0	Shrimps of the genus *Crangon*
	030613 90 0	Other
036.19		Other crustaceans, frozen, including flours, meals and pellets of crustaceans, fit for human consumption
		Rock lobster and other sea crawfish (*Palinurus spp., Panulirus spp., Jasus spp.*)
	030611 10 0	Crawfish tails
	030611 90 0	Other
		Lobsters (*Homarus spp.*)
	030612 10 0	Whole
	030612 90 0	Other
		Crabs
	030614 10 0	Crabs of the species *Paralithodes camchaticus, Chionoecetes spp.* and *Callinectes sapidus*
	030614 30 0	Crabs of the species *Cancer pagurus*
	030614 90 0	Other
		Other
	030619 10 0	Freshwater crayfish
	030619 30 0	Norway lobsters (*Nephrops norvegicus*)
	030619 90 0	Other
036.20		Crustaceans, other than frozen, including flours, meals and pellets of crustaceans, fit for human consumption
	030621 00 0	Rock lobster and other sea crawfish (*Palinurus spp., Panulirus spp., Jasus spp.*)
		Lobsters (*Homarus spp.*)
	030622 10 0	Live
		Other
	030622 91 0	Whole
	030622 99 0	Other
		Shrimps and prawns
	030623 10 0	Of the *Pandalidae* family
		Shrimps of the genus *Crangon*
	030623 31 0	Fresh, chilled or cooked by steaming or by boiling in water
	030623 39 0	Other
	030623 90 0	Other
		Crabs
	030624 10 0	Crabs of the species *Paralithodes camchaticus, Chionoecetes spp.* and *Callinectes sapidus*
	030624 30 0	Crabs of the species *Cancer pagurus*
	030624 90 0	Other
		Other
	030629 10 0	Freshwater crayfish
	030629 30 0	Norway lobsters (*Nephrops norvegicus*)
	030629 90 0	Other

Molluscs, and aquatic invertebrates, fresh, chilled, frozen, dried, salted or in brine; flours, meals and pellets of aquatic invertebrates other than crustaceans, fit for human consumption

036.31		Oysters
	030710 10 0	Flat oysters (of the genus *ostrea*), live and weighing (shell included), not more than 40 g each
	030710 90 0	Other
036.33		Cuttlefish, octopus and squid, fresh or chilled
		Live
	030741 10 0	Cuttle fish (*Sepia officinalis, Rossia macrosoma, Sepiola spp.*)
		Squid (*Ommastrephes spp., Loligo spp., Nototodarus spp., Sepioteuthis spp.*)
	030741 91 0	*Loligo spp., Ommastrephes sagittatus*
	030741 99 0	Other
	030751 00 0	Octopus (*Octopus spp.*)
036.35		Other molluscs and aquatic invertebrates, fresh or chilled
		Scallops, including queen scallops, of the genera *Pecten, Chlamys* or *Placopecten*
	030721 00 0	Live, fresh or chilled
		Mussels (*Mytilus spp., Perna spp.*)
		Live, fresh or chilled
	030731 10 0	*Mytilus spp.*
	030731 90 0	*Perna spp.*

S.I.T.C. (R3)	Commodity Code No	Trade description
cont 036.35		Other
	030791 00 0	Live, fresh or chilled
036.37		**Cuttlefish, octopus and squid, frozen, dried, salted or in brine; flours, meals and pellets thereof, fit for human consumption**
		Cuttle fish (*Sepia officinalis, Rossia macrosoma, Sepiola spp.*) and squid (*Ommastrephes spp., Loligo spp., Nototodarus spp., Sepioteuthis spp.*)
		Frozen
		Cuttle fish (*Sepia officinalis, Rossia macrosoma, Sepiola spp.*)
		Of the genus *Sepiola*
	030749 01 0	Lesser cuttle fish (*Sepiola rondeleti*)
	030749 11 0	Other
	030749 18 0	Other
		Squid (*Ommastrephes spp., Loligo spp., Nototodarus spp., Sepioteuthis spp.*)
		Loligo spp.
	030749 31 0	*Loligo vulgaris*
	030749 33 0	*Loligo pealei*
	030749 35 0	*Loligo patagonica*
	030749 38 0	Other
	030749 51 0	*Ommastrephes sagittatus*
	030749 59 0	Other
		Other
	030749 71 0	Cuttle fish (*Sepia officinalis, Rossia macrosoma, Sepiola spp.*)
		Squid (*Ommastrephes spp., Loligo spp., Nototodarus spp., Sepioteuthis spp.*)
	030749 91 0	*Loligo spp., Ommastrephes sagittatus*
	030749 99 0	Other
		Octopus (*Octopus spp.*)
	030759 10 0	Frozen
	030759 90 0	Other
036.39		**Other molluscs and aquatic invertebrates, frozen, dried, salted or in brine including flours, meals and pellets of aquatic invertebrates other than crustaceans, fit for human consumption**
		Scallops, including queen scallops, of the genera *Pecten, Chlamys* or *Placopecten*
	030729 10 0	Coquilles St. Jacques (*Pecten maximus*), frozen
	030729 90 0	Other
		Mussels (*Mytilus spp., Perna spp.*)
	030739 10 0	*Mytilus spp.*
	030739 90 0	*Perna spp.*
		Other
		Frozen
	030799 11 0	*Illex spp.*
	030799 13 0	Striped venus and other species of the genus *Veneridae*
	030799 15 0	Jellyfish (*Rhopílema spp.*)
	030799 18 0	Other aquatic invertebrates
	030799 90 0	Other

FISH, CRUSTACEANS, MOLLUSCS AND OTHER AQUATIC INVERTEBRATES, PREPARED OR PRESERVED, N.E.S.

Fish, prepared or preserved, n.e.s.; caviar and caviar substitutes prepared from fish eggs

S.I.T.C. (R3)	Commodity Code No	Trade description
037.11	160411 00 0	**Salmon, whole or in pieces, but not minced**
037.12		**Herrings, sardines, sardinella and brislings or sprats, whole or in pieces, but not minced**
		Herrings
	160412 10 0	Fillets, raw, coated with batter or breadcrumbs, deep frozen
		Other
	160412 91 0	In airtight containers
	160412 99 0	Other
		Sardines, sardinella and brisling or sprats
		Sardines
	160413 11 0	In olive oil
	160413 19 0	Other
	160413 90 0	Other
037.13		**Tunas, skipjack and Atlantic bonito, whole or in pieces, but not minced**
		Tunas and skipjack
		In vegetable oil
	160414 12 0	Loins
	160414 14 0	Other
		Other
	160414 16 0	Loins
	160414 18 0	Other
	160414 90 0	Bonito (*Sarda spp.*)
037.14		**Mackerel, whole or in pieces, but not minced**
		Of the species *Scomber scombrus* and *Scomber japonicus*
	160415 11 0	Fillets
	160415 19 0	Other
	160415 90 0	Of the species *Scomber australasicus*

S.I.T.C. (R3)	Commodity Code No	Trade description
037.15		**Other fish, whole or in pieces, but not minced**
	160416 00 0	Anchovies
		Other
	160419 10 0	Salmonidae, other than salmon
		Fish of the genus *Euthynnus*, other than skipjack (*Euthynnus (Katsuwonus) pelamis*)
	160419 31 0	Loins
	160419 39 0	Other
	160419 50 0	Fish of the species *Orcynopsis unicolor*
		Other
	160419 91 0	Fillets, raw, coated with batter or breadcrumbs, deep frozen
		Other
	160419 92 0	Cod (*Gadus morhua, Gadus ogac, Gadus macrocephalus*)
	160419 93 0	Coalfish (*Pollachius virens*)
	160419 94 0	Hake (*Merluccius spp., Urophycis spp.*)
	160419 95 0	Alaska pollack (*Theraga chalcogramma*) and pollack (*Pollachius pollachius*)
	160419 98 0	Other
037.16		**Other fish, prepared or preserved, n.e.s.**
	160420 05 0	Preparations of surimi
		Other
	160420 10 0	Of salmon
	160420 30 0	Of salmonidae, other than salmon
	160420 40 0	Of anchovies
	160420 50 0	Of sardines, bonito, mackerel of the species *Scomber scombrus* and *Scomber japonicus*, fish of the species *Orcynopsis unicolor*
	160420 70 0	Of tunas, skipjack or other fish of the genus *Euthynnus*
	160420 90 0	Of other fish
037.17		**Caviar and caviar substitutes prepared from fish eggs**
	160430 10 0	Caviar (sturgeon roe)
	160430 90 0	Caviar substitutes

Crustaceans, molluscs and other aquatic invertebrates, prepared or preserved, n.e.s.

S.I.T.C. (R3)	Commodity Code No	Trade description
037.21		**Crustaceans, prepared or preserved, n.e.s.**
	160510 00 0	Crab
		Shrimps and prawns
	160520 10 0	In airtight containers
		Other
	160520 91 0	In immediate packings of a net content not exceeding 2 kg
	160520 99 0	Other
	160530 00 0	Lobster
	160540 00 0	Other crustaceans
037.22		**Molluscs and other aquatic invertebrates, prepared or preserved**
		Molluscs
		Mussels (*Mytilus spp., Perna spp.*)
	160590 11 0	In airtight containers
	160590 19 0	Other
	160590 30 0	Other
	160590 90 0	Other aquatic invertebrates

DIVISION 04

CEREALS AND CEREAL PREPARATIONS

WHEAT (INCLUDING SPELT) AND MESLIN, UNMILLED

S.I.T.C. (R3)	Commodity Code No	Trade description
041.10	100110 00 0	**Durum wheat, unmilled**
041.20		**Other wheat (including spelt) and meslin, unmilled**
	100190 10 0	Spelt for sowing
		Other spelt, common wheat and meslin
	100190 91 0	Common wheat and meslin seed
	*100190 99 0	Other

RICE

S.I.T.C. (R3)	Commodity Code No	Trade description
042.10		**Rice in the husk (paddy or rough rice)**
	100610 10 0	For sowing
		Other
		Parboiled
	100610 21 0	Round grain
	100610 23 0	Medium grain
		Long grain
	100610 25 0	Of a length/width ratio greater than 2 but less than 3

S.I.T.C. (R3)	Commodity Code No	Trade description
cont 042.10	100610 27 0	Of a length/width ratio equal to or greater than 3
		Other
	100610 92 0	Round grain
	100610 94 0	Medium grain
		Long grain
	100610 96 0	Of a length/width ratio greater than 2 but less than 3
	100610 98 0	Of a length/width ration equal to or greater than 3
042.20		**Rice husked but not further prepared (cargo rice or brown rice)**
		Parboiled
	100620 11 0	Round grain
	100620 13 0	Medium grain
		Long grain
	100620 15 0	Of a length/width ratio greater than 2 but less than 3
	100620 17 0	Of a length/width ratio equal to or greater than 3
		Other
	100620 92 0	Round grain
	100620 94 0	Medium grain
		Long grain
	100620 96 0	Of a length/width ratio greater than 2 but less than 3
	100620 98 0	Of a length/width ratio equal to or greater than 3

Rice, semi-milled or wholly milled, whether or not polished, glazed, parboiled or converted (including broken rice)

S.I.T.C. (R3)	Commodity Code No	Trade description
042.31		**Rice, semi-milled or wholly milled, whether or not polished, glazed, parboiled or converted (excluding broken rice)**
		Semi-milled rice
		Parboiled
	100630 21 0	Round grain
	100630 23 0	Medium grain
		Long grain
	100630 25 0	Of a length/width ratio greater than 2 but less than 3
	100630 27 0	Of a length/width ratio equal to or greater than 3
		Other
	100630 42 0	Round grain
	100630 44 0	Medium grain
		Long grain
	100630 46 0	Of a length/width ratio greater than 2 but less than 3
	100630 48 0	Of a length/width ratio equal to or greater than 3
		Wholly-milled rice
		Parboiled
	100630 61 0	Round grain
	100630 63 0	Medium grain
		Long grain
	100630 65 0	Of a length/width ratio greater than 2 but less than 3
	100630 67 0	Of a length/width ratio equal to or greater than 3
		Other
	100630 92 0	Round grain
	100630 94 0	Medium grain
		Long grain
	100630 96 0	Of a length/width ratio greater than 2 but less than 3
	100630 98 0	Of a length/width ratio equal to or greater than 3
042.32	100640 00 0	Broken rice

BARLEY, UNMILLED

S.I.T.C. (R3)	Commodity Code No	Trade description
043.00		Barley unmilled
	100300 10 0	Seed
	100300 90 0	Other

MAIZE (NOT INCLUDING SWEET CORN) UNMILLED

S.I.T.C. (R3)	Commodity Code No	Trade description
044.10		Seed
		Hybrid
	100510 11 0	Double hybrids and top cross hybrids
	100510 13 0	Three-cross hybrids
	100510 15 0	Simple hybrids
	100510 19 0	Other
	100510 90 0	Other
044.90	100590 00 0	Other

CEREALS, UNMILLED (OTHER THAN WHEAT, RICE, BARLEY AND MAIZE)

S.I.T.C. (R3)	Commodity Code No	Trade description
045.10	100200 00 0	Rye, unmilled
045.20	100400 00 0	Oats, unmilled

S.I.T.C. (R3)	Commodity Code No	Trade description
045.30		**Grain sorghum, unmilled**
	100700 10 0	Hybrids for sowing
	100700 90 0	Other
		Buckwheat, millet, canary seed and other cereals, unmilled, n.e.s.
045.91	100820 00 0	Millet, unmilled
045.92	100810 00 0	Buckwheat, unmilled
045.93	100830 00 0	Canary seed, unmilled
045.99		Cereals, unmilled, n.e.s.
	100890 10 0	Triticale
	100890 90 0	Other

MEAL AND FLOUR OF WHEAT AND FLOUR OF MESLIN

046.10		**Flour of wheat or of meslin**
		Wheat flour
	110100 11 0	Of durum wheat
	110100 15 0	Of common wheat and spelt
	110100 90 0	Meslin flour
046.20		**Groats, meal and pellets, of wheat**
		Groats and meal
	110311 10 0	Durum wheat
	110311 90 0	Common wheat and spelt
	110321 00 0	Pellets

OTHER CEREAL MEALS AND FLOURS

Cereal flours (other than of wheat or meslin)

047.11		**Maize (corn) flour**
	110220 10 0	Of a fat content not exceeding 1.5 % by weight
	110220 90 0	Other
047.19		**Other**
	110210 00 0	Rye flour
	110230 00 0	Rice flour
	110290 10 0	Barley flour
	110290 30 0	Oat flour
	110290 90 0	Other

Cereal groats, meal and pellets (other than of wheat)

047.21		**Groats and meal of maize (corn)**
	110313 10 0	Of a fat content not exceeding 1.5 % by weight
	110313 90 0	Other
047.22		**Groats and meal of other cereals**
	110312 00 0	Of oats
	110314 00 0	Of rice
	110319 10 0	Of rye
	110319 30 0	Of barley
	110319 90 0	Other
047.29		**Pellets of cereals other than wheat**
	110329 10 0	Of rye
	110329 20 0	Of barley
	110329 30 0	Of oats
	110329 40 0	Of maize
	110329 50 0	Of rice
	110329 90 0	Other

CEREAL PREPARATIONS AND PREPARATIONS OF FLOUR OR STARCH OF FRUITS OR VEGETABLES

Cereal grains, worked or prepared in a manner not elsewhere specified (including 'prepared breakfast foods')

048.11		**Prepared foods obtained by the swelling or roasting of cereals or cereal products (e.g., corn flakes)**
	*190410 10 0	Obtained from maize
	*190410 30 0	Obtained from rice
	*190410 90 0	Other

S.I.T.C. (R3)	Commodity Code No	Trade description
cont 048.11		Prepared foods obtained from unroasted cereal flakes or from mixtures of unroasted cereal flakes and roasted cereal flakes or swelled cereals:
	*190420 91 0	Obtained from maize
	*190420 95 0	Obtained from rice
	*190420 99 0	Other
048.12		Cereals other than maize(corn), in grain form, precooked or otherwise prepared
	190490 10 0	Rice
	190490 90 0	Other
048.13		Other rolled or flaked cereal grains, except rice of heading 042.3
		Of barley
	110411 10 0	Rolled
	110411 90 0	Flaked
		Of oats
	110412 10 0	Rolled
	110412 90 0	Flaked
	110419 10 0	Of wheat
	110419 30 0	Of rye
	110419 50 0	Of maize
	110419 91 0	Flaked rice
	110419 99 0	Other
048.14		Other worked cereal grains (e.g. hulled, pearled, clipped, sliced or kibbled), except rice of heading 042.3
		Of barley
	110421 10 0	Hulled (shelled or husked)
	110421 30 0	Hulled and sliced or kibbled ("Grutze" or "grutten")
	110421 50 0	Pearled
	110421 90 0	Not otherwise worked than kibbled
	110421 99 0	Other
		Of oats
	*110422 20 0	Hulled (shelled or husked)
	110422 30 0	Hulled and sliced or kibbled ("Grutze" or "grutten")
	110422 50 0	Pearled
	110422 90 0	Not otherwise worked than kibbled
	110422 99 0	Other
		Of maize (corn)
	110423 10 0	Hulled (shelled or husked), whether or not sliced or kibbled
	110423 30 0	Pearled
	110423 90 0	Not otherwise worked than kibbled
	*110422 92 0	Clipped
	110423 99 0	Other
		Of other cereals
		Hulled (shelled or husked), whether or not sliced or kibbled
	110429 11 0	Of wheat
	110429 15 0	Of rye
	110429 19 0	Other
		Pearled
	110429 31 0	Of wheat
	110429 35 0	Of rye
	110429 39 0	Other
		Not otherwise worked than kibbled
	110429 51 0	Of wheat
	110429 55 0	Of rye
	110429 59 0	Other
		Other
	110429 81 0	Of wheat
	110429 85 0	Of rye
	110429 89 0	Other
048.15		Germ of cereals, whole, rolled, flaked or ground
	110430 10 0	Of wheat
	110430 90 0	Of other cereals
048.20		Malt, whether or not roasted (including malt flour)
		Not roasted
		Of wheat
	110710 11 0	In the form of flour
	110710 19 0	Other
		Other
	110710 91 0	In the form of flour
	110710 99 0	Other
	110720 00 0	Roasted
048.30		Macaroni, spaghetti and similar products (pasta), uncooked, not stuffed or otherwise prepared); couscous, whether or not prepared
	190211 00 0	Containing eggs
		Other
	190219 10 0	Containing no common wheat flour or meal

S.I.T.C. (R3)	Commodity Code No	Trade description
cont 048.30	190219 90 0	Other

Bread, pastry, cakes, biscuits and other bakers' wares, whether or not containing cocoa in any proportion; communion wafers, empty cachets of a kind suitable for pharmaceutical use, sealing wafers, rice paper and similar products

048.41		Crispbread, rusks, toasted bread and similar products
	190510 00 0	Crispbread
		Rusks, toasted bread and similar toasted products
	190540 10 0	Rusks
	190540 90 0	Other
048.42		Sweet biscuits, waffles and wafers, gingerbread and the like
		Gingerbread and the like
	190520 10 0	Containing by weight of sucrose less than 30 % (including invert sugar expressed as sucrose)
	190520 30 0	Containing by weight of sucrose 30 % or more but less than 50 % (including invert sugar expessed as sucrose)
	190520 90 0	Containing by weight of sucrose 50 % or more (including invert sugar expressed as sucrose)
		Sweet biscuits; waffles and wafers
		Completely or partially coated or covered with chocolate or other preparations containing cocoa
	190530 11 0	In immediate packings of a net content not exceeding 85 g
	190530 19 0	Other
		Other
		Sweet biscuits
	190530 30 0	Containing 8 % or more by weight of milk fats
		Other
	190530 51 0	Sandwich biscuits
	190530 59 0	Other
		Waffles and wafers
	190530 91 0	Salted, whether or not filled
	190530 99 0	Other
048.49		Other
	190590 10 0	Matzos
	190590 20 0	Communion wafers, empty cachets of a kind suitable for pharmaceutical use, sealing wafers, rice paper and similar products
		Other
	190590 30 0	Bread, not containing added honey, eggs, cheese or fruit, and containing by weight in the dry matter state not more than 5 % of sugar and not more than 5 % of fat
	190590 40 0	Waffles and wafers with a water content exceeding 10 % by weight
	190590 45 0	Biscuits
	190590 55 0	Extruded or expanded products, savoury or salted
		Other
	190590 60 0	With added sweetening matter
	190590 90 0	Other
048.50	190120 00 0	Mixes and doughs for the preparation of bakers' wares of heading 048.4

DIVISION 05

VEGETABLES AND FRUIT

VEGETABLES, FRESH, CHILLED, FROZEN OR SIMPLY PRESERVED (INCLUDING DRIED LEGUMINOUS VEGETABLES); ROOTS, TUBERS AND OTHER EDIBLE VEGETABLE PRODUCTS, N.E.S., FRESH OR DRIED

054.10		Potatoes, fresh or chilled (not including sweet potatoes)
	070110 00 0	Seed
		Other
	070190 10 0	For the manufacture of starch
		Other
		New
	070190 51 0	From 1 January to 15 May
	070190 59 0	From 16 May to 30 June
	070190 90 0	Other

Leguminous vegetables, dried, shelled, whether or not skinned or split

054.21		Peas
	071310 10 0	For sowing
	071310 90 0	Other
054.22		Chickpeas
	071320 10 0	For sowing
	071320 90 0	Other

S.I.T.C. (R3)	Commodity Code No	Trade description
054.23		**Beans, other than broad beans and horse beans**
		Beans of the species *Vigna mungo (L.) Hepper* or *Vigna radiata (L.) Wilczek*
	071331 10 0	For sowing
	071331 90 0	Other
		Small red (Adzuki) beans (*Phaseolus* or *Vigna angularis*)
	071332 10 0	For sowing
	071332 90 0	Other
		Kidney beans, including white pea beans (*Phaseolus vulgaris*)
	071333 10 0	For sowing
	071333 90 0	Other
		Other
	071339 10 0	For sowing
	071339 90 0	Other
054.24		**Lentils**
	071340 10 0	For sowing
	071340 90 0	Other
054.25		**Broad beans and horse beans**
	071350 10 0	For sowing
	071350 90 0	Other
054.29		**Other**
	071390 10 0	For sowing
	071390 90 0	Other
054.40		**Tomatoes, fresh or chilled**
	070200 15 0	From 1 January to 31 March
	070200 20 0	From 1 to 30 April
	070200 25 0	From 1 to 14 May
	070200 30 0	From 15 to 31 May
	070200 35 0	From 1 June to 30 September
	070200 40 0	From 1 to 31 October
	070200 45 0	From 1 November to 20 December
	070200 50 0	From 21 to 31 December
		Other fresh or chilled vegetables
054.51		**Onions and shallots, fresh or chilled**
		Onions
	070310 11 0	Seed
	070310 19 0	Other
	070310 90 0	Shallots
054.52		**Garlic, leeks and other alliaceous vegetables**
	070320 00 0	Garlic
	070390 00 0	Leeks and other alliaceous vegetables
054.53		**Cabbage and similar edible brassicas, fresh or chilled**
		Cauliflowers and headed broccoli
	*070410 05 0	From 1 January to 14 April
	070410 10 0	From 15 April to 30 November
	*070410 80 0	From 1 December to 31 December
	070420 00 0	Brussels sprouts
		Other
	070490 10 0	White cabbages and red cabbages
	070490 90 0	Other
054.54		**Lettuce and chicory (including endive), fresh or chilled**
		Lettuce
		Cabbage lettuce (head lettuce)
	*070511 05 0	From 1 January to 31 March
	070511 10 0	From 1 April to 30 November
	*070511 80 0	From 1 December to 31 December
	070519 00 0	Other
		Chicory
	070521 00 0	Witloof chicory (*Cichorium intybus var. foliosum*)
	070529 00 0	Other
054.55		**Carrots, turnips, salad beetroot, salsify, celeriac, radishes and similar edible roots, fresh or chilled**
	070610 00 0	Carrots and turnips
		Other
		Celeriac (rooted celery or German celery)
	*070690 05 0	From 1 January to 30 April
	070690 11 0	From 1 May to 30 September
	*070690 17 0	From 1 October to 31 December
	070690 30 0	Horse-radish (*Cochlearia armoracia*)
	070690 90 0	Other

S.I.T.C. (R3)	Commodity Code No	Trade description
054.56		Cucumbers and gherkins, fresh or chilled
		Cucumbers
	070700 10 0	From 1 January to end February
	070700 15 0	From 1 March to 30 April
	070700 20 0	From 1 to 15 May
	070700 25 0	From 16 May to 30 September
	070700 30 0	From 1 to 31 October
	070700 35 0	From 1 to 10 November
	070700 40 0	From 11 November to 31 December
	070700 90 0	Gherkins
054.57		Leguminous vegetables, fresh or chilled
		Peas (*Pisum sativum*)
	*070810 20 0	From 1 January to 31 May
	070810 90 0	From 1 June to 31 August
	*070810 95 0	From 1 September to 31 December
		Beans (*Vigna spp., Phaseolus spp.*)
	*070820 20 0	From 1 January to 30 June
	070820 90 0	From 1 July to 30 September
	*070820 95 0	From 1 October to 31 December
	070890 00 0	Other leguminous vegetables
054.58		Mushrooms and truffles
		Mushrooms
	070951 10 0	Cultivated mushrooms
	070951 30 0	Chantarelles
	070951 50 0	Flap mushrooms
	070951 90 0	Other
	070952 00 0	Truffles
054.59		Other vegetables, fresh or chilled
		Globe artichokes
	070910 10 0	From 1 January to 31 May
	070910 20 0	From 1 to 30 June
	070910 30 0	From 1 July to 31 October
	070910 40 0	From 1 November to 31 December
	070920 00 0	Asparagus
	070930 00 0	Aubergines (egg-plants)
	070940 00 0	Celery other than celeriac
		Fruits of the genus *Capsicum* or of the genus *Pimenta*
	070960 10 0	Sweet peppers
		Other
	070960 91 0	Of the genus *Capsicum*, for the manufacture of capsicin or *Capsicum* oleoresin dyes
	070960 95 0	For the industrial manufacture of essential oils or resinoids
	070960 99 0	Other
	070970 00 0	Spinach, New Zealand spinach and orache spinach (garden spinach)
		Other
	070990 10 0	Salad vegetables, other than lettuce (*Lactuca sativa*) and chicory (*cichorium spp*)
	070990 20 0	Chard (or white beet) and cardoons
		Olives
	070990 31 0	For uses other than the production of oil
	070990 39 0	Other
	070990 40 0	Capers
	070990 50 0	Fennel
	070990 60 0	Sweet corn
		Courgettes
	070990 71 0	From 1 to 31 January
	070990 73 0	From 1 February to 31 March
	070990 75 0	From 1 April to 31 May
	070990 77 0	From 1 June to 31 July
	070990 79 0	From 1 August to 31 December
	070990 90 0	Other
		Vegetables (uncooked or cooked by steaming or boiling in water), frozen
054.61	071040 00 0	Sweet corn
054.69		Other vegetables and mixtures of vegetables
	071010 00 0	Potatoes
		Leguminous vegetables, shelled or unshelled
	071021 00 0	Peas (*Pisum sativum*)
	071022 00 0	Beans (*Vigna spp., Phaseolus spp.*)
	071029 00 0	Other
	071030 00 0	Spinach, New Zealand spinach and orache spinach (garden spinach)
		Other vegetables
	071080 10 0	Olives
		Fruits of the genus *Capsicum* or of the genus *Pimenta*
	071080 51 0	Sweet pepper
	071080 59 0	Other

S.I.T.C. (R3)	Commodity Code No	Trade description
cont 054.69		Mushrooms
	*071080 61 0	Of the genus Agaricus
	*071080 69 0	Other
	071080 70 0	Tomatoes
	071080 80 0	Globe artichokes
	071080 85 0	Asparagus
	071080 95 0	Other
	071090 00 0	Mixtures of vegetables
054.70		Vegetables provisionally preserved (e.g., by sulphur dioxide gas, in brine, in sulphur water or in other preservative solutions), but unsuitable in that state for immediate consumption
	071110 00 0	Onions
		Olives
	071120 10 0	For uses other than the production of oil
	071120 90 0	Other
	071130 00 0	Capers
	071140 00 0	Cucumbers and gherkins
		Other vegetables; mixtures of vegetables
		Vegetables
	071190 10 0	Fruits of the genus *Capsicum* or of the genus *Pimenta*, excluding sweet peppers
	071190 30 0	Sweet corn
		Mushrooms
	071190 40 0	Of the genus *Agaricus*
	071190 60 0	Other
	071190 70 0	Other
	071190 90 0	Mixtures of vegetables

Vegetable products, roots and tubers, chiefly for human food, n.e.s., fresh or dried

S.I.T.C. (R3)	Commodity Code No	Trade description
054.81		Manioc (cassava) fresh or dried, whether or not sliced or in the form of pellets
	071410 10 0	Pellets of flour and meal
		Other
	071410 91 0	Of a kind used for human consumption in immediate packings of a net content not exceeding 28 kg either fresh and whole or without skin and frozen whether or not sliced
	071410 99 0	Other
054.83		Arrowroot, salep, Jerusalem artichokes, sweet potatoes and similar roots and tubers (other than manioc) with high starch or inulin content, fresh or dried, whether or not sliced or in the form of pellets; sago pith
		Sweet potatoes
	071420 10 0	Fresh, whole, intended for human consumption
	071420 90 0	Other
		Other
		Arrowroot, salep and other similar roots and tubers with high starch content
	071490 11 0	Of a kind used for human consumption in immediate packings of a net content not exceeding 28 kg either fresh and whole or without skin, whether or not sliced
	071490 19 0	Other
	071490 90 0	Other
054.84		Hop cones and lupulin
	121010 00 0	Hop cones, neither ground nor powdered nor in the form of pellets
		Hop cones, ground, powdered or in the form of pellets; lupulin
	121020 10 0	Hop cones, ground, powdered or in the form of pellets, with higher lupulin content; lupulin
	121020 90 0	Other
054.85	121230 00 0	Apricot, peach or plum stones and kernels, fresh or dried, whether or not ground
054.87		Sugar beet, fresh or dried, whether or not ground
	*121291 20 0	Dried, whether or not ground
	*121291 80 0	Other
054.88	121292 00 0	Sugar cane, fresh or dried, whether or not ground
054.89		Vegetable products of a kind used chiefly for human foods, n.e.s.
		Locust beans, including locust bean seeds
	121210 10 0	Locust beans
		Locust bean seeds
	121210 91 0	Not decorticated, crushed or ground
	121210 99 0	Other
		Other
	121299 10 0	Chicory roots
	121299 90 0	Other

VEGETABLES, ROOTS AND TUBERS, PREPARED OR PRESERVED, N.E.S.

Vegetables, dried (excluding leguminous vegetables), whole, cut, sliced, broken or in powder, but not further prepared

S.I.T.C. (R3)	Commodity Code No	Trade description
056.11	*071290 05 0	Potatoes, whether or not cut or sliced but not further prepared

S.I.T.C. (R3)	Commodity Code No	Trade description
056.12	071220 00 0	Onions
056.13	071230 00 0	Mushrooms and truffles
056.19		Other vegetables; mixtures of vegetables
		Sweet corn (zea mays var. saccharata)
	071290 11 0	Hybrid, for sowing
	071290 19 0	Other
	071290 30 0	Tomatoes
	071290 50 0	Carrots
	071290 90 0	Other
		Flours, meals, flakes, granules and pellets of potatoes, fruits and vegetables, n.e.s.
056.41	110510 00 0	Flour and meal of potato
056.42	110520 00 0	Flakes, granules and pellets of potato
056.45	190300 00 0	Tapioca and substitutes therefor prepared from starch, in the form of flakes, grains, pearls, siftings or similar forms.
056.46	110610 00 0	Flour and meal of the dried leguminous vegetables of heading 054.2
056.47		Flour and meal of sago, roots or tubers of headings 054.81 and 054.83
	110620 10 0	Denatured
	110620 90 0	Other
056.48		Flour, meal and powder of the products of any heading of group 057
	110630 10 0	Of bananas
	110630 90 0	Other
		Vegetable prepared or preserved otherwise than by vinegar or acetic acid, n.e.s. frozen
056.61		Potatoes prepared or preserved otherwise than by vinegar or acetic acid, frozen
	200410 10 0	Cooked, not otherwise prepared
		Other
	200410 91 0	In the form of flour, meal or flakes
	200410 99 0	Other
056.69		Other vegetables and mixtures of vegetables prepared or preserved otherwise than by vinegar or acetic acid, frozen
	200490 10 0	Sweet corn (Zea mays var. saccharata)
	200490 30 0	Sauerkraut, capers and olives
	200490 50 0	Peas (Pisum sativum) and immature beans of the species Phaseolus spp., in pod
		Other, including mixtures
	200490 91 0	Onions, cooked, not otherwise prepared
	*200490 98 0	Other
		Vegetables, prepared or preserved, n.e.s.
056.71		Vegetables, fruit, nuts and other edible parts of plants, prepared or preserved by vinegar or acetic acid
	200110 00 0	Cucumbers and gherkins
	200120 00 0	Onions
		Other
	200190 10 0	Mango chutney
	200190 20 0	Fruit of the genus Capsicum other than sweet peppers or pimentos
	200190 30 0	Sweet corn (Zea mays var. saccharata)
	200190 40 0	Yams, sweet potatoes and similar edible parts of plants containing 5 % or more by weight of starch
	200190 50 0	Mushrooms
	200190 60 0	Palm hearts
	200190 65 0	Olives
	200190 70 0	Sweet peppers
	200190 75 0	Salad beetroot (Beta vulgaris var. Conditiva)
	200190 85 0	Red cabbage
	200190 91 0	Tropical fruit and tropical nuts
	200190 96 0	Other
056.72		Tomatoes prepared or preserved otherwise than by vinegar or acetic acid, whole or in pieces
	200210 10 0	Peeled
	200210 90 0	Other
056.73		Tomatoes, prepared or preserved otherwise than by vinegar or acetic acid, n.e.s.
		With a dry matter content of less than 12 % by weight
	200290 11 0	In immediate packings of a net content exceeding 1 kg
	200290 19 0	In immediate packings of a net content not exceeding 1 kg
		With a dry matter content of not less than 12 % but not more than 30 % by weight
	200290 31 0	In immediate packings of a net content exceeding 1 kg
	200290 39 0	In immediate packings of a net content not exceeding 1 kg

S.I.T.C. (R3)	Commodity Code No	Trade description

cont
056.73

    With a dry matter content of more than 30 % by weight

        200290 91 0 — In immediate packings of a net content exceeding 1 kg

        200290 99 0 — In immediate packings of a net content not exceeding 1 kg

056.74   Mushrooms and truffles prepared or preserved otherwise than by vinegar or acetic acid

    Mushrooms

      Of the genus *Agaricus*

        200310 20 0 — Provisionally preserved, completely cooked

        200310 30 0 — Other

        200310 80 0 — Other

        200320 00 0 Truffles

056.75   *200590 75 0   Sauerkraut prepared or preserved otherwise than by vinegar or acetic acid, not frozen

056.76   Potatoes prepared or preserved otherwise than by acetic acid, not frozen

        200520 10 0 In the form of flour, meal or flakes

    Other

        200520 20 0 — Thinly sliced, fried or baked, whether or not salted or flavoured, in airtight packings, suitable for immediate consumption

        200520 80 0 — Other

056.77   200580 00 0   Sweet corn

056.79   Other vegetables prepared or preserved otherwise than by vinegar or acetic acid, not frozen

        200540 00 0 Peas (*Pisum sativum*)

    Beans (*Vigna spp.*, *Phaseolus spp.*)

        200551 00 0 — Shelled

        200559 00 0 — Other

        200560 00 0 Asparagus

    Olives

        200570 10 0 — In immediate packings of a net content not exceeding 5 kg

        200570 90 0 — Other

    Other vegetables and mixtures of vegetables

        200590 10 0 — Fruit of the genus *Capsicum* other than sweet peppers or pimentos

        200590 30 0 — Capers

        200590 50 0 — Globe artichokes

        200590 60 0 — Carrots

        200590 70 0 — Mixtures of vegetables

        200590 80 0 — Other

FRUIT AND NUTS (NOT INCLUDING OIL NUTS), FRESH OR DRIED

Oranges, mandarins, clementines and similar citrus hybrids, fresh or dried

057.11   Oranges, fresh or dried

    Sweet oranges, fresh

      From 1 January to 31 March

        080510 01 0 — Sanguines and semi-sanguines

      Other

        080510 05 0 — Navels, Navelines, Navelates, Salustianas, Vernas, Valencia lates, Maltese, Shamoutis, Ovalis, Trovita and Hamlins

        080510 09 0 — Other

      From 1 to 30 April

        080510 11 0 — Sanguines and semi-sanguines

        080510 15 0 — Navels, Navelines, Navelates, Salustianas, Vernas, Valencia lates, Maltese, Shamoutis, Ovalis, Trovita and Hamlins

        080510 19 0 — Other

      From 1 to 15 May

        080510 21 0 — Sanguines and semi-sanguines

        080510 25 0 — Navels, Navelines, Navelates, Salustianas, Vernas, Valencia lates, Maltese, Shamoutis, Ovalis, Trovita and Hamlins

        080510 29 0 — Other

      From 16 May to 31 May

        *080510 31 0 — Sanguines and semi-sanguines

      Other

        *080510 33 0 — Navels, Navelines, Navelates, Salustianas, Vernas, Valencia lates, Maltese, Shamoutis, Ovalis, Trovita and Hamlins

        *080510 35 0 — Other

      From 1 June to 30 September

        *080510 37 0 — Sanguines and semi-sanguines

      Other

        *080510 38 0 — Navels, Navelines, Navelates, Salustianas, Vernas, Valencia lates, Maltese, Shamoutis, Ovalis, Trovita and Hamlins

        *080510 39 0 — Other

      From 1 to 15 October

        080510 42 0 — Sanguines and semi-sanguines

      Other

        080510 44 0 — Navels, Navelines, Navelates, Salustianas, Vernas, Valencia lates, Maltese, Shamoutis, Ovalis, Trovita and Hamlins

S.I.T.C. (R3)	Commodity Code No	Trade description
cont 057.11	080510 46 0	Other
		From 16 October to 30 November
	080510 51 0	Sanguines and semi-sanguines
		Other
	080510 55 0	Navels, Navelines, Navelates, Salustianas, Vernas, Valencia lates, Maltese, Shamoutis, Ovalis, Trovita and Hamlins
	080510 59 0	Other
		From 1 to 31 December
	080510 61 0	Sanguines and semi-sanguines
		Other
	080510 65 0	Navels, Navelines, Navelates, Salustianas, Vernas, Valencia lates, Maltese, Shamoutis, Ovalis, Trovita and Hamlins
	080510 69 0	Other
		Other
	080510 82 0	From 1 January to 31 March
	080510 84 0	From 1 April to 15 October
	080510 86 0	From 16 October to 31 December
057.12		**Mandarins (including tangerines and satsumas); clementines, wilkings and similar citrus hybrids, fresh or dried**
		From 1st January to end February
	080520 11 0	Clementines
	080520 13 0	Monreales and satsumas
	080520 15 0	Mandarins and wilkings
	080520 17 0	Tangerines
	080520 19 0	Other
		From 1 March 31 October
	080520 21 0	Clementines
	080520 23 0	Monreales and satsumas
	080520 25 0	Mandarins and wilkings
	080520 27 0	Tangerines
	080520 29 0	Other
		From 1 November to 31 December
	080520 31 0	Clementines
	080520 33 0	Monreales and satsumas
	080520 35 0	Mandarins and wilkings
	080520 37 0	Tangerines
	080520 39 0	Other
		Other citrus fruit, fresh or dried
057.21		**Lemons and limes, fresh or dried**
		Lemons (*Citrus limon, Citrus limonum*)
	080530 20 0	From 1 January to 31 May
	080530 30 0	From 1 June to 31 October
	080530 40 0	From 1 November to 31 December
	080530 90 0	Limes (*Citrus aurantifolia*)
057.22		**Grapefruit, fresh or dried**
	*080540 20 0	From 1 January to 30 April
	080540 10 0	From 1 May to 31 October
	*080540 90 0	From 1 November 1 to 31 December
057.29	080590 00 0	**Citrus fruit, n.e.s., fresh or dried**
057.30		**Bananas (including plantains), fresh or dried**
		Fresh
	080300 11 0	Plantains
	080300 19 0	Other
	080300 90 0	Dried
057.40		**Apples, fresh**
	080810 10 0	Cider apples, in bulk, from 16 September to 15 December
		Other
		From 1 January to 31 March
	080810 51 0	Of the variety Golden Delicious
	080810 53 0	Of the variety Granny Smith
	080810 59 0	Other
		From 1 April to 30 June
	080810 61 0	Of the variety Golden Delicious
	080810 63 0	Of the variety Granny Smith
	080810 69 0	Other
		From 1 to 31 July
	080810 71 0	Of the variety Golden Delicious
	080810 73 0	Of the variety Granny Smith
	080810 79 0	Other
		From 1 August to 31 December
	080810 92 0	Of the variety Golden Delicious

S.I.T.C. (R3)	Commodity Code No	Trade description
cont 057.40	080810 94 0 080810 98 0	Of the variety Granny Smith Other

Grapes, fresh or dried

057.51		Grapes, fresh
		Table grapes
		From 1 January to 14 July
	080610 21 0	Of the variety Emperor (*Vitis vinifera cv.*) from 1 to 31 January
	080610 29 0	Other
	080610 30 0	From 15 to 20 July
	080610 40 0	From 21 July to 31 October
	080610 50 0	From 1 to 20 November
		From 21 November to 31 December
	080610 61 0	Of the variety Emperor (*Vitis vinifera cv.*) from 1 to 31 December
	*080610 69 0	Other
		Other
	*080610 93 0	From 1 January to 14 July
	*080610 95 0	From 15 July to 31 October
	*080610 97 0	From 1 November to 31 December

057.52		Grapes, dried (e.g., raisins)
		In immediate containers of a net capacity not exceeding 2 kg
	080620 11 0	Currants
	080620 12 0	Sultanas
	080620 18 0	Other
		Other
	080620 91 0	Currants
	080620 92 0	Sultanas
	080620 98 0	Other

057.60		Figs, fresh or dried
	080420 10 0	Fresh
	080420 90 0	Dried

Edible nuts (excluding nuts chiefly used for the extraction of oil), fresh or dried, whether or not shelled or peeled

057.71		Coconuts
	*080111 00 0	Desiccated coconut
	*080119 00 0	Other

		Brazil nuts
057.72	*080120 00 0	In shelled
	*080122 00 0	Shelled

		Cashew nuts
057.73	*080131 00 0	In shell
	*080132 00 0	Shelled

057.74		Almonds
		In shell
	080211 10 0	Bitter
	080211 90 0	Other
		Shelled
	080212 10 0	Bitter
	080212 90 0	Other

057.75		Hazelnuts or filberts
	080221 00 0	In shell
	080222 00 0	Shelled

057.76		Walnuts
	080231 00 0	In shell
	080232 00 0	Shelled

057.77	080240 00 0	Chestnuts

057.78	080250 00 0	Pistachios

057.79		Edible nuts (excl. mixtures), fresh or dried, n.e.s. whether or not shelled or peeled
	080290 10 0	Pecans
	080290 30 0	Areca (or betel) and cola
	080290 50 0	Pine nuts
	080290 60 0	Macadamia nuts
	080290 85 0	Other

S.I.T.C. (R3)	Commodity Code No	Trade description
		Fruit, fresh or dried, n.e.s.
057.91		Melons (incl. water melons) and papaws (papayas), fresh
		Melons (including watermelons)
	*080711 00 0	Watermelons
	*080719 00 0	Other
	080720 00 0	Papaws (papayas)
057.92		Pears and quinces, fresh
		Pears
	080820 10 0	Perry pears, in bulk, from 1 August to 31 December
		Other
	080820 31 0	From 1 January to 31 March
	080820 37 0	From 1 to 30 April
	080820 41 0	From 1 May to 30 June
	080820 47 0	From 1 to 15 July
	080820 51 0	From 16 to 31 July
	080820 57 0	From 1 August to 31 October
	080820 67 0	From 1 November to 31 December
	080820 90 0	Quinces
057.93		Apricots, cherries, peaches (including nectarines), plums and sloes, fresh
		Apricots
	080910 10 0	From 1 January to 31 May
	080910 20 0	From 1 to 20 June
	080910 30 0	From 21 to 30 June
	080910 40 0	From 1 to 31 July
	080910 50 0	From 1 August to 31 December
		Cherries
		From 1 January to 30 April
	080920 11 0	Sour cherries (*Prunus cerasus*)
	080920 19 0	Other
		From 1 to 20 May
	080920 21 0	Sour cherries (*Prunus cerasus*)
	080920 29 0	Other
		From 21 to 31 May
	080920 31 0	Sour cherries (*Prunus cerasus*)
	080920 39 0	Other
		From 1 June to 15 July
	080920 41 0	Sour cherries (*Prunus cerasus*)
	080920 49 0	Other
		From 16 to 31 July
	080920 51 0	Sour cherries (*Prunus cerasus*)
	080920 59 0	Other
		From 1 to 10 August
	080920 61 0	Sour cherries (*Prunus cerasus*)
	080920 69 0	Other
		From 11 August to 31 December
	080920 71 0	Sour cherries (*Prunus cerasus*)
	080920 79 0	Other
		Peaches, including nectarines
		From 1 January to 10 June
	080930 11 0	Nectarines
	080930 19 0	Other
		From 11 to 20 June
	080930 21 0	Nectarines
	080930 29 0	Other
		From 21 June to 31 July
	080930 31 0	Nectarines
	080930 39 0	Other
		From 1 August to 30 September
	080930 41 0	Nectarines
	080930 49 0	Other
		From 1 October to 31 December
	080930 51 0	Nectarines
	080930 59 0	Other
		Plums and sloes
		Plums
	080940 10 0	From 1 January to 10 June
	080940 20 0	From 11 to 30 June
	080940 30 0	From 1 July to 30 September
	080940 40 0	From 1 October to 31 December
	080940 90 0	Sloes
057.94		Berries, fresh
		Strawberries
	*081010 05 0	From 1 January to 30 April
	*081010 80 0	May to 31 July

S.I.T.C. (R3)	Commodity Code No	Trade description
cont 057.94		Raspberries, blackberries, mulberries and loganberries
	081020 10 0	Raspberries
	081020 90 0	Other
		Black, white or red currants and gooseberries
	081030 10 0	Black currants
	081030 30 0	Red currants
	081030 90 0	Other
		Cranberries, bilberries and other fruits of the genus *Vaccinium*
	081040 10 0	Cowberries, foxberries or mountain cranberries (fruit of the species *Vaccinium vitis-idaea*)
	081040 30 0	Fruit of the species *Vaccinium myrtillus*
	081040 50 0	Fruit of the species *Vaccinium macrocarpum* and *Vaccinium corymbosum*
	081040 90 0	Other
057.95	080430 00 0	Pineapples, fresh or dried
057.96	080410 00 0	Dates, fresh or dried
057.97		Avocados, guavas, mangoes and mangosteens, fresh or dried
		Avocados
	*080440 20 0	From 1 January to 31 May
	*080440 90 0	From 1 June to 30 November
	080440 95 0	From 1 December to 31 December
	080450 00 0	Guavas, mangoes and mangosteens
057.98		Other fresh fruit
	*081050 00 0	Kiwifruit
	081090 30 0	Tamarinds, cashew apples, lychees, jackfruit, sapodillo plums
	081090 40 0	Passion fruit, carambola and pitahaya
	081090 85 0	Other
057.99		Fruit, dried, n.e.s., and mixtures, n.e.s., of nuts or dried fruits of group 057
	081310 00 0	Apricots
	081320 00 0	Prunes
	081330 00 0	Apples
	081340 10 0	Peaches, including nectarines
	081340 30 0	Pears
	081340 50 0	Papaws (papayas)
	081340 60 0	Tamarinds
	081340 70 0	Cashew apples, lychees, jackfruit, sapodillo plums, passion fruit, carambola and pitahaya
	081340 95 0	Other
		Mixtures of nuts or dried fruits of this Chapter
		Fruit salads of dried fruit, other than that of headings 08.01 to 08.06
		Not containing prunes
	081350 12 0	Of papaws (papayas), tamarinds, cashew apples, lychees, jackfruit, sapodillo plums, passion fruit, carambola and pitahaya
	081350 15 0	Other
	081350 19 0	Containing prunes
		Mixtures exclusively of dried nuts of headings 08.01 and 08.02 inclusive
	081350 31 0	Of tropical nuts
	081350 39 0	Other
		Other mixtures
	081350 91 0	Not containing prunes or figs
	081350 99 0	Other

FRUIT, PRESERVED, AND FRUIT PREPARATIONS (EXCLUDING FRUIT JUICES)

S.I.T.C. (R3)	Commodity Code No	Trade description
058.10		Jams, fruit jellies, marmalades, fruit or nut puree and fruit or nut pastes, being cooked preparations, whether or not containing added sugar or other sweetening matter, not including homogenized preparations
		Citrus fruit
	200791 10 0	With a sugar content exceeding 30 % by weight
	200791 30 0	With a sugar content exceeding 13 % but not exceeding 30 % by weight
	200791 90 0	Other
		Other
		With a sugar content exceeding 30 % by weight
	200799 10 0	Plum purée and paste and prune purée and paste, in immediate packings of a net content exceeding 100 kg, for industrial processing
	200799 20 0	Chestnut purée and paste
		Other
	200799 31 0	Of cherries
	200799 33 0	Of strawberries
	200799 35 0	Of raspberries
	200799 39 0	Other
		With a sugar content exceeding 13 % but not exceeding 30 %
	200799 51 0	Chestnut purée and paste
	200799 55 0	Apple purée, including compotes
	200799 58 0	Other
		Other
	200799 91 0	Apple purée, including compotes

S.I.T.C. (R3)	Commodity Code No	Trade description
cont 058.10	200799 93 0	Of tropical fruit and tropical nuts
	200799 98 0	Other

Fruit and nuts provisionally preserved; peel of citrus fruit or melons.

S.I.T.C. (R3)	Commodity Code No	Trade description
058.21		**Fruit and nuts provisionally preserved (e.g., by sulphur dioxide gas, in brine, in sulphur water or in other preservative solutions), but unsuitable in that state for immediate consumption**
	081210 00 0	Cherries
	081220 00 0	Strawberries
	081290 10 0	Apricots
	081290 20 0	Oranges
	081290 30 0	Papaws (papayas)
	081290 40 0	Fruit of the species *Vaccinium myrtillus*
	081290 50 0	Black currants
	081290 60 0	Raspberries
	081290 70 0	Guavas, mangoes, mangosteens, tamarinds, cashew apples, lychees, jackfruit, sapodillo plums, passion fruit, carambola, pitahaya and tropical nuts
	081290 95 0	Other
058.22	081400 00 0	**Peel of citrus fruit or melons, fresh, frozen, dried or provisionally preserved in brine, in sulphur water or in other preservative solutions**

Fruit and nuts, uncooked or cooked by steaming or boiling in water, frozen, whether or not containing added sugar or other sweetening matter

S.I.T.C. (R3)	Commodity Code No	Trade description
058.31		**Strawberries**
		Containing added sugar or other sweetening matter
	081110 11 0	With a sugar content exceeding 13 % by weight
	081110 19 0	Other
	081110 90 0	Other
058.32		**Raspberries, blackberries, mulberries, loganberries, black, white or red currants and gooseberries**
		Containing added sugar or other sweetening matter
	081120 11 0	With a sugar content exceeding 13 % by weight
	081120 19 0	Other
		Other
	081120 31 0	Raspberries
	081120 39 0	Black currants
	081120 51 0	Red currants
	081120 59 0	Blackberries and mulberries
	081120 90 0	Other
058.39		**Other**
		Containing added sugar or other sweetening matter
		With a sugar content exceeding 13 % by weight
	081190 11 0	Tropical fruit and tropical nuts
	081190 19 0	Other
		Other
	081190 31 0	Tropical fruit and tropical nuts
	081190 39 0	Other
		Other
	081190 50 0	Fruit of the species *Vaccinium myrtillus*
	081190 70 0	Fruit of the species *Vaccinium myrtilloides* and *Vaccinium angustifolium*
		Cherries
	081190 75 0	Sour cherries (*Prunus cerasus*)
	081190 80 0	Other
	081190 85 0	Tropical fruit and tropical nuts
	081190 95 0	Other

Fruit, nuts and other edible parts of plants otherwise prepared or preserved, n.e.s., whether or not containing added sugar or other sweetening matter or spirit

S.I.T.C. (R3)	Commodity Code No	Trade description
058.92		**Nuts, groundnuts and other seeds, prepared or preserved, n.e.s.**
		Ground-nuts
	200811 10 0	Peanut butter
		Other, in immediate packings of a net content
		Exceeding 1 kg
	*200811 92 0	Roasted
	*200811 94 0	Other
		Not exceeding 1 kg
	200811 96 0	Roasted
	200811 98 0	Other
		Other, including mixtures
		In immediate packings of a net content exceeding 1 kg
	200819 11 0	Tropical nuts; mixtures containing 50 % or more by weight of tropical nuts and tropical fruit
		Other
	200819 13 0	Roasted almonds and pistachios

S.I.T.C. (R3)	Commodity Code No	Trade description

cont
058.92 200819 19 0 — Other
    — In immediate packings of a net content not exceeding 1 kg
      — Tropical nuts; mixtures containing 50 % or more by weight of tropical nuts and tropical fruit
*200819 51 0 — Roasted tropical nuts
*200819 59 0 — Other
    — Other
      — Roasted nuts
200819 93 0 — Almonds and pistachios
200819 95 0 — Other
200819 99 0 — Other

058.93   **Pineapples**
    — Containing added spirit
      — In immediate packings of a net content exceeding 1 kg
200820 11 0 — With a sugar content exceeding 17 % by weight
200820 19 0 — Other
      — In immediate packings of a net content not exceeding 1 kg
200820 31 0 — With a sugar content exceeding 19 % by weight
200820 39 0 — Other
    — Not containing added spirit
      — Containing added sugar, in immediate packings of a net content exceeding 1 kg
200820 51 0 — With a sugar content exceeding 17 % by weight
200820 59 0 — Other
      — Containing added sugar, in immediate packings of a net content not exceeding 1 kg
200820 71 0 — With a sugar content exceeding 19 % by weight
200820 79 0 — Other
      — Not containing added sugar, in immediate packings of a net content
200820 91 0 — Of 4.5 kg or more
200820 99 0 — Of less than 4.5 kg

058.94   **Citrus fruit**
    — Containing added spirit
      — With a sugar content exceeding 9 % by weight
200830 11 0 — Of an actual alcoholic strength by mass not exceeding 11.85 % mas
200830 19 0 — Other
      — Other
200830 31 0 — Of an actual alcoholic strength by mass not exceeding 11.85 % mas
200830 39 0 — Other
    — Not containing added spirit
      — Containing added sugar, in immediate packings of a net content exceeding 1 kg
200830 51 0 — Grapefruit segments
200830 55 0 — Mandarins (including tangerines and satsumas); clementines, wilkings and other similar citrus hybrids
200830 59 0 — Other
      — Containing added sugar, in immediate packings of a net content not exceeding 1 kg
200830 71 0 — Grapefruit segments
200830 75 0 — Mandarins (including tangerines and satsumas); clementines, wilkings and other similar citrus hybrids
200830 79 0 — Other
      — Not containing added sugar, in immediate packings of a net content
200830 91 0 — Of 4.5 kg or more
200830 99 0 — Of less than 4.5 kg

058.95   **Apricots, cherries and peaches**
    — Apricots
      — Containing added spirit
        — In immediate packings of a net content exceeding 1 kg
        — With a sugar content exceeding 13 % by weight
200850 11 0 — Of an actual alcoholic strength by mass not exceeding 11.85 % mas
200850 19 0 — Other
        — Other
200850 31 0 — Of an actual alcoholic strength by mass not exceeding 11.85 % mas
200850 39 0 — Other
        — In immediate packings of a net content not exceeding 1 kg
200850 51 0 — With a sugar content exceeding 15 % by weight
200850 59 0 — Other
      — Not containing added spirit
        — Containing added sugar, in immediate packings of a net content exceeding 1 kg
200850 61 0 — With a sugar content exceeding 13 % by weight
200850 69 0 — Other
        — Containing added sugar, in immediate packings of a net content not exceeding 1 kg
200850 71 0 — With a sugar content exceeding 15 % by weight
200850 79 0 — Other
        — Not containing added sugar, in immediate packings of a net content
200850 92 0 — Of 5 kg or more
200850 94 0 — Of less than 5 kg, but not less than 4.5 kg
200850 99 0 — Of less than 4.5 kg
    — Cherries
      — Containing added spirit
        — With a sugar content exceeding 9 % by weight

S.I.T.C. (R3)	Commodity Code No	Trade description
cont 058.95	200860 11 0	Of an actual alcoholic strength by mass not exceeding 11.85 % mas
	200860 19 0	Other
		Other
	200860 31 0	Of an actual alcoholic strength by mass not exceeding 11.85 % mas
	200860 39 0	Other
		Not containing added spirit
		Containing added sugar, in immediate packings of a net content exceeding 1 kg
	200860 51 0	Sour cherries (*prunus cerasus*)
	200860 59 0	Other
		Containing added sugar, in immediate packings of a net content not exceeding 1 kg
	200860 61 0	Sour cherries (*prunus cerasus*)
	200860 69 0	Other
		Not containing added sugar, in immediate packings of a net content
		Of 4.5 kg or more
	200860 71 0	Sour cherries (*prunus cerasus*)
	200860 79 0	Other
		Of less than 4.5 kg
	200860 91 0	Sour cherries (*prunus cerasus*)
	200860 99 0	Other
		Peaches
		Containing added spirit
		In immediate packings of a net content exceeding 1 kg
		With a sugar content exceeding 13 % by weight
	200870 11 0	Of an actual alcoholic strength by mass not exceeding 11.85 % mas
	200870 19 0	Other
		Other
	200870 31 0	Of an actual alcoholic strength by mass not exceeding 11.85 % mas
	200870 39 0	Other
		In immediate packings of a net content not exceeding 1 kg
	200870 51 0	With a sugar content exceeding 15 % by weight
	200870 59 0	Other
		Not containing added spirit
		Containing added sugar, in immediate packings of a net content exceeding 1 kg
	200870 61 0	With a sugar content exceeding 13 % by weight
	200870 69 0	Other
		Containing added sugar, in immediate packings of a net content not exceeding 1 kg
	200870 71 0	With a sugar content exceeding 15 % by weight
	200870 79 0	Other
		Not containing added sugar, in immediate packings of a net content
	200870 92 0	Of 5 kg or more
	200870 94 0	Of less than 5 kg, but not less than 4.5 kg
	200870 99 0	Of less than 4.5 kg
058.96		**Fruits or edible parts of plants, prepared or preserved, n.e.s.**
		Pears
		Containing added spirit
		In immediate packings of a net content exceeding 1 kg
		With a sugar content exceeding 13 % by weight
	200840 11 0	Of an actual alcoholic strength by mass not exceeding 11.85 % mas
	200840 19 0	Other
		Other
	200840 21 0	Of an actual alcoholic strength by mass not exceeding 11.85 % mas
	200840 29 0	Other
		In immediate packings of a net content not exceeding 1 kg
	200840 31 0	With a sugar content exceeding 15 % by weight
	200840 39 0	Other
		Not containing added spirit
		Containing added sugar, in immediate packings of a net content exceeding 1 kg
	200840 51 0	With a sugar content exceeding 13 % by weight
	200840 59 0	Other
		Containing added sugar, in immediate packings of a net content not exceeding 1 kg
	200840 71 0	With a sugar content exceeding 15 % in weight
	200840 79 0	Other
		Not containing added sugar, in immediate packings of a net content
	200840 91 0	Of 4.5 kg or more
	200840 99 0	Of less than 4.5 kg
		Strawberries
		Containing added spirit
		With a sugar content exceeding 9 % by weight
	200880 11 0	Of an actual alcoholic strength by mass not exceeding 11.85 % mas
	200880 19 0	Other
		Other
	200880 31 0	Of an actual alcoholic strength by mass not exceeding 11.85 % mas
	200880 39 0	Other
		Not containing added spirit
	200880 50 0	Containing added sugar, in immediate packings of a net content exceeding 1 kg
	200880 70 0	Containing added sugar, in immediate packings of a net content not exceeding 1 kg
		Not containing added sugar, in immediate packings of a net content

S.I.T.C. (R3)	Commodity Code No	Trade description
cont 058.96	200880 91 0	Of 4.5 kg or more
	200880 99 0	Of less than 4.5 kg
		Other, including mixtures other than those of subheading No. 2008.19
	200891 00 0	Palm hearts
		Other
		Containing added spirit
		Ginger
	200899 11 0	Of an actual alcoholic strength by mass not exceeding 11.85 % mas
	200899 19 0	Other
		Grapes
	200899 21 0	With a sugar content exceeding 13 % by weight
	200899 23 0	Other
		Other
		With a sugar content exceeding 9 % by weight
		Of an actual alcoholic strength by mass not exceeding 11.85 % mas
	200899 25 0	Passion fruit and guavas
	200899 26 0	Mangoes, mangosteens, papaws (papayas), tamarinds, cashew apples, lychees, jackfruit, sapodillo plums, carambola and pitahaya
	200899 28 0	Other
		Other
	200899 32 0	Passion fruit and guavas
	200899 33 0	Mangoes, mangosteens, papaws (papayas), tamarinds, cashew apples, lychees, jackfruit, sapodillo plums, carambola and pitahaya
	200899 34 0	Other
		Other
		Of an actual alcoholic strength by mass not exceeding 11.85 % mas
	200899 36 0	Tropical fruit
	200899 37 0	Other
		Other
	200899 38 0	Tropical fruit
	200899 40 0	Other
		Not containing added spirit
		Containing added sugar, in immediate packings of a net content exceeding 1 kg
	200899 41 0	Ginger
	200899 43 0	Grapes
	200899 45 0	Plums and prunes
	200899 46 0	Passion fruit, guavas and tamarinds
	200899 47 0	Mangoes, mangosteens, papaws (papayas), tamarinds, cashew apples, lychees, jackfruit, sapodillo plums, carambola and pitahaya
	200899 49 0	Other
		Containing added sugar, in immediate packings of a net content not exceeding 1 kg
	200899 51 0	Ginger
	200899 53 0	Grapes
	200899 55 0	Plums and prunes
	200899 61 0	Passion fruit and guavas
	200899 62 0	Mangoes, mangosteens, papaws (papayas), tamarinds, cashew apples, lychees, jackfruit, sapodillo plums, carambola and pitahaya
	200899 68 0	Other
		Not containing added sugar
		Plums and prunes, in immediate packings of a net content
	200899 72 0	Of 5 kg or more
	200899 74 0	Of less than 5 kg, but not less than 4.5 kg
	200899 79 0	Of less than 4.5 kg
	200899 85 0	Maize (corn) other than sweet corn (*Zea mays var. Saccharata*)
	200899 91 0	Yams, sweet potatoes and similar edible parts of plants, containing 5 % or more by weight of starch
	200899 99 0	Other
058.97		**Mixtures of fruits or other edible parts of plants, prepared or preserved, n.e.s.**
		Containing added spirit
		With a sugar content exceeding 9 % by weight
		Of an actual alcoholic strength by mass not exceeding 11.85 % mas
	200892 12 0	Of tropical fruit (including mixtures containing 50 % or more by weight of tropical nuts and tropical fruit
	200892 14 0	Other
		Other
	200892 16 0	Of tropical fruit (including mixtures containing 50 % or more by weight of tropical nuts and tropical fruit)
	200892 18 0	Other
		Other
		Of an actual alcoholic strength by mass not exceeding 11.85 % mas
	200892 32 0	Of tropical fruit (including mixtures containing 50 % or more by weight of tropical nuts and tropical fruit)
	200892 34 0	Other
		Other
	200892 36 0	Of tropical fruit (including mixtures containing 50 % or more by weight of tropical nuts and tropical fruit)
	200892 38 0	Other
		Not containing added spirit
	*190420 10 0	Preparation of the Musli type based on unroasted cereal flakes

S.I.T.C. (R3)	Commodity Code No	Trade description
cont 058.97		Other
		Containing added sugar
		In immediate packings of a net content exceeding 1 kg
	200892 51 0	Of tropical fruit (including mixtures containing 50 % or more by weight of tropical nuts and tropical fruit)
	200892 59 0	Other
		Other
		Mixtures of fruit in which no single fruit exceeds 50 % of the total weight of the fruits
	200892 72 0	Of tropical fruit (including mixtures containing 50 % or more by weight of tropical nuts and tropical fruit)
	200892 74 0	Other
		Other
	200892 76 0	Of tropical fruit (including mixtures containing 50 % or more by weight of tropical nuts and tropical fruit)
	200892 78 0	Other
		Not containing added sugar, in immediate packings of a net content
		Of 5 kg or more
	200892 92 0	Of tropical fruit (including mixtures containing 50 % or more by weight of tropical nuts and tropical fruit)
	200892 93 0	Other
		Of less than 5 kg, but not less than 4.5 kg
	200892 94 0	Of tropical fruit (including mixtures containing 50 % or more by weight of tropical nuts and tropical fruit)
	200892 96 0	Other
		Of less than 4.5 kg
	200892 97 0	Of tropical fruit (including mixtures containing 50 % or more by weight of tropical nuts and tropical fruit)
	200892 98 0	Other
		FRUIT JUICES (INCLUDING GRAPE MUST) AND VEGETABLE JUICES, UNFERMENTED AND NOT CONTAINING ADDED SPIRIT, WHETHER OR NOT CONTAINING ADDED SUGAR OR OTHER SWEETENING MATTER
059.10		**Orange juice**
		Frozen
		Of a density exceeding 1.33 g/cm^3 at 20 °C
	200911 11 0	Of a value not exceeding 30 ECU per 100 kg net weight
	200911 19 0	Other
		Of a density not exceeding 1.33 g/cm^3 at 20 °C
	200911 91 0	Of a value not exceeding 30 ECU per 100 kg net weight and with an added sugar content exceeding 30 % by weight
	200911 99 0	Other
		Other
		Of a density exceeding 1.33 g/cm^3 at 20 °C
	200919 11 0	Of a value not exceeding 30 ECU per 100 kg net weight
	200919 19 0	Other
		Of a density not exceeding 1.33 g/cm^3 at 20 °C
	200919 91 0	Of a value not exceeding 30 ECU per 100 kg net weight and with an added sugar content exceeding 30 % by weight
	200919 99 0	Other
059.20		**Grapefruit juice**
		Of a density exceeding 1.33 g/cm^3 at 20 °C
	200920 11 0	Of a value not exceeding 30 ECU per 100 kg net weight
	200920 19 0	Other
		Of a density not exceeding 1.33 g/cm^3 at 20 °C
	200920 91 0	Of a value not exceeding 30 ECU per 100 kg net weight and with an added sugar content exceeding 30 % by weight
	200920 99 0	Other
059.30		**Juice of any other single citrus fruit**
		Of a density exceeding 1.33 g/cm^3 at 20 °C
	200930 11 0	Of a value not exceeding 30 ECU per 100 kg net weight
	200930 19 0	Other
		Of a density not exceeding 1.33 g/cm^3 at 20 °C
		Of a value exceeding 30 ECU per 100 kg net weight
	200930 31 0	Containing added sugar
	200930 39 0	Other
		Of a value not exceeding 30 ECU per 100 kg net weight
		Lemon juice
	200930 51 0	With an added sugar content exceeding 30 % by weight
	200930 55 0	With an added sugar content not exceeding 30 % by weight
	200930 59 0	Not containing added sugar
		Other citrus fruit juices
	200930 91 0	With an added sugar content exceeding 30 % by weight
	200930 95 0	With an added sugar content not exceeding 30 % by weight
	200930 99 0	Not containing added sugar

S.I.T.C. (R3)	Commodity Code No	Trade description
		Juice of any single fruit (other than citrus) or vegetable; mixtures of fruit or vegetable juices
059.91		Pineapple juice
		Of a density exceeding 1.33 g/cm^3 at 20 °C
	200940 11 0	Of a value not exceeding 30 ECU per 100 kg net weight
	200940 19 0	Other
		Of a density not exceeding 1.33 g/cm^3 at 20 °C
	200940 30 0	Of a value exceeding 30 ECU per 100 kg net weight, containing added sugar
		Other
	200940 91 0	With an added sugar content exceeding 30 % by weight
	200940 93 0	With an added sugar content not exceeding 30 % by weight
	200940 99 0	Not containing added sugar
059.92		Tomato juice
	200950 10 0	Containing added sugar
	200950 90 0	Other
059.93		Grape juice (incl. grape must)
		Of a density exceeding 1.33 g/cm^3 at 20 °C
	200960 11 0	Of a value not exceeding 22 ECU per 100 kg net weight
	200960 19 0	Other
		Of a density not exceeding 1.33 g/cm^3 at 20 °C
		Of a value exceeding 18 ECU per 100 kg net weight
	200960 51 0	Concentrated
	200960 59 0	Other
		Of a value not exceeding 18 ECU per 100 kg net weight
		With an added sugar content exceeding 30% by weight
	200960 71 0	Concentrated
	200960 79 0	Other
	200960 90 0	Other
059.94		Apple juice
		Of a density exceeding 1.33 g/cm^3 at 20 °C
	200970 11 0	Of a value not exceeding 22 ECU per 100 kg net weight
	200970 19 0	Other
		Of a density not exceeding 1.33 g/cm^3 at 20 °C
	200970 30 0	Of a value exceeding 18 ECU per 100 kg net weight, containing added sugar
		Other
	200970 91 0	With an added sugar content exceeding 30 % by weight
	200970 93 0	With an added sugar content not exceeding 30 % by weight
	200970 99 0	Not containing added sugar
059.95		Juice of any other single fruit or vegetable
		Of a density exceeding 1.33 g/cm^3 at 20 °C
		Pear juice
	200980 11 0	Of a value not exceeding 22 ECU per 100 kg net weight
	200980 19 0	Other
		Other
		Of a value not exceeding 30 ECU per 100 kg net weight
	200980 32 0	Juices of passion fruit and guavas
	200980 33 0	Juices of mangoes, mangosteens, papaws (papayas), tamarinds, cashew apples, lychees, jackfruit, sapodillo plums, carambola and pitahaya
	200980 35 0	Other
		Other
	200980 36 0	Juices of tropical fruit
	200980 38 0	Other
		Of a density not exceeding 1.33 g/cm^3 at 20 °C
		Pear juice
	200980 50 0	Of a value exceeding 18 ECU per 100 kg net weight, containing added sugar
		Other
	200980 61 0	With an added sugar content exceeding 30 % by weight
	200980 63 0	With an added sugar content not exceeding 30 % by weight
	200980 69 0	Not containing added sugar
		Other
		Of a value exceeding 30 ECU per 100 kg net weight, containing added sugar
	200980 71 0	Cherry juice
	200980 73 0	Juices of tropical fruit
	200980 79 0	Other
		Other
		With an added sugar content exceeding 30 % by weight
	200980 83 0	Juices of passion fruit and guavas
	200980 84 0	Juices of mangoes, mangosteens, papaws (papayas), tamarinds, cashew apples, lychees, jackfruit, sapodillo plums, carambola and pitahaya
	200980 86 0	Other
		With an added sugar content not exceeding 30 % by weight
	200980 88 0	Juices of tropical fruit
	200980 89 0	Other
		Not containing added sugar
	200980 95 0	Juice of the fruit of the species Vaccinium marcocarpon
	200980 96 0	Cherry juice

S.I.T.C. (R3)	Commodity Code No	Trade description
cont 059.95	200980 97 0	Juices of tropical fruit
	200980 98 0	Other
059.96		**Mixtures of fruit or vegetable juices**
		Of a density exceeding 1.33 g/cm^3 at 20 °C
		Mixtures of apple and pear juice
	200990 11 0	Of a value not exceeding 22 ECU per 100 kg net weight
	200990 19 0	Other
		Other
	200990 21 0	Of a value not exceeding 30 ECU per 100 kg net weight
	200990 29 0	Other
		Of a density not exceeding 1.33 g/cm^3 at 20 °C
		Mixtures of apple and pear juice
	200990 31 0	Of a value not exceeding 18 ECU per 100 kg net weight and with an added sugar content exceeding 30 % by weight
	200990 39 0	Other
		Other
		Of a value exceeding 30 ECU per 100 kg net weight
		Mixtures of citrus fruit juices and pineapple juice
	200990 41 0	Containing added sugar
	200990 49 0	Other
		Other
	200990 51 0	Containing added sugar
	200990 59 0	Other
		Of a value not exceeding 30 ECU per 100 kg net weight
		Mixtures of citrus fruit juices and pineapple juice
	200990 71 0	With an added sugar content exceeding 30 % by weight
	200990 73 0	With an added sugar content not exceeding 30 % by weight
	200990 79 0	Not containing added sugar
		Other
		With an added sugar content exceeding 30 % by weight
	200990 92 0	Mixtures of juices of tropical fruit
	200990 94 0	Other
		With an added sugar content not exceeding 30 % by weight
	200990 95 0	Mixtures of juices of tropical fruit
	200990 96 0	Other
		Not containing added sugar
	200990 97 0	Mixtures of juices of tropical fruit
	200990 98 0	Other

DIVISION 06

SUGARS, SUGAR PREPARATIONS AND HONEY

SUGARS, MOLASSES AND HONEY

Sugars, beet or cane, raw, in solid form, not containing added flavouring or colouring matter

S.I.T.C. (R3)	Commodity Code No	Trade description
061.11		**Cane sugar, raw**
	170111 10 0	For refining
	170111 90 0	Other
061.12		**Beet sugar, raw**
	170112 10 0	For refining
	170112 90 0	Other

Other beet or cane sugar and chemically pure sucrose in solid form

S.I.T.C. (R3)	Commodity Code No	Trade description
061.21	170191 00 0	**Containing added flavouring or colouring matter**
061.29		**Other**
	*170199 10 0	White sugar
	*170199 90 0	Other

Molasses resulting from the extraction or refining of sugar

S.I.T.C. (R3)	Commodity Code No	Trade description
061.51	170310 00 0	**Cane molasses**
061.59	170390 00 0	**Beet sugar molasses and other molasses (e.g., corn molasses) resulting from the extraction or refining of sugar**
061.60	040900 00 0	**Natural honey**

Other sugars (including pure lactose, maltose, glucose and fructose), in solid form; sugar syrups not containing added flavouring or colouring matter; artificial honey (whether or not mixed with natural honey); caramel

S.I.T.C. (R3)	Commodity Code No	Trade description
061.91		**Lactose and lactose syrup**
	*170211 00 0	Containing by weight 99% or more lactose, expressed as anhydrous lactose, calculated on the dry matter
	*170219 00 0	Other
061.92		**Maple sugar and maple syrup**
	170220 10 0	Maple sugar in solid form, containing added flavouring or colouring matter
	170220 90 0	Other
061.93		**Glucose (dextrose) and glucose syrup, not containing fructose or containing, in the dry state, less than 20% by weight of fructose**
	170230 10 0	Isoglucose
		Other
		Containing in the dry state, 99 % or more by weight of glucose
	170230 51 0	In the form of white crystalline powder, whether or not agglomerated
	170230 59 0	Other
		Other
	170230 91 0	In the form of white crystalline powder, whether or not agglomerated
	170230 99 0	Other
061.94		**Glucose and glucose syrup, containing, in the dry state, at least 20% but not more than 50% by weight of fructose**
	170240 10 0	Isoglucose
	170240 90 0	Other
061.95	170250 00 0	**Pure fructose**
061.96		**Other fructose and fructose syrup, containing in the dry state more than 50% by weight of fructose**
	170260 10 0	Isoglucose
	170260 90 0	Other
061.99		**Other (incl. invert sugar)**
	170290 10 0	Chemically pure maltose
	170290 30 0	Isoglucose
	170290 50 0	Maltodextrine and maltodextrine syrup
	170290 60 0	Artificial honey, whether or not mixed with natural honey
		Caramel
	170290 71 0	Containing 50 % or more by weight of sucrose in the dry matter
		Other
	170290 75 0	In the form of powder, whether or not agglomerated
	170290 79 0	Other
	170290 80 0	Inulin syrup
	170290 99 0	Other

SUGAR CONFECTIONERY

S.I.T.C. (R3)	Commodity Code No	Trade description
062.10		**Fruit, nuts, fruit-peel and other parts of plants, preserved by sugar or other sweetening matter (drained, glace or crystallized)**
	200600 10 0	Ginger
		Other
		With a sugar content exceeding 13 % by weight
	200600 31 0	Cherries
	200600 35 0	Tropical fruit and tropical nuts
	200600 38 0	Other
		Other
	200600 91 0	Tropical fruit and tropical nuts
	200600 99 0	Other

Sugar confectionery (including white chocolate), not containing cocoa

S.I.T.C. (R3)	Commodity Code No	Trade description
062.21		**Chewing gum, whether or not sugar-coated**
		Containing less than 60 % by weight of sucrose (including invert sugar expressed as sucrose)
	170410 11 0	Gum in strips
	170410 19 0	Other
		Containing 60 % or more by weight of sucrose (including invert sugar expressed as sucrose)
	170410 91 0	Gum in strips
	170410 99 0	Other
062.29		**Other**
	170490 10 0	Liquorice extract containing more than 10 % by weight of sucrose but not containing other added substances
	170490 30 0	White chocolate
		Other
	170490 51 0	Pastes, including marzipan, in immediate packings of a net content of 1 kg or more
	170490 55 0	Throat pastilles and cough drops
	170490 61 0	Sugar coated (panned) goods
		Other
	170490 65 0	Gum confectionery and jelly confectionery including fruit pastes in the form of sugar confectionery
	170490 71 0	Boiled sweets whether or not filled

S.I.T.C. (R3)	Commodity Code No	Trade description
cont 062.29	170490 75 0	Toffees, caramels and similar sweets
		Other
	170490 81 0	Compressed tablets
	170490 99 0	Other

DIVISION 07

COFFEE, TEA, COCOA, SPICES, AND MANUFACTURES THEREOF

COFFEE AND COFFEE SUBSTITUTES

Coffee, not roasted, whether or not decaffeinated; coffee husks and skins

071.11	090111 00 0	Coffee, not roasted, not decaffeinated
071.12	090112 00 0	Coffee, not roasted, decaffeinated
071.13	*090190 10 0	Coffee husks and skins
071.20		**Coffee, roasted**
	090121 00 0	Not decaffeinated
	090122 00 0	Decaffeinated

Extracts, essences and concentrates of coffee and preparations with a basis of these products or with a basis of coffee; coffee substitutes and extracts, essences and concentrates thereof

071.31		**Extracts, essences and concentrates of coffee and preparations with a basis of these products or with a basis of coffee**
		Extracts, essences or concentrates
	*210111 11 0	With a coffee-based dry matter content of 95 % or more by weight
	*210111 19 0	Other
		Preparations with a basis of these extracts, essences or concentrates of coffee:
	*210112 92 0	Preparations with a basis of these extracts, essences or concentrates of coffee
	*210112 98 0	Other
071.32	*090190 90 0	Coffee substitutes containing coffee in any proportion
071.33		**Roasted chicory and other roasted coffee substitutes (not containing coffee) and extracts, essences and concentrates thereof**
		Roasted chicory and other roasted coffee substitutes
	210130 11 0	Roasted chicory
	210130 19 0	Other
		Extracts, essences and concentrates of roasted chicory and other roasted coffee substitutes
	210130 91 0	Of roasted chicory
	210130 99 0	Other

COCOA

072.10	180100 00 0	Cocoa beans, whole or broken, raw or roasted
072.20	180500 00 0	Cocoa powder not containing added sugar or other sweetening matter
		Cocoa paste, whether or not defatted
072.31	180310 00 0	....not defatted (licor)
072.32	180320 00 0	....wholly or partly defatted (cocoa cake)
072.40	180400 00 0	Cocoa butter, fat or oil
072.50	180200 00 0	Cocoa shells, husks, skins and other cocoa waste

CHOCOLATE AND OTHER FOOD PREPARATIONS CONTAINING COCOA, N.E.S.

073.10		**Cocoa powder containing added sugar or other sweetening matter**
	180610 15 0	Containing no sucrose or containing less than 5 % by weight of sucrose (including invert sugar expressed as sucrose)
	180610 20 0	Containing 5 % or more but less than 65 % by weight of sucrose (including invert sugar expressed as sucrose) or isoglucose expressed as sucrose
	180610 30 0	Containing 65 % or more but less than 80 % by weight of sucrose (including invert sugar expressed as sucrose)
	180610 90 0	Containing 80 % or more by weight of sucrose (including invert sugar expressed as sucrose)
073.20		**Other food preparations, containing cocoa, in blocks or slabs weighing more than 2 kg or in liquid, paste, powder, granular or other bulk form in containers or immediate packings of a content exceeding 2 kg**
	180620 10 0	Containing 31 % or more by weight of cocoa butter or containing a combined weight of 31 % or more of cocoa butter and milk fat

S.I.T.C. (R3)	Commodity Code No	Trade description
cont 073.20	180620 30 0	Containing a combined weight of 25 % or more, but less than 31 % of cocoa butter and milk fat
		Other
	180620 50 0	Containing 18 % or more by weight of cocoa butter
	180620 70 0	Chocolate milk crumb
	180620 80 0	Chocolate flavour coating
	180620 95 0	Other
073.30		Other food preparations containing cocoa, in blocks, slabs or bars, whether or not filled
	180631 00 0	Filled
		Not filled
	180632 10 0	With added cereal, fruit or nuts
	180632 90 0	Other
073.90		Food preparations containing cocoa, n.e.s.
		Chocolate and chocolate products
		Chocolates, whether or not filled
	180690 11 0	Containing alcohol
	180690 19 0	Other
		Other
	180690 31 0	Filled
	180690 39 0	Not filled
	180690 50 0	Sugar confectionery and substitutes therefor made from sugar substitution products, containing cocoa
	180690 60 0	Spreads containing cocoa
	180690 70 0	Preparations containing cocoa for making beverages
	180690 90 0	Other

TEA AND MATÉ

Tea, whether or not flavoured

S.I.T.C. (R3)	Commodity Code No	Trade description
074.11	090210 00 0	Green tea (not fermented) in immediate packings of a content not exceeding 3 kg
074.12	090220 00 0	Other green tea (not fermented)
074.13	090230 00 0	Black tea (fermented) and partly fermented tea, in immediate packings of a content not exceeding 3 kg
074.14	090240 00 0	Other black tea (fermented) and other partly fermented tea

Maté; extracts, essences and concentrates of tea or mate, and preparations with a basis of tea, mate, or their extracts, essences or concentrates

S.I.T.C. (R3)	Commodity Code No	Trade description
074.31	090300 00 0	Maté
074.32		Extracts, essences and concentrates of tea or mate, and preparations with a basis of tea, mate, or their extracts, essences or concentrates
	210120 20 0	Extracts, essences or concentrates
		Preparations
	210120 92 0	With a basis of extracts, essences or concentrates of tea or maté
	210120 98 0	Other

SPICES

Pepper of the genus 'piper'; fruits of the genus 'capsicum' or of the genus 'pimenta', dried or crushed or ground

S.I.T.C. (R3)	Commodity Code No	Trade description
075.11		Pepper, neither crushed nor ground.
	090411 10 0	For the industrial manufacture of essential oils or resinoids
	090411 90 0	Other
075.12	090412 00 0	Pepper, crushed or ground
075.13		Fruits of the genus 'Capsicum' or of the genus 'Pimenta', dried or crushed or ground
		Neither crushed nor ground
	090420 10 0	Sweet peppers
		Other
	090420 31 0	Of the genus *Capsicum*, for the manufacture of capsicin or *Capsicum* oleoresin dyes
	090420 35 0	For the industrial manufacture of essential oils or resinoids
	090420 39 0	Other
	090420 90 0	Crushed or ground

Spices (except pepper and pimento)

S.I.T.C. (R3)	Commodity Code No	Trade description
075.21	090500 00 0	Vanilla
075.22	090610 00 0	Cinnamon and cinnamon-tree flowers, neither crushed nor ground
075.23	090620 00 0	Cinnamon and cinnamon-tree flowers, crushed or ground
075.24	090700 00 0	Cloves (whole fruit, cloves and stems)

S.I.T.C. (R3)	Commodity Code No	Trade description
075.25		**Nutmeg, mace and cardamoms**
		Nutmeg
	090810 10 0	Neither crushed nor ground, for the industrial manufacture of essential oils or resinoids
	090810 90 0	Other
		Mace
	090820 10 0	Neither crushed nor ground
	090820 90 0	Crushed or ground
	090830 00 0	Cardamoms
075.26		**Seeds of anise, badian, fennel, coriander, cumin, caraway or juniper**
		Seeds of anise or badian
	090910 10 0	Seeds of anise
	090910 90 0	Seeds of badian
	090920 00 0	Seeds of coriander
		Seeds of cumin
		Neither crushed nor ground
	090930 11 0	For the industrial manufacture of essential oils or resinoids
	090930 19 0	Other
	090930 90 0	Crushed or ground
		Seeds of caraway
		Neither crushed nor ground
	090940 11 0	For the industrial manufacture of essential oils or resinoids
	090940 19 0	Other
	090940 90 0	Crushed or ground
		Seeds of fennel: juniper berries
		Neither crushed nor ground
	090950 11 0	For the industrial manufacture of essential oils or resinoids
	090950 19 0	Other
	090950 90 0	Crushed or ground
075.27		**Ginger (excluding ginger preserved in sugar or conserved in syrup)**
		Whole roots, pieces or slices
	091010 11 0	For the industrial manufacture of essential oils or resinoids
	091010 19 0	Other
	091010 90 0	Other
075.28		**Thyme, saffron and bay leaves**
		Saffron
	091020 10 0	Neither crushed nor ground
	091020 90 0	Crushed or ground
		Thyme; bay leaves
		Thyme
		Neither crushed nor ground
	091040 11 0	Wild thyme (*Thymus serpyllum*)
	091040 13 0	Other
	091040 19 0	Crushed or ground
	091040 90 0	Bay leaves
075.29		**Other spices; mixtures of two or more of the products of different headings of group 075**
	091030 00 0	Turmeric (curcuma)
	091050 00 0	Curry
		Other spices
		Mixtures
	091091 10 0	Neither crushed nor ground
	091091 90 0	Crushed or ground
		Other
	091099 10 0	Fenugreek seed
		Other
	091099 91 0	Neither crushed nor ground
	091099 99 0	Crushed or ground

DIVISION 08

FEEDING STUFF FOR ANIMALS (NOT INCLUDING UNMILLED CEREALS)

FEEDING STUFF FOR ANIMALS (NOT INCLUDING UNMILLED CEREALS)
Hay and fodder, green or dry

S.I.T.C. (R3)	Commodity Code No	Trade description
081.11	121300 00 0	Cereal straw and husks, unprepared, whether or not chopped, ground, pressed or in the form of pellets
081.12	121410 00 0	Lucerne (alfalfa) meal and pellets
081.13		Swedes, mangolds, fodder roots, hay, clover, sainfoin, forage kale, lupines, vetches and similar forage products, whether or not in the form of pellets
	121490 10 0	Mangolds, swedes and other fodder roots

S.I.T.C. (R3)	Commodity Code No	Trade description
cont 081.13		Other
	121490 91 0	In the form of pellets
	121490 99 0	Other
081.19		Vegetable residues and by-products, vegetable waste, whether or not in the form of pellets, of a kind used for animal food, n.e.s.
	230810 00 0	Acorns and horse-chestnuts
		Other
		Grape marc
	230890 11 0	Having a total alcoholic strength by mass not exceeding 4.3 % mas and a dry matter content not less than 40 % by weight
	230890 19 0	Other
	230890 30 0	Pomace or marc of fruit, other than grapes
	230890 90 0	Other
		Bran, sharps and other residues, whether or not in the form of pellets, derived from the sifting, milling or other working of cereals or of leguminous plants
081.23	230250 00 0	....of leguminous plants
081.24		....of maize (corn)
	230210 10 0	With a starch content not exceeding 35 % by weight
	230210 90 0	Other
081.25		....of rice
	230220 10 0	With a starch content not exceeding 35 % by weight
	230220 90 0	Other
081.26		....of wheat
	230230 10 0	Of which the starch content does not exceed 28 % by weight, and of which the proportion that passes through a sieve with an aperture of 0.2 mm does not exceed 10 % by weight or alternatively the proportion that passes through the sieve has an ash content, calculated on the dry product, equal to or more than 1.5 % by weight
	230230 90 0	Other
081.29		....of other cereals
	230240 10 0	Of which the starch content does not exceed 28 % by weight, and of which the proportion that passes through a sieve with an aperture of 0.2 mm does not exceed 10 % by weight or alternatively the proportion that passes through the sieve has an ash content, calculated on the dry product, equal to or more than 1.5 % by weight
	230240 90 0	Other
		Oil-cake and other solid residues (except dregs), whether or not ground or in the form of pellets, resulting from the extraction of fats or oils from oilseeds, oleaginous fruits and germs of cereals
081.31	230400 00 0	....of soya beans
081.32	230500 00 0	....of groundnuts
081.33	230610 00 0	....of cotton seed
081.34	230620 00 0	....of linseed
081.35	230630 00 0	....of sunflower seeds
081.36	230640 00 0	....of rape or colza seeds
081.37	230650 00 0	....of coconut or copra
081.38	230660 00 0	....of palm nuts or kernels
081.39		....of other oil seeds and oleaginous fruits
		Oil-cake and other residues resulting from the extraction of olive oil
	230690 11 0	Containing 3 % or less by weight of olive oil
	230690 19 0	Containing more than 3 % by weight of olive oil
	*230670 00 0	Of maize (corn) germ
		Other
	230690 93 0	Of sesame seeds
	230690 99 0	Other
		Flours, meals and pellets, of meat or meat offal, of fish or of crustaceans, molluscs or other aquatic invertebrates, unfit for human consumption; greaves
081.41	230110 00 0	Flours, meals and pellets, of meat or meat offal (including tankage), unfit for human consumption; greaves
081.42	230120 00 0	Flours, meals and pellets, of fish or of crustaceans, molluscs or other aquatic invertebrates, unfit for human consumption

S.I.T.C. (R3)	Commodity Code No	Trade description
		Residues of starch manufacture and similar residues, beet-pulp, bagasse and other waste of sugar manufacture, brewing or distilling dregs and waste, whether or not in the form of pellets
081.51		**Residues of starch manufacture and similar residues**
		Residues from the manufacture of starch from maize (excluding concentrated steeping liquors), of a protein content, calculated on the dry product
	230310 11 0	Exceeding 40 % by weight
	230310 19 0	Not exceeding 40 % by weight
	230310 90 0	Other
081.52		**Beet-pulp, bagasse and other waste of sugar manufacture**
		Beet-pulp having a dry matter content of
	230320 11 0	Not less than 87 % by weight
	230320 18 0	Less than 87 % by weight
	230320 90 0	Other
081.53	230330 00 0	**Brewing or distilling dregs and waste**
		Food wastes and prepared animal feeds, n.e.s.
081.94		**Wine lees; argol**
		Wine lees
	230700 11 0	Having a total alcoholic strength by mass not exceeding 7.9 % mas and a dry matter content not less than 25 % by weight
	230700 19 0	Other
	230700 90 0	Argol
081.95		**Dog or cat food, put up for retail sale**
		Containing starch, glucose, glucose syrup, maltodextrine or maltodextrine syrup falling within subheadings 1702.30-51 to 1702.30-99, 1702.40-90, 1702.90-50 and 2106.90-55 or milk products
		Containing starch, glucose, glucose syrup, maltodextrine or maltodextrine syrup
		Containing no starch or containing 10 % or less by weight of starch
	230910 11 0	Containing no milk products or containing less than 10 % by weight of such products
	230910 13 0	Containing not less than 10 % but less than 50 % by weight of milk products
	230910 15 0	Containing not less than 50 % but less than 75 % by weight of milk products
	230910 19 0	Containing not less than 75 % by weight of milk products
		Containing more than 10 % but not more than 30 % by weight of starch
	230910 31 0	Containing no milk products or containing less than 10 % by weight of such products
	230910 33 0	Containing not less than 10 % but less than 50 % by weight of milk products
	230910 39 0	Containing not less than 50 % by weight of milk products
		Containing more than 30 % by weight of starch
	230910 51 0	Containing no milk products or containing less than 10 % by weight of such products
	230910 53 0	Containing not less than 10 % but less than 50 % by weight of milk products
	230910 59 0	Containing not less than 50 % by weight of milk products
	230910 70 0	Containing no starch, glucose, glucose syrup, maltodextrine or maltodextrine syrup but containing milk products
	230910 90 0	Other
081.99		**Preparations of a kind used for animal food, n.e.s.**
	230990 10 0	Fish or marine mammal solubles
		Other
		Containing starch, glucose, glucose syrup, maltodextrine or maltodextrine syrup falling within subheadings 1702.30-51 to 1702.30-99, 1702.40-90, 1702.90-50 and 2106.90-55 or milk products
		Containing starch, glucose, glucose syrup, maltodextrine or maltodextrine syrup
		Containing no starch or containing 10 % or less by weight of starch
	230990 31 0	Containing no milk products or containing less than 10 % by weight of such products
	230990 33 0	Containing not less than 10 % but less than 50 % by weight of milk products
	230990 35 0	Containing not less than 50 % but less than 75 % by weight of milk products
	230990 39 0	Containing not less than 75 % by weight of milk products
		Containing more than 10 % but not more than 30 % by weight of starch
	230990 41 0	Containing no milk products or containing less than 10 % by weight of such products
	230990 43 0	Containing not less than 10 % but less than 50 % by weight of milk products
	230990 49 0	Containing not less than 50 % by weight of milk products
		Containing more than 30 % by weight of starch
	230990 51 0	Containing no milk products or containing less than 10 % by weight of such products
	230990 53 0	Containing not less than 10 % but less than 50 % by weight of milk products
	230990 59 0	Containing not less than 50 % by weight of milk products
	230990 70 0	Containing no starch, glucose, glucose syrup, maltodextrine or maltodextrine syrup but containing milk products
		Other
	230990 91 0	Beet-pulp with added molasses
	230990 93 0	Premixtures
	230990 98 0	Other

S.I.T.C. (R3)	Commodity Code No	Trade description

MISCELLANEOUS EDIBLE PRODUCTS AND PREPARATIONS

MARGARINE AND SHORTENING

Margarine; edible mixtures or preparations of animal or vegetable fats or oils or of fractions of different such fats or oils, other than vegetable fats or oils or their fractions of heading 431.2

091.01		Margarine (excl. liquid margarine)
	151710 10 0	Containing more than 10 % but not more than 15 % by weight of milk fats
	151710 90 0	Other
091.09		Other
	151790 10 0	Containing more than 10 % but not more than 15 % by weight of milk fats
		Other
	151790 91 0	Fixed vegetable oils, fluid, mixed
	151790 93 0	Edible mixtures or preparations of a kind used as mould release preparations
	151790 99 0	Other

EDIBLE PRODUCTS AND PREPARATIONS, N.E.S.

Homogenized food preparations

098.11	160210 00 0	Homogenized preparations from meat and edible meat offal
098.12	200510 00 0	Homogenized vegetables
098.13		Cooked fruit preparations, homogenized
	200710 10 0	With a sugar content exceeding 13 % by weight
		Other
	200710 91 0	Of tropical fruit
	200710 99 0	Other
098.14	210420 00 0	Homogenized composite food preparations

Sauces and preparations therefor; mixed condiments and mixed seasonings; mustard flour and meal and prepared mustard; vinegar and substitutes for vinegar obtained from acetic acid

098.41	210310 00 0	Soya sauce
098.42	210320 00 0	Tomato ketchup and other tomato sauces
098.43		Mustard flour and meal and prepared mustard
	210330 10 0	Mustard flour
	210330 90 0	Prepared mustard
098.44		Vinegar and substitutes for vinegar obtained from acetic acid
		Wine vinegar, in containers holding
	220900 11 0	2 l or less
	220900 19 0	More than 2 l
		Other, in containers holding
	220900 91 0	2 l or less
	220900 99 0	More than 2 l
098.49		Other sauces and preparations therefor; mixed condiments and mixed seasonings
	210390 10 0	Mango chutney, liquid
	210390 30 0	Aromatic bitters of an alcoholic strength by volume of 44.2 to 49.2 % vol. containing from 1.5 to 6 % by weight of gentian, spices and various ingredients and from 4 to 10 % of sugar, in containers holding 0.5 litre or less
	210390 90 0	Other
098.50		Soups and broths and preparations therefor
	210410 10 0	Dried
	210410 90 0	Other
098.60		Yeasts (active or inactive); other single-cell micro-organisms, dead (but not including vaccines of heading 541.63); prepared baking powders.
		Active yeasts
	210210 10 0	Culture yeast
		Bakers' yeast
	210210 31 0	Dried
	210210 39 0	Other
	210210 90 0	Other
		Inactive yeasts; other single-cell micro-organisms, dead
		Inactive yeasts
	210220 11 0	In tablet, cube or similar form, or in immediate packings of a net content not exceeding 1 kg
	210220 19 0	Other
	210220 90 0	Other
	210230 00 0	Prepared baking powders

Food preparations, n.e.s.

S.I.T.C. (R3)	Commodity Code No	Trade description
098.91		**Pasta, cooked or stuffed; couscous, whether or not prepared**
	190220 10 0	Containing more than 20 % by weight of fish, crustaceans, molluscs or other aquatic invertebrates
	190220 30 0	Containing more than 20 % by weight of sausages and the like, of meat and meat offal of any kind, including fats of any kind or origin
		Other
	190220 91 0	Cooked
	190220 99 0	Other
		Other pasta
	190230 10 0	Dried
	190230 90 0	Other
		Couscous
	190240 10 0	Unprepared
	190240 90 0	Other
098.92	041000 00 0	Edible products of animal origin, n.e.s.
098.93	190110 00 0	Food preparations for infant use, put up for retail sale, of flour, meal, starch or malt extract (not containing cocoa powder or containing cocoa powder in a proportion by weight of less than 50%) or of goods of headings 022.4 and 022.1 through 022.32 (not containing cocoa powder or containing cocoa powder in a proportion by weight of less than 10%) n.e.s.
098.94		Malt extract; food preparations of flour, meal, starch or malt extract (not containing cocoa powder or containing cocoa powder in a proportion by weight of less than 50%) n.e.s., or of goods of headings 022.4 and 022.1 through 022.32 (not containing cocoa powder or containing cocoa powder in a proportion by weight of less than 10%) n.e.s.
		Malt extract
	190190 11 0	With a dry extract content of 90 % or more by weight
	190190 19 0	Other
		Other
	190190 91 0	Containing no milk fats, sucrose, isoglucose, glucose or starch or containing less than 1.5 % milkfat, 5 % sucrose (including invert sugar) or isoglucose, 5 % glucose or starch, excluding food preparations in powder form of goods of headings 022.11 to 022.49
	190190 99 0	Other
098.99		**Other food preparations**
		Protein concentrates and textured protein substances
	210610 20 0	Containing no milk fats, sucrose, isoglucose, glucose or starch or containing less than 1.5% milk fats, 5% sucrose or isoglucose, 5% glucose or starch
	210610 80 0	Other
		Other
	210690 10 0	Cheese fondues
		Flavoured or coloured sugar syrups
	210690 30 0	Isoglucose syrups
		Other
	210690 51 0	Lactose syrup
	210690 55 0	Glucose syrup and maltodextrine syrup
	210690 59 0	Other
		Other
	210690 92 0	Containing no milk fats, sucrose, isoglucose, glucose or starch or containing less than 1.5% milk fats, 5% sucrose or isoglucose, 5% glucose or starch
	210690 98 0	Other

S.I.T.C. (R3)	Commodity Code No	Trade description

SECTION: 1

**DIVISION
11**   **BEVERAGES**

NON-ALCOHOLIC BEVERAGES, N.E.S.

111.01   **Waters, including natural or artificial mineral waters and aerated waters) not containing added sugar or other sweetening matter nor flavoured; ice and snow**
Mineral waters and aerated waters
    Natural mineral waters:

	220110 11 0	Not carbonated
	220110 19 0	Other
		Other:
	220110 91 0	Not carbonated
	220110 99 0	Other
	220190 00 0	Other

111.02   **Waters (including mineral waters and aerated waters) containing added sugar or other sweetening matter or flavoured, and other non-alcoholic beverages, n.e.s.**

	220210 00 0	Waters, including mineral waters and aerated waters, containing added sugar or other sweetening matter or flavoured
		Other
	220290 10 0	Not containing products of heading 022 or fat obtained from products of heading 022
		Other, containing by weight of fat obtained from products of heading 022
	220290 91 0	Less than 0.2 %
	220290 95 0	0.2 % or more but less than 2 %
	220290 99 0	2 % or more

ALCOHOLIC BEVERAGES

Wine of fresh grapes (including fortified wine); grape must in fermentation or with fermentation arrested

112.11   **Grape must in fermentation or with fermentation arrested otherwise than by the addition of alcohol**

	*220430 10 0	In fermentation or with fermentation arrested otherwise than by the addition of alcohol
		Other
		Of a density of 1.33 g/cm^3 or less at 20°C and of an actual alcoholic strength by volume not exceeding 1 % vol.
	220430 92 0	Concentrated
	220430 94 0	Other
		Other
	220430 96 0	Concentrated
	220430 98 0	Other

112.13   **Vermouth and other wines of fresh grapes flavoured with plants or aromatic substances.**
In containers holding 2 l or less

	*220510 10 0	Of an actual alcoholic strength by volume of 18 % vol. or less
	*220510 90 0	Of an actual alcoholic strength by volume exceeding 18 % vol.
		Other
	*220590 10 0	Of an actual alcoholic strength by volume exceeding 18% vol. or less
	*220590 90 0	Of an actual alcoholic strength by volume exceeding 18% vol.

112.15   **Sparkling wine**
Of an actual alcoholic strength by volume of not less than 8.5 % vol.

	220410 11 0	Champagne
	*220410 19 0	Other
		Other
	220410 91 0	Asti spumante
	*220410 99 0	Other

112.17[1]   Other wine; grape must with fermentation prevented or arrested by the addition of alcohol:
In containers holding 2 l or less

	*220421 10 0	Wine other than that referred to in No. 112.15 in bottles with "mushroom" stoppers held in place by ties or fastenings; wine otherwise put up with an excess pressure due to carbon dioxide in solution of not less than one bar but less than three bars, measured at a temperature of 20°C
		Other
		Of an actual alcoholic strength by volume not exceeding 13 % vol.
		Quality wines produced in specified regions
		White
	220421 11 0	Alsace

---

1. If the total dry extract of a product exceeds the maximum quantities set out in Additional Note 3(B) of Chapter 22 of the Combined Nomenclature, the product is classified in the higher category of the Combined Nomenclature.
For full classification details see the HM Customs and Excise Tariff Chapter 22 Notes.

S.I.T.C. (R3)	Commodity Code No	Trade description
cont 112.17[2]	220421 12 0	Bordeaux
	220421 13 0	Bourgogne (Burgundy)
	220421 17 0	Val de Loire (Loire valley)
	220421 18 0	Mosel-Saar-Ruwer
	220421 19 0	Pfalz
	220421 22 0	Rheinhessen
	220421 24 0	Lazio (Latium)
	220421 26 0	Toscana (Tuscany)
	220421 27 0	Trentino, Alto Adige and Friuli
	220421 28 0	Veneto
	220421 32 0	Vinho Verde
	220421 34 0	Penedés
	220421 36 0	Rioja
	220421 37 0	Valencia
	220421 38 0	Other
		Other
	220421 42 0	Bordeaux
	220421 43 0	Bourgogne (Burgundy)
	220421 44 0	Beaujolais
	220421 46 0	Côtes-du-Rhône
	220421 47 0	Languedoc-Roussillon
	220421 48 0	Val de Loire (Loire valley)
	220421 62 0	Piemonte (Piedmont)
	220421 66 0	Toscana (Tuscany)
	220421 67 0	Trentino and Alto Adige
	220421 68 0	Veneto
	220421 69 0	Dão, Bairrada and Douro
	220421 71 0	Navarra
	220421 74 0	Penedés
	220421 76 0	Rioja
	220421 77 0	Valdepeñas
	220421 78 0	Other
		Other
	220421 79 0	White
	220421 80 0	Other
		Of an actual alcoholic strength by volume exceeding 13 % vol. but not exceeding 15 % vol.
		Quality wines produced in specified regions
	220421 81 0	White
	220421 82 0	Other
		Other
	220421 83 0	White
	220421 84 0	Other
		Of an actual alcoholic strength by volume exceeding 15 % vol. but not exceeding 18 % vol.
	220421 87 0	Marsala
	220421 88 0	Samos and Muscat de Lemnos
	220421 89 0	Port
	220421 91 0	Madeira and Sebutal muscatel
	220421 92 0	Sherry
	220421 93 0	Tokay (Aszu and Szamorodni)
	220421 94 0	Other
		Of an actual alcoholic strength by volume exceeding 18 % vol. but not exceeding 22 % vol.
	220421 95 0	Port
	220421 96 0	Madeira, sherry and Sebutal muscatel
	220421 97 0	Tokay (Aszu and Szamorodni)
	220421 98 0	Other
	220421 99 0	Of an actual alcoholic strength by volume exceeding 22 % vol.
		Other
	*220429 10 0	Wine other than that referred to in No. 112.15 in bottles with "mushroom" stoppers held in place by ties or fastenings; wine otherwise put up with an excess pressure due to carbon dioxide in solution of not less than one bar but less than three bars, measured at a temperature of 20°C
		Other
		Of an actual alcoholic strength by volume not exceeding 13 % vol.
		Quality wines produced in specified regions
		White
	220429 12 0	Bordeaux
	220429 13 0	Bourgogne (Burgundy)
	220429 17 0	Val de Loire (Loire valley)
	220429 18 0	Other
		Other
	220429 42 0	Bordeaux
	220429 43 0	Bourgogne (Burgundy)
	220429 44 0	Beaujolais

---

2. If the total dry extract of a product exceeds the maximum quantities set out in Additional Note 3(B) of Chapter 22 of the Combined Nomenclature, the product is classified in the higher category of the Combined Nomenclature.

For full classification details see the HM Customs and Excise Tariff Chapter 22 Notes.

S.I.T.C. (R3)	Commodity Code No	Trade description
cont 112.17	220429 46 0	Côtes-du-Rhône
	220429 47 0	Languedoc-Roussillon
	220429 48 0	Val de Loire (Loire valley)
	220429 58 0	Other
		Other
		White
	220429 62 0	Sicilia (Sicily)
	220429 64 0	Veneto
	220429 65 0	Other
		Other
	220429 71 0	Puglia (Apuglia)
	220429 72 0	Sicilia (Sicily)
	220429 75 0	Other
		Of an actual alcoholic strength by volume exceeding 13 % vol. but not exceeding 15 % vol.
		Quality wines produced in specified regions
	220429 81 0	White
	220429 82 0	Other
		Other
	220429 83 0	White
	220429 84 0	Other
		Of an actual alcoholic strength by volume exceeding 15 % vol. but not exceeding 18 % vol.
	220429 87 0	Marsala
	220429 88 0	Samos and Muscat de Lemnos
	220429 89 0	Port
	220429 91 0	Madeira and Setubal muscatel
	220429 92 0	Sherry
	220429 93 0	Tokay (Aszu and Szamorodni)
	220429 94 0	Other
		Of an actual alcoholic strength by volume exceeding 18 % vol. but not exceeding 22 % vol.
	220429 95 0	Port
	220429 96 0	Madeira, sherry and Setubal muscatel
	220429 97 0	Tokay (Aszu and Szamorodni)
	220429 98 0	Other
	220429 99 0	Of an actual alcoholic strength by volume exceeding 22 % vol.
112.20		**Fermented beverages (e.g., cider, perry, mead); mixtures of fermented beverages and mixtures of fermented beverages and non-alcoholic beverages, n.e.s.**
	220600 10 0	Piquette
		Other
		Sparkling
	220600 31 0	Cider and perry
	*220600 39 0	Other
		Still, in containers holding
		2 l or less
	220600 51 0	Cider and perry
	*220600 59 0	Other
		More than 2 l
	220600 81 0	Cider and perry
	*220600 89 0	Other
112.30		**Beer made from malt (including ale, stout and porter)**
		In containers holding 10 litres or less
	*220300 01 0	In bottles
	*220300 09 0	Other
	*220300 10 0	In containers holding more than 10 litres
		Spirits (other than those of heading 512.16); liqueurs and other spirituous beverages, n.e.s.; compound alcoholic preparations of a kind used for the manufacture of beverages
112.41		**Whisky**
		Bourbon whisky, in containers holding
	220830 11 0	2 l or less
	220830 19 0	More than 2 l
		Scotch whisky
		Malt whisky, in containers holding
	220830 32 0	2 l or less
	220830 38 0	More than 2 l
		Blended whisky, in containers holding
	220830 52 0	2 l or less
	220830 58 0	More than 2 l
		Other, in containers holding
	220830 72 0	2 l or less
	220830 78 0	More than 2 l
		Other, in litres holding
	220830 82 0	2 l or less
	220830 88 0	More than 2 l
112.42		**Spirits obtained by distilling grape wine or grape marc**
		In containers holding 2 l or less

S.I.T.C. (R3)	Commodity Code No	Trade description
cont 112.42	220820 12 0	Cognac
	220820 14 0	Armagnac
	220820 26 0	Grappa
	*220820 27 0	Brandy de Jerez
	*220820 29 0	Other
		In containers holding more than 2 l
	220820 40 0	Raw distillate
		Other
	220820 62 0	Cognac
	220820 64 0	Armagnac
	220820 86 0	Grappa
	*220820 87 0	Brandy de Jerez
	*220820 89 0	Other
112.43		**Compound alcoholic preparations of a kind used for the manufacture of beverages**
	*220690 20 0	Other than those based on odoriferous substances
112.44		**Rum and tafia**
	220840 10 0	In containers holding 2 l or less
	220840 90 0	In containers holding more than 2 l
112.45		**Gin and Geneva**
		Gin, in containers holding
	220850 11 0	2 l or less
	220850 19 0	More than 2 l
		Geneva, in containers holding
	220850 91 0	2 l or less
	220850 99 0	More than 2 l
112.49		**Spirits and distilled alcoholic beverages, n.e.s.**
		Vodka
		Of an alcoholic strength by volume of 45.4 % vol. or less in containers holding:
	*220860 11 0	2 litres or less
	*220860 19 0	More than 2 litres
		Of an alcoholic strength by volume of more than 45.4 % vol. in containers holding:
	*220860 91 0	2 litres or less
	*220860 99 0	More than 2 litres
		Liqueurs and cordials
	*220870 10 0	In containers holding 2 litres or less
	*220870 90 0	In containers holding more than 2 litres
		Other
		Arrack, in containers holding
	220890 11 0	2 l or less
	220890 19 0	More than 2 l
		Plum, pear or cherry spirit (excluding liqueurs) in containers holding:
	220890 33 0	2 litres or less
	220890 38 0	More than 2 l
		Other spirits, liqueurs and other spirituous beverages, in containers holding:
		2 l or less
	220890 41 0	Ouzo
		Other
		Spirits (excluding liqueurs)
		Distilled from fruit
	220890 45 0	Calvados
	220890 48 0	Other
		Other
	220890 52 0	Korn
	*220890 57 0	Other
	220890 69 0	Other spirituous beverages
		More than 2 l
		Spirits (excluding liqueurs)
	220890 71 0	Distilled from fruit
	*220890 74 0	Other
	*220890 78 0	Other spirituous beverages
		Undenatured ethyl alcohol of an alcoholic strength by volume of less than 80 % vol. in containers holding
	220890 91 0	2 l or less
	220890 99 0	More than 2 l

DIVISION 12

TOBACCO AND TOBACCO MANUFACTURES

TOBACCO, UNMANUFACTURED; TOBACCO REFUSE.

S.I.T.C. (R3)	Commodity Code No	Trade description
121.10		**Tobacco, not stemmed/stripped**
		Flue-cured Virginia type and light air-cured Burley type tobacco (including Burley hybrids); light air-cured Maryland type and fire-cured tobacco
	240110 10 0	Flue-cured Virginia type
	240110 20 0	Light air-cured Burley type (including Burley hybrids)

S.I.T.C. (R3)	Commodity Code No	Trade description
cont 121.10	240110 30 0	Light air-cured Maryland type
		Fire-cured tobacco
	240110 41 0	Kentucky type
	240110 49 0	Other
		Other
	240110 50 0	Light air-cured tobacco
	240110 60 0	Sun-cured Oriental type tobacco
	240110 70 0	Dark air-cured tobacco
	240110 80 0	Flue-cured tobacco
	240110 90 0	Other tobacco
121.20		**Tobacco, wholly or partly stemmed/stripped**
		Flue-cured Virginia type and light air-cured Burley type tobacco (including Burley hybrids); light air-cured Maryland type and fire-cured tobacco
	240120 10 0	Flue-cured Virginia type
	240120 20 0	Light air-cured Burley type (including Burley hybrids)
	240120 30 0	Light air-cured Maryland type
		Fire-cured tobacco
	240120 41 0	Kentucky type
	240120 49 0	Other
		Other
	240120 50 0	Light air-cured tobacco
	240120 60 0	Sun-cured Oriental type tobacco
	240120 70 0	Dark air-cured tobacco
	240120 80 0	Flue-cured tobacco
	240120 90 0	Other tobacco
121.30	240130 00 0	**Tobacco refuse**
		TOBACCO, MANUFACTURED (WHETHER OR NOT CONTAINING TOBACCO SUBSTITUTES)
122.10	240210 00 0	**Cigars, cheroots and cigarillos, containing tobacco**
122.20		**Cigarettes containing tobacco**
	240220 10 0	Containing cloves
	240220 90 0	Other
		Other manufactured tobacco (including smoking and chewing tobacco, snuff); tobacco extracts and essences
122.31	240290 00 0	**Cigars, cheroots, cigarillos and cigarettes, of tobacco substitutes**
122.32		**Smoking tobacco, whether or not containing tobacco substitutes in any proportion**
	240310 10 0	In immediate packings of a net content not exceeding 500 g
	240310 90 0	Other
122.39		**Manufactured tobacco, extracts and essence, n.e.s.**
	240391 00 0	"Homogenised" or "reconstituted" tobacco
		Other
	240399 10 0	Chewing tobacco and snuff
	240399 90 0	Other

SECTION: 2

**DIVISION
21**

HIDES, SKINS AND FURSKINS, RAW

HIDES AND SKINS (EXCEPT FURSKINS), RAW

Bovine or equine hides and skins (other than those of heading 211.2), raw (fresh or salted, dried, limed, pickled or otherwise preserved, but not tanned, parchment-dressed or further prepared), whether or not dehaired or split

211.11		Hides and skins (excluding those of heading 211.2) of bovine animals, fresh or wet-salted.
	410121 00 0	Whole
	410122 00 0	Butts and bends
	410129 00 0	Other
211.12		Other hides and skins of bovine animals, otherwise preserved
	410130 10 0	Dried or dry-salted
	410130 90 0	Other
211.13	410140 00 0	Hides and skins of equine animals
211.20		Whole hides and skins of bovine animals, weighing per skin not more than 8 kg when simply dried, not more than 10 kg when dry-salted, and not more than 14 kg when fresh, wet-salted or otherwise preserved
	410110 10 0	Fresh or wet-salted
	410110 90 0	Other
211.40		Goat skins and kid skins (including dehaired Yemen, Mongolian or Tibetan goat or kid skins), raw (fresh, or salted, dried, limed, pickled or otherwise preserved, but not tanned, parchment-dressed or further prepared), whether or not dehaired or split
	410310 10 0	Fresh, salted or dried
	410310 90 0	Other
211.60		Sheep skins and lamb skins (not those of Astrakhan, Broadtail, Caracul, Persian or similar lambs, Indian, Chinese, Mongolian or Tibetan lambs) with the wool on, raw (fresh or salted, dried, limed, pickled or otherwise preserved, but not tanned, parchment- dressed or further prepared),whether or not split.
	410210 10 0	Of lambs
	410210 90 0	Other
211.70		Sheep skins and lamb skins without wool on, raw (fresh, or salted, dried, limed, pickled or otherwise preserved, but not tanned, parchment-dressed or further prepared), whether or not split.
	410221 00 0	Pickled
	410229 00 0	Other

Hides and skins, n.e.s.; waste and used leather

211.91	411000 00 0	Parings and other waste of leather or of composition leather, not suitable for the manufacture of leather articles; leather dust, powder and flour
211.99		Hides and skins, n.e.s., raw (fresh, or salted, dried, limed, pickled or otherwise preserved, but not tanned, parchment-dressed or further prepared), whether or not dehaired or split
	410320 00 0	Of reptiles
	410390 00 0	Other

FURSKINS, RAW (INCLUDING HEADS, TAILS, PAWS AND OTHER PIECES OR CUTTINGS, SUITABLE FOR FURRIERS' USE), OTHER THAN HIDES AND SKINS OF GROUP 211

212.10	430110 00 0	Mink skins, raw, whole, with or without head, tail or paws.

Raw furskins, other than of mink, whole

212.21	430120 00 0	Of rabbit or hare, whole, with or without head, tail or paws
212.22	430130 00 0	Of lamb, the following: Astrakhan, Broadtail, Caracul, Persian and similar lambs, Indian, Chinese, Mongolian or Tibetan lambs, whole, with or without head, tail or paws
212.23	430140 00 0	Of beaver, whole, with or without head, tail or paws
212.24	430150 00 0	Of muskrat, whole, with or without head, tail or paws
212.25	430160 00 0	Of fox, whole, with or without head, tail or paws

S.I.T.C. (R3)	Commodity Code No	Trade description
212.26		Of seal, whole, with or without head, tail or paws
	430170 10 0	Of whitecoat pups of harp seal and of pups of hooded seal (blue-backs)
	430170 90 0	Other
212.29		Other furskins, whole, with or without head, tail or paws
	430180 10 0	Of sea-otter or of nutria (coypu)
	430180 30 0	Of marmot
	430180 50 0	Of wild felines
	430180 90 0	Other
212.30	430190 00 0	Heads, tails, paws and other pieces or cuttings, suitable for furriers' use

DIVISION 22

OIL SEEDS AND OLEAGINOUS FRUITS

OIL SEEDS AND OLEAGINOUS FRUITS OF A KIND USED FOR THE EXTRACTION OF 'SOFT' FIXED VEGETABLE OILS (EXCLUDING FLOURS AND MEALS).

Groundnuts (peanuts), not roasted or otherwise cooked, whether or not shelled or broken

S.I.T.C. (R3)	Commodity Code No	Trade description
222.11		In shell
	120210 10 0	For sowing
	120210 90 0	Other
222.12	120220 00 0	Shelled
222.20		Soya beans
	120100 10 0	For sowing
	120100 90 0	Other
222.30		Cotton seeds
	120720 10 0	For sowing
	120720 90 0	Other
222.40		Sunflower seeds
	120600 10 0	For sowing
		Other
	120600 91 0	Shelled; in grey and white striped shell
	120600 99 0	Other
222.50		Sesame (sesamum) seeds
	120740 10 0	For sowing
		Other

Rape, colza and mustard seeds

S.I.T.C. (R3)	Commodity Code No	Trade description
222.61		Rape or colza seeds
	120500 10 0	For sowing
	120500 90 0	Other
222.62		Mustard seeds
	120750 10 0	For sowing
	120750 90 0	Other
222.70		Safflower seeds
	120760 10 0	For sowing
	120760 90 0	Other

OIL SEEDS AND OLEAGINOUS FRUITS, WHOLE OR BROKEN, OF A KIND USED FOR THE EXTRACTION OF OTHER FIXED VEGETABLE OILS (INCLUDING FLOURS AND MEALS OF OIL SEEDS OR OLEAGINOUS FRUIT, N.E.S.)

S.I.T.C. (R3)	Commodity Code No	Trade description
223.10	120300 00 0	Copra
223.20		Palm nuts and palm kernels
	120710 10 0	For sowing
	120710 90 0	Other
223.40		Linseed
	120400 10 0	For sowing
	120400 90 0	Other
223.50		Castor oil seeds
	120730 10 0	For sowing
	120730 90 0	Other
223.70		Oil seeds and oleaginous fruits, n.e.s.
		Poppy seeds
	120791 10 0	For sowing

S.I.T.C. (R3)	Commodity Code No	Trade description
cont 223.70	120791 90 0	Other
		Shea nuts (karite nuts)
	120792 10 0	For sowing
	120792 90 0	Other
		Other
	120799 10 0	For sowing
		Other
	120799 91 0	Hemp seeds
	120799 99 0	Other
223.90		Flours and meals of oil seeds or oleaginous fruits (excluding mustard flour), non-defatted, partially defatted, or defatted and wholly or partially refatted with their original oils
	120810 00 0	Of soya beans
	120890 00 0	Other

DIVISION 23

CRUDE RUBBER (INCLUDING SYNTHETIC AND RECLAIMED)

NATURAL RUBBER, BALATA, GUTTA PERCHA, GUAYULE, CHICLE AND SIMILAR NATURAL GUMS, IN PRIMARY FORMS (INCLUDING LATEX) OR IN PLATES, SHEETS OR STRIP

S.I.T.C. (R3)	Commodity Code No	Trade description
231.10	400110 00 0	Natural rubber latex, whether or not prevulcanized
		Natural rubber (other than latex)
231.21	400121 00 0	Smoked sheets
231.25	400122 00 0	Technically specified natural rubber (tsnr)
231.29		Other
	400129 10 0	Crepe
	400129 90 0	Other
231.30	400130 00 0	Balata, gutta-percha, guayule, chicle and similar natural gums

SYNTHETIC RUBBER; RECLAIMED RUBBER; WASTE, PARINGS AND SCRAP OF UNHARDENED RUBBER

Synthetic rubber and factice derived from oils, in primary forms or in plates, sheets or strip; mixtures of any product of group 231 with any product of this heading, in primary forms or in plates, sheets or strip

S.I.T.C. (R3)	Commodity Code No	Trade description
232.11		Styrene-butadiene rubber (SBR); carboxylated styrene-butadiene rubber (XSBR)
	400211 00 0	Latex
	400219 00 0	Other
232.12	400220 00 0	Butadiene rubber (BR)
232.13		Isobutene-isoprene (butyl) rubber (IIR); halo-isobutene-isoprene rubber (CIIR or BIIR)
	400231 00 0	Isobutene-isoprene (butyl) rubber (IIR)
	400239 00 0	Other
232.14		Chloroprene (chlorobutadiene) rubber (CR)
	400241 00 0	Latex
	400249 00 0	Other
232.15		Acrylonitrile-butadiene rubber (NBR)
	400251 00 0	Latex
	400259 00 0	Other
232.16	400260 00 0	Isoprene rubber
232.17	400270 00 0	Ethylene-propylene-non-conjugated diene rubber (EPDM)
232.18	400280 00 0	Mixtures of any product of group 231 with any product of heading 232.1
232.19		Other synthetic rubbers and factice derived from oils
	400291 00 0	Latex
		Other
	400299 10 0	Products modified by the incorporation of plastic
	400299 90 0	Other
		Reclaimed rubber; waste and scrap of unhardened rubber
232.21	400300 00 0	Reclaimed rubber in primary forms or in plates, sheets or strip
232.22	400400 00 0	Waste, parings and scrap of unhardened rubber and powders and granules obtained therefrom

S.I.T.C. (R3)	Commodity Code No	Trade description

DIVISION 24

CORK AND WOOD

CORK, NATURAL, RAW AND WASTE (INCLUDING NATURAL CORK IN BLOCKS OR SHEETS)

S.I.T.C. (R3)	Commodity Code No	Trade description
244.02	450200 00 0	Cork, natural, debacked or roughly squared, or in rectangular blocks, plates, sheets or strip (including sharp-edged blanks for corks and stoppers)
244.03	450110 00 0	Cork, natural, raw or simply prepared
244.04	450190 00 0	Waste cork; crushed, granulated or ground cork

FUEL WOOD (EXCLUDING WOOD WASTE) AND WOOD CHARCOAL

245.01	440110 00 0	Fuel wood, in logs, in billets, in twigs, in faggots or in similar forms (excluding wood waste)
245.02	440200 00 0	Wood charcoal (including shell or nut charcoal), whether or not agglomerated

WOOD IN CHIPS OR PARTICLES AND WOOD WASTE

Wood in chips or particles

246.11	440121 00 0	Coniferous
246.15	440122 00 0	Non-coniferous
246.20		Sawdust and wood waste and scrap, whether or not agglomerated in logs, briquettes, pellets or similar forms
	440130 10 0	Sawdust
	440130 90 0	Other

WOOD IN THE ROUGH OR ROUGHLY SQUARED

247.30		Wood in the rough (whether or not stripped of bark or sapwood) or roughly squared, treated with paint, stains or other preservatives
	440310 10 0	Poles of coniferous wood, injected or otherwise impregnated to any degree, not less than 6 m nor more than 18 m in length and with a circumference at the butt end of more than 45 cm but not more than 90 cm
	*440310 90 0	Other
247.40		Wood, of coniferous species, in the rough (whether or not stripped of bark or sapwood) or roughly squared, but not treated with paint, stains or preservatives
	*440320 10 0	Spruce of the kind "Picea abies Karst." or silver fir (Abies alba Mill.)"
	*440320 30 0	Pine of the kind "Pinus sylvestrris L."
	*440320 90 0	Other

Wood, of non-coniferous species, in the rough (whether or not stripped of bark or sapwood) or roughly squared, but not treated with paint, stains or preservatives

247.51		....of the following tropical wood:
	*440341 00 0	Dark Red Meranti, Light Red Meranti and Meranti Bakau
		Other
	*440349 10 0	Sapelli, acajou d'Afrique and iroko
	*440349 20 0	Okoume
	*440349 30 0	Obeche
	*440349 40 0	Sipo
	*440349 50 0	Limba
	*440349 60 0	Tiama, mansonia, Ilomba, dibétou, limba and azobé
	*440349 70 0	Virola, mahogany (Swietenia spp.), imbuia, balsa, palissandre de Rio, palissandre de Para and palissandre de Rose
	*440349 90 0	Other
247.52		....of other non-coniferous species.
	440391 00 0	Of oak (Quercus spp.)
	440392 00 0	Of beech(Fagus spp.)
		Other
	440399 10 0	Of poplar
	440399 20 0	Of chestnut
	440399 30 0	Of eucalyptus
	*440399 50 0	Of birch
	*440399 99 0	Other

WOOD, SIMPLY WORKED, AND RAILWAY SLEEPERS OF WOOD

Railway or tramway sleepers (cross-ties) of wood.

248.11	440610 00 0	Not impregnated

S.I.T.C. (R3)	Commodity Code No	Trade description
248.19	440690 00 0	Other
248.20		Wood of coniferous species, sawn or chipped lengthways, sliced or peeled, whether or not planed, sanded or finger-jointed, of a thickness exceeding 6 mm
	440710 10 0	Finger-jointed, whether or not planed or sanded
		Other
		Planed
	*440710 31 0	Spruce of the kind "Picea abies Karst" or silver fir (Abies alba Mill)
	*440710 39 0	Other
	440710 50 0	Sanded
		Other
	440710 71 0	Small boards for the manufacture of pencils
	440710 79 0	Wood of a length of 125 cm or less and of a thickness of less than 12.5 mm
		Other
	*440710 91 0	Spruce of the kind "Picea abies Karst." or silver fir (Abies alba Mill.)
	*440710 93 0	Pine of the kind of "Pinus sylvestris L."
	*440710 99 0	Other
248.30		Wood of coniferous species (including strips and friezes for parquet flooring, not assembled), continuously shaped (tongued, grooved, rebated, chamfered, V-jointed, beaded, moulded, rounded or the like, along any of its edges or faces, whether or not planed, sanded or finger jointed
		Beadings and mouldings including moulded skirting and other moulded boards
	440910 11 0	Mouldings for frames for paintings, photographs, mirrors or similar objects
	440910 19 0	Other
	440910 90 0	Other
248.40		Wood of non-coniferous species, sawn or chipped lengthways, sliced or peeled, whether or not planed, sanded or finger-jointed, of a thickness exceeding 6 mm
		Of the following tropical woods
		Virola, mahogany (Swietenia spp.), imbuia and balsa
	*440724 10 0	Finger-jointed, whether or not planed or sanded
		Other
	*440724 30 0	Planed
	*440724 50 0	Sanded
	*440724 90 0	Other
		Dark red meranti, light red meranti, meranti bakau
	*440725 10 0	Finger-jointed, whether or not planed or sanded
		Other
		Planed
	*440725 31 0	Blocks, strips and friezes for parquet or wood block flooring, not assembled
	*440725 39 0	Other
	*440725 50 0	Sanded
		Other
	*440725 60 0	Dark red meranti and light red meranti
	*440725 80 0	Meranti bakau
		White lauan, white meranti, white seraya, yellow meranti and alan
	*440726 10 0	Finger-jointed, whether or not planed or sanded
		Other
		Planed
	*440726 31 0	Blocks, strips and friezes for parquet or wood block flooring, not assembled
	*440726 39 0	Other
	*440726 50 0	Sanded
		Other
	*440726 70 0	White lauan and white meranti
	*440726 80 0	White seraya, yellow meranti and alan
		Other
		Keruing, ramin, kapur, teak, jongkong, merbau, jelutong, kempas, okoume, obeche, sapelli, sipo, acajou d'Afrique, makore, iroko, tiama, mansinia. ilomba. dibetou, limba, azobe, palissandre de Rio, palissandre de Para and palissandre de Rose
	*440729 10 0	Finger-jointed, whether or not planed or sanded
		Other
		Planed
	*440729 20 0	Palissandre de Rio, palissandre de Para and palissandre de Rose
		Other
	*440729 31 0	Blocks, strips and friezes for parquet or wood block flooring, not assembled
	*440729 39 0	Other
	*440729 50 0	Sanded
		Other
	*440729 61 0	Azobe
	*440729 69 0	Other
		Other
	*440729 70 0	Finger-jointed, whether or not planed or sanded
		Other
	*440729 83 0	Planed
	*440729 85 0	Sanded
	*440729 99 0	Other
		Other
		Of oak (Quercus spp.)

S.I.T.C. (R3)	Commodity Code No	Trade description
cont 248.40	440791 10 0	Finger-jointed, whether or not planed or sanded
		Other
		Planed
	440791 31 0	Blocks, strips and friezes for parquet or wood block flooring, not assembled
	440791 39 0	Other
	440791 50 0	Sanded
	440791 90 0	Other
		Of beech (*Fagus spp.*)
	440792 10 0	Finger-jointed, whether or not planed or sanded
		Other
	440792 30 0	Planed
	440792 50 0	Sanded
	440792 90 0	Other
		Other
	*440799 10 0	Finger-jointed, whether or not planed or sanded
		Other
	*440799 30 0	Planed
	*440799 50 0	Sanded
		Other
	440799 91 0	Of poplar
	440799 93 0	Of walnut
	*440799 98 0	Other
248.50		Wood of non-coniferous species (including strips and friezes for parquet flooring, not assembled), continuously shaped (tongued, grooved, rebated, chamfered, V-jointed, beaded, moulded, rounded or the like) along any of its edges or faces, whether or not planed, sanded or finger jointed
		Beadings and mouldings including moulded skirting and other moulded boards
	440920 11 0	Mouldings for frames for paintings, photographs, mirrors or similar objects
	440920 19 0	Other
		Other
	440920 91 0	Blocks, strips and friezes for parquet or wood block flooring, not assembled
	440920 99 0	Other

DIVISION 25

PULP AND WASTE PAPER

S.I.T.C. (R3)	Commodity Code No	Trade description
		Waste and scrap of paper or paperboard
251.11	470710 00 0	....of unbleached kraft paper or paperboard or of corrugated paper
251.12	470720 00 0	....of other paper or paperboard made mainly of bleached chemical
251.13		....of paper or paperboard made mainly of mechanical pulp (e.g. newspapers, journals and similar printed matter
	470730 10 0	Old and unsold newspapers and magazines, telephone directories, brochures and printed advertising material
	470730 90 0	Other
251.19		....other (including unsorted waste and scrap)
	470790 10 0	Unsorted
	470790 90 0	Sorted
251.20		Mechanical wood pulp
	470100 10 0	Thermo-mechanical wood pulp
	470100 90 0	Other
251.30	470200 00 0	Chemical wood pulp, dissolving grades
		Chemical wood pulp, soda or sulphate, other than dissolving grades, unbleached.
251.41	470311 00 0	....coniferous
251.42	470319 00 0	....non-coniferous
		Chemical wood pulp, soda or sulphate, semi-bleached or bleached (other than dissolving grades)
251.51	470321 00 0	....coniferous
251.52	470329 00 0	....non-coniferous
		Chemical wood pulp, sulphite (other than dissolving grades)
251.61		....unbleached
	470411 00 0	Coniferous
	470419 00 0	Non-coniferous

S.I.T.C. (R3)	Commodity Code No	Trade description
251.62		....semi-bleached or bleached (other than dissolving grades)
	470421 00 0	Coniferous
	470429 00 0	Non-coniferous
		Semi-chemical wood pulp and pulps of other fibrous cellulosic material
251.91	470500 00 0	Semi-chemical wood pulp
251.92		Pulps of other fibrous cellulosic material
	470610 00 0	Cotton linters pulp
	*470620 00 0	Pulp of fibres derived from recovered (waste and scrap) paper or paperboard
		Other
	*470691 00 0	Mechanical
	*470692 00 0	Chemical
	*470693 00 0	Semi-chemical

DIVISION 26

TEXTILE FIBRES (OTHER THAN WOOL TOPS AND OTHER COMBED WOOL) AND THEIR WASTES (NOT MANUFACTURED INTO YARN OR FABRIC)

SILK

S.I.T.C. (R3)	Commodity Code No	Trade description
261.30	500200 00 0	Raw silk (not thrown)
		Silk worm cocoons and silk waste
261.41	500100 00 0	Silk worm cocoons suitable for reeling
261.42	500310 00 0	Silk waste (including cocoons unsuitable for reeling, yarn waste and garnetted stock) not carded or combed
261.49	500390 00 0	Other silk waste
		COTTON
263.10		Cotton (other than linters), not carded or combed.
	520100 10 0	Rendered absorbent or bleached
	520100 90 0	Other
263.20	140420 00 0	Cotton linters
		Cotton waste (including yarn waste and garnetted stock).
263.31	520210 00 0	Yarn waste (including thread waste)
263.32	520291 00 0	Garnetted stock
263.39	520299 00 0	Other cotton waste
263.40	520300 00 0	Cotton, carded or combed

JUTE AND OTHER TEXTILE BAST FIBRES, N.E.S., RAW OR PROCESSED BUT NOT SPUN; TOW AND WASTE OF THESE FIBRES (INCLUDING YARN WASTE AND GARNETTED STOCK)

S.I.T.C. (R3)	Commodity Code No	Trade description
264.10	530310 00 0	Jute and other textile bast fibres, raw or retted
264.90	530390 00 0	Other

VEGETABLE TEXTILE FIBRES (OTHER THAN COTTON AND JUTE), RAW OR PROCESSED BUT NOT SPUN; WASTE OF THESE FIBRES

Flax, raw or processed but not spun; flax tow and waste (including yarn waste and garnetted stock)

S.I.T.C. (R3)	Commodity Code No	Trade description
265.11	530110 00 0	Flax, raw or retted
265.12		Flax, broken, scutched, hackled or otherwise processed, but not spun
	530121 00 0	Broken or scutched
	530129 00 0	Other
265.13		Flax tow and waste (including yarn waste and garnetted stock)
	530130 10 0	Tow
	530130 90 0	Flax waste

True hemp (Cannabis sativa L.), raw or processed but not spun; tow and waste of true hemp (including yarn waste and garnetted stock)

S.I.T.C. (R3)	Commodity Code No	Trade description
265.21	530210 00 0	True hemp, raw or retted

S.I.T.C. (R3)	Commodity Code No	Trade description
265.29	530290 00 0	Other

Sisal and other textile fibres of the genus agave, raw or processed but not spun; tow and waste of these fibres (including yarn waste and garnetted stock)

265.41	530410 00 0	Sisal and other textile fibres of the genus agave, raw
265.49	530490 00 0	Other

Abaca (Manila hemp or musa textilis nee), raw or processed but not spun; tow and waste of Manila hemp (including yarn waste and garnetted stock)

265.51	530521 00 0	Abaca (Manila hemp or musa textilis nee), raw
265.59	530529 00 0	Other

Coconut fibres (coir) and waste of these fibres (including yarn waste and garnetted stock)

265.71	530511 00 0	Coconut fibres (coir), raw
265.79	530519 00 0	Other

Vegetable textile fibres, n.e.s., raw or processed but not spun; waste of these fibres (including yarn waste and garnetted stock)

265.81	530591 00 0	Vegetable textile fibres, n.e.s., raw
265.89	530599 00 0	Other

SYNTHETIC FIBRES SUITABLE FOR SPINNING

Synthetic staple fibres, not carded, combed or otherwise processed for spinning

266.51		.... of nylon or other polyamides
		Of aramids
	550310 11 0	High tenacity
	550310 19 0	Other
	550310 90 0	Other
266.52	550320 00 0	.... of polyesters
266.53	550330 00 0	.... acrylic or modacrylic
266.59		Synthetic staple fibres, not processed for spinning, n.e.s.
	550340 00 0	Of polypropylene
		Other
	550390 10 0	Chlorofibres
	550390 90 0	Other

Synthetic filament tow

266.61	550110 00 0	....of nylon or other polyamides
266.62	550120 00 0	....of polyesters
266.63	550130 00 0	....acrylic or modacrylic
266.69	550190 00 0	Synthetic filament tow, n.e.s.

Synthetic staple fibres, carded, combed or otherwise processed for spinning

266.71	550610 00 0	....of nylon or other polyamides
266.72	550620 00 0	....of polyesters
266.73	550630 00 0	....acrylic or modacrylic
266.79		Synthetic staple fibres processed for spinning, n.e.s.
	550690 10 0	Chlorofibres
		Other
	550690 91 0	Of polypropylene
	550690 99 0	Other

S.I.T.C. (R3)	Commodity Code No	Trade description
		OTHER MAN-MADE FIBRES SUITABLE FOR SPINNING AND WASTE OF MAN-MADE FIBRES
		Artificial fibres suitable for spinning
267.11		Artificial staple fibres, not carded, combed or otherwise processed for spinning
	550410 00 0	Of viscose rayon
	550490 00 0	Other
267.12		Artificial filament tow
	550200 10 0	Of viscoe rayon
	550200 90 0	Other
267.13	550700 00 0	Artificial staple fibres, carded, combed or otherwise processed for spinning
		Waste (including noils, yarn waste and garnetted stock), of man-made fibres.
267.21		....of synthetic fibres
	550510 10 0	Of nylon or other polyamides
	550510 30 0	Of polyesters
	550510 50 0	Acrylic or modacrylic
	550510 70 0	Of polypropylene
	550510 90 0	Other
267.22	550520 00 0	....of artificial fibres
		WOOL AND OTHER ANIMAL HAIR (INCLUDING WOOL TOPS)
		Wool, greasy (including fleece-washed wool)
268.11	*510111 00 0	Shorn wool
268.19	510119 00 0	Other
		Other wool, not carded or combed
268.21		Degreased, not carbonised
	*510121 00 0	Shorn wool
	510129 00 0	Other
268.29	510130 00 0	Carbonised
268.30		Fine animal hair, not carded or combed
	510210 10 0	Of Angora rabbit
	510210 30 0	Of alpaca, llama and vicuna
	*510210 50 0	Of camel or yak, or of Angora, Tibetan, Kashmir or similar goats
	510210 90 0	Of rabbit (other than Angora rabbit), hare, beaver, nutria and musk rat
		Horsehair and other coarse animal hair, not carded or combed
268.51	050300 00 0	Horsehair and horsehair waste, whether or not put up as a layer with or without supporting material
268.59	510220 00 0	Other coarse animal hair, not carded or combed
		Waste of wool or of fine or coarse animal hair, other than horsehair, (including yarn waste and garnetted stock)
268.62	510400 00 0	Garnetted stock of wool or of fine or coarse animal hair
268.63		Noils of wool or of fine animal hair, not garnetted
	510310 10 0	Not carbonised
	510310 90 0	Carbonised
268.69		Other waste of wool or of fine or coarse animal hair (other than horsehair)
		Waste of wool of fine animal hair
	510320 10 0	Yarn waste
		Other
	510320 91 0	Not carbonised
	510320 99 0	Carbonised
	510330 00 0	Waste of coarse animal hair
		Wool or other animal hair, fine or coarse, carded or combed
268.71		Carded wool; combed wool in fragments
	510510 00 0	Carded wool
	510521 00 0	Combed wool in fragments
268.73	*510529 00 0	Wool tops and other combed wool

S.I.T.C. (R3)	Commodity Code No	Trade description
268.77		Fine or coarse animal hair, carded or combed
		Fine animal hair, carded or combed
	510530 10 0	Carded
	510530 90 0	Combed
	510540 00 0	Coarse animal hair, carded or combed

WORN CLOTHING AND OTHER WORN TEXTILE ARTICLES; RAGS

Worn clothing and other worn textile articles; rags

269.01	630900 00 0	Clothing, clothing accessories, travelling rugs and blankets, household linen and furnishing articles (other than articles falling within headings 658.9, 659.2 through 659.6 or 821), of textile materials, footwear and headgear of any material other than of asbestos, showing signs of appreciable wear and traded in bulk or in bales, sacks or similar bulk packings
269.02		Used or new rags, scrap twine, cordage, rope and cables and worn out articles of twine, cordage, rope or cables of textile materials
		Sorted
	631010 10 0	Of wool or fine or coarse animal hair
	631010 30 0	Of flax or cotton
	631010 90 0	Of other textile materials
	631090 00 0	Other

DIVISION 27
CRUDE FERTILISERS, OTHER THAN THOSE OF DIVISION 56, AND CRUDE MINERALS (EXCLUDING COAL, PETROLEUM AND PRECIOUS STONES)

FERTILISERS, CRUDE, OTHER THAN THOSE OF DIVISION 56

272.10	310100 00 0	Animal or vegetable fertilisers, whether or not mixed together or chemically treated; fertilisers produced by the mixing or chemical treatment of animal or vegetable products
272.20		Sodium nitrate
	310250 10 0	Natural sodium nitrate
	310250 90 0	Other

Natural calcium phosphates; natural aluminium calcium phosphates and phosphatic chalk

272.31	251010 00 0	....unground
272.32	251020 00 0	....ground
272.40	310410 00 0	Carnallite, sylvite and other crude natural potassium salts

STONE, SAND AND GRAVEL

Building or monumental (dimension) stone, not further worked than roughly trimmed or merely cut, by sawing or otherwise, into blocks or slabs of a square or rectangular shape

273.11	251400 00 0	Slate, whether or not roughly trimmed or merely cut, by sawing or otherwise, into blocks or slabs of a square or rectangular shape
273.12		Marble, travertine, ecaussine and other calcareous monumental or building stone of an apparent specific gravity of 2.5 or more, and alabaster, whether or not roughly trimmed or merely cut, by sawing or otherwise, into blocks or slabs of a square or rectangular shape
		Marble and travertine
	251511 00 0	Crude or roughly trimmed
		Merely cut, by sawing or otherwise, into blocks or slabs of a rectangular (including square) shape
	251512 20 0	Of a thickness not exceeding 4 cm
	251512 50 0	Of a thickness exceeding 4 cm but not exceeding 25 cm
	251512 90 0	Other
	251520 00 0	Ecaussine and other calcareous monumental or building stone; alabaster
273.13		Granite, porphyry, basalt, sandstone and other monumental or building stone, n.e.s., whether or not roughly trimmed or merely cut, by sawing or otherwise, into blocks or slabs of a square or rectangular shape
		Granite
	251611 00 0	Crude or roughly trimmed
		Merely cut, by sawing or otherwise, into blocks or slabs of a rectangular (including square) shape
	251612 10 0	Of a thickness not exceeding 25 cm
	251612 90 0	Other
		Sandstone
	251621 00 0	Crude or roughly trimmed
		Merely cut, by sawing or otherwise, into blocks or slabs of a rectangular (including square) shape
	251622 10 0	Of a thickness not exceeding 25 cm
	251622 90 0	Other

S.I.T.C. (R3)	Commodity Code No	Trade description
cont 273.13		
	251690 10 0	Other monumental or building stone Porphyry, syenite, lava, basalt, gneiss, trachyte and other similar hard rocks, merely cut, by sawing or other wise, into blocks or slabs of a rectangular (including square) shape, of a thickness not exceeding 25 cm
	251690 90 0	Other
		Gypsum, plasters, limestone flux, limestone and other calcareous stone of a kind used for the manufacture of lime or cement
273.22	252100 00 0	Limestone flux; limestone and other calcareous stone of a kind used for the manufacture of lime or cement
273.23	252010 00 0	Gypsum and anhydrite
273.24		**Plasters (consisting of calcined gypsum or calcined sulphate), whether or not coloured, with or without small quantities of accelerators or retarders (including plasters specially prepared for use in dentistry)**
	252020 10 0	Building
	252020 90 0	Other
		Sands, natural, of all kinds, whether or not coloured (other than metal bearing sands of division 28)
273.31	250510 00 0	Silica sands and quartz sands
273.39	250590 00 0	Other sands
273.40		**Pebbles, gravel, broken or crushed stone, of a kind commonly used for concrete aggregates, for road metalling or for railway or other ballast, shingle and flint, whether or not heat-treated; macadam of slag, dross or similar industrial waste, whether or not incorporating materials cited in the first part of the heading; tarred macadam; granules, chippings and powder of stones of heading 273.12 or 273.13, whether or not heat-treated** Pebbles, gravel, broken or crushed stone, of a kind commonly used for concrete aggregates, for road metalling or for railway or other ballast, shingle and flint, whether or not heat-treated
	251710 10 0	Pebbles, gravel, shingle and flint
	*251710 20 0	Limestone, dolomite and other calcereous stone, broken or crushed
	*251710 80 0	Other
	251720 00 0	Macadam of slag, dross or similar industrial waste, whether or not incorporating the materials cited in subheading No. 2517.10
	251730 00 0	Tarred macadam Granules, chippings and powder, of stones of heading 273.12,13, whether or not heat-treated
	251741 00 0	Of marble
	251749 00 0	Other
		SULPHUR AND UNROASTED IRON PYRITES **Sulphur of all kinds (other than sublimed, precipitated or colloidal sulphur)**
274.11	*250300 10 0	Crude or unrefined sulphur
274.19	*250300 90 0	Other
274.20	250200 00 0	Iron pyrites, unroasted
		NATURAL ABRASIVES, N.E.S. (INCLUDING INDUSTRIAL DIAMONDS) **Industrial diamonds, sorted, whether or not worked**
277.11	710221 00 0	Unworked or simply sawn, cleaved or bruted
277.19	710229 00 0	Otherwise worked **Natural abrasives, n.e.s.**
277.21		**Dust and powder of natural or synthetic precious or semi-precious stones**
	710510 00 0	Of diamonds
	710590 00 0	Other
277.22		**Pumice stone; emery; natural corundum, natural garnet and other natural abrasives, crude or in irregular pieces, including crushed pumice ("bimskies")**
	251311 00 0	Pumice stone
	*251320 00 0	Emery, natural corundum, natural garnet and other natural abrasives (crude or in irregular pieces)
277.29		**Pumice stone; emery; natural corundum, natural garnet and other natural abrasives, other than crude, whether or not heat-treated**
	251319 00 0	Pumice stone
	*251320 00 0	Emery, natural corundum, natural garnet and other natural abrasives (other than crude or in regular pieces)

S.I.T.C. (R3)	Commodity Code No	Trade description
		OTHER CRUDE MINERALS
		Clays and other refractory minerals, n.e.s.
278.22		Graphite, natural
	250410 00 0	In powder or in flakes
	250490 00 0	Other
278.23		Dolomite, whether or not calcined; dolomite roughly trimmed or merely cut, by sawing or otherwise, into blocks or slabs of a square or rectangular shape; agglomerated dolomite (including tarred dolomite)
	251810 00 0	Dolomite not calcined
	251820 00 0	Calcined dolomite
	251830 00 0	Agglomerated dolomite (including tarred dolomite)
278.24	251910 00 0	Natural magnesium carbonate (magnesite)
278.25		Fused magnesia; dead-burned (sintered) magnesia; other magnesium oxide, whether or not pure
	251990 10 0	Magnesium oxide, other than calcined natural magnesium carbonate
	251990 30 0	Dead-burned (sintered) magnesia
	251990 90 0	Other
278.26		Kaolin and other kaolinic clays, whether or not calcined
	*250700 20 0	Kaolin
	*250700 80 0	Other kaolinic clays
278.27	250810 00 0	Bentonite
278.29		Other clays, not including expanded clays of heading 663.5; andalusite, kyanite and sillimanite, whether or not calcined; mullite; chamotte and dinas earths
	250820 00 0	Decolourising earths and fuller's earth
	250830 00 0	Fire-clay
	250840 00 0	Other clays
	250850 00 0	Andalusite, kyanite and sillimanite
	250860 00 0	Mullite
		Chamotte or dinas earths
	250870 10 0	Chamotte earth
	250870 90 0	Dinas earth
278.30		Sodium chloride, pure, and common salt (including table salt and denatured salt), whether or not in aqueous solution or containing added anticaking or free-flowing agents; sea water
	250100 10 0	Sea water and salt liquors
		Common salt (including table salt and denatured salt) and pure sodium chloride, whether or not in aqueous solution
	250100 31 0	For chemical transformation (separation of Na from Cl) for the manufacture of other products
		Other
	250100 51 0	Denatured or for industrial uses (including refining) other than the preservation or preparation of foodstuffs for human or animal consumption
		Other
	250100 91 0	Salt suitable for human consumption
	250100 99 0	Other
278.40		Asbestos
	252400 30 0	Fibres, flakes or powder
	252400 80 0	Other
		Quartz, mica, felspar, fluorspar, cryolite and chiolite
278.51		Quartz (other than natural sands); quartzite, whether or not roughly trimmed or merely cut, by sawing or otherwise, into blocks or slabs of a square or rectangular shape
	250610 00 0	Quartz
		Quartzite
	250621 00 0	Crude or roughly trimmed
	250629 00 0	Other
278.52		Mica (including splittings); mica waste
	252510 00 0	Crude mica and mica rifted into sheets or splittings
	252520 00 0	Mica powder
	252530 00 0	Mica waste
278.53		Felspar; leucite; nepheline and nepheline syenite
	252910 00 0	Felspar
	252930 00 0	Leucite; nepheline and nepheline syenite
278.54		Fluorspar
	252921 00 0	Containing by weight 97 % or less of calcium fluoride
	252922 00 0	Containing by weight more than 97 % of calcium fluoride

S.I.T.C. (R3)	Commodity Code No	Trade description
278.55	252700 00 0	Cryolite, natural, chiolite, natural
		Slag, dross, scalings and similar waste, n.e.s.
278.61	261800 00 0	Granulated slag (slag sand) from the manufacture of iron or steel
278.62		Slag, dross (other than granulated slag), scalings and other waste from the manufacture of iron or steel
	261900 10 0	Blast-furnace dust (ECSC)
		Other
	261900 91 0	Waste suitable for the recovery of iron or manganese
	261900 93 0	Slag suitable for the extraction of titanium oxide
	261900 95 0	Waste suitable for the extraction of vanadium
	261900 99 0	Other
278.69	262100 00 0	Slag and ash, n.e.s., including seaweed ash (kelp)
		Minerals, crude, n.e.s.
278.91	250900 00 0	Chalk
278.92		Natural barium sulphate (barytes); natural barium carbonate (witherite), whether or not calcined (other than barium oxide of heading 522.65)
	251110 00 0	Natural barium sulphate (barytes)
	251120 00 0	Natural barium carbonate (witherite)
278.93		Steatite, natural, whether or not roughly trimmed or merely cut, by sawing or otherwise, into blocks or slabs of a square or rectangular shape; talc
	252610 00 0	Not crushed, not powdered
	252620 00 0	Crushed or powdered
278.94		Natural borates and concentrates thereof (calcined or not) but not including borates separated from natural brine; natural boric acid containing not more than 85% of H_3BO_3 calculated on the dry weight
	252810 00 0	Natural sodium borates and concentrates thereof (whether or not calcined)
	252890 00 0	Other
278.95	251200 00 0	Siliceous fossil meals (e.g., kieselguhr, tripolite and diatomite) and similar siliceous earths, whether or not calcined, of an apparent specific gravity of 1 or less
278.96	271410 00 0	Bituminous shale and tar sands
278.97	271490 00 0	Bitumen and asphalt, natural; asphaltites and asphaltic rocks
278.98		Vermiculite, perlite and chlorites, unexpanded
	253010 10 0	Perlite
	253010 90 0	Vermiculite and chlorites
278.99		Mineral substances, n.e.s.
	253020 00 0	Kieserite, epsomite (natural magnesium sulphates)
	253040 00 0	Natural micaceous iron oxides
		Other
	253090 20 0	Sepiolite
	*253090 95 0	Other

DIVISION 28

METALLIFEROUS ORES AND METAL SCRAP

IRON ORE AND CONCENTRATES

S.I.T.C. (R3)	Commodity Code No	Trade description
281.40	260120 00 0	Roasted iron pyrites (pyrites cinders), whether or not agglomerated
281.50	260111 00 0	Iron ore and concentrates, not agglomerated (ECSC)
281.60	260112 00 0	Iron ore agglomerates (sinters, pellets, briquettes, etc.) (ECSC)
		FERROUS WASTE AND SCRAP; REMELTING INGOTS OF IRON OR STEEL
282.10	720410 00 0	Waste and scrap of cast iron
		Waste and scrap of alloy steel
282.21		....of stainless steel
	*720421 10 0	Containing by weight 8 % or more of nickel
	*720421 90 0	Other
282.29	720429 00 0	....of other alloy steel

S.I.T.C. (R3)	Commodity Code No	Trade description
		Other ferrous waste and scrap
282.31	720430 00 0	Waste and scrap of tinned iron or steel
282.32		Turnings, shavings, chips, milling waste, sawdust, filings, trimmings and stampings, whether or not in bundles
	720441 10 0	Turnings, shavings, chips, milling waste, sawdust and filings
		Trimmings and stampings
	720441 91 0	In bundles
	720441 99 0	Other
282.33		Remelting ingots of iron or steel
	720450 10 0	Of alloy steel (ECSC)
	720450 90 0	Other (ECSC)
282.39		Ferrous waste and scrap, n.e.s.
	720449 10 0	Fragmentised (shredded)
		Other
	720449 30 0	In bundles
		Other
	720449 91 0	Neither sorted nor graded
	720449 99 0	Other
	*854810 90 0	Waste and scrap of primary cells, primary batteries and electric accumulators
		COPPER ORES AND CONCENTRATES; COPPER MATTES, CEMENT COPPER
283.10	260300 00 0	Copper ores and concentrates
		Copper mattes; cement copper (precipitated copper)
283.21	740110 00 0	Copper mattes
283.22	740120 00 0	Cement copper (precipitated copper)
		NICKEL ORES AND CONCENTRATES; NICKEL MATTES, NICKEL OXIDE SINTERS AND OTHER INTERMEDIATE PRODUCTS OF NICKEL METALLURGY
284.10	260400 00 0	Nickel ores and concentrates
		Nickel mattes, nickel oxide sinters and other intermediate products of nickel metallurgy
284.21	750110 00 0	Nickel mattes
284.22	750120 00 0	Nickel oxide sinters and other intermediate products of nickel metallurgy
		ALUMINIUM ORES AND CONCENTRATES (INCLUDING ALUMINA)
285.10	260600 00 0	Aluminium ores and concentrates
285.20	*281820 00 0	Alumina (aluminium oxide) other than artificial corundum
		ORES AND CONCENTRATES OF URANIUM OR THORIUM
286.10		Uranium ores and concentrates
	261210 10 0	Uranium ores and pitchblende, and concentrates thereof, with a uranium content of more than 5 % by weight (*Euratom*)
	261210 90 0	Other
286.20		Thorium ores and concentrates
	261220 10 0	Monazite; urano-thorianite and other thorium ores and concentrates, with a thorium content of more than 20 % by weight (*Euratom*)
	261220 90 0	Other
		ORES AND CONCENTRATES OF BASE METALS, N.E.S.
287.40	260700 00 0	Lead ores and concentrates
287.50	260800 00 0	Zinc ores and concentrates
287.60	260900 00 0	Tin ores and concentrates
287.70	260200 00 0	Manganese ores and concentrates (including manganiferous iron ores and concentrates with a manganese content of 20% or more calculated on the dry weight)
		Ores and concentrates of molybdenum, niobium, tantalum, titanium, vanadium and zirconium
287.81	261310 00 0	Molybdenum ores and concentrates, roasted
287.82	261390 00 0	Molybdenum ores and concentrates, other than roasted

S.I.T.C. (R3)	Commodity Code No	Trade description
287.83		Titanium ores and concentrates
	261400 10 0	Ilmenite and concentrates thereof
	261400 90 0	Other
287.84	261510 00 0	Zirconium ores and concentrates
287.85		Niobium, tantalum or vanadium ores and concentrates
	261590 10 0	Niobium and tantalum ores and concentrates
	261590 90 0	Vanadium ores and concentrates

Ores and concentrates of other non-ferrous base metals

287.91	261000 00 0	Chromium ores and concentrates
287.92	261100 00 0	Tungsten (or wolfram) ores and concentrates
287.93	260500 00 0	Cobalt ores and concentrates
287.99		Base metal ores and concentrates, n.e.s.
	261710 00 0	Antimony ores and concentrates
	261790 00 0	Other

NON-FERROUS BASE METAL WASTE AND SCRAP, N.E.S.

288.10		Ash and residues (other than from the manufacture of iron or steel) containing metals or metallic compounds, n.e.s.
		Containing mainly zinc
	262011 00 0	Hard zinc spelter
	262019 00 0	Other
	262020 00 0	Containing mainly lead
	262030 00 0	Containing mainly copper
	262040 00 0	Containing mainly aluminium
	262050 00 0	Containing mainly vanadium
		Other
	262090 10 0	Containing mainly nickel
	262090 20 0	Containing mainly niobium and tantalum
	262090 30 0	Containing mainly tungsten
	262090 40 0	Containing mainly tin
	262090 50 0	Containing mainly molybdenum
	262090 60 0	Containing mainly titanium
	262090 70 0	Containing mainly antimony
	262090 80 0	Containing mainly cobalt
	262090 91 0	Containing mainly zirconium
	262090 99 0	Other
288.21		Other non-ferrous base metal waste and scrap, n.e.s.
		Copper waste and scrap
	740400 10 0	Of refined copper
		Of copper alloys
	740400 91 0	Of copper-zinc base alloys (brass)
	740400 99 0	Other
288.22		Nickel waste and scrap
	750300 10 0	Of nickel, not alloyed
	750300 90 0	Of nickel alloys
288.23		Aluminium waste and scrap
		Waste
	760200 11 0	Turnings, shavings, chips, milling waste, sawdust and filings; waste of coloured, coated or bonded sheets and foil, of a thickness (excluding any backing) not exceeding 0.2 mm
	760200 19 0	Other (including factory rejects)
	760200 90 0	Scrap
288.24	*780200 00 0	Lead waste and scrap
288.25	790200 00 0	Zinc waste and scrap (other than dust)
288.26	800200 00 0	Tin waste and scrap

ORES AND CONCENTRATES OF PRECIOUS METALS; WASTE, SCRAP AND SWEEPINGS OF PRECIOUS METALS (OTHER THAN OF GOLD)

Ores and concentrates of precious metals

289.11	261610 00 0	Silver ores and concentrates
289.19	*261690 00 0	Ores and concentrates of other precious metals

S.I.T.C. (R3)	Commodity Code No	Trade description
		Waste and scrap of precious metal (other than gold) or of metals clad with precious metal (other than gold)
289.21	711220 00 0	Waste and scrap of platinum, including metal clad with platinum but excluding sweepings containing other metals
289.29	711290 00 0	Waste and scrap of precious metal, n.e.s., or of metal clad with such precious metal

DIVISION 29

CRUDE ANIMAL AND VEGETABLE MATERIALS, N.E.S.

CRUDE ANIMAL MATERIALS, N.E.S.

Bones, horns, ivory, hooves, claws, coral, shells and similar products

S.I.T.C. (R3)	Commodity Code No	Trade description
291.11		Bones (including bones of whales, of seals and of other air- breathing aquatic vertebrates) and horn-cores, unworked, de- fatted, simply prepared (but not cut to shape), treated with acid or degelatinized; powder and waste of these products
	050610 00 0	Ossein and bones treated with acid
	050690 00 0	Other
291.15	050800 00 0	Coral and similar materials, unworked or simply prepared but not otherwise worked; shells and cuttle-bone, unworked or simply prepared but not cut to shape, powder and waste thereof
291.16		Ivory, tortoise-shell, whalebone and whalebone hair, horns, antlers, hooves, nails, claws and beaks, unworked or simply prepared but not cut to shape; waste and powder of these products
	050710 00 0	Ivory; ivory powder and waste
	050790 00 0	Other

Materials of animal origin, n.e.s.

S.I.T.C. (R3)	Commodity Code No	Trade description
291.91	050100 00 0	Human hair, unworked, whether or not washed or scoured; waste of human hair
291.92		Pigs', hogs' or boars' bristles and hair; badger hair and other brush making hair; waste of such bristles or hair
	050210 00 0	Pigs', hogs' or boars' bristles and hair and waste thereof
	050290 00 0	Other
291.93	050400 00 0	Guts, bladders and stomachs of animals (other than fish), whole and pieces thereof
291.94	051110 00 0	Bovine semen
291.95		Skins and other parts of birds, with their feathers or down, feathers and parts of feathers (whether or not with trimmed edges) and down, not further worked than cleaned, disinfected or treated for preservation; powder and waste of feathers or parts of feathers
		Feathers of a kind used for stuffing; down
	050510 10 0	Raw
	050510 90 0	Other
	050590 00 0	Other
291.96		Products of fish or crustaceans, molluscs or other aquatic invertebrates; dead animals of division 03, unfit for human consumption
	051191 10 0	Fish waste
	051191 90 0	Other
291.97		Natural sponges of animal origin
	050900 10 0	Raw
	050900 90 0	Other
291.98		Ambergris, castoreum, civet and musk; cantharides; bile, whether or not dried; glands and other animal products used in the preparation of pharmaceutical products, fresh, chilled, frozen or otherwise provisionally preserved
	051000 10 0	Glands and other organs for organo-therapeutic uses
	051000 90 0	Other
291.99		Animal products, n.e.s.
	051199 10 0	Sinews or tendons; parings and similar waste of raw hides or skins
	051199 50 0	Embryos of bovine animals
	051199 80 0	Other

CRUDE VEGETABLE MATERIALS, N.E.S.

Lac; natural gums, resins, gum-resins, and balsams

S.I.T.C. (R3)	Commodity Code No	Trade description
292.21	130110 00 0	Lac
292.22	130120 00 0	Gum Arabic

S.I.T.C. (R3)	Commodity Code No	Trade description
292.29		Other natural gums, resins, gum-resins and balsams
	130190 10 0	Chios mastic (mastic of the tree of the species *Pistacia lentiscus*)
	130190 90 0	Other

Vegetable materials of a kind used primarily for plaiting (e.g., bamboos, rattans, reeds, rushes, oster, raffia, cleaned, bleached or dyed cereal straw, and lime bark)

292.31	140110 00 0	Bamboos
292.32	140120 00 0	Rattans
292.39	140190 00 0	Vegetable materials, other than bamboos or rattans, of a kind used primarily for plaiting

Plants and parts of plants (including seeds and fruits) of a kind used primarily in perfumery, in pharmacy, or for insecticidal, fungicidal or similar purposes, fresh or dried, whether or not cut, crushed or powdered

292.41	121110 00 0	Liquorice roots
292.42	121120 00 0	Ginseng roots
292.49		Other
	121190 10 0	Pyrethum (flowers, leaves, stems, peels and roots)
	121190 30 0	Tonquin beans
	121190 40 0	Mint (stems and leaves)
	121190 60 0	Linden (flowers and leaves)
	121190 65 0	Verbena (leaves and tops)
	121190 70 0	Wild marjoram (*Origanum vulgare*) (branches, stems and leaves)
	121190 75 0	Sage (*Salvia officinalis*) (leaves and flowers)
	121190 80 0	Other

Seeds, fruit and spores, n.e.s., of a kind used for sowing

292.51	120911 00 0	Sugar beet seed
292.52		Seeds of forage plants (other than beet seed)
	120921 00 0	Lucerne (alfalfa) seed
		Clover (*Trifolium spp.*) seed
	120922 10 0	Red clover (*Trifolium pratense L.*)
	120922 80 0	Other
		Fescue seed
	120923 11 0	Meadow fescue (*Festuca pratensis Huds.*) seed
	120923 15 0	Red fescue (*Festuca rubra L.*) seed
	120923 80 0	Other
	120924 00 0	Kentucky blue grass (*Poa pratensis L.*) seed
		Rye grass (*Lolium multiflorum Lam.*, *Lolium perenne L.*) seed
	120925 10 0	Italian ryegrass (including westerwolds) (*Lolium multiflorum Lam.*)
	120925 90 0	Perennial ryegrass (*Lolium perenne L.*)
	120926 00 0	Timothy grass seed
		Other
	120929 10 0	Vetch seed; Seeds of the genus *Poa* (*Poa palustris L.*, *Poa trivialis L.*); Cocksfoot grass (*Dactylis glomerata L.*); Bent grass (*Agrostis*)
	120929 50 0	Lupine seed
	120929 80 0	Other
292.53	120930 00 0	Seeds of herbaceous plants cultivated principally for their flowers
292.54		Other vegetable seeds
	120919 00 0	Beet seed
		Other
	120991 10 0	Kohlrabi seeds (*Brassica oleracea, caulorapa* and *gongylodes L.* varieties)
	120991 90 0	Other
292.59		Seeds, fruit and spores, n.e.s.
	120999 10 0	Forest-tree seeds
		Other
	120999 91 0	Seeds of plants cultivated principally for their flowers, other than those heading 292.53
	120999 99 0	Other

Bulbs, tubers and rhizomes of flowering or of foliage plants; cuttings, slips, live trees and other plants

292.61		Bulbs, tubers, tuberous roots, corms, crowns and rhizomes, dormant, in growth or in flower; chicory plants and roots(other than roots of heading 054.8)
		Bulbs, tubers, tuberous roots, corms, crowns and rhizomes, dormant
	060110 10 0	Hyacinths
	060110 20 0	Narcissi
	060110 30 0	Tulips
	060110 40 0	Gladioli
	060110 90 0	Other

S.I.T.C. (R3)	Commodity Code No	Trade description
cont 292.61		Bulbs, tubers, tuberous roots, corms, crowns and rhizomes, in growth or in flower; chicory plants and roots
	060120 10 0	Chicory plants and roots
	060120 30 0	Orchids, hyacinths, narcissi and tulips
	060120 90 0	Other
292.69		Other live plants (including their roots), cuttings and slips; mushroom spawn
		Unrooted cuttings and slips
	060210 10 0	Of vines
	060210 90 0	Other
		Trees, shrubs and bushes, grafted or not, of kinds which bear edible fruit or nuts
	060220 10 0	Vine slips, grafted or rooted
	060220 90 0	Other
	060230 00 0	Rhododendrons and azaleas, grafted or not
		Roses, grafted or not
	060240 10 0	Neither budded nor grafted
	060240 90 0	Budded or grafted
		Other
	*060290 10 0	Mushroom spawn
		Other
	*060290 20 0	Pineapple plants
		Other
	*060290 30 0	Vegetable and strawberry plants
		Other
		Outdoor plants
		Trees, shrubs and bushes
	*060290 41 0	Forest trees
		Other
	*060290 45 0	Rooted cuttings and young plant
	*060290 49 0	Other
		Other outdoor plants
	*060290 51 0	Perennial plants
	*060290 59 0	Other
		Indoor plants
	*060290 70 0	Rooted cuttings and young plants, excluding cacti
		Other
	*060290 91 0	Flowering plants with buds or flowers, excluding cacti
	*060290 99 0	Other

Cut flowers and foliage

S.I.T.C. (R3)	Commodity Code No	Trade description
292.71		Cut flowers and flower buds of a kind suitable for bouquets or for ornamental purposes, fresh, dried, dyed, bleached, impregnated or otherwise prepared
		Fresh
		From 1 June to 31 October
	060310 11 0	Roses
	060310 13 0	Carnations
	060310 15 0	Orchids
	060310 21 0	Gladioli
	060310 25 0	Chrysanthemums
	060310 29 0	Other
		From 1 November to 31 May
	060310 51 0	Roses
	060310 53 0	Carnations
	060310 55 0	Orchids
	060310 61 0	Gladioli
	060310 65 0	Chrysanthemums
	060310 69 0	Other
	060390 00 0	Other
292.72		Foliage, branches and other parts of plants, without flowers or flower buds, and grasses, mosses and lichens, being goods of a kind suitable for bouquets or for ornamental purposes, fresh, dried, dyed, bleached, impregnated or otherwise prepared
		Mosses and lichens
	060410 10 0	Reindeer moss
	060410 90 0	Other
		Other
		Fresh
		Christmas trees
	060491 21 0	Nordmann's firs (*Abies nordmanniana (Stev.) Spach*) and noble firs (*Abies procera Rehd.*)
	060491 29 0	Other
		Conifer branches
	060491 41 0	Of Nordmann's firs (*Abies nordmanniana (Stev.) Spach*) and of noble firs (*Abies procera Rehd.*)
	060491 49 0	Other
	060491 90 0	Other
		Other
	060499 10 0	Not further prepared than dried
	060499 90 0	Other

S.I.T.C. (R3)	Commodity Code No	Trade description
		Materials of vegetable origin, n.e.s.
292.92		Vegetable materials of a kind used primarily as stuffing or as padding (e.g., kapok, vegetable hair and eel-grass), whether or not put up as a layer with or without supporting material
		Kapok
	*140210 10 0	Raw
		Other
	*140210 91 0	Put up as a layer with supporting material
	*140210 99 0	Other
	*140290 00 0	Other
292.93		Vegetable materials of a kind used primarily in brooms or in brushes (e.g., broomcorn, piassava, couch-grass and istle), whether or not in hanks or bundles
	140310 00 0	Broomcorn (Sorghum vulgare var. technicum)
	140390 00 0	Other
292.94		Vegetable saps and extracts
	130211 00 0	Opium
	130212 00 0	Of liquorice
	130213 00 0	Of hops
	130214 00 0	Of pyrethrum or of the roots of plants containing rotenone
		Other
	*130219 05 0	Vanilla oleoresin
	130219 10 0	Of quassia amara; aloes and manna
	130219 30 0	Intermixtures of vegetable extracts, for the manufacture of beverages or of food preparations
		Other
	130219 91 0	Medicinal
	130219 99 0	Other
292.95		Pectic substances, pectinates and pectates
	130220 10 0	Dry
	130220 90 0	Other
292.96		Mucilages and thickeners, whether or not modified, derived from vegetable products
	130231 00 0	Agar-agar
		Mucilages and thickeners, whether or not modified, derived from locust beans, locust bean seeds or guar seeds
	130232 10 0	Of locust beans or locust bean seeds
	130232 90 0	Of guar seeds
	130239 00 0	Other
292.97	121220 00 0	Seaweeds and other algae
292.99		Vegetable materials and vegetable products, n.e.s.
	140410 00 0	Raw vegetable materials of a kind used primarily in dyeing or tanning
	140490 00 0	Other

SECTION: 3

DIVISION 32

COAL, COKE AND BRIQUETTES

COAL, WHETHER OR NOT PULVERIZED, BUT NOT AGGLOMERATED

321.10 — Anthracite, whether or not pulverized, but not agglomerated
- *270111 10 0 — Having a volatile matter limit (on a dry, mineral-matter-free basis) not exceeding 10 %
- 270111 90 0 — Other

Other coal, whether or not pulverized

321.21 — Bituminous coal, not agglomerated
- 270112 10 0 — Coking coal
- *270112 90 0 — Other

321.22 — 270119 00 0 — Other coal, not agglomerated

BRIQUETTES, LIGNITE AND PEAT

322.10 — 270120 00 0 — Briquettes, ovoids and similar solid fuels manufactured from coal

Lignite, whether or not pulverized (excluding jet)

322.21 — 270210 00 0 — Lignite, not agglomerated

322.22 — 270220 00 0 — Lignite, agglomerated

322.30 — 270300 00 0 — Peat (including peat litter), whether or not agglomerated

COKE AND SEMI-COKE (INCLUDING CHAR) OF COAL, OF LIGNITE OR OF PEAT, WHETHER OR NOT AGGLOMERATED; RETORT CARBON

325.00 — Coke and semi-coke (including char) of coal, of lignite or of peat, whether or not agglomerated; retort carbon
- Coke and semi-coke of coal
- 270400 11 0 — For the manufacture of electrodes
- 270400 19 0 — Other (ECSC)
- 270400 30 0 — Coke and semi-coke of lignite (ECSC)
- 270400 90 0 — Other

DIVISION 33

PETROLEUM, PETROLEUM PRODUCTS AND RELATED MATERIALS

333.00 — PETROLEUM OILS AND OILS OBTAINED FROM BITUMINOUS MINERALS, CRUDE
- 270900 10 0 — Natural gas condensates
- 270900 90 0 — Other

PETROLEUM OILS AND OILS OBTAINED FROM BITUMINOUS MINERALS (OTHER THAN CRUDE); PREPARATIONS, N.E.S., CONTAINING BY WEIGHT 70% OR MORE OF PETROLEUM OILS OR OF OILS OBTAINED FROM BITUMINOUS MINERALS, THESE OILS BEING THE BASIC CONSTITUENTS OF THE PREPARATIONS

Motor spirit

334.11 — Motor spirit (gasolene) including aviation spirit
- 271000 26 0 — Aviation spirit
- Other, with a lead content
- Not exceeding 0.013 g per litre
- 271000 27 0 — With an octane number of less than 95
- 271000 29 0 — With an octane number of 95 or more but less than 98
- 271000 32 0 — With an octane number of 98 or more
- Exceeding 0.013 g per litre
- 271000 34 0 — With an octane number of less than 98
- 271000 36 0 — With an octane number of 98 or more

334.12 — 271000 37 0 — Spirit type (gasolene type) jet fuel

334.19 — Other light petroleum oils and light oils obtained from bituminous minerals (other than crude); light preparations, n.e.s., containing not less than 70 per cent by weight of petroleum oils or oils obtained from bituminous minerals(other than crude), these oils being the basic constituents of the preparations.
- Light oils
- 271000 11 0 — For undergoing a specific process

S.I.T.C. (R3)	Commodity Code No	Trade description
Cont 334.19	271000 15 0	For undergoing chemical transformation by a process other than those specified in respect of subheading No. 271000 11 0
		For other purposes
		Special spirits
	271000 21 0	White spirit
	271000 25 0	Other
		Other
		Motor spirit
	271000 26 0	Aviation spirit
		Other, with a lead content
		Not exceeding 0.013 g per litre
	271000 27 0	With an octane number of less than 95
	271000 29 0	With an octane number of 95 or more but less than 98
	271000 32 0	With an octane number of 98 or more
		Exceeding 0.013 g per litre
	271000 34 0	With an octane number of less than 98
	271000 36 0	With an octane number of 98 or more
	271000 37 0	Spirit type jet fuel
	271000 39 0	Other light oils

Kerosene and other medium oils (not including gas oils)

334.21		Kerosene (including kerosene type jet fuel)
	271000 51 0	Jet fuel
	271000 55 0	Other
334.29		Other medium petroleum oils and medium oils obtained from bituminous minerals (not kerosene), other than crude; medium preparations, n.e.s., containing not less than 70 per cent by weight of petroleum oils or oils obtained from bituminous minerals (other than crude), these oils being the basic constituents of the preparations
	271000 41 0	For undergoing a specific process
	271000 45 0	For undergoing chemical transformation by a process other than those specified in respect of subheading No.271000 41 0
	271000 59 0	Other
334.30		Gas oils
	271000 61 0	For undergoing a specific process
	271000 65 0	For undergoing chemical transformation by a process other than those specified in respect of subheading No.271000 61 0
	271000 69 0	For other purposes
334.40		Fuel oils, n.e.s.
	271000 71 0	For undergoing a specific process
	271000 72 0	For undergoing chemical transformation by a process other than those specified in respect of subheading 271000 71 0
		For other purposes
	271000 74 0	With a sulphur content not exceeding 1 % by weight
	271000 76 0	With a sulphur content exceeding 1 % by weight but not exceeding 2 % by weight
	271000 77 0	With a sulphur content exceeding 2 % by weight but not exceeding 2.8 % by weight
	271000 78 0	With a sulphur content exceeding 2.8 % by weight
334.50		Lubricating petroleum oils and oils obtained from bituminous minerals, other heavy petroleum oils and heavy oils obtained from bituminous minerals (other than crude), and heavy preparations, n.e.s., containing no less than 70 per cent by weight of petroleum oils or oils obtained from bituminous minerals (other than crude, these oils being the basic constituents of the preparation
	271000 81 0	For undergoing a specific process
	271000 83 0	For undergoing chemical transformation by a process other than those specified in respect of subheading No.271000 81 0
	271000 85 0	To be mixed in accordance with the terms of additional note 6 to chapter 27 of the Combined Nomenclature
		For other purposes
	271000 87 0	Motor oils, compressor lube oils, turbine lube oils
	271000 88 0	Liquids for hydraulic purposes
	271000 89 0	White oils, liquid paraffin
	271000 92 0	Gear oils and reductor oils
	271000 94 0	Metal-working compounds, mould release oils, anti-corrosion oils
	271000 96 0	Electrical insulating oils
	271000 98 0	Other lubricating oils and other oils

RESIDUAL PETROLEUM PRODUCTS, N.E.S. AND RELATED MATERIALS

Petroleum jelly; paraffin wax, micro-crystalline petroleum wax, slack wax, ozokerite, lignite wax, peat wax, other mineral waxes, and similar products obtained by synthesis or by other processes, whether or not coloured

335.11		Petroleum jelly (petrolatum)
	271210 10 0	Crude
	271210 90 0	Other

S.I.T.C. (R3)	Commodity Code No	Trade description
335.12		Paraffin wax, micro-crystalline petroleum wax, slack wax, ozokerite, lignite wax, peat wax and other mineral waxes, and similar products obtained by synthesis or by other processes, whether or not coloured
	271220 00 0	Paraffin wax containing by weight less than 0.75 % of oil
		Other
		Ozokerite, lignite wax or peat wax (natural products)
	271290 11 0	Crude
	271290 19 0	Other
		Other
		Crude
	271290 31 0	For undergoing a specific process
	271290 33 0	For undergoing chemical transformation by a process other than those specified in respect of subheading No. 271290 31 0
	271290 39 0	For other purposes
	271290 90 0	Other
		Mineral tars and products of their distillation (including similar products obtained by processing petroleum or by any other process)
335.21	270600 00 0	Tar distilled from coal, from lignite or from peat, and other mineral tars, whether or not dehydrated or partially distilled (including reconstituted tars)
335.22		Benzole
	270710 10 0	For use as a power or heating fuel
	270710 90 0	For other purposes
335.23		Toluole
	270720 10 0	For use as a power or heating fuel
	270720 90 0	For other purposes
335.24		Xylole
	270730 10 0	For use as a power or heating fuel
	270730 90 0	For other purposes
335.25		Oils and other products, n.e.s., of the distillation of high temperature coal tar; similar products in which the weight of the aromatic constituents exceeds that of the non-aromatic constituents
	270740 00 0	Naphthalene
		Other aromatic hydrocarbon mixtures of which 65 % or more by volume (including losses) distils at 250°C by the ASTM D 86 method
	270750 10 0	For use as power or heating fuels
		For other purposes
	270750 91 0	Solvent naphtha
	270750 99 0	Other
	270760 00 0	Phenols
		Other
	270791 00 0	Creosote oils
		Other
		Crude oils
	270799 11 0	Crude light oils of which 90 % or more by volume distils at temperatures of up to 200°C
	270799 19 0	Other
	270799 30 0	Sulphuretted toppings
	270799 50 0	Basic products
	270799 70 0	Anthracene
		Other
	270799 91 0	For the manufacture of the products of heading 522.1
	270799 99 0	Other
		Pitch and pitch coke obtained from coal tar or from other mineral tars
335.31	270810 00 0	Pitch obtained from coal tar or from other mineral tars
335.32	270820 00 0	Pitch coke
		Petroleum bitumen, petroleum coke and bituminous mixtures, n.e.s.
335.41		Petroleum bitumen and other residues of petroleum oils or of oils obtained from bituminous minerals
	271320 00 0	Petroleum bitumen
		Other residues of petroleum oils or of oils obtained from bituminous minerals
	271390 10 0	For the manufacture of the products of heading 522.1
	271390 90 0	Other
335.42		Petroleum coke
	271311 00 0	Not calcined
	271312 00 0	Calcined

S.I.T.C. (R3)	Commodity Code No	Trade description
335.43		Bituminous mixtures based on natural asphalt, on natural bitumen, on petroleum bitumen, on mineral tar or on mineral tar pitch (e.g., bituminous mastics, cut-backs)
	271500 10 0	Bituminous mastics
	271500 90 0	Other

DIVISION 34

GAS, NATURAL AND MANUFACTURED

LIQUEFIED PROPANE AND BUTANE

Propane, liquefied

342.10		Propane of a purity not less than 99 %
	271112 11 0	For use as a power or heating fuel
	271112 19 0	For other purposes
		Other
	271112 91 0	For undergoing a specific process
	271112 93 0	For undergoing chemical transformation by a process other than those specified in respect of subheading No. 271112 91 0
		For other purposes
	271112 94 0	Of a purity exceeding 90 % but less than 99 %
	271112 96 0	Mixtures of propane and butane containing more than 50 % but not more than 70 % of propane
	271112 98 0	Other
342.50		Butanes, liquefied
	271113 10 0	For undergoing a specific process
	271113 30 0	For undergoing chemical transformation by a process other than those specified in respect of subheading No. 271113 10 0
		For other purposes
	271113 91 0	Of a purity exceeding 90 % but less than 95 %
	271113 93 0	Mixtures of butane and propane containing more than 50 % but not more than 65 % of butane
	271113 98 0	Other

NATURAL GAS, WHETHER OR NOT LIQUEFIED

343.10	271111 00 0	Natural gas, liquefied
343.20	271121 00 0	Natural gas, in the gaseous state

PETROLEUM GASES AND OTHER GASEOUS HYDROCARBONS, N.E.S.

344.10	271114 00 0	Ethylene, propylene, butylene and butadiene, liquefied
344.20	271119 00 0	Gaseous hydrocarbons, liquefied, n.e.s.
344.90	271129 00 0	Gaseous hydrocarbons in the gaseous state, n.e.s.

COAL GAS, WATER GAS, PRODUCER GAS AND SIMILAR GASES, OTHER THAN PETROLEUM GASES AND OTHER GASEOUS HYDROCARBONS

345.00	270500 00 0	Coal gas, water gas, producer gas and similar gases, other than petroleum gases and other gaseous hydrocarbons

DIVISION 35

ELECTRIC CURRENT

351.00	271600 00 0	Electric energy

SECTION: 4

DIVISION 41

ANIMAL OILS AND FATS

Fats and oils and their fractions, of fish or marine mammals, whether or not refined, but not chemically modified

411.11 Fish liver oils and their fractions
150410 10 0   Of a vitamin A content not exceeding 2 500 international units per gram
  Other
150410 91 0   Of halibut
150410 99 0   Other

411.12 Fats and oils and their fractions, of fish, other than liver oils
150420 10 0   Solid fractions
150420 90 0   Other

411.13 Fats and oils and their fractions, of marine mammals
  Solid fractions
150430 11 0   Whale oil and sperm oil
150430 19 0   Other
150430 90 0   Other

411.20 Lard; other pig fat and poultry fat, rendered, whether or not pressed or solvent-extracted
  Lard and other pig fat
150100 11 0   For industrial uses other than the manufacture of foodstuffs for human consumption
150100 19 0   Other
150100 90 0   Poultry fat

Animal oils, fats and greases, n.e.s.

411.31 Pig fat free of lean meat and poultry fat (not rendered), fresh, chilled, frozen, salted, in brine, dried or smoked
  Sub-cutaneous pig fat
020900 11 0   Fresh, chilled, frozen, salted or in brine
020900 19 0   Dried or smoked
020900 30 0   Pig fat, other than that falling within subheadings 020900 11 and 020900 19
020900 90 0   Poultry fat

411.32 Fats of bovine animals, sheep or goats, raw or rendered, whether or not pressed or solvent-extracted
150200 10 0   For industrial uses other than the manufacture of foodstuffs for human consumption
150200 90 0   Other

411.33 Lard stearin, lard oil, oleostearin, oleo-oil and tallow oil, not emulsified or mixed or otherwise prepared
  Lard stearin and oleostearin
150300 11 0   For industrial uses
150300 19 0   Other
150300 30 0   Tallow oil for industrial uses other than the manufacture of foodstuffs for human consumption
150300 90 0   Other

411.34 150510 00 0   Wool grease, crude

411.35 150590 00 0   Wool grease (other than crude) and fatty substances derived from wool grease (including lanolin)

411.39 150600 00 0   Animal oils and fats and their fractions, n.e.s., whether or not refined, but not chemically modified

DIVISION 42

FIXED VEGETABLE FATS AND OILS, "SOFT", CRUDE, REFINED OR FRACTIONATED

Soya bean oil and its fractions

421.11 Crude oil, whether or not degummed
150710 10 0   For technical or industrial uses other than the manufacture of foodstuffs for human consumption
150710 90 0   Other

421.19 Refined oil and fractions
150790 10 0   For technical or industrial uses other than the manufacture of foodstuffs for human consumption
150790 90 0   Other

S.I.T.C. (R3)	Commodity Code No	Trade description
		Cotton seed oil and its fractions
421.21		Crude oil, whether or not gossypol has been removed
	151221 10 0	For technical and industrial uses other than the manufacture of foodstuffs for human consumption
	151221 90 0	Other
421.29		Refined oil and fractions
	151229 10 0	For technical or industrial uses other than the manufacture of foodstuffs for human consumption
	151229 90 0	Other
		Groundnut (peanut) oil and its fractions
421.31		Crude oil
	150810 10 0	For technical or industrial uses other than the manufacture of foodstuffs for human consumption
	150810 90 0	Other
421.39		Refined oil and fractions
	150890 10 0	For technical or industrial uses other than the manufacture of foodstuffs for human consumption
	150890 90 0	Other
		Olive oil and other oil obtained from olives
421.41		Virgin oil
	150910 10 0	Lampante virgin olive oil
	150910 90 0	Other
421.42	150990 00 0	Other olive oil and its fractions
421.49		Oils and their fractions obtained solely from olives (other than olive oil of heading 421.41 or 421.42) including blends of these oils or fractions with oils or fractions of heading 421.41 or 421.42
	151000 10 0	Crude oils
	151000 90 0	Other
		Sunflower seed or safflower oil and their fractions
421.51		Crude oil
	151211 10 0	For technical or industrial uses other than the manufacture of foodstuffs for human consumption
		Other
	151211 91 0	Sunflower-seed oil
	151211 99 0	Safflower oil
421.59		Refined oil and fractions
	151219 10 0	For technical or industrial uses other than the manufacture of foodstuffs for human consumption
		Other
	151219 91 0	Sunflower-seed oil
	151219 99 0	Safflower oil
		Maize (corn) oil and its fractions
421.61		Crude oil
	151521 10 0	For technical or industrial uses other than the manufacture of foodstuffs for human consumption
	151521 90 0	Other
421.69		Refined oil and its fractions
	151529 10 0	For technical or industrial uses other than the manufacture of foodstuffs for human consumption
	151529 90 0	Other
		Rape, colza or mustard oil and their fractions
421.71		Crude oil
	151410 10 0	For technical and industrial uses other than the manufacture of foodstuffs for human consumption
	151410 90 0	Other
421.79		Refined oil and fractions
	151490 10 0	For technical and industrial uses other than the manufacture of foodstuffs for human consumption
	151490 90 0	Other
421.80		Sesame (sesamum) oil and its fractions
		Crude oil
	151550 11 0	For technical or industrial uses other than the manufacture of foodstuffs for human consumption
	151550 19 0	Other
		Other
	151550 91 0	For technical or industrial uses other than the manufacture of foodstuffs for human consumption
	151550 99 0	Other

S.I.T.C. (R3)	Commodity Code No	Trade description
		FIXED VEGETABLE FATS AND OILS, CRUDE, REFINED OR FRACTIONATED, OTHER THAN "SOFT"
		Linseed oil and its fractions
422.11	151511 00 0	Crude oil
422.19		**Refined oil and fractions**
	151519 10 0	For technical or industrial uses other than the manufacture of foodstuffs for human consumption
	151519 90 0	Other
		Palm oil and its fractions
422.21		Crude oil
	151110 10 0	For technical or industrial uses other than the manufacture of foodstuffs for human consumption
	151110 90 0	Other
422.29		**Refined oil and fractions**
		Solid fractions
	151190 11 0	In immediate packings of a net capacity of 1 kg or less
	151190 19 0	Other
		Other
	151190 91 0	For technical or industrial uses other than the manufacture of foodstuffs for human consumption
	151190 99 0	Other
		Coconut (copra) oil and its fractions
422.31		Crude oil
	151311 10 0	For technical and industrial uses other than the manufacture of foodstuffs for human consumption
		Other
	151311 91 0	In immediate packings of a net capacity of 1 kg or less
	151311 99 0	Other
422.39		**Refined oil and fractions**
		Solid fractions
	151319 11 0	In immediate packings of a net capacity of 1 kg or less
	151319 19 0	Other
		Other
	151319 30 0	For technical and industrial uses other than the manufacture of foodstuffs for human consumption
		Other
	151319 91 0	In immediate packings of a net capacity of 1 kg or less
	151319 99 0	Other
		Palm kernel or babassu oil and their fractions
422.41		Crude oil
		For technical or industrial uses other than the manufacture of foodstuffs for human consumption
	151321 11 0	Palm kernel oil
	151321 19 0	Babassu oil
		Other
	151321 30 0	In immediate packings of a net capacity of 1 kg or less
	151321 90 0	Other
422.49		**Refined oil and fractions**
		Solid fractions
	151329 11 0	In immediate packings of a net capacity of 1 kg or less
	151329 19 0	Other
		Other
	151329 30 0	For technical or industrial uses other than the manufacture of foodstuffs for human consumption
		Other
	151329 50 0	In immediate packings of a net capacity of 1 kg or less
		Other
	151329 91 0	Palm kernel oil
	151329 99 0	Babassu oil
422.50		**Castor oil and its fractions**
	151530 10 0	For the production of aminoundecanoic acid for use in the manufacture of synthetic textile fibres or of artificial plastic materials
	151530 90 0	Other
		Other fixed vegetable fats, crude, refined or fractionated, other than "soft"
422.91	151540 00 0	**Tung oil and its fractions**
422.99		**Fixed vegetable fats and oils, crude, refined or fractionated, n.e.s.**
		Jojoba oil and its fractions
	151560 10 0	Raw oil
	151560 90 0	Other
		Other

S.I.T.C. (R3)	Commodity Code No	Trade description

Cont
422.99

151590 10 0   Oiticica oils; myrtle wax and Japan wax; their fractions

Tobacco-seed oil and its fractions
  Crude oil

151590 21 0   For technical or industrial uses other than the manufacture of foodstuffs for human consumption

151590 29 0   Other

  Other

151590 31 0   For technical or industrial uses other than the manufacture of foodstuffs for human consumption

151590 39 0   Other

Other oils and their fractions
  Crude oils

151590 40 0   For technical or industrial uses other than the manufacture of foodstuffs for human consumption

    Other

151590 51 0   Solid, in immediate packings of a net capacity of 1 kg or less

151590 59 0   Solid, other; fluid

  Other

151590 60 0   For technical or industrial uses other than the manufacture of foodstuffs for human consumption

    Other

151590 91 0   Solid, in immediate packings of a net capacity of 1 kg or less

151590 99 0   Solid, other; fluid

DIVISION 43

ANIMAL OR VEGETABLE FATS AND OILS, PROCESSED; WAXES OF ANIMAL OR VEGETABLE ORIGIN; INEDIBLE MIXTURES OR PREPARATIONS OF ANIMAL OR VEGETABLE FATS OR OILS, N.E.S.

431.10

Fats and oils and their fractions, animal or vegetable, boiled, oxidized, dehydrated, sulphurized, blown, polymerized by heat in vacuum or in inert gas or otherwise chemically modified (excluding those of heading 431.2); inedible mixtures or preparations of animal or vegetable fats or oils, or of fractions of different such fats or oils, n.e.s.

151800 10 0   Linoxyn

  Fixed vegetable oils, fluid, mixed, for technical or industrial uses other than the manufacture of foodstuffs for human consumption

151800 31 0   Crude

151800 39 0   Other

  Other

151800 91 0   Animal or vegetable fats and oils and their fractions boiled, oxidised, dehydrated, sulphurised, blown, polymerised by heat in vacuum or in inert gas or otherwise chemically modified, excluding those of headings 431.21 & 431.22

    Other

151800 95 0   Inedible mixtures of preparations of animal or of animal and vegetable fats and oils and their fractions

151800 99 0   Other

Animal or vegetable fats or oils and their fractions, partly or wholly hydrogenated, inter-esterified, re-esterified or elaidinised, whether or not refined, but not further prepared.

431.21   **Animal fats and oils and their fractions**

151610 10 0   In immediate packings of a net capacity of 1 kg or less

151610 90 0   Other

431.22   **Vegetable fats and oils and their fractions.**

151620 10 0   Hydrogenated castor oil, so called "opal-wax"

  Other

151620 91 0   In immediate packings of a net capacity of 1 kg or less

    Other

151620 95 0   Colza, linseed, rape seed, sunflower seed, illipe, karite, makore, touloucouna or babassu oils, for technical or industrial uses other than the manufacture of foodstuffs for human consumption

      Other

151620 96 0   Ground-nut, cotton seed, soya beans or sunflower seed oils; other oils containing less than 50 % by weight of free fatty acids and excluding palm kernel, illipe, coconut, colza, rape seed or copaiba oils

151620 98 0   Other

Fatty acids, acid oils, and residues resulting from the treatment of fatty substances or animal or vegetable waxes; degras

431.31   **Fatty acids; acid oils from refining Industrial monocarboxylic fatty acids; acid oils from refining**

*382311 00 0   Stearic acid

*382312 00 0   Oleic acid

*382313 00 0   Tall oil fatty acids

  Other

*382319 10 0   Distilled fatty acids

*382319 30 0   Fatty acid distillate

*382319 90 0   Other

431.33   **Degras; residues resulting from the treatment of fatty substances or animal or vegetable waxes.**

152200 10 0   Degras

S.I.T.C. (R3)	Commodity Code No	Trade description
Cont 431.33		Residues resulting from the treatment of fatty substances or animal or vegetable waxes
		Containing oil having the characteristics of olive oil
	152200 31 0	Soapstocks
	152200 39 0	Other
		Other
	152200 91 0	Oil foots and dregs; soapstocks
	152200 99 0	Other

Waxes of animal or vegetable origin

S.I.T.C. (R3)	Commodity Code No	Trade description
431.41		Vegetable waxes (other than triglycerides) whether ornot refined or coloured
	152110 10 0	Raw
	152110 90 0	Other
431.42		Beeswax, other insect waxes and spermaceti, whether or not refined or coloured
	152190 10 0	Spermaceti, whether or not refined or coloured
		Beeswax and other insect waxes, whether or not refined or coloured
	152190 91 0	Raw
	152190 99 0	Other

SECTION: 5

DIVISION 51   **ORGANIC CHEMICALS**

HYDROCARBONS, N.E.S., AND THEIR HALOGENATED, SULPHONATED, NITRATED OR NITROSATED DERIVATIVES

Acyclic hydrocarbons

511.11   **Ethylene**
- 290121 10 0   For use as a power or heating fuel
- 290121 90 0   For other purposes

511.12   **Propene (propylene)**
- 290122 10 0   For use as a power or heating fuel
- 290122 90 0   For other purposes

511.13   **Butene (butylene) and isomers thereof**
       But-1-ene and but-2-ene
- 290123 11 0   For use as power or heating fuels
- 290123 19 0   For other purposes
       Other
- 290123 91 0   For use as power or heating fuels
- 290123 99 0   For other purposes

     Buta-1,3-diene and isoprene
       Buta-1,3-diene
- 290124 11 0   For use as a power or heating fuel
- 290124 19 0   For other purposes
       Isoprene
- 290124 91 0   For use as a power or heating fuel
- 290124 99 0   For other purposes

511.14   **Saturated acyclic hydrocarbons**
- 290110 10 0   For use as power or heating fuels
- 290110 90 0   For other purposes

511.19   **Acyclic hydrocarbons, n.e.s.**
- 290129 20 0   For use as power or heating fuels
- 290129 80 0   For other purposes

Cyclic hydrocarbons

511.21   **Cyclohexane**
- 290211 10 0   For use as a power or heating fuel
- 290211 90 0   For other purposes

511.22   **Benzene, pure**
- 290220 10 0   For use as a power or heating fuel
- 290220 90 0   For other purposes

511.23   **Toluene, pure**
- 290230 10 0   For use as a power or heating fuel
- 290230 90 0   For other purposes

511.24   **Xylenes, pure**
- 290241 00 0   o- Xylene
- 290242 00 0   m- Xylene
- 290243 00 0   p-Xylene
       Mixed xylene isomers
- 290244 10 0   For use as power or heating fuels
- 290244 90 0   For other purposes

511.25   290250 00 0   **Styrene**

511.26   290260 00 0   **Ethylbenzene**

511.27   290270 00 0   **Cumene**

511.29   **Cyclic hydrocarbons, n.e.s.**
- 290219 10 0   Cycloterpenes
- 290219 30 0   Azulene and its alkyl derivatives
       Other
- 290219 91 0   For use as power or heating fuels
- 290219 99 0   For other purposes
     Other

S.I.T.C. (R3)	Commodity Code No	Trade description
cont 511.29	290290 10 0	Naphthalene and anthracene
	290290 30 0	Biphenyl and terphenyls
		Other
	290290 90 0	Hydrocarbon oil

Halogenated derivatives of hydrocarbons

511.31	290321 00 0	**Vinyl chloride (chloroethylene)**
511.32	290322 00 0	**Trichloroethylene**
511.33	290323 00 0	**Tetrachloroethylene (perchloroethylene)**
511.34	290329 00 0	**Other unsaturated chlorinated derivatives of acyclic hydrocarbons**
511.35	290315 00 0	**1,2-Dichloroethane (ethylene dichloride)**
511.36		**Other saturated chlorinated derivatives of acyclic hydrocarbons**
	290311 00 0	Chloromethane (methyl chloride) and chloroethane (ethyl chloride)
	290312 00 0	Dichloromethane (methylene chloride)
	290313 00 0	Chloroform (trichloromethane)
	290314 00 0	Carbon tetrachloride
	290316 00 0	1,2-Dichloropropane (propylene dichloride) and dichlorobutanes
		Other:
	290319 10 0	1,1,1-Trichloroethane (methylchloroform)
	290319 90 0	Other
511.37		**Fluorinated, brominated or iodinated derivatives of acyclic hydrocarbons**
	290330 10 0	Fluorides
		Bromides
	290330 31 0	Dibromoethane and vinyl bromide
	290330 33 0	Bromomethane (methyl bromide)
	290330 38 0	Other
	290330 90 0	Iodides
511.38		**Halogenated derivatives of acyclic hydrocarbons containing two or more different halogens**
	*290341 10 0	Trichlorofluoromethane
	*290342 20 0	Dichlorodifluoromethane
	*290343 30 0	Trichlorotrifluoroethanes
		Dichlorodifluoromethanes and chloropentafluoroethane:
	*290344 10 0	Dichlorotetrafluoroethanes
	*290344 90 0	Chloropentafluoroethane
		Other derivatives perhalogenated only with fluorine and chlorine
	*290345 10 0	Chlorotrifluoromethane
	*290345 15 0	Pentachlorofluoroethane
	*290345 20 0	Tetrachlorodifluoroethanes
	*290345 25 0	Heptachlorofluoropropanes
	*290345 30 0	Hexachlorodifluoropropanes
	*290345 35 0	Pentachlorotrifluoropropanes
	*290345 40 0	Tetrachlorotetrafluoropropanes
	*290345 45 0	Trichloropentafluoropropanes
	*290345 50 0	Dichlorohexafluoropropanes
	*290345 55 0	Chloroheptafluoropropanes
	*290345 90 0	Other
		Bromochlorodifluoromethane, bromotrifluoromethane and dibromotetrafluoroethanes
	*290346 10 0	Bromochlorodifluoromethane
	*290346 20 0	Bromotrifluoromethane
	*290346 90 0	Dibromotetrafluoroethanes
	*290347 00 0	Other perhalogenated derivatives
		Other
		Halogenated only with fluorine and chlorine:
	*290349 10 0	Of methane, ethane or propane
	*290349 20 0	Other
	*290349 90 0	Other
511.39		**Halogenated derivatives of hydrocarbons, n.e.s.**
		1,2,3,4,5,6-Hexachlorocyclohexane
	290351 10 0	Lindane (ISO)
	290351 90 0	Other
		Other
	290359 10 0	Dibromoethyldibromocyclohexane
	290359 30 0	Tetrabromocyclooctane
	290359 90 0	Other
		Halogenated derivatives of aromatic hydrocarbons
	290361 00 0	Chlorobenzene, o-dichlorobenzene and p-dichlorobenzen
	290362 00 0	Hexachlorobenzene and DDT (1,1,1-trichloro-2,2- bis(p-chlorophenyl)ethane)
		Other

S.I.T.C. (R3)	Commodity Code No	Trade description
cont 511.39	290369 10 0	Pentabromethylbenzene
	290369 90 0	Other
511.40		**Sulphonated, nitrated or nitrosated derivatives of hydrocarbons, whether or not halogenated**
	290410 00 0	Derivatives containing only sulpho groups, their salts and ethyl esters
		Derivatives containing only nitro or only nitroso groups
	290420 10 0	Trinitrotoluenes and dinitronaphthalenes
	290420 90 0	Other
		Other
	*290490 20 0	Sulphohalogenated derivatives
	*290490 80 0	Other

ALCOHOLS, PHENOLS, PHENOL-ALCOHOLS, AND THEIR HALOGENATED, SULPHONATED, NITRATED OR NITROSATED DERIVATIVES

Acyclic monohydric alcohols

512.11	290511 00 0	**Methanol (methyl alcohol)**
512.12	290512 00 0	**Propan-1-ol (propyl alcohol) and propan-2-ol (isopropyl alcohol)**
512.13		**Butanols**
	290513 00 0	Butan-1-ol (*n*-butyl alcohol)
		Other butanols
	290514 10 0	2-Methylpropan-2-ol (*tert*-butyl alcohol)
	290514 90 0	Other
512.14		**Octanol (octyl alcohol) and isomers thereof**
	290516 10 0	2-Ethylhexan-1-ol
	290516 90 0	Other
512.15	220710 00 0	**Undenatured ethyl alcohol of an alcoholic strength by volume of 80% or higher**
512.16	220720 00 0	**Ethyl alcohol and other spirits, denatured, of any strength**
512.17	*382370 00 0	**Industrial fatty alcohols**
512.19		**Other monohydric alcohols**
	290515 00 0	Pentanol (amyl alcohol) and isomers thereof
	290517 00 0	Dodecan-1-ol (lauryl alcohol), hexadecan-1-ol (cetyl alcohol) and octadecan-1-ol(stearyl alcohol)
		Other
	290519 10 0	Metal alcoholates
	290519 90 0	Other
		Unsaturated monohydric alcohols
		Acyclic terpene alcohols
	290522 10 0	Geraniol, citronellol, linalol, rhodinol and nerol
	290522 90 0	Other
		Other
	*290529 10 0	Allyl alcohol
	*290529 90 0	Other

Other acyclic alcohols, and the halogenated, sulphonated, nitrated or nitrosated derivatives of acyclic alcohols

512.21	290531 00 0	**Ethylene glycol (ethanediol)**
512.22		**Glycerol (glycerine), glycerol waters and glycerol lyes**
	*152000 00 0	Glycerol (glycerine), crude; glycerol waters and glycerol lyes
	*290545 00 0	Glycerol (including synthetic glycerol)
512.23	290542 00 0	**Pentaerythritol**
512.24	290543 00 0	**Mannitol**
512.25		**D-glucitol (sorbitol)**
		In aqueous solution
	290544 11 0	Containing 2 % or less by weight of mannitol, calculated on the D -glucitol content
	290544 19 0	Other
		Other
	290544 91 0	Containing 2 % or less by weight of mannitol, calculated on the D -glucitol content
	290544 99 0	Other
512.29		**Other acyclic alcohols**
	290532 00 0	Propylene glycol (propane-1,2-diol)
		Other
	290539 10 0	2-Methylpentane-2,4-diol (hexylene glycol)
	290539 90 0	Other

S.I.T.C. (R3)	Commodity Code No	Trade description
cont 512.29		Other polyhydric alcohols
	290541 00 0	2-Ethyl-2-(hydroxymethyl) propane-1,3-diol (trimethylolpropane)
		Other
	290549 10 0	Triols; tetraols
		Other
		Esters of glycerol formed with acid-function compounds of heading 511.40:
	*290549 51 0	With sulphohalogenated derivatives
	*290549 59 0	Other
	290549 90 0	Other
		Halogenated, sulphonated, nitrated or nitrosated derivatives of acyclic alcohols
	290550 10 0	Of saturated monohydric alcohols
	290550 30 0	Of unsaturated monohydric alcohols
		Of polyhydric alcohols
	290550 91 0	Dibromoneopentylglycol
	290550 99 0	Other

Cyclic alcohols and their halogenated, sulphonated, nitrated or nitrosated deravatives

512.31		**Cyclanic, cyclenic, or cycloterpenic alcohols and their halogenated, sulphonated, nitrated or nitrosated derivatives**
	290611 00 0	Menthol
	290612 00 0	Cyclohexanol, methylcyclohexanols and dimethylcyclohexanols
		Sterols and inositols
	290613 10 0	Sterols
	290613 90 0	Inositols
	290614 00 0	Terpineols
	290619 00 0	Other

512.35		**Aromatic cyclic alcohols and their halogenated, sulphonated, nitrated or nitrosated derivatives**
	290621 00 0	Benzyl alcohol
		Other
	290629 10 0	Cinnamyl alcohol
	290629 90 0	Other

Phenols and phenol-alcohols, and their halogenated, sulphonated, nitrated or nitrosated derivatives

512.41	290711 00 0	**Phenol (hydroxybenzene), pure, and its salts**
512.42	290712 00 0	**Cresoles,n.e.s., and their salts**
512.43		**Other phenols and phenol-alcohols**
		Monophenols
	290713 00 0	Octylphenol, nonylphenol and their isomers; salts thereof
	290714 00 0	Xylenols and their salts
	290715 00 0	Naphthols and their salts
		Other
	290719 10 0	P-tert-Butylphenol
	290719 90 0	Other
		Polyphenols
	290721 00 0	Resorcinol and its salts
		Hydroquinone (quinol) and its salts
	290722 10 0	Hydroquinone (quinol)
	290722 90 0	Other
		4,4'-Isopropylidenediphenol (bisphenol A, diphenylolpropane) and its salts
	290723 10 0	4,4'-Isopropylidenediphenol (bisphenol A, diphenylolpropane)
	290723 90 0	Other
		Other
	290729 10 0	Dihydroxynaphthalenes and their salts
	290729 90 0	Other
	290730 00 0	Phenol-alcohols
512.44		**Halogenated, sulphonated, nitrated or nitrosated derivatives of phenols or phenol-alcohols**
		Derivatives containing only halogen substituents and their salts
	290810 10 0	Brominated derivatives
	290810 90 0	Other
	290820 00 0	Derivatives containing only sulpho groups, their salts and esters
	290890 00 0	Other

CARBOXYLIC ACIDS AND THEIR ANHYDRIDES, HALIDES, PEROXIDES AND PEROXYACIDS; THEIR HALOGENATED, SULPHONATED, NITRATED OR NITROSATED DERIVATIVES

Monocarboxylic acids and their anhydrides, halides, peroxides and peroxyacids; their halogenated, sulphonated, nitrated or nitrosated derivatives

513.71		**Acetic acid and its salts**
	291521 00 0	Acetic acid

S.I.T.C. (R3)	Commodity Code No	Trade description
cont		
513.71	291522 00 0	Sodium acetate
	291523 00 0	Cobalt acetates
	291529 00 0	Other
513.72		**Esters of acetic acid**
	291531 00 0	Ethyl acetate
	291532 00 0	Vinyl acetate
	291533 00 0	n-Butyl acetate
	291534 00 0	Isobutyl acetate
	291535 00 0	2-Ethoxyethyl acetate
		Other
	291539 10 0	Propyl acetate and isopropyl acetate
	291539 30 0	Methyl acetate, pentyl acetate (amyl acetate), isopentyl acetate (isoamyl acetate) and glycerol acetates
	291539 50 0	p- Tolyl acetate, phenylpropyl acetates, benzyl acetate, rhodinyl acetate, santalyl acetate and the acetates of phenylethane-1,2-diol
	291539 90 0	Other
513.73		**Methacrylic acid and its salts and esters**
		Unsaturated acyclic monocarboxylic acids, their anhydrides, halides, peroxides, peroxyacids and their derivatives
	291613 00 0	Methacrylic acid and its salts
		Esters of methacrylic acid
	291614 10 0	Methyl methacrylate
	291614 90 0	Other
513.74		**Formic acid,its salts and esters**
	291511 00 0	Formic acid
	291512 00 0	Salts of formic acid
	291513 00 0	Esters of formic acid
513.75		**Butyric acids, valeric acids, their slats and esters**
	291560 10 0	Butyric acid and isobutyric acid and their salts and esters
	291560 90 0	Valeric acids and their salts and esters
513.76		**Palmitic acid, stearic acid, their salts and esters**
	291570 15 0	Palmitic acid
	291570 20 0	Salts and esters of palmitic acid
	291570 25 0	Stearic acid
	291570 30 0	Salts of stearic acid
	291570 80 0	Esters of stearic acid
513.77		**Saturated acyclic monocarboxylic acids, n.e.s.; anhydrides, halides, peroxides and peroxyacids of saturatedacyclic mono-carboxylic acids and their halogenated,sulphonated, nitrated or nitrosated derivatives**
	291524 00 0	Acetic anhydride
	291540 00 0	Mono-, di- or trichloroacetic acids, their salts and esters
	291550 00 0	Propionic acid, its salts and esters
		Other
	291590 10 0	Lauric acid
	291590 20 0	Chloroformates
	291590 80 0	Other
513.78	291615 00 0	**Oleic, linoleic or linolenic acids, their salts and esters**
513.79		**Other unsaturated acyclic monocarboxylic acids; cyclic monocarboxylic acids, their anhydrides, halides, peroxides, peroxyacids and their derivatives**
		Acrylic acid and its salts
	291611 10 0	Acrylic acid
	291611 90 0	Salts of acrylic acid
		Esters of acrylic acid
	291612 10 0	Methyl acrylate
	291612 20 0	Ethyl acrylate
	291612 90 0	Other
		Other
	291619 10 0	Undecenoic acids and their salts and esters
	291619 30 0	Hexa-2,4-dienoic acid (sorbic acid)
	291619 90 0	Other
	291620 00 0	Cyclanic, cyclenic or cycloterpenic monocarboxylic acids, their anhydrides, halides, peroxides, peroxyacids and their derivatives
		Aromatic monocarboxylic acids, their anhydrides, halides, peroxides, peroxyacids and their derivatives
	291631 00 0	Benzoic acid, its salts and esters
		Benzoyl peroxide and benzoyl chloride
	291632 10 0	Benzoyl peroxide
	291632 90 0	Benzoyl chloride
	*291634 00 0	Phenylacetic acid and its salts

S.I.T.C. (R3)	Commodity Code No	Trade description

cont
513.79 `*291635 90 0` Esters of phenylacetic acid
`291639 00 0` Other

Polycarboxylic acids and their anhydrides, halides, peroxides and peroxyacids; their halogenated, sulphonated, nitrated or nitrosated derivatives

513.81 291714 00 0 **Maleic anhydride**

513.82 291735 00 0 **Phthalic anhydride**

513.83 291732 00 0 **Dioctyl orthophthalates**

513.84 291737 00 0 **Dimethyl terephthalate**

513.85 291720 00 0 **Cyclanic, cyclenic or cycloterpenic polycarboxylic acids, their anhydrides, halides, peroxides, peroxyacids and their derivatives**

513.89 **Polycarboxylic acids, n.e.s.;anhydrides, halides, peroxides and peroxyacids of polycarbolic acids; their halogenated, sulphonated, nitrated or nitrosated derivatives**
291711 00 0 Oxalic acid, its salts and esters
Adipic acid, its salts and esters
291712 10 0 Adipic acid and its salts
291712 90 0 Esters of adipic acid
291713 00 0 Azelaic acid, sebacic acid, their salts and esters
Other
291719 10 0 Malonic acid, its salts and esters
291719 90 0 Other
Aromatic polycarboxylic acids, their anhydrides, halides, peroxides, peroxyacids and their derivatives
291731 00 0 Dibutyl orthophthalates
291733 00 0 Dinonyl or didecyl orthophthalates
Other esters of orthophthalic acid
291734 10 0 Diisooctyl-, diisononyl- and diisodecyl orthophthalates
291734 90 0 Other
291736 00 0 Terephthalic acid and its salts
Other
291739 10 0 Brominated derivatives
291739 90 0 Other

Carboxylic acids with additional oxygen function and their anhydrides, halides, peroxides and peroxyacids; their halogenated, sulphonated, nitrated or nitrosated derivatives

513.91 **Lactic acid, tartaric acid, citric acid and their salts and esters**
291811 00 0 Lactic acid, its salts and esters
291812 00 0 Tartaric acid
291813 00 0 Salts and esters of tartaric acid
291814 00 0 Citric acid
291815 00 0 Salts and esters of citric acid

513.92 **Other carboxylic acids with alcohol function but without other oxygen function, their anhydrides, halides, peroxides and peroxyacids of carboxylic acids with alochol function but without other oxygen function: derivatives, n.e.s., of carboxylic acids with alcohol functin but without other oxygen function and of their anhydides, halides, peroxides and peroxyacids**
291816 00 0 Gluconic acid, its salts and esters
291817 00 0 Phenylglycolic acid (mandelic acid), its salts and esters
Other
291819 10 0 Malic acid and its salts and esters;
291819 30 0 Cholic acid and 3 alpha, 12 alpha-dihydroxy-5 beta-cholan-24-oic acid (deoxycholic acid), their salts and esters
291819 90 0 Other

513.93 **Salicylic acid and its salts and esters**
291821 00 0 Salicylic acid and its salts
291822 00 0 O-Acetylsalicylic acid, its salts and esters
Other esters of salicylic acid and their salts
291823 10 0 Methyl salicylate and phenyl salicylate (salol)
291823 90 0 Other

513.94 **Other carboxylic acids with phenol function but without other oxygen function and their anhydrides, halides,peroxides and peroxyacids of carboxylic acids with phenol function but without other oxygen function: halogenated, sulphonated, nitrated and nitrosated derivatives of carboxylic acids with phenol function but without other oxygen function and their anhydrides, halides, peroxides and peroxyacids**
291829 10 0 Sulphosalicylic acids, hydroxynaphthoic acids; their salts and esters
291829 30 0 4-Hydroxybenzoic acid, its salts and esters
291829 50 0 Gallic acid, its salts and esters
291829 90 0 Other

S.I.T.C. (R3)	Commodity Code No	Trade description
513.95	291830 00 0	**Carboxylic acids with aldehyde or ketone function but without other oxygen function, their anhydrides, halides, peroxides peroxyacids and their derivatives**
513.96	291890 00 0	**Carboxylic acids with additional oxygen functions, n.e.s., their anhydrides, halides, peroxides, peroxyacids and their derivatives**

NITROGEN-FUNCTION COMPOUNDS

Amine-function compounds

S.I.T.C. (R3)	Commodity Code No	Trade description
514.51		**Acyclic monoamines and their derivatives; salts thereof**
		Methylamine, di- or trimethylamine and their salts
	292111 10 0	Methylamine, di- or trimethylamine
	292111 90 0	Salts
	292112 00 0	Diethylamine and its salts
		Other
	292119 10 0	Triethylamine and its salts
	292119 30 0	Isopropylamine and its salts
	292119 90 0	Other
514.52		**Acyclic polyamines and their derivatives; salts thereof**
	292121 00 0	Ethylenediamine and its salts
	292122 00 0	Hexamethylenediamine and its salts
	292129 00 0	Other
514.53		**Cyclanic, cyclenic or cycloterpenic mono- or polyamines, and their derivatives; salts thereof**
	292130 10 0	Cyclohexylamine and cyclohexyldimethylamine, and their salts
	292130 90 0	Other
514.54		**Aromatic monoamines and their derivatives; salts thereof**
	292141 00 0	Aniline and its salts
		Aniline derivatives and their salts
	292142 10 0	Halogenated, sulphonated, nitrated and nitrosated derivatives and their salts
	292142 90 0	Other
		Toluidines and their derivatives; salts thereof
	292143 10 0	Toluidines and their salts
	292143 90 0	Other
	292144 00 0	Diphenylamine and its derivatives; salts thereof
	292145 00 0	1-Naphthylamine (*alpha*-naphthylamine), 2-naphthylamine (*beta*-naphthylamine) and their derivatives; salts thereof
		Other
	292149 10 0	Xylidines and their derivatives; salts thereof
	292149 90 0	Other
514.55		**Aromatic polyamines and their derivatives; salts thereof**
		o-, m-, p-Phenylenediamine, diaminotoluenes, and their derivatives; salts thereof
	292151 10 0	o-, m-, p- Phenylenediamine, diaminotoluenes and their halogenated, sulphonated, nitrated and nitrosated derivatives; salts thereof
	292151 90 0	Other
	292159 00 0	Other

Oxygen-function amino-compounds

S.I.T.C. (R3)	Commodity Code No	Trade description
514.61		**Amino-alcohols, their ethers and esters (other than those containing more than one kind of oxygen-function); salts thereof**
	292211 00 0	Monoethanolamine and its salts
	292212 00 0	Diethanolamine and its salts
	292213 00 0	Triethanolamine and its salts
	292219 00 0	Other
514.62		**Amino-naphthols and other amino-phenols, their ethers and esters (other than those containing more than one kind of oxygen-function); salts thereof**
	292221 00 0	Aminohydroxynaphthalenesulphonic acids and their salts
	292222 00 0	Anisidines, dianisidines, phenetidines, and their salts
	292229 00 0	Other
514.63	292230 00 0	**Amino-aldehydes, amino-ketones and amino-quinones (other than those containing more than one kind of oxygen function); salts thereof**
514.64		**Lysine and its esters; salts thereof; glutamic acid and its salts**
	292241 00 0	Lysine and its esters; salts thereof
		Glutamic acid and its salts
	292242 10 0	Monosodium glutamate
	292242 90 0	Other

S.I.T.C. (R3)	Commodity Code No	Trade description
514.65		**Amino-acids and their esters (other than those containing more than one kind of oxygen function), n.e.s.; salts thereof**
	*292243 00 0	Anthranilic acid and its salts
		Other
	292249 10 0	Glycine
	292249 80 0	Other
514.67	292250 00 0	**Amino-alcohol-phenols, amino-acid-phenols and other amino- compounds with oxygen function**
		Carboxyamide-function compounds; amide-function compounds of carbonic acid (excluding urea)
514.71	292410 00 0	**Acyclic amides (incl. acyclic carbamates) and their derivatives; salts thereof**
514.73		**Ureines and their derivatives; salts thereof**
	292421 10 0	Isoproturon (ISO)
	292421 90 0	Other
514.79		**Other cyclic amides (incl. cyclic carbamates) and their derivatives; salts thereof**
	*292422 00 0	2-Acetamidobenzoic acid
		Other
	292429 10 0	Lidocaine (INN)
	292429 30 0	Paracetamol (INN)
	292429 90 0	Other
		Other nitrogen-function compounds
514.81		**Quaternary ammonium salts and hydroxides; lecithins and other phosphoaminolipids**
		Choline and its salts
	292310 10 0	Choline chloride
	292310 90 0	Other
	292320 00 0	Lecithins and other phosphoaminolipids
	292390 00 0	Other
514.82		**Carboxyimide-function compounds (including saccharin and its salts) and amine-function compounds**
		Imides and their derivatives; salts thereof
	292511 00 0	Saccharin and its salts
		Other
	292519 10 0	3,3',4,4',5,5',6,6'-Octabromo-N,N'-ethylenediphthalimide
	292519 30 0	Ethylenebisdibromonorbornanedicarboximide
	292519 80 0	Other
	292520 00 0	Imines and their derivatives; salts thereof
514.83	292610 00 0	**Acrylonitrile**
514.84		**Other nitrile-function compounds**
	292620 00 0	1-Cyanoguanidine (dicyandiamide)
		Other
	292690 10 0	2-Hydroxy-2-methylpropiononitrile (acetone cyanohydrin)
	292690 90 0	Other
514.85	292700 00 0	**Diazo-, azo-, and azoxy-compounds**
514.86	292800 00 0	**Organic derivatives of hydrazine or of hydroxylamine**
514.89		**Compounds with other nitrogen function**
		Isocyanates
	292910 10 0	Methylphenylene diisocyanates (toluene diisocyanates)
	292910 90 0	Other
	292990 00 0	Other

ORGANO-INORGANIC COMPOUNDS, HETEROCYCLIC COMPOUNDS, NUCLEIC ACIDS AND THEIR SALTS AND SULPHONAMIDES

Organo-sulphur compounds

S.I.T.C. (R3)	Commodity Code No	Trade description
515.41	293010 00 0	**Dithiocarbonates (xanthates)**
515.42	293020 00 0	**Thiocarbamates and dithiocarbamates**
515.43	293030 00 0	**Thiuram mono-, di- or tetrasulphides**
515.44	293040 00 0	**Methionine**

S.I.T.C. (R3)	Commodity Code No	Trade description
515.49		**Other**
	*293090 12 0	Cysteine
	*293090 14 0	Cystine
	*293090 16 0	Derivatives of cysteine or cystine
	293090 20 0	Thiodislycol (INN)(2,2'- thiodiethanol)
	293090 30 0	DL-2-hydroxy-4-(methylthio)butyric acid
	293090 95 0	Other
515.50		**Other organo-inorganic compounds**
	293100 10 0	Dimethyl methylphosphonate
	293100 20 0	Methylphosphonyl difluoride (methylphosphonic difluoride)
	293100 30 0	Methylphosphonyl dichloride (methylphosphonic dichloride)
	293100 40 0	2-Chloroethylphosphonic acid
	293100 50 0	Organo-silicon compounds
	293100 80 0	Other

Lactams; heterocyclic compounds with oxygen hetero-atom(s) only

S.I.T.C. (R3)	Commodity Code No	Trade description
515.61		**Lactams**
	293371 00 0	6-Hexanelactam (epsilon-caprolactam)
	293379 00 0	Other lactams
515.62	293221 00 0	**Coumarin, methylcoumarins and ethylcoumarins**
515.63		**Other lactones**
	293229 10 0	Phenolphthalein
	293229 90 0	Other
515.69		**Heterocyclic compounds with oxygen hetero-atom(s) only, n.e.s.**
	293211 00 0	Tetrahydrofuran
	293212 00 0	2-Furaldehyde (furfuraldehyde)
	293213 00 0	Furfuryl alcohol and tetrahydrofurfuryl alcohol
	293219 00 0	Other
	*293291 00 0	Isosafrole
	*293292 00 0	1-(1,3-Benzodioxol-5-yl)propane-2-one
	*293293 00 0	Piperonal
	*293294 00 0	Safrole
		Other
	*293299 10 0	Benzofuran (coumarone)
	*293299 30 0	Internal ethers
	*293299 50 0	Epoxides with a four-membered ring
	*293299 70 0	Other cyclic acetals and internal hemiacetals, whether or not with other oxygen functions, and their halogenated, sulphonated, nitrated or nitrosated derivatives
	*293299 90 0	Other

Other heterocyclic compounds; nucleic acids

S.I.T.C. (R3)	Commodity Code No	Trade description
515.71		**Heterocyclic compounds,with nitrogen hetero-atom(s) only,containing an unfused pyrazole ring, whether or not hydrogenated, in the structure**
		Phenazone (antipyrin) and its derivatives
	293311 10 0	Propyphenazone (INN)
	293311 90 0	Other
		Other
	293319 10 0	Phenylbutazone (INN)
	293319 90 0	Other
515.72	293321 00 0	**Hydantoin and its derivatives**
515.73		**Other heterocyclic compounds containing an unfused imidazole ring (whether or not hydrogenated) in the structure**
	293329 10 0	Naphazoline hydrochloride (INNM) and naphazoline nitrate (INNM); phentolamine (INN); tolazoline hydrochloride (INNM)
	293329 90 0	Other
515.74		**Heterocyclic compounds with nitrogen hetero-atom(s) only, containing an unfused pyridine ring, whether or not hydrogenated,in the structure**
	293331 00 0	Pyridine and its salts
	*293332 00 0	Piperidine and its salts
		Other
	293339 10 0	Iproniazid (INN); ketobemidone hydrochloride (INNM); pyridostigmine bromide (INN)
	293339 80 0	Other
515.75		**Heterocyclic compounds with nitrogen hetero-atom(s) only, containing a quinoline or isoquinoline ring-system, whether or not hydrogenated, not further fused.**
	293340 10 0	Halogen derivatives of quinoline; quinolinecarboxylic acid derivatives

S.I.T.C. (R3)	Commodity Code No	Trade description
cont 515.75	293340 30 0	Dextromethorphan (INN) and its salts
	293340 90 0	Other
515.76		**Heterocyclic compounds with nitrogen hetero-atom(s) only, containing a pyrimidine ring, whether or not hydrogenated, or piperazine ring, or an unfused triazine ring, whether or not hydrogenated, in the structure; nucleic acids and their salts.**
		Malonylurea (barbituric acid) and its derivatives; salts thereof
	293351 10 0	Phenobarbital (INN) and its salts
	293351 30 0	Barbital (INN) and its salts
	293351 90 0	Other
		Other
	293359 10 0	Diazinon (ISO)
	*293359 80 0	Other
		Compounds containing an unfused triazine ring (whether or not hydrogenated) in the structure
	293361 00 0	Melamine
		Other
	293369 10 0	Atrazine (ISO); propazine (ISO); simazine (ISO); hexahydro-1,3,5-trinitro-1,3,5-triazine (hexogen, trimethylenetrinitramine)
	293369 20 0	Methenamine (INN) (hexamethylenetetramine)
	293369 90 0	Other
515.77		**Other heterocyclic compounds with nitrogen hetero-atom(s) only**
	293390 20 0	Benzimidazole-2-thiol (mercaptobenzimidazole)
	293390 40 0	Indole, 3-methylindole (skatole), 6-allyl-6,7-dihydro-5H-dibenz]c,e[azepine (azapetine), chlordiazepoxide (INN), phenindamine (INN) and their salts; imipramine hydrochloride (INNM)
	293390 50 0	Monoazepines
	293390 60 0	Diazepines
	293390 80 0	Other
515.78		**Heterocyclic compounds containing a phenothiazine ring-system (whether or not hydrogenated), not further fused**
	293430 10 0	Thiethylperazine (INN); thioridazine (INN) and its salts
	293430 90 0	Other
515.79		**Heterocyclic compounds, n.e.s.**
	293410 00 0	Compounds containing an unfused thiazole ring (whether or not hydrogenated) in the structure
		Compounds containing a benzothiazole ring-system (whether or not hydrogenated), not further fused
	293420 20 0	Di(benzothiazol-2-yl)disulphide; benzothiazole-2-thiol (mercaptobenzothiazole) and its salts
	293420 50 0	Benzothiazole-2-thiol (mercaptobenzothiazole) derivatives (other than salts)
	293420 90 0	Other
		Other
	293490 10 0	Thiophene
	293490 30 0	Chlorprothixene (INN); thenalidine (INN) and its tartrates and maleates
	293490 40 0	Furazolidone (INN)
	293490 50 0	Monothiamonoazepines, whether or not hydrogenated
	293490 60 0	Monothioles, whether or not hydrogenated
	293490 70 0	Monooxamonoazines, whether or not hydrogenated
	293490 80 0	Monothiines
	293490 85 0	7-Aminocephalosporanic acid
	*293490 89 0	Nucleic acids and their salts
	293490 99 0	Other
515.80	293500 00 0	**Sulphonamides**
		OTHER ORGANIC CHEMICALS
		Ethers, alcohol peroxides, ether peroxides, epoxides,acetals and hemiacetals, and their halogenated, sulphonated, nitrated or nitrosated derivatives
516.12	291100 00 0	**Acetals and hemiacetals, whether or not with other oxygen-function, and their halogenated, sulphonated, nitrated and nitrosated derivatives**
516.13	291010 00 0	**Oxirane (ethylene oxide)**
516.14	291020 00 0	**Methyloxirane (propylene oxide)**
516.15		**Other epoxides, epoxyalcohols, epoxyphenols and epoxyethers, with a three-member ring, and the halogenated,sulphonated, nitrated or nitrosated derivatives of epoxides, epoxyalcohols, epoxy- phenols and epoxyethers, with a three-member ring**
	291030 00 0	1-Chloro-2,3-epoxypropane (epichlorohydrin)
	291090 00 0	Other
516.16		**Acyclic, cyclanic, cyclenic, cycloterpenic and aromatic ethers; their halogenated, sulphonated, nitrated or nitrosated derivatives.**
	290911 00 0	Diethyl ether
	290919 00 0	Other

S.I.T.C. (R3)	Commodity Code No	Trade description
cont 516.16	290920 00 0	Cyclanic, cyclenic or cycloterpenic ethers and their halogenated, sulphonated, nitrated or nitrosated derivatives
		Aromatic ethers and their halogenated, sulphonated, nitrated or nitrosated derivatives
	290930 10 0	Diphenyl ether
		Brominated derivatives
	290930 31 0	Pentabromodiphenyloxyde; tetradecabromodiphenoxybenzene
	290930 39 0	Other
	290930 90 0	Other
516.17		**Ether-alcohols, ether phenols, ether-alcohol-phenols; alcohol, ether, ketone peroxides; their halogenated, sulphonated , nitrated or nitrosated derivatives**
	290941 00 0	2,2'-Oxydiethanol (diethylene glycol, digol)
	290942 00 0	Monomethyl ethers of ethylene glycol or of diethylene glycol
	290943 00 0	Monobutyl ethers of ethylene glycol or of diethylene glycol
	290944 00 0	Other monoalkylethers of ethylene glycol or of diethylene glycol
		Other
	290949 10 0	Acyclic
	290949 90 0	Cyclic
		Ether-phenols, ether-alcohol-phenols and their halogenated, sulphonated, nitrated or nitrosated derivatives
	290950 10 0	Guaiacol and guaiacol suphonates of potassium
	290950 90 0	Other
	290960 00 0	Alcohol peroxides, ether peroxides, ketone peroxides and their halogenated, sulphonated, nitrated or nitrosated derivatives
		Aldehyde-, ketone- and quinone-function compounds
516.21		**Acyclic aldehydes without other oxygen function**
	291211 00 0	Methanal (formaldehyde)
	291212 00 0	Ethanal (acetaldehyde)
	291213 00 0	Butanal (butyraldehyde, normal isomer)
	291219 00 0	Other
516.22		**Other aldehydes, whether or not with other oxygen function; cyclic polymers of aldehydes; paraformaldehyde**
	291221 00 0	Benzaldehyde
	291229 00 0	Other
	291230 00 0	Aldehyde-alcohols
		Aldehyde-ethers, aldehyde-phenols and aldehydes with other oxygen function
	291241 00 0	Vanillin (4-hydroxy-3-methoxybenzaldehyde)
	291242 00 0	Ethylvanillin (3-ethoxy-4-hydroxybenzaldehyde)
	291249 00 0	Other
	291250 00 0	Cyclic polymers of aldehydes
	291260 00 0	Paraformaldehyde
516.23	291411 00 0	**Acetone**
516.24	291412 00 0	**Butanone (ethyl methyl ketone)**
516.25		**Other acyclic ketones without other oxygen function**
	291413 00 0	4-Methylpentan-2-one (methyl isobutyl ketone)
	291419 00 0	Other
516.26	291300 00 0	**Halogenated, sulphonated, nitrated or nitrosated derivatives of the products of headings 516.21 and 516.22**
516.27	291421 00 0	**Camphor**
516.28		**Other cyclanic, cyclenic or cycloterpenic ketones without other oxygen function**
	291422 00 0	Cyclohexanone and methylcyclohexanones
	291423 00 0	Ionones and methylionones
	291429 00 0	Other
516.29		**Aromatic ketones without other oxygen function; ketone alcohols, ketone-aldehydes, ketone phenols and ketones with other oxygen function; quinones; halogenated, sulphonated, nitrated or nitrosated derivatives of ketones and quinones**
		Aromatic ketones without other oxygen function
	*291431 00 0	Phenylacetone (phenylpropan-2-one)
	*291439 00 0	Other
		Ketone-alcohols and ketone-aldehydes
	*291440 10 0	4-Hydroxy-4-methylpentan-2-one (diacetone alcohol)
	*291440 90 0	Other
	291450 00 0	Ketone-phenols and ketones with other oxygen function
		Quinones
	291461 00 0	Anthraquinone
	291469 00 0	Other
		Halogenated, sulphonated, nitrated or nitrosated derivatives

S.I.T.C. (R3)	Commodity Code No	Trade description
cont 516.29	291470 10 0	4'-*tert*-Butyl-2',6'-dimethyl-3',5'-dinitroacetophenone (muskketone)
	291470 90 0	Other

Esters of inorganic acids and their salts, and their halogenated, sulphonated, nitrated or nitrosated derivatives

516.31		**Phosphoric esters and their salts (including lactophosphates); their halogenated, sulphonated, nitrated or nitrosated derivatives**
	291900 10 0	Tributyl phosphates, triphenyl phosphate, tritolyl phosphates, trixylyl phosphates, and
		tris (2-chloroethyl) phosphate
	291900 90 0	Other
516.39		**Esters of other inorganic acids (excluding esters of hydrogen halides) and their salts; their halogenated, sulphonated, nitrated or nitrosated derivatives**
	292010 00 0	Thiophosphoric esters (phosphorothioates) and their salts; their halogenated, sulphonated, nitrated or nitrosated derivatives
		Other
	292090 10 0	Sulphuric esters and carbonic esters and their salts, and their halogenated, sulphonated, nitrated or nitrosated derivatives
	292090 20 0	Dimethyl phosphonate (dimethyl phosphite)
	292090 30 0	Trimethyl phosphite (trimethoxyphosphine)
	292090 80 0	Other products

Organic chemicals, n.e.s.

516.91		**Enzymes; prepared enzymes, n.e.s.**
	350710 00 0	Rennet and concentrates thereof
	350790 00 0	Other
516.92		**Sugars, pure (other than sucrose, lactose, maltose, glucose and fructose); sugar ethers and sugar esters, and their salts (other than products of headings 541.4, 541.5 or 541.61)**
	294000 10 0	Rhamnose, raffinose and mannose
	294000 90 0	Other
516.99	294200 00 0	**Other organic compounds**

DIVISION 52

INORGANIC CHEMICALS

INORGANIC CHEMICAL ELEMENTS, OXIDES AND HALOGEN SALTS

522.10		**Carbon (including carbon black), n.e.s.**
	280300 10 0	Methane black
	280300 30 0	Acetylene black
	280300 90 0	Other
522.21		**Hydrogen, rare gases, nitrogen and oxygen**
	280410 00 0	Hydrogen
		Rare gases
	280421 00 0	Argon
	280429 00 0	Other
	280430 00 0	Nitrogen
	280440 00 0	Oxygen
522.22		**Selenium, tellurium, phosphorus, arsenic and boron**
	280450 10 0	Boron
	280450 90 0	Tellurium
	280470 00 0	Phosphorus
	280480 00 0	Arsenic
	280490 00 0	Selenium
522.23		**Silicon**
	280461 00 0	Containing by weight not less than 99.99 % of silicon
	280469 00 0	Other
522.24	280110 00 0	**Chlorine**
522.25		**Fluorine, bromine and iodine**
	280120 00 0	Iodine
	280130 10 0	Fluorine
	280130 90 0	Bromine
522.26	280200 00 0	**Sulphur, sublimed or precipitated; colloidal sulphur**

S.I.T.C. (R3)	Commodity Code No	Trade description
522.27		**Mercury**
	280540 10 0	In flasks of a net capacity of 34.5 kg (standard weight), of a fob value, per flask, not exceeding 224 ECU
	280540 90 0	Other
522.28	280511 00 0	**Sodium and other alkali metals**
522.29		**Calcium, strontium and barium; rare earth metals, scandium and yttrium, whether or not intermixed or interalloyed**
	280519 00 0	Alkali metals
		Alkaline-earth metals
	280521 00 0	Calcium
	280522 00 0	Strontium and barium
		Rare-earth metals, scandium and yttrium, whether or not intermixed or interalloyed
	280530 10 0	Intermixtures or interalloys
	280530 90 0	Other

Inorganic acids and inorganic oxygen compounds of non-metals

S.I.T.C. (R3)	Commodity Code No	Trade description
522.31		**Hydrogen chloride (hydrochloric acid); chlorosulphuric acid**
	280610 00 0	Hydrogen chloride (hydrochloric acid)
	280620 00 0	Chlorosulphuric acid
522.32		**Sulphuric acid; oleum**
	280700 10 0	Sulphuric acid
	280700 90 0	Oleum
522.33	280800 00 0	**Nitric acid; sulphinitric acids**
522.34		**Diphosphorus pentoxide; phosphoric acid and polyphosphoric acids**
	280910 00 0	Diphosphorus pentaoxide
	280920 00 0	Phosphoric acid and polyphosphoric acids
522.35	281000 00 0	**Oxides of boron; boric acids**
522.36		**Other inorganic acids**
	281111 00 0	Hydrogen fluoride (hydrofluoric acid)
		Other
	281119 10 0	Hydrobromic acid
	281119 90 0	Other
522.37	281122 00 0	**Silicon dioxide**
522.38	281123 00 0	**Sulphur dioxide**
522.39		**Other inorganic oxygen compounds of non-metals**
	281121 00 0	Carbon dioxide
		Other
	281129 10 0	Sulphur trioxide (sulphuric anhydride); diarsenic trioxide
	281129 30 0	Nitrogen oxides
	281129 90 0	Other

Halogen or sulphur compounds of non-metals

S.I.T.C. (R3)	Commodity Code No	Trade description
522.41		**Halides and halide oxides of non-metals.**
		Chlorides and chloride oxides
		Of phosphorus
	281210 11 0	Phosphorus trichloride oxide (phosphoryl trichloride)
	281210 15 0	Phosphorus trichloride
	281210 19 0	Other
	281210 90 0	Other
	281290 00 0	Other
522.42		**Sulphides of non-metals; commercial phosphorus trisulphide**
	281310 00 0	Carbon disulphide
		Other
	281390 10 0	Phosphorus sulphides; commercial phosphorus trisulphide
	281390 90 0	Other

Oxides of zinc, chromium, manganese, iron, cobalt, titanium and lead

S.I.T.C. (R3)	Commodity Code No	Trade description
522.51	281700 00 0	**Zinc oxide; zinc peroxide**
522.52		**Chromium oxides and hydroxides**
	281910 00 0	Chromium trioxide
	281990 00 0	Other

S.I.T.C. (R3)	Commodity Code No	Trade description
522.53		**Manganese oxides**
	282010 00 0	Manganese dioxide
	282090 00 0	Other
522.54		**Iron oxides and hydroxides; earth colours containing 70% or more by weight of combined iron evaluated as Fe2O3**
	282110 00 0	Iron oxides and hydroxides
	282120 00 0	Earth colours
522.55	282200 00 0	**Cobalt oxides and hydroxides; commercial cobalt oxides**
522.56	282300 00 0	**Titanium oxides**
522.57		**Lead oxides; red lead and orange lead**
	282410 00 0	Lead monoxide (litharge, massicot)
	282420 00 0	Red lead and orange lead
	282490 00 0	Other
		Other inorganic bases and metallic oxides, hydroxides and peroxides
522.61		**Ammonia, anhydrous, or in aqueous solution**
	281410 00 0	Anhydrous ammonia
	281420 00 0	Ammonia in aqueous solution
522.62	281511 00 0	**Sodium hydroxide (caustic soda), solid**
522.63	281512 00 0	**Sodium hydroxide in aqueous solution (soda lye or liquid soda)**
522.64		**Potassium hydroxide (caustic potash); peroxides of sodium or potassium**
		Potassium hydroxide (caustic potash)
	281520 10 0	Solid
	281520 90 0	In aqueous solution (potassium lye or liquid potassium)
	281530 00 0	Peroxides of sodium or potassium
522.65		**Hydroxide and peroxide of magnesium; oxides, hydroxides and peroxides, of strontium or barium**
	281610 00 0	Hydroxide and peroxide of magnesium
	281620 00 0	Oxide, hydroxide and peroxide of strontium
	281630 00 0	Oxide, hydroxide and peroxide of barium
522.66	281830 00 0	**Aluminium hydroxide**
522.67	281810 00 0	**Artificial corundum**
522.68	282510 00 0	**Hydrazine and hydroxylamine and their inorganic salts**
522.69		**Other inorganic bases; other metal oxides, hydroxides and peroxides**
	282520 00 0	Lithium oxide and hydroxide
	282530 00 0	Vanadium oxides and hydroxides
	282540 00 0	Nickel oxides and hydroxides
	282550 00 0	Copper oxides and hydroxides
	282560 00 0	Germanium oxides and zirconium dioxide
	282570 00 0	Molybdenum oxides and hydroxides
	282580 00 0	Antimony oxides
		Other
	282590 10 0	Calcium oxide, hydroxide and peroxide
	282590 20 0	Beryllium oxide and hydroxide
	282590 30 0	Tin oxides
	282590 40 0	Tungsten oxides and hydroxides
	282590 50 0	Mercury oxides
	282590 60 0	Cadmium oxide
	282590 80 0	Other

METALLIC SALTS AND PEROXYSALTS, OF INORGANIC ACIDS

S.I.T.C. (R3)	Commodity Code No	Trade description
523.10		**Fluorides; fluorosilicates, fluoroaluminates and other complex fluorine salts**
		Fluorides
	282611 00 0	Of ammonium or of sodium
	282612 00 0	Of aluminium
	282619 00 0	Other
	282620 00 0	Fluorosilicates of sodium or of potassium
	282630 00 0	Sodium hexafluoroaluminate (synthetic cryolite)
		Other
	282690 10 0	Dipotassium hexafluorozirconate
	282690 90 0	Other

S.I.T.C. (R3)	Commodity Code No	Trade description
		Chlorides, chloride oxides and chloride hydroxides; bromides and bromide oxides; iodides and iodide oxides
523.21	282710 00 0	**Ammonium chloride**
523.22	282720 00 0	**Calcium chloride**
523.29		**Other chlorides, chloride oxides and chloride hydroxides; bromides and bromide oxides; iodides and iodide oxides**
		Other chlorides
	282731 00 0	Of magnesium
	282732 00 0	Of aluminium
	282733 00 0	Of iron
	282734 00 0	Of cobalt
	282735 00 0	Of nickel
	282736 00 0	Of zinc
	282738 00 0	Of barium
		Other
	*282739 10 0	Of tin
	*282739 90 0	Other
		Chloride oxides and chloride hydroxides
	282741 00 0	Of copper
		Other
	282749 10 0	Of lead
	282749 90 0	Other
		Bromides and bromide oxides
	282751 00 0	Bromides of sodium or of potassium
	282759 00 0	Other
	282760 00 0	Iodides and iodide oxides
		Hypochlorites; commercial calcium hypochlorite; chlorites; hypobromites; chlorates and perchlorates; bromates and perbromates; iodates and periodates
523.31		**Hypochlorites; commercial calcium hypochlorite; chlorites; hypo-bromites**
	282810 00 0	Commercial calcium hypochlorite and other calcium hypochlorites
	282890 00 0	Other
523.32	282911 00 0	**Chlorates of sodium**
523.39		**Other chlorates and perchlorates; bromates and perbromates; iodates and periodates**
	282919 00 0	Chlorates
		Other
	282990 10 0	Perchlorates
	282990 50 0	Potassium bromate
	282990 60 0	Sodium bromate
	282990 80 0	Other
		Sulphides polysulphides, dithionites, sulphoxylates, sulphites, thiosulphates and alums
523.41	283010 00 0	**Sodium sulphide**
523.42		**Other sulphides; polysulphides**
	283020 00 0	Zinc sulphide
	283030 00 0	Cadmium sulphide
		Other
		Sulphides
	283090 11 0	Of calcium; of antimony; of iron
	283090 19 0	Other
	283090 90 0	Polysulphides
523.43		**Dithionites and sulphoxylates**
	283110 00 0	Of sodium
	283190 00 0	Other
523.44		**Sulphites; thiosulphates**
	283210 00 0	Sodium sulphites
	283220 00 0	Other sulphites
	283230 00 0	Thiosulphates
523.45		**Sodium sulphates**
	283311 00 0	Disodium sulphate
	283319 00 0	Other
523.49		**Other sulphates; alums**
		Other sulphates
	283321 00 0	Of magnesium
	283322 00 0	Of aluminium

S.I.T.C. (R3)	Commodity Code No	Trade description
cont		
523.49	283323 00 0	Of chromium
	283324 00 0	Of nickel
	283325 00 0	Of copper
	283326 00 0	Of zinc
	283327 00 0	Of barium
	283329 10 0	Of cadmium
	283329 30 0	Of cobalt; of titanium
	283329 50 0	Of iron
	283329 70 0	Of mercury; of lead
	283329 90 0	Other
		Alums
	283330 10 0	Aluminium ammonium bis(sulphate)
	283330 90 0	Other
	283340 00 0	Peroxosulphates (persulphates)
		Nitrites; nitrates
523.51	283410 00 0	**Nitrites**
523.52	283421 00 0	**Potassium nitrate**
523.59		**Other nitrates**
	283422 00 0	Of bismuth
		Other
	283429 10 0	Of barium; of beryllium; of cadmium; of cobalt; of nickel
	283429 30 0	Of copper; of mercury
	283429 50 0	Of lead
	283429 90 0	Other
		Phosphinates (hypophosphites), phosphonates(phospites), phosphates and polyphosphates
523.61	283510 00 0	**Phosphinates (hypophosphites) and phosphonates (phosphites)**
523.62		**Triammonium phosphate**
	*283529 10 0	Of triammonium
	*283529 90 0	Other
523.63		**Other phosphates**
	283522 00 0	Of mono- or disodium
	283523 00 0	Of trisodium
	283524 00 0	Of potassium
		Calcium hydrogenorthophosphate ("dicalcium phosphate")
	283525 10 0	With a fluorine content of less than 0.005% by weight on the dry anhydrous product
	283525 90 0	With a fluorine content of 0.005% or more by weight on the dry anhydrous product
		Other phosphates of calcium
	283526 10 0	With a fluorine content of less than 0.005% by weight on the dry anhydrous product
	283526 90 0	With a fluorine content of 0.005% or more by weight on the dry anhydrous product
	283529 00 0	Other
523.64	283531 00 0	**Sodium triphosphate (sodium tripolyphosphate)**
523.65		**Other polyphosphates**
	283539 10 0	Of ammonium
	283539 30 0	Of sodium
	283539 70 0	Other
		Carbonates; Peroxocarbonates (percarbonates); commercial ammonium carbonate containing ammonium carbamate
523.71	283610 00 0	**Commercial ammonium carbonate and other ammonium carbonates**
523.72	283620 00 0	**Neutral sodium carbonate (disodium carbonate)**
523.73	283630 00 0	**Sodium hydrogencarbonate (sodium bicarbonate)**
523.74	283640 00 0	**Potassium carbonates**
523.75	283670 00 0	**Lead carbonate**
523.79		**Other carbonates**
	283650 00 0	Calcium carbonate
	283660 00 0	Barium carbonate
		Other
	283691 00 0	Lithium carbonates
	283692 00 0	Strontium carbonate
		Other
		Carbonates

S.I.T.C. (R3)	Commodity Code No	Trade description
cont		
523.79	283699 11 0	Of magnesium; of copper
	*283699 18 0	Other
	283699 90 0	Peroxocarbonates (percarbonates)
		Other metallic salts and peroxysalts of inorganic acids
523.81		**Cyanides, cyanide oxides and complex cyanides**
		Cyanides and cyanide oxides
	283711 00 0	Of sodium
	283719 00 0	Other
	283720 00 0	Complex cyanides
523.82	283800 00 0	**Fulminates, cyanates and thiocyanates**
523.83		**Silicates; commercial alkali metal silicates**
		Of sodium
	283911 00 0	Sodium metasilicates
	283919 00 0	Other
	283920 00 0	Of potassium
	283990 00 0	Other
523.84		**Borates; peroxoborates (perborates)**
		Disodium tetraborate (refined borax)
	284011 00 0	Anhydrous
	284019 00 0	Other
		Other borates
	284020 10 0	Borates of sodium, anhydrous
	284020 90 0	Other
	284030 00 0	Peroxoborates (perborates)
523.89		**Other salts of inorganic acids or peroxoacids (excluding azides)**
	284210 00 0	Double or complex silicates
		Other
	284290 10 0	Salts, double salts or complex salts of selenium or tellurium acids
	284290 90 0	Other
		OTHER INORGANIC CHEMICALS; ORGANIC AND INORGANIC COMPOUNDS OF PRECIOUS METALS
		Salts of metallic acids; organic and inorganic compounds of precious metals
524.31		**Salts of oxometallic or peroxometallic acids**
	284110 00 0	Aluminates
	284120 00 0	Chromates of zinc or of lead
	284130 00 0	Sodium dichromate
	284140 00 0	Potassium dichromate
	284150 00 0	Other chromates and dichromates; peroxochromates
		Manganites, manganates and permanganates
	*284161 00 0	Potassium permanganate
	*284169 00 0	Other
	284170 00 0	Molybdates
	284180 00 0	Tungstates (wolframates)
		Other
	284190 10 0	Antimonates
	284190 30 0	Zincates and vanadates
	284190 90 0	Other
524.32		**Colloidal precious metals; compounds, inorganic or organic, of precious metals, whether or not chemically defined; amalgams of precious metals**
		Colloidal precious metals
	284310 10 0	Silver
	284310 90 0	Other
		Silver compounds
	284321 00 0	Silver nitrate
	284329 00 0	Other
	284330 00 0	Gold compounds
		Other compounds; amalgams
	284390 10 0	Amalgams
	284390 90 0	Other
		Inorganic chemical products, n.e.s.
524.91	284700 00 0	**Hydrogen peroxide, whether or not solidified with urea**
524.92	*284800 00 0	**Phosphides, whether or not chemically defined (excluding ferrophosphorus)**
524.93	284910 00 0	**Calcium carbide, whether or not chemically defined**

S.I.T.C. (R3)	Commodity Code No	Trade description
524.94		**Carbides (other than calcium carbide), whether or not chemically defined**
	284920 00 0	Of silicon
		Other
	284990 10 0	Of boron
	284990 30 0	Of tungsten
	284990 50 0	Of aluminium; of chromium; of molybdenum; of vanadium; of tantalum; of titanium
	284990 90 0	Other
524.95		**Hydrides, nitrides, azides, silicides and borides, whether or not chemically defined other than compounds which are also carbides of headings 524.93 or 524.94**
	285000 10 0	Hydrides
	285000 30 0	Nitrides
	285000 50 0	Azides
	285000 70 0	Silicides
	285000 90 0	Borides
524.99		**Inorganic compounds, n.e.s. (including distilled or conductivity water and water of similar purity); liquid air (whether or not rare gases have been removed); compressed air; amalgams (other than amalgams of precious metals)**
	285100 10 0	Distilled and conductivity water and water of similar purity
	285100 30 0	Liquid air (whether or not rare gases have been removed); compressed air
	285100 90 0	Other

RADIO-ACTIVE AND ASSOCIATED MATERIALS

Radio-active chemical elements and isotopes (including the fissile and fertile elements and isotopes) and their compounds; mixtures and residues containing these products

S.I.T.C. (R3)	Commodity Code No	Trade description
525.11		**Natural uranium and its compounds; alloys, dispersions (incl. cermets), ceramic products and mixtures containing natural uranium or natural uranium compounds**
		Natural uranium:
	284410 10 0	Crude; waste and scrap (*Euratom*)
		Worked
	284410 31 0	Bars, rods, angles, shapes and sections, wire, sheets and strips (*Euratom*)
	284410 39 0	Other
	284410 50 0	Ferro-uranium
	284410 90 0	Other (*Euratom*)
525.13		**Uranium enriched in U235 and its compounds; plutonium and its compounds; alloys, dispersions (incl. cermets), ceramic products and mixtures containing uranium enriched in U235, plutonium or compounds of these products**
		Uranium enriched in U 235 and its compounds; alloys, dispersions (including cermets), ceramic products and mixtures containing uranium enriched in U 235 or compounds of these products, of a U 235 content of
		Less than 20 % by weight
	284420 21 0	Ferro-uranium
	284420 29 0	Other (*Euratom*)
		20 % or more by weight
	284420 31 0	Ferro-uranium
	284420 39 0	Other (*Euratom*)
		Plutonium and its compounds; alloys, dispersions (including cermets), ceramic products and mixtures containing plutonium or compounds of these products
		Mixtures of uranium and plutonium
	284420 51 0	Ferro-uranium
	284420 59 0	Other
		Other
	284420 81 0	Ferro-uranium
	284420 89 0	Other
525.15		**Uranium depleted in U235 and its compounds; thorium and its compounds; alloys, dispersions (incl. cermets), ceramic products and mixtures containing uranium depleted in U235, thorium or compounds of these products**
		Uranium depleted in U 235; alloys, dispersions (including cermets), ceramic products and mixtures containing uranium depleted in U 235 or compounds of this product
	284430 11 0	Cermets
	284430 19 0	Other
		Thorium; alloys, dispersions (including cermets), ceramic products and mixtures containing thorium or compounds of this product
	284430 51 0	Cermets
		Other (Euratom)
	284430 55 0	Crude, waste and scrap
		Worked
	284430 61 0	Bars, rods, angles, shapes and sections, sheets and strips
	284430 69 0	Other

S.I.T.C. (R3)	Commodity Code No	Trade description

cont
525.15

		Compounds of uranium depleted in U 235 or of thorium, whether or not mixed together
	284430 91 0	Of thorium or of uranium depleted in U 235, whether or not mixed together (*Euratom*), other than thorium salts
	284430 99 0	Other

525.17	284450 00 0	**Spent (irradiated) fuel elements (cartridges) of nuclear reactors (Euratom)**

525.19

Radio-active elements and isotopes and their compounds, n.e.s.; alloys, dispersions (incl. cermets), ceramic products and mixtures containing these elements, isotopes or compounds; radio-active residues

Uranium derived from U 233 and its compounds; alloys dispersions (including cermets), ceramic products and mixtures and compounds derived from U 233 or compounds of this product

	284440 11 0	Ferro-uranium
	284440 19 0	Other
		Other
	284440 20 0	Artificial radioactive isotopes (*Euratom*)
	284440 30 0	Compounds of artificial radioactive isotopes (*Euratom*)
	284440 40 0	Inorganic products of a kind used as 'luminophores' activated by radioactive compounds
	284440 90 0	Other

Stable isotopes and their compounds; compounds, inorganic or organic, of rare-earth metals, of yttrium or of scandium or of mixtures of these metals

525.91

Isotopes (other than those of heading 525.1); compounds, inorganic or organic, of such isotopes, whether or not chemically defined

	284510 00 0	Heavy water (deuterium oxide)(Euratom)
		Other
	284590 10 0	Deuterium and compounds thereof; hydrogen and compounds thereof, enriched in deuterium; mixtures and solutions containing these products (Euratom)
	284590 90 0	Other

525.95

Compounds, inorganic or organic, of rare-earth metals, of yttrium or of scandium or of mixtures of these metals

	284610 00 0	Cerium compounds
	284690 00 0	Other

DIVISION 53

DYEING, TANNING AND COLOURING MATERIALS

SYNTHETIC ORGANIC COLOURING MATTER AND COLOUR LAKES, AND PREPARATIONS BASED THEREON

Synthetic organic colouring matter and preparations based thereon

531.11	320411 00 0	**Disperse dyes and preparations based thereon**
531.12	*320412 00 0	**Acid dyes, whether or not premetallized, and preparations based thereon; mordant dyes, and preparations based thereon.**
531.13	320413 00 0	**Basic dyes and preparations based thereon**
531.14	320414 00 0	**Direct dyes and preparations based thereon**
531.15	320415 00 0	**Vat dyes (incl. those usable in that state as pigments) and preparations based thereon**
531.16	320416 00 0	**Reactive dyes and preparations based thereon**
531.17	320417 00 0	**Pigments and preparations based thereon**
531.19	*320419 00 0	**Other synthetic organic colouring matter (incl. mixtures of colouring matter falling within two or more of the headings of subgroup 531.1)**

Synthetic organic products of a kind used as flourescent brightening agents or luminophores, whether or not chemically defined; colour lakes and preparations based thereon

531.21

Synthetic organic products of a kind used as fluorescent brightening agents or as luminophores, whether or not chemically defined

	320420 00 0	Synthetic organic products of a kind used as fluorescent brightening agents
	320490 00 0	Other

531.22	320500 00 0	**Colour lakes; preparations based on colour lakes**

S.I.T.C. (R3)	Commodity Code No	Trade description

DYEING AND TANNING EXTRACTS, AND SYNTHETIC TANNING MATERIALS

Tanning extracts of vegetable origin; tannins and their derivatives; colouring matter of vegetable or animal origin and preparations based thereon

532.21		**Tanning extracts of vegetable origin; tannins and their salts, ethers, esters and other derivatives**
	320110 00 0	Quebracho extract
	320120 00 0	Wattle extract
		Other
	*320190 20 0	Sumach extract, vallonia extract
	320190 90 0	Other
	320190 90 0	Other
532.22		**Colouring matter of vegetable or animal origin (including dyeing extracts but excluding animal black), whether or not chemically defined; preparations based on colouring matter of vegetable or animal origin**
		Colouring matter of vegetable origin and preparations based thereon
	320300 11 0	Black cutch (Acacia catechu)
	320300 19 0	Other
	320300 90 0	Colouring matter of animal origin and preparations based thereon

Synthetic organic tanning substances; inorganic tanning substances; tanning preparations, whether or not containing natural tanning substances; enzymatic preparations for pre-tanning

532.31	320210 00 0	**Synthetic organic tanning substances**
532.32	320290 00 0	**Inorganic tanning substances; tanning preparations, whether or not containing natural tanning substances; enzymatic preparations for pre-tanning**

PIGMENTS, PAINTS, VARNISHES AND RELATED MATERIALS

Other colouring matter; preparations based on colouring matter, n.e.s.; luminophores, whether or not chemically defined

533.11		**Pigments and preparations based on titanium dioxide**
	*320611 00 0	Containing not less than 80% by weight of titanium dioxide calculated on the dry weight
	*320619 00 0	Other
533.12	320620 00 0	**Pigments and preparations based on chromium compounds**
533.13	320630 00 0	**Pigments and preparations based on cadmium compounds**
533.14	320641 00 0	**Ultramarine and preparations based thereon**
533.15	320642 00 0	**Lithopone and other pigments and preparations based on zinc sulphide**
533.16	320643 00 0	**Pigments and preparations based on hexacyanoferrates (ferrocyanides and ferricyanides)**
533.17		**Colouring matter and other preparations, n.e.s.**
	320649 10 0	Magnetite
	320649 90 0	Other
533.18	320650 00 0	**Inorganic products of a kind used as luminophores**

Printing ink

533.21	321511 00 0	....black
533.29	321519 00 0	....other

Paints and varnishes (including enamels, lacquers and distempers); plastics in solution; prepared water pigments of a kind used for finishing leather; pigments (including metallic powders and flakes) dispersed in non-aqueous media, in liquid or paste form, of a kind used in the manufacture of paints (including enamels); foils; dyes and other colouring matter put up in forms or packings for retail sale

533.41		**Paints and varnishes (incl. enamels and lacquers) based on synthetic polymers or chemically modified natural polymers, dispersed or dissolved in an aqueous medium.**
	320910 00 0	Based on acrylic or vinyl polymers
	320990 00 0	Other
533.42		**Paints and varnishes (including enamels and lacquers) based on synthetic polymers or chemically modified natural polymers, dispersed or dissolved in a non-aqueous medium; plastics in solution.**
		Based on polyesters
	320810 10 0	Solutions
	320810 90 0	Other

S.I.T.C. (R3)	Commodity Code No	Trade description
cont 533.42		Based on acrylic or vinyl polymers
	320820 10 0	Solutions
	320820 90 0	Other
		Other
	320890 10 0	Solutions
		Other
	320890 91 0	Based on synthetic polymers
		Based on chemically modified natural polymers
	320890 99 0	Cellulose varnishes, lacquers, paints and enamels
533.43		**Other paints and varnishes (incl. enamels, lacquers and distempers); prepared water pigments of a kind used for finishing leather**
	321000 10 0	Oil paints and varnishes (including enamels and lacquers)
	321000 90 0	Other
	321290 10 0	Pearl essence
533.44		**Pigments (including metallic powders and flakes) dispersed in non- aqueous media, in liquid or paste form, of a kind used in the manufacture of paints (including enamels); stamping foils; dyes and other colouring matter put up in forms or packings for retail sale.**
		Stamping foils
	321210 10 0	With a basis of base metal
	321210 90 0	Other
		Other
		Pigments (including metallic powders and flakes) dispersed in non-aqueous media, in liquid or paste form, of a kind used in the manufacture of paints (including enamels)
	321290 31 0	With a basis of aluminium powder
	321290 39 0	Other
	321290 90 0	Dyes and other colouring matter put up in forms or packings for retail sale
		Colouring preparations of a kind used in the ceramic, enamelling and glass industries; artists' colours, paint driers and mastics
533.51		**Prepared pigments, prepared opacifiers and prepared colours, vitrifiable enamels and glazes, engobes (slips), liquid lustres and similar preparations, of a kind used in the ceramic, enamelling or glass industry; glass frit and other glass, in the form of powder, granules or flakes**
	320710 00 0	Prepared pigments, prepared opacifiers, prepared colours and similar preparations
		Vitrifiable enamels and glazes, engobes (slips) and similar preparations
	320720 10 0	Engobes (slips)
	320720 90 0	Other
	320730 00 0	Liquid lustres and similar preparations
		Glass frit and other glass, in the form of powder, granules or flakes
	320740 10 0	Glass of the variety known as "enamel" glass
	320740 90 0	Other
533.52		**Artists', students' or signboard painters' colours, modifying tints, amusement colours and the like, in tablets, tubes, jars, bottles, pans or in similar forms or packings**
	321310 00 0	Colours in sets
	321390 00 0	Other
533.53	321100 00 0	**Prepared driers**
533.54		**Glaziers' putty; grafting putty; resin cements, caulking compounds and other mastics; painters' fillings; non-refractory surfacing preparations for facades, indoor walls, floors, ceilings or the like**
		Mastics; painters' fillings
	321410 10 0	Mastics
	321410 90 0	Painters' fillings
	321490 00 0	Other
533.55		**Organic composite solvents and thinners, n.e.s.; prepared paint or varnish removers**
	381400 10 0	Based on butyl acetate
	381400 90 0	Other

DIVISION 54

MEDICINAL AND PHARMACEUTICAL PRODUCTS

MEDICINAL AND PHARMACEUTICAL PRODUCTS, OTHER THAN MEDICAMENTS OF GROUP 542

Provitamins and vitamins, natural or reproduced by synthesis (including natural concentrates), derivatives thereof used primarily as vitamins, and intermixtures of the foregoing, whether or not in any solvent, not put up as medicaments of heading 542

541.11	293610 00 0	**Provitamins, unmixed**
541.12	293621 00 0	**Vitamins A and their derivatives, unmixed**

S.I.T.C. (R3)	Commodity Code No	Trade description
541.13		**Vitamins B and their derivatives, unmixed**
	293622 00 0	Vitamin B$_1$ and its derivatives
	293623 00 0	Vitamin B$_2$ and its derivatives
	293624 00 0	D- or DL-Pantothenic acid (Vitamin B$_3$ or Vitamin B$_5$) and its derivatives
	293625 00 0	Vitamin B$_6$ and its derivatives
	293626 00 0	Vitamin B$_{12}$ and its derivatives
541.14	293627 00 0	**Vitamin C and its derivatives, unmixed**
541.15	293628 00 0	**Vitamin E and its derivatives, unmixed**
541.16		**Other vitamins and their derivatives, unmixed**
	293629 10 0	Vitamin B$_9$ and its derivatives
	293629 30 0	Vitamin H and its derivatives
	293629 90 0	Other
541.17		**Intermixtures of provitamins and vitamins (incl. natural concentrates), whether or not in any solvent**
		Other, including natural concentrates
		Natural concentrates of vitamins
	293690 11 0	Natural concentrates of vitamins A + D
	293690 19 0	Other
	293690 90 0	Intermixtures, whether or not in any solvent
		Antibiotics, not put up as medicaments of heading 542
541.31		**Penicillins and their derivatives with a penicillanic acid structure; salts thereof**
	294110 10 0	Amoxicillin (INN) and its salts
	294110 20 0	Ampicillin (INN), metampicillin (INN), pivampicillin (INN), and their salts
	294110 90 0	Other
541.32		**Streptomycins and their derivatives; salts thereof**
	294120 10 0	Dihydrostreptomycin
	294120 20 0	Salts, esters and hydrates of dihydrostreptomycin
	294120 80 0	Other
541.33	294130 00 0	**Tetracyclines and their derivatives; salts thereof**
541.39		**Other antibiotics**
	294140 00 0	Chloramphenicol and its derivatives; salts thereof
	294150 00 0	Erythromycin and its derivatives; salts thereof
	294190 00 0	Other
		Vegetable alkaloids, natural or reproduced by synthesis, and their salts, ethers, esters and other derivatives, not put up as medicaments of heading 542
541.41	293910 00 0	**Alkaloids of opium and their derivatives; salts thereof**
541.42		**Alkaloids of cinchona and their derivatives; salts thereof**
		Quinine and its salts
	293921 10 0	Quinine and quinine sulphate
	293921 90 0	Other
	293929 00 0	Other
541.43	293930 00 0	**Caffeine and its salts**
541.44		**Ephedrines and their salts**
	*293941 00 0	Ephedrine and its salts
	*293942 00 0	Pseudoephedrine (INN) and its salts
	*293949 00 0	Other
541.45		**Theophylline and aminophylline (theophylline-ethylenediamine) and their derivatives; salts thereof**
	293950 10 0	Theophylline and aminophylline (theophylline-ethylenediamine); salts thereof
	293950 90 0	Other
541.46		**Alkaloids of rye ergot and their derivatives; salts thereof**
	*293961 00 0	Ergometrine (INN) and its salts
	*293962 00 0	Ergotamine (INN) and its salts
	*293963 00 0	Lysergic acid and its salts
	*293969 00 0	Other
541.47	293970 00 0	**Nicotine and its salts**
541.49		**Other vegetable alkaloids and their salts; derivatives of of alkaloids, n.e.s., and their salts**
		Cocaine and its salts
	293990 11 0	Crude cocaine
	293990 19 0	Other

S.I.T.C. (R3)	Commodity Code No	Trade description
cont 541.49	293990 30 0	Emetine and its salts
	293990 90 0	Other

Hormones, natural or reproduced by synthesis; derivatives thereof used primarily as hormones; other steroids used primarily as hormones, not put up as medicaments of heading 542

S.I.T.C. (R3)	Commodity Code No	Trade description
541.51	293791 00 0	**Insulin and its salts**
541.52		**Pituitary (anterior) or similar hormones, and their derivatives.**
	293710 10 0	Gonadotrophic hormones
	293710 90 0	Other
541.53		**Adrenal cortical hormones and their derivatives**
	293721 00 0	Cortisone, hydrocortisone, prednisone (dehydrocortisone) and prednisolone (dehydrohydrocortisone)
	293722 00 0	Halogenated derivatives of adrenal cortical hormones
		Other
	293729 10 0	Acetates of cortisone or hydrocortisone
	293729 90 0	Other
541.59		**Other hormones and other hormone derivatives; other steroids used primarily as hormones, not put up as medicaments of heading 542**
	293792 00 0	Oestrogens and progestogens
	293799 00 0	Other

Glycosides; glands or other organs and their extracts; antisera, vaccines and similar products

S.I.T.C. (R3)	Commodity Code No	Trade description
541.61		**Glycosides, natural or reproduced by synthesis, and their salts, ethers, esters and other derivatives**
	293810 00 0	Rutoside (rutin) and its derivatives
		Other
	293890 10 0	Digitalis glycosides
	293890 30 0	Glycyrrhizic acid and glycyrrhizates
	293890 90 0	Other
541.62		**Glands and other organs, for organo-therapeutic uses, dried, whether or not powdered; extracts of glands or other organs or of their secretions for organo-therapeutic uses; heparin and its salts; other human or animal substances prepared for therapeutic or prophylacticuses, n.e.s**
		Glands and other organs, dried, whether or not powdered
	300110 10 0	Powdered
	300110 90 0	Other
		Extracts of glands or other organs or of their secretions
	300120 10 0	Of human origin
	300120 90 0	Other
		Other
	300190 10 0	Of human origin
		Other
	300190 91 0	Heparin and its salts
	300190 99 0	Other
541.63		**Antisera and other blood fractions; vaccines**
		Antisera and other blood fractions
	300210 10 0	Antisera
		Other blood fractions
	300210 91 0	Haemoglobin, blood globulins and serum globulins
		Other
	300210 95 0	Of human origin
	300210 99 0	Other
	300220 00 0	Vaccines for human medicine
	*300230 00 0	Vaccines for veterinary medicine
541.64		**Human blood; animal blood prepared for therapeutic, prophylactic or diagnostic uses; toxins, cultures of micro-organisms (excluding yeasts) and similar products**
	300290 10 0	Human blood
	300290 30 0	Animal blood prepared for therapeutic, prophylactic or diagnostic uses
	300290 50 0	Cultures of micro-organisms
	300290 90 0	Other

Pharmaceutical goods, other than medicaments

S.I.T.C. (R3)	Commodity Code No	Trade description
541.91		**Wadding, gauze, bandages and similar articles (e.g., dressings, adhesive plasters, poultices), impregnated or coated with pharmaceutical substances or put up in forms or packings for retail sale for medical, surgical, dental or veterinary purposes, n.e.s.**
	300510 00 0	Adhesive dressings and other articles having an adhesive layer
		Other
	300590 10 0	Wadding and articles of wadding
		Other
		Of textile materials

S.I.T.C. (R3)	Commodity Code No	Trade description
cont 541.91	300590 31 0	Gauze and articles of gauze Other
	300590 51 0	Of "non-woven" fabrics
	300590 55 0	Other
	300590 99 0	Other
541.92	300620 00 0	**Blood-grouping reagents**
541.93	300630 00 0	**Opacifying preparations for x-ray examinations; diagnostic reagents designed to be administered to the patient**
541.99		**Other pharmaceutical goods** Sterile surgical catgut, similar sterile suture materials and sterile tissue adhesives for surgical wound closure; sterile laminaria and sterile laminaria tents;sterile absorbable surgical or dental haemostatics
	300610 10 0	Sterile surgical catgut
	300610 90 0	Other
	300640 00 0	Dental cements and other dental fillings; bone reconstruction cements
	300650 00 0	First-aid boxes and kits Chemical contraceptive preparations based on hormones or spermicides Based on hormones
	300660 11 0	Put up in forms or in packings of a kind sold by retail
	300660 19 0	Other
	300660 90 0	Based on spermicides
		MEDICAMENTS (INCLUDING VETERINARY MEDICAMENTS)
		Medicaments containing antibiotics or derivatives thereof
542.11	300310 00 0	**....containing penicillins or derivatives thereof, with a penicillanic acid structure, or streptomycins or their derivatives, not put up in measured doses or in forms or packings for retail sale**
542.12	300320 00 0	**....containing other antibiotics, not put up in measured doses or in forms or packings for retail sale**
542.13		**....containing penicillins or derivatives thereof, with a penicillanic acid structure, or streptomycins or their derivatives put up in measured doses or in forms or packings for retail sale**
	300410 10 0	Containing, as active substances, only penicillins or derivatives thereof with a penicillanic acid structure
	300410 90 0	Other
542.19		**....containing other antibiotics, put up in measured doses or in forms or packings for retail sale**
	300420 10 0	Put up in forms or packings for retail sale
	300420 90 0	Other
		Medicaments containing hormones or other products of heading 541.5, but not containing antibiotics or derivatives thereof
542.21	300331 00 0	**....containing insulin, not put up in measured doses or in forms or packings for retail sale**
542.22	300339 00 0	**....containing other hormones or other products of heading 541.45, put up in measured doses or in forms or packings for retail sale**
542.23		**....containing insulin, put up in measured doses or in forms or packings for retail sal** Containing insulin
	300431 10 0	Put up in forms or in packings of a kind sold by retail
	300431 90 0	Other
542.24		**....containing adrenal cortex hormones, put up in measured doses or in forms or packings for retail sale**
	300432 10 0	Put up in forms or in packings of a kind sold by retail
	300432 90 0	Other
542.29		**....containing other hormones or other products of heading 541.5 put up in measured doses or in forms or packings for retail sale**
	300439 10 0	Put up in forms or in packings of a kind sold by retail
	300439 90 0	Other
		Medicaments containing alkaloids or derivatives thereof, but not containing hormones, other products of heading 541.5, or antibiotics or derivatives of antibiotics
542.31	300340 00 0	**....not put up in measured doses or in forms or packings for retail sale**

S.I.T.C. (R3)	Commodity Code No	Trade description
542.32		....put up in measured doses or in forms or packings for retail sale
		Containing alkaloids or derivatives thereof but not containing hormones, other products of heading 541.5 or antibiotics
	300440 10 0	Put up in forms or in packings of a kind sold by retail
	300440 90 0	Other
		Medicaments, n.e.s.
542.91		**Medicaments, n.e.s., not put up in measured doses or in forms or or packings for retail sale**
	300390 10 0	Containing iodine or iodine compounds
	300390 90 0	Other
542.92		**Medicaments containing vitamins or other products of heading 541.1, put up in measured doses or in forms or packings for retail sale**
	300450 10 0	Put up in forms or in packings of a kind sold by retail
	300450 90 0	Other
542.93		**Medicaments, n.e.s., put up in measured doses or in forms or packings for retail sale**
		Put up in forms or in packings of a kind sold by retail
	300490 11 0	Containing iodine or iodine compounds
	*300490 19 0	Other
		Other
	300490 91 0	Containing iodine or iodine compounds
	*300490 99 0	Other

DIVISION 55		**ESSENTIAL OILS AND RESINOIDS AND PERFUME MATERIALS; TOILET, POLISHING AND CLEANSING PREPARATIONS**
		ESSENTIAL OILS, PERFUME AND FLAVOUR MATERIALS
		Essential oils (terpeneless or not), including concretes and absolutes; resinoids; concentrates of essential oils in fats, in fixed oils, in waxes or the like, obtained by enfleurage or by maceration; terpenic by-products of the deterpenation of essential oils; aqueous distillates and aqueous solutions of essential oils
551.31		**Essential oils of citrus fruit**
		Of bergamot
	330111 10 0	Not deterpenated
	330111 90 0	Deterpenated
		Of orange
	330112 10 0	Not deterpenated
	330112 90 0	Deterpenated
		Of lemon
	330113 10 0	Not deterpenated
	330113 90 0	Deterpenated
		Of lime
	330114 10 0	Not deterpenated
	330114 90 0	Deterpenated
		Other
	330119 10 0	Not deterpenated
	330119 90 0	Deterpenated
551.32		**Other essential oils**
		Of geranium
	330121 10 0	Not deterpenated
	330121 90 0	Deterpenated
		Of jasmin
	330122 10 0	Not deterpenated
	330122 90 0	Deterpenated
		Of lavender or of lavandin
	330123 10 0	Not deterpenated
	330123 90 0	Deterpenated
		Of peppermint (*Mentha piperita*)
	330124 10 0	Not deterpenated
	330124 90 0	Deterpenated
		Of other mints
	330125 10 0	Not deterpenated
	330125 90 0	Deterpenated
		Of vetiver
	330126 10 0	Not deterpenated
	330126 90 0	Deterpenated
		Other
		Of clove, niaouli and ylang-ylang
	330129 11 0	Not deterpenated

S.I.T.C. (R3)	Commodity Code No	Trade description
cont		
551.32	330129 31 0	Deterpenated
		Other
	330129 61 0	Not deterpenated
	330129 91 0	Deterpenated
551.33	330130 00 0	**Resinoids**
551.35		**Concentrates of essential oils in fats, in fixed oils, in waxes or the like, obtained by enfleurage or by maceration; terpenic by- products of the deterpenation of essential oils; aqueous distillates and aqueous solutions of essential oils**
	330190 10 0	Terpenic by-products of the deterpenation of essential oils
		Extracted oleoresins
	*330190 21 0	Of liquorice and hops
	*330190 29 0	Of pyrethrum or of the roots of plants containing rotenone; intermixtures of vegetable extracts for the manufacture of beverages or of food preparations
		Other
	*330190 31 0	Medicinal
	*330190 39 0	Other
	330190 90 0	Other
		Mixtures of odoriferous substances and mixtures (including alcoholic solutions) with a basis of one or more of these substances, of a kind used as raw materials in industry
551.41		**....of a kind used in the food or drink industries**
		Of a kind used in the drinks industries
		Preparations containing all flavouring agents characterizing a beverage:
	*330210 10 0	Of an actual strength by volume exceeding 0.5%
		Other
	*330210 21 0	Containing no milkfats, sucrose, isoglucose, glucose or starch or containing less than 1.5% milkfat, 5% sucrose or isoglucose, 5% glucose or starch
	*330210 29 0	Other
	*330210 40 0	Other
	*330210 90 0	Of a kind used in the food industries
551.49		**....other**
	330290 10 0	Alcoholic solutions
	330290 90 0	Other
		PERFUMERY, COSMETICS OR TOILET PREPARATIONS (EXCLUDING SOAPS)
553.10		**Perfumes and toilet waters**
	330300 10 0	Perfumes
	330300 90 0	Toilet waters
553.20		**Beauty or make-up preparations for the care of the skin (other than medicaments), including sunscreen or suntan preparations; manicure or pedicure preparations**
	330410 00 0	Lip make-up preparations
	330420 00 0	Eye make-up preparations
	330430 00 0	Manicure or pedicure preparations
		Other
	330491 00 0	Powders, whether or not compressed
	330499 00 0	Other
553.30		**Preparations for use on the hair**
	330510 00 0	Shampoos
	330520 00 0	Preparations for permanent waving or straightening
	330530 00 0	Hair lacquers
		Other
	330590 10 0	Hair lotions
	330590 90 0	Other
553.40		**Preparations for oral or dental hygiene, including denture fixative pastes and powders**
	330610 00 0	Dentifrices
	*330620 00 0	Yarn used to clean between the teeth (dental floss)
	330690 00 0	Other
		Pre-shave, shaving or after-shave preparations, personal deodorants, bath preparations, depilatories and other perfumery, cosmetic or toilet preparations, n. e.s.; prepared room deodorizers, whether or not perfumed or having disinfectant properties
553.51	330710 00 0	**Pre-shave, shaving or after-shave preparations**
553.52	330720 00 0	**Personal deodorants and anti-perspirants**
553.53	330730 00 0	**Perfumed bath salts and other bath preparations**

S.I.T.C. (R3)	Commodity Code No	Trade description
553.54		**Preparations for perfuming or deodorizing rooms (including odoriferous preparations used during religious rites)**
	330741 00 0	"Agarbatti" and other odoriferous preparations which operate by burning
	330749 00 0	Other
553.59	330790 00 0	**Depilatories and perfumery, cosmetic or toilet preparations, n.e.s.**

SOAP, CLEANSING AND POLISHING PREPARATIONS

Soap; organic surface-active products and preparations for use as soap, in the form of bars, cakes or moulded pieces or shapes, whether or not containing soap; paper, wadding, felt and nonwovens, impregnated, coated or covered with soap or detergent

554.11	340111 00 0	**Soap and organic surface-active products and preparations, in the form of bars, cakes, moulded pieces or shapes, and paper, wadding, felt and nonwovens, impregnated, coated or covered with soap or detergent, for toilet use (incl. medicated products)**
554.15	340119 00 0	**Soap and organic surface-active products and preparations, in the form of bars, cakes, moulded pieces or shapes, and paper, wadding, felt and nonwovens, impregnated, coated or covered with soap or detergent, for other uses**
554.19		**Soap in other forms**
	340120 10 0	Flakes, wafers, granules or powders
	340120 90 0	Other

Organic surface-active agents (other than soap); surface-active preparations, washing preparations (including auxiliary washing preparations) and cleaning preparations, whether or not containing soap, n.e.s.

554.21		**Organic surface-active agents, whether or not put up for retail sale**
	340211 00 0	Anionic
	340212 00 0	Cationic
	340213 00 0	Non-ionic
	340219 00 0	Other
554.22		**Surface-active, washing or cleaning preparations,n.e.s.,put up for retail sale.**
	340220 10 0	Surface-active preparations
	*340220 90 0	Washing preparations and cleaning preparations
554.23		**Surface-active, washing or cleaning preparations, n.e.s., not put up for retail sale.**
	340290 10 0	Surface-active preparations
	340290 90 0	Washing preparations and cleaning preparations

Polishes and creams, for footwear, furniture, floors, coachwork, glass or metal, scouring pastes and powders and similar preparations (whether or not in the form of paper, wadding, felt, nonwovens, cellular plastic materials or cellular rubber, impregnated, coated or covered with such preparations) not including items of heading 598.3

554.31	340510 00 0	**Polishes, creams and similar preparations, for footwear or leather (incl. paper, wadding, felt, nonwovens, cellular plastic materials or cellular rubber, impregnated,coated or covered with such preparations)**
554.32	340520 00 0	**Polishes, creams and similar preparations, for the maintenance of wooden furniture, floors and other woodwork (incl. paper, wadding, felt, nonwovens, cellular plastic materials or cellular impregnated, coated or covered with such preparations)**
554.33	340530 00 0	**Polishes and similar preparations, for coachwork, other than metal polishes (incl. paper, wadding, felt, nonwovens,cellular plastic materials or cellular rubber, impregnated, coated or covered with such preparations)**
554.34	340540 00 0	**Scouring pastes and powders and other scouring preparations (incl. paper, wadding, felt, nonwovens, cellular plastic materials or cellular rubber, impregnated, coated or covered with such preparations)**
554.35		**Polishes, creams and similar preparations, for glass or metal, (incl. paper,wadding, felt, nonwovens, cellular plastic materials or cellular rubber impregnated, coated or covered with such preparations)**
	340590 10 0	Metal polishes
	340590 90 0	Other

S.I.T.C. (R3)	Commodity Code No	Trade description

FERTILIZERS (OTHER THAN THOSE OF GROUP 272)

Mineral or chemical fertilizers, nitrogenous

562.11   **Ammonium nitrate, whether or not in aqueous solution**
310230 10 0   In aqueous solution
310230 90 0   Other

562.12   310229 00 0   **Double salts and mixtures of ammomium sulphate and ammonium nitrate**

562.13   310221 00 0   **Ammonium sulphate**

562.14   310260 00 0   **Double salts and mixtures of calcium nitrate and ammonium nitrate**

562.15   **Calcium cyanamide**
*310270 10 0   For the manufacture of pharmaceutical products (1)
*310270 90 0   Other

562.16   **Urea, whether or not in aqueous solution**
310210 10 0   Urea containing more than 45 % by weight of nitrogen on **the dry anhydrous product**
310210 90 0   Other

562.17   310280 00 0   **Mixtures of urea and ammonium nitrate in aqueous or ammoniacal solution**

562.19   **Other nitrogenous fertilizers (incl. mixtures, n.e.s.)**
310240 10 0   With a nitrogen content not exceeding 28 % by weight
310240 90 0   With a nitrogen content exceeding 28 % by weight
310290 00 0   Other, including mixtures not specified in the foregoing subheadings

Mineral or chemical fertilizers, phosphatic

562.21   310320 00 0   **Basic slag (Thomas slag)**

562.22   **Superphosphates**
310310 10 0   Containing more than 35 % by weight of diphosphorous pentaoxide
310310 90 0   Other

562.29   310390 00 0   **Mineral or chemical fertilizers, phosphatic, n.e.s.**

Mineral or chemical fertilizers, potassic (other than crude natural potassium salts

562.31   **Potassium chloride**
310420 10 0   With a K_2O content, by weight, not exceeding 40% on the dry anhydrous product
310420 50 0   With a K_2O content, by weight, exceeding 40 % but not exceeding 62 % on the dry anhydrous product
310420 90 0   With a K_2O content, by weight, exceeding 62 % on the dry anhydrous product

562.32   310430 00 0   **Potassium sulphate**

562.39   310490 00 0   **Mineral or chemical fertilizers, potassic, n.e.s.**

Fertilizers, n.e.s.

562.91   **Fertilizers, n.e.s., containing the three fertilizing elements: nitrogen, phosphorus and potassium**
310520 10 0   With a nitrogen content exceeding 10 % by weight on the dry anhydrous product
310520 90 0   Other

562.92   **Mineral or chemical fertilizers containing the two fertilizing elements phosphorus and potassium**
310560 10 0   Potassic superphosphates
310560 90 0   Other

562.93   **Diammonium hydrogenorthophosphate (diammonium phosphate)**
310530 10 0   With an iron content not exceeding 0.03 % by weight on the dry anhydrous product
310530 90 0   With an iron content exceeding 0.03 % by weight on the dry anhydrous product

562.94   **Ammonium dihydrogenorthophosphate (monoammonium phosphate) and mixtures thereof with diammonium hydrogenorthop (diammonium phosphate)**
310540 10 0   With an iron content not exceeding 0.03 % by weight on the dry anhydrous product
310540 90 0   With an iron content exceeding 0.03 % by weight on the dry anhydrous product

562.95   **Fertilizers, n.e.s., containing the two fertilizing elements: nitrogen and phosphorus**
310551 00 0   Containing nitrates and phosphates
310559 00 0   Other

562.96   310510 00 0   **Goods of heading 272.1, 272.2, 272.4 or 562, in tablets or similar forms or in packages of a gross weight not exceeding 10 kg**

S.I.T.C. (R3)	Commodity Code No	Trade description
562.99		**Other**
	310590 10 0	Natural potassic sodium nitrate, consisting of a natural mixture of sodium nitrate and potassium nitrate (the proportion of potassium nitrate may be as high as 44 %), of a total nitrogen content not exceeding 16.3 % by weight on the dry anhydrous product
		Other
	310590 91 0	With a nitrogen content exceeding 10 % by weight on the dry anhydrous product
	310590 99 0	Other

DIVISION 57

PLASTICS IN PRIMARY FORMS

POLYMERS OF ETHYLENE, IN PRIMARY FORMS

Polyethylene

S.I.T.C. (R3)	Commodity Code No	Trade description
571.11		**....having a specific gravity of less than 0.94**
	390110 10 0	Linear polyethylene
	390110 90 0	Other
571.12	390120 00 0	**....having a specific gravity of 0.94 or more**
571.20	390130 00 0	**Ethylene-vinyl acetate copolymers**
571.90	390190 00 0	**Other polymers of ethylene, in primary forms**

POLYMERS OF STYRENE, IN PRIMARY FORMS

Polystyrene

S.I.T.C. (R3)	Commodity Code No	Trade description
572.11	390311 00 0	**....expansible**
572.19	390319 00 0	**....other**

Other styrene polymers

S.I.T.C. (R3)	Commodity Code No	Trade description
572.91	390320 00 0	**Styrene-acrylonitrile (san) copolymers**
572.92	390330 00 0	**Acrylonitrile-butadiene-styrene (abs) copolymers**
572.99	390390 00 0	**Other**

POLYMERS OF VINYL CHLORIDE OR OF OTHER HALOGENATED OLEFINS, IN PRIMARY FORMS

Polyvinyl chloride

S.I.T.C. (R3)	Commodity Code No	Trade description
573.11	390410 00 0	**....not mixed with any other substances**
573.12	390421 00 0	**....other, non-plasticized**
573.13	390422 00 0	**....other, plasticized**

Other vinyl chloride copolymers and polymers of other halogenated olefins

S.I.T.C. (R3)	Commodity Code No	Trade description
573.91	390430 00 0	**Vinyl chloride-vinyl acetate copolymers**
573.92	390440 00 0	**Other vinyl chloride copolymers**
573.93	390450 00 0	**Vinylidene chloride polymers**
573.94		**Fluoro-polymers**
		Polytetrafluoroethylene
	*390461 10 0	For the manufacture of pharmaceutical products
	*390469 90 0	Other
573.99	390490 00 0	**Other polymers of vinyl chloride or of other halogenated olefins**

POLYACETALS, OTHER POLYETHERS AND EPOXIDE RESINS, IN PRIMARY FORMS; POLYCARBONATES, ALKYD RESINS AND OTHER POLYESTERS, IN PRIMARY FORMS

Polyacetals and other polyethers

S.I.T.C. (R3)	Commodity Code No	Trade description
574.11	390710 00 0	**Polyacetals**
574.19		**Other polyethers**
		Polyether alcohols
		Polyethelene glycols
	*390720 12 0	For the manufacture of pharmaceutical products

S.I.T.C. (R3)	Commodity Code No	Trade description
cont 574.19	*390760 90 0	Other
		Other
	390720 21 0	With a hydroxyl number not exceeding 100
	390720 29 0	Other
	390720 90 0	Other
574.20	390730 00 0	**Epoxide resins**
		Polycarbonates, alkyd resins and other polyesters
574.31	390740 00 0	**Polycarbonates**
574.32	390750 00 0	**Alkyd resins**
574.33		**Polyethylene terephthalate**
	*390760 10 0	For the manufacture of pharmaceutical products
	*390760 90 0	Other
574.34		**Other polyesters, unsaturated**
	390791 10 0	Liquid
	390791 90 0	Other
574.39		**Polyesters in primary forms, n.e.s**
	390799 10 0	With a hydroxyl number not exceeding 100
	390799 90 0	Other
		OTHER PLASTICS, IN PRIMARY FORMS
		Polymers of propylene or of other olefins
575.11	390210 00 0	**Polypropylene**
575.12	390220 00 0	**Polyisobutylene**
575.13	390230 00 0	**Propylene copolymers**
575.19	390290 00 0	**Other olefins**
		Acrylic polymers
575.21	390610 00 0	**Polymethyl methacrylate**
575.29	390690 00 0	**Other acrylic polymers**
		Polyamides
575.31	390810 00 0	**Polyamide-6, -11, -12, -6,6, -6,9, -6,10 or -6,12**
575.39	390890 00 0	**Other polyamides**
		Amino-resins, phenolic resins and polyurethanes
575.41	390910 00 0	**Urea resins; thiourea resins**
575.42	390920 00 0	**Melamine resins**
575.43	390930 00 0	**Other amino-resins**
575.44	390940 00 0	**Phenolic resins**
575.45	390950 00 0	**Polyurethanes**
		Cellulose and its chemical derivatives, n.e.s.
575.51	391211 00 0	**Cellulose acetates, non-plasticised**
575.52	391212 00 0	**Cellulose acetates, plasticised**
575.53		**Cellulose nitrates (including collodions)**
		Non-plasticised
	391220 11 0	Collodions and celloidin
	391220 19 0	Other
	391220 90 0	Plasticised
575.54		**Cellulose ethers**
	391231 00 0	Carboxymethylcellulose and its salts

S.I.T.C. (R3)	Commodity Code No	Trade description
cont 575.54		Other
	391239 10 0	Ethylcellulose
	391239 90 0	Other
575.59		**Other**
	391290 10 0	Cellulose esters
	391290 90 0	Other
		Plastics, n.e.s.
575.91		**Polymers of vinyl acetate**
		Polyvinyl acetate
	*390512 00 0	In aqueous dispersion
	*390519 00 0	Other
		Vinyl acetate copolymers:
	*390521 00 0	In aquaeous dispersion
	*390529 00 0	Other
575.92		**Polymers of other vinyl esters; other vinyl polymers**
	*390530 00 0	Polyvinyl alcohols, whether or not containing unhydrolysed acetate groups
		Other
	*390591 00 0	Copolymers
	*390599 00 0	Other
575.93	391000 00 0	**Silicones in primary forms**
575.94	391310 00 0	**Alginic acid, its salts and esters**
575.95		**Natural polymers and modified natural polymers (eg.,hardened proteins, chemical derivatives of natural rubber), n.e.s**
	391390 10 0	Chemical derivatives of natural rubber
	391390 20 0	Amylopectin
	391390 30 0	Amylose
	391390 80 0	Other
575.96		**Petroleum resins, coumarone-indene resins, polyterpenes, polysulphides, polysulphones and plastics, n.e.s.**
	391110 00 0	Petroleum resins, coumarone, indene or coumarone-indene resins and polyterpenes
		Other
	391190 10 0	Condensation or rearrangement polymerisation products whether or not chemically modified
	391190 90 0	Other
575.97	391400 00 0	**Ion exchangers based on polymers of headings 571 to 575.9**
		WASTE, PARINGS AND SCRAP, OF PLASTICS
579.10	391510 00 0	**....of polymers of ethylene**
579.20	391520 00 0	**....of polymers of styrene**
579.30	391530 00 0	**....of polymers of vinyl chloride**
579.90		**....other**
		Of addition polymerisation products
	391590 11 0	Of polymers of propylene
	391590 13 0	Of acrylic polymers
	391590 19 0	Other
		Other
	391590 91 0	Of epoxide resins
	391590 93 0	Of cellulose and its chemical derivatives
	391590 99 0	Other
DIVISION 58		**PLASTICS IN NON-PRIMARY FORMS**
		TUBES, PIPES AND HOSES OF PLASTICS
581.10		**Artificial guts (sausage casings) of hardened protein or of cellulosic materials**
	391710 10 0	Of hardened protein
	391710 90 0	Of cellulosic materials
581.20		**Tubes, pipes and hoses, rigid**
		Of polymers of ethylene
	391721 10 0	Seamless and cut to a length exceeding the maximum cross-sectional dimension, whether or not surface-worked, but not otherwise worked

S.I.T.C. (R3)	Commodity Code No	Trade description
cont 581.20		Other
	391721 91 0	With fittings attached, for use in civil aircraft
	391721 99 0	Other
		Of polymers of propylene
	391722 10 0	Seamless and cut to a length exceeding the maximum cross-sectional dimension, whether or not surface-worked, but not otherwise worked
		Other
	391722 91 0	With fittings attached, for use in civil aircraft
	391722 99 0	Other
		Of polymers of vinyl chloride
	391723 10 0	Seamless and cut to a length exceeding the maximum cross-sectional dimension, whether or not surface-worked, but not otherwise worked
		Other
	391723 91 0	With fittings attached, for use in civil aircraft
	391723 99 0	Other
		Of other plastics
		Seamless and cut to a length exceeding the maximum cross-sectional dimension, whether or not surface-worked, but not otherwise worked
		Of condensation, or rearrangement polymerisation products, whether or not chemically modified
	391729 11 0	Of epoxide resins
	391729 13 0	Other
	391729 15 0	Of addition polymerisation products
	391729 19 0	Other
		Other
	391729 91 0	With fittings attached, for use in civil aircraft
	391729 99 0	Other
581.30		**Flexible tubes, pipes and hoses, having a minimum burst pressure of 27.6 mpa**
	391731 10 0	With fittings attached, for use in civil aircraft
	391731 90 0	Other
581.40		**Other, not reinforced or otherwise combined with other materials, without fittings**
		Seamless and cut to a length exceeding the maximum cross-sectional dimension, whether or not surface-worked, but not otherwise worked
		Of condensation or rearrangement polymerisation products, whether or not chemically modified
	391732 11 0	Of epoxide resins
	391732 19 0	Other
		Of addition polymerisation products
	391732 31 0	Of polymers of ethylene
	391732 35 0	Of polymers of vinyl chloride
	391732 39 0	Other
	391732 51 0	Other
		Other
	391732 91 0	Artificial sausage casings
	391732 99 0	Other
581.50		**Tubes, pipes and hoses, not reinforced or otherwise combined with other other materials, with fittings**
	391733 10 0	With fittings attached, for use in civil aircraft
	391733 90 0	Other
581.60		**Other tubes, pipes and hoses**
		Seamless and cut to a length exceeding the maximum cross-sectional dimension, whether or not surface-worked, but not otherwise worked
		Of condensation or rearrangement polymerisation products, whether or not chemically modified
	391739 11 0	Of epoxide resins
	391739 13 0	Other
	391739 15 0	Of addition polymerisation products
	391739 19 0	Other
		Other
	391739 91 0	With fittings attached, for use in civil aircraft
	391739 99 0	Other
581.70		**Fittings for tubes, pipes and hoses (eg., joints,elbows flanges), of plastics**
	391740 10 0	For use in civil aircraft
	391740 90 0	Other

PLATES, SHEETS, FILM, FOIL AND STRIP, OF PLASTICS

Plates, sheets, film, foil, tape, strip and other flat shapes, self- adhesive, of plastics, whether or not in rolls, other than floor, wall and ceiling coverings of heading 893.31

582.11		**....in rolls of a width not exceeding 20 cm**
		Strips, the coating of which consists of unvulcanised natural or synthetic rubber
	391910 11 0	Of plasticized polyvinyl chloride or of polyethylene
	391910 13 0	Of non-plasticized polyvinyl chloride
	391910 15 0	Of polypropylene

S.I.T.C. (R3)	Commodity Code No	Trade description

cont
582.11

391910 19 0 — Other
— Other
— — Of condensation or rearrangement polymerisation products, whether or not chemically modified
391910 31 0 — — — Of polyesters
391910 35 0 — — — Of epoxide resins
391910 39 0 — — — Other
— — Of addition polymerisation products
391910 61 0 — — — Of plasticized polyvinyl chloride or of polyethylene
391910 69 0 — — — Other
391910 90 0 — — Other

582.19
....other
391990 10 0 — Further worked than surface-worked, or into rectangles (including squares)
— — Of condensation or rearrangement polymerisation products, whether or not chemically modified
391990 31 0 — — — Of polycarbonates, alkyd resins, polyallyl esters or other polyesters
391990 35 0 — — — Of epoxide resins
391990 39 0 — — — Other
— — Of addition polymerisation products
391990 61 0 — — — Of plasticized polyvinyl chloride or of polyethylene
391990 69 0 — — — Other
391990 90 0 — — Other

Other plates, sheets, film, foil and strip, of plastics, non-cellular and not reinforced, laminated, supported or similarly combined with other materials

582.21
....of polymers of ethylene
— Of a thickness not exceeding 0.125 mm
— — Of polyethylene having a specific gravity of
392010 22 0 — — — Less than 0.94
392010 28 0 — — — 0.94 or more
392010 40 0 — — Other
392010 80 0 — Of a thickness exceeding 0.125 mm

582.22
....of polymers of propylene
— Of a thickness not exceeding 0.10 mm
392020 21 0 — — Biaxially Oriented
392020 29 0 — — Other
— Of a thickness exceeding 0.10 mm
— — Strips of a width exceeding 5 mm but not exceeding 20mm of the kind used for packaging
392020 71 0 — — — Decorative strips
392020 79 0 — — — Other
392020 90 0 — — Other

582.23 392030 00 0 ....of polymers of styrene

582.24
....of polymers of vinyl chloride
— Rigid
— — Non-plasticized, of a thickness:
392041 11 0 — — — Not exceeding 1 mm:
392041 19 0 — — — Exceeding 1 mm
— — Plasticized, of a thickness:
392041 91 0 — — — Not exceeding 1 mm
392041 99 0 — — — Exceeding 1 mm
— Flexible
— — Non-plasticized, of a thickness:
392042 11 0 — — — Not exceeding 1 mm
392042 19 0 — — — Exceeding 1 mm
— — Plasticized, of a thickness:
392042 91 0 — — — Not exceeding 1 mm:
392042 99 0 — — — Exceeding 1 mm

582.25
....of acrylic polymers
392051 00 0 — Of polymethyl methacrylate
392059 00 0 — Other

582.26
....of polycarbonates, alkyd resins or other polyesters
392061 00 0 — Of polycarbonates
— Of polyethylene terephthalate
392062 10 0 — — Of a thickness not exceeding 0,35 mm
392062 90 0 — — Of a thickness exceeding 0,35 mm
392063 00 0 — Of unsaturated polyesters
392069 00 0 — Of other polyesters

582.27 392072 00 0 ....of vulcanized fibre

S.I.T.C. (R3)	Commodity Code No	Trade description
582.28		....of cellulose or its chemical derivatives, n.e.s.
		Of regenerated cellulose
		Sheets, film or strip, coiled or not, of a thickness of less than 0.75 mm
	392071 11 0	Not printed
	392071 19 0	Printed
	392071 90 0	Other
		Of cellulose acetate
	392073 10 0	Film in rolls or in strips, for cinematography or photography
	392073 50 0	Sheets, film or strip, coiled or not, of a thickness of less than 0.75 mm
	392073 90 0	Other
	392079 00 0	Of other cellulose derivatives
582.29		....of other plastics
	392091 00 0	Of polyvinyl butyral
	392092 00 0	Of polyamides
	392093 00 0	Of amino-resins
	392094 00 0	Of phenolic resins
		Of other plastics
		Of condensation or rearrangement polymerisation products, whether or not chemically modified
	392099 11 0	Of epoxide resins
	392099 19 0	Other
	392099 50 0	Of addition polymerisation products
	392099 90 0	Other

Other plates, sheets, film, foil and strip, of plastics

S.I.T.C. (R3)	Commodity Code No	Trade description
582.91		....cellular
	392111 00 0	Of polymers of styrene
	392112 00 0	Of polymers of vinyl chloride
		Of polyurethanes
	392113 10 0	Flexible
	392113 90 0	Other
	392114 00 0	Of regenerated cellulose
		Of other plastics
	392119 10 0	Of epoxide resins
	392119 90 0	Other
582.99		....other
		Of condensation or rearrangement polymerisation products, whether or not chemically modified
		Of polyesters
	392190 11 0	Corrugated sheet and plates
	392190 19 0	Other
	392190 20 0	Of epoxide resins
	392190 30 0	Of phenolic resins
		Of amino-resins
		Laminated
	392190 41 0	High pressure laminates with a decorative surface on one or both sides
	392190 43 0	Other
	392190 49 0	Other
	392190 50 0	Other
	*392190 60 0	Of addition polymerisation products
	392190 90 0	Other

MONOFILAMENT OF WHICH ANY CROSS-SECTIONAL DIMENSION EXCEEDS 1 MM, RODS, STICKS AND PROFILE SHAPES, WHETHER OR NOT SURFACE-WORKED BUT NOT OTHERWISE WORKED, OF PLASTICS

S.I.T.C. (R3)	Commodity Code No	Trade description
583.10	391610 00 0	....of polymers of ethylene
583.20		....of polymers of vinyl chloride
	391620 10 0	Of polyvinyl chloride
	391620 90 0	Other
583.90		....of other plastics
		Of condensation, or rearrangement polymerisation products, whether or not chemically modified
	391690 11 0	Of polyesters
	391690 13 0	Of polyamides
	391690 15 0	Of epoxide resins
	391690 19 0	Other
		Of addition polymerisation products
	391690 51 0	Of polymers of propylene
	391690 59 0	Other
	391690 90 0	Other

S.I.T.C. (R3)	Commodity Code No	Trade description

DIVISION 59

CHEMICAL MATERIALS AND PRODUCTS, N.E.S.

INSECTICIDES, RODENTICIDES, FUNGICIDES, HERBICIDES, ANTI-SPROUTING PRODUCTS AND PLANT-GROWTH REGULATORS, DISINFECTANTS AND SIMILAR PRODUCTS, PUT UP IN FORMS OR PACKINGS FOR RETAIL SALE OR AS PREPARATIONS OR ARTICLES (E.G., SULPHUR-TREATED BANDS, WICKS AND CANDLES, AND FLY-PAPERS)

591.10 **Insecticides put up in forms or packings for retail sale or as preparations or articles**
	380810 10 0	Based on pyrethroids
	380810 20 0	Based on chlorinated hydrocarbons
	380810 30 0	Based on carbamates
	380810 40 0	Based on organophosphorous compounds
	380810 90 0	Other

591.20 **Fungicides put up in forms or packings for retail sale or as preparations or articles**
Inorganic
| | 380820 10 0 | Preparations based on copper compounds |
| | 380820 15 0 | Other |
Other
	380820 30 0	Based on dithiocarbamates
	380820 40 0	Based on benzimidazoles
	380820 50 0	Based on diazoles or triazoles
	380820 60 0	Based on diazines or morpholines
	380820 80 0	Other

591.30 **Weed killers (herbicides), anti-sprouting products and plant-growth regulators, put up in forms or packings for retail sale or as preparations or articles**
Herbicides, anti-sprouting products and plant-growth regulators
    Herbicides
	380830 11 0	Based on phenoxy-phytohormones
	380830 13 0	Based on triazines
	380830 15 0	Based on amides
	380830 17 0	Based on carbamates
	380830 21 0	Based on dinitroaniline derivatives
	380830 23 0	Based on derivatives of urea, of uracil or of sulphonylurea
	380830 27 0	Other
	380830 30 0	Anti-sprouting products
	380830 90 0	Plant-growth regulators

Disinfectants, rodenticides and similar products, put up in forms or packings for retail sale or as preparations or articles

591.41 **Disinfectants put up in forms or packings for retail sale or as preparations or articles**
	380840 10 0	Based on quaternary ammonium salts
	380840 20 0	Based on halogenated compounds
	380840 90 0	Other

591.49 **Rodenticides and other products of group 591, put up in forms or packings for retail sale or as preparations or articles**
| | 380890 10 0 | Rodenticides |
| | 380890 90 0 | Other |

STARCHES, INULIN AND WHEAT GLUTEN; ALBUMINOIDAL SUBSTANCES; GLUES

Starches, inulin and wheat gluten

592.11 | 110811 00 0 | **Wheat starch** |

592.12 | 110812 00 0 | **Maize (corn) starch** |

592.13 | 110813 00 0 | **Potato starch** |

592.14 | 110814 00 0 | **Manioc (cassava) starch** |

592.15 **Other starches**
| | 110819 10 0 | Rice starch |
| | 110819 90 0 | Other |

592.16 | 110820 00 0 | **Inulin** |

592.17 | 110900 00 0 | **Wheat gluten, whether or not dried** |

Albuminoidal substances, modified starches and glues

592.21 **Casein**
| | 350110 10 0 | For the manufacture of regenerated textile fibres |

S.I.T.C. (R3)	Commodity Code No	Trade description
cont 592.21	350110 50 0	For industrial uses other than the manufacture of food stuffs or fodder
	350110 90 0	Other
592.22		**Caseinates and other casein derivatives; casein glues**
	350190 10 0	Casein glues
	350190 90 0	Other
592.23		**Albumins, other than egg albumin; albuminates and other albumin derivatives**
		Milk albumin, including concentrates of two or more whey proteins:
	*350220 10 0	Unfit, or to be rendered unfit, for human consumption
		Other
	*350220 91 0	Dried (for example, in sheets, scales, flakes, powder)
	*350220 99 0	Other
		Other
		Albumins, other than egg albumin and milk albumin (lactalbumin):
	*350290 20 0	Unfit, or to be rendered unfit, for human consumption
	350290 70 0	Other
	350290 90 0	Albuminates and other albumin derivatives
592.24		**Gelatin (including gelatin in rectangular sheets, whether or not surface-worked or coloured) and gelatin derivatives; isinglass; other glues of animal origin, n.e.s.**
	*350300 10 0	Gelatin and derivatives thereof
	350300 80 0	Other
592.25	350400 00 0	**Peptones and their derivatives; other protein substances and their derivatives, n.e.s.; hide powder, whether or not chromed**
592.26		**Dextrins and other modified starches**
	350510 10 0	Dextrins
		Other modified starches
	350510 50 0	Starches, esterified or etherified
	350510 90 0	Other
592.27		**Glues based on starches, or on dextrins or other modified starches**
	350520 10 0	Containing, by weight, less than 25 % of starches or dextrins or other modified starches
	350520 30 0	Containing, by weight, 25 % or more but less than 55 % of starches or dextrins or other modified starches
	350520 50 0	Containing, by weight, 55 % or more but less than 80 % of starches or dextrins or other modified starches
	350520 90 0	Containing by weight 80 % or more of starches or dextrins or other modified starches
592.29		**Prepared glues and other prepared adhesives, n.e.s.; products suitable for use as glues or adhesives, put up for retail sale as glues or adhesives, not exceeding a net weight of 1 kg**
	350610 00 0	Products suitable for use as glues or adhesives, put up for retail sale as glues or adhesives, not exceeding a net weight of 1kg
	350691 00 0	Adhesives based on rubber or plastics (including artificial resins)
	350699 00 0	Other

EXPLOSIVES AND PYROTECHNIC PRODUCTS

Propellent powders and other prepared explosives

S.I.T.C. (R3)	Commodity Code No	Trade description
593.11	360100 00 0	**Propellent powders**
593.12	360200 00 0	**Prepared explosives (other than propellent powders)**
593.20		**Safety fuses; detonating fuses; percussion or detonating caps; igniters; electric detonators**
	360300 10 0	Safety fuses; detonating fuses
	360300 90 0	Other

Fireworks,signalling flares, rain rockets, fog signals and other pyrotechnic articles

S.I.T.C. (R3)	Commodity Code No	Trade description
593.31	360410 00 0	**Fireworks**
593.33	360490 00 0	**Signalling flares, rain rockets, fog signals and other pyrotechnic articles**

PREPARED ADDITIVES FOR MINERAL OILS AND THE LIKE; PREPARED LIQUIDS FOR HYDRAULIC TRANSMISSION; ANTI-FREEZING PREPARATIONS AND PREPARED DE-ICING FLUIDS; LUBRICATING PREPARATIONS

Anti-knock preparations, oxidation inhibitors, gum inhibitors, viscosity improvers, anti-corrosive preparations and other prepared additives, for mineral oils (including gasolene) or for other liquids used for the same purposes as mineral oils

S.I.T.C. (R3)	Commodity Code No	Trade description
597.21		**Anti-knock preparations**
		Based on lead compounds
	381111 10 0	Based on tetraethyl-lead

S.I.T.C. (R3)	Commodity Code No	Trade description

cont
597.21

| | 381111 90 0 | Other |
| | 381119 00 0 | Other |

597.25   **Additives for lubricating oils**
| | 381121 00 0 | Containing petroleum oils or oils obtained from bituminous minerals |
| | 381129 00 0 | Other |

597.29   *381190 00 0   **Prepared additives for other liquids used for the same purposes as mineral oils, n.e.s**

Prepared liquids for hydraulic transmission; anti-freezing preparations

597.31   381900 00 0   **Hydraulic brake fluids and other prepared liquids for hydraulic transmission, not containing or containing less than 70% by weight of petroleum oils or oils obtained from bitumous minerals**

597.33   382000 00 0   **Anti-freezing preparations and prepared de-icing fluids**

Lubricating preparations (including cutting-oil preparations, bolt or nut release preparations, anti-rust or anti-corrosion preparations and mould release preparations, based on lubricants) and preparations of a kind used for the oil or grease treatment of textile materials, leather, furskins or other materials, but excluding preparations containing, as basic constituents, 70% or more by weight of petroleum oils or of oils obtained from bituminous minerals

597.71   340311 00 0   **Preparations for the treatment of textile materials, leather, furskins or other materials, containing petroleum oils or oils obtained from bituminous minerals**

597.72   **Lubricating preparations containing petroleum oils or oils obtained from bituminous minerals**
	340319 10 0	Containing 70% or more by weight of petroleum oils or of oils obtained from bituminous minerals but not as the basic constituents
		Other
	340319 91 0	Preparations for lubricating machines, appliances and vehicles
	340319 99 0	Other

597.73   340391 00 0   **Preparations for the treatment of textile materials, leather, furskins or other materials, containing oils or greases other than of petroleum or bituminous minerals**

597.74   **Lubricating preparations containing oils or greases other than of petroleum or bituminous minerals.**
| | 340399 10 0 | Preparations for lubricating machines, appliances and vehicles |
| | 340399 90 0 | Other |

MISCELLANEOUS CHEMICAL PRODUCTS, N.E.S.

Wood- and resin-based chemical products

598.11   **Tall oil, whether or not refined**
| | 380300 10 0 | Crude |
| | 380300 90 0 | Other |

598.12   **Residual lyes from the manufacture of wood pulp, whether or not concentrated, desugared or chemically treated (incl. lignin sulphonates, but excl. tall oil)**
| | 380400 10 0 | Concentrated sulphite lye |
| | 380400 90 0 | Other |

598.13   **Gum, wood or sulphate turpentine and other terpenic oils produced by the distillation or other treatment of coniferous woods; crude dipentene; sulphite turpentine and other crude para-cymene; pine oil containing alpha-terpineol as the main constituent**
		Gum, wood or sulphate turpentine oils
	380510 10 0	Gum turpentine
	380510 30 0	Wood turpentine
	380510 90 0	Sulphate turpentine
	380520 00 0	Pine oil
	380590 00 0	Other

598.14   **Rosin and resin acids, and derivatives thereof; rosin spirit and rosin oils**
		Rosin and resin acids
	380610 10 0	Obtained from fresh oleoresins
	380610 90 0	Other
	*380620 00 0	Salts of rosin or of resin acids or of derivatives of rosin or resin acids, other than salts of rosin adducts
	380630 00 0	Ester gums
	*380690 00 0	Other

598.18   **Wood tar; wood tar oils; wood creosote; wood naphtha; vegetable pitch; brewers' pitch and similar preparations based on rosin, resin acids or on vegetable pitch**
| | 380700 10 0 | Wood tar |
| | 380700 90 0 | Other |

S.I.T.C. (R3)	Commodity Code No	Trade description
		Artificial waxes and prepared waxes
598.31	340410 00 0	**Artificial waxes and prepared waxes of chemically modified lignite**
598.35	340420 00 0	**Artificial waxes and prepared waxes of polyethylene glycol**
598.39		**Other artificial waxes and other prepared waxes**
	340490 10 0	Prepared waxes, including sealing wax
	340490 90 0	Other
		Mixed alkylbenzenes and mixed alkylnaphthalenes, n.e.s
598.41		**Mixed alkylbenzenes, n.e.s.**
	381710 10 0	Dodecylbenzene
	381710 50 0	Linear alkylbenzene
	381710 80 0	Other
598.45	381720 00 0	**Mixed alkylnaphthalenes, n.e.s.**
598.50		**Chemical elements doped for use in electronics, in the form of discs, wafers or similar forms; chemical compounds doped for use in electronics**
	381800 10 0	Doped silicon
	381800 90 0	Other
		Organic chemical products, n.e.s.
598.61		**Artificial graphite; colloidal or semi-colloidal graphite; preparations based on graphite or other carbon in the form of pastes, blocks, plates or other semi-manufactures**
	380110 00 0	Artificial graphite
		Colloidal or semi-colloidal graphite
	380120 10 0	Colloidal graphite in suspension in oil; semi-colloidal graphite
	380120 90 0	Other
	380130 00 0	Carbonaceous pastes for electrodes and similar pastes for furnace linings
	380190 00 0	Other
598.63	381210 00 0	**Prepared rubber accelerators**
598.64	380210 00 0	**Activated carbon**
598.65	380290 00 0	**Activated natural mineral products; animal black, including spent animal black**
598.67	382100 00 0	**Prepared culture media for development of micro-organisms**
598.69		**Composite diagnostic or laboratory reagents, n.e.s.**
	*382200 00 0	Diagnostic or laboratory reagenets on a backing and prepared diagnostic or laboratory reagents whetheror not on a backing, other than those of heading 514
		Catalysts and catalytic preparations, n.e.s.
598.81	381511 00 0	**Supported catalysts with nickel or nickel compounds as the active substances**
598.83	*381512 00 0	**Supported catalysts with precious metal or precious metal compounds as the active substances**
598.85	381519 00 0	**Other supported catalysts**
598.89	381590 00 0	**Other catalyts and catalytic preparations**
		Chemical products and preparations, n.e.s.
598.91		**Finishing agents, dye carriers to accelerate dyeing or fixing dyestuffs and other products and preparations (e.g., dressings and mordants), of a kind used in the textile, paper, leather or like industries, n.e.s.**
		With a basis of amylaceous substances
	380910 10 0	Containing by weight of such substances less than 55 %
	380910 30 0	Containing by weight of such substances 55 % or more but less than 70 %
	380910 50 0	Containing by weight of such substances 70 % or more but less than 83 %
	380910 90 0	Containing by weight of such substances 83 % or more
		Other
	380991 00 0	Of a kind used in the textile or like industries
	380992 00 0	Of a kind used in the paper or like industries
	380993 00 0	Of a kind used in the leather or like industries
598.93		**Compound plasticizers for rubber or plastics, n.e.s.; anti-oxidizing preparations and other compound stabilizers for rubber or plastics**
	381220 00 0	Compound plasticisers for rubber or plastics
		Anti-oxidising preparations and other compound stabilisers for rubber or plastics
	381230 20 0	Anti-oxidising preparations
	381230 80 0	Other

S.I.T.C. (R3)	Commodity Code No	Trade description
598.94	381300 00 0	**Preparations and charges for fire-extinguishers; charged fire-extinguishing grenades**
598.95	340700 00 0	**Modelling pastes (including those put up for children's amusement); preparations known as compounds', put up in sets, in plates, horseshoe shapes, preparations for use in dentistry, with a basis of plaster (of calcined gypsum or calcium sulphate)**
598.96		**Pickling preparations for metal surfaces; fluxes and other auxiliary preparations for soldering, brazing or welding; soldering, brazing or welding powders and pastes consisting of metal and other materials; preparations of a kind used electrodes or rods**
	381010 00 0	Pickling preparations for metal surfaces; soldering, brazing or welding powders and pastes consisting of metal and other materials
		Other
	381090 10 0	Preparations of a kind used as cores or coatings for welding electrodes and rods
	381090 90 0	Other
598.97	*382440 00 0	**Prepared additives for cements, mortars or concretes**
598.98		**Non-refractory mortars and concretes**
	*382450 10 0	Concrete ready to pour
	*382450 90 0	Other
598.99		**Other chemical products and preparations**
	*382410 00 0	Prepared binders for foundry moulds or cores
	*382420 00 0	Naphthenic acids, their water-insoluble salts and their esters
	*382430 00 0	Non-agglomerated metal carbides mixed together or with metallic binders
		Sorbitol other than that of heading 512.25
		In aqueous solution:
	*382460 11 0	Containing 2 % or less by weight of D-mannitol, calculated on the D-glucitol content
	*382460 19 0	Other
		Other
	*382460 91 0	Containing 2 % or less by weight of D-mannitol, calculated on the D-glucitol content
	*382460 99 0	Other
		Mixtures containing perhalogenated drivatives of acyclic hydrocarbons containing two or more different halogens:
	*382471 00 0	Containing acyclic hydrocarbons perhalgenated only with fluorine and chlorine
	*382479 00 0	Other
	*382490 10 0	Petroleum sulphonates, excluding petroleum sulphonates of alkili metals, of ammonium or of ethanolamines; thiophenated sulphonic acids of oils obtained from bituminous minerals, and their salts
	*382490 15 0	Ion exchangers
	*382490 20 0	Getters for vacuum tubes
	*382490 25 0	Pyrolignites (for example, of calcium); crude calcium tartrate; crude calcium citrate
	*382490 30 0	Alkaline iron oxide for the purification of gas
	*382490 35 0	Anti-rust preparations containing amines as active elements
	*382490 40 0	Inorganic composite solvents and thinners for varnishes and similar products
		Other
	*382490 45 0	Anti-scaling and similar compounds
	*382490 50 0	Preparations for electroplating
	*382490 55 0	Mixtures of mono-, di-, and tri, fatty acid esters of glycerol (emulsifiers for fats)
	*382490 60 0	Products and preparations for pharmaceutical or surgical uses
	*382490 65 0	Auxiliary products for foundries (other than those falling within subheading No. 3823.10)
	*382490 70 0	Fire-proofing, water-proofing and similar protective preparations used in the building industry
	*382490 90 0	Other

SECTION: 6

DIVISION 61   **LEATHER, LEATHER MANUFACTURES, N.E.S., AND DRESSED FURSKINS**

LEATHER

611.20	411100 00 0	**Composition leather with a basis of leather or leather fibre, in slabs, sheets or strap, whether or not in rolls**
611.30		**Whole bovine skin leather, without hair on, of a unit surface area not exceeding 28 square feet (2.6 m^2), except leather of heading 611.8**
	410410 10 0	East India kip, whole, whether or not the heads and legs have been removed, each of a net weight of not more than 4.5 kg, not further prepared than vegetable tanned, whether or not having undergone certain treatments, but obviously unsuitable for immediate use for the manufacture of leather articles
	410410 30 0	Other skin leather not further prepared than chrome-tanned, in the wet-blue state
		Other
	410410 91 0	Not further prepared than tanned
		Otherwise prepared
	410410 95 0	Boxcalf
	410410 99 0	Other

Other bovine leather and equine leather, without hair on (other than leather of heading 611.8)

611.41		**Other bovine leather and equine leather, tanned or retanned but not further prepared, whether or not split**
	410421 00 0	Bovine leather, vegetable pre-tanned
		Bovine leather, otherwise pre-tanned
	410422 10 0	Not further prepared than chrome-tanned in the wet-blue state
	410422 90 0	Other
	410429 00 0	Other
611.42		**Other bovine leather and equine leather, parchment-dressed or prepared after tanning**
		Full grains and grain splits
		Bovine leather
		Full grains
	410431 11 0	Sole leather
	410431 19 0	Other
	410431 30 0	Grain splits
	410431 90 0	Equine leather
		Other
	410439 10 0	Bovine leather
	410439 90 0	Equine leather

Sheep or lamb skin leather, without wool on (other than leather of heading 611.8)

611.51		**Tanned or retanned but not further prepared, whether or not split**
		Vegetable pre-tanned
	410511 10 0	Of Indian hair sheep, whether or not having undergone certain treatments, but obviously unsuitable for immediate use for the manufacture of leather articles
		Other
	410511 91 0	Not split
	410511 99 0	Split
		Otherwise pre-tanned
	410512 10 0	Not split
	410512 90 0	Split
		Other
	410519 10 0	Not split
	410519 90 0	Split
611.52	*410520 00 0	**Parchment-dressed or prepared after tanning**

Goat or kid skin leather, without hair on (other than leather of heading 611.8)

611.61		**Tanned or retanned but not further prepared, whether or not split**
		Vegetable pre-tanned
	410611 10 0	Of Indian goat or kid, whether or not having undergone certain treatments, but obviously unsuitable for immediate use for the manufacture of leather articles
	410611 90 0	Other
	410612 00 0	Otherwise pre-tanned
	410619 00 0	Other
611.62	410620 00 0	**Parchment-dressed or prepared after tanning**

S.I.T.C. (R3)	Commodity Code No	Trade description
		Leather of other animals, without hair on, other than leather of heading 611.8
611.71		....of swine
	410710 10 0	Not further prepared than tanned
	410710 90 0	Other
611.72		....of reptiles
	410721 00 0	Vegetable pre-tanned
		Other
	410729 10 0	Not further prepared than tanned
	410729 90 0	Other
611.79		....of other animals
	410790 10 0	Not further prepared than tanned
	410790 90 0	Other
		Leather, specially dressed or finished, n.e.s.
611.81		Chamois (including combination chamois) leather
	410800 10 0	Of sheep and lambs
	410800 90 0	Of other animals
611.83	410900 00 0	Patent leather and patent laminated leather; metallized leather
		MANUFACTURES OF LEATHER OR OF COMPOSITION LEATHER, N.E.S.; SADDLERY AND HARNESS
612.10		Articles of leather or of composition leathers of a kind used in machinery or mechanical appliances or for other technical uses
	420400 10 0	Conveyor or transmission belts or belting
	420400 90 0	Other
612.20	420100 00 0	Saddlery and harness for any animal (including traces, leads, knee-pads, muzzles, saddle cloths, saddle bags, dog coats and the like), of any material
612.90	420500 00 0	Other articles of leather or of composition leather
		FURSKINS, TANNED OR DRESSED (INCLUDING HEADS, TAILS, PAWS AND OTHER PIECES OR CUTTINGS), UNASSEMBLED, OR ASSEMBLED (WITHOUT THE ADDITION OF OTHER MATERIALS), OTHER THAN THOSE OF HEADING 848.3
		Whole furskins, with or without head, tail or paws, not assembled
613.11	430211 00 0	Whole furskins of mink with or without head, tail or paws, not assembled
613.12	430212 00 0	Whole furskins, of rabbit or hare, with or without head, tail or paws, not assembled
613.13	430213 00 0	Whole furskins of lamb, the following: Astrakhan, Broadtail, Caracul, Persian and similar lamb, Indian, Chinese, Mongolian or Tibetan lamb, with or without head, tail or paws, not assembled
613.19		Other furskins, whole, with or without head, tail or paws, not assembled
	430219 10 0	Of beaver
	430219 20 0	Of muskrat
	430219 30 0	Of fox
		Of seal
	430219 41 0	Of whitecoat pups of harp seal and of pups of hooded seal (blue-backs)
	430219 49 0	Other
	430219 50 0	Of sea-otter or of nutria (coypu)
	430219 60 0	Of marmot
	430219 70 0	Of wild felines
	430219 80 0	Of sheep or lambs
	430219 95 0	Other
613.20	430220 00 0	Heads, tails, paws and other pieces or cuttings, not assembled
613.30		Whole furskins and pieces or cuttings thereof, assembled
	430230 10 0	'Dropped' furskins
		Other
	430230 21 0	Of mink
	430230 25 0	Of rabbit or hare
	430230 31 0	Of lamb, the following: Astrakhan, Broadtail, Caracul, Persian and similar lamb, Indian, Chinese, Mongolian or Tibetan lamb
	430230 35 0	Of beaver
	430230 41 0	Of muskrat
	430230 45 0	Of fox
		Of seal
	430230 51 0	Of whitecoat pups of harp seal and of pups of hooded seal (blue-backs)
	430230 55 0	Other
	430230 61 0	Of sea-otter or of nutria (coypu)
	430230 65 0	Of marmot

S.I.T.C. (R3)	Commodity Code No	Trade description
cont 613.30	430230 71 0	Of wild felines
	430230 75 0	Other

DIVISION 62

RUBBER MANUFACTURES, N.E.S.

MATERIALS OF RUBBER (E.G., PASTES, PLATES, SHEETS, RODS, THREAD, TUBES, OF RUBBER)

Compounded rubber, unvulcanized, in primary forms or in plates, sheets or strip

S.I.T.C. (R3)	Commodity Code No	Trade description
621.11	400510 00 0	**Compounded with carbon black or silica**
621.12	400520 00 0	**Solutions; dispersions (other than those of heading 621.11)**
621.19		**Other**
	400591 00 0	Plates, sheets and strip
	400599 00 0	Other

Other forms (e.g., rods, tubes and profile shapes) and articles (e.g., discs and rings), of unvulcanized rubber

S.I.T.C. (R3)	Commodity Code No	Trade description
621.21	400610 00 0	**'Camel-back' strips for retreading rubber tyres**
621.29	400690 00 0	**Other**

Vulcanized rubber thread and cord; plates, sheets, strip, rods and profile shapes, of unhardened vulcanised rubber

S.I.T.C. (R3)	Commodity Code No	Trade description
621.31	400700 00 0	**Vulcanized rubber thread and cord**
621.32		**Plates, sheets, strip, rods and profile shapes, of unhardened vulcanized cellular rubber**
	400811 00 0	Plates, sheets and strip
	400819 00 0	Other
621.33		**Plates, sheets, strip, rods and profile shapes, of unhardened vulcanized non-cellular rubber**
		Plates, sheets and strip
	400821 10 0	Floor coverings and mats
	*400821 90 0	Other
		Other
	400829 10 0	Profile shapes, cut to size, for use in civil aircraft
	400829 90 0	Other

Tubes, pipes and hoses, of unhardened vulcanized rubber, with or without their fittings (e.g., joints, elbows, flanges)

S.I.T.C. (R3)	Commodity Code No	Trade description
621.41	400910 00 0	**....not reinforced or otherwise combined with other materials, without fittings**
621.42	400920 00 0	**....reinforced or otherwise combined only with metal, without fittings**
621.43	400930 00 0	**....reinforced or otherwise combined only with textile materials, without fittings**
621.44	400940 00 0	**....reinforced or otherwise combined with other materials, without fittings**
621.45		**....with fittings**
	400950 10 0	Suitable for conducting gases or liquids, for use in civil aircraft
		Other
	400950 30 0	Not reinforced or otherwise combined with other materials
	400950 50 0	Reinforced or otherwise combined only with metal
	400950 70 0	Reinforced or otherwise combined only with textile materials
	400950 90 0	Reinforced or otherwise combined with other materials

RUBBER TYRES, INTERCHANGEABLE TYRE TREADS, TYRE FLAPS AND INNER TUBES FOR WHEELS OF ALL KINDS

S.I.T.C. (R3)	Commodity Code No	Trade description
625.10	*401110 00 0	**Tyres, pneumatic, new, of a kind used on motor cars (including station wagons and racing cars)**
625.20		**Tyres, pneumatic, new, of a kind used on buses or lorries**
	401120 10 0	With a load index not exceeding 121
	401120 90 0	With a load index exceeding 121
625.30		**Tyres, pneumatic, new, of a kind used on aircraft**
	401130 10 0	For use on civil aircraft
	401130 90 0	Other
		Tyres, pneumatic, new, of a kind used on motorcycles and bicycles
625.41		**....of a kind used on motorcycles**
	401140 10 0	For rims with diameter not exceeding 30.5 cm

S.I.T.C. (R3)	Commodity Code No	Trade description
cont 625.41		Other, of a weight
	401140 91 0	Not exceeding 1.4 kg
	401140 99 0	Exceeding 1.4 kg
625.42		....of a kind used on bicycles
	401150 10 0	Tyre cases with sewn-in inner tubes
	401150 90 0	Other
		Other new pneumatic tyres
625.51		....having a 'herring-bone' or similar tread
	401191 10 0	Of a kind used on agricultural and forestry vehicles
	401191 30 0	Of the kind used on civil engineering vehicles
	401191 90 0	Other
625.59		....other
	401199 10 0	Of the kind used on agricultural and forestry vehicles
	401199 30 0	Of a kind used on civil engineering vehicles
	401199 90 0	Other
		Other tyres (including retreaded tyres), interchangeable tyre treads, tyre flaps and inner tubes
625.91		**Inner tubes**
		Of a kind used on motor cars (including station wagons and racing cars), buses or lorries
	401310 10 0	Of the kind used on motor cars (including station wagons and racing cars)
	401310 90 0	Of the kind used on buses or lorries
	401320 00 0	Of a kind used on bicycles
		Other
	401390 10 0	Of a kind used on motorcycles
	401390 90 0	Other
625.92		**Retreaded tyres**
	401210 10 0	For use on civil aircraft
		Other
	401210 30 0	Of a kind used on motor cars (including station wagons and racing cars)
	401210 50 0	Of a kind used on buses or lorries
	401210 80 0	Other
625.93		**Used pneumatic tyres**
	401220 10 0	For use on civil aircraft
	401220 90 0	Other
625.94		**Solid or cushion tyres, interchangeable tyre treads and tyre flaps**
	401290 10 0	Solid or cushion tyres and interchangeable tyre treads
	401290 90 0	Tyre flaps
		ARTICLES OF RUBBER, N.E.S.
		Hygienic or pharmaceutical articles (including teats), of unhardened vulcanized rubber, with or without fittings of hard rubber
629.11	401410 00 0	**Sheath contraceptives**
629.19		**Other hygienic or pharmaceutical articles of unhardened vulcanized rubber**
	401490 10 0	Teats, nipple shields, and similar articles for babies
	401490 90 0	Other
		Conveyor or transmission belts or belting, of vulcanized rubber
629.21		....of trapezoidal cross-section (V-belts and V-belting)
	*401021 00 0	Endless transmission belts of trapezoidal cross-section (V-belts), whether or not grooved, of a circumference exceeding 60 cm but not exceeding 180 cm
	*401022 00 0	Endless transmission belts of trapezoidal cross-section (V-belts), whether or not grooved, of a circumference exceeding 180 cm but not exceeding 240 cm
	*401029 00 0	Other
629.29		....other
	*401011 00 0	Reinforced only with metal
	*401012 00 0	Reinforced only with textile materials
	*401013 00 0	Reinforced only with plastics
	*401019 00 0	Other
	*401023 00 0	Endless synchronous belts, of a circumference exceeding 60 cm but not exceeding 150 cm
	*401024 00 0	Endless synchronous belts, of a circumference exceeding 150 cm but not exceeding 198 cm
		Hard rubber; articles of hardened rubber or of unhardened vulcanized rubber, n.e.s.
629.91		**Hard rubber (eg., ebonite), in all forms (including waste and scrap); articles of hard rubber**
		Hard rubber (for example, ebonite) in any form, scrap and waste included
	401700 11 0	In bulk or blocks, in plates, sheets or strip, in rods, profile shapes or tubes

S.I.T.C. (R3)	Commodity Code No	Trade description
cont 629.91	401700 19 0	Scrap, waste and powder, of hardened rubber
		Articles of hard rubber
	401700 91 0	Piping and tubing, with fittings attached, suitable for conducting gases or liquids, for use in civil aircraft
	401700 99 0	Other
629.92		**Articles of unhardened cellular vulcanized rubber, n.e.s**
	401610 10 0	For technical uses, for use in civil aircraft
	401610 90 0	Other
629.99		**Articles of unhardened non-cellular vulcanized rubber, n.e.s.**
	401691 00 0	Floor coverings and mats
	401692 00 0	Erasers
		Gaskets, washers and other seals
	401693 10 0	For technical uses, for use in civil aircraft
	401693 90 0	Other
	401694 00 0	Boat or dock fenders, whether or not inflatable
	401695 00 0	Other inflatable articles
		Other
	401699 10 0	For technical uses, for use in civil aircraft
		Other
	401699 30 0	Expander sleeves
		Other
		For motor vehicles of headings 722.41 to 782.29
	401699 52 0	Rubber-to-metal bonded parts
	401699 58 0	Other
		Other
	401699 82 0	Rubber-to-metal bonded parts
	401699 88 0	Other

DIVISION 63

CORK AND WOOD MANUFACTURES (EXCLUDING FURNITURE)

CORK MANUFACTURES

Articles of natural cork

633.11		**Corks and stoppers**
	450310 10 0	Cylindrical
	450310 90 0	Other
633.19	450390 00 0	**Other**

Agglomerated cork (with or without a binding substance) and articles of agglomerated cork

633.21		**Blocks, plates, sheets, strip, tiles and solid cylinders**
		Corks and stoppers
	450410 11 0	For sparkling wine, including those with discs of natural cork
	450410 19 0	Other
		Other
	450410 91 0	With a binding substance
	450410 99 0	Other
633.29		**Other**
	450490 10 0	Gaskets, washers and other seals, for use in civil aircraft
		Other
	450490 91 0	Corks and stoppers
	450490 99 0	Other

VENEERS, PLYWOOD, PARTICLE BOARD, AND OTHER WOOD, WORKED, N.E.S.

Veneer sheets and sheets for plywood (whether or not spliced) and other wood sawn lengthwise, sliced or peeled, whether or not planed, sanded or finger-jointed, of a thickness not exceeding 6 mm

634.11		**Coniferous**
	440810 10 0	Finger-jointed, whether or not planed or sanded
		Other
	440810 30 0	Planed
	440810 50 0	Sanded
		Other
	440810 91 0	Small boards for the manufacture of pencils
		Other
	440810 93 0	Of a thickness not exceeding 1 mm
	440810 99 0	Of a thickness exceeding 1 mm

S.I.T.C. (R3)	Commodity Code No	Trade description
634.12		**Non-coniferous**
		Of the following tropical woods: Dark Red Meranti, Light Red Meranti, White Lauan, Sipo, Limba, Okoumé, Obeche, Acajou d'Afrique, Sapelli, Baboen, Mahogany (*Swietenia spp.*), Palissandre du Brésil and Bois de Rose femelle
		Dark red meranti, light red meranti and meranti bakau
	*440831 11 0	Finger jointed, whether or not planed or sanded
		Other
	*440831 21 0	Planed
	*440831 25 0	Sanded
	*440831 30 0	Other
		Other
		White lauan, sipo, limba, okoume, obeche, acajou d'Afrique, sapelli, virola, mahogany (*Swietenia spp.*), palissandre de Rio, palissandre de Para and palissandre de Rose
	*440839 11 0	Finger jointed, whether or not planed or sanded
		Other
	*440839 21 0	Planed
	*440839 25 0	Sanded
		Other
	*440839 31 0	Of a thickness not exceeding 1 mm
	*440839 35 0	Of a thickness exceeding 1 mm
		Other
	*440839 51 0	Finger jointed, whether or not planed or sanded
		Other
	*440839 61 0	Planed
	*440839 65 0	Sanded
		Other
	*440839 70 0	Small boards for the manufacture of pencils
		Other
		Of a thickness not exceeding 1 mm
	*440839 81 0	Makore, iroko, tiama, mansonia, ilomba, dibetou, azobe, white merantis, white seraya, yellow meranti, alan, keruing, ramin, kapur, teak, jongkong, merbau, jelutong, kempas, imbuia and balsa
	*440839 89 0	Other
		Of a thickness exceeding 1 mm
	*440839 91 0	Makore, iroko, tiama, mansonia, ilomba, dibetou, azobe, white merantis, white seraya, yellow meranti, alan, keruing, ramin, kapur, teak, jongkong, merbau, jelutong, kempas, imbuia and balsa
	*440839 99 0	Other
		Other
	*440890 11 0	Finger-jointed, whether or not planed or sanded
		Other
	*440890 21 0	Planed
	*440890 25 0	Sanded
		Other
	*440890 35 0	Small boards for the manufacture of pencils
		Other
	*440890 81 0	Of a thickness not exceeding 1 mm
	*440890 89 0	Of a thickness exceeding 1 mm
		Densified wood and reconstituted wood
634.21	441300 00 0	**Densified wood, in blocks, plates, strips or profile shapes**
634.22		**Particle board and similar board of wood, whether or not agglomerated with resins or other organic binding substances**
	*441011 00 0	Waferboard, including oriented strand board
		Other
	*441019 10 0	Unworked or not further worked than sanded
	*441019 30 0	Surfaced with high pressure decorative laminates
	*441019 50 0	Surfaced with melamine resin impregnated paper
	*441019 90 0	Other
634.23	441090 00 0	**Particle board and similar board of ligneous materials other than wood, whether or not agglomerated with resins or other organic binding substances**
		Plywood consisting solely of sheets of wood, each ply not exceeding 6 mm thickness
634.31		**....with at least one outer ply of tropical or non-coniferous wood**
		With at least one outer ply of tropical woods specified in subheading note 1 to this chapter:
	*441213 11 0	With at least one outer ply of okoumé
	*441213 19 0	Of dark red meranti, light red meranti, white lauan, sipo, limba, obeche, acajou d'Afrique, sapelli, virola, mahogany (*Swietenia spp.*), palissandre de Rio, palissandre de Para and palissandre de Rose
	*441213 90 0	Other
	*441214 00 0	Other, with at least one outer ply of non-coniferous wood
634.39	441219 00 0	**....other**
		Other plywood, veneered panels and similar laminated wood

S.I.T.C. (R3)	Commodity Code No	Trade description
634.41		....with at least one outer ply of non-coniferous wood
		With at least one ply of tropical wood specified in subheading note 1 to this chapter
	*441222 10 0	Containing at least one layer of particle board
		Other
	*441222 91 0	Blockboard, laminboard, battenboard and similar laminated wood products
	*441222 99 0	Other
	*441223 00 0	Other, containing at least one layer of particle board
		Other
	*441229 20 0	Blockboard, laminboard and battenboard
	*441229 80 0	Other
634.49		Plywood, veneered panels and similar laminated wood, n.e.s.
		With at least one ply of tropical wood specified in subheading note 1 to this chapter
	*441292 10 0	Containing at least one layer of particle board
		Other
	*441292 91 0	Blockboard, laminboard and battenboard
	*441292 99 0	Other
	*441293 00 0	Other containing at least one layer of particle board
		Other
	*441299 20 0	Blockboard, laminboard, battenboard and similar laminated wood products
	*441299 80 0	Other
		Fibreboard of wood or other ligneous materials, whether or not bonded with resins or other organic substances
634.51		....of a density exceeding 0.80 g/cm^3
	441111 00 0	Not mechanically worked or surface covered
	441119 00 0	Other
634.52		....of a density exceeding 0.50 g/cm3 but not exceeding 0.80g/cm3
	441121 00 0	Not mechanically worked or surface covered
	441129 00 0	Other
634.53		....of a density exceeding 0.35 g/cm3 but not exceeding 0.50 g/cm3
	441131 00 0	Not mechanically worked or surface covered
	441139 00 0	Other
634.59		Fibreboard of wood or other ligneous material, n.e.s.
	441191 00 0	Not mechanically worked or surface covered
	441199 00 0	Other
		Wood, simply shaped, n.e.s.
634.91		Hoopwood; split poles; piles, pickets and stakes of wood, pointed but not sawn lengthwise; wooden sticks, roughly turned, bent or otherwise worked, suitable for the manufacture of walking-sticks, umbrellas, tool handles or the like; chipwood and the like
	440410 00 0	Coniferous
	440420 00 0	Non-coniferous
634.93	440500 00 0	Wood wool; wood flour
		WOOD MANUFACTURES, N.E.S.
		Packings and cable drums of wood; wooden box pallets and the like
635.11		Packing cases, boxes, crates, drums and similar packings, of wood; cable-drums of wood
	441510 10 0	Cases, boxes, crates, drums and similar packings
	441510 90 0	Cable-drums
635.12		Pallets, box pallets and other load boards
	*441520 20 0	Flat pallets
	441520 90 0	Other
635.20		Casks, barrels, vats, tubs and other coopers' products and parts thereof, of wood (including staves)
	441600 10 0	Riven staves of wood, not further prepared than sawn on one principal surface; sawn staves of wood, of which at least one principal surface has been cylindrically sawn, not further prepared than sawn
	441600 90 0	Other
		Builders' joinery and carpentry of wood (including cellular wood panels and assembled parquet panels)
635.31		Windows, French-windows and their frames
	*441810 10 0	Of tropical wood, as specified in additional note 2 to this chapter
	*441810 50 0	Coniferous
	*441810 90 0	Other
635.32		Doors and their frames and thresholds
	*441820 10 0	Of tropical wood, as specified in additional note 2 to this chapter
	*441820 50 0	Coniferous
	*441820 80 0	Of other wood

S.I.T.C. (R3)	Commodity Code No	Trade description
635.33	441850 00 0	**Shingles and shakes**
635.39		**Other builders' joinery and carpentry of wood**
		Parquet panels
	441830 10 0	For mosaic floors
		Other
	441830 91 0	Composed of two or more layers of wood
	441830 99 0	Other
	441840 00 0	Shuttering for concrete constructional work
		Other
	*441890 10 0	Glue-laminated timber
	*441890 90 0	Other

Manufactures of wood for domestic or decorative use (excluding furniture)

S.I.T.C. (R3)	Commodity Code No	Trade description
635.41		**Wooden frames for paintings, photographs, mirrors or similar objects**
	441400 10 0	Of tropical wood
	441400 90 0	Of other wood
635.42		**Tableware and kitchenware, of wood**
	441900 10 0	Of tropical wood
	441900 90 0	Of other wood
635.49		**Wood marquetry and inlaid wood; caskets and cases for jewellery or cutlery, and similar articles, of wood; statuettes and other ornaments, of wood; wooden articles of furniture not falling within division 82.**
		Statuettes and other ornaments, of wood
	442010 11 0	Of tropical wood
	442010 19 0	Of other wood
		Other
		Wood marquetry and inlaid wood
	442090 11 0	Of tropical wood
	442090 19 0	Of other wood
		Other
	442090 91 0	Of tropical wood
	442090 99 0	Other

Manufactured articles of wood, n.e.s.

S.I.T.C. (R3)	Commodity Code No	Trade description
635.91		**Tools, tool bodies, tool handles, broom or brush bodies and handles, of wood; boot or shoe lasts and trees, of wood**
	*441700 20 0	Handles for articles of cutlery (other than for table-knives, forks or spoons); brush bodies
	*442190 70 0	Handles for table-knives, forks or spoons
	441700 90 0	Other
635.99		**Other articles of wood**
	442110 00 0	Clothes hangers
		Other
	*441520 00 0	Pallet collars
	442190 10 0	Spools, cops, bobbins, sewing thread reels and the like, of turned wood
	442190 30 0	Blind rollers, whether or not fitted with springs
	442190 50 0	Match splints; wooden pegs or pins for footwear
		Other
	442190 91 0	Of fibreboard
	442190 99 0	Other

DIVISION 64

PAPER, PAPERBOARD, AND ARTICLES OF PAPER PULP, OF PAPER OR OF PAPERBOARD

PAPER AND PAPERBOARD

S.I.T.C. (R3)	Commodity Code No	Trade description
641.10		**Newsprint, in rolls or sheets**
	*480100 10 0	Mentioned in additional note 1 to this chapter
	*480100 90 0	Other

Paper and paperboard, uncoated, of a kind used for writing, printing or other graphic purposes, and punch card stock and punch tape paper, in rolls or sheets (other than paper of heading 641.1 or 641.63); hand-made paper and paperboard

S.I.T.C. (R3)	Commodity Code No	Trade description
641.21	480210 00 0	**Hand-made paper and paperboard**
641.22	480220 00 0	**Paper and paperboard of a kind used as a base for photo-sensitive, heat-sensitive or electro-sensitive paper or paperboard**
641.23	480230 00 0	**Carbonizing base paper**

S.I.T.C. (R3)	Commodity Code No	Trade description
641.24		**Wallpaper base**
	480240 10 0	Not containing fibres obtained by a mechanical process or of which not more than 10 % by weight of the total fibre content consists of such fibres
	480240 90 0	Other
641.25		**Other paper and paperboard, weighing less than 40g/m^2, not containing fibres obtained by a mechanical process or of which not more than 10% by weight of the total fibre content consists of such fibres**
	480251 10 0	Paper weighing not more than 15 g/m^2 for use in stencil making
	480251 90 0	Other
641.26		**Other paper and paperboard, weighing 40g/m^2 or more but not more than 150g/m2, not containing fibres obtained by a mechanical process or of which not more than 10% by weight of the total fibre content consists of such fibres**
	*480252 20 0	In rolls
	480252 80 0	In sheets
641.27		**Other paper and paper board, weighing more than 150 g/m^2, not containing fibres obtained by a mechanical process or of which not more than 10% by weight of the total fibre content consists of such fibres**
	480253 20 0	In rolls
	480253 80 0	In sheets
641.29		**Other paper and paperboard, of which more than 10 % by weight of the total fibre content consists of fibres obtained by a mechanical process**
		Weighing less than 72 g/m^2 and of which more than 50 % by weight of the total fibre content consists of fibres obtained by a mechanical process
	480260 11 0	In rolls
	480260 19 0	In sheets
		Other
	480260 91 0	In rolls
	480260 99 0	In sheets
		Paper and paperboard, of a kind used for writing, printing or other graphic purposes, coated, impregnated, decorated or printed (not group 892), in rolls or sheets
641.31		**Carbon paper, self-copy paper and other copying or transfer papers (including coated or impregnated paper for duplicator stencils or offset plates), whether or not printed, in rolls of a width exceeding 36 cm or in rectangular sheets with at least one side exceeding 36 cm in unfolded state**
	480910 00 0	Carbon or similar copying papers
		Self-copy paper
	480920 10 0	In rolls
	480920 90 0	In sheets
	480990 00 0	Other
641.32		**Paper and paperboard of a kind used for writing, printing or other graphic purposes, coated on one or both sides with kaolin (China clay) or other inorganic substances, with or without a binder, and with no other coating, whether or not surface-coloured, surface- decorated or printed, not containing fibres obtained by a mechanical process or of which not more than 10% by weight of the total fibre content consists of such fibres, in rolls or sheets, weighing not more than 150 g/m^2**
	481011 10 0	Paper and paperboard of a kind used as a base for photo-sensitive, heat-sensitive or electro-sensitive paper or paperboard
		Other
	*481011 91 0	In rolls
	*481011 99 0	In sheets
641.33	*481012 00 0	**Paper and paperboard of a kind used for writing, printing or other graphic purposes, coated on one or both sides with kaolin (China clay) or other inorganic substances, with or without a binder, and with no other coating, whether or not surface-coloured, surface- decorated or printed, not containing fibres obtained by a mechanical process or of which not more than 10% by weight of the total fibre content consists of such fibres, in rolls or sheets, weighing more than 150 g/m2**
641.34		**Paper and paperboard of a kind used for writing, printing or other graphic purposes, coated on one or both sides with kaolin (China clay) or other inorganic substances, with or without a binder, and with no other coating, whether or not surface-coloured, surface- decorated or printed, of which more than 10% by weight of the total fibre content consists of fibres obtained by a mechanical process, in rolls or sheets**
	481021 00 0	Light-weight coated paper
		Other
		In rolls
	481029 11 0	Wallpaper base
	*481029 19 0	Other
	*481029 90 0	In sheets
	481029 90 1	One side coated
	481029 90 9	Coated both sides

S.I.T.C. (R3)	Commodity Code No	Trade description
		Kraft paper and paperboard, uncoated, n.e.s., in rolls or sheets
641.41		**Kraft paper, uncoated, in rolls or sheets**
		Of which not less than 80% by weight of the total fibre content consists of coniferous fibres obtained by the chemical sulphate or soda process
		Kraftliner
		Unbleached
	480411 11 0	Weighing less than 150g/m^2
	480411 15 0	Weighing 105g/m^2 or more but less than 175g/m^2
	*480411 19 0	Weighing 175g/m2 or more
		Other
		Composed of one or more layers unbleached and an outside layer bleached, semi-bleached or coloured, weighing per g/m^2
	480419 11 0	Less than 150g
	480419 15 0	150g or more but less than 175g
	480419 19 0	175g or more
		Other, weighing per m^2
	480419 31 0	Less than 150g
	480419 35 0	150g or more but less than 175g
	480419 39 0	175g or more
641.42		**Sack kraft paper, uncoated, in rolls or sheets**
		Of which not less than 80% by weight of the total fibre content consists of coniferous fibres obtained by the chemical sulphate or soda process
	480421 10 0	Unbleached
	480429 10 0	Other
641.46		**Kraft paper and paperboard, uncoated, in rolls or sheets, n.e.s., weighing 150 g/m2 or less**
		Unbleached
	480431 10 0	For the manufacture of paper yarn of heading 651.99 or of paper yarn reinforced with metal of heading 657.51
		Other
		Of which not less than 80% by weight of the total fibre content consists of coniferous fibres obtained by the chemical sulphate or soda process
	480431 51 0	Kraft electro-technical insulating paper
	*480431 59 0	Other
		Other
	480439 10 0	For the manufacture of paper yarn of heading 651.99 or of paper yarn reinforced with metal of heading 657.51
		Other
		Of which not less than 80% by weight of the total fibre content consists of coniferous fibres obtained by the chemical sulphate or soda process
	*480439 51 0	Bleached uniformly throughout the mass
	480439 59 0	Other
641.47		**Kraft paper and paperboard, uncoated, in rolls or sheets, n.e.s., weighing more than 150 g/m^2 but less than 225 g/m^2**
		Of which not less than 80% by weight of the total fibre content consists of coniferous fibres obtained by the chemical sulphate or soda process
	480441 10 0	Unbleached
		Bleached uniformly throughout the mass and of which more than 95 % by weight of the total fibre content consists of wood fibres obtained by a chemical process
	480442 10 0	Other
	480449 10 0	Other
641.48		**Kraft paper and paperboard, uncoated, in rolls or sheets, n.e.s., weighing 225 g/m^2 or more**
		Of which not less than 80% by weight of the total fibre content consists of coniferous fibres obtained by the chemical sulphate of soda process
	480451 10 0	Unbleached
	480452 10 0	Bleached uniformly throughout the mass and of which more than 95 % by weight of the total fibre content consists of wood fibres obtained by a chemical process
	480459 10 0	Other
		Paper and paperboard, uncoated, in rolls or sheets, n.e.s.
641.51	480510 00 0	**Semi-chemical fluting paper, uncoated (corrugating medium), in rolls or sheets**
641.52		**Sulphite wrapping paper, uncoated, in rolls or sheets**
	480530 10 0	Weighing less than 30 g/m^2
	480530 90 0	Weighing 30 g/m^2 or more
641.53		**Vegetable parchment, greaseproof papers, tracing papers and glassine and other glazed transparent or translucent papers, in rolls or sheets**
	480610 00 0	Vegetable parchment
	480620 00 0	Greaseproof papers
	480630 00 0	Tracing papers
		Glassine and other glazed transparent or translucent papers
	480640 10 0	Glassine paper
	480640 90 0	Other

S.I.T.C. (R3)	Commodity Code No	Trade description
641.54		**Multi-ply paper and paperboard, uncoated, in rolls or sheets**
		Kraftliner (other than of heading 641.41)
	*480411 90 0	Unbleached
	480419 90 0	Other
		Other
	480521 00 0	Each layer bleached
		With only one outer layer bleached
	480522 10 0	Testliner
	480522 90 0	Other
	480523 00 0	Having three or more layers, of which only the two outer layers are bleached
		Other
	480529 10 0	Testliner
	480529 90 0	Other
641.55		**Cigarette paper, n.e.s.**
	481390 10 0	Not impregnated, in rolls of a width exceeding 15 cm, or in rectangular (including square) sheets with one side exceeding 36 cm
	481390 90 0	Other
641.56		**Filter paper and paperboard, uncoated; felt paper and paperboard, uncoated**
	480540 00 0	Filter paper and paperboard
	480550 00 0	Felt paper and paperboard
641.57		**Other paper and paperboard, uncoated, weighing 150 g/m^2 or less**
		Sack kraft paper (other than of heading 641.42)
	480421 90 0	Unbleached
	480429 90 0	Other
		Other kraft paper and paperboard (other than of heading 641.42)
	480431 90 0	Unbleached
	480439 90 0	Other
	480560 10 0	Strawpaper and strawboard
		Paper and paperboard for corrugated paper and paperboard
	480560 20 0	Wellenstoff
	480560 40 0	Testliner
	480560 60 0	Other
	480560 90 0	Other
641.58		**Other paper and paperboard, uncoated, weighing more than 150 g/m^2 but less than 225 g/m2**
		Other kraft paper and paperboard (other than of heading 641.47)
		Unbleached
	480441 91 0	Saturating kraft
	480441 99 0	Other
	480442 90 0	Bleached uniformly throughout the mass and of which more than 95% by weight of the total fibre content consists of wood fibres obtained by a chemical process
	480449 90 0	Other
		Paper and paperboard for corrugated paper and paperboard
	480570 11 0	Testliner
	480570 19 0	Other
	480570 90 0	Other
641.59		**Other paper and paperboard, uncoated, weighing 225 g/m^2 or more**
		Other kraft paper and paperboard (other than of heading 641.48)
	480451 90 0	Unbleached
	480452 90 0	Bleached uniformly throughout the mass and of which more than 95% by weight of the total fire content consists of wood fibres obtained by a chemical process
	480459 90 0	Other
		Other
		Made from wastepaper
	480580 11 0	Testliner
	480580 19 0	Other
	480580 90 0	Other
		Paper and paperboard, corrugated, creped, crinkled, embossed or perforated, in rolls or sheets
641.61	480820 00 0	**Sack kraft paper, creped or crinkled, whether or not embossed or perforated, in rolls or sheets**
641.62	480830 00 0	**Other kraft paper, in rolls or sheets, creped or crinkled, whether or not embossed or perforated**
641.63		**Toilet or facial tissue stock, towel or napkin stock and similar paper of a kind used for household or sanitary purposes, cellulose wadding and webs of cellulose fibres, whether or not creped, crinkled, embossed, perforated, surface-coloured, surface-decorated or printed, in rolls of a width exceeding 36 cm or in rectangular sheets with at least one side exceeding 36 cm in unfolded state**
	480300 10 0	Cellulose wadding
		Creped paper and webs of cellulose fibres (tissues), weighing, per ply
	480300 31 0	Not more than 25 g/m^2
	480300 39 0	More than 25 g/m^2
	480300 90 0	Other
641.64	480810 00 0	**Paper and paperboard, corrugated (with or without glued flat surface sheets), whether or not perforated, in rolls or sheets**

S.I.T.C. (R3)	Commodity Code No	Trade description
641.69	480890 00 0	Paper, creped, crinkled, embossed or perforated, in rolls or sheets, n.e.s
		Paper, paperboard, cellulose wadding and webs of cellulose fibres, coated, impregnated, covered, surface-coloured, surface-decorated or printed, not constituting printed matter within group 892, in rolls or sheets, n.e.s.
641.71		Paper and paperboard, coated, impregnated or covered with plastics (excluding adhesives), in rolls or sheets, bleached, weighing more than 150 g/m^2
	*481131 00 0	Bleached, weighing more than 150 g/m2
641.72	*481139 00 0	Other paper and paperboard, coated, impregnated or covered with plastics (excluding adhesives), in rolls or sheets
641.73	481110 00 0	Paper and paperboard, tarred, bituminized or asphalted, in rolls or sheets
641.74	481031 00 0	Kraft paper and paperboard, coated on one or both sides with kaolin (China clay) or other inorganic substances, with or without a binder, and with no other coating, whether or not surface-coloured, surface-decorated or printed, in rolls or sheets, other than that of a kind used for writing, printing or other graphic purposes, bleached uniformly throughout the mass and of which more than 95% by weight of the total fibre content consists of wood fibres obtained by a chemical process, and weighing 150 g/m^2 or less
641.75		Kraft paper and paperboard, coated on one or both sides with kaolin (China clay) or other inorganic substances, with or without a binder, and with no other coating, whether or not surface-coloured, surface- decorated or printed, in rolls or sheets, other than that of a kind used for writing, printing or other graphic purposes, bleached uniformly throughout the mass and of which more than 95% by weight of the total fibre content consists of wood fibres obtained by a chemical process, and weighing more than 150 g/m^2
	481032 10 0	Coated with kaolin
	481032 90 0	Other
641.76	481039 00 0	Other kraft paper and paperboard, coated on one or both sides with kaolin (China clay) or other inorganic substances, with or without a binder, and with no other coating, whether or not surface-coloured, surface-decorated or printed, in rolls or sheets, other than that of a kind used for writing, printing or other graphic purposes
641.77		Other paper and paperboard coated on one or both sides with kaolin (China clay) or other inorganic substances, with or without a binder, and with no other coating, whether or not surface-coloured, surface-decorated or printed, in rolls or sheets, other than that of a kind used for writing, printing or other graphic purposes
		Multi-ply
	481091 10 0	Each layer bleached
	*481091 30 0	With only one outer layer bleached
	481091 90 0	Other
		Other
	481099 10 0	Bleached paper and paperboard, coated with kaolin
	481099 30 0	Coated with mica powder
	481099 90 0	Other
641.78		Gummed or adhesive paper and paperboard
	481121 00 0	Self-adhesive
	481129 00 0	Other
641.79		Other paper, paperboard, cellulose wadding and webs of cellulose fibres, coated, impregnated, covered, surface-coloured, surface- decorated or printed, in rolls or sheets
	481140 00 0	Paper and paperboard, coated, impregnated or covered with wax, paraffin wax, stearin, oil or glycerol
		Other paper, paperboard, cellulose wadding and webs of soft cellulose
	481190 10 0	Continuous forms
	481190 90 0	Other
		Converted paper and paperboard, n.e.s.
641.91	480710 00 0	Paper and paperboard, laminated internally with bitumen, tar or asphalt
641.92		Other composite paper and paperboard (made by sticking flat layers of paper or paperboard together with an adhesive) not surface-coated or impregnated, whether or not internally reinforced, in rolls or sheets
	*480790 10 0	Straw paper and paperboard, whether or not covered with paper other than straw paper
		Other
	*480790 50 0	Made from wastepaper, whether or not covered with paper
	*480790 90 0	Other
641.93	481200 00 0	Filter blocks, slabs and plates, of paper pulp
641.94		Wallpaper and similar wall coverings, window transparencies of paper
	481410 00 0	"Ingrain" paper
	481420 00 0	Wallpaper and similar wall coverings, consisting of paper coated or covered, on the face side, with a grained, embossed, coloured, design-printed or otherwise decorated layer of plastics
	481430 00 0	Wallpaper and similar wall coverings, consisting of paper covered, on the face side, with plaiting material, whether or not bound together in parallel strands or woven

S.I.T.C. (R3)	Commodity Code No	Trade description
cont 641.94		Other
	481490 10 0	Wallpaper and similar wall coverings, consisting of grained, embossed, surface-coloured, design-printed or otherwise surface-decorated paper, coated or covered with transparent protective plastics
	481490 90 0	Other

PAPER AND PAPERBOARD, CUT TO SIZE OR SHAPE, AND ARTICLES OF PAPER OR PAPERBOARD

Cartons, boxes, cases, bags and other packing containers, of paper, paperboard, cellulose wadding or webs of cellulose fibres; box files, letter trays and similar articles, of paper or paperboard, of a kind used in offices, shops or the like

642.11	481910 00 0	**Cartons, boxes and cases, of corrugated paper or paperboard**
642.12		**Folding cartons, boxes and cases, of non-corrugated paper or paperboard**
	481920 10 0	With a weight of the paper or the paperboard of less than 600 g/m^2
	481920 90 0	With a weight of the paper or the paperboard of 600 g/m^2 or more
642.13	481930 00 0	**Sacks and bags, having a base of a width of 40 cm or more**
642.14	481940 00 0	**Other sacks and bags (incl. cones)**
642.15	481950 00 0	**Other packing containers (incl. record sleeves)**
642.16	481960 00 0	**Box files, letter trays, storage boxes and similar articles, of a kind used in offices, shops or the like**

Envelopes, letter cards, plain postcards and correspondence cards, of paper or paperboard; boxes, pouches, wallets and writing compendiums, of paper or paperboard, containing an assortment of paper stationery

642.21	481710 00 0	**Envelopes**
642.22	481720 00 0	**Letter cards, plain postcards and correspondence cards**
642.23	481730 00 0	**Boxes, pouches, wallets and writing compendiums, of paper or paperboard, containing an assortment of paper stationery**

Registers, account books, note books, order books, receipt books, letter pads, memorandum pads, diaries and similar articles, exercise books, blotting-pads, binders (loose-leaf or other), folders, file covers, manifold business forms, interleaved carbon sets and other articles of stationery, of paper or paperboard; albums for samples or for collections and book covers, of paper or paperboard

642.31		**Registers, account books, note books, order books, receipt books, letter pads, memorandum pads, diaries and similar articles**
	482010 10 0	Registers, account books, order books and receipt books
	482010 30 0	Note books, letter pads and memorandum pads
	482010 50 0	Diaries
	482010 90 0	Other
642.32	482020 00 0	**Exercise-books**
642.33	482030 00 0	**Binders (other than book covers), folders and file covers**
642.34		**Manifold business forms and interleaved carbon sets**
	482040 10 0	Continuous forms
	482040 90 0	Other
642.35	482050 00 0	**Albums for samples or for collections**
642.39	482090 00 0	**Book covers; blotting pads and other articles of stationery, n.e.s**

Paper and paperboard, cut to size or shape, n.e.s.

642.41		**Cigarette paper, cut to size, whether or not in the form of booklets or tubes**
	481310 00 0	In the form of booklets or tubes
	*481320 00 0	In rolls of a width not exceeding 5 cm
642.42		**Carbon paper, self-copy paper and other copying or transfer papers, cut to size, whether or not put up in boxes**
	481610 00 0	Carbon or similar copying papers
	481620 00 0	Self-copy paper
	481630 00 0	Duplicator stencils
	481690 00 0	Other
642.43		**Toilet paper, cut to size, in rolls or in sheets**
	481810 10 0	Weighing, per ply, 25 g/m^2 or less
	481810 90 0	Weighing, per ply, more than 25 g/m^2

S.I.T.C. (R3)	Commodity Code No	Trade description
642.44		**Gummed or adhesive paper, in strips or rolls**
		Self-adhesive
		Strips of a width not exceeding 10 cm, the coating of which consists of unvulcanised natural or synthetic rubber
	482311 11 0	Self-adhesive on one side
	482311 19 0	Self-adhesive on both sides
	482311 90 0	Other
	482319 00 0	Other
642.45	482320 00 0	**Filter paper and paperboard**
642.48		**Paper and paperboard, of a kind used for writing, printing or other graphic purposes, n.e.s.**
		Printed, embossed or perforated
	482351 10 0	Continuous forms
	482351 90 0	Other
		Other
	482359 10 0	In strips or rolls for office machines and the like
	*482359 90 0	Other
		Articles of paper pulp, paper, paperboard or cellulose wadding, n.e.s.
642.91		**Bobbins, spools, cops and similar supports of paper pulp, paper or paperboard (whether or not perforated or hardened)**
	482210 00 0	Of a kind used for winding textile yarn
	482290 00 0	Other
642.92	*482390 15 0	**Cards, not punched, for punch card machines, whether or not in strips**
642.93		**Trays, dishes, plates, cups and the like, of paper or paperboard**
	482360 10 0	Trays, dishes and plates
	482360 90 0	Other
642.94		**Handkerchiefs, cleansing tissues, towels, serviettes, tablecloths, bed sheets and other paper linen; paper garments and clothing accessories**
		Handkerchiefs, cleansing or facial tissues and towels
	481820 10 0	Handkerchiefs and cleansing or facial tissues
		Hand towels
	481820 91 0	In rolls
	481820 99 0	Other
	481830 00 0	Tablecloths and serviettes
	481850 00 0	Articles of apparel and clothing
		Other
	481890 10 0	Articles of a kind used for surgical, medical or hygienic purposes, not put up for retail sale
	481890 90 0	Other
642.95		**Sanitary towels and tampons, napkins (diapers) and napkin liners for babies and similar sanitary articles, of paper pulp, paper, cellulose wadding or webs of cellulose fibres**
		Sanitary towels, tampons and similar articles
	481840 11 0	Sanitary towels
	481840 13 0	Tampons
	481840 19 0	Other
		Napkins and napkin liners for babies and similar sanitary articles
	481840 91 0	Not put up for retail sale
	481840 99 0	Other
642.99		**Other articles of paper pulp, paper, paperboard, cellulose wadding or webs of cellulose fibres, n.e.s.**
	482340 00 0	Rolls, sheets and dials, printed for self-recording apparatus
		Moulded or pressed articles of paper pulp
	482370 10 0	Moulded trays and boxes for packing eggs
	482370 90 0	Other
		Other
	482390 10 0	Gaskets, washers and other seals, for use in civil aircraft
		Other
	482390 20 0	Perforated paper and paperboard for Jacquard and similar machines
	482390 30 0	Fans and hand screens; frames therefor and parts of such frames
		Other
	*482390 50 0	Cut to size or shape
	*482390 90 0	Other

DIVISION 65

TEXTILE YARN, FABRICS, MADE-UP ARTICLES, N.E.S., AND RELATED PRODUCTS

TEXTILE YARN

Yarn of wool or animal hair (excluding wool tops)

S.I.T.C. (R3)	Commodity Code No	Trade description
651.12		**Yarn of carded wool, containing 85% or more by weight of wool not put up for retail sale.**
	510610 10 0	Unbleached

S.I.T.C. (R3)	Commodity Code No	Trade description
cont 651.12	510610 90 0	Other
651.13		**Yarn of combed wool, containing 85% or more by weight of wool not put up for retail sale**
	510710 10 0	Unbleached
	510710 90 0	Other
651.14		**Yarn of fine animal hair (carded or combed), not put up for retail sale**
		Carded
	510810 10 0	Unbleached
	510810 90 0	Other
		Combed
	510820 10 0	Unbleached
	510820 90 0	Other
651.15	511000 00 0	**Yarn of coarse animal hair or of horsehair (including gimped horsehair yarn), whether or not put up for retail sale**
651.16		**Yarn containing 85% or more by weight of wool or of fine animal hair, put up for retail sale**
	510910 10 0	In balls, hanks or skeins, of a weight exceeding 125 g but not exceeding 500 g
	510910 90 0	Other
651.17		**Yarn of carded wool containing less than 85% by weight of wool, not put up for retail sale**
		Containing 85 % or more by weight of wool and fine animal hair
	510620 11 0	Unbleached
	510620 19 0	Other
		Other
	510620 91 0	Unbleached
	510620 99 0	Other
651.18		**Yarn of combed wool containing less than 85% by weight of wool, not put up for retail sale**
		Containing 85 % or more by weight of wool and fine animal hair
	510720 10 0	Unbleached
	510720 30 0	Other
		Other
		Mixed solely or mainly with synthetic staple fibres
	510720 51 0	Unbleached
	510720 59 0	Other
		Otherwise mixed
	510720 91 0	Unbleached
	510720 99 0	Other
651.19		**Yarn of wool or fine animal hair, containing less than 85% by weight of wool or of fine animal hair, put up for retail sale**
	510990 10 0	In balls, hanks or skeins, of a weight exceeding 125 g but not exceeding 500 g
	510990 90 0	Other
		Cotton sewing thread, whether or not put up for retail sale
651.21		**Cotton sewing thread, not put up for retail sale**
	520411 00 0	Containing 85 % or more by weight of cotton
	520419 00 0	Other
651.22	520420 00 0	**Cotton sewing thread put up for retail sale**
		Cotton yarn, other than sewing thread
651.31	520710 00 0	**Cotton yarn (other than sewing thread) put up for retail sale, containing 85% or more by weight of cotton**
651.32	520790 00 0	**Other cotton yarn, put up for retail sale**
651.33		**Cotton yarn (other than sewing thread), containing 85% or more by weight of cotton , not put up for retail sale**
		Single yarn, of uncombed fibres
	520511 00 0	Measuring 714.29 decitex or more (not exceeding 14 metric number)
	520512 00 0	Measuring less than 714.29 decitex but not less than 232.56 decitex (exceeding 14 metric number but not exceeding 43 metric number)
	520513 00 0	Measuring less than 232.56 decitex but not less than 192.31 decitex (exceeding 43 metric number but not exceeding 52 metric number)
	520514 00 0	Measuring less than 192.31 decitex but not less than 125 decitex (exceeding 52 metric number but not exceeding 80 metric number)
		Measuring less than 125 decitex (exceeding 80 metric number)
	520515 10 0	Measuring less than 125 decitex but not less than 83.33 decitex (exceeding 80 metric number but not exceeding 120 metric number)
	520515 90 0	Measuring less than 83.33 decitex (exceeding 120 metric number)
		Single yarn, of combed fibres
	520521 00 0	Measuring 714.29 decitex or more (not exceeding 14 metric number)
	520522 00 0	Measuring less than 714.29 decitex but not less than 232.56 decitex (exceeding 14 metric number but not exceeding 43 metric number)

S.I.T.C. (R3)	Commodity Code No	Trade description
cont 651.33	520523 00 0	Measuring less than 232.56 decitex but not less than 192.31 decitex (exceeding 43 metric number but not exceeding 52 metric number)
	520524 00 0	Measuring less than 192.31 decitex but not less than 125 decitex (exceeding 52 metric number but not exceeding 80 metric number)
		Measuring less than 125 decitex (exceeding 80 metric number)
	*520526 00 0	Measuring less than 125 decitex but not less than 106.38 decitex (exceeding 80 metric number but not exceeding 94 metric number)
	*520527 00 0	Measuring less than 106.38 decitex but not less than 83.33 decitex (exceeding 94 metric number but not exceeding 120 metric number)
	*520528 00 0	Measuring less than 83.33 decitex (exceeding 120 metric number)
		Multiple (folded) or cabled yarn, of uncombed fibres
	520531 00 0	Measuring per single yarn 714.29 decitex or more (not exceeding 14 metric number per single yarn)
	520532 00 0	Measuring per single yarn less than 714.29 decitex but not less than 232.56 decitex (exceeding 14 metric number but not exceeding 43 metric number per single yarn)
	520533 00 0	Measuring per single yarn less than 232.56 decitex but not less than 192.31 decitex (exceeding 43 metric number but not exceeding 52 metric number per single yarn)
	520534 00 0	Measuring per single yarn less than 192.31 decitex but not less than 125 decitex (exceeding 52 metric number but not exceeding 80 metric number per single yarn)
		Measuring per single yarn less than 125 decitex (exceeding 80 metric number per single yarn)
	520535 10 0	Measuring per single yarn less than 125 decitex but not less than 83.33 decitex (exceeding 80 metric number but not exceeding 120 metric number per single yarn)
	520535 90 0	Measuring per single yarn less than 83.33 decitex (exceeding 120 metric number per single yarn)
		Multiple (folded) or cabled yarn, of combed fibres
	520541 00 0	Measuring per single yarn 714.29 decitex or more (not exceeding 14 metric number per single yarn)
	520542 00 0	Measuring per single yarn less than 714.29 decitex but not less than 232.56 decitex (exceeding 14 metric number but not exceeding 43 metric number per single yarn)
	520543 00 0	Measuring per single yarn less than 232.56 decitex but not less than 192.31 decitex (exceeding 43 metric number but not exceeding 52 metric number per single yarn)
	520544 00 0	Measuring per single yarn less than 192.31 decitex but not less than 125 decitex (exceeding 52 metric number but not exceeding 80 metric number per single yarn)
	*520546 00 0	Measuring per single yarn less than 125 decitex but not less than 106.38 decitex (exceeding 80 metric number but not exceeding 94 metric number per single yarn)
	*520547 00 0	Measuring per single yarn less than 106.38 decitex but not less than 83.33 decitex (exceeding 94 metric number but not exceeding 120 metric number per single yarn)
	*520548 00 0	Measuring per single yarn less than 83.33 decitex (exceeding 120 metric number per single yarn)
651.34		**Cotton yarn (other than sewing thread), containing less than 85% by weight of cotton, not put up for retail sale**
		Single yarn, of uncombed fibres
	520611 00 0	Measuring 714.29 decitex or more (not exceeding 14 metric number)
	520612 00 0	Measuring less than 714.29 decitex but not less than 232.56 decitex (exceeding 14 metric number but not exceeding 43 metric number)
	520613 00 0	Measuring less than 232.56 decitex but not less than 192.31 decitex (exceeding 43 metric number but not exceeding 52 metric number)
	520614 00 0	Measuring less than 192.31 decitex but not less than 125 decitex (exceeding 52 metric number but not exceeding 80 metric number)
		Measuring less than 125 decitex (exceeding 80 metric number)
	520615 10 0	Measuring less than 125 decitex but not less than 83.33 decitex (exceeding 80 metric number but not exceeding 120 metric number)
	520615 90 0	Measuring less than 83.33 decitex (exceeding 120 metric number)
		Single yarn, of combed fibres
	520621 00 0	Measuring 714.29 decitex or more (not exceeding 14 metric number)
	520622 00 0	Measuring less than 714.29 decitex but not less than 232.56 decitex (exceeding 14 metric number but not exceeding 43 metric number)
	520623 00 0	Measuring less than 232.56 decitex but not less than 192.31 decitex (exceeding 43 metric number but not exceeding 52 metric number)
	520624 00 0	Measuring less than 192.31 decitex but not less than 125 decitex (exceeding 52 metric number but not exceeding 80 metric number)
		Measuring less than 125 decitex (exceeding 80 metric number)
	520625 10 0	Measuring less than 125 decitex but not less than 83.33 decitex (exceeding 80 metric number but not exceeding 120 metric number)
	520625 90 0	Measuring less than 83.33 decitex (exceeding 120 metric number)
		Multiple (folded) or cabled yarn, of uncombed fibres
	520631 00 0	Measuring per single yarn 714.29 decitex or more (not exceeding 14 metric number per single yarn)
	520632 00 0	Measuring per single yarn less than 714.29 decitex but not less than 232.56 decitex (exceeding 14 metric number but not exceeding 43 metric number per single yarn)
	520633 00 0	Measuring per single yarn less than 232.56 decitex but not less than 192.31 decitex (exceeding 43 metric number but not exceeding 52 metric number per single yarn)
	520634 00 0	Measuring per single yarn less than 192.31 decitex but not less than 125 decitex (exceeding 52 metric number but not exceeding 80 metric number per single yarn)
		Measuring per single yarn less than 125 decitex (exceeding 80 metric number per single yarn)
	520635 10 0	Measuring per single yarn less than 125 decitex but not less than 83.33 decitex (exceeding 80 metric number but not exceeding 120 metric number per single yarn)
	520635 90 0	Measuring per single yarn less than 83.33 decitex (exceeding 120 metric number per single yarn)
		Multiple (folded) or cabled yarn, of combed fibres
	520641 00 0	Measuring per single yarn 714.29 decitex or more (not exceeding 14 metric number per single yarn)
	520642 00 0	Measuring per single yarn less than 714.29 decitex but not less than 232.56 decitex (exceeding 14 metric number but not exceeding 43 metric number per single yarn)
	520643 00 0	Measuring per single yarn less than 232.56 decitex but not less than 192.31 decitex (exceeding 43 metric number but not exceeding 52 metric number per single yarn)

S.I.T.C. (R3)	Commodity Code No	Trade description
cont 651.34	520644 00 0	Measuring per single yarn less than 192.31 decitex but not less than 125 decitex (exceeding 52 metric number but not exceeding 80 metric number per single yarn)
		Measuring per single yarn less than 125 decitex (exceeding 80 metric number per single yarn)
	520645 10 0	Measuring per single yarn less than 125 decitex but not less than 83.33 decitex (exceeding 80 metric number but not exceeding 120 metric number per single yarn)
	520645 90 0	Measuring per single yarn less than 83.33 decitex (exceeding 120 metric number per single yarn)

Sewing thread of man-made fibres, whether or not put up for retail sale

651.41		**....of synthetic filaments**
		Not put up for retail sale
	540110 11 0	Core yarn
	540110 19 0	Other
	540110 90 0	Put up for retail sale
651.42		**....of artificial filaments**
	540120 10 0	Not put up for retail sale
	540120 90 0	Put up for retail sale
651.43		**....of synthetic staple fibres**
		Not put up for retail sale
	550810 11 0	Of polyesters
	550810 19 0	Other
	550810 90 0	Put up for retail sale
651.44		**....of artificial staple fibres**
	550820 10 0	Not put up for retail sale
	550820 90 0	Put up for retail sale

Synthetic filament yarn (other than sewing thread) textured, not put up for retail sale, including monofilament of less than 67 decitex

651.51		**Filament yarn (other than sewing thread), of nylon or other polyamides**
		Of nylon or other polyamides, measuring per single yarn not more than 50 tex
	540231 10 0	Measuring, per single yarn, not more than 5 tex
	540231 30 0	Measuring, per single yarn, more than 5 tex but not more than 33 tex
	540231 90 0	Measuring, per single yarn, more than 33 tex but not more than 50 tex
	540232 00 0	Of nylon or other polyamides, measuring per single yarn more than 50 tex
651.52		**Filament yarn (other than sewing thread) of polyesters**
		Of polyesters
	540233 10 0	Measuring, per single yarn, not more than 14 tex
	540233 90 0	Measuring, per single yarn, more than 14 tex
651.59		**Other synthetic filament yarn (other than sewing thread)**
	540239 10 0	Of polypropylene
	540239 90 0	Other

Other synthetic filament yarn (other than sewing thread) including monofilament of less than 67 decitex

651.61	540610 00 0	**Yarn of synthetic filaments, put up for retail sale**
651.62		**High tenacity yarn of nylon, other polyamides or of polyesters, not put up for retail sale**
	540210 10 0	Of aramids
	540210 90 0	Other
	540220 00 0	High tenacity yarn of polyesters
651.63		**Other yarn, single, untwisted or with a twist not exceeding 50 turns per metre, not put up for retail sale**
		Of nylon or other polyamides
	540241 10 0	Measuring, per single yarn, not more than 7 tex
	540241 30 0	Measuring, per single yarn, more than 7 tex but not more than 33 tex
	540241 90 0	Measuring, per single yarn, more than 33 tex
	540242 00 0	Of polyesters, partially oriented
		Of polyesters, other
	540243 10 0	Measuring, per single yarn, not more than 14 tex
	540243 90 0	Measuring, per single yarn, more than 14 tex
		Other
	540249 10 0	Elastomeric
		Other
	540249 91 0	Of polypropylene
	540249 99 0	Other
651.64		**Other yarn, single, with a twist exceeding 50 turns per metre, not put up for retail sale**
		Of nylon or other polyamides
	540251 10 0	Measuring, per single yarn, not more than 7 tex
	540251 30 0	Measuring, per single yarn, more than 7 tex but not more than 33 tex
	540251 90 0	Measuring, per single yarn, more than 33 tex
		Of polyesters

S.I.T.C. (R3)	Commodity Code No	Trade description
cont 651.64	540252 10 0	Measuring, per single yarn, not more than 14 tex
	540252 90 0	Measuring, per single yarn, more than 14 tex
		Other
	540259 10 0	Of polypropylene
	540259 90 0	Other
651.69		**Other yarn, multiple (folded) or cabled, not put up for retail sale**
		Of nylon or other polyamides
	540261 10 0	Measuring, per single yarn, not more than 7 tex
	540261 30 0	Measuring, per single yarn, more than 7 tex but not more than 33 tex
	540261 90 0	Measuring, per single yarn, more than 33 tex
		Of polyesters
	540262 10 0	Measuring, per single yarn, not more than 14 tex
	540262 90 0	Measuring, per single yarn, more than 14 tex
		Other
	540269 10 0	Of polypropylene
	540269 90 0	Other
		Artificial filament yarn (other than sewing thread); artificial monofilament, n.e.s.; strip and the like of artificial textile materials, n.e.s.
651.71	540620 00 0	**Yarn (other than sewing thread) of artificial filaments, put up for retail sale**
651.72		**Textured yarn, not put up for retail sale**
	540320 10 0	Of cellulose acetate
	540320 90 0	Other
651.73	540310 00 0	**High tenacity yarn of viscose rayon, not put up for retail sale**
651.74	540331 00 0	**Other yarn, single, of viscose rayon, untwisted or with a twist not exceeding 120 turns per metre, not put up for retail sale**
651.75		**Other yarn, single**
	540332 00 0	Of viscose rayon, with a twist exceeding 120 turns per metre
		Of cellulose acetate
	540333 10 0	Single, untwisted or with a twist not exceeding 250 turns per metre
	540333 90 0	Other
	540339 00 0	Other
651.76		**Other artificial filament yarn (other than sewing thread), not put up for retail sale (including monofilament of less than 67 decitex)**
	540341 00 0	Of viscose rayon
	540342 00 0	Of cellulose acetate
	540349 00 0	Other
651.77	540500 00 0	**Artificial monofilament of 67 decitex or more and of which no cross-sectional dimension exceeds 1 mm; strip and the like (eg., artificial straw) of artificial textile materials of an apparent width not exceeding 5 mm**
		Yarn (other than sewing thread) of staple fibres; synthetic monofilament, n.e.s.; strip and the like of synthetic textile materials of an apparent width not exceeding 5 mm
651.81	551110 00 0	**Yarn (other than sewing thread) containing 85% or more by weight of synthetic staple fibres, put up for retail sale**
651.82		**Yarn (other than sewing thread) containing 85% or more by weight of synthetic staple fibres, not put up for retail sale**
		Containing 85 % or more by weight of staple fibres of nylon or other polyamides
	550911 00 0	Single yarn
	550912 00 0	Multiple (folded) or cabled yarn
		Containing 85 % or more by weight of polyester staple fibres
		Single yarn
	550921 10 0	Unbleached or bleached
	550921 90 0	Other
		Multiple (folded) or cabled yarn
	550922 10 0	Unbleached or bleached
	550922 90 0	Other
		Containing 85 % or more by weight of acrylic or modacrylic staple fibres
		Single yarn
	550931 10 0	Unbleached or bleached
	550931 90 0	Other
		Multiple (folded) or cabled yarn
	550932 10 0	Unbleached or bleached
	550932 90 0	Other
		Other yarn, containing 85 % or more by weight of synthetic staple fibres
		Single yarn
	550941 10 0	Unbleached or bleached
	550941 90 0	Other

S.I.T.C. (R3)	Commodity Code No	Trade description
cont 651.82		Multiple (folded) or cabled yarn
	550942 10 0	Unbleached or bleached
	550942 90 0	Other
651.83	551120 00 0	**Yarn (other than sewing thread) of synthetic staple fibres, containing less than 85% by weight of such fibres, put up for retail sale**
651.84		**Yarn (other than sewing thread) of synthetic staple fibres, containing less than 85% by weight of these fibres, not put up for retail sale**
		Other yarn, of polyester staple fibres
	550951 00 0	Mixed mainly or solely with artificial staple fibres
		Mixed mainly or solely with wool or fine animal hair
	550952 10 0	Unbleached or bleached
	550952 90 0	Other
	550953 00 0	Mixed mainly or solely with cotton
	550959 00 0	Other
		Other yarn, of acrylic or modacrylic staple fibres
		Mixed mainly or solely with wool or fine animal hair
	550961 10 0	Unbleached or bleached
	550961 90 0	Other
	550962 00 0	Mixed mainly or solely with cotton
	550969 00 0	Other
		Other yarn
		Mixed mainly or solely with wool or fine animal hair
	550991 10 0	Unbleached or bleached
	550991 90 0	Other
	550992 00 0	Mixed mainly or solely with cotton
	550999 00 0	Other
651.85	551130 00 0	**Yarn of artificial staple fibres, put up for retail sale**
651.86		**Yarn (other than sewing thread) containing 85% or more by weight of artificial staple fibres, not put up for retail sale**
	551011 00 0	Single yarn
	551012 00 0	Multiple (folded) or cabled yarn
651.87		**Yarn (other than sewing thread) of artificial staple fibres containing less than 85% by weight of these fibres, not put up for retail sale**
	551020 00 0	Other yarn, mixed mainly or solely with wool or fine animal hair
	551030 00 0	Other yarn, mixed mainly or solely with cotton
	551090 00 0	Other yarn
651.88		**Synthetic monofilament of 67 decitex or more and of which no cross- sectional dimension exceeds 1 mm; strip and the like (for example, artificial straw) of synthetic textile materials of an apparent width not exceeding 5 mm**
		Monofilament
	540410 10 0	Elastomeric
	540410 90 0	Other
		Other
		Of polypropylene
	540490 11 0	Decorative strips of the kind used for packaging
	540490 19 0	Other
	540490 90 0	Other

Yarn of textile fibres, n.e.s. (including paper yarn and yarn, slivers and rovings of glass fibre)

S.I.T.C. (R3)	Commodity Code No	Trade description
651.91	560500 00 0	**Metallized yarn, being textile yarn, or strip or the like of heading 651.77 or 651.88, combined with metal in the form of thread, strip or powder or covered with metal.**
651.92		**Silk yarn (other than yarn spun from silk waste) not put up for retail sale**
	500400 10 0	Unbleached, scoured or bleached
	500400 90 0	Other
651.93		**Yarn spun from silk waste, not put up for retail sale**
	500500 10 0	Unbleached, scoured or bleached
	500500 90 0	Other
651.94		**Silk yarn and yarn spun from silk waste, put up for retail sale; silkworm gut**
	500600 10 0	Silk yarn
	500600 90 0	Yarn spun from noil or other silk waste; silk worm gut
651.95		**Slivers, rovings, yarn and chopped strands, of glass fibres**
	*701911 00 0	Chopped strands, of a length of not more than 50 mm
	*701912 00 0	Rovings
		Other
	*701919 10 0	Of filaments
	*701919 90 0	Other

S.I.T.C. (R3)	Commodity Code No	Trade description
651.96		**Flax yarn**
		Single
		Not put up for retail sale
		Measuring 833.3 decitex or more (not exceeding 12 metric number)
	530610 11 0	Unbleached
	530610 19 0	Other
		Measuring less than 833.3 decitex but not less than 277.8 decitex (exceeding 12 metric number but not exceeding 36 metric number)
	530610 31 0	Unbleached
	530610 39 0	Other
	530610 50 0	Measuring less than 277.8 decitex (exceeding 36 metric number)
	530610 90 0	Put up for retail sale
		Multiple (folded) or cabled
		Not put up for retail sale
	530620 11 0	Unbleached
	530620 19 0	Other
	530620 90 0	Put up for retail sale
651.97		**Yarn of jute or of other textile bast fibres of heading 264**
		Single
	530710 10 0	Measuring 1 000 decitex or less (10 metric number or more)
	530710 90 0	Measuring more than 1 000 decitex (less than 10 metric number)
	530720 00 0	Multiple (folded) or cabled
651.99		**Yarn of other vegetable textile fibres; paper yarn**
	530810 00 0	Coir yarn
		True hemp yarn
	530820 10 0	Not put up for retail sale
	530820 90 0	Put up for retail sale
	530830 00 0	Paper yarn
		Other
		Ramie yarn
	530890 11 0	Measuring 833.3 decitex or more (not exceeding 12 metric number)
	530890 13 0	Measuring less than 833.3 decitex but not less than 277.8 decitex (exceeding 12 metric number but not exceeding 36 metric number)
	530890 19 0	Measuring less than 277.8 decitex (exceeding 36 metric number)
	530890 90 0	Other

COTTON FABRICS, WOVEN (NOT INCLUDING NARROW OR SPECIAL FABRICS)

Cotton gauze, pile and chenille fabrics, woven

S.I.T.C. (R3)	Commodity Code No	Trade description
652.11	580310 00 0	**Cotton gauze (other than narrow fabrics of heading 656)**
652.12	580211 00 0	**Terry towelling and similar woven terry fabrics, of cotton(other than fabrics of heading 656), unbleached**
652.13	580219 00 0	**Other terry towelling and similar woven terry fabrics, of cotton other than fabrics of heading 656**
652.14		**Pile fabrics, woven, of cotton (other than terry towelling or similar woven terry fabrics of headings 652.12, 652.13 and 656.1), uncut**
		Of cotton
	580121 00 0	Uncut weft pile fabrics
	580124 00 0	Warp pile fabrics, épinglé (uncut)
652.15		**Other pile fabrics and chenille fabrics, woven, of cotton (other than terry towelling or similar terry fabrics of headings 652.12, 652.13 and 656.1)**
	580122 00 0	Cut corduroy
	580123 00 0	Other weft pile fabrics
	580125 00 0	Warp pile fabrics, cut
	580126 00 0	Chenille fabrics

Cotton fabrics, woven, unbleached (other than gauze and pile and chenille fabrics)

S.I.T.C. (R3)	Commodity Code No	Trade description
652.21		**Woven fabrics containing 85% or more by weight of cotton, unbleached, weighing not more than 200 g/m^2**
		Plain weave, weighing not more than 100 g/m^2
	520811 10 0	Fabrics for the manufacture of bandages, dressings and medical gauzes
	520811 90 0	Other
		Plain weave, weighing more than 100 g/m^2
		Plain weave, weighing more than 100 g/m^2 but not more than 130 g/m^2 and of a width
	520812 11 0	Not exceeding 115 cm
	520812 13 0	Exceeding 115 cm but not exceeding 145 cm
	520812 15 0	Exceeding 145 cm but not exceeding 165 cm
	520812 19 0	Exceeding 165 cm
		Plain weave, weighing more than 130 g/m^2 and of a width
	520812 91 0	Not exceeding 115 cm
	520812 93 0	Exceeding 115 cm but not exceeding 145 cm
	520812 95 0	Exceeding 145 cm but not exceeding 165 cm
	520812 99 0	Exceeding 165 cm

S.I.T.C. (R3)	Commodity Code No	Trade description
cont		
652.21	520813 00 0	3-thread or 4-thread twill, including cross twill
	520819 00 0	Other fabrics
652.22		**Woven fabrics containing 85% or more by weight of cotton, unbleached, weighing more than 200 g/m^2**
	520911 00 0	Plain weave
	520912 00 0	3-thread or 4-thread twill, including cross twill
	520919 00 0	Other fabrics
652.23		**Woven cotton fabrics, containing less than 85% by weight of cotton, unbleached, mixed mainly or solely with man-made fibres, weighing not more than 200 g/m^2**
		Plain weave
	521011 10 0	Of a width not exceeding 165 cm
	521011 90 0	Of a width exceeding 165 cm
	521012 00 0	3-thread or 4-thread twill, including cross twill
	521019 00 0	Other fabrics
652.24		**Woven cotton fabrics, containing less than 85% by weight of cotton, unbleached, mixed mainly or solely with man-made fibres, weighing more than 200 g/m^2**
	521111 00 0	Plain weave
	521112 00 0	3-thread or 4-thread twill, including cross twill
	521119 00 0	Other fabrics
652.25		**Other woven fabrics of cotton, unbleached, weighing not more than 200 g/m^2**
	521211 10 0	Mixed mainly or solely with flax
	521211 90 0	Otherwise mixed
652.26		**Other woven fabrics of cotton, unbleached, weighing more than 200 g/m^2**
	521221 10 0	Mixed mainly or solely with flax
	521221 90 0	Otherwise mixed
		Other woven fabrics, containing 85% or more by weight of cotton, bleached, dyed, printed or otherwise finished, weighing not more than 200 g/m^2
652.31		....bleached
		Plain weave, weighing not more than 100 g/m^2
	520821 10 0	Fabrics for the manufacture of bandages, dressings and medical gauzes
	520821 90 0	Other
		Plain weave, weighing more than 100 g/m^2
		Plain weave, weighing more than 100 g/m^2 but not more than 130 g/m^2 and of a width
	520822 11 0	Not exceeding 115 cm
	520822 13 0	Exceeding 115 cm but not exceeding 145 cm
	520822 15 0	Exceeding 145 cm but not exceeding 165 cm
	520822 19 0	Exceeding 165 cm
		Plain weave, weighing more than 130 g/m^2 and of a width
	520822 91 0	Not exceeding 115 cm
	520822 93 0	Exceeding 115 cm but not exceeding 145 cm
	520822 95 0	Exceeding 145 cm but not exceeding 165 cm
	520822 99 0	Exceeding 165 cm
	520823 00 0	3-thread or 4-thread twill, including cross twill
	520829 00 0	Other fabrics
652.32		....dyed
	520831 00 0	Plain weave, weighing not more than 100 g/m^2
		Plain weave, weighing more than 100 g/m^2
		Plain weave, weighing more than 100 g/m^2 but not more than 130 g/m^2 and of a width
	520832 11 0	Not exceeding 115 cm
	520832 13 0	Exceeding 115 cm but not exceeding 145 cm
	520832 15 0	Exceeding 145 cm but not exceeding 165 cm
	520832 19 0	Exceeding 165 cm
		Plain weave, weighing more than 130 g/m^2 and of a width
	520832 91 0	Not exceeding 115 cm
	520832 93 0	Exceeding 115 cm but not exceeding 145 cm
	520832 95 0	Exceeding 145 cm but not exceeding 165 cm
	520832 99 0	Exceeding 165 cm
	520833 00 0	3-thread or 4-thread twill, including cross twill
	520839 00 0	Other fabrics
652.33		....of yarns of different colour
	520841 00 0	Plain weave, weighing not more than 100 g/m^2
	520842 00 0	Plain weave, weighing more than 100 g/m^2
	520843 00 0	3-thread or 4-thread twill, including cross twill
	520849 00 0	Other fabrics
652.34		....printed
	520851 00 0	Plain weave, weighing not more than 100 g/m^2
		Plain weave, weighing more than 100 g/m^2
	520852 10 0	Plain weave, weighing more than 100 g/m^2 but not more than 130 g/m^2
	520852 90 0	Plain weave, weighing more than 130 g/m^2

S.I.T.C. (R3)	Commodity Code No	Trade description
cont 652.34	520853 00 0	3-thread or 4-thread twill, including cross twill
	520859 00 0	Other fabrics

Other woven fabrics, containing 85% or more by weight of cotton, bleached, dyed, printed or otherwise finished, weighing more than 200 g/m^2

652.41		....bleached
	520921 00 0	Plain weave
	520922 00 0	3-thread or 4-thread twill, including cross twill
	520929 00 0	Other fabrics
652.42		....dyed
	520931 00 0	Plain weave
	520932 00 0	3-thread or 4-thread twill, including cross twill
	520939 00 0	Other fabrics
652.43	520942 00 0	....denim
652.44		....of yarns of different colours (other than denim)
	520941 00 0	Plain weave
	520943 00 0	Other fabrics of 3-thread or 4-thread twill, including cross twill
		Other fabrics
	520949 10 0	Jacquard fabrics of a width of more than 115 cm but less than 140 cm
	520949 90 0	Other
652.45		....printed
	520951 00 0	Plain weave
	520952 00 0	3-thread or 4-thread twill, including cross twill
	520959 00 0	Other fabrics

Other woven cotton fabrics, containing less than 85% by weight of cotton, mixed mainly or solely with man-made fibres, bleached, dyed, printed or otherwise finished, weighing not more than 200 g/m^2

652.51		....bleached
		Plain weave
	521021 10 0	Of a width not exceeding 165 cm
	521021 90 0	Of a width exceeding 165 cm
	521022 00 0	3-thread or 4-thread twill, including cross twill
	521029 00 0	Other fabrics
652.52		....dyed
		Plain weave
	521031 10 0	Of a width not exceeding 165 cm
	521031 90 0	Of a width exceeding 165 cm
	521032 00 0	3-thread or 4-thread twill, including cross twill
	521039 00 0	Other fabrics
652.53		....of yarns of different colours
	521041 00 0	Plain weave
	521042 00 0	3-thread or 4-thread twill, including cross twill
	521049 00 0	Other fabrics
652.54		....printed
	521051 00 0	Plain weave
	521052 00 0	3-thread or 4-thread twill, including cross twill
	521059 00 0	Other fabrics

Other woven cotton fabrics, containing less than 85% by weight of cotton, mixed mainly or solely with man-made fibres, bleached, dyed printed or otherwise finished, weighing more than 200 g/m^2

652.61		....bleached
	521121 00 0	Plain weave
	521122 00 0	3-thread or 4-thread twill, including cross twill
	521129 00 0	Other fabrics
652.62		....dyed
	521131 00 0	Plain weave
	521132 00 0	3-thread or 4-thread twill, including cross twill
	521139 00 0	Other fabrics
652.63	521142 00 0	....denim
652.64		....of yarns of different colours(other than denim)
	521141 00 0	Plain weave
	521143 00 0	Other fabrics of 3-thread or 4-thread twill, including cross twill
		Other fabrics
	*521149 10 0	Jacquard fabrics
	521149 90 0	Other

S.I.T.C. (R3)	Commodity Code No	Trade description
652.65		....printed
	521151 00 0	Plain weave
	521152 00 0	3-thread or 4-thread twill, including cross twill
	521159 00 0	Other fabrics
		Other woven fabrics of cotton
652.91		....bleached, weighing not more than 200 g/m^2
	521212 10 0	Mixed mainly or solely with flax
	521212 90 0	Otherwise mixed
652.92		....dyed, weighing not more than 200 g/m^2
	521213 10 0	Mixed mainly or solely with flax
	521213 90 0	Otherwise mixed
652.93		....of yarns of different colours, weighing not more than 200g/m^2
	521214 10 0	Mixed mainly or solely with flax
	521214 90 0	Otherwise mixed
652.94		....printed, weighing not more than 200 g/m^2
	521215 10 0	Mixed mainly or solely with flax
	521215 90 0	Otherwise mixed
652.95		....bleached, weighing more than 200 g/m^2
	521222 10 0	Mixed mainly or solely with flax
	521222 90 0	Otherwise mixed
652.96		....dyed, weighing more than 200 g/m^2
	521223 10 0	Mixed mainly or solely with flax
	521223 90 0	Otherwise mixed
652.97		....of different colours, weighing more than 200 g/m^2
	521224 10 0	Mixed mainly or solely with flax
	521224 90 0	Otherwise mixed
652.98		....printed, weighing more than 200 g/m^2
	521225 10 0	Mixed mainly or solely with flax
	521225 90 0	Otherwise mixed

FABRICS, WOVEN, OF MAN-MADE TEXTILE MATERIALS (NOT INCLUDING NARROW OR SPECIAL FABRICS)

Fabrics, woven, of synthetic filament yarn (including woven fabrics obtained from materials of heading 651.88), other than pile and chenille fabrics

S.I.T.C. (R3)	Commodity Code No	Trade description
653.11	540710 00 0	**Woven fabrics obtained from high tenacity yarn of nylon or other polyamides or of polyesters**
653.12		**Woven fabrics obtained from strip or the like**
		Of polyethylene or polypropylene, of a width of
	540720 11 0	Less than 3 m
	540720 19 0	3 m or more
	540720 90 0	Other
653.13	540730 00 0	**Fabrics consisting of layers of parallel synthetic filament yarns superimposed on each other at acute or right angles, the layers bonded at the intersections of the yarns by an adhesive or by thermal bonding**
653.14		**Other woven fabrics, containing 85% or more by weight of filaments of nylon or other polyamides**
	540741 00 0	Unbleached or bleached
	*540742 00 0	Dyed
	540743 00 0	Of yarns of different colours
	*540744 00 0	Printed
653.15		**Other woven fabrics, containing 85% or more by weight of textured polyester filaments**
	*540751 00 0	Unbleached or bleached
	*540752 00 0	Dyed
	*540753 00 0	Of yarns of different colours
	*540754 00 0	Printed
653.16		**Other woven fabrics, containing 85% or more by weight of non-textured polyester filaments**
	540761 10 0	Unbleached or bleached
	540761 30 0	Dyed
	540761 50 0	Of yarns of different colours
	540761 90 0	Printed
653.17		**Other woven fabrics, containing 85% or more by weight of synthetic filaments, n.e.s.**
	540771 00 0	Unbleached or bleached
	540772 00 0	Dyed
	*540773 00 0	Of yarns of different colours
	540774 00 0	Printed

S.I.T.C. (R3)	Commodity Code No	Trade description
653.18		**Other woven fabrics, containing less than 85% by weight of synthetic filaments, mixed mainly or solely with cotton**
	540781 00 0	Unbleached or bleached
	540782 00 0	Dyed
	*540783 00 0	Of yarns of different colours
	540784 00 0	Printed
653.19		**Woven fabrics of synthetic filaments, n.e.s**
	540791 00 0	Unbleached or bleached
	540792 00 0	Dyed
	*540793 00 0	Of yarns of different colours
	540794 00 0	Printed
		Fabrics, woven, of synthetic staple fibres, containing 85% or more by weight of such fibres, other than pile and chenille fabrics
653.21		**....of polyester staple fibres**
	551211 00 0	Unbleached or bleached
		Other
	551219 10 0	Printed
	551219 90 0	Other
653.25		**....of acrylic or modacrylic staple fibres**
	551221 00 0	Unbleached or bleached
		Other
	551229 10 0	Printed
	551229 90 0	Other
653.29		**....of other synthetic staple fibres**
	551291 00 0	Unbleached or bleached
		Other
	551299 10 0	Printed
	551299 90 0	Other
		Fabrics, woven, of synthetic staple fibres, containing less than 85% by weight of such fibres, mixed mainly or solely with cotton (other than pile and chenille fabrics)
653.31		**....of a weight not exceeding 170 g/m^2, of polyester staple fibres**
		Unbleached or bleached
		Of polyester staple fibres, plain weave
	551311 10 0	Of a width of 135 cm or less
	551311 30 0	Of a width of more than 135 cm but not more than 165 cm
	551311 90 0	Of a width of more than 165 cm
	551312 00 0	3-thread or 4-thread twill, including cross twill, of polyester staple fibres
	551313 00 0	Other woven fabrics of polyester staple fibres
		Dyed
		Of polyester staple fibres, plain weave
	551321 10 0	Of a width of 135 cm or less
	551321 30 0	Of a width of more than 135 cm but not more than 165 cm
	551321 90 0	Of a width of more than 165 cm
	551322 00 0	3-thread or 4-thread twill, including cross twill, of polyester staple fibres
	551323 00 0	Other woven fabrics of polyester staple fibres
		Of yarns of different colours
	551331 00 0	Of polyester staple fibres, plain weave
	551332 00 0	3-thread or 4-thread twill, including cross twill, of polyester staple fibres
	551333 00 0	Other woven fabrics of polyester staple fibres
		Printed
	551341 00 0	Of polyester staple fibres, plain weave
	551342 00 0	3-thread or 4-thread twill, including cross twill, of polyester staple fibres
	551343 00 0	Other woven fabrics of polyester staple fibres
653.32		**....of a weight not exceeding 170 g/m^2, of other synthetic staple**
		Unbleached or bleached
	551319 00 0	Other woven fabrics
		Dyed
	551329 00 0	Other woven fabrics
		Of yarns of different colours
	551339 00 0	Other woven fabrics
		Printed
	551349 00 0	Other woven fabrics
653.33		**....of a weight exceeding 170 g/m^2, of polyester staple fibres**
		Unbleached or bleached
	551411 00 0	Of polyester staple fibres, plain weave
	551412 00 0	3-thread or 4-thread twill, including cross twill, of polyester staple fibres
	551413 00 0	Other woven fabrics of polyester staple fibres
		Dyed
	551421 00 0	Of polyester staple fibres, plain weave
	551422 00 0	3-thread or 4-thread twill, including cross twill, of polyester staple fibres
	551423 00 0	Other woven fabrics of polyester staple fibres

S.I.T.C. (R3)	Commodity Code No	Trade description
cont 653.33		Of yarns of different colours
	551431 00 0	Of polyester staple fibres, plain weave
	551432 00 0	3-thread or 4-thread twill, including cross twill, of polyester staple fibres
	551433 00 0	Other woven fabrics of polyester staple fibres
		Printed
	551441 00 0	Of polyester staple fibres, plain weave
	551442 00 0	3-thread or 4-thread twill, including cross twill, of polyester staple fibres
	551443 00 0	Other woven fabrics of polyester staple fibres
653.34		....of a weight exceeding 170 g/m^2, of other synthetic staple
		Unbleached or bleached
	551419 00 0	Other woven fabrics
		Dyed
	551429 00 0	Other woven fabrics
		Of yarns of different colours
	551439 00 0	Other woven fabrics
		Printed
	551449 00 0	Other woven fabrics
		Fabrics, woven, of synthetic staple fibres, containing less than 85% by weight of such fibres, mixed mainly or solely with fibres other than cotton (other than pile and chenille fabrics)
653.41		....mixed mainly or solely with wool or fine animal hair
		Of polyester staple fibres
		Mixed mainly or solely with carded wool or fine animal hair (woollen)
	551513 11 0	Unbleached or bleached
	551513 19 0	Other
		Mixed mainly or solely with combed wool or fine animal hair (worsted)
	551513 91 0	Unbleached or bleached
	551513 99 0	Other
		Of acrylic or modacrylic staple fibres
		Mixed mainly or solely with carded wool or fine animal hair (woollen)
	551522 11 0	Unbleached or bleached
	551522 19 0	Other
		Mixed mainly or solely with combed wool or fine animal hair (worsted)
	551522 91 0	Unbleached or bleached
	551522 99 0	Other
		Other woven fabrics
		Mixed mainly or solely with carded wool or fine animal hair (woollen)
	551592 11 0	Unbleached or bleached
	551592 19 0	Other
		Mixed mainly or solely with combed wool or fine animal hair (worsted)
	551592 91 0	Unbleached or bleached
	551592 99 0	Other
653.42		....mixed mainly or solely with man-made filaments
		Of polyester staple fibres
	551512 10 0	Unbleached or bleached
	551512 30 0	Printed
	551512 90 0	Other
		Of acrylic or modacrylic staple fibres
		Mixed mainly or solely with man-made filaments
	551521 10 0	Unbleached or bleached
	551521 30 0	Printed
	551521 90 0	Other
		Other woven fabrics
	551591 10 0	Unbleached or bleached
	551591 30 0	Printed
	551591 90 0	Other
653.43		....mixed mainly or solely with fibres other than cotton, wool,
		Of polyester staple fibres
		Mixed mainly or solely with viscose rayon staple fibres
	551511 10 0	Unbleached or bleached
	551511 30 0	Printed
	551511 90 0	Other
		Other
	551519 10 0	Unbleached or bleached
	551519 30 0	Printed
	551519 90 0	Other
		Of acrylic or modacrylic staple fibres
	551529 10 0	Unbleached or bleached
	551529 30 0	Printed
	551529 90 0	Other
		Other woven fabrics
	551599 10 0	Unbleached or bleached
	551599 30 0	Printed
	551599 90 0	Other

S.I.T.C. (R3)	Commodity Code No	Trade description
		Fabrics, woven, of artificial filament yarn (including woven fabrics obtained from materials of heading 651.77)
653.51	540810 00 0	**Woven fabrics obtained from high tenacity yarn of viscose rayon**
653.52		**Other fabrics, woven, containing 85% or more by weight of artificial filaments or strip or the like (other than pile and chenille fabrics)**
	540821 00 0	Unbleached or bleached
		Dyed
	540822 10 0	Of a width exceeding 135 cm but not exceeding 155 cm, plain weave, twill weave, cross twill weave or satin weave
	540822 90 0	Other
		Of yarns of different colours
	540823 10 0	Jacquard fabrics of a width of more than 115 cm but less than 140 cm, of a weight exceeding 250 g/m^2
	540823 90 0	Other
	540824 00 0	Printed
653.59		**Fabrics, woven, of artificial filament yarn, n.e.s.**
	540831 00 0	Unbleached or bleached
	540832 00 0	Dyed
	540833 00 0	Of yarns of different colours
	540834 00 0	Printed
653.60		**Fabrics, woven, containing 85% or more by weight of artificial staple fibres (other than pile and chenille fabrics)**
	551611 00 0	Unbleached or bleached
	551612 00 0	Dyed
	551613 00 0	Of yarns of different colours
	551614 00 0	Printed
		Fabrics, woven, of artificial staple fibres, containing less than 85% by weight of such fibres (other than pile and chenille fabrics)
653.81		**....mixed mainly or solely with cotton**
	551641 00 0	Unbleached or bleached
	551642 00 0	Dyed
	551643 00 0	Of yarns of different colours
	551644 00 0	Printed
653.82		**....mixed mainly or solely with wool or fine animal hair**
	551631 00 0	Unbleached or bleached
	551632 00 0	Dyed
	551633 00 0	Of yarns of different colours
	551634 00 0	Printed
653.83		**....mixed mainly or solely with man-made filaments**
	551621 00 0	Unbleached or bleached
	551622 00 0	Dyed
		Of yarns of different colours
	551623 10 0	Jacquard fabrics of a width of 140 cm or more (mattress tickings)
	551623 90 0	Other
	551624 00 0	Printed
653.89		**....mixed mainly or solely with fibres other than cotton,**
	551691 00 0	Unbleached or bleached
	551692 00 0	Dyed
	551693 00 0	Of yarns of different colours
	551694 00 0	Printed
		Pile fabrics and chenille fabrics, woven, of man-made fibres other than fabrics of heading 652 or 656)
653.91		**Pile fabrics, uncut**
	580131 00 0	Uncut weft pile fabrics
	580134 00 0	Warp pile fabrics, épinglé (uncut)
653.93		**Other pile fabrics and chenille fabrics**
	580132 00 0	Cut corduroy
	580133 00 0	Other weft pile fabrics
	580135 00 0	Warp pile fabrics, cut
	580136 00 0	Chenille fabrics
		OTHER TEXTILE FABRICS, WOVEN
		Fabrics, woven, of silk or of silk waste
654.11	500710 00 0	**Fabrics of noil silk**

S.I.T.C. (R3)	Commodity Code No	Trade description
654.13		**Other silk fabrics containing 85% or more by weight of silk or of silk waste (other than noil silk)**
		Crêpes
	500720 11 0	Unbleached, scoured or bleached
	500720 19 0	Other
		Pongee, habutai, honan, shantung, corah and similar Far Eastern fabrics, wholly of silk (not mixed with noil or other silk waste or other textile materials)
	500720 21 0	Plain-woven, unbleached or not further processed than scoured
		Other
	500720 31 0	Plain-woven
	500720 39 0	Other
		Other
	500720 41 0	Diaphanous fabrics (open weave)
		Other
	500720 51 0	Unbleached, scoured or bleached
	500720 59 0	Dyed
		Of yarns of different colours
	500720 61 0	Of a width exceeding 57 cm but not exceeding 75 cm
	500720 69 0	Other
	500720 71 0	Printed
654.19		**Other silk fabrics**
	500790 10 0	Unbleached, scoured or bleached
	500790 30 0	Dyed
	500790 50 0	Of yarns of different colours
	500790 90 0	Printed
		Fabrics, woven, containing 85% or more by weight of wool or of fine animal hair (other than pile and chenille fabrics)
654.21		**....of carded wool or of carded fine animal hair**
		Of a weight not exceeding 300 g/m^2
		Loden fabrics
	511111 11 0	Of a value of ECU 2.50 or more per m^2
	511111 19 0	Other
		Other fabrics
	511111 91 0	Of woollen yarn, of a value of ECU 2.50 or more per m^2
	511111 99 0	Other
		Other
		Of a weight exceeding 300 g/m^2 but not exceeding 450 g/m^2
		Loden fabrics
	511119 11 0	Of a value of ECU 2.50 or more per m^2
	511119 19 0	Other
		Other fabrics
	511119 31 0	Of woollen yarn, of a value of ECU 2.50 or more per m^2
	511119 39 0	Other
		Of a weight exceeding 450 g/m^2
	511119 91 0	Of woollen yarn, of a value of ECU 2.50 or more per m^2
	511119 99 0	Other
654.22		**....of combed wool or of combed fine animal hair**
		Of a weight not exceeding 200 g/m^2
	*511211 10 0	Of a value of ECU 3 or more per m2
	*511211 90 0	Other
		Other
		Of a weight exceeding 200 g/m^2 but not exceeding 375 g/m^2
	*511219 11 0	Of a value of ECU 3 or more per m2
	*511219 19 0	Other
		Of a weight exceeding 375 g/m^2
	511219 91 0	Of a value of ECU 3 or more per m^2
	511219 99 0	Other
		Fabrics, woven, of wool or of fine animal hair, n.e.s.
654.31		**Fabrics, woven, of carded wool or of carded fine animal hair, containing less than 85% by weight of wool or fine animal hair, mixed mainly or solely with man-made filaments or man-made staple fibres**
	511120 00 0	Other, mixed mainly or solely with man-made filaments
		Other, mixed mainly or solely with man-made staple fibres
	511130 10 0	Of a weight not exceeding 300 g/m^2
	511130 30 0	Of a weight exceeding 300 g/m^2 but not exceeding 450 g/m^2
	511130 90 0	Of a weight exceeding 450 g/m^2
654.32		**Fabrics, woven, of combed wool or of combed fine animal hair, containing less than 85% by weight of wool or fine animal hair, mixed mainly or solely with man-made filaments or man-made staple fibres**
	511220 00 0	Other, mixed mainly or solely with man-made filaments
		Other, mixed mainly or solely with man-made staple fibres
	511230 10 0	Of a weight not exceeding 200 g/m^2
	511230 30 0	Of a weight exceeding 200 g/m^2 but not exceeding 375 g/m^2
	511230 90 0	Of a weight exceeding 375 g/m^2

S.I.T.C. (R3)	Commodity Code No	Trade description
654.33		**Fabrics, woven, of carded wool or of carded fine animal hair, containing less than 85% by weight of wool or fine animal hair, mixed mainly or solely with fibres other than man-made filaments or staple fibres**
	511190 10 0	Containing a total of more than 10 % by weight of textile materials of Chapter 50
		Other
	511190 91 0	Of a weight not exceeding 300 g/m^2
	511190 93 0	Of a weight exceeding 300 g/m^2 but not exceeding 450 g/m^2
	511190 99 0	Of a weight exceeding 450 g/m^2
654.34		**Fabrics, woven, of combed wool or of combed fine animal hair, containing less than 85% by weight of wool of fine animal hair, mixed mainly or solely with fibres other than man-made filaments or staple fibres**
	511290 10 0	Containing a total of more than 10 % by weight of textile materials of Chapter 50
		Other
	511290 91 0	Of a weight not exceeding 200 g/m^2
	511290 93 0	Of a weight exceeding 200 g/m^2 but not exceeding 375 g/m^2
	511290 99 0	Of a weight exceeding 375 g/m^2
654.35	580110 00 0	**Pile fabrics and chenille fabrics, woven, of wool or fine animal hair (other than fabrics of heading 652.1,654.9 or 656.1)**
		Fabrics, woven, of flax
654.41		**....containing 85% or more by weight of flax**
		Unbleached or bleached
		Unbleached, of a weight
	530911 11 0	Not exceeding 400 g/m^2
	530911 19 0	Exceeding 400 g/m^2
	530911 90 0	Bleached
		Other
	530919 10 0	Dyed or of yarns of different colours
	530919 90 0	Printed
654.42		**....containing less than 85% by weight of flax**
		Unbleached or bleached
	530921 10 0	Unbleached
	530921 90 0	Bleached
		Other
	530929 10 0	Dyed or of yarns of different colours
	530929 90 0	Printed
654.50		**Fabrics, woven, of jute or of other textile bast fibres of heading 264**
		Unbleached
	531010 10 0	Of a width not exceeding 150 cm
	531010 90 0	Of a width exceeding 150 cm
	531090 00 0	Other
654.60		**Fabrics, woven, of glass fibre (including narrow fabrics)**
	*701940 00 0	Made from rovings
		Other, of a width not exceeding 30 cm
	*701051 10 0	Of filaments
	*701051 90 0	Of staple fibres
	*701052 00 0	Of a width exceeding 30 cm, plain weave, weighing less than 250 g/m^2 of filaments measuring per single yarn not more than 136 tex
		Other
	*701059 10 0	Of filaments
	*701059 90 0	Of staple fibres
		Fabrics, woven, n.e.s.
654.91	580900 00 0	**Fabrics, woven, of metal thread or of metallized yarn of heading 651.91, of a kind used in apparel, as furnishing fabrics or for similar purposes, n.e.s.**
654.92	511300 00 0	**Fabrics, woven, of coarse animal hair or of horsehair**
654.93		**Fabrics, woven, of vegetable textile fibres, n.e.s.; woven fabrics of paper yarn**
	531100 10 0	Of ramie
	531100 90 0	Other
654.94		**Gauze (other than narrow fabrics) of textile materials (other than cotton)**
	580390 10 0	Of silk or silk waste
	580390 30 0	Of synthetic fibres
	580390 50 0	Of artificial fibres
	580390 90 0	Other
654.95		**Pile and chenille fabrics, n.e.s., of textile materials (other than wool, cotton and man-made fibres)**
	580190 10 0	Of flax
	580190 90 0	Other
654.96	580220 00 0	**Terry towelling and similar woven terry fabrics of textile materials (other than cotton)**

S.I.T.C. (R3)	Commodity Code No	Trade description
654.97	580230 00 0	**Tufted textile fabrics**
		KNITTED OR CROCHETED FABRICS (INCLUDING TUBULAR KNIT FABRICS, N.E.S., PILE FABRICS AND OPEN-WORK FABRICS), N.E.S.
		Pile fabrics (including 'long pile' fabrics and terry fabrics), knitted or crocheted, whether or not impregnated, coated, covered, or laminated.
655.11	600110 00 0	**'Long pile' fabrics**
655.12		**Looped pile fabrics**
	600121 00 0	Of cotton
	600122 00 0	Of man-made fibres
		Of other textile materials
	600129 10 0	Of wool or fine animal hair
	600129 90 0	Other
655.19		**Other pile fabrics, knitted or crocheted**
		Of cotton
	600191 10 0	Unbleached or bleached
	600191 30 0	Dyed
	600191 50 0	Of yarns of different colours
	600191 90 0	Printed
		Of man-made fibres
	600192 10 0	Unbleached or bleached
	600192 30 0	Dyed
	600192 50 0	Of yarns of different colours
	600192 90 0	Printed
		Of other textile materials
	600199 10 0	Of wool or fine animal hair
	600199 90 0	Other
		Other knitted or crocheted fabrics, not impregnated, coated, covered or laminated
655.21		**....of a width not exceeding 30 cm**
		Of a width not exceeding 30 cm containing by weight 5% or more of elastomeric yarn or rubber thread
	600210 10 0	Containing by weight 5 % or more of elastomeric yarn, but not containing rubber thread
	600210 90 0	Other
		Other of a width not exceeding 30 cm
	600220 10 0	Of wool or fine animal hair
		Of synthetic fibres
	600220 31 0	Raschel lace
	600220 39 0	Other
	600220 50 0	Of artificial fibres
	600220 70 0	Of cotton
	600220 90 0	Other
655.22		**Of a width exceeding 30 cm, containing 5% or more by weight of elastomeric yarn or rubber thread**
	600230 10 0	Containing by weight 5 % or more of elastomeric yarn, but not containing rubber thread
	600230 90 0	Other
655.23		**Other fabrics, warp knit (including those made on galloon knitting machines)**
	600241 00 0	Of wool or fine animal hair
		Of cotton
	600242 10 0	Unbleached or bleached
	600242 30 0	Dyed
	600242 50 0	Of yarns of different colours
	600242 90 0	Printed
		Of man-made fibres
		Of synthetic fibres
	600243 11 0	For curtains, including net curtain fabric
	600243 19 0	Raschel lace
		Other
	600243 31 0	Unbleached or bleached
	600243 33 0	Dyed
	600243 35 0	Of yarns of different colours
	600243 39 0	Printed
		Of artificial fibres
	600243 50 0	For curtains, including net curtain fabric
		Other
	600243 91 0	Unbleached or bleached
	600243 93 0	Dyed
	600243 95 0	Of yarns of different colours
	600243 99 0	Printed
	600249 00 0	Other
655.29		**Knitted or crocheted fabrics, n.e.s.**
	600291 00 0	Of wool or fine animal hair
		Of cotton
	600292 10 0	Unbleached or bleached

S.I.T.C. (R3)	Commodity Code No	Trade description
cont 655.29	600292 30 0	Dyed
	600292 50 0	Of yarns of different colours
	600292 90 0	Printed
		Of man-made fibres
		Of synthetic fibres
	600293 10 0	For curtains, including net curtain fabric
		Other
	600293 31 0	Unbleached or bleached
	600293 33 0	Dyed
	600293 35 0	Of yarns of different colours
	600293 39 0	Printed
		Of artificial fibres
	600293 91 0	For curtains, including net curtain fabric
	600293 99 0	Other
	600299 00 0	Other

TULLES, LACE, EMBROIDERY, RIBBONS, TRIMMINGS AND OTHER SMALL WARES

Narrow woven fabrics (other than goods of heading 656.2); narrow fabrics consisting of warp without weft assembled by means of an adhesive (bolducs)

S.I.T.C. (R3)	Commodity Code No	Trade description
656.11	580610 00 0	**Woven pile fabrics (incl. terry towelling and similar woven terry fabrics) and chenille fabrics**
656.12	580620 00 0	**Other woven fabrics containing by weight 5% or more of elastomeric yarn or rubber thread**
656.13		**Other woven fabrics**
		Of cotton
	580631 10 0	With real selvedges
	580631 90 0	Other
		Of man-made fibres
	580632 10 0	With real selvedges
	580632 90 0	Other
	580639 00 0	Of other textile materials
656.14	580640 00 0	**Fabrics consisting of warp without weft assembled by means of an adhesive (bolducs)**

Labels, badges and similar articles of textile materials, in the piece, in strips or cut to shape or size, not embroidered

S.I.T.C. (R3)	Commodity Code No	Trade description
656.21		**....woven**
	580710 10 0	With woven inscription
	580710 90 0	Other
656.29		**....other**
	580790 10 0	Of felt or nonwovens
	580790 90 0	Other

Gimped yarn, and strip and the like of heading 651.77 or 651.88, gimped (other than metallized yarn and gimped horsehair yarn); chenille yarn (including flock chenille yarn); loop-wale yarn; braids in the piece; ornamental trimmimgs in the piece (containing no embroidery, knitting or crochet); tassels, pompoms and similar articles

S.I.T.C. (R3)	Commodity Code No	Trade description
656.31		**Gimped yarn, and strip and the like of heading 651.77 or 651.88, gimped (other than metallized yarn and gimped horsehair yarn); chenille yarn (incl. flock chenille yarn); loop-wale yarn**
	560600 10 0	Loop wale-yarn
		Other
	560600 91 0	Gimped yarn
	560600 99 0	Other
656.32		**Braids in the piece; ornamental trimmings in the piece, without embroidery, other than knitted or crocheted; tassels, pompoms and similar articles**
	580810 00 0	Braids in the piece
	580890 00 0	Other

Tulles and other net fabrics (not including woven, knitted or crocheted fabrics); lace, in the piece, in strips or in motifs

S.I.T.C. (R3)	Commodity Code No	Trade description
656.41		**Tulles and other net fabrics**
		Plain
	580410 11 0	Knotted net fabrics
	580410 19 0	Other
	580410 90 0	Other
656.42		**Lace, mechanically made**
		Of man-made fibres
	580421 10 0	Made on mechanical bobbin machines
	580421 90 0	Other
		Of other textile materials
	580429 10 0	Made on mechanical bobbin machines
	580429 90 0	Other

S.I.T.C. (R3)	Commodity Code No	Trade description
656.43	580430 00 0	Lace, hand-made

Embroidery, in the piece, in strips or in motifs

S.I.T.C. (R3)	Commodity Code No	Trade description
656.51		**Embroidery without visible ground**
	581010 10 0	Of a value exceeding 35 ECU/kg (net weight)
	581010 90 0	Other
656.59		**Other embroidery**
		Of cotton
	581091 10 0	Of a value exceeding 17.5 ECU/kg (net weight)
	581091 90 0	Other
		Of man-made fibres
	581092 10 0	Of a value exceeding 17.5 ECU/kg (net weight)
	581092 90 0	Other
		Of other textile materials
	581099 10 0	Of a value exceeding 17.5 ECU/kg (net weight)
	581099 90 0	Other

SPECIAL YARNS, SPECIAL TEXTILE FABRICS AND RELATED PRODUCTS

Felt, whether or not impregnated, coated, covered or laminated, n.e.s.

S.I.T.C. (R3)	Commodity Code No	Trade description
657.11		**Needleloom felt and stitch-bonded fibre fabrics**
		Not impregnated, coated, covered or laminated
		Needleloom felt
	560210 11 0	Of jute or other textile bast fibres of heading 264
	560210 19 0	Of other textile materials
		Stitch-bonded fibre fabrics
	560210 31 0	Of wool or fine animal hair
	560210 35 0	Of coarse animal hair
	560210 39 0	Of other textile materials
	560210 90 0	Impregnated, coated, covered or laminated
657.12		**Other felt, not impregnated, coated, covered or laminated**
	560221 00 0	Of wool or fine animal hair
		Of other textile materials
	560229 10 0	Of coarse animal hair
	560229 90 0	Of other textile materials
657.19	560290 00 0	**Felt, impregnated, coated, covered or laminated, n.e.s.**
657.20		**Nonwovens, whether or not impregnated, coated, covered or laminated, n.e.s.**
		Of man-made filaments
		Weighing not more than 25 g/m^2
	*560311 10 0	Coated or covered
	*560311 90 0	Other
		Weighing more than 25 g/m^2 but not more than 70 g/m^2
	*560312 10 0	Coated or covered
	*560312 90 0	Other
		Weighing more than 70 g/m^2 but not more than 150 g/m^2
	*560313 10 0	Coated or covered
	*560313 90 0	Other
		Weighing more than 150 g/m^2
	*560314 10 0	Coated or covered
	*560314 90 0	Other
		Other
		Weighing not more than 25 g/m^2
	*560391 10 0	Coated or covered
	*560391 90 0	Other
		Weighing more than 25 g/m^2 but not more than 70 g/m^2
	*560392 10 0	Coated or covered
	*560392 90 0	Other
		Weighing more than 70 g/m^2 but not more than 150 g/m^2
	*560393 10 0	Coated or covered
	*560393 90 0	Other
		Weighing more than 150 g/m^2
	*560394 10 0	Coated or covered
	*560394 90 0	Other

Coated or impregnated textile fabrics and products, n.e.s.

S.I.T.C. (R3)	Commodity Code No	Trade description
657.31		**Textile fabrics coated with gum or amylaceous substances, of a kind used for the outer covers of books or the like; tracing cloth; prepared painting canvas; buckram and similar stiffened textile fabrics of a kind used for hat foundations**
	590110 00 0	Textile fabrics coated with gum or amylaceous substances, of a kind used for the outer covers of books or the like
	590190 00 0	Other

S.I.T.C. (R3)	Commodity Code No	Trade description
657.32		**Textile fabrics impregnated, coated, covered or laminated with plastics, other than those of heading 657.93**
		With polyvinyl chloride
	590310 10 0	Impregnated
	590310 90 0	Coated, covered or laminated
		With polyurethane
	590320 10 0	Impregnated
	590320 90 0	Coated, covered or laminated
		Other
	590390 10 0	Impregnated
		Coated, covered or laminated
	590390 91 0	With cellulose derivatives or other plastics, with the fabric forming the right side
	590390 99 0	Other
657.33		**Rubberized textile fabrics, other than those of heading 657.93**
		Adhesive tape of a width not exceeding 20 cm
	590610 10 0	Of a width not exceeding 10 cm
	590610 90 0	Of a width exceeding 10 cm but not exceeding 20 cm
		Other
	590691 00 0	Knitted or crocheted
		Other
	590699 10 0	Fabrics composed of parallel textile yarns agglomerated with rubber
	590699 90 0	Other
657.34		**Textile fabrics otherwise impregnated, coated or covered; painted canvas being theatrical scenery, studio back-cloths or the like**
	590700 10 0	Oil cloth and other textile fabrics coated with preparations with a basis of drying oil
	590700 90 0	Other
657.35		**Textile wall coverings**
	590500 10 0	Consisting of parallel yarns, fixed on a backing of any material
		Other
		Of flax
	590500 31 0	Unbleached
	590500 39 0	Other
	590500 50 0	Of jute
	590500 70 0	Of man-made fibres
	590500 90 0	Other
657.40	581100 00 0	**Quilted textile products in the piece composed of one or more layers of textile materials assembled with padding by stitching or otherwise, n.e.s**
		Twine, cordage, ropes and cables and manufactures thereof (e.g., fishing nets, ropemakers' wares)
657.51		**Twine, cordage, ropes and cables, whether or not plaited or braided and whether or not impregnated, coated, covered or sheathed with rubber or plastics**
	560710 00 0	Of jute or other textile bast fibres of heading 264
		Of sisal or other textile fibres of the genus *Agave*
	560721 00 0	Binder or baler twine
		Other
	560729 10 0	Measuring more than 100 000 decitex (10 g/m)
	560729 90 0	Measuring 100 000 decitex (10 g/m) or less
	560730 00 0	Of abaca (Manila hemp or *Musa textilis Nee*) or other hard (leaf) fibres
		Of polyethylene or polypropylene
	560741 00 0	Binder or baler twine
		Other
		Measuring more than 50 000 decitex (5 g/m)
	560749 11 0	Plaited
	560749 19 0	Other
	560749 90 0	Measuring 50 000 decitex (5 g/m) or less
		Of other synthetic fibres
		Of nylon or of other polyamides or polyesters
		Measuring more than 50 000 decitex (5 g/m)
	560750 11 0	Plaited
	560750 19 0	Other
	560750 30 0	Measuring 50 000 decitex or less
	560750 90 0	Of other synthetic fibres
	560790 00 0	Other
657.52		**Knotted netting of twine, cordage or rope; made up fishing nets and other made up nets, of textile materials**
		Of man-made textile materials
		Made up fishing nets
		Of nylon or other polyamides
	560811 11 0	Of twine, cordage, rope or cable
	560811 19 0	Of yarn
		Other
	560811 91 0	Of twine, cordage, rope or cable
	560811 99 0	Of yarn

S.I.T.C. (R3)	Commodity Code No	Trade description
cont 657.52		Other
		Made up nets
		Of nylon or other polyamides
	560819 11 0	Of twine, cordage or rope
	560819 19 0	Other
		Other
	560819 31 0	Of twine, cordage or rope
	560819 39 0	Other
		Other
	560819 91 0	Of nylon or other polyamides
	560819 99 0	Other
	560890 00 0	Other
657.59	560900 00 0	**Articles of yarn, strip or the like of heading 651.77 or 651.88, twine, cordage, rope or cables, n.e.s.**
		Hat-shapes, hat-forms, hat bodies and hoods
657.61	650100 00 0	**Hat-forms, hat bodies and hoods of felt, neither blocked to shape nor with made brims; plateaux and manchons (including slit manchons), of felt**
657.62	650200 00 0	**Hat-shapes, plaited or made by assembling strips of any material, neither blocked to shape nor with made brims, nor lined nor trimmed**
		Wadding, wicks, and textile fabrics and articles for use in machinery or plant
657.71		**Wadding of textile materials and articles thereof; textile fibres not exceeding 5 mm in length (flock), textile dust and mill neps**
		Sanitary towels and tampons, napkins and napkin liners for babies and similar sanitary articles, of wadding
	560110 10 0	Of man-made fibres
	560110 90 0	Of other textile materials
		Wadding; other articles of wadding
		Of cotton
	560121 10 0	Absorbent
	560121 90 0	Other
		Of man-made fibres
	560122 10 0	Rolls of a diameter not exceeding 8 mm
		Other
	560122 91 0	Of synthetic fibres
	560122 99 0	Of artificial fibres
	560129 00 0	Other
	560130 00 0	Textile flock and dust and mill neps
657.72	590800 00 0	**Textile wicks, woven, plaited or knitted, for lamps, stoves lighters, candles or the like; incandescent gas mantles and tubular knitted fabric therefor, whether or not impregnated**
657.73		**Textile products and articles, for technical uses**
	591110 00 0	Textile fabrics, felt and felt-lined woven fabrics, coated, covered or laminated with rubber, leather or other material, of a kind used for card clothing, and similar fabric for other technical uses
	591120 00 0	Bolting cloth, whether or not made up
		Textile fabrics and felts, endless or fitted with linking devices, of a kind used in paper-making or similar machines (for example, for pulp or asbestos-cement)
		Weighing less than 650 g/m^2
		Of silk or of man-made fibres
	591131 11 0	Woven fabrics, felted or not, of synthetic fibres, of a kind used in paper-making machines
	591131 19 0	Other
	591131 90 0	Of other textile materials
		Weighing 650 g/m^2 or more
	591132 10 0	Of silk or man-made fibres
	591132 90 0	Of other textile materials
	591140 00 0	Straining cloth of a kind used in oil presses or the like, including that of human hair
		Other
	591190 10 0	Of felt
	591190 90 0	Other
		Rubber thread and cord, textile covered; textile yarn, and strip and the like of heading 651.77 or 651.88, impregnated, coated, covered or sheathed with rubber or plastics
657.81	560410 00 0	**Rubber thread and cord, textile covered**
657.85	560420 00 0	**High tenacity yarn of polyesters, of nylon or other polyamides or of viscose rayon, impregnated**
657.89	560490 00 0	**Other**
		Special products of textile materials
657.91		**Textile hosepiping and similar textile tubing, with or without lining, armour or accessories of other materials**
	590900 10 0	Of synthetic fibres
	590900 90 0	Of other textile materials

S.I.T.C. (R3)	Commodity Code No	Trade description
657.92	591000 00 0	Transmission or conveyor belts or belting, of textile material, whether or not reinforced with metal or other material
657.93		Tyre cord fabric of high tenacity yarn of nylon or other polyamides, polyesters or viscose rayon
		Of nylon or other polyamides
	590210 10 0	Impregnated with rubber
	590210 90 0	Other
		Of polyesters
	590220 10 0	Impregnated with rubber
	590220 90 0	Other
		Other
	590290 10 0	Impregnated with rubber
	590290 90 0	Other

MADE-UP ARTICLES, WHOLLY OR CHIEFLY OF TEXTILE MATERIALS, N.E.S.

Sacks and bags, of textile materials, of a kind used for the packing of goods

S.I.T.C. (R3)	Commodity Code No	Trade description
658.11		....of jute or of other textile bast fibres of heading 264
	630510 10 0	Used
	630510 90 0	Other
658.12	630520 00 0	....of cotton
658.13		....of man-made textile materials
		Flexible intermediate bulk containers
		Of polyethylene or polypropylene strip or the like
	*630532 11 0	Knitted or crocheted
		Other
	*630532 81 0	Of fabric weighing 120 g/m^2 or less
	*630532 89 0	Of fabric weighing more than 120 g/m^2
		Other
		Other, of polyethylene or polypropylene strip or the like
	*630533 10 0	Knitted or crocheted
		Other
	*630533 91 0	Of fabric weighing 120 g/m^2 or less
	*630533 99 0	Of fabric weighing more than 120 g/m^2
	*630539 00 0	Other
658.19	630590 00 0	....of other textile materials

Tarpaulins, awnings and sunblinds; tents; sails for boats, sailboards or landcraft; camping goods

S.I.T.C. (R3)	Commodity Code No	Trade description
658.21		**Tarpaulins, awnings and sunblinds**
	630611 00 0	Of cotton
	630612 00 0	Of synthetic fibres
	630619 00 0	Of other textile materials
658.22		**Tents**
	630621 00 0	Of cotton
	630622 00 0	Of synthetic fibres
	630629 00 0	Of other textile materials
658.23		**Sails**
	630631 00 0	Of synthetic fibres
	630639 00 0	Of other textile materials
658.24		**Pneumatic mattresses**
	630641 00 0	Of cotton
	630649 00 0	Of other textile materials
658.29		**Camping goods, n.e.s.**
	630691 00 0	Of cotton
	630699 00 0	Of other textile materials

Blankets and travelling rugs (other than electric)

S.I.T.C. (R3)	Commodity Code No	Trade description
658.31		....of wool or fine animal hair
	630120 10 0	Knitted or crocheted
		Other
	630120 91 0	Wholly of wool or fine animal hair
	630120 99 0	Other
658.32		....of cotton
	630130 10 0	Knitted or crocheted
	630130 90 0	Other
658.33		....of synthetic fibres
	630140 10 0	Knitted or crocheted
	630140 90 0	Other

S.I.T.C. (R3)	Commodity Code No	Trade description
658.39		....of other textile materials
	630190 10 0	Knitted or crocheted
	630190 90 0	Other
		Bed linen, table linen, toilet linen and kitchen linen
658.41		**Bed linen, knitted or crocheted**
	630210 10 0	Of cotton
	630210 90 0	Of other textile materials
658.42		**Bed linen, not knitted nor crocheted, of cotton**
		Printed
	630221 00 0	Of cotton
		Other bed linen
		Of cotton
	630231 10 0	Mixed with flax
	*630231 90 0	Other
658.43		**Bed linen, not knitted nor crocheted, of other textile materials**
		Printed
		Of man-made fibres
	630222 10 0	Nonwovens
	630222 90 0	Other
		Of other textile materials
	630229 10 0	Of flax or ramie
	630229 90 0	Of other textile materials
		Other bed linen
		Of man-made fibres
	630232 10 0	Nonwovens
	630232 90 0	Other
		Of other textile materials
	630239 10 0	Of flax
	630239 30 0	Of ramie
	630239 90 0	Of other textile materials
658.44	630240 00 0	**Table linen, knitted or crocheted**
658.45		**Table linen, not knitted nor crocheted, of cotton**
	630251 10 0	Mixed with flax
	630251 90 0	Other
658.46		**Table linen, not knitted nor crocheted, of other textile materials**
	630252 00 0	Of flax
		Of man-made fibres
	630253 10 0	Nonwovens
	630253 90 0	Other
	630259 00 0	Of other textile materials
658.47		**Toilet and kitchen linen of cotton**
	630260 00 0	Toilet linen and kitchen linen, of terry towelling or similar terry fabrics, of cotton
	630291 10 0	Mixed with flax
	630291 90 0	Other
658.48		**Toilet and kitchen linen of other fibres**
	630292 00 0	Of flax
		Of man-made fibres
	630293 10 0	Nonwovens
	630293 90 0	Other
	630299 00 0	Of other textile materials
		Curtains and other furnishing articles, n.e.s., of textile materials
658.51		**Curtains (including drapes) and interior blinds; curtain or bed valences**
		Knitted or crocheted
	630311 00 0	Of cotton
	630312 00 0	Of synthetic fibres
	630319 00 0	Of other textile materials
		Other
	630391 00 0	Of cotton
		Of synthetic fibres
	630392 10 0	Nonwovens
	630392 90 0	Other
		Of other textile materials
	630399 10 0	Nonwovens
	630399 90 0	Other
658.52		**Bedspreads**
	630411 00 0	Knitted or crocheted
		Other
	630419 10 0	Of cotton

S.I.T.C. (R3)	Commodity Code No	Trade description
cont 658.52	630419 30 0	Of flax or of ramie
	630419 90 0	Of other textile materials
658.59		**Furnishing articles, n.e.s.**
	630491 00 0	Knitted or crocheted
	630492 00 0	Not knitted or crocheted, of cotton
	630493 00 0	Not knitted or crocheted, of synthetic fibres
	630499 00 0	Not knitted or crocheted, of other textile materials
		Made-up articles of textile materials, n.e.s.
658.91	580500 00 0	**Tapestries, hand-woven, of the type Gobelins, Flanders, Aubusson, Beauvais and the like, and needle-worked tapestries (e.g., petit point, cross stitch), whether or not made up**
658.92		**Floor-cloths, dish-cloths, dusters and similar cleaning cloths**
	630710 10 0	Knitted or crocheted
	630710 30 0	Nonwovens
	630710 90 0	Other
658.93		**Life-jackets and life-belts and other made up articles, including dress patterns**
	630720 00 0	Life-jackets and life-belts
		Other
	630790 10 0	Knitted or crocheted
		Other
	630790 91 0	Of felt
	630790 99 0	Other
658.99	630800 00 0	**Sets consisting of woven fabric and yarn, with or without accessories, for making up into rugs, tapestries, tablecloths or similar textile articles, put up in packings for retail sale**
		FLOOR COVERINGS, ETC.
		Linoleum and similar floor coverings
659.11	481500 00 0	**Floor coverings on a base of paper or of paperboard, whether or not cut to size**
659.12		**Linoleum, whether or not cut to shape; floor coverings consisting of a coating or covering applied on a textile backing, whether or not cut to shape**
	590410 00 0	Linoleum
		Other
		With a base consisting of needleloom felt or nonwovens
	590491 10 0	With a base consisting of needleloom felt
	590491 90 0	With a base consisting of nonwovens
	590492 00 0	With other textile base
		Carpets and other textile floor coverings, knotted, whether or not made up
659.21		**....of wool or fine animal hair**
	570110 10 0	Containing a total of more than 10 % by weight of silk or of waste silk other than noil
		Other
	570110 91 0	Comprising not more than 350 knots per metre of warp
	570110 93 0	Comprising more than 350 but not more than 500 knots per metre of warp
	570110 99 0	Comprising more than 500 knots per metre of warp
659.29		**....of other textile materials**
	570190 10 0	Of silk, of waste silk other than noil, of synthetic fibres, of yarn falling within heading 651.91 or of textile materials containing metal threads
	570190 90 0	Of other textile materials
659.30	570210 00 0	**'Kelem', 'Schumacks', 'Karamanie' and similar hand-woven rugs**
		Carpets and other textile floor coverings, tufted, whether or not made up
659.41		**....of wool or fine animal hair**
	570310 10 0	Printed tufted
	570310 90 0	Other
659.42		**....of nylon or other polyamides**
		Printed tufted
	570320 11 0	Tiles, having a maximum surface area of $0.3m^2$
	570320 19 0	Other
		Other
	570320 91 0	Tiles, having a maximum surface area of $0.3m^2$
	570320 99 0	Other
659.43		**....of other man-made textile fibres**
		Of polypropylene
	570330 11 0	Tiles, having a maximum surface area of $0.3m^2$
	570330 19 0	Other

S.I.T.C. (R3)	Commodity Code No	Trade description
cont 659.43		Other
		Printed tufted
	570330 51 0	Tiles, having a maximum surface area of $0.3m^2$
	570330 59 0	Other
		Other
	570330 91 0	Tiles, having a maximum surface area of $0.3m^2$
	570330 99 0	Other
659.49		....of other textile materials
	570390 10 0	Tiles, having a maximum surface area of $0.3m^2$
	570390 90 0	Other
		Carpets and other textile floor coverings, woven, n.e.s., whether or not made up
659.51		....of wool or fine animal hair
		Of pile construction, not made up
	570231 10 0	Axminster
	570231 30 0	Wilton
	570231 90 0	Other
		Of pile construction, made up
	570241 10 0	Axminster
	570241 90 0	Other
	570251 00 0	Not of pile construction, not made up
	570291 00 0	Not of pile construction, made up
659.52		....of man-made textile materials
		Of pile construction, not made up
	570232 10 0	Axminster
	570232 90 0	Other
		Of pile construction, made up
	570242 10 0	Axminster
	570242 90 0	Other
	570252 00 0	Not of pile construction, not made up
	570292 00 0	Not of pile construction, made up
659.59		....of other textile materials
	570220 00 0	Floor coverings of coconut fibres (coir)
		Of pile construction, not made up
	570239 10 0	Of cotton
	570239 90 0	Other
		Of pile construction, made up
	570249 10 0	Of cotton
	570249 90 0	Other
	570259 00 0	Not of pile construction, not made up
	570299 00 0	Not of pile construction, made up
		Carpets and other textile floor coverings, n.e.s.
659.61		**Carpets and other textile floor coverings, of felt, not tufted or flocked, whether or not made up**
	570410 00 0	Tiles, having a maximum surface area of $0.3m^2$
	570490 00 0	Other
659.69		**Other carpets and other textile floor coverings, whether or not made up**
	570500 10 0	Of wool or fine animal hair
		Of man-made textile materials
	570500 31 0	Tiles, having a maximum surface area of $0.3m^2$
	570500 39 0	Other
	570500 90 0	Of other textile materials

DIVISION 66

NON-METALLIC MINERAL MANUFACTURES, N.E.S.

LIME, CEMENT, AND FABRICATED CONSTRUCTION MATERIALS (EXCEPT GLASS AND CLAY MATERIALS)

Quicklime, slaked lime and hydraulic lime (other than calcium oxide and hydroxide of heading 522.6)

661.11	252210 00 0	**Quicklime**
661.12	252220 00 0	**Slaked lime**
661.13	252230 00 0	**Hydraulic lime**

Portland cement, aluminous cement, slag cement, supersulphate cement and similar hydraulic cements, whether or not coloured or in the form of clinkers

661.21	252310 00 0	**Cement clinkers**

S.I.T.C. (R3)	Commodity Code No	Trade description
661.22		**Portland cement**
	252321 00 0	White cement, whether or not artificially coloured
	252329 00 0	Other
661.23	252330 00 0	**Aluminous cement**
661.29		**Other hydraulic cements**
	252390 10 0	Blast furnace cement
	252390 30 0	Pozzolanic cement
	252390 90 0	Other

Monumental or building stone, worked, and articles thereof

S.I.T.C. (R3)	Commodity Code No	Trade description
661.31	680100 00 0	**Setts, curbstones and flagstones, of natural stone (except slate)**
661.32		**Slate, worked, and articles of slate or of agglomerated slate**
	680300 10 0	Roofing and wall slates
	680300 90 0	Other
661.33	680210 00 0	**Tiles, cubes and similar articles of natural stone, whether or not rectangular, the largest surface area of which is capable of being enclosed in a square, the side of which is less than 7 cm ; artificially coloured granules, chippings, and powder of natural stone (including slate)**
661.34	680221 00 0	**Marble, travertine and alabaster and articles thereof, simply cut or sawn, with a flat or even surface**
661.35		**Monumental or building stone (except slate) and articles thereof, n.e.s., simply cut or sawn, with a flat or even surface.**
	680222 00 0	Other calcareous stone
	680223 00 0	Granite
	680229 00 0	Other stone
661.36		**Marble, travertine and alabaster and articles thereof, moulded, turned, polished, decorated, carved or otherwise worked**
	680291 10 0	Polished alabaster, decorated or otherwise worked, but not carved
	680291 90 0	Other
661.39		**Other monumental or building stone (except slate) and articles thereof (other than goods of heading 661.31), moulded, turned, polished, decorated, carved or otherwise worked**
		Other calcareous stone
	680292 10 0	Polished, decorated or otherwise worked, but not carved
	680292 90 0	Other
		Granite
	680293 10 0	Polished, decorated or otherwise worked, but not carved; of a net weight of 10 kg or more
	680293 90 0	Other
		Other stone
	680299 10 0	Polished, decorated or otherwise worked, but not carved; of a net weight of 10 kg or more
	680299 90 0	Other

Construction materials of asbestos-cement and fibre-cement and of unfired non-metallic minerals, n.e.s.

S.I.T.C. (R3)	Commodity Code No	Trade description
661.81		**Articles of asphalt or of similar material (e.g., petroleum bitumen or coal tar pitch)**
		In rolls
	680710 10 0	Roofing and facing products
	680710 90 0	Other
	680790 00 0	Other
661.82	680800 00 0	**Panels, boards, tiles, blocks and similar articles of vegetable fibre, of straw or of shavings, chips, particles, sawdust or other waste, of wood, agglomerated with cement, plaster or other mineral binders**
661.83		**Articles of asbestos-cement, of cellulose fibre-cement or the like**
	681110 00 0	Corrugated sheets
		Other sheets, panels, tiles and similar articles
	681120 11 0	Sheets for roofing walls, not exceeding 40 x 60 cm
	681120 80 0	Other
	681130 00 0	Tubes, pipes and tube or pipe fittings
	681190 00 0	Other articles

CLAY CONSTRUCTION MATERIALS AND REFRACTORY CONSTRUCTION MATERIALS

Refractory bricks and other refractory construction materials

S.I.T.C. (R3)	Commodity Code No	Trade description
662.31		**Bricks, blocks, tiles and other ceramic goods, of siliceous fossil meals (e.g., kieselguhr, tripolite or diatomite) or of similar siliceous earths**
	690100 10 0	Bricks weighing more than 650 kg/m^3
	690100 90 0	Other

S.I.T.C. (R3)	Commodity Code No	Trade description
662.32		**Refractory bricks, blocks, tiles and similar refractory ceramic constructional goods (other than goods of heading 662.31)**
	690210 00 0	Containing, by weight, singly or together, more than 50 % of the elements Mg, Ca or Cr, expressed as MgO, CaO or Cr_2O_3
		Containing, by weight, more than 50 % of alumina (Al_2O_3), of silica SiO^2) or of a mixture or compound of these products
	690220 10 0	Containing, by weight, 93 % or more of silica (SiO_2)
		Other
	690220 91 0	Containing, by weight, more than 7 % but less than 45% of alumina (Al_2O_3)
	690220 99 0	Other
	690290 00 0	Other
662.33	381600 00 0	**Refractory cements, mortars, concretes and similar compositions, n.e.s.**
		Non-refractory ceramic bricks, tiles, pipes and similar products
662.41		**Ceramic building bricks, flooring blocks, support or filler tiles and the like**
	690410 00 0	Building bricks
	690490 00 0	Other
662.42		**Roofing tiles, chimney-pots, cowls, chimney liners, architectural ornaments and other ceramic constructional goods**
	690510 00 0	Roofing tiles
	690590 00 0	Other
662.43	690600 00 0	**Ceramic pipes, conduits, guttering and pipe fittings**
662.44		**Unglazed ceramic flags and paving, hearth or wall tiles; unglazed ceramic mosaic cubes and the like, whether or not on a backing**
	690710 00 0	Tiles, cubes and similar articles, whether or not rectangular, the largest surface area which is capable of being enclosed in a square the side of which is less than 7 cm
		Other
	690790 10 0	Double tiles of the "Spaltplatten" type
		Other
	690790 91 0	Stoneware
	690790 93 0	Earthenware or fine pottery
	690790 99 0	Other
662.45		**Glazed ceramic flags and paving, hearth or wall tiles; glazed ceramic mosaic cubes and the like, whether or not on a backing**
		Tiles, cubes and similar articles, whether or not rectangular, the largest surface area of which is capable of being enclosed in a square the side of which is less than 7 cm
	690810 10 0	Of common pottery
	690810 90 0	Other
		Other
		Of common pottery
	690890 11 0	Double tiles of the "Spaltplatten" type
		Other, of a maximum thickness
	690890 21 0	Not exceeding 15 mm
	690890 29 0	Exceeding 15 mm
		Other
	690890 31 0	Double tiles of the "Spaltplatten" type
		Other
	690890 51 0	With a face of not more than 90 cm^2
		Other
	690890 91 0	Stoneware
	690890 93 0	Earthenware or fine pottery
	690890 99 0	Other

MINERAL MANUFACTURES, N.E.S.

Millstones, grindstones, grinding wheels and the like, without frameworks, for grinding, sharpening, polishing, trueing or cutting, hand sharpening or polishing stones, and parts thereof, of natural stone, of agglomerated natural or artificial abrasives or of ceramics, with or without parts of other materials

S.I.T.C. (R3)	Commodity Code No	Trade description
663.11	680410 00 0	**Millstones and grindstones for milling, grinding or pulping**
663.12		**Other millstones, grindstones, grinding wheels and the like**
	680421 00 0	Of agglomerated synthetic or natural diamond
		Of other agglomerated abrasives or of ceramics
		Of artificial abrasives, with binder
		Of synthetic or artificial resin
	680422 12 0	Not reinforced
	680422 18 0	Reinforced
	680422 30 0	Of ceramics or silicates
	680422 50 0	Of other materials
	680422 90 0	Other
	680423 00 0	Of natural stone
663.13	680430 00 0	**Hand sharpening or polishing stones**

S.I.T.C. (R3)	Commodity Code No	Trade description
		Natural or artificial abrasive powder or grain, on a base of textile material, of paper, of paperboard or of other materials, whether or not cut to shape or sewn or otherwise made up
663.21	680510 00 0	....on a base of woven textile fabric only
663.22	680520 00 0	....on a base of paper or paperboard only
663.29		....on a base of other materials
	680530 10 0	On a base of woven textile fabric combined with paper or paperboard
	680530 20 0	On a base of vulcanized fibre
	680530 80 0	Other
		Manufactures of mineral materials, n.e.s. (other than ceramic)
663.31		**Articles of plaster or of compositions based on plaster**
		Boards, sheets, panels, tiles and similar articles, not ornamented
	680911 00 0	Faced or reinforced with paper or paperboard only
	680919 00 0	Other
	680990 00 0	Other articles
663.32		**Building blocks and bricks, tiles, flagstones and similar articles**
		Building blocks and bricks
	681011 10 0	Of light concrete (with a basis of crushed pumice, granulated slag, etc.)
	681011 90 0	Other
		Other
	681019 10 0	Roofing tiles
		Other tiles and paving
	681019 31 0	Of concrete
	681019 39 0	Other
	681019 90 0	Other
663.33		**Prefabricated structural components for building or civil engineering**
	681091 10 0	Floor components
	681091 90 0	Other
663.34	*681099 00 0	**Other articles of cement, of concrete or of artificial stone, reinforced or not**
663.35		**Mica, worked, and articles of mica (including agglomerated or reconstituted mica), whether or not on a support of paper, paperboard or other materials**
	681410 00 0	Plates, sheets and strips of agglomerated or reconstituted mica, whether or not on a support
		Other
	681490 10 0	Sheets or splittings of mica
	681490 90 0	Other
663.36		**Non-electrical articles of graphite or other carbon**
	681510 10 0	Carbon fibres and articles of carbon fibres
	681510 90 0	Other
663.37	681520 00 0	**Articles of peat**
663.38	681591 00 0	**Articles of other mineral substances containing magnesite, dolomite or chromite**
663.39		**Articles of stone or other mineral substances, n.e.s.**
	681599 10 0	Of refractory materials, chemically bonded
	681599 90 0	Other
		Slag wool, rock wool and similar mineral wools; exfoliated vermiculite, expanded clays, foamed slag and similar expanded mineral materials; mixtures and articles of heat-insulating, sound-insulating or sound-absorbing mineral materials (other than those of heading 661.83 or 663.81, or ceramic goods)
663.51	680610 00 0	**Slag wool, rock wool and similar mineral wools (including intermixtures thereof), in bulk, sheets or rolls**
663.52		**Exfoliated vermiculite, expanded clays, foamed slag and similar expanded mineral materials (including intermixtures thereof)**
	680620 10 0	Expanded clays
	680620 90 0	Other
663.53	680690 00 0	**Mixtures and articles of heat-insulating, sound-insulating, sound- absorbing mineral materials**
663.70		**Refractory ceramic goods (e.g., retorts, crucibles, muffles, nozzles, plugs, supports, cupels, tubes, pipes, sheaths and rods), n.e.s.**
	690310 00 0	Containing, by weight, more than 50 % of graphite or other forms of carbon or of a mixture of these products
		Containing, by weight, more than 50% of alumina (Al_2O_3) or of a mixture or compound of alumina and of silica (SiO_2)
	690320 10 0	Containing, by weight, less than 45 % of alumina (Al_2O_3)
	690320 90 0	Containing, by weight, 45 % or more of alumina (Al_2O_3)
		Other

S.I.T.C. (R3)	Commodity Code No	Trade description
cont 663.70	690390 10 0	Containing, by weight, more than 25 % but not more than 50 % of graphite or other forms of carbon or of a mixture of these products
	690390 20 0	Containing by weight, singly or together, more than 50 % of the elements Mg, Ca or Cr, expressed as MgO, CaO or Cr_2O_3
	690390 80 0	Other

Manufactures of asbestos; friction materials

663.81		**Fabricated asbestos fibres; mixtures with a basis of asbestos or with a basis of asbestos and magnesium carbonate; articles of such mixtures or of asbestos (e.g., thread, woven fabric, clothing, headgear, footgear, gaskets), reinforced or not (other than goods of heading 661.83 or 663.82)**
	681210 00 0	Fabricated asbestos fibres; mixtures with a basis of asbestos or with a basis of asbestos and magnesium carbonate
	681220 00 0	Yarn and thread
	681230 00 0	Cords and string, whether or not plaited
	681240 00 0	Woven or knitted fabric
	681250 00 0	Clothing, clothing accessories, footwear and headgear
	681260 00 0	Paper, millboard and felt
	681270 00 0	Compressed asbestos fibre jointing, in sheets or rolls
		Other
	681290 10 0	For use in civil aircraft
	681290 90 0	Other
663.82		**Friction material and articles thereof (e.g., sheets, rolls, strips, segments, discs, washers, pads), not mounted, for brakes, for clutches or the like, with a basis of asbestos, of other mineral substances or of cellulose, whether or not combined with other materials**
		Brake linings and pads
	681310 10 0	With a basis of asbestos or other mineral substances, for use in civil aircraft
	681310 90 0	Other
		Other
	681390 10 0	With a basis of asbestos or other mineral substances, for use in civil aircraft
	681390 90 0	Other

Articles of ceramic materials, n.e.s.

663.91		**Laboratory, chemical or industrial ceramic wares, non-refractory; ceramic troughs, tubs and similar receptacles of a kind used in agriculture; ceramic pots, jars and similar articles of a kind used for the conveyance or packing of goods**
		Ceramic wares for laboratory, chemical or other technical uses
	690911 00 0	Of porcelain or china
	*690912 00 0	Articles having a hardness equivalent to 9 or more on the Mohs scale
	*690919 00 0	Other
	690990 00 0	Other
663.99		**Ceramic articles, n.e.s.**
	691410 00 0	Of porcelain or china
		Other
	691490 10 0	Of common pottery
	691490 90 0	Other

GLASS

Glass in the mass, in balls, rods or tubes (unworked); waste and scrap of glass

664.11		**Glass in the mass; cullet and other waste and scrap of glass**
	700100 10 0	Cullet and other waste and scrap of glass
		Glass in the mass
	700100 91 0	Optical glass
	700100 99 0	Other
664.12		**Glass in balls (other than microspheres of heading 665.93), rods or tubes, unworked**
	700210 00 0	Balls
		Rods
	700220 10 0	Of optical glass
	700220 90 0	Other
		Tubes
	700231 00 0	Of fused quartz or other fused silica
	700232 00 0	Of other glass having a linear coefficient of expansion not exceeding 5 x 10^{-6} per Kelvin within a temperature range of 0 °C to 300 °C
	700239 00 0	Other

Drawn glass and blown glass, in sheets, whether or not having an absorbent or reflecting layer, but not otherwise worked

664.31		**Glass, coloured throughout the mass (body tinted), opacified, flashed or having an absorbent or reflecting layer**
	*700420 10 0	Optical glass
	*700420 99 0	Other

S.I.T.C. (R3)	Commodity Code No	Trade description
664.39		**Other glass**
	700490 10 0	Optical glass
	700490 70 0	Horticultural sheet glass
		Other, of a thickness
	700490 92 0	Not exceeding 2.5 mm
	700490 98 0	Exceeding 2.5 mm

Float glass and surface ground or polished glass, in sheets, whether or not having an absorbent or reflecting layer, but not otherwise worked

664.41		**Non-wired glass**
		Non-wired glass, having an absorbent or reflecting layer
		Of a thickness
	*700510 25 0	Not exceeding 3.5 mm
	*700510 30 0	Exceeding 3.5 mm but not exceeding 4.5 mm
	*700510 80 0	Exceeding 4.5 mm
		Other non-wired glass
		Coloured throughout the mass (body tinted), opacified, flashed or merely surface ground
	*700521 25 0	Of a thickness not exceeding 3.5 mm
	700521 30 0	Of a thickness exceeding 3.5 mm but not exceeding 4.5 mm
	*700521 80 0	Of a thickness exceeding 4.5 mm
		Other
	*700529 25 0	Not exceeding 3.5 mm
	700529 35 0	Exceeding 3.5 mm but not exceeding 4.5 mm
	*700529 80 0	Exceeding 4.5 mm
664.42	700530 00 0	**Wired glass**

Cast glass and rolled glass, in sheets or profiles, whether or not having an absorbent or reflecting layer, but not otherwise worked

664.51		**Non-wired sheets**
		Coloured throughout the mass (body tinted), opacified, flashed or having an absorbent or reflecting layer
	*700312 10 0	Of optical glass
	*700312 99 0	Other
		Other
	700319 10 0	Of optical glass
	700319 90 0	Other
664.52	700320 00 0	**Wired sheets**
664.53	700330 00 0	**Profiles**

Safety glass consisting of toughened (tempered) or laminated glass

664.71		**Toughened (tempered) safety glass**
		Of size and shape suitable for incorporation in vehicles, aircraft, spacecraft or vessels
	700711 10 0	Of size and shape suitable for incorporation in motor vehicles
	700711 90 0	Other
		Other
	700719 10 0	Enamelled
	700719 20 0	Coloured throughout the mass (body tinted), opacified, flashed or having an absorbent or reflecting layer
	700719 80 0	Other
664.72		**Laminated safety glass**
		Of size and shape suitable for incorporation in vehicles, aircraft, spacecraft or vessels
	700721 10 0	Windshields, not framed, for use in civil aircraft
		Other
	700721 91 0	Of size and shape suitable for incorporation in motor vehicles
	700721 99 0	Other
	700729 00 0	Other

Glass mirrors, whether or not framed (including rear-view mirrors)

664.81	700910 00 0	**Rear-view mirrors for vehicles**
664.89		**Other glass mirrors, whether or not framed**
	700991 00 0	Unframed
	700992 00 0	Framed

Glass, n.e.s.

664.91		**Glass of heading 664.3, 664.4 or 664.5, bent, edge-worked, engraved, drilled, enamelled or otherwise worked, but not framed or fitted with other materials**
	*700510 05 0	Having a non-reflecting layer
	*700600 10 0	Optical glass
	700560 90 0	Other

S.I.T.C. (R3)	Commodity Code No	Trade description
664.92		**Multiple-walled insulating units of glass**
	700800 20 0	Coloured throughout the mass (body tinted), opacified, flashed or having an absorbent or reflecting layer
		Other
	700800 81 0	Consisting of two panels of glass sealed around the edges by an airtight joint and separated by a layer of air, other gases or a vacuum
	700800 89 0	Other
664.93		**Glass envelopes (including bulbs and tubes), open, and glass parts thereof without fittings, for electric lamps, cathode-ray tubes or the like**
		For electric lighting
	701110 10 0	Bulbs for filament lamps with a greatest external diameter of 25 mm or more but not exceeding 70 mm
	701110 90 0	Other
	701120 00 0	For cathode-ray tubes
	701190 00 0	Other
664.94		**Clock and watch glasses and similar glasses, glass for non- corrective or corrective spectacles, curved, bent, hallowed or the like, not optically worked; hollow glass spheres and their segments, for the manufacture of such glasses**
	701510 00 0	Glasses for corrective spectacles
	701590 00 0	Other
664.95		**Glass fibres (including glass wool) and articles thereof, n.e.s.**
		Thin sheets (voiles), webs, mats, mattresses, boards and similar nonwoven products
	701931 00 0	Mats
	701932 00 0	Thin sheets (voiles)
		Other
	701939 10 0	Covered with paper or metal
	701939 90 0	Other
		Other
	701990 10 0	Non-textile fibres in bulk or flocks
	701990 30 0	Pads and casings for insulating tubes and pipes
		Other
	701990 91 0	Of textile fibres
	701990 99 0	Other
664.96		**Paving blocks, slabs, bricks, squares, tiles and other articles of pressed or moulded glass, whether or not wired, of a kind used for building or construction purposes; leaded lights and the like; multicellular glass or foam glass, in blocks, panels, plates, shells or similar forms**
	701690 10 0	Leaded lights and the like
	701690 30 0	Multicellular glass or foam glass
	701690 90 0	Other

GLASSWARE

Containers, of glass, of a kind used for the conveyance or packing of goods; stoppers and closures, of glass; glass inners for vacuum vessels

S.I.T.C. (R3)	Commodity Code No	Trade description
665.11		**Carboys, bottles, flasks, jars, pots, phials and other containers, of glass, of a kind used for the conveyance or packing of goods; preserving jars of glass; stoppers, lids and other closures, of glass**
	*701020 00 0	Stoppers, lids and other closures
		Other, of a capacity
		Exceeding 1 l
	*701091 10 0	Preserving jars (sterilizing jars)
		Other
		For beverages and foodstuffs
		Bottles
	*701091 21 0	Of colourless glass
	*701091 29 0	Of coloured glass
	*701091 60 0	Other
	*701091 90 0	For other products
		Exceeding 0.33 l but not exceeding 1 l
	*701092 10 0	Preserving jars (sterilising jars)
		Other
		For beverages and foodstuffs
		Bottles
	*701092 21 0	Of colourless glass
	*701092 29 0	Of coloured glass
	*701092 60 0	Other
	*701092 90 0	For other products
		Exceeding 0.15 l but not exceeding 0.33 l
	*701093 10 0	Preserving jars (sterilising jars)
		Other
		For beverages and foodstuffs
		Bottles
	*701093 21 0	Of colourless glass
	*701093 29 0	Of coloured glass
		Other, of a capacity
	*701093 61 0	0.25 l or more but not exceeding 0,33 l

S.I.T.C. (R3)	Commodity Code No	Trade description
cont 665.11	*701093 69 0	Exceeding 0.15 l but less than 0.25 l
	*701093 70 0	For pharmaceutical products
	*701093 90 0	For other products
		Not exceeding 0.15 l
	*701094 10 0	Preserving jars (sterilising jars)
		Other
		For beverages and foodstuffs
	*701094 20 0	Bottles
	*701094 60 0	Other
		For pharmaceutical products, of a capacity
	*701094 71 0	Exceeding 0.055 l but not exceeding 0.15 l
	*701094 79 0	Not exceeding 0.055 l
	*701094 90 0	For other products
665.12		**Glass inners for vacuum flasks or for other vacuum vessels**
	701200 10 0	Unfinished
	701200 90 0	Finished
		Glassware of a kind used for table, kitchen, toilet, office, indoor decoration or similar purposes (other than that of heading 665.11, 665.92 or 665.93
665.21	701310 00 0	**Glassware of glass-ceramics**
665.22		**Drinking glasses other than of glass-ceramics**
		Of lead crystal
		Gathered by hand
	701321 11 0	Cut or otherwise decorated
	701321 19 0	Other
		Gathered mechanically
	701321 91 0	Cut or otherwise decorated
	701321 99 0	Other
		Other
	701329 10 0	Of toughened glass
		Other
		Gathered by hand
	701329 51 0	Cut or otherwise decorated
	701329 59 0	Other
		Gathered mechanically
	701329 91 0	Cut or otherwise decorated
	701329 99 0	Other
665.23		**Glassware of a kind used for table (other than drinking glasses) or kitchen purposes other than of glass-ceramics**
		Of lead crystal
	701331 10 0	Gathered by hand
	701331 90 0	Gathered mechanically
	701332 00 0	Of glass having a linear coefficient of expansion not exceeding 5×10^{-6} per Kelvin within a temperature range of 0 °C to 300 °C
		Other
	701339 10 0	Of toughened glass
		Other
	701339 91 0	Gathered by hand
	701339 99 0	Gathered mechanically
665.29		**Other glassware**
		Of lead crystal
	701391 10 0	Gathered by hand
	701391 90 0	Gathered mechanically
		Other
	701399 10 0	Gathered by hand
	701399 90 0	Gathered mechanically
		Articles made of glass, n.e.s.
665.91		**Laboratory, hygienic or pharmaceutical glassware, whether or not graduated or calibrated**
	701710 00 0	Of fused quartz or other fused silica
	701720 00 0	Of other glass having a linear coefficient of expansion not exceeding 5×10^{-6} per Kelvin within a temperature range of 0 °C to 300 °C
	701790 00 0	Other
665.92	701010 00 0	**Glass ampoules**
665.93		**Glass beads, imitation pearls, imitation precious or semi-precious stones and similar glass smallwares, and articles thereof (other than imitation jewellery); glass eyes (other than prosthetic articles); ornaments and other fancy articles of lamp-worked glass (other than imitation jewellery); glass microspheres not exceeding 1 mm in diameter**
		Glass beads, imitation pearls, imitation precious or semi-precious stones and similar glass smallwares
		Glass beads
	701810 11 0	Cut and mechanically polished
	701810 19 0	Other

S.I.T.C. (R3)	Commodity Code No	Trade description
cont 665.93	701810 30 0	Imitation pearls
		Imitation precious and semi-precious stones
	701810 51 0	Cut and mechanically polished
	701810 59 0	Other
	701810 90 0	Other
	701820 00 0	Glass microspheres not exceeding 1 mm in diameter
		Other
	701890 10 0	Glass eyes; articles of smallware
	701890 90 0	Other
665.94	701610 00 0	**Glass cubes and other glass smallwares, whether or not on a backing, for mosaics or similar decorative purposes**
665.95	701400 00 0	**Signalling glassware and optical elements of glass (other than those of heading 664.94), not optically worked**
665.99		**Other articles of glass**
	702000 10 0	Of fused quartz or other fused silica
	702000 30 0	Of glass having a linear coefficient of expansion not exceeding 5×10^{-6} per Kelvin within a temperature range of 0 °C to 300 °C
	702000 90 0	Other

POTTERY

Ceramic tableware, kitchenware and other ceramic household and toilet articles

S.I.T.C. (R3)	Commodity Code No	Trade description
666.11	691110 00 0	**Tableware and kitchenware of porcelain or china**
666.12	691190 00 0	**Other household or toilet articles of porcelain or china**
666.13		**Ceramic tableware, kitchenware, other household articles and toilet articles (other than porcelain or china)**
	691200 10 0	Of common pottery
	691200 30 0	Stoneware
	691200 50 0	Earthenware or fine pottery
	691200 90 0	Other

Statuettes and other ornamental ceramic articles.

S.I.T.C. (R3)	Commodity Code No	Trade description
666.21	691310 00 0	**....of porcelain or china**
666.29		**....other**
	691390 10 0	Of common pottery
		Other
	691390 91 0	Stoneware
	691390 93 0	Earthenware or fine pottery
	691390 99 0	Other

PEARLS, PRECIOUS AND SEMI-PRECIOUS STONES, UNWORKED OR WORKED

Pearls (natural or cultured), whether or not worked or graded but not strung, mounted or set; ungraded pearls (natural or cultured) temporarily strung for convenience of transport

S.I.T.C. (R3)	Commodity Code No	Trade description
667.11	710110 00 0	**Natural pearls**
667.12	710121 00 0	**Cultured pearls, unworked**
667.13	710122 00 0	**Cultured pearls, worked**

Diamonds (other than sorted industrial diamonds), whether or not worked, but not mounted or set

S.I.T.C. (R3)	Commodity Code No	Trade description
667.21	710210 00 0	**Diamonds, rough, unsorted**
667.22	710231 00 0	**Diamonds, sorted (other than industrial diamonds), unworked or simply sawn, cleaved or bruted**
667.29	710239 00 0	**Diamonds (other than industrial diamonds), otherwise worked, but not mounted or set**

Precious stones (other than diamonds) and semi-precious stones, whether or not worked or graded but not strung, mounted or set; ungraded precious stones (other than diamonds) and semi-precious stones, temporarily strung for convenience of transport

S.I.T.C. (R3)	Commodity Code No	Trade description
667.31	710310 00 0	**....unworked or simply sawn or roughly shaped**
667.39		**....otherwise worked**
	710391 00 0	Rubies, sapphires and emeralds
	710399 00 0	Other

S.I.T.C. (R3)	Commodity Code No	Trade description
		Synthetic or reconstituted precious or semi-precious stones, whether or not worked or graded but not strung, mounted or set; ungraded synthetic or reconstructed precious or semi- precious stones, temporarily strung for convenience of transport
667.41	710410 00 0	**Piezo-electric quartz**
667.42	710420 00 0	**Synthetic or reconstituted precious or semi-precious stones, other than piezo-electric quartz, unworked or simply sawn or roughly shaped**
667.49	710490 00 0	**Synthetic or reconstituted precious or semi-precious stones, n.e.s.**

DIVISION 67

IRON AND STEEL

PIG IRON, SPIEGELEISEN, SPONGE IRON, IRON OR STEEL GRANULES AND POWDERS AND FERRO-ALLOYS

Pig iron and spiegeleisen, in pigs, blocks or other primary forms

S.I.T.C. (R3)	Commodity Code No	Trade description
671.21		**Non-alloyed pig iron containing by weight 0.50% or less of phosphorus**
		Containing by weight not less than 0.4 % of manganese
	720110 11 0	Containing by weight 1 % or less of silicon
	720110 19 0	Containing by weight more than 1 % of silicon
	720110 30 0	Containing by weight not less than 0.1 % but less than 0.4 % of manganese
	720110 90 0	Containing by weight less than 0.1 % of manganese
671.22	720120 00 0	**Non-alloyed pig iron containing by weight more than 0.50% of phosphorus**
671.23		**Alloy pig iron and spiegeleisen**
		Alloy pig iron
	*720150 10 0	Alloy pig iron containing by weight not less than 0.3 % but not more than 1 % of titanium and not less than 0.5% but not more than 1% of vanadium (ECSC)
	*720150 90 0	Other (ECSC)

Granules and powders, of pig iron, spiegeleisen, iron or steel; ferrous products obtained by direct reduction of iron ore and other spongy ferrous products, in lumps, pellets or similar forms; iron having a minimum purity of 99.94%, in lumps, pellets or similar forms

S.I.T.C. (R3)	Commodity Code No	Trade description
671.31	720510 00 0	**Granules of pig iron, spiegeleisen, iron or steel**
671.32		**Powders of pig iron, spiegeleisen, iron or steel**
	720521 00 0	Of alloy steel
	720529 00 0	Other
671.33		**Ferrous products obtained by direct reduction of iron ore and other spongy ferrous products, in lumps, pellets or similar forms; iron having a minimum purity of 99.94%, in lumps, pellets or similar forms**
	720310 00 0	Ferrous products obtained by direct reduction of iron ore (ECSC)
	720390 00 0	Other (ECSC)
		Ferro-manganese
671.41		**....containing by weight more than 2% of carbon**
	720211 20 0	With a granulometry not exceeding 5 mm and a manganese content by weight exceeding 65 %
	720211 80 0	Other
671.49	720219 00 0	**....other**
		Other ferro-alloys (excl. radio-active ferro-alloys)
671.51		**Ferro-silicon**
		Containing by weight more than 55 % of silicon
	720221 10 0	Containing by weight more than 55 % but not more than 80 % of silicon
	720221 90 0	Containing by weight more than 80 % of silicon
	720229 00 0	Other
671.52	720230 00 0	**Ferro-silico-manganese**
671.53		**Ferro-chromium**
		Containing by weight more than 4 % of carbon
	720241 10 0	Containing by weight more than 4 % but not more than 6 % of carbon
		Containing by weight more than 6 % of carbon
	720241 91 0	Containing by weight not more than 60 % of chromium
	720241 99 0	Containing by weight more than 60 % of chromium
		Other
	720249 10 0	Containing by weight not more than 0.05 % of carbon
	720249 50 0	Containing by weight more than 0.05 % but not more than 0.5 % of carbon
	720249 90 0	Containing by weight more than 0.5 % but not more than 4 % of carbon
671.54	720250 00 0	**Ferro-silico-chromium**

S.I.T.C. (R3)	Commodity Code No	Trade description
671.55	720260 00 0	**Ferro-nickel**
671.59		**Ferro-alloys, n.e.s.**
	720270 00 0	Ferro-molybdenum
	720280 00 0	Ferro-tungsten and ferro-silico-tungsten
		Other
	720291 00 0	Ferro-titanium and ferro-silico-titanium
	720292 00 0	Ferro-vanadium
	720293 00 0	Ferro-niobium
		Other
		Ferro-phosphorus
	720299 11 0	Containing by weight more than 3 % but less than 15 % of phosphorus (ECSC)
	720299 19 0	Containing by weight 15 % or more of phosphorus
	720299 30 0	Ferro-silico-magnesium
	720299 80 0	Other

INGOTS AND OTHER PRIMARY FORMS, OF IRON OR STEEL; SEMI-FINISHED PRODUCTS OF IRON OR STEEL

Ingots and other primary forms, of iron (other than iron of heading 671.33) or steel

S.I.T.C. (R3)	Commodity Code No	Trade description
672.41	720610 00 0	**Ingots of iron (other than iron of heading 671.33) or non-alloy steel**
672.45	720690 00 0	**Other primary forms of iron (other than iron of heading 671.33) or non-alloy steel**
672.47	721810 00 0	**Ingots and other primary forms, of stainless steel**
672.49	722410 00 0	**Ingots and other primary forms, of other alloy steel**

Semi-finished products of iron or non-alloy steel containing by weight less than 0.25% of carbon

S.I.T.C. (R3)	Commodity Code No	Trade description
672.61		**....of rectangular (including square) cross-section, the width measuring less than twice the thickness**
		Rolled or obtained by continuous casting (ECSC)
	720711 11 0	Of free-cutting steel
		Other
	720711 14 0	Of a thickness not exceeding 130 mm
	720711 16 0	Of a thickness exceeding 130 mm
	720711 90 0	Forged
672.62		**....other, of rectangular (other than square) cross-section**
	720712 10 0	Rolled or obtained by continuous casting (ECSC)
	720712 90 0	Forged
672.69		**....other**
		Of circular or polygonal cross-section
		Rolled or obtained by continuous casting
	720719 11 0	Of free-cutting steel (ECSC)
		Other (ECSC)
	720719 14 0	Obtained by continuous casting
	720719 16 0	Other
	720719 19 0	Forged
		Blanks for angles, shapes and sections
	720719 31 0	Rolled or obtained by continuous casting (ECSC)
	720719 39 0	Forged
	720719 90 0	Other
672.70		**Semi-finished products of iron or non-alloy steel containing by weight 0.25% or more of carbon**
		Of rectangular (including square) cross-section, the width measuring less than twice the thickness
		Rolled or obtained by continuous casting (ECSC)
	720720 11 0	Of free-cutting steel
		Other, containing by weight
	720720 15 0	0.25 % or more but less than 0.6 % of carbon
	720720 17 0	0.6 % or more of carbon
	720720 19 0	Forged
		Other, of rectangular (other than square) cross-section
	720720 32 0	Rolled or obtained by continuous casting (ECSC)
	720720 39 0	Forged
		Of circular or polygonal cross-section
		Rolled or obtained by continuous casting
	720720 51 0	Of free-cutting steel (ECSC)
		Other (ECSC)
	720720 55 0	Containing by weight 0.25 % or more but less than 0.6% of carbon
	720720 57 0	Containing by weight 0.6 % or more of carbon
	720720 59 0	Forged
		Blanks for angles, shapes and sections
	720720 71 0	Rolled or obtained by continuous casting (ECSC)
	720720 79 0	Forged
	720720 90 0	Other

S.I.T.C. (R3)	Commodity Code No	Trade description

Semi-finished products of alloy steel

672.81 ....**of stainless steel**
Of rectangular (including square) cross-section
Rolled or obtained by continuous casting:
  *721891 11 0   Containing by weight 2.5 % or more of nickel (ECSC)
  *721891 19 0   Containing by weight less than 2.5 % of nickel (ECSC)
  *721891 90 0   Forged
Other
Of square cross-section:
  *721899 11 0   Rolled or obtained by continuous casting (ECSC)
  *721899 19 0   Forged
Other
  *721899 20 0   Rolled or obtained by continuous casting (ECSC)
Forged:
  *721899 91 0   Of circular or polygonal cross-section
  *721899 99 0   Other

672.82 ....**of other alloy steel**
Of rectangular (including square) cross-section
Hot-rolled or obtained by continuous casting (ECSC)
The width measuring less than twice the thickness :
  722490 01 0   Of high-speed steel
  722490 05 0   Containing by weight not more than 0.7 % of carbon, 0.5 % or more but not more than 1.2 % of manganese and 0.6 % or more but not more than 2.3 % of silicon; containing by weight 0.0008 % or more of boron with any other element less than the minimum content referred to in note 1 f) to chapter 72 of the Combined Nomenclature
  722490 08 0   Other
  722490 15 0   Other
  722490 19 0   Forged
Other
  722490 30 0   Hot-rolled or obtained by continuous casting (ECSC)
  722490 31 0   Containing by weight not less than 0.9 % but not more than 1.15 % of carbon, not less than 0.5 % but not more than 2 % of chromium and, if present, not more than 0.5 % of molybdenum
  722490 39 0   Other
Forged
  722490 91 0   Of circular or polygonal cross-section
  722490 99 0   Other

FLAT-ROLLED PRODUCTS, OF IRON OR NON-ALLOY STEEL, NOT CLAD, PLATED OR COATED

Flat-rolled products of iron or non-alloy steel, not clad, plated or coated

673.10 **of a width of 600 mm or more, in coils**
  *720810 00 0   In coils, not further worked than hot-rolled, with patterns in relief (ECSC)

Flat-rolled products of iron or non-alloy steel, not clad, plated or coated, not further worked than hot-rolled

673.21 ....**of a width of 600 mm or more and of a thickness of 4.75 mm or more, in coils**
Other, in coils, not further worked than hot-rolled, pickled:
  *720825 00 0   Of a thickness of 4.75 mm or more (ECSC)
Other, in coils, not further worked than hot-rolled:
  *720836 00 0   Of a thickness exceeding 10 mm
Of a thickness of 4.75 mm or more but not exceeding 10 mm:
  *720837 10 0   Intended for re-rolling (ECSC)
  *720837 90 0   Other (ECSC)

673.22 ....**of a width of 600 mm or more and of a thickness of less than 4.75 mm, in coils**
Other, in coils, not further worked than hot-rolled, pickled:
  *720826 00 0   Of a thickness of 3 mm or more but less than 4.75 mm (ECSC)
  *720827 00 0   Of a thickness of less than 3 mm (ECSC)
Other, in coils, not further worked than hot-rolled:
Of a thickness of 3 mm or more but less than 4.75 mm:
  *720838 10 0   Intended for re-rolling (ECSC)
  *720838 90 0   Other (ECSC)
Of a thickness of less than 3 mm:
  *720839 10 0   Intended for re-rolling (ECSC)
  *720839 90 0   Other (ECSC)

673.23 ....**rolled on four faces or in a closed box pass, of a width of 600 mm or more but not exceeding 1250 mm, and of a thickness of not less than 4 mm, not in coils and without patterns of relief**
Of a thickness exceeding 10 mm:
  *720851 10 0   Rolled on four faces or in a closed box pass, of a width not exceeding 1250 mm (ECSC)
Of a thickness of 4.75 mm or more but not exceeding 10 mm
  *720852 10 0   Rolled on four faces or in a closed box pass, of a width not exceeding 1250 mm (ECSC)
Of a thickness of 3 mm or more but less than 4.75
  *720853 10 0   Rolled on four faces or in a closed box pass, of a width not exceeding 1250 mm (ECSC)

S.I.T.C. (R3)	Commodity Code No	Trade description
673.24		....other, of a width of 600 mm or more and of a thickness of 4.75 mm or more, not in coils
		Not further worked than hot-rolled, with patterns in relief:
	*720840 10 0	Of a thickness of 2 mm or more (ECSC)
		Other
		Other, of a thickness exceeding 10 mm:
	*720851 30 0	Exceeding 20 mm (ECSC)
	*720851 50 0	Exceeding 15 mm but not exceeding 20 mm (ECSC)
		Exceeding 10 mm but not exceeding 15 mm, of a width of:
	*720851 91 0	2050 mm or more (ECSC)
	*720851 99 0	Less than 2050 mm (ECSC)
		Of a thickness of 4.75 mm or more but not exceeding 10 mm:
	*720852 91 0	2050 mm or more (ECSC)
	*720852 99 0	Less than 2050 mm (ECSC)
673.25		....other, of a width of 600 mm or more and of a thickness of less than 4.75 mm, not in coils
		Not in coils, not further worked than hot-rolled, with patterns in relief:
	*720840 90 0	Of a thickness of less than 2 mm (ECSC)
		Other, not in coils, not further worked than hot-rolled:
	*720853 90 0	Of a thickness of 3 mm or more but less than 4.75 mm
		Of a thickness of less than 3 mm:
	*720854 10 0	Of a thickness of 2 mm or more (ECSC)
	*720854 90 0	Of a thickness of less than 2 mm (ECSC)
673.26	*721113 00 0	....rolled on four faces or in a closed box pass, of a width exceeding 150 mm but not exceeding 600 mm, and of a thickness of not less than 4 mm, not in coils and without patterns of relief (ECSC)
673.27		....other, of a width of less than 600 mm and of a thickness of 4.75 mm, or more
	*721114 10 0	Of a width exceeding 500 mm (ECSC)
	*721114 90 0	Of a width not exceeding 500 mm (ECSC)
673.29		....other, of a width of less than 600 mm
	*721119 20 0	Of a width exceeding 500 mm (ECSC)
	*721119 90 0	Of a width not exceeding 500 mm (ECSC)

Flat-rolled products of iron or non-alloy steel, not clad, plated or coated, not further worked than cold-rolled (cold-reduced) of a thickness of less than 3 mm and having a minimum yield point of 275 MPa or of a thickness of 3 mm or more and yield point of 355 MPa

Flat-rolled products of iron or non-alloy steel, not clad, plated or coated, not further worked than cold-rolled (cold-reduced)

S.I.T.C. (R3)	Commodity Code No	Trade description
673.41	*720915 00 0	....of a width of 600 mm or more and of a thickness of 3 mm or more, in coils
673.42		....of a width of 600 mm or more and a thickness exceeding 1 mm but less than 3 mm in coils
	*720916 10 0	"Electrical" (ECSC)
	*720916 90 0	Other (ECSC)
673.43		....of a width of 600 mm or more and of a thickness of 0.50 mm or more but not exceeding 1 mm, in coils
	*720917 10 0	"Electrical" (ECSC)
	*720917 90 0	Other (ECSC)
673.44		....of a width of 600 mm or more and a thickness of less than 0.50 mm, in coils
	*720918 10 0	"Electrical" (ECSC)
		Other (ECSC)
	*720918 91 0	Of a thickness of 0.35 mm or more but less than 0.5 mm
	*720918 99 0	Of a thickness of less than 0.35 mm
673.45	*720925 00 0	....of a width of 600 mm or more and of a thickness of 3 mm or more, not in coils
673.46		....of a width of 600 mm or more and of a thickness exceeding 1 mm but less than 3 mm, not in coils
	*720926 10 0	"Electrical" (ECSC)
	*720926 90 0	Other (ECSC)
673.47		....of a width of 600 mm or more and of a thickness of 0.50 mm or more but not exceeding 1 mm, not in coils
	*720927 10 0	"Electrical" (ECSC)
	*720927 90 0	Other (ECSC)
673.48		....of a width of 600 mm or more and of a thickness of less than 0.5 mm, not in coils
	*720928 10 0	"Electrical" (ECSC)
	*720928 90 0	Other (ECSC)
673.49		....of a width of less than 600 mm
		Containing by weight less than 0.25 % of carbon
	*721123 10 0	Of a width exceeding 500 mm (ECSC)
		Of a width not exceeding 500 mm
	*721123 51 0	In coils intended for the manufacture of tinplate (ECSC)

S.I.T.C. (R3)	Commodity Code No	Trade description
cont 673.49		Other
	*721123 91 0	"Electrical"
	*721123 99 0	Other
		Other
	*721129 20 0	Of a width exceeding 500 mm (ECSC)
		Of a width not exceeding 500 mm
	*721129 50 0	Containing by weight 0.25 % or more but less than 0.6% of carbon
	*721129 90 0	Containing by weight 0.6 % or more of carbon

Flat-rolled products of iron or non-alloy steel, not clad, plated or coated, n.e.s.

673.51		....of a width of 600 mm or more, hot-rolled
	720890 10 0	Not further worked than surface-treated or simply cut into shapes other than rectangular (including square) (ECSC)
	720890 90 0	Other
673.52		....of a width of 600 mm or more, cold-rolled
	720990 10 0	Not further worked than surface-treated or simply cut into shapes other than rectangular (including square) (ECSC)
	720990 90 0	Other
673.53		....of a width of less than 600 mm
		Of a width exceeding 500 mm
	721190 11 0	Not further worked than surface-treated (ECSC)
	721190 19 0	Other
	721190 90 0	Of a width not exceeding 500 mm

FLAT-ROLLED PRODUCTS OF IRON OR NON-ALLOY STEEL, CLAD, PLATED OR COATED

Flat-rolled products of iron or non-alloy steel, plated or coated with zinc

674.11		....electrolytically plated or coated of a width of 600 mm or more
	*721030 10 0	Not further worked than surface-treated or simply cut into shapes other than rectangular (including square) (ECSC)
	*721030 90 0	Other
674.12		....electrolytically plated or coated, of a width of less than 600 mm
		Of a width exceeding 500 mm
	*721220 11 0	Not further worked than surface-treated (ECSC)
	*721220 19 0	Other
	*721220 90 0	Of a width not exceeding 500 mm
674.13		....otherwise plated or coated, of a width of 600 mm or more
		Corrugated
	721041 10 0	Not further worked than surface-treated or simply cut into shapes other than rectangular (including square) (ECSC)
	721041 90 0	Other
		Other
	721049 10 0	Not further worked than surface-treated or simply cut into shapes other than rectangular (including square) (ECSC)
	721049 90 0	Other
674.14		....otherwise plated or coated, of a width of less than 600 mm
		Of a width exceeding 500 mm
	721230 11 0	Not further worked than surface-treated (ECSC)
	721230 19 0	Other
	721230 90 0	Of a width not exceeding 500 mm

Flat-rolled products of iron or non-alloy steel, plated or coated with tin

674.21		....of a width of 600 mm or more
		Of a thickness of 0.5 mm or more
	721011 10 0	Not further worked than surface-treated or simply cut into shapes other than rectangular (including square) (ECSC)
	721011 90 0	Other
		Of a thickness of less than 0.5 mm
		Not further worked than surface-treated or simply cut into shapes other than rectangular (including square)
	721012 11 0	Tinplate (ECSC)
	721012 19 0	Other (ECSC)
	721012 90 0	Other
674.22		....of a width of less than 600 mm
	721210 10 0	Tinplate, not further worked than surface-treated (ECSC)
		Other
	721210 91 0	Not further worked than surface-treated (ECSC)
	721210 93 0	Other
	721210 99 0	Of a width not exceeding 500 mm

S.I.T.C. (R3)	Commodity Code No	Trade description
		Flat-rolled products of iron or non-alloy steel, painted, varnished or coated with plastics
674.31		**....of a width of 600 mm or more**
		Not further worked than surface-treated or simply cut into shapes other than rectangular (including square)
	721070 31 0	Tinplate and products, plated or coated with chromium oxides or with chromium and chromium oxides, varnished (ECSC)
	721070 39 0	Other (ECSC)
	721070 90 0	Other
674.32		**....of a width of less than 600 mm**
	721240 10 0	Tinplate, not further worked than varnished (ECSC)
		Other
		Of a width exceeding 500 mm
	721240 91 0	Not further worked than surface-treated (ECSC)
	721240 93 0	Other
		Of a width not exceeding 500 mm
	721240 95 0	Plated or coated with chromium oxides or with chromium and chromine oxides, varnished
	721240 98 0	Other
		Flat-rolled products of iron or non-alloy steel, clad, painted or coated, n.e.s., of a width of 600 mm or more
674.41		**....plated or coated with lead, including terne-plate**
	721020 10 0	Not further worked than surface-treated or simply cut into shapes other than rectangular (including square) (ECSC)
	721020 90 0	Other
674.42		**....plated or coated with chromium oxides or with chromium and chromium oxides**
	721050 10 0	Not further worked than surface-treated or simply cut into shapes other than rectangular (including square) (ECSC)
	721050 90 0	Other
674.43		**....plated or coated with aluminium**
	*721061 10 0	Not further worked than surface-treated or simply cut into shapes other than rectangle (including square) (ECSC)
	*721061 90 0	Other
		Other
	*721069 10 0	Not further worked than surface-treated or simply cut into shapes other than rectangle (including square) (ECSC)
	*721069 90 0	Other
674.44		**....other**
	721090 10 0	Silvered, gilded, platinum-plated or enamelled
		Other
		Not further worked than surface-treated, including cladding, or simply cut into shapes other than rectangular (including square) (ECSC)
	721090 31 0	Clad
	721090 33 0	Tinned and printed
	*721090 38 0	Other
	721090 90 0	Other
		Flat-rolled products of iron or non-alloy steel, clad, plated or coated, n.e.s., of a width of less than 600 mm
674.51		**....Plated or coated otherwise than by electrolysis**
		Of a width exceeding 500 mm
	721250 10 0	Silvered, gilded, platinum-plated or enamelled
		Other:
		Not further worked than surface-treated:
	721250 31 0	Lead-coated (ECSC)
	721250 51 0	Other (ECSC)
	*721250 58 0	Other
		Of a width not exceeding 500 mm
	721250 75 0	Plated or coated with copper
	721250 91 0	Plated or coated with chromium or nickel
		Plated or coated with aluminium
	721250 93 0	Plated or coated with aluminium-zinc alloys
	721250 97 0	Other
	*721250 99 0	Other
674.52		**....clad**
		Of a width exceeding 500 mm
	721260 11 0	Not further worked than surface-treated (ECSC)
	721260 19 0	Other
		Of a width not exceeding 500 mm
		Not further worked than surface-treated
	721260 91 0	Hot-rolled, not further worked than clad (ECSC)
	721260 93 0	Other
	721260 99 0	Other

S.I.T.C. (R3)	Commodity Code No	Trade description
		FLAT-ROLLED PRODUCTS OF ALLOY STEEL
		Flat-rolled products of silicon-electrical steel
675.11		**....of a width of 600 mm or more**
	*722511 00 0	Grain-oriented (ECSC)
		Other
	*722519 10 0	Hot-rolled
	*722519 90 0	Cold-rolled
675.12		**....of a width of less than 600 mm**
		Grain-orientated
	*722611 10 0	Of a width exceeding 500 mm (ECSC)
	*722611 90 0	Of a width not exceeding 500 mm
		Other:
	*722619 10 0	Not further worked than hot-rolled (ECSC)
		Other:
	*722619 30 0	Of a width exceeding 500 mm (ECSC)
	*722619 90 0	Of a width not exceeding 500 mm
		Flat-rolled products of high speed steel
675.21		**....of a width of 600 mm or more**
	722520 20 0	Not further worked than rolled; not further worked than surface-treated, including cladding or simply cut into shapes other than rectangular (including square) (ECSC)
	722520 90 0	Other
675.22		**....of a width of less than 600 mm**
	722620 20 0	Not further worked than hot-rolled; of a width not exceeding 500 mm, hot-rolled, not further worked than clad; of a width exceeding 500 mm, not further worked than cold-rolled (cold-reduced) or not further worked than surface-treated, including cladding (ECSC)
	722620 80 0	Other
		Flat-rolled products of stainless steel, not further worked than hot-rolled
675.31		**....of a width of 600 mm or more and of a thickness of 4.75 mm or more, in coils**
	*721911 00 0	Of a thickness exceeding 10 mm (ECSC)
		Of a thickness of 4.75 mm or more but not exceeding 10 mm
	721912 10 0	Containing by weight 2.5 % or more of nickel (ECSC)
	721912 90 0	Containing by weight less than 2.5 % of nickel (ECSC)
675.32		**....of a width of 600 mm or more and of a thickness of 3 mm or more but less than 4.75 mm, in coils**
	721913 10 0	Containing by weight 2.5 % or more of nickel
	721913 90 0	Containing by weight less than 2.5 % of nickel
675.33		**....of a width of 600 mm or more and of a thickness of less than 3 mm, in coils**
	721914 10 0	Containing by weight 2.5 % or more of nickel
	721914 90 0	Containing by weight less than 2.5 % of nickel
675.34		**....of a width of 600 mm or more and of a thickness of 4.75 mm or more, not in coils**
		Of a thickness exceeding 10 mm:
	*721921 10 0	Containing by weight 2.5% or more of nickel (ECSC)
	721921 90 0	Containing by weight less than 2.5 % of nickel (ECSC)
		Of a thickness of 4.75 mm or more but not exceeding 10 mm
	721922 10 0	Containing by weight 2.5 % or more of nickel (ECSC)
	721922 90 0	Containing by weight less than 2.5 % of nickel (ECSC)
675.35	*721923 00 0	**....of a width of 600 mm or more and of a thickness of 3 mm or more but less than 4.75 mm, not in coils**
675.36	*721924 10 0	**....of a width of 600 mm or more and of a thickness of less than 3 mm, not in coils**
675.37	722011 00 0	**....of a width of less than 600 mm and of a thickness of 4.75 mm or more**
675.38	722012 00 0	**....of a width of less than 600 mm and of a thickness of less than 4.75 mm**
		Flat-rolled products of other alloy steel, not further worked than hot-rolled
675.41	722530 00 0	**....of a width of 600 mm or more, in coils**
675.42		**....of a width of 600 mm or more, not in coils**
	*722540 20 0	Of a thickness exceeding 15 mm
	722540 50 0	Of a thickness of 4.75 mm or more but not exceeding 15 mm
	*722540 80 0	Of a thickness of less than 4.75 mm
675.43		**....of a width of less than 600 mm**
	722691 10 0	Of a thickness of 4.75 mm or more
	722691 90 0	Of a thickness of less than 4.75 mm

S.I.T.C. (R3)	Commodity Code No	Trade description
		Flat-rolled products of stainless steel, not further worked than cold-rolled (cold-reduced)
675.51	*721931 00 0	....of a width of 600 mm or more and of a thickness of 4.75 mm or more
675.52		....of a width of 600 mm or more and of a thickness of 3 mm or more but less than 4.75 mm
	721932 10 0	Containing by weight 2.5 % or more of nickel
	721932 90 0	Containing by weight less than 2.5 % of nickel
675.53		....of a width of 600 mm or more and of a thickness exceeding 1 mm but less than 3 mm
	721933 10 0	Containing by weight 2.5 % or more of nickel
	721933 90 0	Containing by weight less than 2.5 % of nickel
675.54		....of a width of 600 mm or more and of a thickness of 0.50 mm or more but not exceeding 1 mm
	721934 10 0	Containing by weight 2.5 % or more of nickel
	721934 90 0	Containing by weight less than 2.5 % of nickel
675.55		....of a width of 600 mm or more and of a thickness of less than 0.5 mm
	721935 10 0	Containing by weight 2.5 % or more of nickel
	721935 90 0	Containing by weight less than 2.5 % of nickel
675.56		....of a width of less than 600 mm
	722020 10 0	Of a width exceeding 500 mm (ECSC)
		Of a width not exceeding 500 mm
		Of a thickness of 3 mm or more, containing by weight
	722020 31 0	2.5 % or more of nickel
	722020 39 0	Less than 2.5 % of nickel
		Of a thickness exceeding 0.35 mm but less than 3 mm, containing by weight
	722020 51 0	2.5 % or more of nickel
	722020 59 0	Less than 2.5 % of nickel
		Of a thickness not exceeding 0.35 mm, containing by weight
	722020 91 0	2.5 % or more of nickel
	722020 99 0	Less than 2.5 % of nickel
		Flat-rolled products of other alloy steel, not further worked than cold-rolled (cold-reduced)
675.61	*722550 00 0	....of a width of 600 mm or more
675.62		....of a width of less than 600 mm
	722692 10 0	Of a width exceeding 500 mm (ECSC)
	*722692 90 0	Of a width not exceeding 500 mm
		Flat-rolled products of alloy steel, n.e.s.
675.71		....of stainless steel, of a width of 600 mm or more
	*721990 10 0	Not further worked than surface-treated, including cladding, or simply cut into shapes other than rectangular (including square) (ECSC)
	*721990 90 0	Other
675.72		....of stainless steel, of a width of less than 600 mm
		Of a width exceeding 500 mm
	722090 11 0	Not further worked than surface-treated, including cladding (ECSC)
	722090 19 0	Other
		Of a width not exceeding 500 mm
		Not further worked than surface-treated, including cladding
	722090 31 0	Hot-rolled, not further worked than clad (ECSC)
	722090 39 0	Other
	722090 90 0	Other
675.73		....of other alloy steel, of a width of 600 mm or more
		Electrolytically plated or coated with zinc:
	*722591 10 0	Not further worked than surface-treated, including cladding or simply cut into shapes other than rectangular (including square) (ECSC)
	*722591 90 0	Other
		Otherwise plated or coated with zinc:
	*722592 10 0	Not further worked than surface-treated, including cladding or simply cut into shapes other than rectangular (including square) (ECSC)
	*722592 90 0	Other
		Other
	*722599 10 0	Not further worked than surface-treated, including cladding or simply cut into shapes other than rectangular (including square) (ECSC)
	*722599 90 0	Other
675.74		....of other alloy steel, of a width of less than 600 mm
		Electrolytically plated or coated with zinc:
	*722693 20 0	Of a width not exceeding 500 mm, hot-rolled, not further worked than clad; of a width exceeding 500 mm, not further worked than surface-treated, including cladding (ECSC)
	*722693 80 0	Other
		Otherwise plated or coated with zinc:
	*722694 20 0	Of a width not exceeding 500 mm, hot-rolled, not further worked than clad; of a width exceeding 500 mm, not further worked than surface-treated, including cladding (ECSC)
	*722694 80 0	Other

S.I.T.C. (R3)	Commodity Code No	Trade description
cont 675.74		
	*722699 20 0	Other
		Of a width not exceeding 500 mm, hot-rolled, not further worked than clad; of a width exceeding 500 mm, not further worked than surface-treated, including cladding (ECSC)
	*722699 80 0	Other

IRON AND STEEL BARS, RODS, ANGLES, SHAPES AND SECTIONS (INCLUDING SHEET PILING)

Bars and rods, hot-rolled, in irregularly wound coils, of iron or steel

S.I.T.C. (R3)	Commodity Code No	Trade description
676.11	721310 00 0	**....of iron or non-alloy steel containing indentations, ribs, grooves or other deformations produced during the rolling process**
676.12	721320 00 0	**....of free cutting steel**
676.13		**....other, of iron or non-alloy steel, containing by weight less than 0.60% of carbon**
		Of circular cross-section measuring less than 14 mm in diameter (ECSC)
	*721391 10 0	Of a type used for concrete reinforcement (ECSC)
		Other
	*721391 41 0	Containing by weight 0.06 % or less of carbon
	*721391 49 0	Containing by weight more than 0.06 % but less than 0.25% of carbon (ECSC)
	*721391 70 0	Containing by weight 0.25% or more but not more than 0.75% of carbon (ECSC)
		Other
	*721399 10 0	Containing by weight less than 0.25% or more of carbon (ECSC)
		Other (ECSC)
676.14		**....other, of iron or non-alloy steel, containing by weight 0.60 % of carbon or more**
		Of circular cross-section measuring less than 14 mm in diameter (ECSC)
	*721391 20 0	Of a type used for tyre cord
		Other
	*721391 90 0	Containing by weight more than 0.75 % of carbon
		Other
	*721399 90 0	Containing by weight 0.25 % or more of carbon
676.15		**....of stainless steel**
	722100 10 0	Containing by weight 2.5 % or more of nickel
	722100 90 0	Containing by weight less than 2.5 % of nickel
676.17	722710 00 0	**....of high speed steel**
676.19		**....of other alloy steel**
	722720 00 0	Of silico-manganese steel (ECSC)
		Other:
	722790 10 0	Containing by weight 0.0008 % or more of boron with any other element less than the minimum content referred to in note 1 f) to this chapter (ECSC)
	*722790 50 0	Containing by weight not less than 0.9 % but not more than 1.15 % of carbon, 0.5 % but not more than 2 % of chromium and, if present, not more than 0.5 % of molybdenum
	*722790 95 0	Other

Bars and rods (other than those of heading 676.1) of iron or steel, not further worked than hot-rolled, hot-drawn or hot-extruded, but including those twisted after rolling

S.I.T.C. (R3)	Commodity Code No	Trade description
676.21	721420 00 0	**....of iron or non-alloy steel containing indentations ribs, grooves or other deformations produced during the rolling process**
676.22	721430 00 0	**....of free-cutting steel**
676.23		**....other, of iron or non-alloy steel, containing by weight less than 0.60% of carbon**
		Of rectangular (other than square) cross-section:
	*721491 10 0	Containing by weight less than 0.25% of carbon (ECSC)
		Other
		Containing by weight 0.25% or more of carbon (ECSC)
	*721499 10 0	Of a type used for concrete reinforcement (ECSC)
		Other, of a circular cross-section measuring in diameter
	*721499 31 0	80 mm or more (ECSC)
	*721499 39 0	Less than 80 mm (ECSC)
	*721499 50 0	Other
		Containing by weight 0.25 % or more but less than 0.6 % of carbon (ECSC)
		Of circular cross-section measuring in diameter
	*721499 61 0	80 mm or more
	*721499 69 0	Less than 80 mm
	*721499 80 0	Other
676.24		**....other, of iron or non-alloy steel, containing by weight 0.60% or more**
		Of rectangular (other than square) cross-section:
	*721491 90 0	Containing by weight 0.25% or more of carbon (ECSC)
	*721499 90 0	Other, containing by weight 0.6% or more of carbon (ECSC)
676.25		**....of stainless steel**
		Of circular cross-section

S.I.T.C. (R3)	Commodity Code No	Trade description
cont 676.25		
	*722211 11 0	Of a diameter of 80 mm or more, containing by weight 2.5 % or more of nickel (ECSC)
	*722211 19 0	Less than 2.5 % of nickel (ECSC)
		Of a diameter of 25 mm or more, but less than 80 mm, containing by weight
	*722211 21 0	2.5 % or more of nickel (ECSC)
	*722211 29 0	Less than 2.5 % of nickel (ECSC)
		Of a diameter of less than 25 mm, containing by weight
	*722211 91 0	2.5 % or more of nickel (ECSC)
	*722211 99 0	Less than 2.5 % of nickel (ECSC)
		Other, containing by weight
	*722219 10 0	2.5 % or more of nickel (ECSC)
	*722219 90 0	Less than 2.5 % of nickel (ECSC)
676.29		**....of other alloy steel (except high speed steel or silico-manganese steel**
	722830 20 0	Of tool steel
		Containing by weight not less than 0.9 % but not more than 1.15 % of carbon, not less than 0.5 % but not more than 2 % of chromium and, if present, not more than 0.5 % of molybdenum
	722830 41 0	Of circular cross-section of a diameter of 80 mm or more
	722830 49 0	Other
		Other
		Of circular cross-section, of a diameter of
	722830 61 0	80 mm or more
	722830 69 0	Less than 80 mm
	722830 70 0	Of rectangular (other than square) cross-section, rolled on four faces
	722830 89 0	Other

Bars and rods (other than those of heading 676.1) of iron or steel, not further worked than cold-formed or cold-finished

S.I.T.C. (R3)	Commodity Code No	Trade description
676.31	721510 00 0	**....of free-cutting steel**
676.32		**....other, of iron or non-alloy steel, containing by weight less than 0.60% of carbon**
		Other, not further worked than cold-formed or cold-finished
		Containing by weight less than 0.25 % of carbon
	*721550 11 0	Of rectangular (other than square) cross-section
	*721550 19 0	Other
	*721550 30 0	Containing by weight 0.25 % or more but less than 0.6% of carbon
676.33	*721550 90 0	**....other, of iron or non-alloy steel, containing by weight 0.60% or more**
676.34		**....of stainless steel**
		Of circular cross-section
		Of a diameter of 80 mm or more, containing by weight
	722220 11 0	2.5% or more of nickel
	722220 19 0	Less than 2.5% of nickel
		Of a diameter of 25 mm or more, but less than 80 mm, containing by weight
	722220 21 0	2.5% or more of nickel
	722220 29 0	Less than 2.5% of nickel
		Of a diameter of less than 25 mm, containing by weight
	722220 31 0	2.5% or more of nickel
	722220 39 0	Less than 2.5% of nickel
		Other, containing by weight
	722220 81 0	2.5% or more of nickel
	722220 89 0	Less than 2.5% of nickel
676.39		**....of other alloy steel (except high speed or silico-manganese steel)**
	722850 20 0	Of tool steel
	722850 40 0	Containing by weight not less than 0.9 % but not more than 1.15 % of carbon, not less than 0.5 % but not more than 2 % of chromium and, if present, not more than 0.5% of molybdenum
		Other
		Of circular cross-section, of a diameter of
	722850 61 0	80 mm or more
	722850 69 0	Less than 80 mm
	722850 70 0	Of rectangular (other than square) cross-section, rolled on four faces
	722850 89 0	Other

Other bars and rods of iron and steel

S.I.T.C. (R3)	Commodity Code No	Trade description
676.41		**....of high speed steel**
	722810 10 0	Not further worked than hot-rolled, hot-drawn or extruded (ECSC)
		Other
	722810 30 0	Hot-rolled, hot-drawn or extruded, not further worked than clad (ECSC)
	722810 50 0	Forged
	722810 90 0	Other
676.42		**....of silico-manganese steel**
		Not further worked than hot-rolled, hot-drawn or extruded (ECSC)
	722820 11 0	Of rectangular (other than square) cross-section, rolled on four faces
	722820 19 0	Other

S.I.T.C. (R3)	Commodity Code No	Trade description
cont 676.42		Other
	722820 30 0	Hot-rolled, hot-drawn or extruded, not further worked than clad (ECSC)
	722820 60 0	Other
676.43	721410 00 0	....of iron or non-alloy steel, not further worked than forged
676.44		....of other iron or other non-alloy steel
	721590 10 0	Hot-rolled, hot-drawn or extruded, not further worked than clad (ECSC)
	721590 90 0	Other
676.45		....of stainless steel
	722230 10 0	Hot-rolled, hot-drawn or extruded, not further worked than clad (ECSC)
		Forged, containing by weight:
		Containing by weight:
	722230 51 0	2.5 % or more of nickel
	722230 91 0	Less than 2.5% of nickel
	*722230 98 0	Other
676.46		....of other alloy steel (except high speed or silico-manganese) not further worked than forged
	722840 10 0	Of tool steel
	722840 90 0	Other
676.47		Bars and rods of alloy steel, n.e.s.
	722860 10 0	Hot-rolled, hot-drawn or extruded, not further worked than clad (ECSC)
		Other
	722860 81 0	Of tool steel
	722860 89 0	Other
676.48		Hollow drill bars and rods of alloy or non-alloy steel
	722880 10 0	Of alloy steel (ECSC)
	722880 90 0	Of non-alloy steel (ECSC)
		Angles, shapes and sections (excluding rails) and sheet piling, of iron or steel
676.81		**U, I, H, L or T sections, not further worked than hot-rolled, hot-drawn or extruded, of a height of less than 80 mm, of iron or non-alloy steel**
	721610 00 0	U, I or H sections, not further worked than hot-rolled, hot-drawn or extruded, of a height of less than 80 mm (ECSC)
		L or T sections, not further worked than hot-rolled, hot-drawn or extruded, of a height of less than 80 mm
	721621 00 0	L sections (ECSC)
	721622 00 0	T sections (ECSC)
676.82		**U, I, H, L or T sections, not further worked than hot-rolled, hot-drawn or extruded, of a height of 80 mm or more, of iron or non-alloy steel**
		U, I or H sections, not further worked than hot-rolled, hot-drawn or extrude of a height of 80 mm or more
		U sections (ECSC)
		Of a height of 80 mm or more but not exceeding 220 mm
	721631 11 0	With parallel flange faces
	721631 19 0	Other
		Of a height of more than 220 mm
	721631 91 0	With parallel flange faces
	721631 99 0	Other
		I sections (ECSC)
		Of a height of 80 mm or more but not exceeding 220 mm
	721632 11 0	With parallel flange faces
	721632 19 0	Other
		Of a height of more than 220 mm
	721632 91 0	With parallel flange faces
	721632 99 0	Other
		H sections (ECSC)
	721633 10 0	Of a height of 80 mm or more but not exceeding 180 mm
	721633 90 0	Of a height of more than 180 mm
		L or T sections, not further worked than hot-rolled, hot-drawn or extruded, of a height of 80 mm or more (ECSC)
	721640 10 0	L sections
	721640 90 0	T sections
676.83		**Other angles, shapes and sections, of iron or non-alloy steel, not further worked than hot-rolled, hot-drawn or extruded**
	721650 10 0	With a cross-section which is capable of being enclosed in a square the side of which is 80 mm
		Other
	721650 91 0	Bulb flats
	721650 99 0	Other

S.I.T.C. (R3)	Commodity Code No	Trade description
676.84		**Angles, shapes and sections, not further worked than cold-formed or cold-finished, of iron or non-alloy steel**
		Obtained from flat-rolled products
	*721661 10 0	C, L, U, Z, omega or open-ended sections
	*721661 90 0	Other
	*721669 00 0	Other
676.85		**Other angles, shapes and sections, of iron or non-alloy steel**
		Cold-formed or cold finished from flat-rolled products:
	*721691 10 0	Profiled (ribbed) sheets
		Other:
		Plated or coated with zinc, of a thickness of:
	*721691 30 0	Less than 2.5 mm
	*721691 50 0	2.5 mm or more
	*721691 90 0	Other
		Other
	*721699 10 0	Hot-rolled, hot drawn or extruded, not further worked than clad (ECSC)
	*721699 90 0	Other
676.86		**Sheet piling of iron or steel, whether or not drilled, punched or made from assembled elements; welded angles, shapes and sections, of iron or steel**
	730110 00 0	Sheet piling (ECSC)
	730120 00 0	Angles, shapes and sections
676.87		**Angles, shapes and sections, of stainless steel**
	*722240 10 0	Not further worked than hot-rolled, hot-drawn or extruded (ECSC)
		Other
	722240 30 0	Hot-rolled, hot-drawn or extruded, not further worked than clad (ECSC)
		Other
		Not further worked than cold-formed or cold-finished
	722240 91 0	Obtained from flat-rolled products
	722240 93 0	Other
	722240 99 0	Other
676.88		**Angles, shapes and sections, of other alloy steel**
	722870 10 0	Not further worked than hot-rolled, hot-drawn or extruded (ECSC)
		Other
	722870 31 0	Hot-rolled, hot-drawn or extruded, not further worked than clad (ECSC)
		Other
	722870 91 0	Not further worked than cold-formed or cold-finished
	722870 99 0	Other

RAILS AND RAILWAY TRACK CONSTRUCTION MATERIAL, OF IRON OR STEEL

Railway and tramway track construction material, of iron or steel

S.I.T.C. (R3)	Commodity Code No	Trade description
677.01		**Rails (including check-rails and rack rails), of iron or steel**
	730210 10 0	Current-conducting, with parts of non-ferrous metal
		Other
		New (ECSC)
	730210 31 0	Of a weight per m of 20 kg or more
	730210 39 0	Of a weight per m of less than 20 kg
	730210 90 0	Used (ECSC)
677.09		**Other railway and tramway track construction material of iron or steel (ie., switch blades, crossing frogs, point rods and other crossing pieces, sleepers (cross-ties), fish-plates, chairs, chair wedges, sole plates (base plates), rail clips, bedplates, ties and other material specialised for joining or fixing rails)**
	730220 00 0	Sleepers (cross-ties) (ECSC)
	730230 00 0	Switch blades, crossing frogs, point rods and other crossing pieces
		Fish-plates and sole plates
	730240 10 0	Rolled (ECSC)
	730240 90 0	Other
		Other
	730290 10 0	Check-rails (ECSC)
	730290 30 0	Rail clips, bedplates and ties
	730290 90 0	Other

WIRE OF IRON OR STEEL

Wire of iron or non-alloy steel

S.I.T.C. (R3)	Commodity Code No	Trade description
678.11		**....containing by weight less than 0.25% of carbon**
		Not plated or coated, whether or not polished
	*721710 10 0	With a maximum cross-sectional dimension of less than 0.8 mm
		With a maximum cross-sectional dimension of 0.8 mm or more:
	*721710 31 0	Containing indentations, ribs, grooves or other deformations produced during the rolling process
	*721710 39 0	Other
		Plated or coated with zinc
	*721720 10 0	With a maximum cross-sectional dimension of less than 0.8 mm

S.I.T.C. (R3)	Commodity Code No	Trade description
cont 678.11	*721720 30 0	With a maximum cross-sectional dimension of 0.8 mm or more
		Plated or coated with other base metals
		With a maximum cross-sectional dimension of less than 0.8 mm
	*721730 11 0	Copper-coated
	*721730 19 0	Other
		With a maximum cross-sectional dimension of 0.8 mm or more
	*721730 31 0	Copper-coated
	*721730 39 0	Other
		Other
	*721790 10 0	With a maximum cross-sectional dimension of less than 0.8 mm
	*721790 30 0	With a maximum cross-sectional dimension of 0.8 mm or more
678.12		....containing by weight 0.25% or more but less than 0.60% of carbon
	*721710 50 0	Not plated or coated, whether or not polished
	*721720 50 0	Plated or coated with zinc
	*721730 50 0	Plated or coated with other base metals
	*721790 50 0	Other
678.13		....containing by weight 0.60% or more of carbon
	*721710 90 0	Not plated or coated, whether or not polished
	*721720 90 0	Plated or coated with zinc
	*721730 90 0	Plated or coated with other base metals
	*721790 90 0	Other
		Wire of stainless steel or other alloy steel
678.21		....of stainless steel
		Containing by weight 2.5 % or more of nickel
	722300 11 0	Containing by weight 28 % or more but not more than 31 % of nickel and 20 % or more but not more than 22 % of chromium
	722300 19 0	Other
		Containing by weight less than 2.5 % of nickel
	722300 91 0	Containing by weight 13 % or more but not more than 25 % of chromium and 3.5 % or more but not more than 6 % of aluminium
	722300 99 0	Other
678.29		....of other alloy steel
	722910 00 0	Of high-speed steel
	*722920 00 0	Of silico-manganese steel
		Other
	722990 50 0	Containing by weight not less than 0.9 % but not more than 1.15 % of carbon, not less than 0.5 % but not more than 2 % of chromium and, if present, not more than 0.5 % of molybdenum
	722990 90 0	Other
		TUBES, PIPES AND HOLLOW PROFILES, AND TUBE OR PIPE FITTINGS, OF IRON OR STEEL
		Tubes, pipes and hollow profiles, seamless, of iron or steel
679.11		**Tubes, pipes and hollow profiles, of cast iron**
	730300 10 0	Tubes and pipes of a kind used in pressure systems
	730300 90 0	Other
679.12		**Line pipe (other than cast iron) of a kind used for oil or gas pipelines**
	730410 10 0	Of an external diameter not exceeding 168.3 mm
	730410 30 0	Of an external diameter exceeding 168.3 mm, but not exceeding 406.4 mm
	730410 90 0	Of an external diameter exceeding 406.4 mm
679.13		**Casing, tubing and drill pipe, of a kind used in drilling for oil or gas, of iron (other than cast iron)**
	*730421 00 0	Drill pipe
		Other
	*730429 11 0	Of an external diameter not exceeding 406.4 mm
	*730429 19 0	Of an external diameter exceeding 406.4 mm
679.14		**Other, of circular cross-section, of iron or non-alloy steel**
		Cold-drawn or cold-rolled (cold-reduced)
	730431 10 0	With attached fittings, suitable for conducting gases or liquids, for use in civil aircraft
		Other
	730431 91 0	Precision tubes
	730431 99 0	Other
		Other
	730439 10 0	Unworked, straight and of uniform wall-thickness, for use solely in the manufacture of tubes and pipes with other cross-sections and wall-thicknesses
		Other
	730439 20 0	With attached fittings, suitable for conducting gases or liquids, for use in civil aircraft
		Other
	730439 30 0	Of an external diameter exceeding 421 mm and of a wall-thickness exceeding 10.5 mm
		Other
		Threaded or threadable tubes (gas pipe)
	730439 51 0	Plated or coated with zinc
	730439 59 0	Other

S.I.T.C. (R3)	Commodity Code No	Trade description

cont
679.14

		Other, of an external diameter
	730439 91 0	Not exceeding 168.3 mm
	730439 93 0	Exceeding 168.3 mm, but not exceeding 406.4 mm
	730439 99 0	Exceeding 406.4 mm

679.15

		Other, of circular cross-section, of stainless steel
		Cold-drawn or cold-rolled (cold-reduced)
	730441 10 0	With attached fittings, suitable for conducting gases or liquids, for use in civil aircraft
	730441 90 0	Other
		Other
	730449 10 0	Unworked, straight and of uniform wall-thickness, for use solely in the manufacture of tubes and pipes with other cross-sections and wall-thicknesses
		Other
	730449 30 0	With attached fittings, suitable for conducting gases or liquids, for use in civil aircraft
		Other
	730449 91 0	Of an external diameter not exceeding 406.4 mm
	730449 99 0	Of an external diameter exceeding 406.4 mm

679.16

		Other, of circular cross-section, of other alloy steel
		Cold-drawn or cold-rolled (cold-reduced)
		Straight and of uniform wall-thickness, of alloy steel containing by weight not less than 0.9 % but not more than 1.15 % of carbon, not less than 0.5% but not more than 2 % of chromium and not more than 0.5 % of molybdenum, of a length
	730451 11 0	Not exceeding 4.5 m
	730451 19 0	Exceeding 4.5 m
		Other
	730451 30 0	With attached fittings, suitable for conducting gases or liquids, for use in civil aircraft
		Other
	730451 91 0	Precision tubes
	730451 99 0	Other
		Other
	730459 10 0	Unworked, straight and of uniform wall-thickness, for use solely in the manufacture of tubes and pipes with other cross-sections and wall-thicknesses
		Other, straight and of uniform wall-thickness, of alloy steel containing by weight not less than 0.9 % but not more than 1.15 % of carbon, not less than 0.5 % but not more than 2 % of chromium and not more than 0.5 % of molybdenum of a length
	730459 31 0	Not exceeding 4.5 m
	730459 39 0	Exceeding 4.5 m
		Other
	730459 50 0	With attached fittings, suitable for conducting gases or liquids, for use in civil aircraft
		Other
	730459 91 0	Of an external diameter not exceeding 168.3 mm
	730459 93 0	Of an external diameter exceeding 168.3 mm, but not exceeding 406.4 mm
	730459 99 0	Of an external diameter exceeding 406.4 mm

679.17

		Other seamless tubes, pipes and hollow profiles
	730490 10 0	With attached fittings, suitable for conducting gases or liquids, for use in civil aircraft
	730490 90 0	Other

Other tubes and pipes (eg., welded, riveted or similarly closed), having internal and external circular cross-sections, the external diameter of which exceeds 406.4 mm, of iron or steel

679.31

		Line pipe of a kind used for oil or gas pipelines
	730511 00 0	Longitudinally submerged arc welded
	730512 00 0	Other, longitudinally welded
	730519 00 0	Other

679.32

		Casing of a kind used in drilling for oil or gas
	730520 10 0	Longitudinally welded
	730520 90 0	Other

679.33

		Other, welded
	730531 00 0	Longitudinally welded
	730539 00 0	Other

679.39

	730590 00 0	**Other tubes and pipes**

Other tubes, pipes and hollow profiles (e.g., open seam or welded, riveted or similarly closed), of iron or steel

679.41

		Line pipe of a kind used for oil or gas pipelines
		Longitudinally welded, of an external diameter of
	730610 11 0	Not more than 168.3 mm
	730610 19 0	More than 168.3 mm, but not more than 406.4 mm
	730610 90 0	Spirally welded

679.42

	730620 00 0	**Casing and tubing, of a kind used in drilling for oil or gas**

S.I.T.C. (R3)	Commodity Code No	Trade description
679.43		**Other, welded, of circular cross-section**
		Of iron or non-alloy steel
	730630 10 0	With attached fittings, suitable for conducting gases or liquids, for use in civil aircraft
		Other
		Precision tubes, with a wall thickness
	730630 21 0	Not exceeding 2 mm
	730630 29 0	Exceeding 2 mm
		Other
		Threaded or threadable tubes (gas pipe)
	730630 51 0	Plated or coated with zinc
	730630 59 0	Other
		Other, of an external diameter
		Not exceeding 168.3 mm
	730630 71 0	Plated or coated with zinc
	730630 78 0	Other
	730630 90 0	Exceeding 168.3 mm, but not exceeding 406.4 mm
		Of stainless steel
	730640 10 0	With attached fittings, suitable for conducting gases or liquids, for use in civil aircraft
		Other
	730640 91 0	Cold-drawn or cold-rolled (cold-reduced)
	730640 99 0	Other
		Of other alloy steel
	730650 10 0	With attached fittings, suitable for conducting gases or liquids, for use in civil aircraft
		Other
	730650 91 0	Precision tubes
	730650 99 0	Other
679.44		**Other, welded, of non-circular cross-section**
	730660 10 0	With attached fittings, suitable for conducting gases or liquids, for use in civil aircraft
		Other
		Of rectangular (including square) cross-section, with a wall thickness
	730660 31 0	Not exceeding 2 mm
	730660 39 0	Exceeding 2 mm
	730660 90 0	Of other sections
679.49	730690 00 0	**Other**
		Tube or pipe fittings (eg., couplings, elbows, sleeves), of iron or steel
679.51		**Cast fittings of non-malleable cast iron**
	730711 10 0	Of a kind used in pressure systems
	730711 90 0	Other
679.52		**Other cast fittings**
	730719 10 0	Of malleable cast iron
	730719 90 0	Other
679.53	730721 00 0	**Flanges of stainless steel**
679.54		**Threaded elbows, bends and sleeves of stainless steel**
	730722 10 0	Sleeves
	730722 90 0	Elbows and bends
679.55		**Butt welding fittings of stainless steel**
	730723 10 0	Elbows and bends
	730723 90 0	Other
679.56		**Other tube and pipe fittings of stainless steel**
	730729 10 0	Threaded
	730729 30 0	For welding
	730729 90 0	Other
679.59		**Tube and pipe fittings of iron or steel, n.e.s.**
	730791 00 0	Flanges
		Threaded elbows, bends and sleeves
	730792 10 0	Sleeves
	730792 90 0	Elbows and bends
		Butt welding fittings
		With greatest external diameter not exceeding 609.6 mm
	730793 11 0	Elbows and bends
	730793 19 0	Other
		With greatest external diameter exceeding 609.6 mm
	730793 91 0	Elbows and bends
	730793 99 0	Other
		Other
	730799 10 0	Threaded
	730799 30 0	For welding
	730799 90 0	Other

S.I.T.C. (R3)	Commodity Code No	Trade description

NON-FERROUS METALS

SILVER, PLATINUM AND OTHER METALS OF THE PLATINUM GROUP

Silver (including base metals clad with silver), unwrought, unworked or semi-manufactured

681.12	710700 00 0	**Base metals clad with silver, not further worked than semi- manufactured**
681.13		**Silver (including silver plated with gold or platinum), unwrought**
	710691 10 0	Of a fineness of not less than 999 parts per 1 000
	710691 90 0	Of a fineness of less than 999 parts per 1 000
681.14		**Silver (including silver plated with gold or platinum), in semi-manufactured or in powdered form**
	710610 00 0	Powder
		Other
		Semi-manufactured
	710692 10 0	Purls, spangles and cuttings
		Other
	710692 91 0	Of a fineness of not less than 750 parts per 1000
	710692 99 0	Of a fineness of less than 750 parts per 1000

Platinum and other metals of the platinum group (including metals clad with platinum or other metals of the platinum group), unwrought, unworked or semi-manufactured

681.22	711100 00 0	**Base metals, silver or gold, clad with platinum or other metals of the platinum group, not further worked than semi-manufactured**
681.23	*711011 00 0	**Platinum and platinum alloys, unwrought or in powder form**
681.24		**Other metals of the platinum group and alloys thereof, unwrought or in powder form**
	711021 00 0	Palladium
	711031 00 0	Rhodium
	711041 00 0	Iridium, osmium and ruthenium
681.25		**Platinum and other metals of the platinum group and alloys thereof, in other semi-manufactured forms**
		Platinum
	711019 10 0	Bars, rods, wire and sections; plates; sheets and strips of a thickness, excluding any backing, exceeding 0.15 mm
	711019 30 0	Tubes, pipes and hollow bars
	711019 50 0	Thin sheets and strips (foil) of a thickness, excluding any backing, not exceeding 0.15 mm
	711019 90 0	Other
	711029 00 0	Palladium
	711039 00 0	Rhodium
	711049 00 0	Iridium, osmium and ruthenium

COPPER

Copper, refined and unrefined; copper anodes for electrolytic refining; copper alloys unwrought

682.11	740200 00 0	**Unrefined copper (including blister copper but excluding cement copper); copper anodes for electrolytic refining**
682.12		**Refined copper**
	740311 00 0	Cathodes and sections of cathodes
	740312 00 0	Wire-bars
	740313 00 0	Billets
	740319 00 0	Other
682.13	740500 00 0	**Master alloys of copper**
682.14		**Copper alloys (other than master alloys)**
	740321 00 0	Copper-zinc base alloys (brass)
	740322 00 0	Copper-tin base alloys (bronze)
	740323 00 0	Copper-nickel base alloys (cupro-nickel) or copper-nickel-zinc base alloys (nickel silver)
	740329 00 0	Other copper alloys (other than master alloys of heading 682.13)

Copper bars, rods and profiles

682.31	740710 00 0	....**of refined copper**
682.32		....**of copper alloys**
		Of copper-zinc base alloys (brass)
	740721 10 0	Bars and rods
	740721 90 0	Profiles
		Of copper-nickel base alloys (cupro-nickel) or copper-nickel-zinc base alloys (nickel silver)
	740722 10 0	Of copper-nickel base alloys (cupro-nickel)
	740722 90 0	Of copper-nickel-zinc base alloys (nickel silver)
	740729 00 0	Other

S.I.T.C. (R3)	Commodity Code No	Trade description
		Copper wire
682.41		**....of refined copper**
	740811 00 0	Of which the maximum cross-sectional dimension exceeds 6 mm
		Other
	740819 10 0	Of which the maximum cross-sectional dimension exceeds 0.5 mm
	740819 90 0	Of which the maximum cross-sectional dimension does not exceed 0.5 mm
682.42		**....of copper alloys**
	740821 00 0	Of copper-zinc base alloys (brass)
	740822 00 0	Of copper-nickel base alloys (cupro-nickel) or copper-nickel-zinc base alloys (nickel silver)
	740829 00 0	Other
		Copper plates, sheets and strip, of a thickness exceeding 0.15 mm
682.51		**....of refined copper**
	*740911 00 0	In coils
	740919 00 0	Other
682.52		**....of copper alloys**
		Of copper-zinc base alloys (brass)
	740921 00 0	In coils
	740929 00 0	Other
		Of copper-tin base alloys (bronze)
	740931 00 0	In coils
	740939 00 0	Other
		Of copper-nickel base alloys (cupro-nickel) or copper-nickel-zinc base alloys (nickel silver)
	740940 10 0	Of copper-nickel base alloys (cupro-nickel)
	740940 90 0	Of copper-nickel-zinc base alloys (nickel silver)
		Of other copper alloys
	740990 10 0	In coils
	740990 90 0	Other
		Copper foil (whether or not printed or backed with paper, paperboard, plastics or similar backing materials) of a thickness (excluding any backing) not exceeding 0.15 mm; copper powders and flakes
682.61		**Copper foil (whether or not printed or backed with paper, paperboard, plastics or similar backing materials) of a thickness (excluding any backing) not exceeding 0.15 mm**
		Not backed
	741011 00 0	Of refined copper
	741012 00 0	Of copper alloys
		Backed
	741021 00 0	Of refined copper
	741022 00 0	Of copper alloys
682.62		**Copper powders and flakes**
	740610 00 0	Powders of non-lamellar structure
	740620 00 0	Powders of lamellar structure; flakes
		Copper tubes, pipes and tube or pipe fittings (e.g., couplings, elbows, sleeves)
682.71		**Tubes and pipes**
		Of refined copper
		Straight, of a wall thickness
	741110 11 0	Exceeding 0.6 mm
	741110 19 0	Not exceeding 0.6 mm
	741110 90 0	Other
		Of copper alloys
		Of copper-zinc base alloys (brass)
	*741121 10 0	Straight
	741121 90 0	Other
	741122 00 0	Of copper-nickel base alloys (cupro-nickel) or copper-nickel-zinc base alloys (nickel silver)
		Other
	741129 10 0	Straight
	741129 90 0	Other
682.72		**Tube or pipe fittings**
	741210 00 0	Of refined copper
	741220 00 0	Of copper alloys
		NICKEL
		Nickel and nickel alloys, unwrought (excluding electro-plating anodes)
683.11	750210 00 0	**Nickel, not alloyed**
683.12	750220 00 0	**Nickel alloys**

S.I.T.C. (R3)	Commodity Code No	Trade description
		Nickel and nickel alloys, worked (excluding electro-plating anodes)
683.21		**Nickel bars, rods, profiles and wire**
		Bars, rods and profiles
	750511 00 0	Of nickel, not alloyed
	750512 00 0	Of nickel alloys
		Wire
	750521 00 0	Of nickel, not alloyed
	750522 00 0	Of nickel alloys
683.22		**Nickel tubes, pipes and tube or pipe fittings (e.g., couplings, elbows, sleeves)**
		Tubes and pipes
	750711 00 0	Of nickel, not alloyed
	750712 00 0	Of nickel alloys
	750720 00 0	Tube or pipe fittings
683.23	750400 00 0	**Nickel powders and flakes**
683.24		**Nickel plates, sheets, strip and foil**
	750610 00 0	Of nickel, not alloyed
	750620 00 0	Of nickel alloys
		ALUMINIUM
		Aluminium and aluminium alloys, unwrought
684.11	760110 00 0	**Aluminium, not alloyed**
684.12		**Aluminium alloys**
	760120 10 0	Primary
		Secondary
	*760120 91 0	In ingots or in a liquid state
	*760120 99 0	Other
		Aluminium and aluminium alloys, worked
684.21		**Aluminium bars, rods and profiles**
		Of aluminium, not alloyed
	760410 10 0	Bars and rods
	760410 90 0	Profiles
		Of aluminium alloys
	760421 00 0	Hollow profiles
		Other
	760429 10 0	Bars and rods
	760429 90 0	Profiles
684.22		**Aluminium wire**
		Of aluminium, not alloyed
	760511 00 0	Of which the maximum cross-sectional dimension exceeds 7 mm
	760519 00 0	Other
		Of aluminium alloys
	760521 00 0	Of which the maximum cross-sectional dimension exceeds 7 mm
	760529 00 0	Other
684.23		**Aluminium plates, sheets and strip, of a thickness exceeding 0.20 mm**
		Rectangular (including square)
		Of aluminium, not alloyed
	760611 10 0	Painted, varnished or plastic-coated
		Other, of a thickness of
	760611 91 0	Less than 3 mm
	760611 93 0	Not less than 3 mm but less than 6 mm
	760611 99 0	Not less than 6 mm
		Of aluminium alloys
	760612 10 0	Strip for venetian blinds
		Other
	760612 50 0	Painted, varnished or plastic-coated
		Other, of a thickness of
	760612 91 0	Less than 3 mm
	760612 93 0	Not less than 3 mm but less than 6 mm
	760612 99 0	Not less than 6 mm
		Other
	760691 00 0	Of aluminium, not alloyed
	760692 00 0	Of aluminium alloys
684.24		**Aluminium foil (whether or not printed or backed with paper, paperboard, plastics or similar backing materials) of a thickness (excluding any backing) not exceeding 0.20 mm**
		Not backed
		Rolled but not further worked
	760711 10 0	Of a thickness of less than 0.021 mm
	760711 90 0	Of a thickness of not less than 0.021 mm but not more than 0.2 mm

S.I.T.C. (R3)	Commodity Code No	Trade description
cont 684.24		Other
	760719 10 0	Of a thickness of less than 0.021 mm
		Of a thickness of not less than 0.021 mm but not more than 0.2 mm
	760719 91 0	Self-adhesive
	760719 99 0	Other
		Backed
	760720 10 0	Of a thickness (excluding any backing) of less than 0.021 mm
		Of a thickness (excluding any backing) of not less than 0.021 mm but not more than 0.2 mm
	760720 91 0	Self-adhesive
	760720 99 0	Other
684.25		**Aluminium powders and flakes**
	760310 00 0	Powders of non-lamellar structure
	760320 00 0	Powders of lamellar structure; flakes
684.26		**Aluminium tubes and pipes**
		Of aluminium, not alloyed
	760810 10 0	With attached fittings, suitable for conducting gases or liquids, for use in civil aircraft
	760810 90 0	Other
		Of aluminium alloys
	760820 10 0	With attached fittings, suitable for conducting gases or liquids, for use in civil aircraft
		Other
	760820 30 0	Welded
		Other
	760820 91 0	Not further worked than extruded
	760820 99 0	Other
684.27	760900 00 0	**Aluminium tube and pipe fittings (eg., couplings, elbows, sleeves)**
		LEAD
		Lead and lead alloys, unwrought
685.11		**Unrefined lead and lead alloys**
		Other
	780191 00 0	Containing by weight antimony as the principal other element
		Other
	780199 10 0	For refining, containing 0.02 % or more by weight of silver (bullion lead)
		Other
	780199 91 0	Lead alloys
	780199 99 0	Other
685.12	780110 00 0	**Refined lead**
		Lead and lead alloys, worked
685.21	780300 00 0	**Lead bars, rods, profiles and wire**
685.22		**Lead plates, sheets, strip and foil; lead powders and flakes**
		Plates, sheets, strip and foil
	780411 00 0	Sheets, strip and foil of a thickness (excluding any backing) not exceeding 0.2 mm
	780419 00 0	Other
	780420 00 0	Powders and flakes
685.24	780500 00 0	**Lead tubes, pipes and tube or pipe fittings (e.g., couplings, elbows, sleeves)**
		ZINC
		Zinc and zinc alloys, unwrought
686.11		**Zinc, not alloyed**
	790111 00 0	Containing by weight 99.99 % or more of zinc
		Containing by weight less than 99.99 % of zinc
	790112 10 0	Containing by weight 99.95 % or more but less than 99.99 % of zinc
	790112 30 0	Containing by weight 98.5% or more but less than 99.95% of zinc
	790112 90 0	Containing by weight 97.5% or more but less than 98.5% of zinc
686.12	790120 00 0	**Zinc alloys**
		Zinc and zinc alloys, worked
686.31	790400 00 0	**Zinc bars, rods, profiles and wire**
686.32	790500 00 0	**Zinc plates, sheets, strip and foil**
686.33		**Zinc dust (blue powder), powders and flakes**
	790310 00 0	Zinc dust
	790390 00 0	Other
686.34	790600 00 0	**Zinc tubes, pipes and tube or pipe fittings (e.g., couplings, elbows, sleeves)**

S.I.T.C. (R3)	Commodity Code No	Trade description
		TIN
		Tin and tin alloys, unwrought
687.11	800110 00 0	**Tin, not alloyed**
687.12	800120 00 0	**Tin alloys**
		Tin and tin alloys, worked
687.21	800300 00 0	**Tin bars, rods, profiles and wire**
687.22	800400 00 0	**Tin plates, sheets and strip, of a thickness exceeding 0.20 mm**
687.23		**Tin foil (whether or not printed or backed with paper, paperboard, plastics or similar backing materials), of a thickness (excluding any backing) not exceeding 0.20 mm; tin powders and flakes**
	*800500 10 0	Foil
	*800500 20 0	Powders and flakes
687.24	800600 00 0	**Tin tubes, pipes and tube or pipe fittings (e.g., couplings, elbows sleeves)**
		MISCELLANEOUS NON-FERROUS BASE METALS EMPLOYED IN METALLURGY, AND CERMETS
		Tungsten (wolfram), molybdenum, tantalum and magnesium, unwrought (including waste and scrap)
689.11		**Tungsten (wolfram), unwrought; tungsten waste and scrap**
	810110 00 0	Powders
		Other
		Unwrought tungsten, including bars and rods obtained simply by sintering; waste and scrap
	810191 10 0	Unwrought tungsten, including bars and rods obtained simply by sintering
	810191 90 0	Waste and scrap
689.12		**Molybdenum, unwrought; molybdenum waste and scrap**
	810210 00 0	Powders
		Other
		Unwrought molybdenum, including bars and rods obtained simply by sintering; waste and scrap
	810291 10 0	Unwrought molybdenum, including bars and rods obtained simply by sintering
	810291 90 0	Waste and scrap
689.13		**Tantalum, unwrought (including bars and rods obtained simply by sintering); waste and scrap; powders**
	810310 10 0	Unwrought tantalum, including bars and rods obtained simply by sintering; powders
	810310 90 0	Waste and scrap
689.14	810420 00 0	**Magnesium waste and scrap**
689.15		**Magnesium, unwrought**
	810411 00 0	Containing at least 99.8 % by weight of magnesium
	810419 00 0	Other
		Intermediate products of cobalt metallurgy; cobalt, cadmium, titanium and zirconium, unwrought (including waste and scrap)
689.81		**Cobalt mattes and other intermediate products of cobalt metallurgy; cobalt, unwrought; waste and scrap; powders**
	810510 10 0	Cobalt mattes and other intermediate products of cobalt metallurgy; unwrought cobalt; powders
	810510 90 0	Waste and scrap
689.82		**Cadmium, unwrought; cadmium waste and scrap; powders**
	810710 10 0	Unwrought cadmium; powders
	810710 90 0	Waste and scrap
689.83		**Titanium, unwrought; titanium waste and scrap; powders**
	810810 10 0	Unwrought titanium; powders
	810810 90 0	Waste and scrap
689.84		**Zirconium, unwrought; zirconium waste and scrap; powders**
	810910 10 0	Unwrought zirconium; powders
	810910 90 0	Waste and scrap
		Base metals, n.e.s., and cermets, and articles thereof, n.e.s. (including waste and scrap)
689.91		**Beryllium, unwrought; beryllium waste and scrap; powders**
	811211 10 0	Unwrought; powders
	811211 90 0	Waste and scrap
689.92		**Bismuth and articles thereof (including waste and scrap)**
	810600 10 0	Unwrought bismuth; waste and scrap; powders
	810600 90 0	Other

S.I.T.C. (R3)	Commodity Code No	Trade description
689.93		**Antimony and articles thereof (including waste and scrap)**
		Unwrought antimony; waste and scrap; powders
	811000 11 0	Unwrought antimony; powders
	811000 19 0	Waste and scrap
	811000 90 0	Other
689.94		**Manganese and articles thereof (including waste and scrap)**
		Unwrought manganese; waste and scrap; powders
	811100 11 0	Unwrought manganese; powders
	811100 19 0	Waste and scrap
	811100 90 0	Other
689.95		**Chromium and articles thereof (including waste and scrap)**
		Unwrought; waste and scrap; powders
	811220 10 0	Alloys containing more than 10 % by weight of nickel
		Other
	811220 31 0	Unwrought; powders
	811220 39 0	Waste and scrap
	811220 90 0	Other
689.96		**Germanium and articles thereof (including waste and scrap)**
	811230 20 0	Unwrought; powders
	811230 40 0	Waste and scrap
	811230 90 0	Other
689.97		**Vanadium and articles thereof (including waste and scrap)**
		Unwrought; waste and scrap; powders
	811240 11 0	Unwrought; powders
	811240 19 0	Waste and scrap
	811240 90 0	Other
689.98		**Other base metals, unwrought; waste and scrap; powders**
		Unwrought; waste and scrap; powders
	811291 10 0	Hafnium (celtium)
		Niobium (columbium); Rhenium
	811291 31 0	Unwrought; powders
	811291 39 0	Waste and scrap
		Gallium; indium; thallium
	811291 50 0	Waste and scrap
		Other
	811291 81 0	Indium
	811291 89 0	Gallium; thallium
689.99		**Cermets and articles thereof (including waste and scrap)**
	811300 20 0	Unwrought
	811300 40 0	Waste and scrap
	811300 90 0	Other

DIVISION 69

MANUFACTURES OF METALS, N.E.S.

STRUCTURES AND PARTS OF STRUCTURES, N.E.S., OF IRON, STEEL OR ALUMINIUM

Structures (excluding prefabricated buildings of heading 811) parts of structures (e.g., bridges and bridge-sections, lock-gates, towers, lattice masts, roofs, roofing frameworks, doors and windows and their frames and thresholds for doors, shutters, balustrades, pillars and columns), of iron or steel; plates, rods, angles, shapes, sections, tubes and the like, prepared for use in structures, of iron or steel

S.I.T.C. (R3)	Commodity Code No	Trade description
691.11	730810 00 0	**Bridges and bridge-sections**
691.12	730820 00 0	**Towers and lattice masts**
691.13	730830 00 0	**Doors, windows and their frames and thresholds for doors**
691.14		**Equipment for scaffolding, shuttering or propping pit-propping**
	730840 10 0	Mine supports
	730840 90 0	Other
691.19		**Other**
	730890 10 0	Weirs, sluices, lock-gates, landing stages, fixed docks and other maritime and waterway structures
		Other
		Solely or principally of sheet
	730890 51 0	Panels containing two walls of profiled (ribbed) sheet with an insulating core
	730890 59 0	Other
	730890 99 0	Other

S.I.T.C. (R3)	Commodity Code No	Trade description
		Aluminium structures (excluding prefabricated buildings of heading 811) towers, lattice masts, roofs, roofing frameworks, doors and windows and their frames and thresholds for doors, balustrades, pillars and columns); aluminium plates, rods, profiles, tubes and the like, prepared for use in structures
691.21	761010 00 0	Doors, windows and their frames and thresholds for doors
691.29		Aluminium structures and parts of structures, n.e.s.; aluminium plates, rods, profiles, tubes and the like, prepared for use in structures
	761090 10 0	Bridges and bridge-sections, towers and lattice masts
	761090 90 0	Other
		METAL CONTAINERS FOR STORAGE OR TRANSPORT
		Reservoirs, tanks, vats and similar containers, for any material (other than compressed or liquefied gas), of iron, steel or aluminium, of a capacity exceeding 300 litres, whether or not lined or heat-insulated, but not fitted with mechanical or thermal equipment
692.11		....of iron or steel
	730900 10 0	For gases (other than compressed or liquefied gas)
		For liquids
	730900 30 0	Lined or heat-insulated
		Other, of a capacity
	730900 51 0	Exceeding 100,000 litres
	730900 59 0	Not exceeding 100,000 litres
	730900 90 0	For solids
692.12	761100 00 0	....of aluminium
		Tanks, casks, drums, cans, boxes and similar containers, for any material (including compressed or liquefied gas), of iron, steel or aluminium, of a capacity not exceeding 300 litres, whether or not lined or heat-insulated, but not fitted with mechanical or thermal equipment
692.41		Tanks, casks, drums, cans, boxes and similar containers, for any material (other than compressed or liquefied gas), of iron or steel, of a capacity not exceeding 300 litres, whether or not lined or heat-insulated, but not fitted with mechanical or thermal equipment
	731010 00 0	Of a capacity of 50 l or more
		Of a capacity of less than 50 l
		Cans which are to be closed by soldering or crimping
	731021 10 0	Cans of a kind used for preserving food and drink
		Other, with a wall thickness of
	731021 91 0	Less than 0.5 mm
	731021 99 0	0.5 mm or more
		Other
	731029 10 0	With a wall thickness of less than 0.5 mm
	731029 90 0	With a wall thickness of 0.5 mm or more
692.42		Aluminium casks, drums, cans, boxes and similar containers (including rigid or collapsible tubular containers), for any material (other than compressed or liquefied gas), of a capacity not exceeding 300 litres, whether or not lined or heat-insulated, but not fitted with mechanical or thermal equipment
	761210 00 0	Collapsible tubular containers
		Other
	761290 10 0	Rigid tubular containers
	761290 20 0	Containers of a kind used for aerosols
		Other, with a capacity of
	761290 91 0	50 l or more
	761290 98 0	Less than 50 l
692.43		Containers of iron or steel for compressed or liquefied gas
	731100 10 0	Seamless
		Other, of a capacity of
	731100 91 0	Less than 1,000 l
	731100 99 0	1,000 l or more
692.44	761300 00 0	Containers of aluminium for compressed or liquefied gas
		WIRE PRODUCTS (EXCLUDING INSULATED ELECTRICAL WIRING) AND FENCING GRILLS
		Stranded wire, ropes, cables, plaited bands, slings and the like, of iron, steel, copper or aluminium, not electrically insulated
693.11		....of iron or steel
		Stranded wire, ropes and cables
	731210 10 0	With fittings attached, or made up into articles, for use in civil aircraft
		Other
	731210 30 0	Of stainless steel
		Other, with a maximum cross-sectional dimension
		Not exceeding 3 mm
	731210 51 0	Plated or coated with copper-zinc alloys (brass)
	731210 59 0	Other

S.I.T.C. (R3)	Commodity Code No	Trade description

cont
693.11

		Exceeding 3 mm
		Stranded wire
	731210 71 0	Not coated
		Coated
	731210 75 0	Plated or coated with zinc
	731210 79 0	Other
		Ropes and cables (including locked coil ropes)
		Not coated or only plated or coated with zinc, with a maximum cross-sectional dimension
	731210 82 0	Exceeding 3 mm but not exceeding 12 mm
	731210 84 0	Exceeding 12 mm but not exceeding 24 mm
	731210 86 0	Exceeding 24 mm but not exceeding 48 mm
	731210 88 0	Exceeding 48 mm
	731210 99 0	Other
		Other
	731290 10 0	With fittings attached, or made up into articles for use in civil aircraft
	731290 90 0	Other

693.12

	741300 10 0	....of copper
		With fittings attached, for use in civil aircraft
		Other
	741300 91 0	Of refined copper
	741300 99 0	Of copper alloys

693.13

	761410 00 0	....of aluminium
		With steel core
	761490 00 0	Other

693.20   731300 00 0   **Barbed wire of iron or steel; twisted hoop or single flat wire, barbed or not, and loosely twisted double wire, of a kind used for fencing, of iron or steel**

Cloth (including endless bands), grill, netting and fencing, of iron, steel or copper wire; expanded metal of iron, steel or copper

693.51   **....of iron or steel**

		Woven products
	*731412 00 0	Endless bands, for machinery
	*731413 00 0	Other endless bands, for machinery
	*731414 00 0	Other woven cloth, of stainless steel
	*731419 00 0	Other

Grill, netting and fencing, welded at the intersection, of wire with a maximum cross-sectional dimension of 3 mm or more and having a mesh size of 100 c^{m2} or more

	731420 10 0	Of ribbed wire
	731420 90 0	Other
		Other grill, netting and fencing, welded at the intersection
	*731431 00 0	Plated or coated with zinc
	*731439 00 0	Other
		Other grill, netting and fencing
		Plated or coated with zinc
	731441 10 0	Hexagonal netting
	731441 90 0	Other
		Coated with plastics
	731442 10 0	Hexagonal netting
	731442 90 0	Other
	731449 00 0	Other
	731450 00 0	Expanded metal

693.52

		....of copper
	*741420 00 0	Cloth
	*741490 00 0	Other

NAILS, SCREWS, NUTS, BOLTS, RIVETS AND THE LIKE, OF IRON, STEEL, COPPER

694.10   **Nails, tacks, drawing pins, corrugated nails, staples (other than those of heading 895.12) and similar articles, of iron or steel, whether or not with heads of other material, but excluding such articles with heads of copper or aluminium**

	731700 10 0	Drawing pins
		Other
		Cold-pressed from wire
	731700 20 0	Nails in strips or coils
	731700 40 0	Nails of steel containing by weight 0.5% or more of carbon, hardened
		Other
	731700 61 0	Plated or coated with zinc
	731700 69 0	Other
	731700 90 0	Other

Screws, bolts, nuts, coach screws, screw hooks, rivets, cotters, cotter-pins, washers (including spring washers) and similar articles, of iron or steel

694.21

| | 731811 00 0 | ....threaded |
| | | Coach screws |

S.I.T.C. (R3)	Commodity Code No	Trade description
cont 694.21		Other wood screws
	731812 10 0	Of stainless steel
	731812 90 0	Other
	731813 00 0	Screw hooks and screw rings
		Self-tapping screws
	731814 10 0	Of stainless steel
		Other
	731814 91 0	Spaced-thread screws
	731814 99 0	Other
		Other screws and bolts, whether or not with their nuts or washers
	731815 10 0	Screws, turned from bars, rods, profiles, or wire, of solid section, of a shank thickness not exceeding 6 mm
		Other
	731815 20 0	For fixing railway track construction material
		Other
		Without heads
	731815 30 0	Of stainless steel
		Other, with a tensile strength
	731815 41 0	Of less than 800 MPa
	731815 49 0	Of 800 MPa or more
		With heads
		Slotted and cross-recessed screws
	731815 51 0	Of stainless steel
	731815 59 0	Other
		Hexagon socket head screws
	731815 61 0	Of stainless steel
	731815 69 0	Other
		Hexagon bolts
	731815 70 0	Of stainless steel
		Other, with a tensile strength
	731815 81 0	Of less than 800 MPa
	731815 89 0	Of 800 MPa or more
	731815 90 0	Other
		Nuts
	731816 10 0	Turned from bars, rods, profiles or wire, of solid section, of a hole diameter not exceeding 6 mm
		Other
	731816 30 0	Of stainless steel
		Other
	731816 50 0	Self-locking nuts
		Other, with an inside diameter
	731816 91 0	Not exceeding 12 mm
	731816 99 0	Exceeding 12 mm
	731819 00 0	Other
694.22		**....non-threaded**
	731821 00 0	Spring washers and other lock washers
	731822 00 0	Other washers
	731823 00 0	Rivets
	731824 00 0	Cotters and cotter-pins
	731829 00 0	Other
		Nails, tacks, drawing pins, staples (other than those of heading 895.12) and similar articles, of copper or of iron or steel with heads of copper; screws, bolts, nuts, screw hooks, rivets, cotters, cotter-pins, washers (including spring washers) and similar articles, of copper
694.31	741510 00 0	**Nails and tacks, drawing pins, staples and similar articles**
694.32		**Washers (including spring washers) and similar articles of copper, not threaded**
	741521 00 0	Washers (including spring washers)
	741529 00 0	Other
694.33		**Screws, bolts and nuts and similar articles of copper, threaded**
	741531 00 0	Screws for wood
	741532 00 0	Other screws; bolts and nuts
	741539 00 0	Other
694.40	761610 00 0	**Nails, tacks, staples (other than those of heading 895.12), screws, bolts, nuts, screw hooks, rivets, cotters, cotter-pins, washers and similar articles of aluminium**
		TOOLS FOR USE IN THE HAND OR IN MACHINES
695.10		**Hand tools, the following: spades, shovels, mattocks, picks, hoes, forks and rakes; axes, bill hooks and similar hewing tools; secateurs and pruners of any kind; scythes, sickles, hay knives, hedge shares, timber wedges and other tools of a kind used in agriculture, horticulture or forestry**
	820110 00 0	Spades and shovels
	820120 00 0	Forks
	820130 00 0	Mattocks, picks, hoes and rakes
	820140 00 0	Axes, bill hooks and similar hewing tools
	820150 00 0	Secateurs and similar one-handed pruners and shears (including poultry shears)

S.I.T.C. (R3)	Commodity Code No	Trade description
cont 695.10	820160 00 0	Hedge shears, two-handed pruning shears and similar two-handed shears
	820190 00 0	Other hand tools of a kind used in agriculture, horticulture or forestry
		Hand saws, files, rasps, pliers, pincers, tweezers, metal cutting shares, pipe cutters, bolt croppers, perforating punches and similar hand tools
695.21	820210 00 0	**Hand saws**
695.22	820310 00 0	**Files, rasps and similar tools**
695.23		**Pliers (including cutting pliers), pincers, tweezers, metal-cutting shears, pipe-cutters, bolt croppers, perforating punches and similar tools**
		Pliers (including cutting pliers), pincers, tweezers and similar tools
	820320 10 0	Tweezers
	820320 90 0	Other
	820330 00 0	Metal cutting shears and similar tools
	820340 00 0	Pipe-cutters, bolt croppers, perforating punches and similar tools
695.30		**Spanners and wrenches, hand-operated (including torque meter wrenches but not including tap wrenches); interchangeable spanner sockets, with or without handles**
		Hand-operated spanners and wrenches
	820411 00 0	Non-adjustable
	820412 00 0	Adjustable
	820420 00 0	Interchangeable spanner sockets, with or without handles
		Hand tools (including glaziers' diamonds), n.e.s.; blow lamps; vices, clamps and the like, other than accessories for and parts of, machine tools; anvils; portable forges; hand or pedal-operated grinding wheels with frameworks
695.41	820510 00 0	**Drilling, threading and tapping tools**
695.42	820520 00 0	**Hammers and sledge hammers**
695.43	820530 00 0	**Planes, chisels, gouges and similar cutting tools for working wood**
695.44	820540 00 0	**Screwdrivers**
695.45	820551 00 0	**Household tools, n.e.s**
695.46		**Other hand tools (including glaziers' diamonds); blow lamps**
		Other hand tools (including glaziers' diamonds)
	820559 10 0	Tools for masons, moulders, cement workers, plasterers and painters
	820559 30 0	Cartridge operated riveting, wallplugging, etc., tools
	820559 90 0	Other
	820560 00 0	Blow lamps
695.47	820570 00 0	**Vices, clamps and the like**
695.48	820580 00 0	**Anvils; portable forges; hand or pedal-operated grinding wheels with frameworks**
695.49	820590 00 0	**Sets of articles of two or more of the headings of 695.4**
		Blades for saws of all kinds (including slitting, slotting or toothless saw blades)
695.51	*820220 00 0	**Band saw blades**
		Band saw blades
695.52	*820231 00 0	**Circular saw blades (including slitting or slotting saw blades) with working part of steel**
		With working part of steel
695.53	*820239 00 0	**Circular saw blades (including slitting or slotting saw blades) with working part of other materials**
		Other, including parts
695.54	820240 00 0	**Chain saw blades**
695.55	820291 00 0	**Straight saw blades, for working metal**
695.59		**Other saw blades**
		With working part of steel
	820299 11 0	For working metal
	820299 19 0	For working other materials
	820299 90 0	With working part of other materials
		Knives and cutting blades, for machines or for mechanical appliances; interchangeable tools for hand tools or for machine tools; plates, sticks, tips and the like for tools
695.61		**Knives and cutting blades, for machines or for mechanical appliances**
	820810 00 0	For metal working
	820820 00 0	For wood working

S.I.T.C. (R3)	Commodity Code No	Trade description
cont		
695.61		For kitchen appliances or for machines used by the food industry
	820830 10 0	Circular knives
	820830 90 0	Other
	820840 00 0	For agricultural, horticultural or forestry machines
	820890 00 0	Other
695.62		**Plates, sticks, tips and the like for tools, unmounted, of sintered metal carbides or cermets**
	820900 20 0	Indexable inserts
	820900 80 0	Other
695.63		**Rock drilling or earth boring tools**
	*820713 00 0	With working part of cermets
		Other, including parts
	*820719 10 0	Of diamond or agglomerated diamond
	*820719 90 0	Other
695.64		**Interchangeable tools for hand tools, whether or not power-operated, or for machine-tools (e.g., for pressing, stamping, punching, tapping, threading, drilling, boring, broaching, milling, turning or screw driving), including dies for drawing or extruding metal**
		Dies for drawing or extruding metal
	820720 10 0	With working part of diamond or agglomerated diamond
	820720 90 0	With working part of other materials
		Tools for pressing, stamping or punching
	820730 10 0	For working metal
	820730 90 0	Other
		Tools for tapping or threading
		For working metal
	*820740 10 0	Tools for tapping
	*820740 30 0	Tools for threading
	820740 90 0	Other
		Tools for drilling, other than for rock drilling
	820750 10 0	With working part of diamond or agglomerated diamond
		With working part of other materials
	820750 30 0	Masonry drills
		Other
		For working metal, with working part
	820750 50 0	Of sintered metal carbide
	820750 60 0	Of high speed steel
	820750 70 0	Of other materials
	820750 90 0	Other
		Tools for boring or broaching
	820760 10 0	With working part of diamond or agglomerated diamond
		With working part of other materials
		Tools for boring
	820760 30 0	For working metal
	820760 50 0	Other
		Tools for broaching
	820760 70 0	For working metal
	820760 90 0	Other
		Tools for milling
		For working metal, with working part
	820770 10 0	Of sintered metal carbide
		Of other materials
	820770 31 0	Shank type
	820770 35 0	Hobs
	820770 38 0	Other
	820770 90 0	Other
		Tools for turning
		For working metal, with working part
	820780 11 0	Of cermets
	820780 19 0	Of other materials
	820780 90 0	Other
		Other interchangeable tools
	820790 10 0	With working part of diamond or agglomerated diamond
		With working part of other materials
	820790 30 0	Screwdriver bits
	820790 50 0	Gear-cutting tools
		Other, with working part
		Of sintered metal carbide
	820790 71 0	For working metal
	820790 78 0	Other
		Of other materials
	820790 91 0	For working metal
	820790 99 0	Other
695.70	820600 00 0	**Tools of two or more of the headings of subgroups 695.2 through 695.5 put up in sets for retail sale**

S.I.T.C. (R3)	Commodity Code No	Trade description
		CUTLERY
		Razors and razor blades (including razor blade blanks in strips)
696.31		**Razors, non-electric**
	821210 10 0	Safety razors with non-replaceable blades
	821210 90 0	Other
696.35	821220 00 0	**Safety razor blades (including razor blades blanks in strips)**
696.38	821290 00 0	**Parts, n.e.s., of non-electric razors, other than plastic**
696.40	821300 00 0	**Scissors, tailors' shears and similar shears, and blades therefor**
		Other articles of cutlery (e.g., hair clippers, butchers' or kitchen cleavers, choppers and mincing knives, paper knives); manicure or pedicure sets and instruments (including nail files)
696.51	821410 00 0	**Paper knives, letter openers, erasing knives, pencil sharpeners and blades therefor**
696.55	821420 00 0	**Manicure or pedicure sets and instruments (incl. nail files)**
696.59	821490 00 0	**Articles of cutlery, n.e.s.**
		Spoons, forks, ladles, skimmers, cake-servers, fish-knives, butter- knives, sugar tongs and similar kitchen or tableware
696.61		**Sets of assorted articles containing at least one article plated with precious metal**
	821510 20 0	Containing only articles plated with precious metal
		Other:
	821510 30 0	Of stainless steel
	821510 80 0	Other
696.62		**Other sets of assorted articles**
	821520 10 0	Of stainless steel
	821520 90 0	Other
696.63	821591 00 0	**Articles, not in sets, plated with precious metal**
696.69		**Other articles, not in sets**
	821599 10 0	Of stainless steel
	821599 90 0	Other
696.80		**Knives with cutting blades, serrated or not (including pruning knives), other than knives of heading 695.6, and blades therefor**
	821110 00 0	Sets of assorted articles
		Other
		Table knives having fixed blades
	821191 30 0	Table knives with handle and blade of stainless steel
	821191 80 0	Other
	*821192 00 0	Other knives having fixed blades
	*821193 00 0	Knives having other than fixed blades
	821194 00 0	Blades
	*821195 00 0	Handles of base metal
		HOUSEHOLD EQUIPMENT OF BASE METAL, N.E.S.
		Cooking or heating apparatus of a kind used for domestic purposes, non-electric, and parts thereof, of iron, steel
697.31		**Domestic cooking appliances (e.g., kitchen stoves, ranges, cookers, barbecues, braziers, gas-rings) and plate warmers, non-electric, of iron or steel**
		For gas fuel or for both gas and other fuels
	732111 10 0	With oven, including separate ovens
	732111 90 0	Other
	732112 00 0	For liquid fuel
	732113 00 0	For solid fuel
697.32		**Domestic stoves (other than cooking appliances), grates and similar non-electric space heaters (including those with subsidiary boilers for central heating), of iron or steel**
		For gas fuel or for both gas and other fuels
	732181 10 0	With exhaust outlet
	732181 90 0	Other
		For liquid fuel
	732182 10 0	With exhaust outlet
	732182 90 0	Other
	732183 00 0	For solid fuel
697.33	732190 00 0	**Parts, of iron or steel, of the appliances of headings 697.31 and 697.32**

S.I.T.C. (R3)	Commodity Code No	Trade description
697.34	741700 00 0	Cooking or heating apparatus of a kind used for domestic purposes, non-electric, and parts thereof, of copper

Table, kitchen or other household articles and parts thereof, n.e.s., of iron, steel, copper or aluminium; iron or steel wool; pot scourers and scouring or polishing pads, gloves and the like, of iron, steel, copper or aluminium

S.I.T.C. (R3)	Commodity Code No	Trade description
697.41		**Household articles and parts thereof, n.e.s., of iron or steel**
	732391 00 0	Of cast iron, not enamelled
	732392 00 0	Of cast iron, enamelled
		Of stainless steel
	732393 10 0	Articles for table use
	*732393 90 0	Other
		Of iron (or than cast iron) or steel, enamelled
	732394 10 0	Articles for table use
	732394 90 0	Other
		Other
	732399 10 0	Articles for table use
		Other
	732399 91 0	Varnished or painted
	732399 99 0	Other
697.42		**Household articles and parts thereof, n.e.s., of copper**
	*741811 00 0	Pot scourers and scouring or polishing pads, gloves and the like
	*741819 00 0	Other
697.43		**Household articles and parts thereof, n.e.s., of aluminium**
	*761511 00 0	Pot scourers and scouring or polishing pads, gloves and the like:
		Other
	*761519 10 0	Cast
	*761519 90 0	Other
697.44	732310 00 0	**Iron or steel wool; pot scourers and scouring or polishing pads, gloves and the like**

Sanitary ware and parts thereof, n.e.s., of iron, steel, copper or aluminium

S.I.T.C. (R3)	Commodity Code No	Trade description
697.51		**....of iron or steel**
		Sinks and wash basins, of stainless steel
	732410 10 0	For use in civil aircraft
	732410 90 0	Other
		Baths
	732421 00 0	Of cast iron, whether or not enamelled
	732429 00 0	Other
		Other, including parts
	732490 10 0	Sanitary ware (excluding parts thereof), for use in civil aircraft
	732490 90 0	Other
697.52	741820 00 0	**....of copper**
697.53	761520 00 0	**....of aluminium**

Household appliances, decorative articles, frames and mirrors, of base metal, n.e.s

S.I.T.C. (R3)	Commodity Code No	Trade description
697.81	821000 00 0	**Mechanical appliances, hand-operated, weighing 10 KG or less, used in the preparation, conditioning or serving of food or drink**
697.82		**Statuettes and other ornaments, of base metal; photograph, picture or similar frames, of base metal; mirrors of base metal**
		Statuettes and other ornaments
	830621 00 0	Plated with precious metal
		Other
	830629 10 0	Of copper
	830629 90 0	Of other base metal
	830630 00 0	Photograph, picture or similar frames; mirrors

MANUFACTURES OF BASE METAL, N.E.S.

Locksmiths' wares, safes, strong boxes, etc. and hardware, n.e.s., of base metal

S.I.T.C. (R3)	Commodity Code No	Trade description
699.11		**Padlocks and locks (key, combination or electrically operated), of base metal; clasps and frames with clasps, incorporating locks, of base metal; keys for any of the foregoing articles, of base metal**
	830110 00 0	Padlocks
	830120 00 0	Locks of a kind used for motor vehicles
	830130 00 0	Locks of a kind used for furniture
		Other locks
		Locks of a kind used for doors of buildings
	830140 11 0	Cylinder
	830140 19 0	Other
	830140 90 0	Other locks
	830150 00 0	Clasps and frames with clasps, incorporating locks

S.I.T.C. (R3)	Commodity Code No	Trade description
cont 699.11	830160 00 0	Parts
	830170 00 0	Keys presented separately
699.12		**Armoured or reinforced safes, strong-boxes and doors and safe deposit lockers for strong-rooms, cash and deed boxes and the like, of base metal**
	830300 10 0	Armoured or reinforced safes and strong-boxes
	830300 30 0	Armoured or reinforced doors and safe deposit lockers for strong-rooms
	830300 90 0	Cash or deed boxes and the like
699.13		**Hinges**
	830210 10 0	For use in civil aircraft
	830210 90 0	Other
699.14		**Castors**
	830220 10 0	For use in civil aircraft
	830220 90 0	Other
699.15	830230 00 0	**Other mountings, fittings and similar articles suitable for motor vehicles**
699.16	830241 00 0	**Other mountings, fittings and similar articles suitable for buildings**
699.17		**Other mountings, fittings and similar articles suitable for furniture**
	830242 10 0	For use in civil aircraft
	830242 90 0	Other
699.19		**Other mountings, fittings and similar articles; base metal hat-racks, hat-pegs, brackets and similar fixtures; automatic door closers**
		Other mountings, fittings and similar articles
	830249 10 0	For use in civil aircraft
	830249 90 0	Other
	830250 00 0	Hat-racks, hat-pegs, brackets and similar fixtures
		Automatic door closers
	830260 10 0	For use in civil aircraft
	830260 90 0	Other
		Chain (other than articulated link chain) and parts thereof, of iron or steel
699.21	731520 00 0	**Skid chain**
699.22		**Other chain**
	731581 00 0	Stud-link
		Other, welded link
	731582 10 0	The constituent material of which has a maximum cross-sectional dimension of 16 mm or less
	731582 90 0	The constituent material of which has a maximum cross-sectional dimension of more than 16 mm
	731589 00 0	Other
	731590 00 0	Other parts
		Pins and needles, of iron or steel; base metal beads and spangles; and fittings of base metal, of a kind commonly used for clothing, handbags, travel goods, etc.
699.31		**Sewing needles, knitting needles, bodkins, crochet hooks, embroidery stilettos and similar articles, for use in the hand, of iron or steel**
	731910 00 0	Sewing, darning or embroidery needles
	731990 00 0	Other
699.32		**Safety pins and other pins, of iron or steel, n.e.s.**
	731920 00 0	Safety pins
	731930 00 0	Other pins
699.33		**Clasps, frames with clasps, buckles, buckle-clasps, hooks, eyes, eyelets and the like, of base metal, of a kind used for clothing, footwear, awnings, handbags, travel goods or other made-up articles; tubular or bifurcated rivets, of base metal; beads and spangles, of base metal**
	830810 00 0	Hooks, eyes and eyelets
	830820 00 0	Tubular or bifurcated rivets
	830890 00 0	Other, including parts
		Springs and leaves for springs, of iron, steel or copper
699.41		**Springs and leaves for springs, of iron or steel**
		Leaf-springs and leaves therefor
		Hot worked
	732010 11 0	Laminated springs and leaves therefor
	732010 19 0	Other
	732010 90 0	Other
		Helical springs
	732020 20 0	Hot worked
		Other
	732020 81 0	Coil compression springs
	732020 85 0	Coil tension springs
	732020 89 0	Other

S.I.T.C. (R3)	Commodity Code No	Trade description
cont 699.41		Other
	732090 10 0	Flat spiral springs
	732090 30 0	Discs springs
	732090 90 0	Other
699.42	741600 00 0	**Copper springs**
		Miscellaneous articles of base metal
699.51		**Flexible tubing of base metal, with or without fittings**
		Of iron or steel
	830710 10 0	With fittings attached, for use in civil aircraft
	830710 90 0	Other
		Of other base metal
	830790 10 0	With fittings attached, for use in civil aircraft
	830790 90 0	Other
699.52	830610 00 0	**Bells, gongs and the like, non-electric, and parts thereof, of base metal**
699.53		**Stoppers, caps and lids (including crown corks, screw caps and pouring stoppers), capsules for bottles, threaded bungs, bung covers, seals and other packing accessories, of base metal**
	830910 00 0	Crown corks
		Other
	830990 10 0	Capsules of lead; capsules of aluminium of a diameter exceeding 21 mm
	830990 90 0	Other
699.54	831000 00 0	**Sign-plates, name-plates, address-plates and similar plates, numbers, letters and other symbols, of base metal (excluding those of heading 813)**
699.55		**Wire, rods, tubes, plates, electrodes and similar products, of base metal or of metal carbides, coated or cored with flux material, of a kind used for soldering, brazing, welding or deposition of metal or of metal carbides; wire and rods, of agglomerated base metal powder, used for metal spraying**
		Coated electrodes of base metal, for electric arc-welding
	831110 10 0	Welding electrodes cored with iron or steel and coated with refractory material
	831110 90 0	Other
	831120 00 0	Cored wire of base metal, for electric arc-welding
	831130 00 0	Coated rods and cored wire, of base metal, for soldering, brazing or welding by flame
	831190 00 0	Other, including parts
		Articles of iron or steel, n.e.s.
699.61	731600 00 0	**Anchors, grapnels and parts thereof, of iron or steel**
699.62		**Cast articles of non-malleable cast iron, n.e.s.**
	732510 20 0	Step irons of a kind used in sewers
	732510 50 0	Surface and valve boxes
		Other
	732510 91 0	For sewage, water, etc., systems
	732510 99 0	Other
699.63		**Cast articles of other iron or steel, n.e.s.**
	732591 00 0	Grinding balls and similar articles for mills
		Other
	732599 10 0	Of malleable cast iron
		Other
	732599 91 0	Container corner fittings
	732599 99 0	Other
699.65		**Articles of iron or steel, forged or stamped, but not further worked, n.e.s.**
	732611 00 0	Grinding balls and similar articles for mills
		Other
	732619 10 0	Open-die forged
	732619 90 0	Other
699.67		**Articles of iron or steel wire, n.e.s.**
	732620 10 0	For use in civil aircraft
		Other
	732620 30 0	Small cages and aviaries
	732620 50 0	Wire baskets
	732620 90 0	Other
699.69		**Articles of iron or steel, n.e.s.**
	732690 20 0	Snuff boxes, cigarette cases, cosmetic and powder boxes and cases, and similar pocket articles
	732690 30 0	Ladders and steps
	732690 40 0	Pallets and similar platforms for handling goods
	732690 50 0	Reels for cables, piping and the like
	732690 60 0	Non-mechanical ventilators, guttering, hooks and like articles used in the building industry
	732690 70 0	Perforated buckets and similar articles of sheet used to filter water at the entrance to drains
	732690 80 0	Connectors for optical fibre cables

S.I.T.C. (R3)	Commodity Code No	Trade description
cont 699.69		Other articles of iron or steel
	732690 91 0	Open-die forged
	732690 93 0	Closed-die forged
	732690 95 0	Sintered
	732690 97 0	Other
		Articles, n.e.s., of copper, nickel, aluminium, lead, zinc and tin
699.71	741910 00 0	**Chain of copper and parts thereof**
699.73		**Articles of copper, n.e.s.**
	741991 00 0	Cast, moulded, stamped or forged, but not further worked
	741999 00 0	Other
699.75		**Articles of nickel, n.e.s.**
	*750810 00 0	Cloth, grill, netting and fencing, of nickel wire
	*750890 00 0	Other
699.76		**Articles of lead, n.e.s.**
	780600 10 0	Containers with an anti-radiation lead covering, for the transport or storage of radio-active materials (EURATOM)
	780600 90 0	Other
699.77	*790700 00 0	**Articles of zinc, n.e.s**
699.78	800700 00 0	**Articles of tin, n.e.s**
699.79		**Articles of aluminium, n.e.s**
	*761691 00 0	Cloth, grill, netting and fencing
		Other
	*761699 10 0	Cast
	*761699 90 0	Other
		Semi-manufactures and articles of cobalt, cadmium, titanium and zirconium, n.e.s.
699.81	810590 00 0	**Cobalt, wrought, and articles of cobalt, n.e.s.**
699.83	810790 00 0	**Cadmium, wrought, and articles of cadmium, n.e.s.**
699.85		**Titanium, wrought, and articles of titanium, n.e.s.**
	810890 10 0	Tubes and pipes, with attached fittings, suitable for conducting gases or liquids, for use in civil aircraft
		Other
	810890 30 0	Bars, rods, profiles and wire
	810890 50 0	Plates, sheets, strip and foil
	810890 70 0	Tubes and pipes
	810890 90 0	Other
699.87	810990 00 0	**Zirconium, wrought, and articles of zirconium, n.e.s.**
		Semi-manufactures and articles of tungsten (wolfram), molybdenum, tantalum, magnesium, of other base metals, n.e.s.
699.91		**Tungsten, wrought, and articles of tungsten, n.e.s.**
	810192 00 0	Bars and rods, other than those obtained simply by sintering, profiles, plates, sheets, strip and foil
	810193 00 0	Wire
	810199 00 0	Other
699.92		**Molybdenum, wrought, and articles of molybdenum, n.e.s**
	810292 00 0	Bars and rods, other than those obtained simply by sintering, profiles, plates, sheets, strip and foil
	810293 00 0	Wire
	810299 00 0	Other
699.93		**Tantalum, wrought, and articles of tantalum, n.e.s.**
	810390 10 0	Bars and rods other than those obtained simply by sintering, profiles, wire, plates, sheets, strip and foil
	810390 90 0	Other
699.94		**Magnesium, wrought, and articles of magnesium. n.e.s.**
	810430 00 0	Raspings, turnings and granules, graded according to size; powders
	810490 00 0	Other
699.95	811219 00 0	**Beryllium**
699.99		**Base metals, wrought, n.e.s., and articles of these metals, n.e.s**
	811299 10 0	Hafnium (celtium)
	811299 30 0	Niobium (columbium); Rhenium
	811299 90 0	Gallium; indium; thallium

SECTION: 7

**DIVISION
71**

POWER GENERATING MACHINERY AND EQUIPMENT

STEAM OR OTHER VAPOUR GENERATING BOILERS, SUPER-HEATED WATER BOILERS, AND AUXILIARY PLANT FOR USE THEREWITH; AND PARTS THEREOF

Steam or other vapour generating boilers (excluding central heating hot water boilers capable also of producing low pressure steam); super-heated water boilers

S.I.T.C.	Code No	Trade description
711.11		Steam or other vapour generating boilers
	840211 00 0	Watertube boilers with a steam production exceeding 45 t per hour
	840212 00 0	Watertube boilers with a steam production not exceeding 45 t per hour
		Other vapour generating boilers, including hybrid boilers
	840219 10 0	Firetube boilers
	840219 90 0	Other
711.12	840220 00 0	Super-heated water boilers

Auxiliary plant for use with boilers of heading 711.1 or 812.1 (e.g., economizers, super-heaters, soot removers and gas recoverers); condensers for steam or other vapour power units

711.21	840410 00 0	Auxiliary plant for use with boilers of heading 711.1 or 812.1
711.22	840420 00 0	Condensers for steam or other vapour power units

Parts for the boilers and auxiliary plant of headings 711.1 and 711.2

711.91	840290 00 0	Parts for the boilers of heading 711.1
711.92	840490 00 0	Parts for the apparatus and appliances of heading 711.2

STEAM TURBINES AND OTHER VAPOUR TURBINES AND PARTS THEREOF, N.E.S.

Steam turbines and other vapour turbines

S.I.T.C.	Code No	Trade description
712.11		....for marine propulsion
	*840610 00 0	Turbines for marine propulsion
712.19		....other
		Of an output exceeding 40 MW
	*840681 10 0	Steam turbines for electricity generation
	*840681 90 0	Other
		Of an output not exceeding 40 MW
		Steam turbines for electricity generation, of a power:
	*840682 11 0	Not exceeding 10 MW
	*840682 19 0	Exceeding 10 MW
	*840682 90 0	Other
712.80		Parts for the turbines of heading 712.1
	840690 10 0	Stator blades, rotors and their blades
	840690 90 0	Other

INTERNAL COMBUSTION PISTON ENGINES, AND PARTS THEREOF, N.E.S.

Internal combustion piston engines for aircraft, and parts thereof, n.e.s.

S.I.T.C.	Code No	Trade description
713.11		Spark-ignition reciprocating or rotary internal combustion piston engines for aircraft
	840710 10 0	For use in civil aircraft
	840710 90 0	Other
713.19		Parts, n.e.s., of the aircraft engines of heading 713.11
	840910 10 0	For engines for use in civil aircraft
	840910 90 0	Other

Internal combustion piston engines for propelling vehicles of division 78, group 722 and headings 744.14, 744.15 and 891.11

S.I.T.C.	Code No	Trade description
713.21		Reciprocating piston engines of a cylinder capacity not exceeding 1000 cc
	840731 00 0	Of a cylinder capacity not exceeding 50 cc
		Of a cylinder capacity exceeding 50 cc but not exceeding 250 cc
	840732 10 0	Of a cylinder capacity exceeding 50 cc but not exceeding 125 cc
	840732 90 0	Of a cylinder capacity exceeding 125 cc but not exceeding 250 cc

S.I.T.C. (R3)	Commodity Code No	Trade description
cont 713.21		
	840733 10 0	Of a cylinder capacity exceeding 250 cc but not exceeding 1,000 cc For the industrial assembly of: Pedestrian controlled tractors of heading 722.41; Motor vehicles of headings 781, 782
	840733 90 0	Other
713.22		Reciprocating piston engines of a cylinder capacity exceeding 1000 cc
	840734 10 0	For the industrial assembly of : Pedestrian controlled tractors of heading 722.41; Motor vehicles of heading 781; Motor vehicles of heading 782.1 with an engine of a cylinder capacity of less than 2,800 cc; Motor vehicles of heading 782.2 Other
	840734 30 0	Used New, of a cylinder capacity
	840734 91 0	Not exceeding 1,500 cc
	840734 99 0	Exceeding 1,500 cc
713.23		Compression-ignition engines (diesel or semi-diesel engines)
	840820 10 0	For the industrial assembly of : Pedestrian controlled tractors of heading 722.41; Motor vehicles of heading 781; Motor vehicles of heading 782.1 with an engine of a cylinder capacity of less than 2,500 cc; Motor vehicles of heading 782.2 Other For wheeled agricultural or forestry tractors, of a power
	840820 31 0	Not exceeding 50 kW
	840820 35 0	Exceeding 50 kW but not exceeding 100 kW
	840820 37 0	Exceeding 100 kW For other vehicles of Chapter 87, of a power
	840820 51 0	Not exceeding 50 kW
	840820 55 0	Exceeding 50 kW but not exceeding 100 kW
	840820 57 0	Exceeding 100 kW but not exceeding 200 kW
	840820 99 0	Exceeding 200 kW
		Internal combustion piston engines, marine propulsion
713.31		Outboard motors
	840721 10 0	Of a cylinder capacity not exceeding 325 cc Of a cylinder capacity exceeding 325 cc
	840721 91 0	Of a power not exceeding 30 kW
	840721 99 0	Of a power exceeding 30 kW
713.32		Other spark-ignition reciprocating or rotary engines
	840729 20 0	Of a power not exceeding 200 kW
	840729 80 0	Of a power exceeding 200 kW
713.33		Compression-ignition engines (diesel or semi-diesel engines) Used
	840810 11 0	For sea-going vessels of headings 793.28 to 793.29, tugs of heading 899.96 and warships of heading 793.29
	840810 19 0	Other New, of a power Not exceeding 15 kW
	840810 22 0	For sea-going vessels of headings 793.28 to 793.29, tugs of heading 899.96 and warships of heading 793.29
	840810 24 0	Other Exceeding 15 kW but not exceeding 50 kW
	840810 26 0	For sea-going vessels of headings 793.28 to 793.29, tugs of heading 899.96 and warships of heading 793.29
	840810 28 0	Other Exceeding 50 kW but not exceeding 100 kW
	840810 31 0	For sea-going vessels of headings 793.28 to 793.29, tugs of heading 899.96 and warships of heading 793.29
	890410 39 0	Other Exceeding 100 kW but not exceeding 200 kW
	840810 41 0	For sea-going vessels of headings 793.28 to 793.29, tugs of heading 899.96 and warships of heading 793.29
	840810 49 0	Other Exceeding 200 kW but not exceeding 300 kW
	840810 51 0	For sea-going vessels of headings 793.28 to 793.29, tugs of heading 899.96 and warships of heading 793.29
	840810 59 0	Other Exceeding 300 kW but not exceeding 500 kW
	840810 61 0	For sea-going vessels of headings 793.28 to 793.29, tugs of heading 899.96 and warships of heading 793.29
	840810 69 0	Other Exceeding 500 kW but not exceeding 1,000 kW
	840810 71 0	For sea-going vessels of headings 793.28 to 793.29, tugs of heading 899.96 and warships of heading 793.29
	840810 79 0	Other Exceeding 1,000 kW but not exceeding 5,000 kW

S.I.T.C. (R3)	Commodity Code No	Trade description

S.I.T.C. (R3)	Commodity Code No	Trade description
cont 713.33	840810 81 0	For sea-going vessels of headings 793.28 to 793.29, tugs of heading 899.96 and warships of heading 793.29
	804810 89 0	Other
		Exceeding 5,000 kW
	840810 91 0	For sea-going vessels of headings 793.28 to 793.29, tugs of heading 899.96 and warships of heading 793.29
	840810 99 0	Other
		Internal combustion piston engines, n.e.s.
713.81		**Other spark-ignition reciprocating or rotary internal combustion piston engines**
	840790 10 0	Of a cylinder capacity not exceeding 250 cc
		Of a cylinder capacity exceeding 250 cc
	840790 50 0	For the industrial assembly of: Pedestrian controlled tractors of heading 722.41; Motor vehicles of heading 781; Motor vehicles of heading 782.1 with an engine of a cylinder capacity of less than 2,800 cc; Motor vehicles of heading 782.2
		Other
	840790 80 0	Of a power not exceeding 10 kW
	840790 90 0	Of a power exceeding 10 kW
713.82		**Other compression-ignition internal combustion engines (diesel or semi-diesel engines)**
	840890 10 0	For use in civil aircraft
		Other
	840890 21 0	For rail traction
		Other
	840890 29 0	Used
		New, of a power
	840890 31 0	Not exceeding 15 kW
	840890 33 0	Exceeding 15 kW but not exceeding 30 kW
	840890 36 0	Exceeding 30 kW but not exceeding 50 kW
	840890 37 0	Exceeding 50 kW but not exceeding 100 kW
	840890 51 0	Exceeding 100 kW but not exceeding 200 kW
	840890 55 0	Exceeding 200 kW but not exceeding 300 kW
	840890 57 0	Exceeding 300 kW but not exceeding 500 kW
	*840890 71 0	Exceeding 500 kW but not exceeding 1,000 kW
	840890 75 0	Exceeding 1,000 kW but not exceeding 5,000 kW
	840890 99 0	Exceeding 5,000 kW
		Parts, n.e.s., for the internal combustion piston engines of headings 713.2, 713.3 and 713.8
713.91	840991 00 0	....suitable for use solely or principally with spark-ignition internal combustion piston engines
713.92	*840999 00 0	....suitable for use solely or principally with compression-ignition internal combustion piston engines
		ENGINES AND MOTORS, NON-ELECTRIC (OTHER THAN THOSE OF GROUPS 712, 713 AND 718); PARTS, N.E.S. OF THESE ENGINES AND MOTORS
		Reaction engines
714.41		**Turbo-jets**
		Of a thrust not exceeding 25 kN
	*841111 10 0	For use in civil aircraft
	*841111 90 0	Other
		Of a thrust exceeding 25 kN
		For use in civil aircraft
	*841112 11 0	Of a thrust exceeding 25 kN but not exceeding 44 kN
	*841112 13 0	Of a thrust exceeding 44 kN but not exceeding 132 kN
	*841112 19 0	Of a thrust exceeding 132 kN
	*841112 90 0	Other
714.49		**Other than turbo-jets**
	841210 10 0	For use in civil aircraft
	841210 90 0	Other
		Gas turbines, n.e.s.
714.81		**Turbo-propellers**
		Of a power not exceeding 1,100 kW
	841121 10 0	For use in civil aircraft
	841121 90 0	Other
		Of a power exceeding 1,100 kW
		For use in civil aircraft
	841122 11 0	Of a power exceeding 1,100 kW but not exceeding 3,730 kW
	841122 19 0	Of a power exceeding 3,730 kW
	841122 90 0	Other

S.I.T.C. (R3)	Commodity Code No	Trade description
714.89		Other gas turbines
		Of a power not exceeding 5,000 kW
	841181 10 0	For use in civil aircraft
	841181 90 0	Other
		Of a power exceeding 5,000 kW
	841182 10 0	For use in civil aircraft
		Other
	841182 91 0	Of a power exceeding 5,000 kW but not exceeding 20,000 kW
	841182 93 0	Of a power exceeding 20,000 kW but not exceeding 50,000 kW
	841182 99 0	Of a power exceeding 50,000 kW

Parts of the engines and motors of headings 714.41 and 714.8

S.I.T.C. (R3)	Commodity Code No	Trade description
714.91		Parts for turbo-jets or turbo-propellers
	841191 10 0	For use in civil aircraft
	841191 90 0	Other
714.99		Parts for the gas turbines of heading 714.89
	841199 10 0	Of gas turbines, for use in civil aircraft
	841199 90 0	Other

ROTATING ELECTRIC PLANT AND PARTS THEREOF, N.E.S.

S.I.T.C. (R3)	Commodity Code No	Trade description
716.10		Electric motors of an output not exceeding 37.5 W
	850110 10 0	Synchronous motors of an output not exceeding 18 W
		Other
	850110 91 0	Universal AC/DC motors
	850110 93 0	AC motors
	850110 99 0	DC motors
716.20		Motors (other than motors of an output not exceeding 37.5 W) and generators, direct current
		Of an output not exceeding 750 W
	850131 10 0	Motors of an output exceeding 735 W, DC generators, for use in civil aircraft
	850131 90 0	Other
		Of an output exceeding 750 W but not exceeding 75 kW
	850132 10 0	For use in civil aircraft
		Other
	850132 91 0	Of an output exceeding 750 W but not exceeding 7.5 kW
	850132 99 0	Of an output exceeding 7.5 kW but not exceeding 75 kW
		Of an output exceeding 75 kW but not exceeding 375 kW
	850133 10 0	Motors of an output not exceeding 150 kW and generators, for use in civil aircraft
	850133 90 0	Other
		Of an output exceeding 375 kW
	850134 10 0	Generators for use in civil aircraft
		Other
	850134 50 0	Traction motors
		Other, of an output
	850134 91 0	Exceeding 375 kW but not exceeding 750 kW
	850134 99 0	Exceeding 750 kW
716.31		Motors (other than motors of an output not exceeding 37.5 W) and generators, alternating current AC motors (including universal (AC/DC) motors, but excluding motors of an output not exceeding 37.5 W)
	850120 10 0	Of an output exceeding 735 W but not exceeding 150 kW, for use in civil aircraft
	850120 90 0	Other
		Other AC motors, single-phase
	850140 10 0	Of an output exceeding 750 W but not exceeding 150 kW, for use in civil aircraft
		Other
	850140 91 0	Of an output not exceeding 750 W
	850140 99 0	Of an output exceeding 750 W
		Other AC motors, multi-phase
		Of an output not exceeding 750 W
	850151 10 0	Of an output exceeding 735 W, for use in civil aircraft
	850151 90 0	Other
		Of an output exceeding 750 W but not exceeding 75 kW
	850152 10 0	For use in civil aircraft
		Other
	850152 91 0	Of an output exceeding 750 W but not exceeding 7.5 kW
	850152 93 0	Of an output exceeding 7.5 kW but not exceeding 37 kW
	850152 99 0	Of an output exceeding 37 kW but not exceeding 75 kW
		Of an output exceeding 75 kW
	850153 10 0	Of an output less than 150 kW, for use in civil aircraft
		Other
	850153 50 0	Traction motors
		Other, of an output
	850153 92 0	Exceeding 75 kW but not exceeding 375 kW
	850153 94 0	Exceeding 375 kW but not exceeding 750 kW
	850153 99 0	Exceeding 750 kW

S.I.T.C. (R3)	Commodity Code No	Trade description
716.32		Generators, alternating current
		Of an output not exceeding 75 kVA
	850161 10 0	For use in civil aircraft
		Other
	850161 91 0	Of an output not exceeding 7.5 kVA
	850161 99 0	Of an output exceeding 7.5 kVA but not exceeding 75 kVA
		Of an output exceeding 75 kVA but not exceeding 375 kVA
	850162 10 0	For use in civil aircraft
	850162 90 0	Other
		Of an output exceeding 375 kVA but not exceeding 750 kVA
	850163 10 0	For use in civil aircraft
	850163 90 0	Other
	850164 00 0	Of an output exceeding 750 kVA
716.40		Electric rotary converters.
	850240 10 0	For use in civil aircraft
	850240 90 0	Other

Generating sets

S.I.T.C. (R3)	Commodity Code No	Trade description
716.51		Electric generating sets with internal combustion piston engines
		Generating sets with compression-ignition internal combustion piston engines (diesel or semi-diesel engines)
		Of an output not exceeding 75 kVA
	850211 10 0	For use in civil aircraft
		Other
	850211 91 0	Of an output not exceeding 7.5 kVA
	850211 99 0	Of an output exceeding 7.5 kVA but not exceeding 75 kVA
		Of an output exceeding 75 kVA but not exceeding 375 kVA
	850212 10 0	For use in civil aircraft
	*850212 90 0	Other
		Of an output exceeding 375 kVA
	850213 10 0	For use in civil aircraft
		Other
	850213 91 0	Of an output exceeding 375 kVA but not exceeding 750 kVA
	850213 99 0	Of an output exceeding 750 kVA
		Generating sets with spark-ignition internal combustion piston engines
	850220 10 0	For use in civil aircraft
		Other
	850220 91 0	Of an output not exceeding 7.5 kVA
	850220 99 0	Of an output exceeding 7.5 kVA
716.52		Other generating sets.
	*850231 00 0	Wind-powered
		Other
	*850239 10 0	For use in civil aircraft
		Other
	*850239 91 0	Turbo-generators
	*850239 99 0	Other
716.90		Parts, n.e.s., suitable for use solely or principally with the machines falling within group 716
	850300 10 0	Non-magnetic retaining rings
		Other
	850300 91 0	Of cast iron or cast steel
	850300 99 0	Other

OTHER POWER GENERATING MACHINERY AND PARTS THEREOF, N.E.S.

Hydraulic turbines and water wheels, and parts thereof

S.I.T.C. (R3)	Commodity Code No	Trade description
718.11		Hydraulic turbines and water wheels
	841011 00 0	Of a power not exceeding 1,000 kW
	841012 00 0	Of a power exceeding 1,000 kW but not exceeding 10,000 kW
	841013 00 0	Of a power exceeding 10,000 kW
718.19		Parts, including regulators, of hydraulic turbines and water wheels
	841090 10 0	Of cast iron or cast steel
	841090 90 0	Other

Nuclear reactors, and parts thereof; fuel elements (cartridges) non-irradiated, for nuclear reactors

S.I.T.C. (R3)	Commodity Code No	Trade description
718.71	840110 00 0	Nuclear reactors
718.77	840130 00 0	Fuel elements (cartridges), non-irradiated
718.78		Parts of nuclear reactors
	840140 10 0	Of open-die forged steel
	840140 90 0	Other

S.I.T.C. (R3)	Commodity Code No	Trade description

Engines and motors, n.e.s. (e.g., wind engines and hot air engines); parts of these engines and motors and of the reaction engines of heading 714.49

718.91		Linear acting hydraulic power engines and motors (cylinders)
	841221 10 0	For use in civil aircraft
		Other
	841221 91 0	Hydraulic systems
	841221 99 0	Other
718.92		Linear acting pneumatic power engines and motors (cylinders)
	841231 10 0	For use in civil aircraft
	841231 90 0	Other
718.93		Other engines and motors
		Hydraulic power engines and motors
	841229 10 0	For use in civil aircraft
		Other
	841229 50 0	Hydraulic systems
		Other
	841229 91 0	Hydraulic fluid power motors
	841229 99 0	Other
		Pneumatic power engines and motors
	841239 10 0	For use in civil aircraft
	841239 90 0	Other
		Other
	841280 10 0	Steam or other vapour power engines
		Other
	841280 91 0	For use in civil aircraft
	841280 99 0	Other
718.99		Parts of the engines and motors of headings 714.49, 718.91, 718.92 and 718.93
	841290 10 0	For use in civil aircraft
		Other
	841290 30 0	Of reaction engines other than turbo-jets
	841290 50 0	Of hydraulic power engines and motors
	841290 90 0	Other

DIVISION 72

MACHINERY SPECIALISED FOR PARTICULAR INDUSTRIES

AGRICULTURAL MACHINERY (EXCLUDING TRACTORS) AND PARTS THEREOF

Agricultural, horticultural or forestry machinery for soil preparation or cultivation; lawn or sports ground rollers; and parts thereof

721.11		Ploughs
	843210 10 0	Mouldboard
	843210 90 0	Other
721.12		Seeders, planters, transplanters; fertiliser distributers and manure spreaders
		Seeders, planters and transplanters
		Seeders
	843230 11 0	Central driven precision spacing seeders
	843230 19 0	Other
	843230 90 0	Planters and transplanters
		Manure spreaders and fertiliser distributors
	843240 10 0	Mineral or chemical fertiliser distribution
	843240 90 0	Other
721.13		Scarifiers, cultivators, weeders, hoes and harrows (other than hand tools)
	843221 00 0	Disc harrows
		Other
	843229 10 0	Scarifiers and cultivators
	843229 30 0	Harrows
	843229 50 0	Rotovators
	843229 90 0	Other
721.18	843280 00 0	Other agricultural and horticultural or forestry machinery for soil preparation or cultivation; lawn and sports ground rollers
721.19		Parts of the machinery of sub-group 721.1
	843290 10 0	Ploughshares
		Other
	843290 91 0	Of cast iron or cast steel
	843290 99 0	Other

S.I.T.C. (R3)	Commodity Code No	Trade description
		Harvesting or threshing machinery (including straw or fodder balers); grass or hay mowers; machines for cleaning, sorting or grading seed or grain or for grading eggs, fruit or other agricultural produce (other than milling machinery of heading 727.11); parts thereof, n.e.s.
721.21		Mowers for lawns, parks or sports grounds
		Powered, with the cutting device rotating in a horizontal plane
	843311 10 0	Electric
		Other
		Self-propelled
	843311 51 0	With a seat
	843311 59 0	Other
	843311 90 0	Other
		Other
		With motor
	843319 10 0	Electric
		Other
		Self-propelled
	843319 51 0	With a seat
	843319 59 0	Other
	843319 70 0	Other
	843319 90 0	Without motor
721.22	843351 00 0	Combine harvester-threshers
721.23		Other harvesting and threshing machinery; mowers (other than those of heading 721.21)
		Other mowers, including cutter bars for tractor mounting
	843320 10 0	With motor
		Other
		Designed to be carried on or hauled by a tractor
	843320 51 0	With the cutting device rotating in a horizontal plane
	843320 59 0	Other
	843320 90 0	Other
		Other haymaking machinery
	843330 10 0	Turners, side delivery rakes, and tedders
	843330 90 0	Other
		Straw or fodder balers, including pick-up balers
	843340 10 0	Pick-up balers
	843340 90 0	Other
		Other harvesting machinery; threshing machinery
	843352 00 0	Other threshing machinery
		Root or tuber harvesting machines
	843353 10 0	Potato-diggers and potato harvesters
	843353 30 0	Beet-topping machines and beet harvesters
	843353 90 0	Other
		Other
		Forage harvesters
	843359 11 0	Self-propelled
	843359 19 0	Other
	843359 30 0	Grape harvesters
	843359 80 0	Other
721.26		Machines for cleaning, sorting or grading eggs, fruit or other agricultural produce
	843360 10 0	Machines for sorting or grading eggs
	843360 90 0	Other
721.27	843710 00 0	Machines for cleaning, sorting or grading seed, grain or dried leguminous vegetables(not milling machinery of heading 727.11)
721.29	*843390 00 0	Parts of the machines of headings 721.21 through 721.26
		Milking machines and dairy machinery and parts thereof
721.31	843410 00 0	Milking machines
721.38	843420 00 0	Dairy machinery
721.39	843490 00 0	Parts for milking machines and dairy machinery
		Agricultural, horticultural, forestry, poultry-keeping or bee-keeping machinery, n.e.s., and parts thereof, n.e.s.
721.91		Presses, crushers and similar machinery, used in the manufacture of wine, cider, fruit juices or similar beverages
	843510 10 0	Presses
	843510 90 0	Other
721.95		Poultry-keeping machinery; poultry incubators and brooders
	843621 00 0	Poultry incubators and brooders
	843629 00 0	Other

S.I.T.C. (R3)	Commodity Code No	Trade description
721.96		Other agricultural, horticultural, forestry or bee-keeping machinery (including germination plant fitted with mechanical or thermal equipment)
		Machinery for preparing animal feeding stuffs
	843610 10 0	Crushers and other mills for cereals, beans, peas and the like
	843610 90 0	Other
		Other machinery
	843680 10 0	Forestry machinery
		Other
	843680 91 0	Automatic drinking bowls
	843680 99 0	Other
721.98	843590 00 0	Parts of the machinery at heading 721.91
721.99		Parts of the machinery and appliances of headings 721.95 and 721.96
	843691 00 0	Of poultry-keeping machinery or poultry incubators and brooders
	843699 00 0	Other

TRACTORS (OTHER THAN THOSE OF HEADINGS 744.14 AND 744.15)

S.I.T.C. (R3)	Commodity Code No	Trade description
722.30	870130 00 0	Track-laying tractors
		Wheeled tractors (other than those of headings 744.14 and 744.15
722.41		Pedestrian controlled tractors
	870110 10 0	Of a power not exceeding 4 kW
	870110 90 0	Of a power exceeding 4 kW
722.49		Other wheeled tractors
		Agricultural tractors (excluding pedestrian-controlled tractors) and forestry tractors, wheeled
		New, of an engine power
	870190 11 0	Not exceeding 18 kW
	870190 15 0	Exceeding 18 kW but not exceeding 25 kW
	870190 21 0	Exceeding 25 kW but not exceeding 37 kW
	870190 25 0	Exceeding 37 kW but not exceeding 59 kW
	870190 31 0	Exceeding 59 kW but not exceeding 75 kW
	870190 35 0	Exceeding 75 kW but not exceeding 90 kW
	870190 39 0	Exceeding 90 kW
	870190 50 0	Used
	870190 90 0	Other

CIVIL ENGINEERING AND CONTRACTORS' PLANT AND EQUIPMENT

Bulldozers, angledozers, graders and levellers, self-propelled

S.I.T.C. (R3)	Commodity Code No	Trade description
723.11		Bulldozers and angledozers
	842911 00 0	Track laying
	842919 00 0	Other
723.12	842920 00 0	Graders and levellers

Mechanical shovels, excavators and shovel-loaders, self-propelled

S.I.T.C. (R3)	Commodity Code No	Trade description
723.21		Front-end shovel-loaders
	842951 10 0	Loaders specially designed for underground use
		Other
	842951 91 0	Crawler shovel loaders
	842951 99 0	Other
723.22		Mechanical shovels, excavators and shovel loaders with a 360 degree revolving superstructure
	842952 10 0	Track-laying excavators
	842952 90 0	Other
723.29	*842959 00 0	Other self-propelled mechanical shovels, excavators and shovel-loaders

Moving, grading, levelling, scraping, excavating, tamping, compacting, extracting or boring machinery, for earth, minerals or ores, self-propelled, n.e.s.

S.I.T.C. (R3)	Commodity Code No	Trade description
723.31	842930 00 0	Scrapers
723.33		Tamping machines and road rollers
		Road rollers
	842940 10 0	Vibratory
	842940 30 0	Other
	842940 90 0	Tamping machines
723.35	843031 00 0	Coal or rock cutters and tunnelling machinery
723.37	843041 00 0	Other boring or sinking machinery

S.I.T.C. (R3)	Commodity Code No	Trade description
723.39	843050 00 0	Other moving, grading, levelling, scraping, excavating, compacting or extracting machinery, for earth, minerals or ores, self-propelled

Construction and mining machinery, n.e.s.

S.I.T.C. (R3)	Commodity Code No	Trade description
723.41	843010 00 0	Pile-drivers and pile extractors
723.42	843020 00 0	Snow-ploughs and snow-blowers
723.43	843039 00 0	Coal or rock cutters and tunnelling machinery, not self-propelled
723.44	*843049 00 0	Other boring and sinking machinery, not self-propelled
723.45	843061 00 0	Tamping or compacting machinery, not self-propelled
723.46	843062 00 0	Scrapers, not self-propelled
723.47	843069 00 0	Other moving, grading, levelling, scraping, excavating, compacting or extracting machinery, for earth, minerals or ores, not self-propelled
723.48	847910 00 0	Machinery for public works, building or the like, n.e.s.

Parts, n.e.s., of the machinery of headings 723 and 744.3

S.I.T.C. (R3)	Commodity Code No	Trade description
723.91	843141 00 0	Buckets, shovels, grabs and grips
723.92	843142 00 0	Bulldozer or angledozer blades
723.93	843143 00 0	Parts for boring or sinking machinery of headings 723.37
723.99		Other parts for the machinery of headings 723 and 744.3
	843149 20 0	Of cast iron or cast steel
	843149 80 0	Other

TEXTILE AND LEATHER MACHINERY, AND PARTS THEREOF, N.E.S.

Sewing machines (other than book-sewing machines of heading 726.81); furniture, bases and covers specially designed for sewing machines; sewing machine needles; parts of the machines and furniture of this heading

S.I.T.C. (R3)	Commodity Code No	Trade description
724.33		Sewing machines of the household type
		Sewing machines (lock-stitch only), with heads of a weight not exceeding 16 kg without motor or 17kg including the motor; sewing machine heads (lock-stitch only), of a weight not exceeding 16 kg without motor or 17kg including the motor
	845210 11 0	Sewing machines having a value (not including frames, tables or furniture) of more than 65 ECU each
	845210 19 0	Other
	845210 90 0	Other sewing machines and other sewing machine heads
724.35		Other Sewing machines
	845221 00 0	Automatic units
	845229 00 0	Other
724.39		Sewing machine needles; furniture, bases and covers specially designed for sewing machines; parts of the machines and furniture of sub-group 724.3
		Sewing machine needles
	845230 10 0	With single flat shank
	845230 90 0	Other
	845240 00 0	Furniture, bases and covers for sewing machines and parts thereof
	845290 00 0	Other parts of sewing machines

Machines for extruding, drawing, texturing or cutting textile materials; machines for preparing textile fibres; spinning, doubling or twisting machines and other machinery for producing textile yarns; textile reeling or winding (including weft-winding) machines; parts and accessories thereof

S.I.T.C. (R3)	Commodity Code No	Trade description
724.41		Machines for extruding, drawing, texturing or cutting man-made textile materials
	844400 10 0	Machines for extruding
	844400 90 0	Other
724.42		Machines for preparing textile fibres
	844511 00 0	Carding machines
	844512 00 0	Combing machines
	844513 00 0	Drawing or roving machines
	844519 00 0	Other

S.I.T.C. (R3)	Commodity Code No	Trade description
724.43		Textile spinning, doubling or twisting machines; textile winding (including weft-winding) or reeling machines
	844520 00 0	Textile spinning machines
		Textile doubling or twisting machines
	844530 10 0	Textile doubling machines
	844530 90 0	Textile twisting machines
	844540 00 0	Textile winding (including weft-winding) or reeling machines
724.49		Parts and accessories of machines of heading 724.4 or 724.54 or of their auxiliary machinery
		Parts and accessories of machines of heading 724.41 or of their auxiliary machinery
	844820 10 0	Of cast iron or cast steel
	844820 90 0	Other
		Parts and accessories of machines of heading 724.42, 43 or of their auxiliary machinery
	844831 00 0	Card clothing
	844832 00 0	Of machines for preparing textile fibres, other than card clothing
		Spindles, spindle flyers, spinning rings and ring travellers
	844833 10 0	Spindles and spindle flyers
	844833 90 0	Spinning rings and ring travellers
	844839 00 0	Other

Weaving machines, knitting machines, stitch-bonding machines and machines for making gimped yarn, tulle, lace, embroidery, trimmings, braid or net and machines for tufting or for making nonwovens; machines for preparing yarns for use on the machines of headings 724.51, 724.52 and 724.53; machines for the manufacture or finishing of felt or non-wovens in the piece or in shapes (including machines for making felt hats); blocks for making hats

S.I.T.C. (R3)	Commodity Code No	Trade description
724.51		Weaving machines (looms)
	844610 00 0	For weaving fabrics of a width not exceeding 30 cm
		For weaving fabrics of a width exceeding 30 cm, shuttle type
	844621 00 0	Power looms
	844629 00 0	Other
	844630 00 0	For weaving fabrics of a width exceeding 30 cm, shuttleless type
724.52		Knitting machines and stitch-bonding machines
		Circular knitting machines
		With cylinder diameter not exceeding 165 mm
	844711 10 0	Working with latch needles
	844711 90 0	Other
	844712 00 0	With cylinder diameter exceeding 165 mm
	844712 10 0	Working with latch needles
	844712 90 0	Other
		Flat knitting machines; stitch-bonding machines
	844720 10 0	Hand operated
		Other
	844720 92 0	Warp knitting machines (including Raschel type); stitch bonding machines
	844720 98 0	Other
724.53	844790 00 0	Machines for making gimped yarn, tulle, lace, embroidery, trimmings, braid or net and machines for tufting
724.54	844590 00 0	Machines for preparing textile yarns for use on the machines of headings 724.51 through 724.53
724.55	844900 00 0	Machinery for the manufacture or finishing of felt or nonwovens in the piece or in shapes, including machinery for making felt hats; blocks for making hats

Auxiliary machinery for use with machines of headings 724.4 through 724.53; parts and accessories suitable for use solely or principally with the machines of headings 724.51 through 724.53 or with their auxiliary machinery

S.I.T.C. (R3)	Commodity Code No	Trade description
724.61		Auxiliary machinery for machines of headings 724.41, 724.42, 724.43, 724.51, 724.52 and 724.53
	844811 00 0	Dobbies and Jacquards; card reducing, copying, punching or assembling machines for use therewith
	844819 00 0	Other
724.67		Parts and accessories of weaving machines (looms) of heading 724.51 or of their auxiliary machinery
	844841 00 0	Shuttles
	844842 00 0	Reeds for looms, healds and heald-frames
	844849 00 0	Other
724.68		Parts and accessories of machines of headings 724.52 and 724.53 or of their auxiliary machinery
		Sinkers, needles and other articles used in forming stitches
	844851 10 0	Sinkers
	844851 90 0	Other
	*844859 00 0	Other

S.I.T.C. (R3)	Commodity Code No	Trade description
		Machinery (other than machines of heading 775.1) for washing, cleaning, wringing, drying, ironing, pressing (including fusing presses), bleaching, dyeing, dressing, finishing, coating or impregnating textile yarns, fabrics or made-up textile articles; machines for applying the paste to the base fabric or other support used in the manufacture of floor coverings such as linoleum; machines for reeling, unreeling, folding, cutting or pinking textile fabrics
724.71	845020 00 0	Household or laundry-type washing machines (including machines which both wash and dry), each of a dry linen capacity exceeding 10 kgs.
724.72	845110 00 0	Dry-cleaning machines
724.73	845129 00 0	Drying machines, each of dry-linen capacity exceeding 10 kgs (excluding those of headings 741.8 and 743.5)
724.74		Machinery for washing (other than household or laundry-type machines), cleaning (other than dry-cleaning machines), wringing, pressing (including fusing presses), bleaching, dyeing, dressing, finishing (other than machines for the finishing of felt), coating or impregnating textile yarns, fabrics or made-up textile articles; machines for applying the paste to the base fabric or other support used in the manufacture of floor coverings such as linoleum; machines for reeling, unreeling, folding, cutting or pinking textile fabrics Ironing machines and presses (including fusing presses) 　Electrically heated, of a power
	845130 10 0	Not exceeding 2,500 W
	845130 30 0	Exceeding 2,500 W
	845130 80 0	Other
	845140 00 0	Washing, bleaching or dyeing machines
	845150 00 0	Machines for reeling, unreeling, folding, cutting or pinking textile fabrics Other machinery
	845180 10 0	Machines used in the manufacture of linoleum or other floor coverings for applying the paste to the base fabric or other support
	845180 30 0	Machines for dressing or finishing
	845180 80 0	Other
		Machinery (other than sewing machines) for preparing, tanning, or working hides, skins or leather or for making or repairing footwear or other articles of hides, skins or leather; and parts thereof
724.81	845310 00 0	Machinery for preparing, tanning or working hides, skins or leather
724.83	845320 00 0	Machinery for making or repairing footwear
724.85	845380 00 0	Machinery for making or repairing articles, of hides, skins or leather, other than footwear
724.88	845390 00 0	Parts for the machinery of heading 724.8
		Parts for the machines of headings 724.7 and 775.1
724.91	845090 00 0	....for household or laundry type washing machines of headings
724.92	845190 00 0	....for the machines of headings 724.72, 724.73, 724.74 and 775.12
		PAPER MILL AND PULP MILL MACHINERY, PAPER CUTTING MACHINES AND OTHER MACHINERY FOR THE MANUFACTURE OF PAPER ARTICLES; PARTS THEREOF
		Machinery for making pulp of fibrous cellulosic material or for making or finishing paper or paperboard
725.11	843910 00 0	Machinery for making pulp of fibrous cellulosic material
725.12		Machinery for making or finishing paper or paperboard
	843920 00 0	Machinery for making paper or paperboard
	843930 00 0	Machinery for finishing paper or paperboard
		Other machinery for making up paper pulp, paper or paperboard (including cutting machines of all kinds)
725.21		Cutting machines
	844110 10 0	Combined reel slitting and re-reeling machines
	844110 20 0	Other slitting and cross cutting machines
	844110 30 0	Guillotines
	844110 40 0	Three-knife trimmers
	844110 80 0	Other
725.23	844120 00 0	Machines for making bags, sacks or envelopes
725.25	844130 00 0	Machines for making cartons, boxes, cases, tubes, drums or similar containers, other than by moulding
725.27	844140 00 0	Machines for moulding articles in paper pulp, paper or paperboard

S.I.T.C. (R3)	Commodity Code No	Trade description
725.29	844180 00 0	Other machinery
		Parts of the machines of heading 725
725.91		Parts of the machines of heading 725.1
		Of machinery for making pulp of fibrous cellulosic material
	843991 10 0	Of cast iron or cast steel
	843991 90 0	Other
		Other
	843999 10 0	Of cast iron or cast steel
	843999 90 0	Other
725.99		Parts of the machines of heading 725.2
	844190 10 0	Of cutting machines
	844190 90 0	Other

PRINTING AND BOOKBINDING MACHINERY, AND PARTS THEREOF

Machinery, apparatus and equipment (other than the machine-tools of heading 728.1 or 731) for type-founding or type-setting, for preparing or making printing blocks, plates, cylinders or other printing components; printing type, blocks, plates, cylinders and other printing components; blocks, plates, cylinders and lithographic stones, prepared for printing purposes (e.g., planed, grained or polished)

726.31		Machinery, apparatus and equipment (other than the machine-tools of heading 728.1 or 731) for type-founding or type-setting, for preparing or making printing blocks, plates, cylinders or other printing components
	844210 00 0	Phototype-setting and composing machines
		Machinery, apparatus and equipment for type-setting or composing by other processes, with or without founding device
	844220 10 0	For founding and setting (for example, linotypes, monotypes, intertypes)
	844220 90 0	Other
	844230 00 0	Other machinery, apparatus and equipment
726.35		Printing type, blocks, plates, cylinders and other printing components; blocks, plates, cylinders and lithographic stones prepared for printing purposes (e.g., planed, grained or polished)
		With printing image
	844250 21 0	For relief printing
	844250 23 0	For planographic printing
	844250 29 0	Other
	844250 80 0	Other
		Offset printing machinery
726.51	844311 00 0	Reel fed
726.55	844312 00 0	Sheet fed, office type (sheet size not exceeding 22 x 36 cm)
726.59		Other offset printing machinery
		Sheet fed
	844319 10 0	Used
		New, taking sheets of a size
	844319 31 0	Not exceeding 52 x 74 cm
	844319 35 0	Exceeding 52 x 74 cm but not exceeding 74 x 107 cm
	844319 39 0	Exceeding 74 x 107 cm
	844319 90 0	Other
		Other printing machinery; machines for uses ancillary to printing
726.61		Letterpress printing machinery (excluding flexographic printing)
	844321 00 0	Reel fed
	844329 00 0	Other
726.63	844330 00 0	Flexographic printing machinery
726.65	844340 00 0	Gravure printing machinery
726.67		Other printing machinery
	* 844359 20 0	For printing textile materials
	* 844355 80 0	Other
726.68	844360 00 0	Machines for uses ancillary to printing
		Bookbinding machinery (including book-sewing machines); parts thereof
726.81		Bookbinding machinery (including book-sewing machines)
	844010 10 0	Folding machines
	844010 20 0	Collating machines and gathering machines
	844010 30 0	Sewing, wire stitching and stapling machines

S.I.T.C. (R3)	Commodity Code No	Trade description
cont 726.81	844010 40 0 844010 90 0	Unsewn (perfect) binding machines Other
726.89	844090 00 0	Parts for bookbinding machinery
		Parts for the machines of headings 726.31, 726.5, and 726.6
726.91	844240 00 0	....for the machines of heading 726.31
726.99		....for the machines of headings 726.5 and 726.6
	844390 10 0	Of cast iron or cast steel
	844390 90 0	Other

FOOD-PROCESSING MACHINES (EXCLUDING DOMESTIC)

Machinery used in the milling industry or for the working of cereals or dried leguminous vegetables (other than farm-type machinery)

727.11	843780 00 0	Machinery used in the milling industry or for the working of cereals or dried leguminous vegetables (other than farm-type machinery)
727.19	843790 00 0	Parts for the machines of headings 727.11 and 721.27

Other food-processing machinery and parts thereof, n.e.s.

727.21	847920 00 0	Machinery for the extraction or preparation of animal or fixed vegetable fats and oils
727.22		Machinery, n.e.s., for the industrial preparation or manufacture of food or drink
		Bakery machinery and machinery for the manufacture of macaroni, spaghetti or similar products
	*843810 10 0	Bakery machinery
	843810 90 0	Machinery for the manufacture of macaroni, spaghetti or similar products
	843820 00 0	Machinery for the manufacture of confectionery, cocoa or chocolate
	843830 00 0	Machinery for sugar manufacture
	843840 00 0	Brewery machinery
	843850 00 0	Machinery for the preparation of meat or poultry
	843860 00 0	Machinery for the preparation of fruits, nuts or vegetables
		Other machinery
	843880 10 0	For the preparation of tea or coffee
		Other
	843880 91 0	For the preparation or manufacture of drink
	843880 99 0	Other
727.29	843890 00 0	Parts for the food-processing machinery of heading 727.22

OTHER MACHINERY AND EQUIPMENT SPECIALISED FOR PARTICULAR INDUSTRIES, AND PARTS THEREOF, N.E.S.

Machine-tools specialized for particular industries; parts and accessories thereof

728.11		Machine-tools for working stone, ceramics, concrete, asbestos-cement or like mineral materials or for cold working glass (other than machines of headings 731.1 and 745.1)
		Sawing machines
	846410 10 0	For sawing monocrystal semiconductor boules into slices
	846410 90 0	Other
		Grinding or polishing machines
	846420 05 0	For working semiconductor wafers
		For working glass
	846420 11 0	Optical glass
	846420 19 0	Other
	846420 80 0	Other
		Other
	846490 10 0	For scribing or scoring semiconductor wafers
	846490 90 0	Other
728.12		Machine-tools (including machines for nailing, stapling, glueing or otherwise assembling) for working wood, cork, bone, hard rubber, hard plastics or similar hard materials (other than machines of headings 731.1 and 745.1)
		Machines which can carry out different types of machining operations without tool change between such operations
	846510 10 0	With manual transfer of workpiece between each operations
	846510 90 0	With automatic transfer of workpiece between each operation
		Other
		Sawing machines
	846591 10 0	Band saws
	846591 20 0	Circular saws
	846591 90 0	Other
	846592 00 0	Planing, milling or moulding (by cutting) machines
	846593 00 0	Grinding, sanding or polishing machines

S.I.T.C. (R3)	Commodity Code No	Trade description
cont 728.12	846594 00 0	Bending or assembling machines
	846595 00 0	Drilling or morticing machines
	846596 00 0	Splitting, slicing or paring machines
		Other
	846599 10 0	Lathes
	846599 90 0	Other
728.19		Parts and accessories suitable for use solely or principally with the machine-tools of heading 728.1
		For machines of heading 728.11
	846691 20 0	Of cast iron or cast steel
	846691 80 0	Other
		For machines of heading 728.12
	846692 20 0	Of cast iron or cast steel
	846692 80 0	Other

Machinery (other than machine-tools) for sorting, screening, separating, washing, crushing, grinding, mixing or kneading earth, stone, ores or other mineral substances, in solid (including powder or paste) form; machinery for agglomerating, shaping OR moulding solid mineral fuels, ceramic paste, unhardened cements, plastering materials or other mineral products in powder or paste form; machines for forming foundry moulds of sand; parts thereof

728.31	847410 00 0	Machinery for sorting, screening, separating or washing earth, stone, ores or other mineral substances, in solid (including powder or paste) form
728.32	847420 00 0	Machinery for crushing or grinding earth, stone, ores or other mineral substances in solid (including powder or paste) form
728.33		Machinery for mixing or kneading earth, stone, ores or other mineral substances in solid (including powder or paste) form
	847431 00 0	Concrete or mortar mixers
	847432 00 0	Machines for mixing mineral substances with bitumen
	847439 00 0	Other
728.34		Machinery for agglomerating, shaping or moulding solid mineral fuels, ceramic paste, unhardened cements, plastering materials or other mineral products in powder or paste form, and machines for forming foundry moulds of sand
	*847480 00 0	Other machinery
728.39		Parts of the machinery of heading 728.3
	847490 10 0	Of cast iron or cast steel
	847490 90 0	Other

Machinery and mechanical appliances specialized for particular industries, n.e.s.

728.41		Machines for assembling electric or electronic lamps, tubes or valves or flashbulbs, in glass envelopes; machines for manufacturing or hot working glass or glassware
	847510 00 0	Machines for assembling electric or electronic lamps, tubes or valves or flashbulbs, in glass envelopes
		Machines fro manufacturing or hot working glass or glassware
	*847521 00 0	Machines for making optical fibres and preforms thereof
	*847529 00 0	Other
728.42		Machinery for working rubber or plastics or for the manufacture of Products from these materials, n.e.s.
	847710 00 0	Injection-moulding machines
	847720 00 0	Extruders
	847730 00 0	Blow moulding machines
	847740 00 0	Vacuum moulding machines and other thermoforming machines
		Other machinery for moulding or otherwise forming
	847751 00 0	For moulding or retreading pneumatic tyres or for moulding or otherwise forming inner tubes
		Other
	847759 10 0	Presses
	847759 90 0	Other
		Other machinery
	847780 10 0	Machines for the manufacture of foam products
	847780 90 0	Other
728.43	847810 00 0	Machinery for preparing or making up tobacco, n.e.s.
728.44		Presses for the manufacture of particle board or fibre building board of wood or other ligneous material and other machinery for treating wood or cork, n.e.s.
	847930 10 0	Presses
	847930 90 0	Other
728.46	847981 00 0	Machinery for treating metal (including electric wirecoil-winders), n.e.s.
728.47	840120 00 0	Machinery and apparatus for isotopic separation, and parts thereof, n.e.s.

S.I.T.C. (R3)	Commodity Code No	Trade description
728.49		Machinery having individual functions, n.e.s.
	847940 00 0	Rope or cable-making machines
	*847950 00 0	Industrial robots, not elsewhere specified or included
	*847960 00 0	Evaporative air coolers
		Other machines and mechanical appliances
	847982 00 0	Mixing, kneading, crushing, grinding, screening, sifting, homogenising, emulsifying or stirring machines
		Other
	847989 10 0	The following goods, for use in civil aircraft : Hydropneumatic batteries; Mechanical actuators for thrust reversers; Toilet units specially designed; Air humidifiers and dehumidifiers; Servo-mechanisms, non-electric; non-electric starter motors; Pneumatic starters for turbo-jets, turbo-propellers and other gas turbines; Windscreen wipers, non-electric; Propeller regulators, non-electric
		Other
	847989 30 0	Mobile hydraulic powered mine roof supports
	847989 60 0	Central greasing systems
	847989 65 0	Apparatus for growing or pulling monocrystal semiconductor boules
	847989 70 0	Apparatus for epitaxial deposition on semiconductor wafers
	847989 75 0	Apparatus for wet etching, developing, stripping or cleaning semiconductor wafers
	*847989 95 0	Other
		Parts, n.e.s. of the machines and mechanical appliances of headings 723.48, 727.21 and 728.41 to 728.49
728.51	847590 00 0	Parts for the machines of heading 728.41
728.52		Parts for the machines of heading 728.42
	847790 10 0	Of cast iron or cast steel
	847790 90 0	Other
728.53	847890 00 0	Parts for the machines of heading 728.43
728.55		Parts, n.e.s., for the machines of headings 723.48, 727.21 and 728.44 through 728.49
	847990 10 0	For use in civil aircraft
		Other
	847990 92 0	Of cast iron or cast steel
	847990 98 0	Other

DIVISION 73

METALWORKING MACHINERY

MACHINE-TOOLS WORKING BY REMOVING METAL OR OTHER MATERIAL

Machine-tools for working any material by removal of material, by laser or other light or photon beam, ultra-sonic, electro-discharge, electro-chemical, electron beam, ionic-beam or plasma jet processes

S.I.T.C. (R3)	Commodity Code No	Trade description
731.11	845610 00 0	....operated by laser or other light or photon beam processes
731.12	845620 00 0	....operated by ultra-sonic processes
731.13		....operated by electro-discharge processes
		Numerically controlled
	845630 11 0	Wire-cut
	845630 19 0	Other
	845630 90 0	Other
731.14		Other
	*845691 00 0	For dry-etching patterns on semiconductor materials
		Other
	*845699 10 0	Focused ion beam milling machines for producing or repairing masks and reticles for patterns on semiconductor devices
	*845699 30 0	Apparatus for dry etching, stripping or cleaning semiconductor wafers
	*845699 90 0	Other

Machining centres, unit construction machines (single station) and multi-station transfer machines for working metal

S.I.T.C. (R3)	Commodity Code No	Trade description
731.21		Machining centres
	845710 10 0	Horizontal
	845710 90 0	Other
731.22		Unit construction machines (single station)
	845720 10 0	Numerically controlled
	845720 90 0	Other

S.I.T.C. (R3)	Commodity Code No	Trade description
731.23		Multi-station transfer machines
	845730 10 0	Numerically controlled
	845730 90 0	Other

Lathes for removing metal (other than those of heading 731.1, 731.2 or 733.9)

S.I.T.C. (R3)	Commodity Code No	Trade description
731.31		Horizontal lathes, numerically controlled
	845811 20 0	Turning centres
		Automatic lathes
	845811 41 0	Single spindle
	845811 49 0	Multi-spindle
	845811 80 0	Other
731.35		Other lathes, numerically controlled
	845891 20 0	Turning centres
	845891 80 0	Other
731.37		Other horizontal lathes
	845819 20 0	Centre lathes (engine or tool-room)
	845819 40 0	Automatic lathes
	845819 80 0	Other
731.39	845899 00 0	Lathes, n.e.s.

Way-type unit head machines; other machine-tools for drilling or boring

S.I.T.C. (R3)	Commodity Code No	Trade description
731.41	845910 00 0	Way-type unit head machines
731.42	845921 00 0	Other drilling machines, numerically controlled
731.43	845929 00 0	Drilling machines, n.e.s
731.44	845931 00 0	Other boring-milling machines, numerically controlled
731.45	845939 00 0	Boring-milling machines, n.e.s
731.46		Other boring machines
	845940 10 0	Numerically controlled
	845940 90 0	Other

Machine-tools for milling , threading or tapping by removing metal (other than the lathes of heading 731.3 or the machine- tools of heading 731.1, 731.2 or 731.4)

S.I.T.C. (R3)	Commodity Code No	Trade description
731.51	845951 00 0	Milling machines, knee-type, numerically controlled
731.52	845959 00 0	Other knee-type milling machines
731.53		Other milling machines, numerically controlled
	845961 10 0	Tool milling machines
		Other
	845961 91 0	Plano-milling machines
	845961 99 0	Other
731.54		Milling machines, n.e.s
	845969 10 0	Tool milling machines
		Other
	845969 91 0	Plano-milling machines
	845969 99 0	Other
731.57	845970 00 0	Other threading or tapping machines

Machine-tools for deburring, sharpening, grinding, honing, lapping, polishing or otherwise finishing metal, sintered metal carbides or cermets by means of grinding stones, abrasives or polishing products (other than gear-cutting, gear grinding or gear finishing machines of heading 731.7)

S.I.T.C. (R3)	Commodity Code No	Trade description
731.61	846011 00 0	Flat-surface grinding machines, numerically controlled, in which the positioning in any one axis can be set up to an accuracy of at least 0.01 mm
731.62	846019 00 0	Non-numerically controlled flat-surface grinding machines, in which the positioning in any one axis can be set up to an accuracy of at least 0.01 mm
731.63		Other grinding machines, numerically controlled, in which the positioning in any one axis can be set up to an accuracy of at least 0.01mm
		For cylindrical surfaces
	846021 11 0	Internal cylindrical grinding machines
	846021 15 0	Centreless grinding machines
	846021 19 0	Other
	846021 90 0	Other

S.I.T.C. (R3)	Commodity Code No	Trade description
731.64		Grinding machines, n.e.s., in which the positioning in any one axis can be set up to an accuracy of at least 0.01 mm
		For cylindrical surfaces
	846029 11 0	Internal cylindrical surfaces
	846029 19 0	Other
	846029 90 0	Other
731.65	846031 00 0	Sharpening (tool or cutter grinding) machines, numerically controlled
731.66	846039 00 0	Other sharpening (tool or cutter grinding) machines
731.67		Honing or lapping machines
	846040 10 0	Numerically controlled
	846040 90 0	Other
731.69		Machine-tools for deburring, polishing, or otherwise finishing metal, sintered metal carbides or cermets by means of grinding stones, abrasives or polishing products, n.e.s.
	846090 10 0	Fitted with a micrometric adjusting system, in which the positioning in any one axis can be set up to an accuracy of at least 0.01 mm
	846090 90 0	Other

Machine-tools for planing, shaping, slotting, broaching, gear- cutting, gear grinding or gear finishing, sawing, cutting-off, and other machine-tools working by removing metal, sintered metal carbides or cermets, n.e.s.

S.I.T.C. (R3)	Commodity Code No	Trade description
731.71	846120 00 0	Shaping or slotting machines
731.73		Broaching machines
	846130 10 0	Numerically controlled
	846030 90 0	Other
731.75		Gear-cutting, gear grinding or gear finishing machines
		Gear cutting machines (including abrasive gear-cutting machines)
		For cutting cylindrical gears
	846140 11 0	Numerically controlled
	846140 19 0	Other
		For cutting other gears
	846140 31 0	Numerically controlled
	846140 39 0	Other
		Gear-finishing machines
		Fitted with a micrometric adjusting system, in which the positioning in anyone axis can be set up to an accuracy of at least 0.01 mm
	846140 71 0	Numerically controlled
	846140 79 0	Other
	846140 90 0	Other
731.77		Sawing or cutting-off machines
		Sawing machines
	846150 11 0	Circular saws
	846150 19 0	Other
	846150 90 0	Cutting-off machines
731.78	846110 00 0	Planing machines, metalworking
731.79	846190 00 0	Machine-tools working by removing metal, sintered metal carbides or cermets, n.e.s.

MACHINE-TOOLS FOR WORKING METAL, SINTERED METAL CARBIDES OR CERMETS, WITHOUT REMOVING MATERIAL

Machine-tools (including presses) for working metal by forging, hammering or die-stamping; machines-tools (including presses) for working metal by bending, folding, straightening, flattening, shearing, punching or notching; presses for working metal or metal carbides, n.e.s

S.I.T.C. (R3)	Commodity Code No	Trade description
733.11		Forging or die-stamping machines (including presses) and hammers
	846210 10 0	Numerically controlled
	846210 90 0	Other
733.12		Bending, folding, straightening or flattening machines (including presses), numerically controlled
	846221 10 0	For working flat products
	846221 90 0	Other
733.13		Non-numerically controlled bending, folding, straightening or flattening machines (including presses)
	846229 10 0	For working flat products
		Other
	846229 91 0	Hydraulic
	846229 99 0	Other

S.I.T.C. (R3)	Commodity Code No	Trade description
733.14	846231 00 0	Shearing machines (including presses), numerically controlled, other than combined punching and shearing machines
733.15		Shearing machines (including presses), other than combined punching and shearing machines, not numerically controlled
	846239 10 0	For working flat products
		Other
	846239 91 0	Hydraulic
	846239 99 0	Other
733.16		Punching or notching machines (including presses), including combined punching and shearing machines, numerically controlled
	846241 10 0	For working flat products
	846241 90 0	Other
733.17		Punching or notching machines, n.e.s., (including presses), including combined punching and shearing machines
	846249 10 0	For working flat products
	846249 90 0	Other
733.18		Presses for working metal or metal carbides, n.e.s.
		Hydraulic presses
	846291 10 0	Presses for moulding metallic powders by sintering or presses for compressing scrap metal into bales
		Other
	846291 50 0	Numerically controlled
		Other
	846291 91 0	For making rivets, bolts and screws
	846291 99 0	Other
		Other
	846299 10 0	Presses for moulding metallic powders by sintering or presses for compressing scrap metal into bales
		Other
	846299 50 0	Numerically controlled
		Other
	846299 91 0	For making rivets, bolts and screws
	846299 99 0	Other

Other machine-tools for working metal, sintered metal carbides or cermets, without removing material

S.I.T.C. (R3)	Commodity Code No	Trade description
733.91		Draw-benches for bars, tubes, profiles, wire and the like
	846310 10 0	Draw-benches for wire
	846310 90 0	Other
733.93	846320 00 0	**Thread rolling machines**
733.95	846330 00 0	**Machines for working wire**
733.99		Machine-tools for working metals, sintered metal carbides or cermets, without removing material, n.e.s.
	846390 10 0	For working flat products
	846390 90 0	Other

PARTS, N.E.S., AND ACCESSORIES SUITABLE FOR USE SOLELY OR PRINCIPALLY WITH THE MACHINES FALLING WITHIN HEADINGS 731 AND 733 (INCLUDING WORK OR TOOL HOLDERS, SELF-OPENING DIEHEADS, DIVIDING HEADS AND OTHER SPECIAL ATTACHMENTS FOR MACHINE-TOOLS); TOOL HOLDERS FOR ANY TYPE OF TOOL FOR WORKING IN THE HAND

Work-holders, self-opening dieheads and dividing heads for machine-tools; tool holders

S.I.T.C. (R3)	Commodity Code No	Trade description
735.11		Tool holders and self-opening dieheads
		Tool holders
	846610 10 0	Arbors, collets and sleeves
		Other
	846610 31 0	For lathes
	846610 39 0	Other
	846610 90 0	Self-opening dieheads
735.13		Work holders
	846620 10 0	Jigs and fixtures for specific applications; sets of standard jig and fixture components.
		Other
	846620 91 0	For lathes
	846620 99 0	Other
735.15	846630 00 0	Dividing heads and other special attachments for machine-tools

Parts, n.e.s., and accessories suitable for use solely or principally with the machine-tools of headings 731 and 733

S.I.T.C. (R3)	Commodity Code No	Trade description
735.91		....for machines of heading 731
	846693 20 0	Of cast iron or cast steel
	846693 80 0	Other
735.95	846694 00 0	....for machines of heading 733

METALWORKING MACHINERY (OTHER THAN MACHINE-TOOLS), AND PARTS THEREOF, N.E.S.

Converters, ladles, ingot moulds and casting machines of a kind used in metallurgy or in metal foundries, and parts thereof, n.e.s.

S.I.T.C. (R3)	Commodity Code No	Trade description
737.11		Converters, ingot moulds and ladles
	845410 00 0	Converters
	845420 00 0	Ingot moulds and ladles
737.12		Casting machines
	845430 10 0	For casting under pressure
	845430 90 0	Other
737.19	845490 00 0	Parts

Metal-rolling mills and rolls and other parts therefor

S.I.T.C. (R3)	Commodity Code No	Trade description
737.21		Metal-rolling mills
	845510 00 0	Tube mills
		Other rolling mills
	845521 00 0	Hot or combination hot and cold
	845522 00 0	Cold
737.29		Rolls and other parts for metal rolling mills
		Rolls for rolling mills
	845530 10 0	Of cast iron
		Of open-die forged steel
	845530 31 0	Hot-rolling work-rolls; hot-rolling and cold-rolling back-up rolls
	845530 39 0	Cold-rolling work-rolls
	845530 90 0	Of cast or wrought steel
	845590 00 0	Other parts

Electric (including electrically heated gas), laser or other light or photon beam, ultra-sonic, electron beam, magnetic pulse or plasma arc soldering, brazing or welding machines and apparatus, whether or not capable of cutting; electric machines and apparatus for hot spraying of metals or sintered metal carbides; and parts thereof, n.e.s.

S.I.T.C. (R3)	Commodity Code No	Trade description
737.31	851511 00 0	Soldering irons and guns
737.32	851519 00 0	Other brazing or soldering machines and apparatus
737.33	851521 00 0	Machines and apparatus for resistance welding of metal, fully or partly automatic
737.34		Other machines and apparatus for resistance welding of metal
	851529 10 0	For butt welding
	851529 90 0	Other
737.35	851531 00 0	Machines and apparatus for arc, including plasma arc welding of metal, fully or partly automatic
737.36		Other machines and apparatus for arc welding of metal
		For manual welding with coated electrodes, complete with welding or cutting devices, and consigned with
	851539 13 0	Transformers
	851539 18 0	Generators or rotary convertors or static converters, rectifiers or rectifying apparatus
	851539 90 0	Other
737.37		Other machines and apparatus
		For treating metals
	851580 11 0	For welding
	851580 19 0	Other
		Other
	851580 91 0	For resistance welding of plastics
	851580 99 0	Other
737.39	851590 00 0	Parts for the machines and apparatus of heading 737.3

Machinery and apparatus for soldering, brazing or welding, whether or not capable of cutting (other than those of heading 737.3); gas- operated surface tempering machines and appliances, and parts thereof, n.e.s.

S.I.T.C. (R3)	Commodity Code No	Trade description
737.41	846810 00 0	Hand-held blow pipes

S.I.T.C. (R3)	Commodity Code No	Trade description
737.42	846820 00 0	Other gas-operated machinery and apparatus
737.43	846880 00 0	Other machinery and other apparatus
737.49	846890 00 0	Parts for the machinery and apparatus of heading 737.4

DIVISION 74 — GENERAL INDUSTRIAL MACHINERY AND EQUIPMENT, N.E.S., AND MACHINE PARTS, N.E.S.

HEATING AND COOLING EQUIPMENT AND PARTS THEREOF, N.E.S

Furnace burners for liquid fuel, for pulverized solid fuel or for gas; mechanical stokers, including their mechanical grates, mechanical ash dischargers and similar appliances; and parts thereof, n.e.s.

S.I.T.C. (R3)	Commodity Code No	Trade description
741.21		Furnace burners for liquid fuel
	841610 10 0	Incorporating an automatic control device
	841610 90 0	Other
741.23		Other furnace burners (including combination burners)
	*841620 10 0	Only for gas, monobloc, incorporating a ventilator and a control device
	*841620 90 0	Other
741.25	841630 00 0	Mechanical stokers, including their mechanical grates, mechanical ash dischargers and similar appliances
741.28	841690 00 0	Parts for the burners and other articles of heading 741.2

Industrial or laboratory furnaces and ovens, etc., and parts thereof

S.I.T.C. (R3)	Commodity Code No	Trade description
741.31		Resistance heated furnaces and ovens
	851410 10 0	Bakery and biscuit ovens
	851410 90 0	Other
741.32		Induction or dielectric furnaces and ovens
	851420 10 0	Induction furnaces and ovens
	851420 90 0	Dielectric furnaces and ovens
741.33		Other electric furnaces and ovens
		Infra-red radiation ovens
	851430 11 0	For the manufacture of semiconductor devices on semiconductor wafers
	851430 19 0	Other
		Other
	851430 91 0	For the manufacture of semiconductor devices on semiconductor wafers
	851430 99 0	Other
741.34	851440 00 0	Other induction or dielectric heating equipment
741.35		Parts for the equipment of headings 741.31 through 741.34
	851490 10 0	Of cast iron or cast steel
	851490 90 0	Other
741.36	841710 00 0	Furnaces and ovens for the roasting, melting or other heat-treatment of ores, pyrites or of metals, non-electric
741.37		Bakery ovens (including biscuit ovens), non-electric
	841720 10 0	Tunnel ovens
	841720 90 0	Other
741.38		Other non-electric furnaces and ovens (including incinerators)
	841780 10 0	Furnaces and ovens for the incineration of rubbish
	841780 90 0	Other
741.39	841790 00 0	Parts for the furnaces and ovens of headings 741.36 through 741.38

Refrigerators, freezers and other refrigerating or freezing equipment (electric or other), other than household type refrigerators and freezers; parts of refrigerators, freezers and other refrigerating or freezing equipment

S.I.T.C. (R3)	Commodity Code No	Trade description
741.43		Refrigerating or freezing chests (other than household type), cabinets, display counters, show-cases and similar refrigerating or freezing furniture
		Refrigerated show-cases and counters (incorporating a refrigerating unit or evaporator)
	841850 11 0	For frozen food storage
	841850 19 0	Other
		Other refrigerating furniture
	841850 91 0	For deep-freezing, other than that of heading 775.22
	841850 99 0	Other

S.I.T.C. (R3)	Commodity Code No	Trade description
741.45		Other refrigerating or freezing equipment; heat pumps
		Compression type units whose condensers are heat exchangers
	841861 10 0	For use in civil aircraft
	841861 90 0	Other
		Other
	841869 10 0	For use in civil aircraft
		Other
	841869 91 0	Absorption heat pumps
	841869 99 0	Other
741.49		Parts of refrigerators, freezers and other refrigerating or freezing equipment (electric or other)
	841891 00 0	Furniture designed to receive refrigerating or freezing equipment
		Other
	841899 10 0	Evaporators and condensers, excluding those for refrigerators of the household type
	841899 90 0	Other
		Air conditioning machines comprising a motor-driven fan and elements for changing the temperature and humidity, and parts thereof
741.51	841510 00 0	....window or wall types, self-contained
741.55		....other air conditioning machines
	*841520 00 0	Of a kind used for persons, in motor vehicles
		Other
		Incorporating a refrigerating unit and a valve for reversal of the cooling/heat cycle
	841581 10 0	For use in civil aircraft
	841581 90 0	Other
		Other, incorporating a refrigerating unit
	841582 10 0	For use in civil aircraft
	*841582 80 0	Other
		Not incorporating a refrigerating unit
	841583 10 0	For use in civil aircraft
	841583 90 0	Other
741.59		Parts for the air conditioning machines of heading 741.5
	841590 10 0	Of air conditioning machines of heading 741.55 for use in civil aircraft
	841590 90 0	Other
		Gas generators, distilling or rectifying plant, heat exchange units and machinery for liquifying air or other gases
741.71	840510 00 0	Producer gas or water gas generators, with or without their purifiers; acetylene gas generators and similar water process gas generators, with or without their purifiers
741.72	840590 00 0	Parts for the generators of heading 741.71
741.73	841940 00 0	Distilling or rectifying plant
741.74		Heat exchange units
	841950 10 0	For use in civil aircraft
	841950 90 0	Other
741.75	841960 00 0	Machinery for liquifying air or other gases
		Other machinery, plant and similar laboratory equipment, whether or not electrically heated, for the treatment of materials by a process involving a change of temperature, not being machinery or plant of a kind used for domestic purposes; instantaneous or storage water heaters, non-electric
741.81	841911 00 0	Instantaneous gas water heaters
741.82	841919 00 0	Other instantaneous or storage water heaters, non-electric
741.83	841920 00 0	Medical, surgical or laboratory sterilizers
741.84	841931 00 0	Dryers for agricultural products
741.85	841932 00 0	Dryers for wood, paper pulp, paper or paperboard
741.86	841939 00 0	Dryers, n.e.s
741.87		Machinery for making hot drinks or for cooking or heating food
	841981 10 0	For use in civil aircraft
		Other
	841981 91 0	Percolators and other appliances for making coffee and other hot drinks
	841981 99 0	Other

S.I.T.C. (R3)	Commodity Code No	Trade description
741.89		**Other machinery, plant or equipment**
	841989 10 0	Cooling towers and similar plant for direct cooling (without a separating wall) by means of recirculated water
	841989 15 0	Apparatus for rapid heating of semiconductor wafers
	841989 20 0	Apparatus for chemical vapour deposition on semiconductor wafers
	841989 25 0	Apparatus for physical vapour deposition by electronic beam or evaporation on semiconductor wafers
	841989 30 0	Vacuum-vapour plant for the deposition of metal
	841989 95 0	Other
741.90		**Parts, n.e.s., for the machinery included at headings 741.7 and 741.8**
	841990 10 0	Of heat exchange units, for use in civil aircraft
	841990 20 0	Of heading 741.83
	841990 95 0	Other

PUMPS FOR LIQUIDS, WHETHER OR NOT FITTED WITH A MEASURING DEVICE; LIQUID ELEVATORS: PARTS FOR SUCH PUMPS AND LIQUID ELEVATORS

Pumps fitted or designed to be fitted with a measuring device

S.I.T.C. (R3)	Commodity Code No	Trade description
742.11	841311 00 0	Pumps for dispensing fuel or lubricants, of the type used in filling stations or in garages, fitted or designed to be fitted with a measuring device
742.19		**Other pumps fitted or designed to be fitted with a measuring device**
	841319 10 0	For use in civil aircraft
	841319 90 0	Other
742.20		**Fuel, lubricating or cooling medium pumps for internal combustion piston engines**
	841330 10 0	For use in civil aircraft
		Other
	841330 91 0	Injection pumps
	841330 99 0	Other
742.30	841340 00 0	**Concrete pumps**
742.40		**Reciprocating positive displacement pumps, n.e.s.**
	841350 10 0	For use in civil aircraft
		Other
	841350 30 0	Hydraulic units
	841350 50 0	Dosing and proportioning pumps
		Other
		Piston pumps
	841350 71 0	Hydraulic fluid power
	841350 79 0	Other
	841350 90 0	Other
742.50		**Rotary positive displacement pumps, n.e.s.**
	841360 10 0	For use in civil aircraft
		Other
	841360 30 0	Hydraulic units
		Other
		Gear pumps
	841360 41 0	Hydraulic fluid power
	841360 49 0	Other
		Vane pumps
	841360 51 0	Hydraulic fluid power
	841360 59 0	Other
	841360 60 0	Screw pumps
	841360 90 0	Other
742.60		**Centrifugal pumps, n.e.s.**
	841370 10 0	For use in civil aircraft
		Other
		Submersible pumps
	841370 21 0	Single-stage
	841370 29 0	Multi-stage
	841370 30 0	Glandless impeller pumps for heating systems and warm water supply
		Other, with a discharge outlet diameter
	841370 40 0	Not exceeding 15 mm
		Exceeding 15 mm
	841370 50 0	Channel impeller pumps and side channel pumps
		Radial flow pumps
		Single-stage
		With single entry impeller
	841370 61 0	Monobloc
	841370 69 0	Other
	841370 70 0	With more than one entry impeller
	841370 80 0	Multi-stage
		Other centrifugal pumps

cont 742.60	841370 91 0	Single-stage
	841370 99 0	Multi-stage

Pumps for liquids, n.e.s., and liquid elevators

742.71		Pumps for liquids, n.e.s.
		Hand pumps, other than those of heading 742.11
	841320 10 0	For use in civil aircraft
	841320 90 0	Other
		Other
	841381 10 0	For use in civil aircraft
	841381 90 0	Other
742.75	841382 00 0	Liquid elevators

Parts of the pumps and liquid elevators of group 742

742.91		....of pumps
	841391 10 0	For use in civil aircraft
	841391 90 0	Other
742.95	841392 00 0	....of liquid elevators

PUMPS (OTHER THAN PUMPS FOR LIQUIDS), AIR OR OTHER GAS COMPRESSORS AND FANS; VENTILATING OR RECYCLING HOODS INCORPORATING A FAN, WHETHER OR NOT FITTED WITH FILTERS; CENTRIFUGES; FILTERING OR PURIFYING APPARATUS; AND PARTS THEREOF

Air or vacuum pumps, air or other gas compressors, ventilating or recycling hoods (other than cooker hoods) incorporating a fan

743.11		Vacuum pumps
	841410 10 0	For use in civil aircraft
		Other
	841410 30 0	Rotary piston pumps, sliding vane rotary pumps, molecular drag pumps and Roots pumps
		Other
	841410 50 0	Diffusion pumps, cryopumps and adsorption pumps
	841410 90 0	Other
743.13		Hand-or foot-operated air pumps
	841420 10 0	For use in civil aircraft
		Other
	841420 91 0	Hand pumps for cycles
	841420 99 0	Other
743.15		Compressors of a kind used in refrigerating equipment
	841430 10 0	For use in civil aircraft
		Other
	841430 30 0	Of a power not exceeding 0.4 kw
		Of a power exceeding 0.4 kw
	841430 91 0	Hermetic or semi-hermetic
	841430 99 0	Other
743.17		Air compressors mounted on a wheeled chassis for towing
	841440 10 0	Giving a flow per minute not exceeding 2 m^3
	841440 90 0	Giving a flow per minute exceeding 2 m^3
743.19		Other
	841480 10 0	For use in civil aircraft
		Other
		Turbo-compressors
	841480 21 0	Single-stage
	841480 29 0	Multi-stage
		Reciprocating displacement compressors, having a gauge pressure capacity of
		Not exceeding 15 bar, giving a flow per hour
	841480 31 0	Not exceeding 60 m^3
	841480 39 0	Exceeding 60 m^3
		Exceeding 15 bar, giving a flow per hour
	841480 41 0	Not exceeding 120 m^3
	841480 49 0	Exceeding 120 m^3
		Rotary displacement compressors
	841480 60 0	Single-shaft
		Multi-shaft
	841480 71 0	Screw compressors
	841480 79 0	Other
	841480 90 0	Other

S.I.T.C. (R3)	Commodity Code No	Trade description
		Fans and cooker hoods incorporating a fan
743.41		Table, floor, wall, window, ceiling or roof fans with self-contained electric motor of an output not exceeding 125 W
	841451 10 0	For use in civil aircraft
	841451 90 0	Other
743.43		Other fans
	841459 10 0	For use in civil aircraft
		Other
	841459 30 0	Axial fans
	841459 50 0	Centrifugal fans
	841459 90 0	Other
743.45	841460 00 0	Hoods having a maximum horizontal side not exceeding 120 cms.
		Centrifuges (including centrifugal dryers), n.e.s.
743.51	842111 00 0	Cream separators
743.55	842112 00 0	Clothes-dryers
743.59		Other centrifuges
	842119 10 0	For use in civil aircraft
		Other
	842119 91 0	Centrifuges of a kind used in laboratories
	842119 93 0	Spinners for coating photographic emulsions on semiconductor wafers
	842119 98 0	Other
		Filtering and purifying machinery and apparatus, for liquids or gases
743.61		....for filtering and purifying water
	842121 10 0	For use in civil aircraft
	842121 90 0	Other
743.62	842122 00 0	....for filtering or purifying beverages other than water
743.63		Oil or petrol-filters for internal combustion engines
	842123 10 0	For use in civil aircraft
	842123 90 0	Other
743.64		Intake air filters for internal combustion engines
	842131 10 0	For use in civil aircraft
	842131 90 0	Other
743.67		Filtering or purifying machinery and apparatus for liquids, n.e.s
	842129 10 0	For use in civil aircraft
	842129 90 0	Other
743.69		Filtering or purifying machinery and apparatus for gases, n.e.s
	842139 10 0	For use in civil aircraft
		Other
	842139 30 0	Machinery and apparatus for filtering or purifying air
		Machinery and apparatus for filtering or purifying other gases
	842139 51 0	By a liquid process
	842139 71 0	By a catalytic process
	*842139 98 0	Other
743.80		Parts for the pumps, compressors, fans and hoods of headings 743.1 and 743.4
	841490 10 0	For use in civil aircraft
	841490 90 0	Other
		Parts of the machines and apparatus of headings 743.5 and 743.6
743.91	842191 00 0	....of centrifuges (including centrifugal dryers)
743.95	842199 00 0	....of filtering or purifying machinery and apparatus
		MECHANICAL HANDLING EQUIPMENT, AND PARTS THEREOF, N.E.S.
		Works trucks, of the type used in factories, warehouses, dock areas or airports for short distance transport of goods; tractors of the type used on railway station platforms; parts, n.e.s., of the foregoing vehicles
744.11		Self-propelled trucks powered by an electric motor, fitted with lifting or handling equipment
	842710 10 0	With a lifting height of 1 m or more
	842710 90 0	Other

S.I.T.C. (R3)	Commodity Code No	Trade description
744.12		Other self-propelled trucks fitted with lifting or handling equipment
		With a lifting height of 1 m or more
	842720 11 0	Rough terrain fork-lift and other stacking trucks
	842720 19 0	Other
	842720 90 0	Other
744.13	842790 00 0	Other works trucks fitted with lifting or handling equipment
744.14		Works trucks, electrical, self-propelled, not fitted with lifting or handling equipment
	870911 10 0	Specially designed for the transport of highly radio-active materials (EURATOM)
	870911 90 0	Other
744.15		Other self-propelled works trucks, not fitted with lifting or handling equipment; tractors of the type used on railway station platforms
	870919 10 0	Specially designed for the transport of highly radio-active materials (EURATOM)
	870919 90 0	Other
744.19		Parts of the trucks and tractors of headings 744.14 and 744.15
	870990 10 0	Of cast iron or cast steel
	870990 90 0	Other
		Pulley tackle and hoists (other than skip hoists); winches and capstans
744.21		Pulley tackle and hoists (other than skip hoists or hoists of a kind used for raising vehicles)
		Powered by electric motor
	842511 10 0	For use in civil aircraft
	842511 90 0	Other
		Other
	842519 10 0	For use in civil aircraft
		Other
	842519 91 0	Manually operated chain hoists
	842519 99 0	Other
744.23	842520 00 0	Pit-head winding gear; winches specially designed for use underground
744.25		Other winches; capstans
		Powered by electric motor
	842531 10 0	For use in civil aircraft
	842531 90 0	Other
		Other
	842539 10 0	For use in civil aircraft
		Other
	842539 91 0	Powered by internal combustion piston engines
	842539 99 0	Other
		Ships' derricks; cranes (including cable cranes); mobile lifting frames; straddle carriers and works trucks fitted with a crane
744.31	842611 00 0	Overhead travelling cranes on fixed support
744.32	842612 00 0	Mobile lifting frames on tyres and straddle carriers
744.33	842619 00 0	Other overhead travelling cranes, transporter cranes, gantry cranes, bridge cranes and other mobile lifting frames
744.34	842620 00 0	Tower cranes
744.35	842630 00 0	Portal or pedestal jib cranes
744.37		Other machinery, self-propelled
	842641 00 0	On tyres
	842649 00 0	Other
744.39		Other machinery, not self-propelled
		Designed for mounting on road vehicles
	842691 10 0	Hydraulic cranes designed for the loading and unloading of the vehicle
	842691 90 0	Other
		Other
	842699 10 0	For use in civil aircraft
	842699 90 0	Other
		Jacks; hoists of a kind used for raising vehicles
744.41	842541 00 0	Built-in jacking systems of a type used in garages
744.43		Other jacks and hoists, hydraulic
	842542 10 0	For use in civil aircraft
	842542 90 0	Other

S.I.T.C. (R3)	Commodity Code No	Trade description
744.49		Other
	842549 10 0	For use in civil aircraft
	842549 90 0	Other
		Continuous-action elevators and conveyors, for goods or materials
744.71		Pneumatic elevators and conveyers
	842820 10 0	For use in civil aircraft
		Other
	842820 30 0	Specially designed for use in agriculture
		Other
	842820 91 0	For bulk materials
	842820 99 0	Other
744.72	842831 00 0	Other continuous-action elevators and conveyors, specially designed for underground use
744.73	842832 00 0	Other continuous-action elevators and conveyors, bucket type
744.74		Other continuous-action elevators and conveyors, belt type
	842833 10 0	For use in civil aircraft
	842833 90 0	Other
744.79		Continuous-action elevators and conveyers for goods or materials, n.e.s.
	842839 10 0	For use in civil aircraft
		Other
	842839 91 0	Roller conveyors
	842839 93 0	Automated material handling machines for transport, handling and storage of semiconductor wafers, wafer cassettes, wafer boxes and other material for semiconductor devices
	842839 98 0	Other
		Lifting, handling, loading or unloading machinery, n.e.s.
744.81		Lifts and skip hoists
	842810 10 0	For use in civil aircraft
		Other
	842810 91 0	Electrically operated
	842810 99 0	Other
744.85	842840 00 0	**Escalators and moving walkways**
744.89		Other lifting, handling, loading or unloading machinery
	842850 00 0	Mine wagon pushers, locomotive or wagon traversers, wagon tippers and similar railway wagon handling equipment
	842860 00 0	Teleferics, chair-lifts, ski-draglines; traction mechanisms for funiculars
		Other machinery
	842890 10 0	For use in civil aircraft
		Other
	842890 30 0	Rolling-mill machinery; roller tables for feeding and removing products; tilters and manipulators for ingots, balls, bars and slabs
		Other
	842890 50 0	Feeding equipment (excluding cranes) for blast and other industrial furnaces; forging manipulators
		Loaders specially designed for use in agriculture
	842890 71 0	Designed for attachment to agricultural tractors
	842890 79 0	Other
		Other
	842890 91 0	Mechanical loaders for bulk material
	842890 99 0	Other
		Parts suitable for use solely or principally with the machinery of headings 744.11, 744.12, 744.13, 744.2, 744.4, 744.7 and 744.8
744.91	843110 00 0	....of machinery of headings 744.2 and 744.4
744.92	843120 00 0	....of machinery of headings 744.11 ,744.12 and 744.13
744.93	*843131 00 0	....of lifts, skip hoists or escalators
744.94		....of other lifting, handling, loading or unloading machinery of heading 744.8
	843139 10 0	Of rolling-mill machinery of subheading 8428.90-30
	843139 90 0	Other

S.I.T.C. (R3)	Commodity Code No	Trade description
		OTHER NON-ELECTRICAL MACHINERY, TOOLS AND MECHANICAL APPARATUS, AND PARTS THEREOF, N.E.S.
		Tools for working in the hand, pneumatic or with self-contained non-electric motor, and parts thereof
745.11		Tools for working in the hand, pneumatic
		Rotary type (including combined rotary-percussion)
	846711 10 0	Metal working
	846711 90 0	Other
	846719 00 0	Other
745.12		Tools for working in the hand, with self-contained non-electric motor
	846781 00 0	Chain saws
	*846789 00 0	Other
745.19		Parts of the tools of heading 745.1
	846791 00 0	Of chain saws
	846792 00 0	Of pneumatic tools
	846799 00 0	Other
		Dish washing machines (other than household type); machinery for cleaning or drying bottles or other containers; machinery for filling, closing, sealing, capsuling or labelling bottles, cans, boxes, bags or other containers; other packing or wrapping machinery; machinery for aerating beverages
745.21	842219 00 0	Dish washing machines not of the household type
745.23	842220 00 0	Machinery for cleaning or drying bottles or other containers
745.27		Other packing or wrapping machinery
	842230 00 0	Machinery for filling, closing, sealing, or capsuling
	842240 00 0	Other packing or wrapping machinery (including heat-shrink wrapping machinery)
745.29		Parts of the machinery of headings 745.2 and 775.3
	842290 10 0	Of dish-washing machines
	842290 90 0	Other
		Weighing machinery (excluding balances of a sensitivity of 5 cg or better) including weight-operated counting and checking machines; weighing machine weights of all kinds; parts thereof
745.31		Weighing machinery (excluding balances of a sensitivity of 5 cg or better, personal weighing machines and household scales), including weight-operated counting and checking machines
	842320 00 0	Scales for continuous weighing of goods on conveyors
	842330 00 0	Constant weight scales and scales for discharging a predetermined weight of material into a bag or container, including hopper scales
		Other weighing machinery
		Having a maximum weighing capacity not exceeding 30 kg
	842381 10 0	Check weighers and automatic control machines operating by reference to a pre-determined weight
	842381 30 0	Machinery for weighing and labelling pre-packaged goods
	842381 50 0	Shop-scales
	842381 90 0	Other
		Having a maximum weighing capacity exceeding 30 kg but not exceeding 5,000 kg
	842382 10 0	Check weighers and automatic control machines operating by reference to a pre-determined weight
	842382 90 0	Other
		Other
	842389 10 0	Weighbridges
	842389 90 0	Other
745.32		Personal weighing machines (including baby scales); household scales
	842310 10 0	Household scales
	842310 90 0	Other
745.39	842390 00 0	Weighing machine weights of all kinds; parts of the weighing machinery of heading 745.3
		Mechanical appliances, whether or not hand operated, for projecting, dispersing or spraying liquids or powders; fire extinguishers, whether or not charged; spray guns and similar appliances; steam or sand blasting machines and similar jet projecting machines
745.61		Fire extinguishers, whether or not charged
	842410 10 0	For use in civil aircraft
		Other
	842410 91 0	Of a weight not exceeding 21 Kg
	842410 99 0	Other
745.62	842420 00 0	Spray guns and similar appliances

S.I.T.C. (R3)	Commodity Code No	Trade description
745.63		**Steam or sand blasting machines and similar jet projecting machines**
		Water cleaning appliances, with built-in motor
	842430 01 0	With heating device
		Other, of an engine power
	842430 05 0	Not exceeding 7.5 kw
	842430 09 0	Exceeding 7.5 kw
745.64		**Agricultural or horticultural appliances for projecting, dispersing or spraying liquids or powders**
	842481 10 0	Watering appliances
		Other
		Portable appliances
	842481 31 0	Without motor
	842481 39 0	With motor
		Other
	842481 91 0	Sprayers and powder distributors designed to be mounted on or drawn by agricultural tractors
	842481 99 0	Other
745.65		**Other appliances**
	842489 20 0	Spraying appliances for etching, stripping or cleaning semiconductor wafers
	*842489 80 0	Other
	*844351 00 0	Ink-jet printing machines
745.68	842490 00 0	**Parts of the appliances of heading 745.6**
		Other non-electrical machines and parts thereof
745.91		**Calendering or other rolling machines (other than for metals or glass)**
	842010 10 0	Of a kind used in the textile industry
	842010 30 0	Of a kind used in the paper industry
	842010 50 0	Of a kind used in the rubber or plastics industries
	842010 90 0	Other
745.93		**Cylinders and other parts for the machines of heading**
		Cylinders
	842091 10 0	Of cast iron
	842091 30 0	Of open-die forged steel
	842091 90 0	Other
	842099 00 0	Other
745.95		**Automatic goods-vending machines (eg., food or beverage machines), including money-changing machines**
		Automatic beverage-vending machines:
	*847621 00 0	Incorporating heating or refrigerating devices
	*847629 00 0	Other
		Other machines
	*847681 00 0	Incorporating heating or refrigerating devices
	*847689 00 0	Other
745.97	847690 00 0	**Parts for the machines of heading 745.95**
		BALL OR ROLLER BEARINGS
746.10		**Ball bearings**
	848210 10 0	With greatest external diameter not exceeding 30 mm
	848210 90 0	Other
746.20	848220 00 0	**Tapered roller bearings (including cone and tapered roller assemblies)**
746.30	848230 00 0	**Spherical roller bearings**
746.40	848240 00 0	**Needle roller bearings**
746.50	848250 00 0	**Other cylindrical roller bearings**
746.80	848280 00 0	**Other ball or roller bearings (including combined ball/roller bearings)**
		Parts of ball and roller bearings
746.91		**Balls, needles and rollers**
	848291 10 0	Tapered rollers
	848291 90 0	Other
746.99	848299 00 0	**Other parts of ball and roller bearings**

S.I.T.C. (R3)	Commodity Code No	Trade description
		TAPS, COCKS, VALVES AND SIMILAR APPLIANCES, FOR PIPES, BOILER SHELLS, TANKS, VATS AND THE LIKE (INCLUDING PRESSURE REDUCING VALVES AND THERMOSTATICALLY CONTROLLED VALVES)
747.10		Pressure-reducing valves
		Of cast iron or steel
	848110 11 0	Combined with filters or lubricators
	848110 19 0	Other
		Other:
	848110 91 0	Combined with filters or lubricators
	848110 99 0	Other
747.20		Valves for oleohydraulic or pneumatic transmissions
	848120 10 0	Valves for the control of oleohydraulic power transmission
	848120 90 0	Valves for the control of pneumatic power transmission
747.30		Check valves
	848130 10 0	For pneumatic tyres and inner-tubes
		Other
	848130 91 0	Of cast iron or steel
	848130 99 0	Other
747.40		Safety or relief valves
	848140 10 0	Of cast iron or steel
	848140 90 0	Other
747.80		Taps, cocks, valves and similar appliances, n.e.s.
		Taps, cocks and valves for sinks, wash basins, bidets, water cisterns, baths and similar fixtures
	848180 11 0	Mixing valves
	848180 19 0	Other
		Central heating radiator valves
	848180 31 0	Thermostatic valves
	848180 39 0	Other
		Other
		Process control valves
	848180 51 0	Temperature regulators
	848180 59 0	Other
		Other
		Gate valves
	848180 61 0	Of cast iron
	848180 63 0	Of steel
	848180 69 0	Other
		Globe valves
	848180 71 0	Of cast iron
	848180 73 0	Of steel
	848180 79 0	Other
	848180 81 0	Ball and plug valves
	848180 85 0	Butterfly valves
	848180 87 0	Diaphragm valves
	848180 99 0	Other
747.90	848190 00 0	Parts for the appliances of heading 747
		TRANSMISSION SHAFTS (INCLUDING CAM SHAFTS AND CRANK SHAFTS) AND CRANKS; BEARING HOUSINGS AND PLAIN SHAFT BEARINGS; GEARS AND GEARING; BALL SCREWS; GEAR BOXES AND OTHER SPEED CHANGERS (INCLUDING TORQUE CONVERTERS); FLYWHEELS AND PULLEYS (INCLUDING PULLEY BLOCKS); CLUTCHES AND SHAFT COUPLINGS (INCLUDING UNIVERSAL JOINTS); AND PARTS THEREOF
748.10		Transmission shafts (including cam shafts and crank shafts) and cranks
	848310 10 0	For use in civil aircraft
		Other
		Cranks and crank shafts
	848310 30 0	Crank shafts built up from several parts (composite crank shafts)
		Other
	848310 41 0	Of cast iron or cast steel
	848310 51 0	Of open-die forged steel
	848310 53 0	Of closed-die forged steel
	848310 58 0	Other
	848310 90 0	Other
		Bearing housings and plain shaft bearings
748.21		Bearing housings, incorporating ball or roller bearings
	848320 10 0	Of a kind used in aircraft and spacecraft
	848320 90 0	Other

S.I.T.C. (R3)	Commodity Code No	Trade description
748.22		Bearing housings, not incorporating ball or roller bearings; plain shaft bearings
	848330 10 0	For use in civil aircraft
		Other
		Bearing housings
	848330 31 0	For ball or roller bearings
		Other
	848330 51 0	Of cast iron or cast steel
	848330 59 0	Other
	848330 90 0	Plain shaft bearings
		Articulated link chain and parts thereof, of iron or steel
748.31		Roller chain
	731511 10 0	Of a kind used for cycles and motor-cycles
	731511 90 0	Other
748.32	731512 00 0	Other articulated chain
748.39	731519 00 0	Parts of articulated link chain
748.40		Gears and gearing (excluding toothed wheels, chain sprockets and other transmission elements presented separately); ball screws; gear boxes and other speed changers (including torque converters)
	848340 10 0	For use in civil aircraft
		Other
	848340 91 0	Gear and gearing
	*848340 92 0	Ball or roller screws
	848340 93 0	Gear boxes and other speed changers
	*848340 98 0	Other
748.50		Flywheels and pulleys (including pulley blocks)
	848350 10 0	Pulleys for use in civil aircraft
		Other
	848350 91 0	Of cast iron or cast steel
	848350 99 0	Other
748.60		Clutches and shaft couplings (including universal joints)
	848360 10 0	For use in civil aircraft
		Other
	848360 91 0	Of cast iron or cast steel
	848360 99 0	Other
748.90		Parts, n.e.s., for the articles of heading 748
	848390 10 0	For use in civil aircraft
		Other
	848390 30 0	Of bearing housings
		Other
	848390 92 0	Of cast iron or cast steel
	848390 98 0	Other

NON-ELECTRIC PARTS AND ACCESSORIES OF MACHINERY, N.E.S.

Moulding boxes for metal foundry; mould bases; moulding patterns; moulds for metal (other than ingot moulds), metal carbides, glass, mineral materials, rubber or plastics

S.I.T.C. (R3)	Commodity Code No	Trade description
749.11	848010 00 0	Moulding boxes for metal foundry
749.12	848020 00 0	Mould bases
749.13		Moulding patterns
	848030 10 0	Of wood
	848030 90 0	Other
749.14	848041 00 0	Injection or compression types of moulds for metals or metal carbides
749.15	848049 00 0	Other moulds for metals or metal carbides
749.16	848050 00 0	Moulds for glass
749.17	848060 00 0	Moulds for mineral materials
749.18	848071 00 0	Injection or compression types of moulds for rubber or plastics
749.19	848079 00 0	Other moulds for rubber or plastics

S.I.T.C. (R3)	Commodity Code No	Trade description
749.20		Gaskets and similar joints of metal sheeting combined with other material or of two or more layers of metal; sets or assortments of gaskets and similar joints, dissimilar in composition, put up in pouches, envelopes or similar packings
		Gaskets and similar joints of metal sheeting combined with other material or of two or more layers of metal
	848410 10 0	For use in civil aircraft
	848410 90 0	Other
		Other
	848490 10 0	For use in civil aircraft
	848490 90 0	Other
		Machinery parts, not containing electrical connectors, insulators, coils, contacts or other electrical features, n.e.s.
749.91		Ships' or boats' propellers and blades therefor
	848510 10 0	Of bronze
	848510 90 0	Other
749.99		Other machinery parts, not containing electrical connectors, insulators, coils, contacts or other electrical features
	*848420 00 0	Mechanical seals
		Other
	848590 10 0	Of non-malleable cast iron
	848590 30 0	Of malleable cast iron
		Of iron or steel
	848590 51 0	Of cast steel
	848590 53 0	Of open-die forged iron or steel
	848590 55 0	Of closed-die forged iron or steel
	848590 59 0	Other
	*848590 80 0	Other

DIVISION 75 — OFFICE MACHINES AND AUTOMATIC DATA PROCESSING MACHINES

OFFICE MACHINES

S.I.T.C. (R3)	Commodity Code No	Trade description
		Typewriters (other than typewriters incorporating a calculating device); word-processing machines
751.13		Automatic typewriters; word-processing machines
	*846911 00 0	Word-processing machines
	*846912 00 0	Automatic typewriters
751.15	*846920 00 0	Other electric typewriters
751.18	*846930 00 0	Non-electric typewriters
		Calculating machines; accounting machines, postage-franking machines, ticket-issuing machines and similar machines, incorporating a calculating device; cash registers
751.21		Electronic calculators capable of operation without an external source of electric power and pocket-size data recording, reproducing and displaying machines with calculating functions:
	*847010 10 0	Electronic calculators capable of operating without an external source of power
	*847010 90 0	Pocket-size data recording, reproducing and displaying machines with calculating functions
751.22		Other calculating machines
		Other electronic calculating machines
	847021 00 0	Incorporating a printing device
	847029 00 0	Other
	847030 00 0	Other calculating machines
751.23	847040 00 0	Accounting machines (including bookkeeping machines)
751.24	847050 00 0	Cash registers
751.28	847090 00 0	Postage-franking, ticket-issuing and similar machines, incorporating a calculating device
		Photocopying apparatus incorporating an optical system or of the contact type and thermo-copying apparatus
751.31	900911 00 0	Electrostatic photocopying apparatus operating by reproducing the original image directly onto the copy (direct process)
751.32	900912 00 0	Electrostatic photocopying apparatus operating by reproducing the original image via an intermediate onto the copy (indirect process)

S.I.T.C. (R3)	Commodity Code No	Trade description
751.33	900921 00 0	Non-electrostatic photocopying apparatus incorporating an optical system
751.34		Non-electrostatic photocopying apparatus of the contact type
	900922 10 0	Blueprinters and diazo-copiers
	900922 90 0	Other
751.35	900930 00 0	Thermo-copying apparatus
		Other office machines (e.g., hectograph or stencil duplicating machines, addressing machines, automatic banknote dispensers, coin-sorting machines, coin-counting or wrapping machines, pencil-sharpening machines, perforating or stapling machines)
751.91	847210 00 0	Duplicating machines
751.92	847220 00 0	Addressing machines and address plate embossing machines
751.93	847230 00 0	Machines for sorting or folding mail or for inserting mail in envelopes or bands, machines for opening, closing or sealing mail and machines for affixing or cancelling postage stamps
751.99		Office machines, n.e.s.
	847290 10 0	Coin-sorting, coin-counting or coin-wrapping machines
	847290 90 0	Other

AUTOMATIC DATA PROCESSING MACHINES AND UNITS THEREOF; MAGNETIC OR OPTICAL READERS, MACHINES FOR TRANSCRIBING DATA ONTO DATA MEDIA IN CODED FORM AND MACHINES FOR PROCESSING SUCH DATA, N.E.S.

S.I.T.C. (R3)	Commodity Code No	Trade description
752.10		Analogue or hybrid (analogue-digital) data processing machines
	847110 10 0	For use in civil aircraft
	847110 90 0	Other
752.20		Digital automatic data processing machines containing in the same housing at least a central processing unit and an input and output unit
	*847130 00 0	Portable digital automatic data processing machines, weighing not more than 10 kg, consisting of at least a central processing unit, a keyboard and a display.
		Other digital automatic data processing machines:
	*847141 10 0	For use in civil aircraft
	*847141 90 0	Other
752.30		Digital processing units, whether or not presented with the rest of a system which may contain in the same housing one or two of the following types of unit: storage units, input units, output units
		Presented in the form of systems other than those of 752.2:
	*847149 10 0	For use in civil aircraft
	*847149 90 0	Other
		Other
	*847150 10 0	For use in civil aircraft
	*847150 90 0	Other
752.60		Input or output units, whether or not presented with the rest of a system and whether or not containing storage units in the same housing
	*847160 10 0	For use in civil aircraft
		Other
	*847160 40 0	Printers
	*847160 50 0	Keyboards
	*847160 90 0	Other
752.70		Storage units, whether or not presented with the rest of a system
	*847170 10 0	For use in civil aircraft
		Other
	*847170 40 0	Central storage units
		Other
		Disc storage units
	*847170 51 0	Optical, including magneto-optical
		Other
	*847170 53 0	Hard disk drives
	*847170 59 0	Other
	*847170 60 0	Magnetic tape storage units
	*847170 90 0	Other
752.90		Data processing equipment, n.e.s.
		Other units of automatic data-processing machines
	*847180 10 0	Peripheral units
	*847180 90 0	Other
	*847190 00 0	Other

S.I.T.C. (R3)	Commodity Code No	Trade description
		PARTS AND ACCESSORIES (OTHER THAN COVERS, CARRYING CASES AND THE LIKE) SUITABLE FOR USE SOLELY OR PRINCIPALLY WITH MACHINES FALLING WITHIN GROUPS 751 AND 752
759.10		**Parts and accessories of the photocopying and thermo-copying apparatus of heading 751.3**
	900990 10 0	Of electrostatic photocopying apparatus or other photocopying apparatus incorporating an optical system
	900990 90 0	Other
		Parts and accessories (other than covers, carrying cases and the like) suitable for use solely or principally with machines of sub-groups 751.1, 751.2, 751.9 and group 752
759.91		**....of the machines of sub-group 751.1**
	847310 10 0	Electronic assemblies
	847310 90 0	Other
759.93		**....of the machines of sub-group 751.9**
		Of sub-groups 751.91, 751.92, 751.99
	*847340 10 0	Electronic assemblies
	*847340 90 0	Other
		Other
	*847350 10 0	Electronic assemblies:
	*847350 90 0	Other
759.95		**....of the electronic calculating machines of sub-group 751.2**
		Of the electronic calculating machines of headings 751.21,22
	847321 10 0	Electronic assemblies
	847321 90 0	Other
		Other:
	847329 10 0	Electronic assemblies
	847329 90 0	Other
759.97		**....of the machines of group 752**
	847330 10 0	Electronic assemblies
	847330 90 0	Other

DIVISION 76

TELECOMMUNICATIONS AND SOUND RECORDING AND REPRODUCING APPARATUS AND EQUIPMENT

TELEVISION RECEIVERS (INCLUDING VIDEO MONITORS AND VIDEO PROJECTORS), WHETHER OR NOT INCORPORATING RADIO-BROADCAST RECEIVERS OR SOUND OR VIDEO RECORDING OR REPRODUCING APPARATUS

S.I.T.C. (R3)	Commodity Code No	Trade description
761.10		**Television receivers, colour (including video monitors and video projectors), whether or not incorporating radio-broadcast receivers or sound or video recording or reproducing apparatus**
		Television projection equipment
	*852812 14 0	With scanning parameters not exceeding 625 lines
		With scanning parameters exceeding 625 lines
	*852812 16 0	With a vertical resolution of less than 700 lines
	*852812 18 0	With a vertical resolution of 700 lines or more
		Apparatus incorporating a video recorder or reproducer
	*852812 22 0	With a screen width/height ratio less than 1.5
	*852812 28 0	Other
		Other
		With an integral tube
		With a screen width/height ratio less than 1.5, with a diagonal measurement of the screen
	*852812 52 0	Not exceeding 42 cm
	*852812 54 0	Exceeding 42 cm but not exceeding 52 cm
	*852812 56 0	Exceeding 52 cm but not exceeding 72 cm
	*852812 58 0	Exceeding 72 cm
		Other
		With scanning parameters not exceeding 625 lines, with a diagonal measurement of the screen
	*852812 62 0	Not exceeding 75 cm
	*852812 66 0	Exceeding 75 cm
		With scanning parameters exceeding 625 lines
	*852812 72 0	With a vertical resolution of less than 700 lines
	*852812 76 0	With a vertical resolution of 700 lines or more
		Other
		With screen
	*852812 81 0	With a screen width/height ratio less than 1.5
	*852812 89 0	Other
		Without screen
	*852812 91 0	Video tuners
	*852812 98 0	Other

S.I.T.C. (R3)	Commodity Code No	Trade description

cont
761.10

    Video monitors
        With cathode-ray tube

*852821 14 0   With a screen width/height ratio less than 1.5
           Other
*852821 16 0   With scanning parameters not exceeding 625 lines
*852821 18 0   With scanning parameters exceeding 625 lines
*852821 90 0   Other
*852830 10 0   Colour video projectors

761.20

    Television receivers, black and white or other monochrome (including video monitors and video projectors), whether or not incorporating radio-broadcast receivers or sound or video recording or reproducing apparatus
        Reception apparatus for television, whether or not incorporating radio-broadcast receivers or sound or video recording or reproducing apparatus:
*852813 00 0   Black and white or other monochrome
        Video monitors
*852822 00 0   Black and white or other monochrome
        Video projectors
*852830 90 0   Black and white or other monochrome

RADIO-BROADCAST RECEIVERS, WHETHER OR NOT INCORPORATING SOUND RECORDING OR REPRODUCING APPARATUS OR A CLOCK

Radio-broadcast receivers not capable of operating without an external source of power, of a kind used in motor vehicles (including apparatus capable of receiving also radiotelephony or radiotelegraphy)

762.11

    ....combined with sound recording or reproducing
        Capable of receiving and decoding digital Radio Data System signals
*852721 20 0   With laser reading system
        Other
*852721 52 0   Of the cassette-type with an analogue and digital reading system
*852721 59 0   Other
        Other
*852721 70 0   With laser reading system
        Other
*852721 92 0   Of the cassette-type with an analogue and digital reading system
*852721 98 0   Other

762.12   852729 00 0   ....not combined with sound recording or reproducing apparatus

Radio-broadcast receivers capable of operating without an external source of power (including apparatus capable of receiving also radiotelephony or radiotelegraphy)

762.21

    ....combined with sound recording or reproducing
        Pocket-size radio cassette-players:
*852712 10 0   With an analogue and digital reading system
*852712 90 0   Other
        Other apparatus combined with sound recording or reproducing apparatus:
*852713 10 0   With laser reading system
        Other
*852713 91 0   Of the cassette-type with an analogue and digital reading system
*852713 99 0   Other

762.22   852719 00 0   ....not combined with sound recording or reproducing apparatus

Other radio-broadcast receivers (including apparatus capable of receiving also radiotelephony or radiotelegraphy)

762.81

    ....combined with sound recording or reproducing apparatus
852731 10 0   With in the same housing one or more loudspeakers
        Other
852731 11 0   Of the cassette-type with an analogue and digital reading system
852731 19 0   Other
852731 91 0   With laser optical reading system
        Other
852731 93 0   Of the cassette-type with an analogue and digital reading system
852731 98 0   Other

762.82

    ....not combined with sound recording or reproducing apparatus
        Not combined with sound recording or reproducing apparatus but combined with a clock
852732 10 0   Alarm clock radios
852732 90 0   Other

S.I.T.C. (R3)	Commodity Code No	Trade description
762.89		....not combined with sound recording or reproducing apparatus
	852739 10 0	Within the same housing one or more loudspeakers
		Other
	852739 91 0	Without built-in amplifier
	852739 99 0	With built-in amplifier

SOUND RECORDERS OR REPRODUCERS; TELEVISION IMAGE AND SOUND RECORDERS OR REPRODUCERS; PREPARED UNRECORDED MEDIA

Turntables (record-decks) and record-players, not incorporating a sound recording device

S.I.T.C. (R3)	Commodity Code No	Trade description
763.31	851910 00 0	**Record-players, coin- or disc-operated**
763.33		Other record players
	851921 00 0	Without loudspeaker
	851929 00 0	Other
763.35		Turntables (record-decks)
	851931 00 0	With automatic record changing mechanism
	851939 00 0	Other

Sound recording and other sound reproducing apparatus; video recording or reproducing apparatus, whether or not incorporating a video tuner

S.I.T.C. (R3)	Commodity Code No	Trade description
763.81		Video recording or reproducing apparatus, whether or not incorporating a video tuner
		Magnetic tape-type
	852110 10 0	For use in civil aircraft
		Other
	*852110 30 0	Of a width not exceeding 1.3 cm and allowing recording or reproduction at a tape speed not exceeding 50 mm per second
	852110 80 0	Other
	852190 00 0	Other
	*852540 99 0	Other video camera recorders
763.82	851940 00 0	**Transcribing machines**
763.83		Other sound reproducing apparatus
	*851992 00 0	Pocket-size cassette types
		Of a kind used in motor vehicles
	*851993 31 0	With an analogue and digital reading system
	*851993 39 0	Other
		Other
	*851993 81 0	With an analogue and digital reading system
	*851993 89 0	Other
		Other
		With laser reading system
	*851999 12 0	Of a type used in motor vehicles, of a type using discs of a diameter not exceeding 6.5 cm
	*851999 18 0	Other
	851999 90 0	Other
763.84		Sound recording apparatus, whether or not incorporating a sound reproducing device
	852010 00 0	Dictating machines not capable of operating without an external source of power
	852020 00 0	Telephone answering machines
		Other magnetic tape recorders incorporating sound reproducing apparatus
		Cassette-type
		With built-in amplifier and one or more built-in loudspeakers
	*852032 11 0	Capable of operating without an external source of power
	*852032 19 0	Other
	*852032 30 0	Pocket-size recorders
	*852032 50 0	Other
		Other
	*852032 91 0	Using magnetic tapes on reels, allowing sound recording or reproduction either at a single speed of 19 cm per second or at several speeds if those comprise only 19 cm per second and lower speeds
	*852032 99 0	Other
		Other, cassette type
		With built-in amplifier and one or more built-in loudspeakers
	*852033 11 0	Capable of operating without an external source of power
	*852033 19 0	Other
	*852033 30 0	Pocket-size recorders
	*852033 90 0	Other
		Other
	852039 10 0	Using magnetic tapes on reels, allowing sound recording or reproduction either at a single speed of 19 cm per second or at several speeds if those comprise only 19 cm per second and lower speeds
	852039 90 0	Other
		Other
	852090 10 0	For use in civil aircraft
	852090 90 0	Other

S.I.T.C. (R3)	Commodity Code No	Trade description
		TELECOMMUNICATIONS EQUIPMENT, N.E.S.; AND PARTS, N.E.S., AND ACCESSORIES of APPARATUS FALLING WITHIN DIVISION 76
		Electrical apparatus for line telephony or line telegraphy (including such apparatus for carrier-current line systems)
764.11		**Telephone sets**
	*851711 00 0	Line telephone sets with cordless handsets
		Other
	*851719 90 0	Videophones
764.13	*851722 00 0	**Teleprinters**
764.15	851730 00 0	**Telephonic or telegraphic switching apparatus**
764.17		**Other apparatus for carrier-current line systems**
	*851750 10 0	For carrier-current line systems
764.19		**Other telephonic or telegraphic apparatus**
	*851721 00 0	Facsimile machines
	*851750 90 0	Other apparatus for digital line systems
		Other apparatus
	*851780 10 0	Entry-phone systems
	*851780 90 0	Other
		Microphones and stands therefor; loudspeakers, whether or not mounted in their enclosures; headphones, earphones and combined microphone/ speaker sets; audio-frequency electric amplifiers; electric sound amplifier sets
764.21		**Microphones and stands therefor**
	851810 10 0	For use in civil aircraft
	851810 90 0	Other
764.22		**Loudspeakers, mounted in their enclosures**
		Single loudspeakers, mounted in their enclosures
	851821 10 0	For use in civil aircraft
	*851821 90 0	Other
		Multiple loudspeakers, mounted in the same enclosure
	851822 10 0	For use in civil aircraft
	*851822 90 0	Other
764.23		**Loudspeakers, not mounted in their enclosures**
	851829 10 0	For use in civil aircraft
	851829 90 0	Other
764.24		**Headphones, earphones and combined microphone/speaker sets**
	851830 10 0	For use in civil aircraft
	851830 90 0	Other
764.25		**Audio-frequency electric amplifiers**
	851840 10 0	For use in civil aircraft
		Other
	851840 30 0	Telephonic and measurement amplifiers
		Other
	851840 91 0	With only one channel
	*851840 99 0	Other
764.26		**Electric sound amplifier sets**
	851850 10 0	For use in civil aircraft
	851850 90 0	Other
		Transmission apparatus for radio-telephony, radio-telegraphy, radio- broadcasting or television, whether or not incorporating reception apparatus or sound recording or reproducing apparatus
764.31		**Transmission apparatus**
	852510 10 0	Radio-telegraphic or radio-telephonic apparatus, for use in civil aircraft
	*852510 90 0	Other
764.32		**Transmission apparatus incorporating reception apparatus**
	*851719 10 0	Videophones
	*851719 90 0	Telephone sets not elsewhere specified
	852520 10 0	Radio-telegraphic or radio-telephonic apparatus, for use in civil aircraft
		Other
	*852520 91 0	For cellular networks (mobile telephones)
	*852520 99 0	Other
		Telecommunications equipment, n.e.s.

S.I.T.C. (R3)	Commodity Code No	Trade description
764.81		**Reception apparatus for radiotelephony or radiotelegraphy, n.e.s.**
	852790 10 0	For radiotelephony or radiotelegraphy, for use in civil aircraft
		Other
	852790 91 0	Portable receivers for calling or paging
	*852790 99 0	Other
764.82		**Television cameras**
	852530 10 0	With 3 or more camera tubes
	*852530 90 0	Other
		Still image video cameras and other video camera recorders:
	*852540 10 0	Still image video cameras
		Other video cameras
	*852540 91 0	Only able to record sound and images taken by the television camera
764.83		**Radar apparatus, radio navigational aid apparatus and radio remote control apparatus**
		Radar apparatus
	852610 10 0	For use in civil aircraft
	*852610 90 0	Other
		Other
		Radio navigational aid apparatus
		For use in civil aircraft
	852691 11 0	Radio navigational receivers
	852691 19 0	Other
	852691 90 0	Other
		Radio remote control apparatus
	852692 10 0	For use in civil aircraft
	852692 90 0	Other
		Parts and accessories suitable for use solely or principally with the apparatus of division 76
764.91		**....of the apparatus of heading 764.1**
		Of apparatus of heading 764.17
	851790 11 0	Electronic assemblies
	851790 19 0	Other
		Other:
		Of telephonic apparatus:
	*851790 82 0	Electronic assemblies
	*851790 88 0	Other
764.92	851890 00 0	**....of the apparatus and equipment of heading 764.2**
764.93		**....of the apparatus and equipment of headings 761, 762, 764.3**
		Aerials and aerial reflectors of all kinds; parts suitable for use therewith
	852910 10 0	For use in civil aircraft
		Other
		Aerials
	852910 20 0	Telescopic and whip-type aerials for portable apparatus or for apparatus for fitting in motor vehicles
		Outside aerials for radio or television broadcast receivers
	852910 31 0	For reception via satellite
	852910 39 0	Other
	852910 40 0	Inside aerials for radio or television broadcast receivers, including built-in types
	852910 50 0	Other
	852910 70 0	Aerial filters and separators
	852910 90 0	Other
		Other
	852990 10 0	Assemblies and sub-assemblies consisting of two or more parts or pieces fastened or joined together, for apparatus falling within heading 764.83, for use in civil aircraft
		Other
		Cabinets and cases
	852990 51 0	Of wood
	852990 59 0	Of other materials
	852990 70 0	Electronic assemblies
		Other
	852990 81 0	For television cameras of heading 764.82 and apparatus of headings 761, 762, and 764.81
	852990 89 0	Other
764.99		**....of the apparatus falling within group 763**
	852210 00 0	Pick-up cartridges
		Other
	852290 10 0	Assemblies and sub-assemblies consisting of two or more parts or pieces fastened or joined together, for apparatus falling within heading 763.83, for use in civil aircraft
		Other
	852290 30 0	Styli; diamonds, sapphires and other precious or semi-precious stones (natural, synthetic or reconstructed) for styli, whether or not mounted
		Other
	852290 91 0	Electronic assemblies

S.I.T.C. (R3)	Commodity Code No	Trade description
cont 764.99	852290 93 0	Single cassette-deck assemblies with a total thickness not exceeding 53 mm, of a kind used in the manufacture of sound recording and reproducing apparatus
	852290 98 0	Other

DIVISION 77

ELECTRICAL MACHINERY, APPARATUS AND APPLIANCES, N.E.S., AND ELECTRICAL PARTS THEREOF (INCLUDING NON-ELECTRICAL COUNTERPARTS, N.E.S., OF ELECTRICAL HOUSEHOLD TYPE EQUIPMENT)

ELECTRIC POWER MACHINERY (OTHER THAN ROTATING ELECTRIC PLANT OF HEADING 716), AND PARTS THEREOF

Transformers, electrical

S.I.T.C. (R3)	Commodity Code No	Trade description
771.11		**Liquid dielectric transformers**
	850421 00 0	Having a power handling capacity not exceeding 650 kVA
		Having a power handling capacity exceeding 650 kVA but not exceeding 10,000 kVA
	850422 10 0	Exceeding 650 kVA but not exceeding 1,600 kVA
	850422 90 0	Exceeding 1,600 kVA but not exceeding 10,000 kVA
	850423 00 0	Having a power handling capacity exceeding 10,000 kVA
771.19		**Other electric transformers**
		Having a power handling capacity not exceeding 1 kVA
	850431 10 0	For use in civil aircraft
		Other
		Measuring transformers
	850431 31 0	For voltage measurement
	850431 39 0	Other
	850431 90 0	Other
		Having a power handling capacity exceeding 1 kVA but not exceeding 16 kVA
	850432 10 0	For use in civil aircraft
		Other
	850432 30 0	Measuring transformers
	850432 90 0	Other
		Having a power handling capacity exceeding 16 kVA but not exceeding 500 kVA
	850433 10 0	For use in civil aircraft
	850433 90 0	Other
	850434 00 0	Having a power handling capacity exceeding 500 kVA

Other electric power machinery; parts of the electric power machinery of group 771

S.I.T.C. (R3)	Commodity Code No	Trade description
771.21		**Static converters (e.g., rectifiers)**
	850440 10 0	For use in civil aircraft
		Other
	*850440 30 0	Power supply units of a kind used with automatic data-processing machines
	850440 50 0	Polycrystalline semiconductors
		Other
	850440 93 0	Accumulator chargers
		Other
	850440 94 0	Rectifiers
		Inverters
	850440 96 0	Having a power handling capacity not exceeding 7.5 kVA
	850440 97 0	Having a power handling capacity exceeding 7.5 kVA
	*850440 99 0	Other
771.23		**Ballasts for discharge lamps or tubes**
	850410 10 0	For use in civil aircraft
		Other
	850410 91 0	Inductors, whether or not connected with a capacitor
	850410 99 0	Other
771.25		**Other inductors**
	850450 10 0	For use in civil aircraft
	850450 90 0	Other
771.29		**Parts of the electric power machinery of group 771**
		Of transformers and inductors
	850490 11 0	Ferrite cores
	850490 19 0	Other
	850490 90 0	Of static converters

S.I.T.C. (R3)	Commodity Code No	Trade description

ELECTRICAL APPARATUS FOR SWITCHING OR PROTECTING ELECTRICAL CIRCUITS OR FOR MAKING CONNECTIONS TO OR IN ELECTRICAL CIRCUITS (E.G., SWITCHES, RELAYS, FUSES, LIGHTNING ARRESTERS, VOLTAGE LIMITERS, SURGE SUPPRESSORS, PLUGS AND SOCKETS, LAMPHOLDERS AND JUNCTION BOXES); ELECTRICAL RESISTORS (INCLUDING RHEOSTATS AND POTENTIOMETERS), OTHER THAN HEATING RESISTORS; PRINTED CIRCUITS; BOARDS, PANELS (INCLUDING NUMERICAL CONTROL PANELS), CONSOLES, DESKS, CABINETS AND OTHER BASES, EQUIPPED WITH TWO OR MORE APPARATUS FOR SWITCHING, PROTECTING OR FOR MAKING CONNECTIONS TO OR IN ELECTRICAL CIRCUITS, FOR ELECTRIC CONTROL OR THE DISTRIBUTION OF ELECTRICITY (EXCLUDING SWITCHING APPARATUS OF HEADING 764.1)

772.20   Printed circuits
                                   Consisting only of conductor elements and contacts
           853400 11 0   Multiple circuits
           853400 19 0   Other
           853400 90 0   With other passive elements

Electrical resistors (including rheostats and potentiometers), other than heating resistors; and parts thereof

772.31   853310 00 0   Fixed carbon resistors, composition or film types

772.32   Other fixed resistors
           853321 00 0   For a power handling capacity not exceeding 20 W
           853329 00 0   Other

772.33   Wirewound variable resistors (including rheostats and potentiometers)
           853331 00 0   For a power handling capacity not exceeding 20 W
           853339 00 0   Other

772.35   Other variable resistors (including rheostats and potentiometers)
           853340 10 0   For a power handling capacity not exceeding 20 W
           853340 90 0   Other

772.38   853390 00 0   Parts for the electrical resistors of heading 772.3

Electrical apparatus for switching or protecting electrical circuits, or for making connections to or in electrical circuits, for a voltage exceeding 1000 volts

772.41   853510 00 0   Fuses

772.42   853521 00 0   Automatic circuit breakers for a voltage of less than 72.5 KV

772.43   853529 00 0   Other automatic circuit breakers

772.44   Isolating switches and make-and-break switches
           853530 10 0   For a voltage of less than 72.5 kV
           853530 90 0   Other

772.45   853540 00 0   Lightning arresters, voltage limiters and surge suppressors

772.49   *853590 00 0   Other electrical apparatus for switching or protecting electrical circuits, or for making connections to or in electrical circuits, for a voltage exceeding 1000 volts

772.51   Fuses
           853610 10 0   For a current not exceeding 10 A
           853610 50 0   For a current exceeding 10 A but not exceeding 63 A
           853610 90 0   For a current exceeding 63 A

772.52   Automatic circuit breakers
           853620 10 0   For a current not exceeding 63 A
           853620 90 0   For a current exceeding 63 A

772.53   Other apparatus for protecting electrical circuits
           853630 10 0   For a current not exceeding 16 A
           853630 30 0   For a current exceeding 16 A but not exceeding 125 A
           853630 90 0   For a current exceeding 125 A

772.54   Relays
                                     For a voltage not exceeding 60 volts
           853641 10 0   For a current not exceeding 2 A
           853641 90 0   For a current exceeding 2 A
           853649 00 0   Other

772.55   Other switches
                                     For a voltage not exceeding 60 V
           853650 11 0   Push-button switches
           853650 15 0   Rotary switches

S.I.T.C. (R3)	Commodity Code No	Trade description
cont 772.55	853650 19 0 853650 90 0	Other Other
772.57		Lamp-holders
	853661 10 0 853661 90 0	Edison lamp-holders Other
772.58		Plugs and sockets
	853669 10 0 853669 30 0 853669 90 0	For co-axial cables For printed circuits Other
772.59		Other electrical apparatus for switching or protecting electrical circuits, or for making connections to or in for a voltage not exceeding 1000 volts
	853690 01 0 853690 10 0 853690 20 0 *853690 85 0	Prefabricated elements for electrical circuits Connections and contact elements for wire and cables Wafer probers Other

Boards, panels (including numerical control panels) consoles, desks, cabinets and other bases, equipped with two or more apparatus of heading 772.4 or 772.5, for electric control or the distribution of electricity (including those incorporating instruments or apparatus of groups 774, 881, 884 or of division 87, but excluding the switching apparatus of sub-group 764.1)

S.I.T.C. (R3)	Commodity Code No	Trade description
772.61	853710 10 0	....for a voltage not exceeding 1000 V Numerical control panels with built-in automatic data processing machine Other
	853710 91 0 853710 99 0	Programmable memory controllers Other
772.62	853720 91 0 853720 99 0	....for a voltage exceeding 1000 V For a voltage exceeding 1 000 volts but not exceeding 72.5 kV For a voltage exceeding 72.5 kV

Parts suitable for use solely or principally with the apparatus falling within headings 772.4, 772.5 and 772.6

S.I.T.C. (R3)	Commodity Code No	Trade description
772.81	853810 00 0	Boards, panels, consoles, desks, cabinets and other bases for the goods of heading 772.6, not equipped with their apparatus
772.82	853890 10 0 853890 90 0	Other parts Electronic assemblies Other

EQUIPMENT FOR DISTRIBUTING ELECTRICITY, N.E.S.

Insulated (including enamelled or anodized) wire, cable (including co-axial cable) and other insulated electric conductors, whether or not fitted with connectors; optical fibre cables made up of individually sheathed fibres, whether or not assembled with electric conductors or fitted with connectors

S.I.T.C. (R3)	Commodity Code No	Trade description
773.11		Winding wire Of copper
	854411 10 0 854411 90 0	Lacquered or enamelled Other Other
	854419 10 0 854419 90 0	Lacquered or enamelled Other
773.12	854420 00 0	Co-axial cable and other co-axial conductors
773.13		Ignition wiring sets and other wiring sets of a kind used in vehicles, aircraft or ships
	854430 10 0 854430 90 0	For use in civil aircraft Other
773.14		Other electric conductors, for a voltage not exceeding 80 volts Fitted with connectors
	854441 10 0 854441 90 0	Of a kind used for telecommunications Other Other
	854449 20 0 854449 80 0	Of a kind used for telecommunications Other
773.15		Other electric conductors, for a voltage exceeding 80 V but not exceeding 1000 V Fitted with connectors
	854451 00 0	Other
	854459 20 0 854459 80 0	For a voltage of 1,000 V For a voltage exceeding 80 V but less than 1,000 V

S.I.T.C. (R3)	Commodity Code No	Trade description
773.17		Other electric conductors, for a voltage exceeding 1000 V
	854460 10 0	With copper conductors
	854460 90 0	With other conductors
773.18	854470 00 0	Optical fibre cables
		Electrical insulating equipment
773.22	854610 00 0	Electrical insulators of glass
773.23		Electrical insulators of ceramics
	854620 10 0	With no metal parts
		With metal parts
	854620 91 0	For overhead power transmission or traction lines
	854620 99 0	Other
773.24		Electrical insulators of materials other than glass or ceramics
	854690 10 0	Of plastics
	854690 90 0	Other
773.26		Insulating fittings for electrical machines, appliances or equipment, being fittings wholly of ceramic materials apart from any minor components of metal (e.g., threaded sockets) incorporated during moulding solely for purposes of assembly (but not including insulators of heading 773.23)
	854710 10 0	Containing 80 % or more by weight of metallic oxides
	854710 90 0	Other
773.28	854720 00 0	Insulating fittings for electrical machines, appliances or equipment, being fittings wholly of plastic materials apart from any minor components of metal incorporated during moulding solely for purposes of assembly (but not including insulators of heading 773.24)
773.29	854790 00 0	Insulating fittings for electrical machines, appliances or equipment, being fittings wholly of materials other than ceramics or plastics apart from any minor components of metal incorporated during moulding solely for purposes of assembly (but not including insulators of heading 773.22 , or 773.24); electrical conduit tubing and joints therefor, of base metal lined with insulating material

ELECTRO-DIAGNOSTIC APPARATUS FOR MEDICAL, SURGICAL, DENTAL OR VETERINARY SCIENCES AND RADIOLOGICAL APPARATUS

S.I.T.C. (R3)	Commodity Code No	Trade description
		Electro-diagnostic apparatus (other than radiological apparatus)
774.11	901811 00 0	Electro-cardiographs
774.12		Other electro-diagnostic apparatus (including apparatus for functional exploratory examination or for checking physiological parameters)
	*901812 00 0	Electro-cardiographs
	*901813 00 0	Ultrasonic scanning apparatus
	*901814 00 0	Scintigraphic apparatus
	*901819 00 0	Other
774.13	901820 00 0	Ultra-violet or infra-red ray apparatus
		Apparatus based on the use of x-rays or of alpha, beta or gamma radiations, whether or not for medical, surgical, dental or veterinary uses (including radiography or radiotherapy apparatus), x-ray tubes and other x-ray generators; high tension generators, control panels and desks; screens, examination or treatment tables, chairs and the like; parts, n.e.s., and accessories for the foregoing apparatus and equipment
774.21		Apparatus based on the use of x-rays, whether or not for medical, surgical, dental or veterinary uses (including radiography or radiotherapy apparatus)
	*902212 00 0	Computed tomography apparatus
	*902213 00 0	Other, for dental uses
	*902214 00 0	Other, for medical, surgical or veterinary uses
774.22		Apparatus based on the use of alpha, beta or gamma radiations, whether or not for medical, surgical, dentalor veterinary uses (including radiography or radiotherapy apparatus)
	902221 00 0	For medical, surgical, dental or veterinary uses
	902229 00 0	For other uses
774.23	902230 00 0	X-ray tubes
774.29		Other (including parts and accessories)
	902290 10 0	X-ray fluorescent screens and X-ray intensifying screens; anti-scatter shields and grids
	902290 90 0	Other

S.I.T.C. (R3)	Commodity Code No	Trade description
		HOUSEHOLD TYPE, ELECTRICAL AND NON-ELECTRICAL EQUIPMENT, N.E.S.
		Household type laundry equipment, n.e.s., whether or not electrical
775.11		Household or laundry-type washing machines (including machines which both wash and dry), each of a dry linen capacity not exceeding 10 kg
		Fully-automatic machines
		Each of a dry linen capacity not exceeding 6 kg
	845011 11 0	Front-loading machines
	845011 19 0	Top-loading machines
	845011 90 0	Each of a dry linen capacity exceeding 6 kg but not exceeding 10 kg
	845012 00 0	Other machines, with built-in centrifugal drier
	845019 00 0	Other
775.12		Clothes drying machines, each of a dry linen capacity not exceeding 10 kg (excluding those of heading 743.55)
	845121 10 0	Each of a dry linen capacity not exceeding 6 kg
	845121 90 0	Each of a dry linen capacity exceeding 6 kg but not exceeding 10 kg
		Household type refrigerators and food freezers (electrical and other)
775.21		Refrigerators, household type (electric or other), whether or not containing a deep-freezer compartment
		Combined refrigerator-freezers, fitted with separate external doors
	841810 10 0	For use in civil aircraft
		Other
	841810 91 0	Of a capacity exceeding 340 litres
	841810 99 0	Other
		Compression-type
	841821 10 0	Of a capacity exceeding 340 litres
		Other
	841821 51 0	Table model
	841821 59 0	Building-in type
		Other, of a capacity
	841821 91 0	Not exceeding 250 litres
	841821 99 0	Exceeding 250 litres but not exceeding 340 litres
	841822 00 0	Absorption-type, electrical
	841829 00 0	Other
775.22		Deep-freezers, household type (electric or other)
		Freezers of the chest type, not exceeding 800 litres capacity
	841830 10 0	For use in civil aircraft
		Other
	841830 91 0	Of a capacity not exceeding 400 litres
	841830 99 0	Of a capacity exceeding 400 litres but not exceeding 800 litres
		Freezers of the upright type, not exceeding 900 litres capacity
	841840 10 0	For use in civil aircraft
		Other
	841840 91 0	Of a capacity not exceeding 250 litres
	841840 99 0	Of a capacity exceeding 250 litres but not exceeding 900 litres
775.30	842211 00 0	Dish washing machines of the household type
		Shavers and hair clippers, with self-contained electric motor, and parts thereof (excluding blades and cutting heads)
775.41	851010 00 0	Shavers
775.42	851020 00 0	Hair clippers
775.49	851090 00 0	Parts
		Electro-mechanical, domestic appliances with self-contained electric motor; parts thereof
775.71		Vacuum cleaners and floor polishers, electro-mechanical, domestic, with self-contained electric motor
		Vacuum cleaners
	*850910 10 0	For a voltage of 110 volts or more
	850910 90 0	For a voltage of less than 110 volts
	850920 00 0	Floor polishers
775.72	850940 00 0	Food grinders and mixers; fruit or vegetable juice extractors, electro-mechanical, domestic
775.73		Other electro-mechanical, domestic appliances with self-contained electric motor
	851030 00 0	Hair-removing apparatus
	850930 00 0	Kitchen waste disposers
	850980 00 0	Other appliances

S.I.T.C. (R3)	Commodity Code No	Trade description
775.79		Parts of the electro-mechanical domestic appliances falling within heading 775.7
	850990 10 0	Of vacuum cleaners or floor polishers
	850990 90 0	Other
		Electro-thermic appliances, n.e.s.
775.81		Electric instantaneous or storage water heaters and immersion heaters
		Water heaters
	851610 11 0	Instantaneous water heaters
	851610 19 0	Other
	851610 90 0	Immersion heaters
775.82		Electric space heating apparatus and electric soil heating apparatus
	851621 00 0	Storage heating radiators
		Other
	851629 10 0	Liquid filled radiators
	851629 50 0	Convection heaters
		Other
	851629 91 0	With built-in fan
	851629 99 0	Other
775.83		Electro-thermic hair-dressing or hand-drying apparatus
		Hair dryers
	851631 10 0	Drying hoods
	851631 90 0	Other
	851632 00 0	Other hair-dressing apparatus
	851633 00 0	Hand-drying apparatus
775.84		Electric smoothing irons
	851640 10 0	Steam smoothing irons
	851640 90 0	Other
775.85	630110 00 0	Electric blankets
775.86		Microwave ovens; other ovens; cookers, cooking plates, boiling rings, grillers and roasters
	851650 00 0	Microwave ovens
		Other ovens; cookers, cooking plates, boiling rings; grillers and roasters
	851660 10 0	Cookers (incorporating at least an oven and a hob)
		Cooking plates, boiling rings and hobs
	851660 51 0	Hobs for building-in
	851660 59 0	Other
	851660 70 0	Grillers and roasters
	851660 80 0	Ovens for building-in
	851660 90 0	Other
775.87		Electro-thermic domestic appliances, n.e.s.
	851671 00 0	Coffee or tea makers
	851672 00 0	Toasters
		Other
	851679 10 0	Plate warmers
	851679 20 0	Deep fat fryers
	851679 80 0	Other
775.88		Electric heating resistors (other than of carbon)
	851680 10 0	Assembled only with a simple insulated former and electrical connections, used for anti- icing or de-icing, for use in civil aircraft
		Other
	851680 91 0	Assembled with an insulated former
	851680 99 0	Other
775.89	851690 00 0	Parts of the electro-thermic appliances of sub-group 775.8

THERMIONIC, COLD CATHODE OR PHOTO-CATHODE VALVES AND TUBES(E.G., VACUUM OR VAPOUR OR GAS-FILLED VALVES AND TUBES, MERCURY ARC RECTIFYING VALVES AND TUBES, CATHODE-RAY TUBES, TELEVISION CAMERA TUBES); DIODES, TRANSISTORS AND SIMILAR SEMI-CONDUCTOR DEVICES; PHOTOSENSITIVE SEMI-CONDUCTOR DEVICES; LIGHT EMITTING DIODES; MOUNTED PIEZO-ELECTRIC CRYSTALS; ELECTRONIC INTEGRATED CIRCUITS AND MICROASSEMBLIES; AND PARTS THEREOF

Television picture tubes, cathode ray (including video monitor cathode-ray tubes)

S.I.T.C. (R3)	Commodity Code No	Trade description
776.11		....colour
		With a screen width/height ratio less than 1.5, with a diagonal measurement of the screen
	854011 11 0	Not exceeding 42 cm
	854011 13 0	Exceeding 42 cm but not exceeding 52 cm
	854011 15 0	Exceeding 52 cm but not exceeding 72 cm
	854011 19 0	Exceeding 72 cm

S.I.T.C. (R3)	Commodity Code No	Trade description
cont 776.11		Other with a diagonal measurement of the screen
	854011 91 0	Not exceeding 75 cm
	854011 99 0	Exceeding 75 cm
776.12	854012 00 0	....black and white or other monochrome

Other electronic valves and tubes (including television camera tubes)

776.21		Television camera tubes; image converters and intensifiers; other photo-cathode tubes
	854020 10 0	Television camera tubes
	854020 30 0	Image converters or intensifiers
	854020 90 0	Other photo-cathode tubes
776.23		Other cathode-ray tubes
	*854040 00 0	Data/graphic display tubes, colour , with a phosphor dot screen pitch smaller than 0.4 mm;
	*854050 00 0	Data/graphic display tubes, black and white or other monochrome
	*854060 00 0	Other cathode-ray tubes
776.25		Microwave tubes (excluding grid-controlled tubes)
	*854071 00 0	Magnetrons
	*854072 00 0	Klystrons
	*854079 00 0	Other
776.27		Other valves and tubes
	854081 00 0	Receiver or amplifier valves and tubes
		Other
		Display tubes
	854089 11 0	Vacuum fluorescent
	854089 19 0	Other
	854089 90 0	Other
776.29		Parts of the tubes and valves of sub-groups 776.1 and 776.2
	854091 00 0	Of cathode-ray tubes
	854099 00 0	Other

Diodes, transistors and similar semi-conductor devices; photosensitive semi-conductor devices; light emitting diodes

776.31		Diodes, not photosensitive nor light emitting diodes
	854110 10 0	Wafers not yet cut into chips
		Other
	854110 91 0	Power rectifier diodes
	854110 99 0	Other
776.32		Transistors (excluding photosensitive transistors) with a dissipation rate of less than 1 watt
	854121 10 0	Wafers not yet cut into chips
	854121 90 0	Other
776.33		Transistors (excluding photosensitive transistors) with a dissipation rate of 1 watt or more
	854129 10 0	Wafers not yet cut into chips
	854129 20 0	PowerMOS field effective transistors
	854129 30 0	Insulated gate bipolar transistors (IGBTs)
	854129 80 0	Other
776.35		Thyristors, diacs and triacs (excluding photosensitive devices)
	854130 10 0	Wafers not yet cut into chips
	*854130 90 0	Other
776.37		Photosensitive semi-conductor devices; light emitting diodes
		Light emitting diodes
	854140 11 0	Laser diodes
	854140 19 0	Other
		Other
	854140 91 0	Solar cells whether or not assembled in modules or made up into panels
	854140 93 0	Photodiodes, phototransistors, photothyristors or photocouples
	854140 99 0	Other
776.39		Other semi-conductor devices
	854150 10 0	Wafers not yet cut into chips
	854150 90 0	Other

Electronic integrated circuits and microassemblies

776.41		Monolithic integrated units
	854212 00 0	Cards incorporating an electronic integrated circuit ("smart" cards)
		Metal oxide semiconductors (MOS technology):
	*854213 01 0	Wafers not yet cut into chips
	*854213 05 0	Chips

S.I.T.C. (R3)	Commodity Code No	Trade description
cont 776.41		Other:
		Memories:
		Dynamic random-access memories (D-RAM's):
	*854213 11 0	With a storage capacity not exceeding 4 Mbits
	*854213 13 0	With a storage capacity exceeding 4 Mbits but not exceeding 16 Mbits
	*854213 15 0	With a storage capacity exceeding 16 Mbits but not exceeding 64 Mbits
	*854213 17 0	With a storage capacity exceeding 64 Mbits
		Static random-access memories (S-RAMs), including cache random-access memories (cache RAMs):
	*854213 22 0	With a storage capacity not exceeding 256 Kbits
	*854213 25 0	With a storage capacity exceeding 256 Kbits but not exceeding 1 Mbit
	*854213 27 0	With a storage capacity exceeding 1 Mbit
		UV erasable, programmable , read only memories (EPROMs)
	*854213 32 0	With a storage capacity not exceeding 1Mbit
	*854213 35 0	With a storage capacity exceeding 1 Mbit but not exceeding 4 Mbits
	*854213 37 0	With a storage capacity exceeding 4 Mbits
		Electrically erasable, programmable, read only memories (E^{2}PROMs), including FLASH E^{2}PROMs
		Flash E2PROMS:
	*854213 41 0	With a storage capacity not exceeding 1 Mbit
	*854213 43 0	With a storage capacity exceeding 1 Mbit but not exceeding 4 Mbits
	*854213 45 0	With a storage capacity exceeding 4 Mbits but not exceeding 16 Mbits
	*854213 47 0	With a storage capacity exceeding 16 Mbits
	*854213 49 0	Other
	*854213 51 0	Read only memories, non-programmable (ROMs); content addressable memories (CAMs); first-in/first-out read/write memories (FIFOs); last-in/first-out read/write memories (LIFOs); ferroelectric memories
	*854213 53 0	Other memories
	*854213 55 0	Microprocessors
		Microcontrollers and microcomputers
	*854213 61 0	With a processing capacity not exceeding 4 bits
	*854213 63 0	With a processing capacity exceeding 4 bits but not exceeding 8 bits
	*854213 65 0	With a processing capacity exceeding 8 bits but not exceeding 16 bits
	*854213 67 0	With a processing capacity exceeding 16 bits but not exceeding 32 bits
	*854213 69 0	With a processing capacity exceeding 32 bits
		Other
	*854213 70 0	Microperipherals
		Other
	*854213 72 0	Full custom logic circuits
	*854213 74 0	Gate arrays
	*854213 76 0	Standard cells
	*854213 82 0	Programmable logic circuits
	*854213 84 0	Standard logic circuits
		Other
	*854213 91 0	Control circuits, interface circuits; interface circuits capable of performing control functions
	*854213 99 0	Other
		Circuits obtained by bipolar technology
	*854214 01 0	Wafers not yet cut into chips
	*854214 05 0	Chips
		Other
		Memories
	*854214 10 0	Dynamic random-access memories (D-RAMs)
	*854214 15 0	Static random-access memories (S-RAMs), including cache random-access memories (cache-RAMs); read only memories, non-programmable (ROMs); content addressable memories (CAMs); first-in/first-out read/write memories (FIFOs); last-in/first-out read/write memories (LIFOs); ferroelectric memories
	*854214 20 0	Electrically erasable, programmable, read only memories (E2PROMs), including FLASH E2PROMs
	*854214 25 0	Other memories
	*854214 30 0	Microprocessors
		Microcontrollers and microcomputers
	*854214 42 0	With a processing capacity not exceeding 4 bits
	*854214 44 0	With a processing capacity exceeding 4 bits
		Other
	*854214 50 0	Microperipherals
		Other
	*854214 60 0	Full custom logic circuits
	*854214 65 0	Gate arrays
	*854214 70 0	Standard cells
	*854214 75 0	Programmable logic circuits
	*854214 80 0	Standard logic circuits
		Other
	*854214 91 0	Control circuits
	*854214 99 0	Other

S.I.T.C. (R3)	Commodity Code No	Trade description
cont 776.41		Other, including circuits obtained by a combination of bipolar and MOS technologies (BIMOS technology)
	*854219 01 0	Wafers not yet cut into chips
	*854219 05 0	Chips
		Other:
		Memories
	*854219 15 0	Dynamic random-access memories (D-RAMS)
		Static random-access memories (S-RAMs), including cache random-access memories (cache-RAMS):
	*854219 22 0	With a storage capacity not exceeding 256 Kbits
	*854219 25 0	With a storage capacity exceeding 256 Kbits but not exceeding 1 Mbit
	*854219 27 0	With a storage capacity exceeding 1 Mbit
	*854219 31 0	UV erasable, programmable, read only memories (EPROMs)
	*854219 35 0	Electrically erasable, programmable, read only memories (E2PROMs), including FLASH E2PROMs
	*854219 41 0	Read only memories, non-programmable (ROMs); content addressable memories (CAMs); first- in/first-out read/write memories (FIFOs); last-in/first-out read/write memories (LIFOs); ferroelectric memories
	*854219 49 0	Other memories
	*854219 55 0	Microprocessors
		Microcontrollers and microcomputers
	*854219 62 0	With a processing capacity not exceeding 4 bits
	*854219 68 0	With a processing capacity exceeding 4 bits
		Other
	*854219 71 0	Microperipherals
		Other
	*854219 72 0	Full custom logic circuits
	*854219 74 0	Gate arrays
	*854219 76 0	Standard cells
	*854219 82 0	Programmable logic circuits
	*854219 84 0	Standard logic circuits
		Other
	*854219 92 0	Control circuits; interface circuits; interface circuits capable of performing control functions
	*854219 98 0	Other
776.43		**Non-digital monolithic integrated units**
	*854230 10 0	Wafers not yet cut into chips
	*854230 20 0	Chips
		Other:
	*854230 30 0	Amplifiers
	*854230 50 0	Voltage and current regulators
		Control circuits
	*854230 61 0	Smartpower circuits
		Other
	*854230 65 0	Mixed analogue-digital circuits
	*854230 69 0	Other
	*854230 70 0	Interface circuits; interface circuits capable of performing control functions
		Other
	*854230 91 0	Smartpower circuits
		Other
	*854230 95 0	Mixed analogue-digital circuits
	*854230 99 0	Other
776.45		**Hybrid integrated circuits**
	*854240 10 0	Microprocessors, microcontrollers and microcomputers
	*854240 30 0	Converters
	*854240 50 0	Amplifiers
	*854240 90 0	Other
776.49	*854250 00 0	**Other electronic integrated circuits and microassemblies**
		Piezo-electric crystals, mounted, and parts, n.e.s., of the electronic components of group 776
776.81	854160 00 0	**Piezo-electric crystals, mounted**
776.88	854190 00 0	**Parts of the devices of sub-group piezo-electric crystals of item 776,81**
776.89	854290 00 0	**Parts of the articles of heading 776.4**
		ELECTRICAL MACHINERY AND APPARATUS, N.E.S.
		Batteries and electric accumulators, and parts thereof
778.11		**Primary cells and primary batteries**
		Of an external volume not exceeding 300 cm^3
		Manganese dioxide:
		Alkaline:

S.I.T.C. (R3)	Commodity Code No	Trade description

cont
778.11

	*850610 11 0	Cylindrical cells
	*850610 15 0	Button cells
	*850610 19 0	Other
		Other:
	*850610 91 0	Cylindrical cells
	*850610 95 0	Button cells
	*850610 99 0	Other
		Mercuric oxide:
	*850630 10 0	Cylindrical cells
	*850630 30 0	Button cells
	*850630 90 0	Other
		Silver oxide:
	*850640 10 0	Cylindrical cells
	*850640 30 0	Button cells
	*850640 90 0	Other
		Lithium:
	*850650 10 0	Cylindrical cells
	*850650 30 0	Button cells
	*850650 90 0	Other
		Air-zinc:
	*850660 10 0	Cylindrical cells
	*850660 35 0	Button cells
	*850660 90 0	Other
		Other
	*850680 05 0	Dry zinc-carbon batteries of a voltage of 5.5 V or more but not exceeding 6.5 V
		Other:
	*850680 11 0	Cylindrical cells
	*850680 15 0	Button cells
	*850680 90 0	Other
	*854810 10 0	Spent primary cells, spent primary batteries

778.12		Electric accumulators (storage batteries).
		Lead-acid, of a kind used for starting piston engines
	850710 10 0	For use in civil aircraft
		Other
		Of a weight not exceeding 5 kg:
	850710 31 0	Working with liquid electrolyte
	850710 39 0	Other
		Of a weight exceeding 5 kg:
	850710 81 0	Working with liquid electrolyte
	850710 89 0	Other
		Other lead-acid accumulators
	850720 10 0	For use in civil aircraft
		Other
		Traction accumulators:
	850720 31 0	Working with liquid electrolyte
	850720 39 0	Other
		Other:
	850720 81 0	Working with liquid electrolyte
	850720 89 0	Other
		Nickel-cadmium
	850730 10 0	For use in civil aircraft
		Other
	850730 91 0	Hermetically sealed
		Other:
	850730 93 0	Traction accumulators
	850730 98 0	Other
		Nickel-iron
	850740 10 0	For use in civil aircraft
	850740 90 0	Other
		Other accumulators:
	850780 10 0	For use in civil aircraft
		Other:
	850780 91 0	Nickel-hybrid
	850780 99 0	Other
	*854810 20 0	Spent electric accumulators

| 778.17 | 850690 00 0 | Parts of primary cells and primary batteries |

778.19		Parts of electric accumulators
	850790 10 0	For use in civil aircraft
		Other
	850790 91 0	Plates for accumulators
	850790 93 0	Separators
	850790 98 0	Other

S.I.T.C. (R3)	Commodity Code No	Trade description
		Electric filament or discharge lamps (including sealed beam lamp units and ultra-violet or infra-red lamps); arc-lamps; and parts thereof
778.21		Filament lamps (other than flashbulbs, infra-red and ultra-violet lamps and sealed beam lamp units)
		Other filament lamps, excluding ultra-violet or infra-red lamps
		Tungsten halogen
	853921 30 0	Of a kind used for motor-cycles or other motor vehicles
		Other, for a voltage
	*853921 92 0	Exceeding 100 volts
	*853921 98 0	Not exceeding 100 volts
		Other, of a power not exceeding 200 W and for a voltage exceeding 100 volts
	853922 10 0	Reflector lamps
	853922 90 0	Other
		Other
	*853929 30 0	Of a kind used for motor-cycles or other motor vehicles
		Other, for a voltage
	*853929 92 0	Exceeding 100 volts
	*853929 98 0	Not exceeding 100 volts
778.22		Discharge lamps (other than ultra-violet lamps)
		Fluorescent, hot cathode
	853931 10 0	With double ended cap
	853931 90 0	Other
		Mercury or sodium vapour lamps; metal halide lamps:
	*853932 10 0	Mercury vapour lamps
	*853932 50 0	Sodium lamps
	*853932 90 0	Metal halide lamps
	*853900 00 0	Other
778.23		Sealed beam lamp units
	853910 10 0	For use in civil aircraft
	853910 90 0	Other
778.24		Ultra-violet or infra-red lamps; arc-lamps
	*853941 00 0	Arc-lamps
		Other
	*853949 10 0	Ultra-violet lamps
	*853949 30 0	Infra-red lamps
778.29		Parts of the lamps of sub-group 778.2
	853990 10 0	Lamp bases
	853990 90 0	Other
		Electrical equipment, n.e.s., for internal combustion engines and vehicles; and parts thereof
778.31		Electrical ignition or starting equipment of a kind used for spark- ignition or compression-ignition internal combustion engines (eg., ignition magnetos, magneto-dynamos, ignition coils, sparking plugs and glow plugs, starter motors); generators (eg., dynamos and alternators) and cut-outs of a kind used in conjunction with such engines.
		Sparking plugs
	851110 10 0	For use in civil aircraft
	851110 90 0	Other
		Ignition magnetos; magneto-dynamos; magnetic flywheels
	851120 10 0	For use in civil aircraft
	851120 90 0	Other
		Distributors; ignition coils
	851130 10 0	For use in civil aircraft
	851130 90 0	Other
		Starter motors and dual purpose starter-generators
	851140 10 0	For use in civil aircraft
	851140 90 0	Other
		Other generators
	851150 10 0	For use in civil aircraft
	851150 90 0	Other
		Other equipment
	851180 10 0	For use in civil aircraft
	851180 90 0	Other
778.33	851190 00 0	Parts of the equipment of heading 778.31
778.34		Electrical lighting or signalling equipment (excluding articles of heading 778.2), windscreen wipers, defrosters and demisters of a kind used for cycles or motor vehicles
	851210 00 0	Lighting or visual signalling equipment of a kind used on bicycles
	851220 00 0	Other lighting or visual signalling equipment
	851230 00 0	Sound signalling equipment
	851240 00 0	Windscreen wipers, defrosters and demisters

S.I.T.C. (R3)	Commodity Code No	Trade description
778.35	851290 00 0	Parts of the equipment of heading 778.34
		Electro-mechanical tools for working in the hand, with self- contained electric motor; and parts thereof
778.41		**Drills of all kinds**
	850810 10 0	Capable of operation without an external source of power
		Other
	850810 91 0	Electropneumatic
	850810 99 0	Other
778.43		**Saws**
	850820 10 0	Chainsaws
	850820 30 0	Circular saws
	850820 90 0	Other
778.45		**Other tools**
	850880 10 0	Of a kind used for working textile materials
		Other
	850880 30 0	Capable of operation without an external source of power
		Other
		Grinders and sanders
	850880 51 0	Angle grinders
	850880 53 0	Belt sanders
	850880 59 0	Other
	850880 70 0	Planers
	850880 80 0	Hedge trimmers and lawn edge cutters
	850880 90 0	Other
778.48	850890 00 0	Parts of the electro-mechanical hand tools of sub-group 778.4
		Electrical capacitors, fixed, variable or adjustable (pre-set)
778.61	853210 00 0	Fixed capacitors designed for use in 50/60 Hz circuits and having a reactive power handling capacity of not less than 0.5 kvar (power capacitors)
778.62	853221 00 0	**Tantalum fixed capacitors**
778.63	853222 00 0	**Aluminium electrolytic fixed capacitors**
778.64	853223 00 0	**Ceramic dielectric fixed capacitors, single layer**
778.65		**Ceramic dielectric fixed capacitors, multilayer**
	853224 10 0	With connecting leads
	853224 90 0	Other
778.66	853225 00 0	**Paper or plastics dielectric fixed capacitors**
778.67	853229 00 0	**Other fixed capacitors**
778.68		**Variable or adjustable (pre-set) capacitors**
	853230 10 0	Variable capacitors
	853230 90 0	Other
778.69	853290 00 0	Parts of electrical capacitors
		Electrical machines and apparatus, having individual functions, n.e.s.; parts thereof
778.71		**Particle accelerators**
	*854311 00 0	Ion implanters for doping semiconductor wafers
	*854319 00 0	Other
778.78		**Other electrical machines and apparatus, having individual functions**
	854320 00 0	Signal generators
		Machines and apparatus for electroplating, electrolysis or electrophoresis
	854330 10 0	Apparatus for wet etching, developing, stripping or cleaning semiconductor wafers
	854330 90 0	Other
	*854340 00 0	Electric fence organisers
		Other machines and apparatus
	*854381 00 0	Proximity cards and tags
		Other:
	*854389 10 0	Flight recorders, for use in civil aircraft
	*854389 20 0	Aerial amplifiers
		Sunbeds, sunlamps and similar suntanning equipment
		For fluorescent tubes using ultraviolet A rays
	*854389 51 0	With a maximum tube length of 100 cm
	*854389 55 0	Other
	*854389 59 0	Other

S.I.T.C. (R3)	Commodity Code No	Trade description
cont 778.78	*854389 70 0 *854389 90 0	Apparatus for physical deposition by sputtering on semiconductor wafers Other

778.79	854390 10 0
	
	854390 90 0
		Parts of the electrical machines and apparatus of sub-group 778.7
		    Assemblies and sub-assemblies consisting of two or more parts or pieces fastened or joined
		      together, for flight recorders, for use in civil aircraft
		    Other

Electrical machinery and equipment, n.e.s.

S.I.T.C. (R3)	Commodity Code No	Trade description

778.81	
	
	850511 00 0
	
	850519 10 0
	850519 90 0
	850520 00 0
	850530 00 0
	
	850590 10 0
	850590 30 0
	850590 90 0
		Electro-magnets; permanent magnets and articles intended to become permanent magnets after
		magnetization; electro-magnetic or permanent magnet chucks, clamps and similar holding
		devices; electro-magnetic couplings, clutches and brakes; electro-magnetic lifting heads
		Permanent magnets and articles intended to become permanent magnets after magnetisation
		    Of metal
		    Other
		      Permanent magnets of agglomerated ferrite
		      Other
		Electro-magnetic couplings, clutches and brakes
		Electro-magnetic lifting heads
		Other, including parts
		    Electro-magnets
		    Electro-magnetic or permanent magnet chucks, clamps and similar holding devices
		    Parts

778.82	 853010 00 0 853080 00 0	Electrical signalling, safety or traffic control equipment for railways, tramways, roads, inland water-ways, parking facilities, port installations or airfields (other than those of heading 791.91) Equipment for railways or tramways Other equipment
778.83	853090 00 0	Parts of the equipment of heading 778.82

778.84	
	
	853110 10 0
	
	853110 20 0
	853110 30 0
	853110 80 0
	
	853120 10 0
	
	853120 30 0
	
	853120 51 0
	853120 59 0
	853120 80 0
	
	853180 10 0
	853180 90 0
		Electric sound or visual signalling apparatus (e.g., bells, sirens, indicator panels, burglar and fire
		alarms), other than those of heading 778.33 or 778.82
		Burglar or fire alarms and similar apparatus
		    For use in civil aircraft
		    Other
		      Of a kind used for motor vehicles
		      Of a kind used for buildings
		      Other
		Indicator panels incorporating liquid crystal devices (LCD) or light emitting diodes (LED)
		    For use in civil aircraft
		    Other
		      Incorporating light emitting diodes (LED)
		      Incorporating liquid crystal devices (LCD)
		        Incorporating active matrix liquid crystal devices (LCD)
		          Colour
		          Black and white or other monochrome
		        Other
		Other apparatus
		    For use in civil aircraft
		    Other

778.85	853190 10 0
	853190 90 0
		Parts of the equipment of heading 778.84
		    Of apparatus of heading 778.84
		    Other

778.86	
	
	854511 00 0
	
	854519 10 0
	854519 90 0
	854520 00 0
	
	854590 10 0
	854590 90 0
		Carbon electrodes, carbon brushes, lamp carbons, battery carbons and other carbon articles,
		with or without metal, of a kind used for electrical purposes
		Electrodes
		    Of a kind used for furnaces
		    Other
		      Electrodes for electrolysis installations
		      Other
		Brushes
		Other
		    Heating resistors
		    Other

778.89	*854890 00 0	Electrical parts of machinery or apparatus, n.e.s.

S.I.T.C. (R3)	Commodity Code No	Trade description

DIVISION 78   **ROAD VEHICLES (INCLUDING AIR-CUSHION VEHICLES)**

MOTOR CARS AND OTHER MOTOR VEHICLES PRINCIPALLY DESIGNED FOR THE TRANSPORT OF PERSONS (OTHER THAN PUBLIC-TRANSPORT TYPE VEHICLES), INCLUDING STATION WAGONS AND RACING CARS

781.10   Vehicles specially designed for travelling on snow; golf cars and similar vehicles

870310 10 0   With compression-ignition internal combustion piston engine (diesel or semi-diesel), or with spark-ignition internal combustion piston engine

870310 90 0   With other engines

781.20   Motor vehicles for the transport of persons, n.e.s.

Other vehicles, with spark-ignition internal combustion reciprocating piston engine

Of a cylinder capacity not exceeding 1,000 cc

870321 10 0   New

870321 90 0   Used

Of a cylinder capacity exceeding 1,000 cc but not exceeding 1,500 cc

New

870322 11 0   Motor caravans

*870322 19 0   Other

870322 90 0   Used

Of a cylinder capacity exceeding 1,500 cc but not exceeding 3,000 cc

New

870323 11 0   Motor caravans

*870323 19 0   Other

870323 90 0   Used

Of a cylinder capacity exceeding 3,000 cc

*870324 10 0   New

870324 90 0   Used

Other vehicles, with compression-ignition internal combustion piston engine (diesel or semi-diesel)

Of a cylinder capacity not exceeding 1,500 cc

870331 10 0   New

870331 90 0   Used

Of a cylinder capacity exceeding 1,500 cc but not exceeding 2,500 cc

New

870332 11 0   Motor caravans

*870332 19 0   Other

870332 90 0   Used

Of a cylinder capacity exceeding 2,500 cc

New

870333 11 0   Motor caravans

*870333 19 0   Other

870333 90 0   Used

Other

870390 10 0   With electric motors

870390 90 0   Other

MOTOR VEHICLES FOR THE TRANSPORT OF GOODS AND SPECIAL PURPOSE MOTOR VEHICLES

Motor vehicles for the transport of goods

782.11   Dumpers designed for off-highway use

With compression-ignition internal combustion piston engine (diesel or semi-diesel), or with spark-ignition internal combustion piston engine

870410 11 0   With compression-ignition internal combustion piston engine (diesel or semi-diesel) with a cylinder capacity exceeding 2,500 cc, or with spark-ignition internal combustion piston engine with a cylinder capacity exceeding 2,800 cc

870410 19 0   Other

870410 90 0   Other

782.19   Motor vehicles for the transport of goods, n.e.s.

Other, with compression-ignition internal combustion piston engine (diesel or semi-diesel)

Of a gross vehicle weight not exceeding five tonnes

870421 10 0   Specially designed for the transport of highly radio-active materials (EURATOM)

Other

With engines of a cylinder capacity exceeding 2,500 cc

870421 31 0   New

870421 39 0   Used

With engines of a cylinder capacity not exceeding 2,500 cc

*870421 91 0   New

870421 99 0   Used

Of a gross vehicle weight exceeding five tonnes but not exceeding 20 tonnes

870422 10 0   Specially designed for the transport of highly radio-active materials (EURATOM)

Other

*870422 91 0   New

870422 99 0   Used

S.I.T.C. (R3)	Commodity Code No	Trade description
cont 782.19		Of a gross vehicle weight exceeding 20 tonnes
	870423 10 0	Specially designed for the transport of highly radio-active materials (EURATOM)
		Other
	870423 91 0	New
	870423 99 0	Used
		Other, with spark-ignition internal combustion piston engine
		Of a gross vehicle weight not exceeding five tonnes
	870431 10 0	Specially designed for the transport of highly radio-active materials (EURATOM)
		Other
		With engines of a cylinder capacity exceeding 2,800 cc
	870431 31 0	New
	870431 39 0	Used
		With engines of a cylinder capacity not exceeding 2,800 cc
	*870431 91 0	New
	870431 99 0	Used
		Of a gross vehicle weight exceeding five tonnes
	870432 10 0	Specially designed for the transport of highly radio-active materials (EURATOM)
		Other
	870432 91 0	New
	870432 99 0	Used
	870490 00 0	Other

Special purpose motor vehicles, other than those designed primarily for the transport of persons or goods (e.g., breakdown lorries, crane lorries, fire fighting vehicles, concrete-mixer lorries, road sweeper lorries, spraying lorries, mobile workshops, mobile radiological units)

782.21	870510 00 0	Crane lorries
782.23	870520 00 0	Mobile drilling derricks
782.25	870530 00 0	Fire fighting vehicles
782.27	870540 00 0	Concrete-mixer lorries
782.29		Other special purpose vehicles
	870590 10 0	Breakdown lorries
	870590 30 0	Concrete-pumping vehicles
	870590 90 0	Other

ROAD MOTOR VEHICLES, N.E.S.

Motor vehicles for the transport of ten or more persons, including the driver

783.11		....with compression-ignition internal combustion engine
		Of a cylinder capacity exceeding 2,500 cc
	870210 11 0	New
	870210 19 0	Used
		Of a cylinder capacity not exceeding 2,500 cc
	870210 91 0	New
	870210 99 0	Used
783.19		....other
		With spark-ignition internal combustion piston engine
		Of a cylinder capacity exceeding 2,500 cc
	870290 11 0	New
	870290 19 0	Used
		Of a cylinder capacity not exceeding 2,500 cc
	870290 31 0	New
	870290 39 0	Used
	870290 90 0	With other engines
783.20		Road tractors for semi-trailers
	870120 10 0	New
	870120 90 0	Used

PARTS AND ACCESSORIES OF THE MOTOR VEHICLES OF GROUPS
722, 781, 782 and 783

784.10		Chassis fitted with engines, for the motor vehicles of groups 722, 781, 782 and 783
		Chassis for tractors falling within group 722; chassis for motor vehicles falling within groups 781, 782, 783 with either a compression-ignition internal combustion piston engine (diesel or semi-diesel), with a cylinder capacity exceeding 2,500 cc or with a spark-ignition internal combustion engine with a capacity exceeding 2,800 cc
	870600 11 0	For vehicles of heading 782.1 or 783.1
	870600 19 0	Other
		Other
	870600 91 0	For vehicles of heading 781
	870600 99 0	Other

S.I.T.C. (R3)	Commodity Code No	Trade description
784.21		**Bodies (including cabs), for the motor vehicles of groups 722, 781, 782 and 783**
		....for the vehicles of group 781
	870710 10 0	For industrial assembly purposes
	870710 90 0	Other
784.25		**....for the vehicles of groups 722, 782 and 783**
	870790 10 0	For the industrial assembly of : Pedestrian-controlled tractors falling within heading 722.41 ; Vehicles of heading 782.1 with either a compression-ignition internal combustion piston engine (diesel or semi-diesel),with a cylinder capacity not exceeding 2,800 cc or with spark-ignition internal piston engine with a cylinder capacity not exceeding 2,500 cc; Special purpose motor vehicles of heading 782.2
	870790 90 0	Other

Other parts and accessories of the motor vehicles of groups 722, 781, 782 and 783

S.I.T.C. (R3)	Commodity Code No	Trade description
784.31		**Bumpers and parts thereof**
	870810 10 0	For the industrial assembly of : Vehicles of heading 781; Vehicles of heading 782.1 with either a compression-ignition internal combustion engine (diesel or semi-diesel), with a cylinder capacity not exceeding 2,500 cc or with a spark-ignition internal combustion engine with a cylinder capacity not exceeding 2,800 cc; Vehicles of heading 782.2
	870810 90 0	Other
784.32		**Other parts and accessories of bodies (including cabs)**
		Safety seat belts
	870821 10 0	For the industrial assembly of: Vehicles of heading 781; Vehicles of heading 782.1 with either a compression-ignition internal combustion engine (diesel or semi-diesel), with a cylinder capacity not exceeding 2,500 cc or with a spark-ignition internal combustion engine with a cylinder capacity not exceeding 2,800 cc; Vehicles of heading 782.2
	870821 90 0	Other
		Other
	870829 10 0	For the industrial assembly of: Pedestrian-controlled tractors falling within heading 722.41; Vehicles of heading 781; Vehicles of heading 782.1 with either a compression-ignition internal combustion engine (diesel or semi-diesel), with a cylinder capacity not exceeding 2,500 cc or with a spark-ignition internal combustion engine with a cylinder capacity not exceeding 2,800 cc; Vehicles of heading 782.2
	870829 90 0	Other
784.33		**Brakes and servo-brakes and parts thereof**
		Mounted brake linings
	870831 10 0	For the industrial assembly of: Pedestrian-controlled tractors falling within heading 722.41; Vehicles of heading 781; Vehicles of heading 782.1 with either a compression-ignition internal combustion engine (diesel or semi-diesel), with a cylinder capacity not exceeding 2,500 cc or with a spark-ignition internal combustion engine with a cylinder capacity not exceeding 2,800 cc; Vehicles of heading 782.2
		Other
	870831 91 0	For disc brakes
	870831 99 0	Other
		Other
	870839 10 0	For the industrial assembly of: Pedestrian-controlled tractors falling within heading 722.41; Vehicles of heading 781; Vehicles of heading 782.1 with either a compression-ignition internal combustion engine (diesel or semi-diesel), with a cylinder capacity not exceeding 2,500 cc or with a spark-ignition internal combustion engine with a cylinder capacity not exceeding 2,800 cc; Vehicles of heading 782.2
	870839 90 0	Other
784.34		**Gear boxes**
	870840 10 0	For the industrial assembly of: Pedestrian-controlled tractors falling within heading 722.41; Vehicles of heading 781; Vehicles of heading 782.1 with either a compression-ignition internal combustion engine (diesel or semi-diesel), with a cylinder capacity not exceeding 2,500 cc or with a spark-ignition internal combustion engine with a cylinder capacity not exceeding 2,800 cc; Vehicles of heading 782.2
	870840 90 0	Other
784.35		**Drive-axles with differential, whether or not provided with other transmission components**
	870850 10 0	For the industrial assembly of : Vehicles of heading 781; Vehicles of heading 782.1 with either a compression-ignition internal combustion engine (diesel or semi-diesel), with a cylinder capacity not exceeding 2,500 cc or with a spark-ignition internal combustion engine with a cylinder capacity not exceeding 2,800 cc, Vehicles of heading 782.2
	*870850 90 0	Other
784.36		**Non-driving axles and parts thereof**
	870860 10 0	For the industrial assembly of : Vehicles of heading 781; Vehicles of heading 782.1 with either a compression-ignition internal combustion engine (diesel or semi-diesel), with a cylinder capacity not exceeding 2,500 cc or with a spark-ignition internal combustion engine with a cylinder capacity not exceeding 2,800 cc; Vehicles of heading 782.2
		Other
	870860 91 0	Of closed-die forged steel
	870860 99 0	Other

S.I.T.C. (R3)	Commodity Code No	Trade description
784.39		Other parts and accessories
		Road wheels and parts and accessories thereof
	870870 10 0	For the industrial assembly of : Pedestrian-controlled tractors falling within heading 722.41; Vehicles of heading 781; Vehicles of heading 782.1 with either a compression-ignition internal combustion engine (diesel or semi-diesel), with a cylinder capacity not exceeding 2,500 cc or with a spark-ignition internal combustion engine with a cylinder capacity not exceeding 2,800 cc; Vehicles of heading 782.2
		Other
	870870 50 0	Wheels of aluminium; parts and accessories of wheels of aluminium
	870870 91 0	Wheel centres in star form, cast in one piece, of iron or steel
	870870 99 0	Other
		Suspension shock-absorbers
	870880 10 0	For the industrial assembly of : Vehicles of heading 781; Vehicles of heading 782.1 with either a compression-ignition internal combustion engine (diesel or semi-diesel), with a cylinder capacity not exceeding 2,500 cc or with a spark-ignition internal combustion engine with a cylinder capacity not exceeding 2,800 cc; Vehicles of heading 782.2
	870880 90 0	Other
		Other parts and accessories
		Radiators
	870891 10 0	For the industrial assembly of : Pedestrian-controlled tractors falling within heading 722.41; Vehicles of heading 781; Vehicles of heading 782.1 with either a compression-ignition internal combustion engine (diesel or semi-diesel), with a cylinder capacity not exceeding 2,500 cc or with a spark-ignition internal combustion engine with a cylinder capacity not exceeding 2,800 cc; Vehicles of heading 782.2
	870891 90 0	Other
		Silencers and exhaust pipes
	870892 10 0	For the industrial assembly of: Pedestrian-controlled tractors falling within heading 722.41; Vehicles of heading 781; Vehicles of heading 782.1 with either a compression-ignition internal combustion engine (diesel or semi-diesel), with a cylinder capacity not exceeding 2,500 cc or with a spark-ignition internal combustion engine with a cylinder capacity not exceeding 2,800 cc; Vehicles of heading 782.2
	870892 90 0	Other
		Clutches and parts thereof
	870893 10 0	For the industrial assembly of : Pedestrian-controlled tractors falling within heading 722.41; Vehicles of heading 781; Vehicles of heading 782.1 with either a compression-ignition internal combustion engine (diesel or semi-diesel), with a cylinder capacity not exceeding 2,500 cc or with a spark-ignition internal combustion engine with a cylinder capacity not exceeding 2,800 cc; Vehicles of heading 782.2
	870893 90 0	Other
		Steering wheels, steering columns and steering boxes
	870894 10 0	For the industrial assembly of : Vehicles of heading 781; Vehicles of heading 782.1 with either a compression-ignition internal combustion engine (diesel or semi-diesel), with a cylinder capacity not exceeding 2,500 cc or with a spark-ignition internal combustion engine with a cylinder capacity not exceeding 2,800 cc; Vehicles of heading 782.2
	870894 90 0	Other
		Other
	870899 10 0	For the industrial assembly of : Pedestrian-controlled tractors falling within heading 722.41; Vehicles of heading 781; Vehicles of heading 782.1 with either a compression-ignition internal combustion engine (diesel or semi-diesel), with a cylinder capacity not exceeding 2,500 cc or with a spark-ignition internal combustion engine with a cylinder capacity not exceeding 2,800 cc; Vehicles of heading 782.2
		Other
	870899 30 0	Anti roll bars
	870899 50 0	Other torsion bars
		Other
	870899 92 0	Of closed-die forged steel
	*870899 98 0	Other

MOTORCYCLES (INCLUDING MOPEDS) AND CYCLES, MOTORIZED AND NON-MOTORIZED; INVALID CARRIAGES

Motorcycles (including mopeds) and cycles fitted with an auxiliary motor, with or without side-cars; side cars

S.I.T.C. (R3)	Commodity Code No	Trade description
785.11	871110 00 0	....with reciprocating internal combustion piston engine of a cylinder capacity not exceeding 50 cc
785.13		....with reciprocating internal combustion piston engine of a cylinder capacity exceeding 50 cc but not exceeding 250 cc
	871120 10 0	Scooters
		Other, of a cylinder capacity
	871120 91 0	Exceeding 50 cc but not exceeding 80 cc
	871120 93 0	Exceeding 80 cc but not exceeding 125 cc
	871120 98 0	Exceeding 125 cc but not exceeding 250 cc
785.15		....with reciprocating internal combustion piston engine of a cylinder capacity exceeding 250 cc but not exceeding 500 cc
	871130 10 0	Of a cylinder capacity exceeding 250 cc but not exceeding 380 cc
	871130 90 0	Of a cylinder capacity exceeding 380 cc but not exceeding 500 cc

S.I.T.C. (R3)	Commodity Code No	Trade description
785.16	871140 00 0	....with reciprocating internal combustion piston engine of a cylinder capacity exceeding 500 cc but not exceeding 800 cc
785.17	871150 00 0	....with reciprocating internal combustion piston engine of a cylinder capacity exceeding 800 cc
785.19	871190 00 0	....other
785.20		**Bicycles and other cycles (including delivery tricycles), not motorized**
	871200 10 0	Without ball bearings
		Other
	871200 30 0	Bicycles
	871200 80 0	Other
		Invalid carriages, whether or not motorized or otherwise mechanically propelled; parts of the articles of group 785
785.31		**Invalid carriages, whether or not motorized or otherwise mechanically propelled**
	871310 00 0	Not mechanically propelled
	871390 00 0	Other
785.35		**Parts and accessories of motorcycles (including mopeds)**
	871411 00 0	Saddles
	871419 00 0	Other
785.36	871420 00 0	**Parts and accessories of invalid carriages**
785.37		**Parts and accessories of other vehicles of group 785**
		Frames and forks, and parts thereof
	871491 10 0	Frames
	871491 30 0	Front forks
	871491 90 0	Parts
		Wheel rims and spokes
	871492 10 0	Rims
	871492 90 0	Spokes
		Hubs, other than coaster braking hubs and hub brakes, and free-wheel sprocket-wheels
	871493 10 0	Hubs without freewheel or braking device
	871493 90 0	Free-wheel sprocket-wheels
		Brakes, including coaster braking hubs and hub brakes, and parts thereof
	871494 10 0	Coaster braking hubs and hub brakes
	871494 30 0	Other brakes
	871494 90 0	Parts
	871495 00 0	Saddles
		Pedals and crank-gear, and parts thereof
	871496 10 0	Pedals
	871496 30 0	Crank-gear
	871496 90 0	Parts
		Other
	871499 10 0	Handlebars
	871499 30 0	Luggage carriers
	871499 50 0	Derailleur gears
	871499 90 0	Other; parts

TRAILERS AND SEMI-TRAILERS; OTHER VEHICLES, NOT MECHANICALLY PROPELLED; SPECIALLY DESIGNED AND EQUIPPED TRANSPORT CONTAINERS

S.I.T.C. (R3)	Commodity Code No	Trade description
786.10		**Trailers and semi-trailers of the caravan type, for housing or camping**
	871610 10 0	Folding caravans
		Other, of a weight
	871610 91 0	Not exceeding 750 kg
	871610 94 0	Exceeding 750 kg but not exceeding 1,600 kg
	871610 96 0	Exceeding 1,600 kg but not exceeding 3,500 kg
	871610 99 0	Exceeding 3,500 kg
		Trailers and semi-trailers for the transport of goods.
786.21		**Self-loading or self-unloading trailers and semi-trailers for agricultural purposes.**
	871620 10 0	Manure spreaders
	871620 90 0	Other
786.22	871631 00 0	**Tanker trailers and tanker semi-trailers**
786.29		**Other trailers and semi-trailers for the transport of goods**
	871639 10 0	Specially designed for the transport of highly radio-active materials (EURATOM)
		Other
		New
	871639 30 0	Semi-trailers
		Other
	871639 51 0	With a single axle
	871639 59 0	Other

S.I.T.C. (R3)	Commodity Code No	Trade description
cont 786.29	871639 80 0	Used
786.30		Containers (including containers for the transport of fluids) specially designed and equipped for carriage by one or more modes of transport
	860900 10 0	Containers with an anti-radiation lead covering, for the transport of radio-active materials (Euratom)
	860900 90 0	Other
		Other vehicles, not mechanically propelled; parts of trailers, semi-trailers and of non-mechanically propelled vehicles
786.83	871640 00 0	Trailers and semi-trailers, n.e.s.
786.85	871680 00 0	Vehicles, not mechanically propelled, n.e.s.
786.89		Parts of the trailers and semi-trailers of headings 786.1, 786.2, 786.83 and of the vehicles of heading 786.85
	871690 10 0	Chassis
	871690 30 0	Bodies
	871690 50 0	Axles
	871690 90 0	Other parts

DIVISION 79

OTHER TRANSPORT EQUIPMENT

RAILWAY VEHICLES (INCLUDING HOVERTRAINS) AND ASSOCIATED EQUIPMENT

Rail locomotives powered from an external source of electricity or by electric accumulators

S.I.T.C. (R3)	Commodity Code No	Trade description
791.11	860110 00 0	Powered from an external source of electricity
791.15	860120 00 0	Powered by electric accumulators
		Other rail locomotives; locomotive tenders
791.21	860210 00 0	Diesel-electric locomotives
791.29	860290 00 0	Rail locomotives, n.e.s.; locomotive tenders
791.60		Railway or tramway coaches, vans and trucks, self-propelled (other than maintenance and service vehicles of heading 791.81)
	860310 00 0	Powered from an external source of electricity
	860390 00 0	Other
791.70	860500 00 0	Railway or tramway passenger coaches, not self-propelled; luggage vans, post office coaches and other special purpose railway or tramway coaches, not self-propelled (excluding those of heading 791.81)
		Railway or tramway freight and maintenance cars
791.81	860400 00 0	Railway or tramway maintenance or service vehicles, whether or not self-propelled (e.g., workshops, cranes, ballast tampers, trackliners, testing coaches and track inspection vehicles)
791.82		Railway or tramway goods vans and wagons (freight cars), not self- propelled
	860610 00 0	Tank wagons and the like
	860620 00 0	Insulated or refrigerated vans and wagons, other than those of subheading No. 8606.10
	860630 00 0	Self-discharging vans and wagons, other than those of subheading No. 8606.10 or 8606.20
		Other
		Covered and closed
	860691 10 0	Specially designed for the transport of highly radioactive materials (EURATOM)
	860691 90 0	Other
	860692 00 0	Open, with non-removable sides of a height exceeding 60 cm
	860699 00 0	Other
		Railway or tramway track fixtures and fittings; mechanical (including electro-mechanical) signalling, safety or traffic control equipment for railways, tramways, roads, inland waterways, parking facilities, port installations or airfields; stock, fixtures, fittings and equipment of group 791
791.91		Railway or tramway track fixtures and fittings; mechanical (including electro-mechanical) signalling, safety or traffic control equipment for railways, tramways, roads, inland waterways, parking facilities, port installations or airfields; parts of the foregoing
	860800 10 0	Equipment for railways or tramways
	860800 30 0	Other equipment
		Parts
	860800 91 0	Of cast iron or cast steel
	860800 99 0	Other

S.I.T.C. (R3)	Commodity Code No	Trade description
791.99		Parts of the railway or tramway locomotives or rolling stock of headings 791.1 through 791.82
		Bogies, bissel-bogies, axles and wheels, and parts thereof
	860711 00 0	Driving bogies and bissel-bogies
	860712 00 0	Other bogies and bissel-bogies
		Other, including parts
		Axles, assembled or not; wheels and parts thereof
	860719 01 0	Of cast iron or cast steel
	860719 11 0	Of closed-die forged steel
	860719 18 0	Other
		Parts of bogies, bissel-bogies and the like
	860719 91 0	Of cast iron or cast steel
	860719 99 0	Other
		Brakes and parts thereof
		Air brakes and parts thereof
	860721 10 0	Of cast iron or cast steel
	860721 90 0	Other
		Other
	860729 10 0	Of cast iron or cast steel
	860729 90 0	Other
		Hooks and other coupling devices, buffers, and parts thereof
	860730 01 0	Of cast iron or cast steel
	860730 99 0	Other
		Other
		Of locomotives
	860791 10 0	Axle-boxes and parts thereof
		Other
	860791 91 0	Of cast iron or cast steel
	860791 99 0	Other
		Other
	860799 10 0	Axle-boxes and parts thereof
	860799 30 0	Bodies and parts thereof
	860799 50 0	Chassis and parts thereof
	860799 90 0	Other

AIRCRAFT AND ASSOCIATED EQUIPMENT; SPACECRAFT (INCLUDING SATELLITES) AND SPACECRAFT LAUNCH VEHICLES; AND PARTS THEREOF

Helicopters

S.I.T.C. (R3)	Commodity Code No	Trade description
792.11		....of an unladen weight not exceeding 2000 kg
	*880211 10 0	Civil helicopters
	880211 90 0	Other
792.15		....of an unladen weight exceeding 2000 kg
	*880212 10 0	Civil helicopters
	*880212 90 0	Other
792.20		Aeroplanes and other aircraft, mechanically propelled (other than helicopters), of an unladen weight not exceeding 2000 kg
	*880220 10 0	Civil aircraft
	*880220 90 0	Other
792.30		Aeroplanes and other aircraft, mechanically propelled (other than helicopters), of an unladen weight exceeding 2000 kg but not exceeding 15000 kg
	*880230 10 0	Civil aircraft
	*880230 90 0	Other
792.40		Aeroplanes and other aircraft, mechanically propelled (other than helicopters), of an unladen weight exceeding 15000 kg
	*880240 10 0	Civil aircraft
	*880240 90 0	Other
792.50	*880260 00 0	Spacecraft (including satellites) and spacecraft launch vehicles
		Aircraft, n.e.s. (including dirigibles, balloons, gliders, etc.) and associated equipment
792.81		Gliders and hang gliders
	880110 10 0	For civil use
	880110 90 0	Other
792.82		Balloons, dirigibles and other non-powered aircraft
	880190 10 0	For civil use
		Other
	880190 91 0	Balloons and dirigibles
	880190 99 0	Other

S.I.T.C. (R3)	Commodity Code No	Trade description
792.83		Aircraft launching gear; deck-arrestor or similar gear; ground flying trainers; parts of the foregoing
		Aircraft launching gear and parts thereof; deck-arrestor or similar gear and parts thereof
	880510 10 0	Aircraft launching gear and parts thereof
	880510 90 0	Other
		Ground flying trainers and parts thereof
	880520 10 0	For civil use
	*880520 90 0	Other
		Parts, n.e.s.,(not including tyres, engines and electrical parts) of the goods of group 792
792.91		Propellers and rotors and parts thereof
	880310 10 0	For use in civil aircraft
	880310 90 0	Other
792.93		Under-carriages and parts thereof
	880320 10 0	For use in civil aircraft
	880320 90 0	Other
792.95		Other parts of aeroplanes or helicopters
	880330 10 0	For use in civil aircraft
	880330 90 0	Other
792.97		Other parts of the goods of group 792
	880390 10 0	Of kites
		Other
	880390 91 0	For use in civil aircraft and gliders
	*880390 99 0	Other

SHIPS, BOATS (INCLUDING HOVERCRAFT) AND FLOATING STRUCTURES

Yachts and other vessels for pleasure or sports; rowing boats and canoes

S.I.T.C. (R3)	Commodity Code No	Trade description
793.11		Inflatable vessels (including rowing boats and canoes)
		Of a weight not exceeding 100 kg each
	890310 11 0	Of a weight not exceeding 20 kg each or of a length not exceeding 2.5 m
	890310 19 0	Other
	890310 90 0	Other
793.12		Sailboats, not inflatable, with or without auxiliary motor
	890391 10 0	Sea-going
		Other
	890391 91 0	Of a weight not exceeding 100 kg each
		Other
	890391 93 0	Of a length not exceeding 7.5 m
	890391 99 0	Of a length exceeding 7.5 m
793.19		Non-inflatable rowing boats and canoes and vessels for pleasure or sport, n.e.s.
		Motorboats, other than outboard motorboats
	890392 10 0	Sea-going
		Other
	890392 91 0	Of a length not exceeding 7.5 m
	890392 99 0	Of a length exceeding 7.5 m
		Other
	890399 10 0	Of a weight not exceeding 100 kg each
		Other
	890399 91 0	Of a length not exceeding 7.5 m
	890399 99 0	Of a length exceeding 7.5 m

Ships, boats and other vessels (other than pleasure craft, tugs, pusher craft, special purpose vessels and vessels for breaking up)

S.I.T.C. (R3)	Commodity Code No	Trade description
793.22		Tankers of all kinds
	890120 10 0	Sea-going
	890120 90 0	Other
793.24		Fishing vessels; factory ships and other vessels for processing or preserving fishery products
		Sea-going
	890200 11 0	Of a gross tonnage exceeding 250 tons (GRT)
	890200 19 0	Of a gross tonnage not exceeding 250 tons (GRT)
	890200 90 0	Other
793.26		Refrigerated vessels (other than tankers)
	890130 10 0	Sea-going
	890130 90 0	Other

S.I.T.C. (R3)	Commodity Code No	Trade description
793.27		Other vessels for the transport of goods (including vessels for the transport of both passengers and goods)
	890190 10 0	Sea-going
		Other
	890190 91 0	Not mechanically propelled
	890190 99 0	Mechanically propelled
793.28		Cruise ships, excursion boats and similar vessels designed for the transport of persons; ferry-boats of all kinds
	890110 10 0	Sea-going
	890110 90 0	Other
793.29		Other vessels (including warships and lifeboats other than rowing boats
	890600 10 0	Warships
		Other
	890600 91 0	Sea-going
		Other
	890600 93 0	Of a weight not exceeding 100 kg each
	890600 99 0	Other
793.30	890800 00 0	Vessels and other floating structures for breaking up
		Light vessels, fire-floats, dredgers, floating cranes and other vessels the navigability of which is subsidiary to their main function; floating docks; floating or submersible drilling or production platforms
793.51		Dredgers
	890510 10 0	Sea-going
	890510 90 0	Other
793.55	890520 00 0	Floating or submersible drilling or production platforms
793.59		Light vessels, fire-floats, floating cranes and other vessels, n.e.s., the navigability of which is subsidiary to their main function
	890590 10 0	Sea-going
	890590 90 0	Other
793.70		Tugs and pusher craft
	890400 10 0	Tugs
		Pusher craft
	890400 91 0	Sea-going
	890400 99 0	Other
		Other floating structures (e.g., rafts, tanks, coffer-dams, landing-stages, buoys and beacons)
793.91	890710 00 0	Rafts, inflatable
793.99	890790 00 0	Floating structures, n.e.s.

SECTION: 8

DIVISION 81

PREFABRICATED BUILDINGS; SANITARY, PLUMBING, HEATING AND LIGHTING FIXTURES AND FITTINGS, N.E.S.

811.00   **Prefabricated buildings**

	940600 10 0	Of wood
		Of iron or steel
	940600 31 0	Greenhouses
	940600 39 0	Other
	940600 90 0	Of other materials

SANITARY, PLUMBING AND HEATING FIXTURES AND FITTINGS, N.E.S.

Boilers (other than those of heading 711) and radiators, for central heating, not electrically heated, and parts thereof, of iron or steel; air heaters and hot air distributors (including distributors which can also distribute fresh or conditioned air), not electrically heated, incorporating a motor-driven fan or blower, and parts thereof, of iron or steel

812.11   **Radiators and parts thereof**

	732211 00 0	Of cast iron
	732219 00 0	Other

812.15   **Air heaters and hot air distributors and parts thereof**

	732290 10 0	Air heaters and hot air distributors (excl. their parts) for use in civil aircraft
	732290 90 0	Other

812.17   **Central heating boilers (other than those of heading 711)**

	840310 10 0	Of cast iron
	840310 90 0	Other

812.19   **Parts for the boilers of heading 812.17**

	840390 10 0	Of cast iron
	840390 90 0	Other

Ceramic sinks, wash basins, wash basin pedestals, baths, bidets, water closet pans, flushing cisterns, urinals and similar sanitary fixtures

812.21   691010 00 0   ....of porcelain or china

812.29   691090 00 0   ....other than of porcelain or china

LIGHTING FIXTURES AND FITTINGS, N.E.S.

Lamps and lighting fittings (including searchlights and spotlights), n.e.s.

813.11   **Chandeliers and other electric ceiling and wall lighting fittings (excluding those of a kind used for lighting public open spaces or thoroughfares)**

	940510 10 0	Of base metal or of plastics, for use in civil aircraft
		Other
		Of plastics
	940510 21 0	Of a kind used with filament lamps
	940510 29 0	Other
	940510 30 0	Of ceramic materials
	940510 50 0	Of glass
		Of other materials
	940510 91 0	Of a kind used with filament lamps
	940510 99 0	Other

813.12   851310 00 0   Portable electric lamps designed to function by their own source of energy (e.g., dry batteries, accumulators or magnetos), other than lighting equipment falling within heading 778.34

813.13   **Electric table, desk, bedside or floor-standing lamps**

		Of plastics
	940520 11 0	Of a kind used with filament lamps
	940520 19 0	Other
	940520 30 0	Of ceramic materials
	940520 50 0	Of glass

S.I.T.C. (R3)	Commodity Code No	Trade description
cont 813.13		Of other materials
	940520 91 0	Of a kind used with filament lamps
	940520 99 0	Other
813.15		**Electric lamps and lighting fittings, n.e.s**
	940540 10 0	Searchlights and spotlights
		Other
		Of plastics
	940540 31 0	Of a kind used with filament lamps
	940540 35 0	Of a kind used with tubular fluorescent lamps
	940540 39 0	Other
		Of other materials
	940540 91 0	Of a kind used with filament lamps
	940540 95 0	Of a kind used with tubular fluorescent lamps
	940540 99 0	Other
813.17	940550 00 0	**Non-electrical lamps and lighting fittings**
813.20		**Illuminated signs, illuminated name-plates and the like**
	940560 10 0	Illuminated signs, illuminated name plates and the like, of base metal or of plastics, for use in civil aircraft
		Other
	940560 91 0	Of plastics
	940560 99 0	Of other materials
813.80	851390 00 0	**Parts of the portable electric lamps of heading 813.12**
		Parts, n.e.s. of the goods of headings 813.1 and 813.2
813.91		**....of glass**
		Articles for electrical lighting fittings (excluding searchlights and spotlights)
	940591 11 0	Facetted glass, plates, balls, pear-shaped drops, flower-shaped pieces, pendants and similar articles for trimming chandeliers
	940591 19 0	Other (for example, diffusers, ceiling lights, bowls, cups, lamp-shades, globes , tulip-shaped pieces)
	940591 90 0	Other
813.92		**....of plastics**
	940592 10 0	Parts of the articles of headings 813.11, 813.2, for use in civil aircraft
	940592 90 0	Other
813.99		**....other**
	940599 10 0	Parts of the articles of headings 813.11, 813.2, of base metal, for use in civil aircraft
	940599 90 0	Other

DIVISION 82

FURNITURE AND PARTS THEREOF; BEDDING, MATTRESSES, MATTRESS SUPPORTS, CUSHIONS AND SIMILAR STUFFED FURNISHINGS

Seats (other than those of heading 872.4), whether or not convertible into beds, and parts thereof

S.I.T.C. (R3)	Commodity Code No	Trade description
821.11		**Seats of a kind used for aircraft**
	940110 10 0	Not leather covered, for use in civil aircraft
	940110 90 0	Other
821.12	940120 00 0	**Seats of a kind used for motor vehicles**
821.13	940150 00 0	**Seats of cane, osier, bamboo or similar materials**
821.14		**Swivel seats with variable height adjustment**
	940130 10 0	Upholstered, with backrest and fitted with castors or glides
	940130 90 0	Other
821.15	940140 00 0	**Seats, other than garden seats or camping equipment, convertible into beds**
821.16		**Seats, n.e.s, with wooden frames**
	940161 00 0	Upholstered
	940169 00 0	Other
821.17		**Seats, n.e.s., with metal frames**
	940171 00 0	Upholstered
	940179 00 0	Other
821.18	940180 00 0	**Other seats**

S.I.T.C. (R3)	Commodity Code No	Trade description
821.19		**Parts of the seats of sub-group 821.1**
	940190 10 0	Of seats of a kind used for aircraft
		Other
	940190 30 0	Of wood
	940190 80 0	Other

Mattress supports; articles of bedding or similar furnishings (e.g., mattresses, quilts, eiderdowns, cushions, pouffes and pillows), fitted with springs or stuffed or internally fitted with any material or of cellular rubber or plastics, whether or not covered

S.I.T.C. (R3)	Commodity Code No	Trade description
821.21	940410 00 0	**Mattress supports**
821.23		**Mattresses of cellular rubber or plastics**
	940421 10 0	Of rubber
	940421 90 0	Of plastics
821.25		**Mattresses of other materials**
	940429 10 0	Spring interior
	940429 90 0	Other
821.27		**Sleeping bags**
	940430 10 0	Filled with feathers or down
	940430 90 0	Other
821.29		**Other articles of bedding**
	940490 10 0	Filled with feathers or down
	940490 90 0	Other

Furniture, n.e.s., of metal

S.I.T.C. (R3)	Commodity Code No	Trade description
821.31		**....of a kind used in offices**
	940310 10 0	Drawing tables (other than those of heading 874.22)
		Other
		Not exceeding 80 cm in height
	940310 51 0	Desks
	940310 59 0	Other
		Exceeding 80 cm in height
	940310 91 0	Cupboards with doors, shutters or flaps
	940310 93 0	Filing, card-index and other cabinets
	940310 99 0	Other
821.39		**....other metal furniture**
	940320 10 0	For use in civil aircraft
		Other
	940320 91 0	Beds
	940320 99 0	Other

Furniture, n.e.s., of wood

S.I.T.C. (R3)	Commodity Code No	Trade description
821.51		**....of a kind used in offices**
		Not exceeding 80 cm in height
	940330 11 0	Desks
	940330 19 0	Other
		Exceeding 80 cm in height
	940330 91 0	Cupboards with doors, shutters or flaps; filing, card-index and other cabinets
	940330 99 0	Other
821.53		**....of a kind used in the kitchen**
	940340 10 0	Fitted kitchen units
	940340 90 0	Other
821.55	940350 00 0	**....of a kind used in the bedroom**
821.59		**....other wooden furniture**
	*940360 10 0	Wooden furniture of a kind used the in dining room and the living room
	940360 30 0	Wooden furniture of a kind used in shops
	*940360 90 0	Other wooden furniture

Furniture, n.e.s., of other materials

S.I.T.C. (R3)	Commodity Code No	Trade description
821.71		**Furniture of plastics**
	940370 10 0	For use in civil aircraft
	940370 90 0	Other
821.79	940380 00 0	**Furniture of other materials (including bamboo)**
821.80		**Parts of the furniture of headings 821.3, 821.5 and 821.7**
	940390 10 0	Of metal
	940390 30 0	Of wood

S.I.T.C. (R3)	Commodity Code No	Trade description

cont
821.80   940390 90 0   Of other materials

DIVISION 83

TRAVEL GOODS, HANDBAGS AND SIMILAR CONTAINERS

TRUNKS, SUIT-CASES, VANITY-CASES, EXECUTIVE-CASES, BRIEF-CASES, SCHOOL SATCHELS, BINOCULAR CASES, CAMERA CASES, MUSICAL INSTRUMENT CASES, SPECTACLE CASES, GUN CASES, HOLSTERS AND SIMILAR CONTAINERS; TRAVELLING BAGS, TOILET BAGS, RUCKSACKS, HANDBAGS, SHOPPING-BAGS, WALLETS, PURSES, MAP-CASES, CIGARETTE-CASES, TOBACCO-POUCHES, TOOL BAGS, SPORTS BAGS, BOTTLE-CASES, JEWELLERY BOXES, POWDER-BOXES, CUTLERY CASES AND SIMILAR CONTAINERS, OF LEATHER OR OF COMPOSITION LEATHER, OF SHEETING OF PLASTICS, OF TEXTILE MATERIALS, OF VULCANIZED FIBRE OR OF PAPERBOARD, OR WHOLLY OR MAINLY COVERED WITH SUCH MATERIALS OR WITH PAPER; TRAVEL SETS FOR PERSONAL TOILET, SEWING OR SHOE OR CLOTHES CLEANING

Handbags, whether or not with shoulder strap (including those without handle)

831.11   420221 00 0   ....with outer surface of leather, of composition leather or

831.12   ....with outer surface of sheeting of plastics or of textile materials
         420222 10 0   Of plastic sheeting
         420222 90 0   Of textile materials

831.19   420229 00 0   ....other handbags

Trunks, suit-cases, vanity cases, executive-cases, brief-cases, school satchels and similar containers

831.21   ....with outer surface of leather, of composition leather or of patent leather
         420211 10 0   Executive-cases, brief-cases, school satchels and similar containers
         420211 90 0   Other

831.22   ....with outer surface of plastics or of textile materials
            In the form of plastic sheeting
         420212 11 0   Executive-cases, brief-cases, school satchels and similar containers
         420212 19 0   Other
         420212 50 0   Of moulded plastic material
            Of other materials, including vulcanised fibre
         420212 91 0   Executive-cases, brief-cases, school satchels and similar containers
         420212 99 0   Other

831.29   ....other
         420219 10 0   Of aluminium
         420219 90 0   Of other materials

831.30   960500 00 0   **Travel sets for personal toilet, sewing or shoe or clothes cleaning**

Binocular cases, camera cases, musical instrument cases, spectacle cases, gun cases, holsters and similar cases, n.e.s.; travelling bags, toilet bags, rucksacks, shopping bags, wallets, purses, map-cases, cigarette cases, tobacco-pouches, tool bags, sports bags, bottle-cases, jewellery boxes, powder-boxes, cutlery cases and similar containers, of leather or of composition leather, of sheeting of plastics, of textile materials, of vulcanized fibre or of paperboard, or wholly or mainly covered with such materials or with paper, n.e.s.

831.91   Articles of a kind normally carried in the pocket or handbag
         420231 00 0   With outer surface of leather, of composition leather or of patent leather
            With outer surface of plastic sheeting or of textile materials
         420232 10 0   Of plastic sheeting
         420232 90 0   Of textile materials
         420239 00 0   Other

831.99   Other
            With outer surface of leather, of composition leather or of patent leather
         420291 10 0   Travelling-bags, toilet bags, rucksacks and sports bags
         420291 80 0   Other
            With outer surface of plastic sheeting or of textile materials
               Of plastic sheeting
         420292 11 0   Travelling-bags, toilet bags, rucksacks and sports bags
         420292 15 0   Musical instrument cases
         420292 19 0   Other
               Of textile materials
         420292 91 0   Travelling-bags, toilet bags, rucksacks and sports bags
         420292 98 0   Other
         420299 00 0   Other

S.I.T.C. (R3)	Commodity Code No	Trade description

DIVISION 84

ARTICLES OF APPAREL AND CLOTHING ACCESSORIES

MEN'S OR BOYS' COATS, JACKETS, SUITS, BLAZERS, TROUSERS, SHORTS, SHIRTS, UNDERWEAR, KNITWEAR AND SIMILAR ARTICLES OF TEXTILE FABRICS, NOT KNITTED OR CROCHETED (OTHER THAN THOSE OF HEADING 845.2 or 845.6)

Overcoats, car-coats, capes, cloaks, anoraks (incl. ski-jackets), wind-cheaters, wind-jackets and similar articles (other than those of headings 841.2 or 841.3)

S.I.T.C. (R3)	Commodity Code No	Trade description
841.11	620111 00 0	**Overcoats, raincoats, car-coats, capes, cloaks and similar articles of wool or fine animal hair**
841.12		**Overcoats, raincoats, car-coats, capes, cloaks and similar articles of textile materials other than wool or fine animal hair**
		Of cotton
	620112 10 0	Of a weight, per garment, not exceeding 1 kg
	620112 90 0	Of a weight, per garment, exceeding 1 kg
		Of man-made fibres
	620113 10 0	Of a weight, per garment, not exceeding 1 kg
	620113 90 0	Of a weight, per garment, exceeding 1 kg
	620119 00 0	Of other textile materials
841.19		**Other**
	620191 00 0	Of wool or fine animal hair
	620192 00 0	Of cotton
	620193 00 0	Of man-made fibres
	620199 00 0	Of other textile materials
		Suits and ensembles
841.21	620311 00 0	**Suits of wool or fine animal hair**
841.22		**Suits of textile materials other than wool or fine animal hair**
	620312 00 0	Of synthetic fibres
		Of other textile materials
	620319 10 0	Of cotton
	620319 30 0	Of artificial fibres
	620319 90 0	Other
841.23		**Ensembles**
	620321 00 0	Of wool or fine animal hair
		Of cotton
	620322 10 0	Industrial and occupational
	620322 80 0	Other
		Of synthetic fibres
	620323 10 0	Industrial and occupational
	620323 80 0	Other
		Of other textile materials
		Of artificial fibres
	620329 11 0	Industrial and occupational
	620329 18 0	Other
	620329 90 0	Other
841.30		**Jackets and blazers**
	620331 00 0	Of wool or fine animal hair
		Of cotton
	620332 10 0	Industrial and occupational
	620332 90 0	Other
		Of synthetic fibres
	620333 10 0	Industrial and occupational
	620333 90 0	Other
		Of other textile materials
		Of artificial fibres
	620339 11 0	Industrial and occupational
	620339 19 0	Other
	620339 90 0	Other
841.40		**Trousers, bib and brace overalls, breeches and shorts**
		Of wool or fine animal hair
	620341 10 0	Trousers and breeches
	620341 30 0	Bib and brace overalls
	620341 90 0	Other
		Of cotton
		Trousers and breeches
	620342 11 0	Industrial and occupational
		Other
	620342 31 0	Of denim
	620342 33 0	Of cut corduroy
	620342 35 0	Other

S.I.T.C. (R3)	Commodity Code No	Trade description

cont
841.40

		Bib and brace overalls
	620342 51 0	Industrial and occupational
	620342 59 0	Other
	620342 90 0	Other
		Of synthetic fibres
		Trousers and breeches
	620343 11 0	Industrial and occupational
	620343 19 0	Other
		Bib and brace overalls
	620343 31 0	Industrial and occupational
	620343 39 0	Other
	620343 90 0	Other
		Of other textile materials
		Of artificial fibres
		Trousers and breeches
	620349 11 0	Industrial and occupational
	620349 19 0	Other
		Bib and brace overalls
	620349 31 0	Industrial and occupational
	620349 39 0	Other
	620349 50 0	Other
	620349 90 0	Other

Shirts

841.51	620520 00 0	....of cotton

841.59		....of textile materials other than cotton
	620510 00 0	Of wool or fine animal hair
	620530 00 0	Of man-made fibres
		Of other textile materials
	620590 10 0	Of flax or of ramie
	620590 90 0	Other

Singlets and other vests, underpants, briefs, night-shirts, pyjamas, bathrobes, dressing gowns and similar articles

841.61		**Underpants and briefs**
	620711 00 0	Of cotton
	620719 00 0	Of other textile materials

841.62		**Night-shirts and pyjamas**
	620721 00 0	Of cotton
	620722 00 0	Of man-made fibres
	620729 00 0	Of other textile materials

841.69		**Other**
		Of cotton
	620791 10 0	Bathrobes, dressing gowns and similar articles of terry towelling and similar woven terry fabrics
	620791 90 0	Other
	620792 00 0	Of man-made fibres
	620799 00 0	Of other textile materials

WOMEN'S AND GIRLS' COATS, CAPES, JACKETS, SUITS, TROUSERS, SHORTS, SHIRTS, DRESSES AND SKIRTS, UNDERWEAR, NIGHTWEAR AND SIMILAR ARTICLES OF TEXTILE FABRICS, NOT KNITTED OR CROCHETED (OTHER THAN THOSE OF HEADING 845.2 OR 845.6)

Overcoats, car-coats, capes, cloaks, anoraks (incl. ski-jackets), wind-cheaters, wind-jackets and similar articles (other than those of headings 842.2 or 842.3)

842.11		**Overcoats, raincoats, car-coats, capes, cloaks and similar articles**
	620211 00 0	Of wool or fine animal hair
		Of cotton
	620212 10 0	Of a weight, per garment, not exceeding 1 kg
	620212 90 0	Of a weight, per garment, exceeding 1 kg
		Of man-made fibres
	620213 10 0	Of a weight, per garment, not exceeding 1 kg
	620213 90 0	Of a weight, per garment, exceeding 1 kg
	620219 00 0	Of other textile materials

842.19		**Other**
	620291 00 0	Of wool or fine animal hair
	620292 00 0	Of cotton
	620293 00 0	Of man-made fibres
	620299 00 0	Of other textile materials

S.I.T.C. (R3)	Commodity Code No	Trade description
		Suits and ensembles
842.21		**Suits**
	620411 00 0	Of wool or fine animal hair
	620412 00 0	Of cotton
	620413 00 0	Of synthetic fibres
		Of other textile materials
	620419 10 0	Of artificial fibres
	620419 90 0	Other
842.22		**Ensembles**
	620421 00 0	Of wool or fine animal hair
		Of cotton
	620422 10 0	Industrial and occupational
	620422 80 0	Other
		Of synthetic fibres
	620423 10 0	Industrial and occupational
	620423 80 0	Other
		Of other textile materials
		Of artificial fibres
	620429 11 0	Industrial and occupational
	620429 18 0	Other
	620429 90 0	Other
842.30		**Jackets and blazers**
	620431 00 0	Of wool or fine animal hair
		Of cotton
	620432 10 0	Industrial and occupational
	620432 90 0	Other
		Of synthetic fibres
	620433 10 0	Industrial and occupational
	620433 90 0	Other
		Of other textile materials
		Of artificial fibres
	620439 11 0	Industrial and occupational
	620439 19 0	Other
	620439 90 0	Other
842.40		**Dresses**
	620441 00 0	Of wool or fine animal hair
	620442 00 0	Of cotton
	620443 00 0	Of synthetic fibres
	620444 00 0	Of artificial fibres
		Of other textile materials
	620449 10 0	Of silk or waste silk
	620449 90 0	Other
842.50		**Skirts and divided skirts**
	620451 00 0	Of wool or fine animal hair
	620452 00 0	Of cotton
	620453 00 0	Of synthetic fibres
		Of other textile materials
	620459 10 0	Of artificial fibres
	620459 90 0	Other
842.60		**Trousers, bib and brace overalls, breeches and shorts**
		Of wool or fine animal hair
	620461 10 0	Trousers and breeches
	620461 80 0	Bib and brace overalls
	620461 90 0	Other
		Of cotton
		Trousers and breeches
	620462 11 0	Industrial and occupational
		Other
	620462 31 0	Of denim
	620462 33 0	Of cut corduroy
	620462 39 0	Other
		Bib and brace overalls
	620462 51 0	Industrial and occupational
	620462 59 0	Other
	620462 90 0	Other
		Of synthetic fibres
		Trousers and breeches
	620463 11 0	Industrial and occupational
	620463 18 0	Other
		Bib and brace overalls
	620463 31 0	Industrial and occupational
	620463 39 0	Other
	620463 90 0	Other

S.I.T.C. (R3)	Commodity Code No	Trade description
cont 842.60		Of other textile materials
		Of artificial fibres
		Trousers and breeches
	620469 11 0	Industrial and occupational
	620469 18 0	Other
		Bib and brace overalls
	620469 31 0	Industrial and occupational
	620469 39 0	Other
	620469 50 0	Other
	620469 90 0	Other
842.70		**Blouses, shirts and shirt-blouses**
	620610 00 0	Of silk or silk waste
	620620 00 0	Of wool or fine animal hair
	620630 00 0	Of cotton
	620640 00 0	Of man-made fibres
		Of other textile materials
	620690 10 0	Of flax or of ramie
	620690 90 0	Other

Singlets and other vests, slips, petticoats, briefs, panties, night-dresses, pyjamas, negligees, bathrobes, dressing gowns and similar articles

S.I.T.C. (R3)	Commodity Code No	Trade description
842.81		**Slips and petticoats**
	620811 00 0	Of man-made fibres
		Of other textile materials
	620819 10 0	Of cotton
	620819 90 0	Other
842.82		**Night-dresses and pyjamas**
	620821 00 0	Of cotton
	620822 00 0	Of man-made fibres
	620829 00 0	Of other textile materials
842.89		**Other**
		Of cotton
		Negligées, bathrobes, dressing gowns and similar articles
	620891 11 0	Of terry towelling and similar woven terry fabrics
	620891 19 0	Other
	620891 90 0	Other
		Of man-made fibres
	620892 10 0	Negligées, bathrobes, dressing gowns and similar articles
	620892 90 0	Other
	620899 00 0	Of other textile materials

MEN'S OR BOYS' COATS, CAPES, JACKETS, SUITS, BLAZERS, TROUSERS, SHORTS, SHIRTS, UNDERWEAR, NIGHTWEAR AND SIMILAR ARTICLES OF TEXTILE FABRICS, KNITTED OR CROCHETED (OTHER THAN THOSE OF HEADING 845.2 OR 845.6)

S.I.T.C. (R3)	Commodity Code No	Trade description
843.10		**Overcoats, car-coats, capes, cloaks, anoraks (incl. ski-jackets), wind-cheaters, wind-jackets and similar articles (other than those of heading 843.2)**
		Of wool or fine animal hair
	610110 10 0	Overcoats, car-coats, capes, cloaks and similar articles
	610110 90 0	Anoraks (including ski-jackets), wind-cheaters, wind-jackets and similar articles
		Of cotton
	610120 10 0	Overcoats, car-coats, capes, cloaks and similar articles
	610120 90 0	Anoraks (including ski-jackets), wind-cheaters, wind-jackets and similar articles
		Of man-made fibres
	610130 10 0	Overcoats, car-coats, capes, cloaks and similar articles
	610130 90 0	Anoraks (including ski-jackets), wind-cheaters, wind-jackets and similar articles
		Of other textile materials
	610190 10 0	Overcoats, car-coats, capes, cloaks and similar articles
	610190 90 0	Anoraks (including ski-jackets), wind-cheaters, wind-jackets and similar articles

Suits, ensembles, jackets, blazers, trousers, bib and brace overalls, breeches and shorts

S.I.T.C. (R3)	Commodity Code No	Trade description
843.21		**Suits**
	610311 00 0	Of wool or fine animal hair
	610312 00 0	Of synthetic fibres
	610319 00 0	Of other textile materials
843.22		**Ensembles**
	610321 00 0	Of wool or fine animal hair
	610322 00 0	Of cotton
	610323 00 0	Of synthetic fibres
	610329 00 0	Of other textile materials

S.I.T.C. (R3)	Commodity Code No	Trade description
843.23		**Jackets and blazers**
	610331 00 0	Of wool or fine animal hair
	610332 00 0	Of cotton
	610333 00 0	Of synthetic fibres
	610339 00 0	Of other textile materials
843.24		**Trousers, bib and brace overalls, breeches and shorts.**
		Of wool or fine animal hair
	610341 10 0	Trousers and breeches
	610341 90 0	Other
		Of cotton
	610342 10 0	Trousers and breeches
	610342 90 0	Other
		Of synthetic fibres
	610343 10 0	Trousers and breeches
	610343 90 0	Other
		Of other textile materials
	610349 10 0	Trousers and breeches
		Other
	610349 91 0	Of artificial fibres
	610349 99 0	Other
		Shirts
843.71	610510 00 0	**Of cotton**
843.79		**Of other textile materials**
		Of man-made fibres
	610520 10 0	Of synthetic fibres
	610520 90 0	Of artificial fibres
		Of other textile materials
	610590 10 0	Of wool or fine animal hair
	610590 90 0	Of other textile materials
		Underpants, briefs, night-shirts, pyjamas, bathrobes, dressing gowns and similar articles
843.81		**Underpants and briefs**
	610711 00 0	Of cotton
	610712 00 0	Of man-made fibres
	610719 00 0	Of other textile materials
843.82		**Night-shirts and pyjamas**
	610721 00 0	Of cotton
	610722 00 0	Of man-made fibres
	610729 00 0	Of other textile materials
843.89		**Other**
		Of cotton
	610791 10 0	Of terry fabrics
	610791 90 0	Other
	610792 00 0	Of man-made fibres
	610799 00 0	Of other textile materials

WOMEN'S OR GIRLS' COATS, CAPES, JACKETS, SUITS, TROUSERS, SHORTS, SHIRTS, DRESSES AND SKIRTS, UNDERWEAR, NIGHTWEAR AND SIMILAR ARTICLES OF TEXTILE FABRICS, KNITTED OR CROCHETED (OTHER THAN THOSE OF HEADING 845.2 OR 845.6)

S.I.T.C. (R3)	Commodity Code No	Trade description
844.10		**Overcoats, car-coats, capes, cloaks, anoraks (incl. ski-jackets), wind-cheaters, wind-jackets and similar articles (other than those of headings 844.2)**
		Of wool or fine animal hair
	610210 10 0	Overcoats, car-coats, capes, cloaks and similar articles
	610210 90 0	Anoraks (including ski-jackets), wind-cheaters, wind-jackets and similar articles
		Of cotton
	610220 10 0	Overcoats, car-coats, capes, cloaks and similar articles
	610220 90 0	Anoraks (including ski-jackets), wind-cheaters, wind-jackets and similar articles
		Of man-made fibres
	610230 10 0	Overcoats, car-coats, capes, cloaks and similar articles
	610230 90 0	Anoraks (including ski-jackets), wind-cheaters, wind-jackets and similar articles
		Of other textile materials
	610290 10 0	Overcoats, car-coats, capes, cloaks and similar articles
	610290 90 0	Anoraks (including ski-jackets), wind-cheaters, wind-jackets and similar articles
		Suits, ensembles, jackets, blazers, dresses, skirts, divided skirts, trousers, bib and brace overalls, breeches and shorts
844.21		**Suits**
	610411 00 0	Of wool or fine animal hair
	610412 00 0	Of cotton
	610413 00 0	Of synthetic fibres
	610419 00 0	Of other textile materials

S.I.T.C. (R3)	Commodity Code No	Trade description
844.22		**Ensembles**
	610421 00 0	Of wool or fine animal hair
	610422 00 0	Of cotton
	610423 00 0	Of synthetic fibres
	610429 00 0	Of other textile materials
844.23		**Jackets and blazers**
	610431 00 0	Of wool or fine animal hair
	610432 00 0	Of cotton
	610433 00 0	Of synthetic fibres
	610439 00 0	Of other textile materials
844.24		**Dresses**
	610441 00 0	Of wool or fine animal hair
	610442 00 0	Of cotton
	610443 00 0	Of synthetic fibres
	610444 00 0	Of artificial fibres
	610449 00 0	Of other textile materials
844.25		**Skirts and divided skirts**
	610451 00 0	Of wool or fine animal hair
	610452 00 0	Of cotton
	610453 00 0	Of synthetic fibres
	610459 00 0	Of other textile materials
844.26		**Trousers, bib and brace overalls, breeches and shorts**
		Of wool or fine animal hair
	610461 10 0	Trousers and breeches
	610461 90 0	Other
		Of cotton
	610462 10 0	Trousers and breeches
	610462 90 0	Other
		Of synthetic fibres
	610463 10 0	Trousers and breeches
	610463 90 0	Other
		Of other textile materials
	610469 10 0	Trousers and breeches
		Other
	610469 91 0	Of artificial fibres
	610469 99 0	Of other textile materials
844.70		**Blouses, shirts and shirt-blouses**
	610610 00 0	Of cotton
	610620 00 0	Of man-made fibres
		Of other textile materials
	610690 10 0	Of wool or fine animal hair
	610690 30 0	Of silk or silk waste
	610690 50 0	Of flax or of ramie
	610690 90 0	Of other textile materials
		Slips, petticoats, briefs, panties, night-dresses, pyjamas, negligees, bathrobes, dressing gowns and similar articles
844.81		**Slips and petticoats**
		Of man-made fibres
	610811 10 0	Of synthetic fibres
	610811 90 0	Of artificial fibres
		Of other textile materials
	610819 10 0	Of cotton
	610819 90 0	Of other textile materials
844.82		**Briefs and panties**
	610821 00 0	Of cotton
	610822 00 0	Of man-made fibres
	610829 00 0	Of other textile materials
844.83		**Night-dresses and pyjamas**
		Of cotton
	610831 10 0	Night-dresses
	610831 90 0	Pyjamas
		Of man-made fibres
		Of synthetic fibres
	610832 11 0	Night-dresses
	610832 19 0	Pyjamas
	610832 90 0	Of artificial fibres
	610839 00 0	Of other textile materials

S.I.T.C. (R3)	Commodity Code No	Trade description
844.89		**Other**
		Of cotton
	610891 10 0	Of terry fabrics
	610891 90 0	Other
	610892 00 0	Of man-made fibres
		Of other textile materials
	610899 10 0	Of wool or fine animal hair
	610899 90 0	Of other textile materials

ARTICLES OF APPAREL, OF TEXTILE FABRICS, WHETHER OR NOT KNITTED OR CROCHETED, N.E.S.

Babies' garments and clothing accessories

S.I.T.C. (R3)	Commodity Code No	Trade description
845.11		**....not knitted or crocheted**
	620910 00 0	Of wool or fine animal hair
	620920 00 0	Of cotton
	620930 00 0	Of synthetic fibres
	620990 00 0	Of other textile materials
845.12		**....knitted or crocheted**
		Of wool or fine animal hair
	611110 10 0	Gloves, mittens and mitts
	611110 90 0	Other
		Of cotton
	611120 10 0	Gloves, mittens and mitts
	611120 90 0	Other
		Of synthetic fibres
	611130 10 0	Gloves, mittens and mitts
	611130 90 0	Other
	611190 00 0	Of other textile materials

Garments made up of fabrics of heading 657.1, 657.2, 657.32, 657.33 or 657.34

S.I.T.C. (R3)	Commodity Code No	Trade description
845.21		**Garments made up of fabrics of heading 657.1 or 657.2**
	621010 10 0	Of fabrics of heading 657.1
		Of fabrics of heading 657.2
	621010 91 0	In sterile packs
	621010 99 0	Other
845.22		**Men's and boy's garments of fabrics not knitted or crocheted of heading 657.32, 657.33, or 657.34**
	621020 00 0	Other garments, of the type described in headings 841.11, 841.12
	621040 00 0	Other men's or boys' garments
845.23		**Women's or girls' garments made up of fabrics not knitted or crocheted of heading 657.32, 657.33, or 657.34**
	621030 00 0	Other garments, of the type described in heading 842.1
	621050 00 0	Other women's or girls' garments
845.24		**Garments made up of knitted or crocheted fabrics of heading 657.32, 657.33 or 657.34**
	611300 10 0	Of knitted or crocheted fabrics of heading 657.33
	611300 90 0	Other
845.30		**Jerseys, pullovers, cardigans, waistcoats and similar articles, knitted or crocheted**
		Of wool or fine animal hair
	*611010 10 0	Jerseys and pullovers, containing at least 50 % by weight of wool and weighing 600 g or more per article
		Other
		Men's or boys'
	*611010 31 0	Of wool
		Of fine animal hair
	611010 35 0	Of Kashmir goats
	611010 38 0	Other
		Women's or girls'
	*611010 91 0	Of wool
		Of fine animal hair
	611010 95 0	Of Kashmir goats
	611010 98 0	Other
		Of cotton
	611020 10 0	Lightweight fine knit roll, polo or turtle neck jumpers and pullovers
		Other
	*611020 91 0	Men's or boys'
	*611020 99 0	Women's or girls'
		Of man-made fibres
	611030 10 0	Lightweight fine knit roll, polo or turtle neck jumpers and pullovers
		Other
	*611030 91 0	Men's or boys'
	*611030 99 0	Women's or girls'
		Of other textile materials

S.I.T.C. (R3)	Commodity Code No	Trade description
cont 845.30	611090 10 0	Of flax or ramie
	611090 90 0	Other
845.40		**T-shirts, singlets and other vests, knitted or crocheted**
	610910 00 0	Of cotton
		Of other textile materials
	610990 10 0	Of wool or fine animal hair
	610990 30 0	Of man-made fibres
	610990 90 0	Other
		Brassieres, girdles, corsets, braces, suspenders, garters and similar articles, whether or not knitted or crocheted
845.51	621210 00 0	**Brassieres**
845.52		**Girdles, corsets, braces, suspenders, garters and similar articles**
	621220 00 0	Girdles and panty-girdles
	621230 00 0	Corselettes
	621290 00 0	Other
		Swimwear
845.61	621111 00 0	**Swimwear, men's and boys', not knitted or crocheted**
845.62		**Swimwear, men's and boys', knitted or crocheted**
		Of synthetic fibres
	611231 10 0	Containing by weight 5 % or more of rubber thread
	611231 90 0	Other
		Of other textile materials
	611239 10 0	Containing by weight 5 % or more of rubber thread
	611239 90 0	Other
845.63	621112 00 0	**Swimwear, women's and girls', not knitted or crocheted**
845.64		**Swimwear, women's and girls', knitted or crocheted**
		Of synthetic fibres
	611241 10 0	Containing by weight 5 % or more of rubber thread
	611241 90 0	Other
		Of other textile materials
	611249 10 0	Containing by weight 5 % or more of rubber thread
	611249 90 0	Other
		Other garments, not knitted or crocheted
845.81	621120 00 0	**Ski suits**
845.87		**Articles of apparel, men's or boys', n.e.s.**
	621131 00 0	Of wool or fine animal hair
		Of cotton
	621132 10 0	Industrial and occupational clothing
		Track suits with lining
	621132 31 0	With an outer shell of a single identical fabric
		Other:
	621132 41 0	Upper parts
	621132 42 0	Lower parts
	621132 90 0	Other
		Of man-made fibres
	621133 10 0	Industrial and occupational clothing
		Track suits with lining:
	621133 31 0	With an outer shell of a single identical fabric
		Other:
	621133 41 0	Upper parts
	621133 42 0	Lower parts
	621133 90 0	Other
	621139 00 0	Of other textile materials
845.89		**Articles of apparel, women's or girls', n.e.s.**
	621141 00 0	Of wool or fine animal hair
		Of cotton
	621142 10 0	Aprons, overalls, smock-overalls and other industrial and occupational clothing (whether or not also suitable for domestic use)
		Track suits with lining:
	621142 31 0	With an outer shell of a single fabric
		Other:
	621142 41 0	Upper parts
	621142 42 0	Lower parts
	621142 90 0	Other

S.I.T.C. (R3)	Commodity Code No	Trade description
cont 845.89		
	621143 10 0	Of man-made fibres Aprons, overalls, smock-overalls and other industrial and occupational clothing (whether or not also suitable for domestic use) Track suits with lining:
	621143 31 0	With an outer shell of a single fabric Other:
	621143 41 0	Upper parts
	621143 42 0	Lower parts
	621143 90 0	Other
	621149 00 0	Of other textile materials

Other garments, knitted or crocheted

845.91		**Track suits**
	611211 00 0	Of cotton
	611212 00 0	Of synthetic fibres
	611219 00 0	Of other textile materials
845.92	611220 00 0	**Ski suits**
845.99		**Garments, knitted or crocheted, n.e.s.**
	611410 00 0	Of wool or fine animal hair
	611420 00 0	Of cotton
	611430 00 0	Of man-made fibres
	611490 00 0	Of other textile materials

CLOTHING ACCESSORIES, OF TEXTILE FABRICS, WHETHER OR NOT KNITTED OR CROCHETED (OTHER THAN THOSE FOR BABIES)

Clothing accessories, not for babies, not knitted or crocheted

846.11		**Handkerchiefs**
	621310 00 0	Of silk or silk waste
	621320 00 0	Of cotton
	621390 00 0	Of other textile materials
846.12		**Shawls, scarves, mufflers, mantillas, veils and the like**
	621410 00 0	Of silk or silk waste
	621420 00 0	Of wool or fine animal hair
	621430 00 0	Of synthetic fibres
	621440 00 0	Of artificial fibres Of other textile materials
	621490 10 0	Of cotton
	621490 90 0	Other
846.13		**Ties, bow ties and cravats**
	621510 00 0	Of silk or silk waste
	621520 00 0	Of man-made fibres
	621590 00 0	Of other textile materials
846.14	621600 00 0	**Gloves, mittens and mitts**
846.19		**Other made-up clothing accessories; parts of garments or of clothing other than those of heading 845.5**
	621710 00 0	Accessories
	621790 00 0	Parts

Panty hose, tights, stockings, socks and other hosiery (including stockings for varicose veins and footwear without applied soles), knitted or crocheted

846.21		**Panty hose and tights**
	611511 00 0	Of synthetic fibres, measuring per single yarn less than 67 decitex
	611512 00 0	Of synthetic fibres, measuring per single yarn 67 decitex or more Of other textile materials
	611519 10 0	Of wool or fine animal hair
	611519 90 0	Other
846.22		**Women's full-length or knee-length hosiery, measuring per single yarn less than 67 decitex** Of synthetic fibres
	611520 11 0	Knee-length stockings
	611520 19 0	Other
	611520 90 0	Of other textile materials
846.29		**Other hosiery**
	611591 00 0	Of wool or fine animal hair
	611592 00 0	Of cotton Of synthetic fibres
	611593 10 0	Stockings for varicose veins

S.I.T.C. (R3)	Commodity Code No	Trade description
cont 846.29	611593 30 0	Knee-length stockings (other than stockings for varicose veins)
		Other
	611593 91 0	Women's stockings
	611593 99 0	Other
	611599 00 0	Of other textile materials

Other made up clothing accessories; parts of garments or of clothing accessories

S.I.T.C. (R3)	Commodity Code No	Trade description
846.91		**Gloves, knitted or crocheted, impregnated, coated or covered with plastics or rubber**
	*611610 20 0	Gloves impregnated, coated or covered with rubber
	*611610 80 0	Other
846.92		**Other gloves, mittens and mitts, knitted or crocheted**
	611691 00 0	Of wool or fine animal hair
	611692 00 0	Of cotton
	611693 00 0	Of synthetic fibres
	611699 00 0	Of other textile materials
846.93	611710 00 0	**Shawls, scarves, mufflers, mantillas, veils and the like**
846.94	611720 00 0	**Ties, bow ties and cravats**
846.99		**Made up clothing accessories, n.e.s.; parts of garments or of clothing accessories**
		Other accessories
	611780 10 0	Knitted or crocheted , elasticated or rubberised
	611780 90 0	Other
	611790 00 0	Parts

ARTICLES OF APPAREL AND CLOTHING ACCESSORIES OF OTHER THAN TEXTILE FABRICS; HEADGEAR OF ALL MATERIALS

Articles of apparel and clothing accessories, of leather or of composition leather (not including gloves, mittens and mitts of heading 894.77)

S.I.T.C. (R3)	Commodity Code No	Trade description
848.11	420310 00 0	**Articles of apparel**
848.12		**Gloves, mittens and mitts, not designed for use in sports**
	420329 10 0	Protective for all trades
		Other
	420329 91 0	Men's and boys'
	420329 99 0	Other
848.13	420330 00 0	**Belts and bandoliers**
848.19	420340 00 0	**Other clothing accessories**

Articles of apparel and clothing accessories (including gloves), for all purposes, of plastics or of vulcanized rubber (other than hard rubber)

S.I.T.C. (R3)	Commodity Code No	Trade description
848.21	392620 00 0	**Articles of apparel and clothing accessories, of plastics**
848.22		**Rubber gloves**
	401511 00 0	Surgical
		Other
	401519 10 0	Household gloves
	401519 90 0	Other
848.29	401590 00 0	**Other articles of apparel and clothing accessories, for all purposes, of vulcanized rubber (other than hard rubber)**

Articles of apparel, clothing accessories (not including headgear) and other articles of furskins; artificial fur and articles thereof

S.I.T.C. (R3)	Commodity Code No	Trade description
848.31		**Articles of furskin**
		Articles of apparel and clothing accessories
	430310 10 0	Of furskins of whitecoat pups of harp seals or of pups of hooded seals (blue-backs)
	430310 90 0	Other
	430390 00 0	Other
848.32	430400 00 0	**Artificial fur and articles thereof**

Headgear and fittings therefor, n.e.s.

S.I.T.C. (R3)	Commodity Code No	Trade description
848.41		**Felt hats and other felt headgear, made from the hat bodies, hoods or plateaux of heading 657.61, whether or not lined or trimmed**
	650300 10 0	Of fur felt or of felt of wool and fur
	650300 90 0	Other

S.I.T.C. (R3)	Commodity Code No	Trade description
848.42	650400 00 0	Hats and other headgear, plaited or made by assembling strips of any material, whether or not lined or trimmed
848.43		Hats and other headgear, knitted or crocheted, or made up from lace, felt or other textile fabric in the piece (but not in strips), whether or not lined or trimmed; hair-nets of any material, whether or not lined or trimmed
	650510 00 0	Hair-nets
		Other
	650590 10 0	Berets, bonnets, skull-caps, fezzes, tarbooshes and the like
	650590 30 0	Peaked caps
	650590 90 0	Other
848.44		Safety headgear, whether or not lined or trimmed
	650610 10 0	Of plastics
	650610 80 0	Of other materials
848.45	650691 00 0	Headgear, n.e.s., of rubber or plastics, whether or not lined or trimmed
848.48	650700 00 0	Head-bands, linings, covers, hat foundations, hat frames, peaks and chinstraps, for headgear
848.49		Headgear, n.e.s., of materials other than rubber or plastics
	650692 00 0	Of furskin
	650699 00 0	Of other materials

DIVISION 85

FOOTWEAR

Footwear incorporating a protective metal toe-cap, not including sports footwear

851.11		Waterproof footwear with outer soles and uppers of rubber or of plastics, the uppers of which are neither fixed to the sole nor assembled by stitching, riveting, nailing, screwing, plugging or similar processes
	640110 10 0	With uppers of rubber
	640110 90 0	With uppers of plastics
851.13		Footwear with outer soles and uppers of rubber or plastics
	*640230 00 0	Incorporating a protective metal toe-cap
851.15	640340 00 0	Footwear with outer soles of rubber, plastics, leather or composition leather and uppers of leather

Sports footwear

851.21		Ski-boots and cross country ski footwear with outer soles and uppers of rubber or plastics
	*640212 10 0	Ski-boots and cross country ski footwear
	*640212 90 0	Snowboard boots
851.22		Ski-boots and cross-country ski footwear with outer soles of rubber, plastics, leather or composition leather and uppers of leather
	*640312 00 0	Ski-boots, cross-country ski footwear and snowboard boots
851.23	640219 00 0	Other sports footwear with outer soles and uppers of rubber or plastics
851.24	640319 00 0	Other sports footwear, with outer soles of rubber, plastics, leather or composition leather and uppers of leather
851.25	640411 00 0	Tennis shoes, basketball shoes, gym shoes, training shoes and the like and other sports footwear with outer soles of rubber or plastics and uppers of textile materials

Footwear, n.e.s, with outer soles and uppers of rubber or plastics

851.31		Other waterproof footwear with outer soles and uppers of rubber or of plastics, the uppers of which are neither fixed to the sole nor assembled by stitching, riveting, nailing, screwing, plugging or similar processes
		Covering the knee
	640191 10 0	With uppers of rubber
	640191 90 0	With uppers of plastics
		Covering the ankle but not covering the knee
	640192 10 0	With uppers of rubber
	640192 90 0	With uppers of plastics
		Other
	640199 10 0	With uppers of rubber
	640199 90 0	With uppers of plastics
851.32		Other footwear with outer soles and uppers of rubber or plastics
	640220 00 0	Footwear with upper straps or thongs assembled to the sole by means of plugs
		Other footwear
	*640291 00 0	Covering the ankle

S.I.T.C. (R3)	Commodity Code No	Trade description
cont 851.32		Other
	640299 10 0	With uppers of rubber
		With uppers of plastics
		Footwear with a vamp made of straps or which has one or more pieces cut out
	640299 31 0	With sole and heel combined having a height of more than 3 cm
	640299 39 0	Other
	640299 50 0	Slippers and other indoor footwear
		Other, with in-soles of a length
	640299 91 0	Of less than 24 cm
		Of 24 cm or more
	640299 93 0	Footwear which cannot be identified as men's or women's footwear
		Other
	640299 96 0	For men
	640299 98 0	For women
		Other footwear with uppers of leather or composition leather
851.41	640320 00 0	**Footwear with outer soles of leather, and uppers which consist of leather straps across the instep and around the big toe**
851.42	640330 00 0	**Footwear made on a base or platform of wood, not having an inner sole or a protective metal toe-cap**
851.48		**Footwear, n.e.s., with outer soles of leather**
		Covering the ankle
		Covering the ankle but no part of the calf, with in-soles of a length
	640351 11 0	Of less than 24 cm
		Of 24 cm or more
	640351 15 0	For men
	640351 19 0	For women
		Other, with in-soles of a length
	640351 91 0	Of less than 24 cm
		Of 24 cm or more
	640351 95 0	For men
	640351 99 0	For women
		Other
		Footwear with a vamp made of straps or which has one or several pieces cut out
	640359 11 0	With sole and heel combined having a height of more than 3 cm
		Other, with in-soles of a length
	640359 31 0	Of less than 24 cm
		Of 24 cm or more
	640359 35 0	For men
	640359 39 0	For women
	640359 50 0	Slippers and other indoor footwear
		Other, with in-soles of a length
	640359 91 0	Of less than 24 cm
		Of 24 cm or more
	640359 95 0	For men
	640359 99 0	For women
851.49		**Footwear with uppers of leather or composition leather, n.e.s.**
		Covering the ankle
		Covering the ankle but no part of the calf, with in-soles of a length
	640391 11 0	Of less than 24 cm
		Of 24 cm or more
	640391 13 0	Footwear which cannot be identified as men's or women's footwear
		Other
	640391 16 0	For men
	640391 18 0	For women
		Other, with in-soles of a length
	640391 91 0	Of less than 24 cm
		Of 24 cm or more
	640391 93 0	Footwear which cannot be identified as men's or women's footwear
		Other
	640391 96 0	For men
	640391 98 0	For women
		Other
		Footwear with a vamp made of straps or which has one or several pieces cut out
	640399 11 0	With sole and heel combined having a height of more than 3 cm
		Other, with in-soles of a length
	640399 31 0	Of less than 24 cm
		Of 24 cm or more
	640399 33 0	Footwear which cannot be identified as men's or women's footwear
		Other
	640399 36 0	For men
	640399 38 0	For women
	640399 50 0	Slippers and other indoor footwear

S.I.T.C. (R3)	Commodity Code No	Trade description
cont 851.49		Other, with in-soles of a length
	640399 91 0	Of less than 24 cm
		Of 24 cm or more
	640399 93 0	Footwear which cannot be identified as men's or women's footwear
		Other
	640399 96 0	For men
	640399 98 0	For women
	640510 10 0	With outer soles of wood or cork
	640510 90 0	With outer soles of other materials

Other footwear, with uppers of textile materials

S.I.T.C. (R3)	Commodity Code No	Trade description
851.51		**Footwear with outer soles of rubber or plastics**
	640419 10 0	Slippers and other indoor footwear
	640419 90 0	Other
851.52		**Footwear with outer soles of leather or composition leather**
	640420 10 0	Slippers and other indoor footwear
	640420 90 0	Other
851.59		**Footwear with uppers of textile materials, n.e.s.**
	640520 10 0	With outer soles of wood or cork
		With outer soles of other materials
	640520 91 0	Slippers and other indoor footwear
	640520 99 0	Other
851.70		**Footwear, n.e.s.**
	640590 10 0	With outer soles of rubber, plastics, leather or composition leather
	640590 90 0	With outer soles of other materials
851.90		**Parts of footwear (including uppers, whether or not attached to soles other than outer soles); removable in-soles, heel cushions and similar articles; gaiters, leggings and similar articles, and parts thereof**
		Uppers and parts thereof, other than stiffeners
		Of leather
	640610 11 0	Uppers
	640610 19 0	Parts of uppers
	640610 90 0	Of other materials
		Outer soles and heels, of rubber or plastics
	640620 10 0	Of rubber
	640620 90 0	Of plastics
		Other
	640691 00 0	Of wood
		Of other materials
	640699 10 0	Gaiters, leggings and similar articles and parts thereof
	640699 30 0	Assemblies of uppers affixed to inner soles or to other sole components, but without outer soles
	640699 50 0	Removable in-soles and other removable accessories
	640699 60 0	Outer soles of leather or composition leather
	640699 80 0	Other

DIVISION 87

PROFESSIONAL, SCIENTIFIC AND CONTROLLING INSTRUMENTS AND APPARATUS, N.E.S.

OPTICAL INSTRUMENTS AND APPARATUS, N.E.S.

Binoculars, monoculars, other optical telescopes, and mountings therefor; other astronomical instruments and mountings therefor (not including instruments for radio-astronomy)

S.I.T.C. (R3)	Commodity Code No	Trade description
871.11	900510 00 0	**Binoculars**
871.15	900580 00 0	**Other instruments**
871.19	900590 00 0	**Parts and accessories (including mountings)**

Microscopes (other than optical microscopes); diffraction apparatus; parts and accessories thereof, n.e.s.

S.I.T.C. (R3)	Commodity Code No	Trade description
871.31	901210 00 0	**Microscopes other than optical microscopes and diffraction apparatus**
871.39	901290 00 0	**Parts and accessories**

Compound optical microscopes (including those for photomicrography, cinephotomicrography or microprojection)

S.I.T.C. (R3)	Commodity Code No	Trade description
871.41	901110 00 0	**Stereoscopic microscopes**

S.I.T.C. (R3)	Commodity Code No	Trade description
871.43	901120 00 0	Other microscopes for photomicrography, cinephotomicrography or microprojection
871.45	901180 00 0	Microscopes, n.e.s.
871.49	901190 00 0	Parts and accessories
		Liquid crystal devices, n.e.s.; lasers (other than laser diodes); other optical appliances and instruments, n.e.s.
871.91	*901310 00 0	Telescopic sights for fitting to arms; periscopes; telescopes designed to form parts of machines, appliances, instruments or apparatus of section 7, division 87, group 881 or 884 or sub- group 899.6
871.92	901320 00 0	Lasers (other than laser diodes)
871.93		Other devices, appliances and instruments
		Liquid crystal devices
		Active matrix liquid crystal devices
	901380 11 0	Colour
	901380 19 0	Black and white or other monochrome
	901380 30 0	Other
	901380 90 0	Other
871.99		Parts and accessories of the articles of sub-group 871.9
	901390 10 0	For liquid crystal devices (LCD)
	901390 90 0	Other
		INSTRUMENTS AND APPLIANCES, N.E.S., FOR MEDICAL, SURGICAL, DENTAL OR VETERINARY PURPOSES
		Dental instruments and appliances, n.e.s.
872.11	901841 00 0	Dental drill engines, whether or not combined on a single base with other dental equipment
872.19		Other dental instruments
	901849 10 0	Burrs, discs, drills and brushes, for use in dental drills
	901849 90 0	Other
		Instruments and appliances used in medical, surgical or veterinary sciences (including sight testing instruments, but excluding electro- diagnostic and radiological instruments and apparatus)
872.21		Syringes, needles, catheters, cannulae and the like
		Syringes, with or without needles
	901831 10 0	Of plastics
	901831 90 0	Other
		Tubular metal needles and needles for sutures
	901832 10 0	Tubular metal needles
	901832 90 0	Needles for sutures
	901839 00 0	Other
872.25		Ophthalmic instruments and appliances, n.e.s.
	901850 10 0	Non-optical
	901850 90 0	Optical
872.29		Other instruments and appliances
	901890 10 0	Instruments and apparatus for measuring blood-pressure
	901890 20 0	Endoscopes
	901890 30 0	Renal dialysis equipment (artificial kidneys, kidney machines and dialysers)
		Diathermic apparatus
	901890 41 0	Ultrasonic
	901890 49 0	Other
	901890 50 0	Transfusion apparatus
	901890 60 0	Anaesthetic apparatus and instruments
	901890 70 0	Ultrasonic lithotripsy instruments
	901890 75 0	Apparatus for nerve stimulation
	901890 85 0	Other
		Mechano-therapy appliances; massage apparatus; psychological aptitude-testing apparatus; ozone therapy, oxygen therapy, aerosol therapy, artificial respiration or other therapeutic respiration apparatus; other breathing appliances and gas masks (excluding protective masks having neither mechanical parts nor replaceable filters)
872.31		Mechano-therapy appliances; massage apparatus; psychological aptitude-testing apparatus
	901910 10 0	Electrical vibratory-massage apparatus
	901910 90 0	Other
872.33	901920 00 0	Ozone therapy, oxygen therapy, aerosol therapy, artificial respiration or other therapeutic respiration apparatus

S.I.T.C. (R3)	Commodity Code No	Trade description
872.35		**Other breathing appliances and gas masks (excluding protective masks having neither mechanical parts nor replaceable filters)**
	902000 10 0	Breathing appliances and gas masks (excluding parts thereof), for use in civil aircraft
	902000 90 0	Other
872.40		**Medical, dental, surgical or veterinary furniture (e.g., operating tables, examination tables, hospital beds with mechanical fittings, dentists' chairs); barbers' chairs and similar chairs with rotating, reclining and elevating movements; parts of the foregoing articles**
	940210 00 0	Dentists', barbers' or similar chairs and parts thereof
	940290 00 0	Other

METERS AND COUNTERS, N.E.S

Gas, liquid or electricity supply or production meters, including calibrating meters therefor

S.I.T.C. (R3)	Commodity Code No	Trade description
873.11	902810 00 0	**Gas meters**
873.13	902820 00 0	**Liquid meters**
873.15		**Electricity meters**
		For alternating current
	902830 11 0	For single-phase
	902830 19 0	For multi-phase
	902830 90 0	Other
873.19		**Parts and accessories of gas, liquid or electricity meters**
	902890 10 0	For electricity meters
	902890 90 0	Other

Revolution counters, production counters, taximeters, mileometers, pedometers and the like; speed indicators and tachometers (other than articles of heading 874.1); stroboscopes

S.I.T.C. (R3)	Commodity Code No	Trade description
873.21		**Revolution counters, production counters, taximeters, mileometers, pedometers and the like**
	902910 10 0	Electric or electronic revolution counters, for use in civil aircraft
	902910 90 0	Other
873.25		**Speed indicators and tachometers; stroboscopes**
		Speed indicators and tachometers
	902920 10 0	For use in civil aircraft
		Other
	902920 31 0	Speed indicators for vehicles
	902920 39 0	Other
	902920 90 0	Stroboscopes
873.29		**Parts and accessories of the articles of sub-group 873.1**
	902990 10 0	Of revolution counters, speed indicators and tachometers, for use in civil aircraft
	902990 90 0	Other

MEASURING, CHECKING, ANALYSING AND CONTROLLING INSTRUMENTS AND APPARATUS, N.E.S.

Compasses; other navigational instruments and appliances; surveying (including photogrammetricaL surveying), hydrographic, oceanographic, hydrological, meteorological or geophysical instruments and appliances; rangefinders

S.I.T.C. (R3)	Commodity Code No	Trade description
874.11		**Direction finding compasses; other navigational instruments and appliances**
		Direction finding compasses
	901410 10 0	For use in civil aircraft
	901410 90 0	Other
		Instruments and appliances for aeronautical or space navigation (other than compasses)
		For use in civil aircraft
	901420 13 0	Inertial navigation systems
	901420 18 0	Other
	901420 90 0	Other
	901480 00 0	Other instruments and appliances
874.12		**Parts and accessories of navigational instruments and appliances**
	901490 10 0	Of instruments of heading 874.11 for use in civil aircraft
	901490 90 0	Other
874.13		**Surveying (including photogrammetrical surveying), hydrographic, oceanographic, hydrological, meteorological or geophysical instruments and appliances(excluding compasses); rangefinders**
		Rangefinders
	901510 10 0	Electronic
	901510 90 0	Other
		Theodolites and tacheometers
	901520 10 0	Electronic
	901520 90 0	Other
		Levels

S.I.T.C. (R3)	Commodity Code No	Trade description

cont
874.13

901530 10 0   Electronic
901530 90 0   Other
     Photogrammetrical, surveying instruments and appliances
901540 10 0   Electronic
901540 90 0   Other
     Other instruments and appliances
       Electronic
901580 11 0   Meteorological, hydrological and geophysical instruments and apparatus
901580 19 0   Other
       Other
901580 91 0   Instruments and appliances used in geodesy, topography, surveying or levelling; hydrographic instruments
901580 93 0   Meteorological, hydrological and geophysical instruments and apparatus
901580 99 0   Other

874.14   901590 00 0   **Parts and accessories for the articles of heading 874.13**

Drawing, marking-out or mathematical calculating instruments (e.g., drafting machines, pantographs, protractors, drawing sets, slide rules, disc calculators); instruments for measuring length, for use in the hand (e.g., measuring rods and tapes, micrometers, callipers), n.e.s.; measuring or checking instruments, appliances and machines, n.e.s.; profile projectors; parts and accessories therefor

874.22   **Drafting tables and machines, whether or not automatic, and other drawing, marking-out or mathematical calculating instruments**
      Drafting tables and machines, whether or not automatic
901710 10 0   Parallelogram and track type drafting machines
901710 90 0   Other
      Other drawing, marking-out or mathematical calculating instruments
       Drawing instruments
901720 11 0   Drawing sets
901720 19 0   Other
       Marking-out instruments
901720 31 0   Pattern generating apparatus of a kind used for producing masks or reticles from photoresist coated substrates
901720 39 0   Other
901720 90 0   Mathematical calculating instruments (including slide rules, disc calculators and the like)

874.23   **Instruments for measuring length, for use in the hand (eg., measuring rods and tapes, micrometers, callipers), n.e.s.**
      Micrometers, callipers and gauges
901730 10 0   Micrometers and callipers
901730 90 0   Other
      Other instruments
901780 10 0   Measuring rods and tapes and divided scales
901780 90 0   Other

874.24   901790 00 0   **Parts and accessories for the articles of headings 874.22 and 874.23**

874.25   **Measuring or checking instruments, appliances and machines, n.e.s.; profile projectors**
903110 00 0   Machines for balancing mechanical parts
903120 00 0   Test benches
903130 00 0   Profile projectors
      Other optical instruments and appliances
*903141 00 0   For inspecting semiconductor wafers or devices or for inspecting photomasks or reticles used in manufacturing semiconductor devices
      Other
*903149 10 0   For measuring surface particulate contamination on semiconductor wafers
*903149 90 0   Other
      Other instruments, appliances and machines
903180 10 0   For use in civil aircraft
      Other
       Electronic
903180 31 0   For measuring or checking geometrical quantities
903180 39 0   Other
       Other
        For measuring or checking geometrical quantities
903180 51 0   Gauges without adjustable devices
903180 59 0   Other
903180 99 0   Other

874.26   **Parts and accessories for the articles of heading 874.25**
903190 10 0   Of instruments, appliances and machines of heading 874.25, for use in civil aircraft
903190 90 0   Other

S.I.T.C. (R3)	Commodity Code No	Trade description

Instruments and apparatus for measuring or checking the flow, level, pressure or other variables of liquids or gases (e.g., flow meters, level gauges, manometers, heat meters), excluding instruments and apparatus of headings 873.1, 874.1 and 874.6; parts and accessories

874.31   **Instruments and apparatus for measuring or checking the flow or level of liquids**
902610 10 0   For use in civil aircraft
       Other
         Electronic
902610 51 0   Flow meters
902610 59 0   Other
         Other
902610 91 0   Flow meters
902610 99 0   Other

874.35   **Instruments and apparatus for measuring or checking pressure**
902620 10 0   For use civil aircraft
       Other
902620 30 0   Electronic
       Other
         Spiral or metal diaphragm type pressure gauges
902620 51 0   Appliances for measuring and non-automatically regulating tyre pressure
902620 59 0   Other
902620 90 0   Other

874.37   **Other instruments and apparatus**
902680 10 0   For use in civil aircraft
       Other
902680 91 0   Electronic
902680 99 0   Other

874.39   **Parts and accessories for the articles of sub-group 874.3**
902690 10 0   For use in civil aircraft
902690 90 0   Other

Instruments and apparatus for physical or chemical analysis (e.g., polarimeters, refractometers, spectrometers, gas or smoke analysis apparatus); instruments and apparatus for measuring or checking viscosity, porosity, expansion, surface tension or the like; instruments and apparatus for measuring or checking quantities of heat, sound or light (including exposure meters); microtomes

874.41   **Gas or smoke analysis apparatus**
902710 10 0   Electronic
902710 90 0   Other

874.42   **Chromatographs and electrophoresis instruments**
902720 10 0   Chromatographs
902720 90 0   Electrophoresis instruments

874.43   902730 00 0   **Spectrometers, spectrophotometers and spectrographs using optical radiations (UV, visible, IR)**

874.44   902740 00 0   **Exposure meters**

874.45   902750 00 0   **Other instruments and apparatus using optical radiations (UV, visible, IR)**

874.46   **Instruments and apparatus for physical or chemical analysis, n.e.s.**
       Electronic
902780 11 0   pH meters, rH meters and other apparatus for measuring conductivity
902780 15 0   Apparatus for performing measurements of the physical properties of semiconductor materials or associated insulating and conducting layers during the semiconductor wafer production process
902780 18 0   Other
       Other
902780 91 0   Viscometers, porosimeters and expansion meters
902780 95 0   Apparatus for performing measurements of the physical properties of semiconductor materials or associated insulating and conducting layers during the semiconductor wafer production process
902780 98 0   Other

874.49   **Microtomes; parts and accessories of the articles of sub-group 874.4**
902790 10 0   Microtomes
902790 90 0   Parts and accessories

Measuring, controlling and scientific instruments, n.e.s.

874.51   **Balances of a sensitivity of 5 cg or better, with or without weights**
901600 10 0   Balances
901600 90 0   Parts and accessories

S.I.T.C. (R3)	Commodity Code No	Trade description
874.52		Instruments, apparatus or models, designed for demonstration purposes (e.g., in education or exhibition), unsuitable for other uses
	902300 10 0	Of a type used for teaching physics, chemistry or technical subjects
	902300 80 0	Other
874.53		Machines and appliances for testing the hardness, strength, compressibility, elasticity or other mechanical properties of materials (e.g., metals, wood, textiles, paper, plastics)
		Machines and appliances for testing metals
	902410 10 0	Electronic
		Other
	902410 91 0	Universal or for tensile tests
	902410 93 0	For hardness tests
	902410 99 0	Other
		Other machines and appliances
	902480 10 0	Electronic
		Other
	902480 91 0	For testing textiles, paper or paperboard
	902480 99 0	Other
874.54	902490 00 0	Parts and accessories for the machines and appliances of heading 874.53
874.55		Hydrometers and similar floating instruments, thermometers, pyrometers, barometers, hygrometers, psychrometers, recording or not, and any combination of these instruments
		Thermometers and pyrometers, not combined with other instruments
		Liquid-filled, for direct reading
	902511 10 0	For use in civil aircraft
		Other
	902511 91 0	Clinical or veterinary thermometers
	902511 99 0	Other
		Other
	902519 10 0	For use in civil aircraft
		Other
	902519 91 0	Electronic
	902519 99 0	Other
		Other instruments
	*902580 15 0	For use in civil aircraft
		Other
	*902580 20 0	Barometers, not combined with other instruments
		Other
	902580 91 0	Electronic
	902580 99 0	Other
874.56		Parts and accessories for the instruments of heading 874.55
	902590 10 0	For use in civil aircraft
	902590 90 0	Other
		Automatic regulating or controlling instruments and apparatus
874.61		**Thermostats**
	903210 10 0	For use in civil aircraft
		Other
	903210 30 0	Electronic
		Other
	903210 91 0	With electrical triggering device
	903210 99 0	Other
874.63		**Pressure regulators and controllers (manostats)**
	903220 10 0	For use in civil aircraft
	903220 90 0	Other
874.65		**Other regulating or controlling instruments and apparatus**
		Hydraulic or pneumatic
	903281 10 0	For use in civil aircraft
	903281 90 0	Other
		Other
	903289 10 0	For use in civil aircraft
	903289 90 0	Other
874.69		**Parts and accessories for automatic regulating or controlling instruments and apparatus**
	903290 10 0	For use in civil aircraft
	903290 90 0	Other
		Oscilloscopes, spectrum analysers and other instruments and apparatus for measuring or checking electrical quantities (other than meters of heading 873.1); instruments and apparatus for measuring or detecting alpha, beta, gamma, x-ray, cosmic or other ionizing radiation

S.I.T.C. (R3)	Commodity Code No	Trade description
874.71		**Instruments and apparatus for measuring or detecting ionizing radiations**
	903010 10 0	For use in civil aircraft
	903010 90 0	Other
874.73		**Cathode-ray oscilloscopes and cathode-ray oscillographs**
	903020 10 0	For use in civil aircraft
	903020 90 0	Other
874.75		**Other instruments and apparatus, for measuring or checking voltage, current, resistance or power, without a recording device**
		Multimeters
	903031 10 0	For use in civil aircraft
	903031 90 0	Other
		Other
	903039 10 0	For use in civil aircraft
		Other
	903039 30 0	Electronic
		Other
	903039 91 0	Voltmeters
	903039 99 0	Other
874.77		**Other instruments and apparatus, specially designed for telecommunications (e.g., cross-talk meters, gain measuring instruments, distortion factor meters, psophometers)**
	903040 10 0	For use in civil aircraft
	903040 90 0	Other
874.78		**Other instruments and apparatus for measuring or checking electrical quantities**
	*903082 00 0	For measuring or checking semiconductor wafers or devices
		Other, with a recording device
	*903083 10 0	For use in civil aircraft
	*900383 90 0	Other
		Other
	*903089 10 0	For use in civil aircraft
		Other
	*903089 92 0	Electronic
	*900389 99 0	Other
874.79		**Parts and accessories for the instruments and apparatus of sub-group 874.7**
	903090 10 0	For use in civil aircraft
	903090 90 0	Other
874.90	903300 00 0	**Parts and accessories for machines, appliances, instruments and apparatus, n.e.s.**

DIVISION 88

PHOTOGRAPHIC APPARATUS, EQUIPMENT AND SUPPLIES AND OPTICAL GOODS, N.E.S.; WATCHES AND CLOCKS

PHOTOGRAPHIC APPARATUS AND EQUIPMENT, N.E.S.

Photographic (other than cinematographic) cameras; photographic flashlight apparatus and flashbulbs (other than discharge lamps of heading 778.2); parts and accessories thereof

S.I.T.C. (R3)	Commodity Code No	Trade description
881.11		**Photographic (other than cinematographic) cameras**
		Cameras of a kind used for preparing printing plates or cylinders
	900610 10 0	Pattern generating apparatus of a kind used for producing masks or reticles from photoresist coated substrates
	900610 90 0	Other
	900620 00 0	Cameras of a kind used for recording documents on microfilm, microfiche or other microforms
	900630 00 0	Cameras specially designed for underwater use, for aerial survey or for medical or surgical examination of internal organs; comparison cameras for forensic or criminological purposes
	900640 00 0	Instant print cameras
		Other cameras
	900651 00 0	With a through-the-lens viewfinder (single lens reflex (SLR), for roll film of a width not exceeding 35 mm
	900652 00 0	Other, for roll film of a width less than 35 mm
		Other, for roll film of a width of 35 mm
	900653 10 0	Disposable cameras
	900653 90 0	Other
	900659 00 0	Other
881.12	900662 00 0	**Flashbulbs, flashcubes and the like**
881.13		**Photographic flashlight apparatus (other than discharge lamps of heading 778.2),**
	900661 00 0	Discharge lamp ("electronic") flashlight apparatus
	900669 00 0	Other
881.14	900691 00 0	**Parts and accessories for the photographic cameras of heading 881**
881.15	900699 00 0	**Parts and accessories**

S.I.T.C. (R3)	Commodity Code No	Trade description
		Cinematographic cameras and projectors, whether or not incorporating sound recording or reproducing apparatus; parts and accessories thereof
881.21		Cinematographic cameras
	900711 00 0	For film of less than 16 mm width or for double-8 mm film
	900719 00 0	Other
881.22	*900720 00 0	Cinematographic projectors
881.23	900791 00 0	Parts and accessories for the cinematographic cameras of heading 821.21
881.24	900792 00 0	Parts and accessories for cinematographic projectors
		Photographic and cinematographic apparatus and equipment, n.e.s.
881.31	900820 00 0	Microfilm, microfiche or other microform readers, whether or not capable of producing copies
881.32		Image projectors, n.e.s
	900810 00 0	Slide projectors
	900830 00 0	Other image projectors
881.33	900840 00 0	Photographic (other than cinematographic) enlargers and reducers
881.34	900890 00 0	Parts and accessories for the equipment of headings 881.31 through 881.33
881.35		Apparatus and equipment for photographic (including cinematographic) laboratories, n.e.s.; negatoscopes; projection screens
	901010 00 0	Apparatus and equipment for automatically developing photographic (including cinematographic) film or paper in rolls or for automatically exposing developed film to rolls of photographic paper
		Other apparatus and equipment for photographic (including cinematographic) laboratories; negatoscopes
		Apparatus for the projection or drawing of circuit patterns on sensitised semiconductor material
	*901041 00 0	Direct write-on-wafer apparatus
	*901042 00 0	Step and repeat aligners
	*901049 00 0	Other
	*901050 00 0	Other apparatus and equipment for photographic (including cinematographic) laboratories; negatscopes
	*901060 00 0	Projection screens
881.36	901090 00 0	Parts and accessories for the apparatus and equipment of heading 881.35
		PHOTOGRAPHIC AND CINEMATOGRAPHIC SUPPLIES
882.10		Chemical preparations for photographic uses (other than varnishes, glues, adhesives and similar preparations); unmixed products for photographic uses, put up in measured portions or put up for retail sale in a form ready for use
	370710 00 0	Sensitising emulsions
		Other
		Developers and fixers
		For colour photography (polychrome)
	370790 11 0	For photographic film and plates
	370790 19 0	Other
	370790 30 0	Other
	370790 90 0	Other
882.20		Photographic plates and film in the flat, sensitised, unexposed, of any material other than paper, paperboard or textiles; instant print film in the flat, sensitised, unexposed, whether or not in packs
		For X-ray
	370110 10 0	For medical, dental or veterinary use
	370110 90 0	Other
	370120 00 0	Instant print film
	*370130 00 0	Other plates and film, with any side exceeding 255 mm
		Other
	370191 00 0	For colour photography (polychrome)
	370199 00 0	Other
882.30		Photographic film in rolls, sensitised, unexposed, of any material other than paper, paperboard or textiles; instant print film in rolls, sensitised, unexposed
	370210 00 0	For X-ray
	370220 00 0	Instant print film
		Other film, without sprocket holes, of a width not exceeding 105 mm
		For colour photography (polychrome)
	370231 10 0	Of a length not exceeding 30 m
	370231 90 0	Of a length exceeding 30 m

S.I.T.C. (R3)	Commodity Code No	Trade description
cont 882.30		Other, with silver halide emulsion
		Of a width not exceeding 35 mm
	370232 11 0	Microfilm; film for the graphic arts
	370232 19 0	Other
		Of a width exceeding 35 mm
	370232 31 0	Microfilm
	370232 51 0	Film for the graphic arts
	370232 90 0	Other
	370239 00 0	Other
		Other film, without sprocket holes, of a width exceeding 105 mm
	370241 00 0	Of a width exceeding 610 mm and of a length exceeding 200 m, for colour photography (polychrome)
	370242 00 0	Of a width exceeding 610 mm and of a length exceeding 200 m, other than for colour photography
	370243 00 0	Of a width exceeding 610 mm and of a length not exceeding 200 m
	370244 00 0	Of a width exceeding 105 mm but not exceeding 610 mm
		Other film, for colour photography (polychrome)
	370251 00 0	Of a width not exceeding 16 mm and of a length not exceeding 14 m
		Of a width not exceeding 16 mm and of a length exceeding 14 m
	370252 10 0	Of a length not exceeding 30 m
	370252 90 0	Of a length exceeding 30 m
	370253 00 0	Of a width exceeding 16 mm but not exceeding 35 mm and of a length not exceeding 30 m, for slides
	370254 00 0	Of a width exceeding 16 mm but not exceeding 35 mm and of a length not exceeding 30 m, other than for slides
	370255 00 0	Of a width exceeding 16 mm but not exceeding 35 mm and of a length exceeding 30 m
		Of a width exceeding 35 mm
	370256 10 0	Of a length not exceeding 30 m
	370256 90 0	Of a length exceeding 30 m
		Other
		Of a width not exceeding 16 mm and of a length not exceeding 14 m
	370291 10 0	Film for the graphic arts
	370291 90 0	Other
		Of a width not exceeding 16 mm and of a length exceeding 14 m
	370292 10 0	Film for the graphic arts
	370292 90 0	Other
		Of a width exceeding 16 mm but not exceeding 35 mm and of a length not exceeding 30 m
	370293 10 0	Microfilm; film for the graphic arts
	370293 90 0	Other
		Of a width exceeding 16 mm but not exceeding 35 mm and of a length exceeding 30 m
	370294 10 0	Microfilm; film for the graphic arts
	370294 90 0	Other
	370295 00 0	Of a width exceeding 35 mm
882.40		**Photographic paper, paperboard and textiles, sensitised, unexposed**
	370310 00 0	In rolls of a width exceeding 610 mm
		Other, for colour photography (polychrome)
	370320 10 0	For photographs obtained from reversal type film
	370320 90 0	Other
		Other
	370390 10 0	Sensitised with silver or platinum salts
	370390 90 0	Other
882.50		**Photographic plates, film, paper, paperboard and textiles, exposed but not developed**
	370400 10 0	Plates and film
	370400 90 0	Other
882.60		**Photographic plates and film, exposed and developed, other than cinematographic film**
	370510 00 0	For offset reproduction
	370520 00 0	Microfilms
		Other
	370590 10 0	For the graphic arts
	370590 90 0	Other

CINEMATOGRAPHIC FILM, EXPOSED AND DEVELOPED, WHETHER OR NOT INCORPORATING SOUNDTRACK OR CONSISTING ONLY OF SOUNDTRACK

S.I.T.C. (R3)	Commodity Code No	Trade description
883.10		....of a width of 35 mm or more
		Consisting only of sound track
	370610 11 0	Negatives; intermediate positives
	370610 19 0	Other positives
		Other
	370610 91 0	Negatives; intermediate positives
	370610 99 0	Other positives
883.90		....other
		Consisting only of sound track
	370690 11 0	Negatives; intermediate positives
	370690 19 0	Other positives
		Other
	370690 31 0	Negatives; intermediate positives

S.I.T.C. (R3)	Commodity Code No	Trade description
cont 883.90		Other positives
	370690 51 0	Newsreels
		Other, of a width of
	370690 91 0	Less than 10 mm
	370690 99 0	10 mm or more

OPTICAL GOODS, N.E.S.

Optical fibres and optical fibre bundles ; optical fibre cables other than those of heading 773.1; sheets and plates of polarising material; lenses (including contact lenses), prisms, mirrors and other optical elements, of any material, unmounted, other than such elements of glass not optically worked

S.I.T.C. (R3)	Commodity Code No	Trade description
884.11	900130 00 0	**Contact lenses**
884.15		**Spectacle lenses of glass**
	900140 20 0	Not for the correction of vision
		For the correction of vision
		Both sides finished
	900140 41 0	Single focal
	900140 49 0	Other
	900140 80 0	Other
884.17		**Spectacle lenses of other materials**
	900150 20 0	Not for the correction of vision
		For the correction of vision
		Both sides finished
	900150 41 0	Single focal
	900150 49 0	Other
	900150 80 0	Other
884.19		**Optical fibres and optical fibre bundles and cables; sheets and plates of polarising material; unmounted optical elements, n.e.s.**
		Optical fibres, optical fibre bundles and cables
	900110 10 0	Image conductor cables
	900110 90 0	Other
	900120 00 0	Sheets and plates of polarising material
		Other
	900190 10 0	For use in civil aircraft
	900190 90 0	Other

Spectacles and spectacle frames

S.I.T.C. (R3)	Commodity Code No	Trade description
884.21		**Frames and mountings for spectacles, goggles or the like**
	900311 00 0	Of plastics
		Of other materials
	900319 10 0	Of precious metal or of rolled precious metal
	900319 30 0	Of base metal
	900319 90 0	Of other materials
884.22	900390 00 0	**Parts for frames and mountings of spectacles, goggles and the like**
884.23		**Spectacles, goggles and the like, corrective, protective or other**
		Sunglasses
	900410 10 0	With lenses optically worked
		Other
	900410 91 0	With lenses of plastics
	900410 99 0	Other
		Other
	900490 10 0	With lenses of plastics
	900490 90 0	Other

Lenses, prisms, mirrors and other optical elements, of any material, mounted, being parts of or fittings for instruments or apparatus, other than such elements of glass not optically worked

S.I.T.C. (R3)	Commodity Code No	Trade description
884.31	900211 00 0	**Objective lenses for cameras, projectors or photographic enlargers or reducers**
884.32	900219 00 0	**Other objective lenses**
884.33	900220 00 0	**Filters**
884.39		**Mounted optical elements, n.e.s.**
	900290 10 0	For use in civil aircraft
		Other
	900290 91 0	For cameras, projectors or photographic enlargers or reducers
	900290 99 0	Other

S.I.T.C. (R3)	Commodity Code No	Trade description
		WATCHES AND CLOCKS
		Wrist watches, pocket watches and other watches (including stop watches), with case wholly or partly of precious metal or metal clad with precious metal
885.31		**Wrist watches, battery or accumulator powered, whether or not incorporating a stop watch facility**
	*910111 00 0	With mechanical display only
	*910112 00 0	With opto-electronic display only
	*910119 00 0	Other
885.32		**Other wrist watches, whether or not incorporating a stop watch facility**
	910121 00 0	With automatic winding
	*910129 00 0	Other
885.39		**Pocket-watches and other watches (not wrist-watches)**
	*910191 00 0	Electrically powered
	*910199 00 0	Other
		Wrist watches, pocket watches and other watches (including stop watches), other than those of heading 885.3
885.41		**Wrist watches, battery or accumulator powered, whether or not incorporating a stop watch facility**
	*910211 00 0	With mechanical display only
	*910212 00 0	With opto-electronic display only
	*910219 00 0	Other
885.42		**Other wrist watches, whether or not incorporating a stop watch facility**
	910221 00 0	With automatic winding
	*910229 00 0	Other
885.49		**Pocket-watches and other watches(not wrist-watches)**
	*910291 00 0	Electrically
	*910299 00 0	Other
		Watch movements, complete and assembled
885.51		**Watch movements, battery or accumulator powered** Electrically operated
	910811 00 0	With mechanical display only or with a device to which a mechanical display can be incorporated
	910812 00 0	With opto-electronic display only
	910819 00 0	Other
885.52		**Watch movements, neither battery nor accumulator powered**
	910820 00 0	With automatic winding
		Other
	910891 00 0	Measuring 33.8 mm or less
	910899 00 0	Other
		Clocks
885.71		**Instrument panel clocks and clocks of a similar type, for vehicles, aircraft, spacecraft or vessels**
	910400 10 0	For use in civil aircraft
	910400 90 0	Other
885.72		**Clocks with watch movements (excluding clocks of heading 885.71), battery or accumulator powered**
	*910310 00 0	Electrically operated
	*910390 00 0	Other
885.73	910390 00 0	**Other clocks with watch movements (excluding clocks of heading 885.71)**
885.74		**Alarm clocks, battery, accumulator or mains powered**
	910511 00 0	Electrically operated
885.75	910519 00 0	**Other alarm clocks**
885.76	910521 00 0	**Wall clocks, battery, accumulator or mains powered**
885.77	*910529 00 0	**Other wall clocks**
885.78		**Other clocks, battery, accumulator or mains powered**
	910591 00 0	Electrically operated
885.79		**Clocks, n.e.s.**
	910599 10 0	Table-top or mantelpiece clocks
	910599 90 0	Other

Time measuring equipment and accessories, n.e.s.; parts and accessories for clocks and watches

S.I.T.C. (R3)	Commodity Code No	Trade description
885.91		**Watch cases and parts of watch cases**
	911110 00 0	Cases of precious metal or of metal clad with precious metal
		Cases of base metal, whether or not gold- or silver-plated
	911120 10 0	Gold- or silver-plated
	911120 90 0	Other
	911180 00 0	Other cases
	911190 00 0	Parts
885.92		**Watch straps, watch bands and watch bracelets, and parts** thereof, of metal
		Of precious metal or of metal clad with precious metal
	911310 10 0	Of precious metal
	911310 90 0	Of metal clad with precious metal
	911320 00 0	Of base metal, whether or not gold- or silver-plated
885.93		**Watch straps, watch bands and watch bracelets and parts thereof, of material other than metal**
	911390 10 0	Of leather or of composition leather
	911390 30 0	Of plastic materials
	911390 90 0	Other
885.94		**Time of day recording apparatus and apparatus for measuring, recording or otherwise indicating intervals of time, with clock or watch movement or with synchronous motor (e.g., time-registers, time recorders)**
	910610 00 0	Time-registers; time recorders
	910620 00 0	Parking meters
		Other
	910690 10 0	Process-timers, stop-clocks and the like
	910690 90 0	Other
885.95	910700 00 0	**Time switches with clock or watch movement or with synchronous motor**
885.96		**Clock movements, complete and assembled**
		Electrically operated
	910911 00 0	Of alarm clocks
		Other
	910919 10 0	Of a width or diameter not exceeding 50 mm, for use in civil aircraft
	910919 90 0	Other
		Other
	910990 10 0	Of a width or diameter not exceeding 50 mm, for use in civil aircraft
	910990 90 0	Other
885.97		**Clock cases and cases of a similar type for other goods of group 885, and parts thereof**
	911210 00 0	Cases of metal
	911280 00 0	Other cases
	911290 00 0	Parts
885.98		**Complete watch or clock movements, unassembled or partly assembled (movement sets); incomplete watch or clock movements, assembled; rough watch or clock movements**
		Of watches
		Complete movements, unassembled or partly assembled (movement sets)
	911011 10 0	With balance-wheel and hairspring
	911011 90 0	Other
	911012 00 0	Incomplete movements, assembled
	911019 00 0	Rough movements
	911090 00 0	Other
885.99		**Clock or watch parts. n.e.s.**
	911410 00 0	Springs, including hair-springs
	911420 00 0	Jewels
	911430 00 0	Dials
	911440 00 0	Plates and bridges
	911490 00 0	Other

DIVISION 89

MISCELLANEOUS MANUFACTURED ARTICLES, N.E.S.

ARMS AND AMMUNITION (FOR NON-MILITARY PURPOSES)

Cartridges and other ammunition and projectiles and parts thereof, including shot and cartridge wads (for non-military purposes)

S.I.T.C. (R3)	Commodity Code No	Trade description
891.21	930610 00 0	Cartridges for riveting or similar tools or for captive-bolt humane killers and parts thereof
891.22	930621 00 0	**Cartridges for shotguns**

S.I.T.C. (R3)	Commodity Code No	Trade description
891.23		**Air gun pellets and parts of cartridges for shotguns**
	930629 40 0	Cases
	930629 70 0	Other
891.24		**Other cartridges and parts thereof (for non-military purposes)**
	930630 91 0	Centrefire cartridges
	930630 93 0	Rimfire cartridges
	930630 98 0	Other
891.29	930690 90 0	**Other articles of heading 891.20 (for non-military purposes)**
		Non-military arms
891.31		**Firearms, n.e.s. and similar devices which operate by the firing of an explosive charge (e.g., sporting shotguns and rifles, muzzle- loading firearms, Very pistols and other devices designed to project only signal flares, pistols and revolvers for firing blank ammunition, captive-bolt humane killers, line-throwing guns)**
	930310 00 0	Muzzle-loading firearms
		Other sporting, hunting or target-shooting shotguns, including combination shot gun-rifles
	930320 30 0	Double-barrelled, smooth bore
	930320 80 0	Other
	930330 00 0	Other sporting, hunting or target-shooting rifles
	930390 00 0	Other
891.39	930400 00 0	**Other arms (e.g., spring, air or gas guns and pistols, truncheons) excluding those of heading 891.13 (for non-military purposes)**
		Parts and accessories of articles of heading 891.3
891.93	930521 00 0	**Shotgun barrels of shotguns of heading 891.31**
891.95		**Other parts of shotguns and rifles of heading 891.31**
	930529 10 0	Rifled barrels
	930529 30 0	Roughly shaped gun stock blocks
	930529 80 0	Other
891.99	930590 90 0	**Parts and accessories, n.e.s., of heading 891.39**
		PRINTED MATTER
		Books, pamphlets, maps and globes, printed (not including advertising material)
892.12	490300 00 0	**Children's picture, drawing or colouring books**
892.13	490591 00 0	**Maps and charts in book form**
892.14		**Maps and hydrographic or similar charts of all kinds (including wall maps, topographical plans and globes),printed, not in book form**
	490510 00 0	Globes
	490599 00 0	Other
892.15	490110 00 0	**Printed books, brochures, leaflets and similar printed matter, in single sheets, whether or not folded**
892.16	490191 00 0	**Dictionaries and encyclopaedias, and serial instalments thereof, not in single sheets**
892.19	*490199 00 0	**Other books, brochures and similar printed matter, not in single sheets**
		Newspapers, journals and periodicals, whether or not illustrated or containing advertising material
892.21	490210 00 0	**....appearing at least four times a week**
892.29		**....other**
	490290 10 0	Appearing once a week
	490290 30 0	Appearing once a month
	490290 90 0	Other
		Postcards, personal greeting message or announcement cards and transfers (decalcomanias), printed by any process
892.41		**Transfers (decalcomanias)**
	490810 00 0	Transfers (decalcomanias), vitrifiable
	490890 00 0	Other
892.42		**Printed or illustrated postcards; printed cards bearing personal greetings, messages or announcements, whether or not illustrated, with or without envelopes or trimmings**
	490900 10 0	Printed or illustrated postcards
	490900 90 0	Other

Printed matter, n.e.s.

892.81		**Paper and paperboard labels of all kinds, whether or not printed**
		Printed
	482110 10 0	Self-adhesive
	482110 90 0	Other
		Other
	482190 10 0	Self-adhesive
	482190 90 0	Other
892.82	490600 00 0	**Plans and drawings for architectural, engineering, industrial, commercial, topographical or similar purposes, being originals by hand; hand-written texts; carbon copies and photographic reproductions on sensitised paper of the foregoing**
892.83		**Unused postage, revenue or similar stamps of current or new issue in the country to which they are destined; stamp impressed paper; banknotes; cheque forms; stock, share or bond certificates and similar documents of title**
	490700 10 0	Postage, revenue and similar stamps
	*490700 30 0	Banknotes
		Other
	490700 91 0	Signed and numbered
	490700 99 0	Other
892.84	491000 00 0	**Calendars of any kind, printed (including calendar blocks)**
892.85	490400 00 0	**Music, printed or in manuscript, whether or not bound or illustrated**
892.86		**Trade advertising material, commercial catalogues and the like**
	491110 10 0	Commercial catalogues
	491110 90 0	Other
892.87		**Pictures, designs and photographs**
	491191 80 0	Other
892.89		**Printed matter, n.e.s.**
	491191 10 0	Sheets (not being trade advertising material), not folded, merely with illustrations or pictures not bearing a text or caption, for editions of books or periodicals which are published in different countries in one or more languages
	491199 00 0	Other

ARTICLES, N.E.S. OF PLASTICS

Articles for the conveyance or packing of goods, of plastics; stoppers, lids, caps and other closures, of plastics.

893.11		**Sacks and bags (including cones)**
	392321 00 0	Of polymers of ethylene
		Of other plastics
	392329 10 0	Of polyvinyl chloride
	392329 90 0	Other
893.19		**Articles for the conveyance or packing of goods, n.e.s., of plastics; stoppers, lids, caps and other closures, of plastics**
	392310 00 0	Boxes, cases, crates and similar articles
		Carboys, bottles, flasks and similar articles
	392330 10 0	Of a capacity not exceeding two litres
	392330 90 0	Of a capacity exceeding two litres
		Spools, cops, bobbins and similar supports
	392340 10 0	Spools, reels and similar supports for photographic and cinematographic film or for tapes, films and the like falling within headings 898.4-7
	392340 90 0	Other
		Stoppers, lids, caps and other closure
	392350 10 0	Caps and capsules for bottles
	392350 90 0	Other
		Other
	392390 10 0	Netting extruded in tubular form
	392390 90 0	Other

Builders' ware of plastics

893.21		**Baths, shower-baths, wash-basins, bidets, lavatory pans, seats and covers, flushing cisterns and similar sanitary ware**
	392210 00 0	Baths, shower-baths and wash-basins
	392220 00 0	Lavatory seats and covers
	392290 00 0	Other
893.29		**Other builders' ware**
	392510 00 0	Reservoirs, tanks, vats and similar containers, of a capacity exceeding 300 litres

S.I.T.C. (R3)	Commodity Code No	Trade description
cont 893.29	392520 00 0	Doors, windows and their frames and thresholds for doors
	392530 00 0	Shutters, blinds (including Venetian blinds) and similar articles and parts thereof
		Other
	392590 10 0	Fittings and mountings intended for permanent installation in or on doors, windows, staircases, walls or other parts of buildings
	392590 20 0	Trunking, ducting and cable trays for electrical circuits
	392590 80 0	Other

Floor coverings, wall or ceiling coverings and household and toilet articles of plastics

S.I.T.C. (R3)	Commodity Code No	Trade description
893.31		Floor coverings of plastics, whether or not self-adhesive, in rolls or in the form of tiles; wall or ceiling coverings of plastics
		Of polymers of vinyl chloride
	*391810 10 0	Consisting of a support impregnated, coated or covered with polyvinyl chloride
	*391810 90 0	Other
	391890 00 0	Of other plastics
893.32		Tableware, kitchenware, other household articles and toilet articles
	392410 00 0	Tableware and kitchenware
		Other
		Of regenerated cellulose
	392490 11 0	Sponges
	392490 19 0	Other
	392490 90 0	Other

Articles of plastics, n.e.s.

S.I.T.C. (R3)	Commodity Code No	Trade description
893.94	392610 00 0	Office or school supplies
893.95	392630 00 0	Fittings for furniture, coachwork or the like
893.99		Other articles of plastics
	392640 00 0	Statuettes and other ornamental articles
		Other
	392690 10 0	For technical uses, for use in civil aircraft
		Other
	392690 50 0	Perforated buckets and similar articles used to filter water at the entrance to drains
		Other
	392690 91 0	Made from sheet
	392690 99 0	Other

BABY CARRIAGES; TOYS, GAMES AND SPORTING GOODS

S.I.T.C. (R3)	Commodity Code No	Trade description
894.10		Baby carriages, and parts thereof, n.e.s.
	871500 10 0	Baby carriages
	871500 90 0	Parts

Children's toys

S.I.T.C. (R3)	Commodity Code No	Trade description
894.21		Wheeled toys designed to be ridden by children (e.g., tricycles, scooters and pedal cars, but excluding bicycles); dolls' carriages
	950100 10 0	Dolls' carriages
	950100 90 0	Other
894.22		Dolls representing only human beings, whether or not dressed
	950210 10 0	Of plastics
	950210 90 0	Of other materials
894.23		Parts and accessories of dolls representing only human beings
	950291 00 0	Garments and accessories therefor, footwear and headgear
	950299 00 0	Other
894.24		Construction sets and constructional toys
		Electric trains, including tracks, signals and other accessories therefor:
	950310 10 0	Reduced size ("scale") models
	950310 90 0	Other
		Reduced-size ("scale") model assembly kits, whether or not working models, excluding those of subheading No. 9503.10
	950320 10 0	Of plastics
	950320 90 0	Of other materials
		Other construction sets and constructional toys
	950330 10 0	Of wood
	950330 30 0	Of plastics
	950330 90 0	Of other materials
894.25		Toys representing animals or non-human creatures
	950341 00 0	Stuffed
		Other

S.I.T.C. (R3)	Commodity Code No	Trade description
cont 894.25	950349 10 0	Of wood
	950349 30 0	Of plastics
	950349 90 0	Of other materials
894.26	950350 00 0	**Toy musical instruments and apparatus**
894.27		**Puzzles**
	950360 10 0	Of wood
	950360 90 0	Other
894.29		**Toys, n.e.s.**
	950370 00 0	Other toys, put up in sets or outfits
		Other toys and models, incorporating a motor
	950380 10 0	Of plastics
	950380 90 0	Of other materials
		Other
	950390 10 0	Toy weapons
		Other
		Of plastics
	950390 32 0	Not mechanically operated
	950390 34 0	Other
	950390 35 0	Of rubber
	950390 37 0	Of textile materials
		Of metal
	950390 51 0	Die-cast miniature models
	950390 55 0	Other
	950390 99 0	Of other materials

Articles for funfair, table or parlour games (including pintables, billiards and special tables for casino games and automatic bowling alley equipment)

S.I.T.C. (R3)	Commodity Code No	Trade description
894.31	950410 00 0	**Video games of a kind used with a television receiver**
894.33		**Articles and accessories for billiards**
	950420 10 0	Billiard tables (with or without legs)
	950420 90 0	Other
894.35		**Other games, coin- or disc-operated (not bowling alley equipment)**
	950430 10 0	Games with screen
		Other games
	950430 30 0	Flippers
	950430 50 0	Other
	950430 90 0	Parts
894.37	950440 00 0	**Playing cards**
894.39		**Articles for funfair, table and parlour games, n.e.s**
	950490 10 0	Electric car racing sets, having the character of competitive games
	940360 90 0	Other

Festive, carnival or other entertainment articles (e.g., conjuring tricks and novelty jokes), including Christmas tree decorations and similar articles for Christmas festivities(e.g., artificial Christmas trees, Christmas stockings, imitation yule logs, Nativity scenes and figures thereof

S.I.T.C. (R3)	Commodity Code No	Trade description
894.41	940530 00 0	**Lighting sets of a kind used for Christmas trees**
894.45		**Other articles for Christmas festivities**
	950510 10 0	Of glass
	950510 90 0	Of other materials
894.49	950590 00 0	**Other entertainment articles**
894.60	950800 00 0	**Roundabouts, swings, shooting galleries and other fairground amusements, travelling circuses, travelling menageries and travelling theatres**

Sports goods

S.I.T.C. (R3)	Commodity Code No	Trade description
894.71		**Fishing rods, fish-hooks and other line tackle; fish landing nets, butterfly nets and similar nets; decoy 'birds' (other than those of heading 896.5 or 898.29) and similar hunting or shooting requisites, n.e.s.**
	950710 00 0	Fishing rods
		Fish-hooks, whether or not snelled
	950720 10 0	Fish-hooks, not snelled
	950720 90 0	Other
	950730 00 0	Fishing reels
	950790 00 0	Other

S.I.T.C. (R3)	Commodity Code No	Trade description
894.72		**Ice skates and roller skates (including skating boots with skates attached)**
	950670 10 0	Ice skates
	950670 30 0	Roller skates
	950670 90 0	Parts and accessories
894.73		**Snow-skis and other snow-ski equipment**
		Skis
	950611 10 0	Cross-country skis
	950611 90 0	Other skis
	950612 00 0	Ski-fastenings (ski-bindings)
	950619 00 0	Other
894.74		**Water-skis, surf-boards, sailboards and other water sport equipment**
	950621 00 0	Sailboards
	950629 00 0	Other
894.75		**Golf equipment**
	950631 00 0	Clubs, complete
	950632 00 0	Balls
		Other
	950639 10 0	Parts of golf clubs
	950639 90 0	Other
894.76		**Tennis, badminton or similar rackets, whether or not strung**
	950651 00 0	Lawn-tennis rackets, whether or not strung
	950659 00 0	Other
894.77	420321 00 0	**Gloves, mittens and mitts, specially designed for use in sports**
894.78	*950691 00 0	**Articles and equipment for general physical exercise, gymnastics or athletics**
894.79		**Sports goods, n.e.s.**
		Articles and equipment for table-tennis
	950640 10 0	Bats, balls and nets
	950640 90 0	Other
		Balls, other than golf balls and table-tennis balls
	950661 00 0	Lawn-tennis balls
		Inflatable
	950662 10 0	Of leather
	950662 90 0	Other
		Other
	950669 10 0	Cricket and polo balls
	950669 90 0	Other
		Other
	950699 10 0	Cricket and polo equipment, other than balls
	950699 90 0	Other

OFFICE AND STATIONERY SUPPLIES, N.E.S.

Office and stationery supplies, of base metal

S.I.T.C. (R3)	Commodity Code No	Trade description
895.11	830400 00 0	**Filing cabinets, card-index cabinets, paper trays, paper rests, pen trays, office-stamp stands and similar office or desk equipment, of base metal (other than office furniture of group 821)**
895.12		**Fittings for loose-leaf binders or files, letter clips, letter corners, paper clips, indexing tags and similar office articles, of base metal; staples in strips (e.g., for offices, upholstery, packaging), of base metal**
	830510 00 0	Fittings for loose-leaf binders or files
	830520 00 0	Staples in strips
	830590 00 0	Other, including parts

Pens, pencils and fountain pens

S.I.T.C. (R3)	Commodity Code No	Trade description
895.21		**Ball point pens; felt tipped or other porous-tipped pens and markers; fountain pens, stylograph pens and other pens; duplicating stylos; propelling or sliding pencils; pen-holders, pencil-holders and similar holders; parts (including caps and clips) of the foregoing articles (not including goods of heading 895.22 or 895.23)**
		Ball point pens
	960810 10 0	With liquid ink (rolling ball pens)
		Other
	960810 30 0	With body or cap of precious metal or rolled precious metal
		Other
	960810 91 0	With replaceable refill
	960810 99 0	Other
	960820 00 0	Felt tipped and other porous-tipped pens and markers
		Fountain pens, stylograph pens and other pens
	960831 00 0	Indian ink drawing pens
		Other

S.I.T.C. (R3)	Commodity Code No	Trade description
cont		
895.21	960839 10 0	With body or cap of precious metal or rolled precious metal
	960839 90 0	Other
	960840 00 0	Propelling or sliding pencils
	960850 00 0	Sets of articles from two or more of the foregoing subheadings
		Refills for ball point pens, comprising the ball point and ink-reservoir
	960860 10 0	With liquid ink (for rolling ball pens)
	960860 90 0	Other
		Other
	960899 10 0	Pen-holders, pencil-holders and similar holders
		Other
	960899 30 0	Refills for felt tipped and fibre tipped pens and pencils
		Other
	960899 91 0	Of metal
	960899 99 0	Other
895.22	960891 00 0	**Pen nibs and nib points**
895.23		**Pencils (other than pencils of heading 895.21), crayons, pencil leads, pastels, drawing charcoals, writing or drawing chalks and tailors' chalks**
		Pencils and crayons, with leads encased in a rigid sheath
	960910 10 0	With "leads" of graphite
	960910 90 0	Other
	960920 00 0	Pencil leads, black or coloured
		Other
	960990 10 0	Pastels and drawing charcoals
	960990 90 0	Other
		Other office and stationery supplies
895.91		**Writing or drawing ink and other inks (except printing ink), whether or not concentrated or solid**
	321590 10 0	Writing or drawing ink
	321590 80 0	Other
895.92	961000 00 0	**Slates and boards, with writing or drawing surfaces, whether or not framed**
895.93	961100 00 0	**Date, sealing or numbering stamps, and the like (including devices for printing or embossing labels) designed for operating in the hand; hand-operated composing sticks and hand printing sets incorporating such composing sticks**
895.94		**Typewriter or similar ribbons, inked or otherwise prepared for giving impressions, whether or not on spools or in cartridges; ink pads, whether or not inked, with or without boxes**
		Ribbons
	961210 10 0	Of plastics
	961210 20 0	Of man-made fibres, measuring less than 30 mm in width, permanently put in plastic or metal cartridges of a kind used in automatic typewriters, automatic data-processing equipment and other machines
	961210 80 0	Other
	961220 00 0	Ink-pads
		WORKS OF ART, COLLECTORS' PIECES AND ANTIQUES
		Paintings, drawings and pastels, executed entirely by hand, other than drawings of heading 892.82 and other than hand-painted or hand- decorated manufactured articles; collages and similar decorative plaques
896.11	*970110 00 0	**Paintings, drawings and pastels**
896.12	970190 00 0	**Collages and similar decorative plaques**
896.20	970200 00 0	**Original engravings, prints and lithographs**
896.30	970300 00 0	**Original sculptures and statuary, in any material**
896.40	970400 00 0	**Postage or revenue stamps, stamp-postmarks, first-day covers, postal stationery (stamped paper) and the like, used, or if unused not of current or new issue in the country to which they are destined**
896.50	970500 00 0	**Collections and collectors' pieces of zoological, botanical, mineralogical, anatomical, historical, archaeological, palaeontological, ethnographic or numismatic interest**
896.60	970600 00 0	**Antiques of an age exceeding 100 years**

JEWELLERY, GOLDSMITHS' AND SILVERSMITHS' WARES, AND OTHER ARTICLES OF PRECIOUS OR SEMI-PRECIOUS MATERIALS, N.E.S.

Imitation jewellery

S.I.T.C. (R3)	Commodity Code No	Trade description
897.21		....of base metal, whether or not plated with precious metal
	711711 00 0	Cuff-links and studs
		Other
	711719 10 0	With parts of glass
		Without parts of glass
	711719 91 0	Gilt, silvered or platinum plated
	711719 99 0	Other
897.29	711790 00 0	....of other non-precious materials

Jewellery of gold, silver or platinum group metals (except watches and watch cases) and goldsmiths' or silversmiths' wares (including set gems)

S.I.T.C. (R3)	Commodity Code No	Trade description
897.31		Articles of jewellery and parts thereof, of precious metals or metals clad with precious metals (except watches and watch cases)
	711311 00 0	Of silver, whether or not plated or clad with other precious metal
	*711319 00 0	Of other precious metal, whether or not plated or clad with precious metal
	711320 00 0	Of base metal clad with precious metal
897.32		Articles of goldsmiths' or silversmiths' wares and parts thereof, of precious metals or of metals clad with precious metals (other than goods of heading 897.31)
		Of precious metal whether or not plated or clad with precious metal
	711411 00 0	Of silver, whether or not plated or clad with other precious metal
	711419 00 0	Of other precious metal, whether or not plated or clad with precious metal
	711420 00 0	Of base metal clad with precious metal
897.33		Articles of natural or cultured pearls, precious or semi-precious stones (natural, synthetic or reconstructed)
	711610 00 0	Of natural or cultured pearls
		Of precious or semi-precious stones (natural, synthetic or reconstructed)
		Made wholly of natural precious or semi-precious stones
	711620 11 0	Necklaces, bracelets and other articles of natural precious or semi-precious stones, simply strung without fasteners or other accessories
	711620 19 0	Other
	711620 90 0	Other

Other articles of precious metal or of metal clad with precious metal

S.I.T.C. (R3)	Commodity Code No	Trade description
897.41	711510 00 0	**Catalysts in the form of wire cloth or grill, of platinum or of other metals of the platinum group**
897.49		**Articles of precious metal or of metal clad with precious metal, n.e.s.**
	711590 10 0	Of precious metal
	711590 90 0	Of metal clad with precious metal

MUSICAL INSTRUMENTS AND PARTS AND ACCESSORIES THEREOF; RECORDS, TAPES AND OTHER SOUND OR SIMILAR RECORDINGS (EXCLUDING GOODS OF GROUPS 763 AND 883)

Pianos and other string musical instruments

S.I.T.C. (R3)	Commodity Code No	Trade description
898.13		**Pianos (including automatic pianos); harpsichords and other keyboard stringed instruments**
		Upright pianos
	920110 10 0	New
	920110 90 0	Used
	920120 00 0	Grand pianos
	920190 00 0	Other
898.15		**Other string musical instruments (e.g., guitars, violins, harps)**
		Played with a bow
	920210 10 0	Violins
	920210 90 0	Other
		Other
	920290 10 0	Harps
	920290 30 0	Guitars
	920290 90 0	Other

Musical instruments (other than pianos and other string musical instruments)

S.I.T.C. (R3)	Commodity Code No	Trade description
898.21		**Keyboard pipe organs; harmoniums and similar keyboard instruments with free metal reeds**
	920300 10 0	Keyboard pipe organs
	920300 90 0	Other

S.I.T.C. (R3)	Commodity Code No	Trade description
898.22		**Accordions and similar instruments; mouth organs**
		Accordions and similar instruments
	920410 10 0	With less than 80 basses
	920410 90 0	With 80 basses or more
	920420 00 0	Mouth organs
898.23		**Other wind musical instruments (e.g., clarinets, trumpets, bagpipes)**
	920510 00 0	Brass-wind instruments
	920590 00 0	Other
898.24	920600 00 0	**Percussion musical instruments (e.g., drums, xylophones, cymbals, castanets, maracas)**
898.25		**Keyboard instruments (other than accordions), the sound of which is produced or must be amplified electrically (eg., organs)**
	920710 10 0	Organs
	920710 30 0	Digital-pianos
	920710 50 0	Synthesizers
	920710 80 0	Other
898.26		**Musical instruments, n.e.s., the sound of which is produced or must be amplified electrically (e.g., guitars, accordions)**
	920790 10 0	Guitars
	920790 90 0	Other
898.29		**Musical boxes, fairground organs, mechanical street organs, mechanical singing birds, musical saws and other musical instruments, n.e.s.; decoy calls of all kinds; whistles, call horns and other mouth-blown sound signalling instruments**
	920810 00 0	Musical boxes
	920890 00 0	Other
		Magnetic tapes for sound recording or similar recording of other phenomena
898.41	*852311 00 0	**..Of a width not exceeding 4 mm**
898.43	852312 00 0	**..Of a width exceeding 4 mm but not exceeding 6.5 mm**
898.45	*852313 00 0	**..Of a width exceeding 6.5 mm**
		Other prepared unrecorded media for sound recording or similar recording of other phenomena (excluding products of group 883)
898.51		**Magnetic discs**
		Rigid
	853220 11 0	With a thin film metallic coating, having a coercivity exceeding 600 Oersted and an external diameter not exceeding 231 mm
	853220 19 0	Other
	852320 90 0	Other
898.59	852390 00 0	**Prepared unrecorded media, n.e.s.**
		Magnetic tapes, recorded
		Magnetic tapes for reproducing phenomena other than sound or image:
	*852440 10 0	Bearing data or instructions of a kind used in automatic data processing machines
	*852440 91 0	Other
	*852440 99 0	Of a width exceeding 4 mm but not exceeding 6.5 mm
		Other magnetic tapes:
	*852451 00 0	Of a width not exceeding 4 mm
	*852452 00 0	Of a width exceeding 4 mm but not exceeding 6.5 mm
	*852453 00 0	Of a width exceeding 6.5 mm
		Records and other recorded media (excluding magnetic tapes) for sound or other similarly recorded phenomena (including matrices and masters for the production of records, but excluding products of group 883)
898.71	*852410 00 0	**Gramophone records**
898.79		**Recorded media, n.e.s.**
		Discs for laser reading systems
	*852431 00 0	For reproducing phenomena other than sound or image
	*852432 00 0	For reproducing sound only
	*852439 00 0	Other
		Other:
		For reproducing phenomena other than sound or image
	*852491 10 0	Bearing data or instructions of a kind used in automatic data processing machines
	*852491 90 0	Other
	*852491 99 0	Other

S.I.T.C. (R3)	Commodity Code No	Trade description
898.90		**Parts and accessories of musical instruments (e.g., mechanisms for musical boxes , perforated cards, discs and rolls for mechanical instruments); metronomes, tuning forks and pitch pipes of all kinds.**
	920910 00 0	Metronomes, tuning forks and pitch pipes
	920920 00 0	Mechanisms for musical boxes
	920930 00 0	Musical instrument strings
		Other
	920991 00 0	Parts and accessories for pianos
	920992 00 0	Parts and accessories for the musical instruments of heading 898.15
	920993 00 0	Parts and accessories for the musical instruments of heading 898.21
	920994 00 0	Parts and accessories for the musical instruments of heading 898.25 & 26
		Other
	920999 10 0	Parts and accessories for the musical instruments of heading 898.22
	920999 30 0	Parts and accessories for the musical instruments of heading 898.23
	920999 80 0	Other

MISCELLANEOUS MANUFACTURED ARTICLES, N.E.S.

Articles and manufactures of carving or moulding materials, n.e.s.

S.I.T.C. (R3)	Commodity Code No	Trade description
899.11		**Worked ivory, bone, tortoise-shell, horn, coral, mother of pearl and other animal carving material, and articles of these materials, (including articles obtained by moulding)**
	960110 00 0	Worked ivory and articles of ivory
		Other
	960190 10 0	Worked coral (natural or agglomerated), and articles of coral
	960190 90 0	Other
899.19	960200 00 0	**Worked vegetable or mineral carving material and articles of these materials; moulded or carved articles gums or natural resins or of modelling pastes, and other moulded or carved articles, n.e.s.; worked, unhardened gelatin (except gelatin of heading 592.24) and articles of unhardened gelatin**

Artificial flowers, foliage or fruit and parts thereof; articles made of artificial flowers, foliage or fruit

S.I.T.C. (R3)	Commodity Code No	Trade description
899.21	670210 00 0	**....of plastics**
899.29	670290 00 0	**....of materials other than plastics**

Candles; matches, pyrophoric alloys, articles of combustible materials; smokers' requisites

S.I.T.C. (R3)	Commodity Code No	Trade description
899.31		**Candles, tapers and the like**
		Candles
	340600 11 0	Plain, not perfumed
	340600 19 0	Other
	340600 90 0	Other
899.32	360500 00 0	**Matches, other than pyrotechnic articles of heading 593.3**
899.33		**Cigarette lighters and other lighters, whether or not mechanical or electrical**
	961310 00 0	Pocket lighters, gas fuelled, non-refillable
		Pocket lighters, gas fuelled, refillable
	961320 10 0	With electrical ignition system
	961320 90 0	With other ignition system
	961330 00 0	Table lighters
	961380 00 0	Other lighters
899.34	360610 00 0	**Liquid or liquefied-gas fuels in containers of a kind used for filling or refilling cigarette or similar lighters, of a capacity not exceeding 300 cm^3**
899.35	961390 00 0	**Parts of lighters, n.e.s., other than flints and wicks**
899.36	*961420 20 0	**Roughly shaped blocks of wood or root, for the manufacture of pipes**
899.37		**Smoking pipes (including pipe bowls) and cigar or cigarette holders, and parts thereof, not including articles of heading 899.36**
		Pipes and pipe bowls
	*961420 80 0	Other
	961490 00 0	Other
899.39		**Ferro-cerium and other pyrophoric alloys in all forms; metaldehyde, hexamethylenetetramine and similar substances, put up in forms for use as fuels; fuels with a basis of alcohol, and similar prepared fuels, in solid or semi-solid form; resin torches, firelighters and the like**
	360690 10 0	Ferro-cerium and other pyrophoric alloys in all forms
	360690 90 0	Other

Umbrellas, parasols, walking-sticks and similar articles and parts thereof

S.I.T.C. (R3)	Commodity Code No	Trade description
899.41		**Umbrellas and sun umbrellas (including walking-stick umbrellas, garden umbrellas and similar umbrellas)**
	660110 00 0	Garden or similar umbrellas
		Other
	660191 00 0	Having a telescopic shaft
		Other
		With a cover of textile material
	660199 11 0	Of man-made fibres
	660199 19 0	Of other textile materials
	660199 90 0	Other
899.42	660200 00 0	**Walking sticks, seat sticks, whips, riding-crops and the like**
899.49		**Parts, trimmings and accessories of articles falling within heading 899.41 or 899.42**
	660310 00 0	Handles and knobs
	660320 00 0	Umbrella frames, including frames mounted on shafts (sticks)
	660390 00 0	Other
		Orthopaedic appliances (including crutches, surgical belts and trusses); splints and other fracture appliances; artificial parts of the body; hearing aids and other appliances which are worn or carried or implanted in the body, to compensate for a defect or disability
899.61	902140 00 0	**Hearing aids (excluding parts and accessories)**
899.63		**Orthopaedic or fracture appliances**
		Artificial joints and other orthopaedic or fracture appliances
	902111 00 0	Artificial joints
		Other
	902119 10 0	Orthopaedic appliances
	902119 90 0	Splints and other fracture appliances
899.65		**Artificial teeth and dental fittings**
		Artificial teeth
	902121 10 0	Of plastics
	902121 90 0	Of other materials
		Other
	902129 10 0	Of precious metals or rolled precious metals
	902129 90 0	Other
899.66		**Other artificial parts of the body**
	902130 10 0	Artificial eyes
	902130 90 0	Other
899.67	902150 00 0	**Pacemakers for stimulating heart muscles (excluding parts and accessories)**
899.69		**Appliances, n.e.s., which are worn or carried, or implanted in the body, to compensate for a defect or a disability**
	902190 10 0	Parts and accessories of hearing aids
	902190 90 0	Other
		Basketware, wickerwork and other articles of plaiting materials, n.e.s., brooms, brushes, paint rollers, squeegees and mops
899.71		**Basketware, wickerwork and other articles made directly to shape from plaiting materials or made up from goods 899.74 or 899.79; articles of loofah**
		Of vegetable materials
	460210 10 0	Straw envelopes for bottles
		Other
	460210 91 0	Basketwork, wickerwork and other articles, made directly to shape from plaiting materials
	460210 99 0	Other
		Other
	460290 10 0	Basketwork, wickerwork and other articles, made directly to shape from plaiting materials
	460290 90 0	Other
899.72		**Brooms, brushes (including brushes constituting parts of machines, appliances or vehicles), hand-operated mechanical floor sweepers, not motorized, mops and feather dusters; prepared knots and tufts for broom or brush making; paint pads and rollers; squeegees (other than roller squeegees)**
	960310 00 0	Brooms and brushes, consisting of twigs or other vegetable materials bound together, with or without handles
		Tooth brushes, shaving brushes, hair brushes, nail brushes, eyelash brushes and other toilet brushes for use on the person, including such brushes constituting parts of appliances
	960321 00 0	Tooth brushes, including dental-plate brushes
		Other
	960329 10 0	Shaving brushes
	960329 30 0	Hair brushes
	960329 90 0	Other
		Artists' brushes, writing brushes and similar brushes for the application of cosmetics
	960330 10 0	Artists' and writing brushes

S.I.T.C. (R3)	Commodity Code No	Trade description
cont 899.72	960330 90 0	Brushes for the application of cosmetics
		Paint, distemper, varnish or similar brushes (other than brushes of subheading No. 9603.30); paint pads and rollers
	960340 10 0	Paint, distemper, varnish or similar brushes
	960340 90 0	Paint pads and rollers
	960350 00 0	Other brushes constituting parts of machines, appliances or vehicles
		Other
	960390 10 0	Hand-operated mechanical floor sweepers, not motorised
		Other
	960390 91 0	Road-sweeping brushes; household type brooms and brushes, including shoe brushes and clothes brushes; brushes for grooming animals
	960390 99 0	Other
899.73		**Plaits and similar products of plaiting materials, whether or not assembled into strips**
	460110 10 0	Of unspun vegetable materials
	460110 90 0	Other
899.74		**Mats, matting and screens of vegetable materials**
	460120 10 0	Of plaits or similar products of heading 899.73
	460120 90 0	Other
899.79		**Plaiting materials, plaits and similar products of plaiting materials, n.e.s., bound together in parallel strands or woven, in sheet form, whether or not being finished articles**
		Of vegetable materials
	460191 10 0	Of plaits or similar products of heading 899.73
	460191 90 0	Other
		Other
	460199 10 0	Of plaits or similar products of heading 899.73
	460199 90 0	Other
		Small-wares and toilet articles, n.e.s.; sieves; tailors' dummies, etc.
899.81	960400 00 0	**Hand sieves and hand riddles**
899.82	961620 00 0	**Powder puffs and pads for the application of cosmetics or toilet preparations**
899.83		**Press-fasteners, snap-fasteners and press-studs and parts therefor; buttons**
	960610 00 0	Press-fasteners, snap-fasteners and press-studs and parts therefor
		Buttons
	960621 00 0	Of plastics, not covered with textile material
	960622 00 0	Of base metal, not covered with textile material
	960629 00 0	Other
899.84	960630 00 0	**Button moulds and other parts of buttons; button blanks**
899.85		**Slide fasteners**
	960711 00 0	Fitted with chain scoops of base metal
	960719 00 0	Other
899.86		**Parts of slide fasteners**
	960720 10 0	Of base metal, including narrow strips mounted with chain scoops of base metal
	960720 90 0	Other
899.87		Scent sprays and similar toilet sprays, and mounts and heads therefor
	961610 10 0	Toilet sprays
	961610 90 0	Mounts and heads
899.88	961800 00 0	**Tailors' dummies and other lay figures; automata and other animated displays used for shop window dressing**
899.89		**Combs, hair-slides and the like; hairpins, curling pins, curling grips, hair-curlers and the like (other than those of heading 775.8), and parts thereof**
		Combs, hair-slides and the like
	961511 00 0	Of hard rubber or plastics
	961519 00 0	Other
	961590 00 0	Other
		Manufactured goods, n.e.s.
899.91		**Articles of gut (other than silkworm gut), of goldbeater's skin, of bladders or of tendons**
	420610 00 0	Catgut
	420690 00 0	Other
899.92	670100 00 0	**Skins and other parts of birds with their feathers or down, feathers, parts of feathers, down and articles thereof (other than goods of heading 291.95)**
899.94	670300 00 0	**Human hair, dressed, thinned, bleached or otherwise worked; wool or other animal hair, or other textile materials, prepared for use in making wigs or the like**

S.I.T.C. (R3)	Commodity Code No	Trade description
899.95		**Wigs, false beards, eyebrows and eyelashes, switches and the like, of human or animal hair or of textile materials; articles of human hair, n.e.s.**
		Of synthetic textile materials
	670411 00 0	Complete wigs
	670419 00 0	Other
	670420 00 0	Of human hair
	670490 00 0	Of other materials
899.96	880400 00 0	**Parachutes (including dirigible parachutes) and rotochutes; parts thereof and accessories thereto**
899.97		**Vacuum flasks and other vacuum vessels, complete with cases; parts thereof (other than glass inners)**
		Vacuum flasks and other vacuum vessels, complete with cases, having a capacity
	961700 11 0	Not exceeding 0.75 litre
	961700 19 0	Exceeding 0.75 litre
	961700 90 0	Parts (other than glass inners)

S.I.T.C. (R3)	Commodity Code No	Trade description

SECTION: 9

COMMODITIES AND TRANSACTIONS NOT CLASSIFIED ELSEWHERE IN THE SITC

911.00	992099 00 8	Postal packages not classified according to kind
931.00		Special transactions and commodities not classified according to kind
	999099 02 8	Continental shelf transactions
	999099 02 9	Transactions of low value
961.00		Coin (other than gold coin), not being legal tender
	711810 10 0	Of silver
	711810 90 0	Other
962.00	711890 00 9	Coin (other than gold coin), of legal tender

Gold, non-monetary (excluding gold ores and concentrates)

971.01		Gold (including gold plated with platinum), non-monetary, unwrought or in semi-manufactured forms or in powder form
		Non-monetary
	710811 00 0	Powder
	*710812 00 0	Other unwrought forms
		Other semi-manufactured forms
	710813 10 0	Bars, rods, wire and sections; plates; sheets and strips of a thickness, excluding any backing, exceeding 0.15 mm
	710813 30 0	Tubes, pipes and hollow bars
	710813 50 0	Thin sheets and strips (foil) of a thickness, excluding any backing, not exceeding 0.15 mm
	710813 90 0	Other
971.02	710900 00 0	Base metals or silver, clad with gold, not further worked than semi-manufactured
971.03	711210 00 0	Waste and scrap, of gold (including metal clad with gold but excluding sweepings containing other precious metals)

Parts and accessories of articles of headings 981.12 and 981.14

ARMS AND AMMUNITION (FOR MILITARY PURPOSES)

Armoured fighting vehicles and arms of war

981.11	*871000 00 0	Tanks and other armoured fighting vehicles, motorised, whether or not fitted with weapons, and parts of such vehicles
981.12	930100 00 0	Military weapons (other than revolvers, pistols and the arms of heading 981.13)
981.13	930700 00 0	Swords, cutlasses, bayonets, lances and similar arms, and parts thereof and scabbards and shields therefor
981.14		Revolvers and pistols (other than those of heading 891.3)
	930200 10 0	9 mm calibre and higher
	930200 90 0	Other

Bombs, grenades, torpedoes, mines, missiles and similar munitions of war and parts thereof

981.24		Cartridges and parts thereof, for military purposes
	930630 10 0	For revolvers and pistols falling within heading 981.14 and for sub-machine-guns falling within heading 981.12
		Other
	*930630 30 0	For military weapons
981.29	*930690 10 0	Munitions of war and parts thereof, n.e.s.

Parts and accessories, n.e.s of articles of headings 981.12 and 981.14

981.91	930510 00 0	Parts and accessories of revolvers or pistols
981.99		Parts and accessories, n.e.s.,
	*930590 10 0	For military weapons falling within 981.12

S.I.T.C. (R3)	Commodity Code No	Trade description
		GOLD, MONETARY; GOLD COIN AND CURRENT COIN
	*710820 00 0	Monetary
	*710890 00 0	Other

HS	SITC(R3)	HS	SITC(R3)	HS	SITC(R3)	HS	SITC(R3)
0101 11	001.51	0207 27	012.36	0303 60	034.25	0404 10	022.41
0101 19	001.51	0207 27	012.35	0303 71	034.24	0404 90	022.49
0101 20	001.52	0207 32	012.31	0303 72	034.28	0405 10	023.00
0102 10	001.11	0207 33	012.32	0303 73	034.28	0405 20	023.00
0102 90	001.19	0207 34	012.33	0303 74	034.26	0405 90	023.00
0103 10	001.31	0207 35	012.34	0303 75	034.28	0406 10	024.91
0103 91	001.39	0207 36	012.36	0303 76	034.28	0406 20	024.10
0103 92	001.39	0207 36	012.35	0303 77	034.28	0406 30	024.20
0104 10	001.21	0208 10	012.91	0303 78	034.27	0406 40	024.30
0104 20	001.22	0208 20	012.92	0303 79	034.28	0406 90	024.99
0105 11	001.41	0208 90	012.99	0303 80	034.29	0407 00	025.10
0105 12	001.41	0209 00	411.31	0304 10	034.51	0408 11	025.21
0105 19	001.41	0210 11	016.11	0304 20	034.40	0408 19	025.22
0105 92	001.49	0210 12	016.12	0304 90	034.55	0408 91	025.21
0105 93	001.49	0210 19	016.19	0305 10	035.50	0408 99	025.22
0105 99	001.49	0210 20	016.81	0305 20	035.40	0409 00	061.60
0106 00	001.90	0210 90	016.89	0305 30	035.12	0410 00	098.92
0201 10	011.11	0301 10	034.11	0305 41	035.30	0499 00	099.99
0201 20	011.11	0301 91	034.11	0305 42	035.30	0501 00	291.91
0201 30	011.12	0301 92	034.11	0305 49	035.30	0502 10	291.92
0202 10	011.21	0301 93	034.11	0305 51	035.11	0502 90	291.92
0202 20	011.21	0301 99	034.11	0305 59	035.13	0503 00	268.51
0202 30	011.22	0302 11	034.12	0305 61	035.29	0504 00	291.93
0203 11	012.21	0302 12	034.12	0305 62	035.21	0505 10	291.95
0203 12	012.21	0302 19	034.12	0305 63	035.22	0505 90	291.95
0203 19	012.21	0302 21	034.13	0305 69	035.29	0506 10	291.11
0203 21	012.22	0302 22	034.13	0306 11	036.19	0506 90	291.11
0203 22	012.22	0302 23	034.13	0306 12	036.19	0507 10	291.16
0203 29	012.22	0302 29	034.13	0306 13	036.11	0507 90	291.16
0204 10	012.11	0302 31	034.14	0306 14	036.19	0508 00	291.15
0204 21	012.11	0302 32	034.14	0306 19	036.19	0509 00	291.97
0204 22	012.11	0302 33	034.14	0306 21	036.20	0510 00	291.98
0204 23	012.11	0302 39	034.14	0306 22	036.20	0511 10	291.94
0204 30	012.12	0302 40	034.15	0306 23	036.20	0511 91	291.96
0204 41	012.12	0302 50	034.16	0306 24	036.20	0511 99	291.99
0204 42	012.12	0302 61	034.15	0306 29	036.20	0601 10	292.61
0204 43	012.12	0302 62	034.18	0307 10	036.31	0601 20	292.61
0204 50	012.13	0302 63	034.18	0307 29	036.39	0602 10	292.69
0205 00	012.40	0302 64	034.17	0307 31	036.33	0602 20	292.69
0206 10	012.51	0302 65	034.18	0307 39	036.39	0602 30	292.69
0206 21	012.52	0302 66	034.18	0307 41	036.33	0602 40	292.69
0206 22	012.52	0302 69	034.18	0307 49	036.37	0602 90	292.69
0206 29	012.52	0302 70	034.19	0307 59	036.37	0603 10	292.71
0206 30	012.53	0303 10	034.21	0307 60	012.93	0603 90	292.71
0206 41	012.54	0303 21	034.21	0307 91	036.33	0604 10	292.72
0206 49	012.54	0303 22	034.21	0307 99	036.39	0604 91	292.72
0206 80	012.55	0303 29	034.21	0401 10	022.11	0604 99	292.72
0206 90	012.56	0303 31	034.22	0401 20	022.12	0701 10	054.10
0207 11	012.31	0303 32	034.22	0401 30	022.13	0701 90	054.10
0207 12	012.32	0303 33	034.22	0402 10	022.21	0702 00	054.40
0207 13	012.34	0303 39	034.22	0402 21	022.22	0703 10	054.51
0207 14	012.36	0303 41	034.23	0402 29	022.22	0703 20	054.52
0207 14	012.35	0303 42	034.23	0402 91	022.23	0703 90	054.52
0207 24	012.31	0303 43	034.23	0402 99	022.24	0704 10	054.53
0207 25	012.32	0303 49	034.23	0403 10	022.31	0704 20	054.53
0207 26	012.34	0303 50	034.24	0403 90	022.32	0704 90	054.53

HS	SITC(R3)	HS	SITC(R3)	HS	SITC(R3)	HS	SITC(R3)
0705 11	054.54	0802 21	057.75	0903 00	074.31	1104 23	048.14
0705 19	054.54	0802 22	057.75	0904 11	075.11	1104 29	048.14
0705 21	054.54	0802 31	057.76	0904 12	075.12	1104 30	048.15
0705 29	054.54	0802 32	057.76	0904 20	075.13	1105 10	056.41
0706 10	054.55	0802 40	057.77	0905 00	075.21	1105 20	056.42
0706 90	054.55	0802 50	057.78	0906 10	075.22	1106 10	056.46
0707 00	054.56	0802 90	057.79	0906 20	075.23	1106 20	056.47
0708 10	054.57	0803 00	057.30	0907 00	075.24	1106 30	056.48
0708 20	054.57	0804 10	057.96	0908 10	075.25	1107 10	048.20
0708 90	054.57	0804 20	057.60	0908 20	075.25	1107 20	048.20
0709 10	054.59	0804 30	057.95	0908 30	075.25	1108 11	592.11
0709 20	054.59	0804 40	057.97	0909 10	075.26	1108 12	592.12
0709 30	054.59	0804 50	057.97	0909 20	075.26	1108 13	592.13
0709 40	054.59	0805 10	057.11	0909 30	075.26	1108 14	592.14
0709 51	054.58	0805 20	057.12	0909 40	075.26	1108 19	592.15
0709 52	054.58	0805 30	057.21	0909 50	075.26	1108 20	592.16
0709 60	054.59	0805 40	057.22	0910 10	075.27	1109 00	592.17
0709 70	054.59	0805 90	057.29	0910 20	075.28	1201 00	222.20
0709 90	054.59	0806 10	057.51	0910 30	075.29	1202 10	222.11
0710 10	054.69	0806 20	057.52	0910 40	075.28	1202 20	222.12
0710 21	054.69	0807 11	057.91	0910 50	075.29	1203 00	223.10
0710 22	054.69	0807 19	057.91	0910 91	075.29	1204 00	223.40
0710 29	054.69	0807 20	057.91	0910 99	075.29	1205 00	222.61
0710 30	054.69	0808 10	057.40	1001 10	041.10	1206 00	222.40
0710 40	054.61	0808 20	057.92	1001 90	041.20	1207 10	223.20
0710 80	054.69	0809 10	057.93	1002 00	045.10	1207 20	222.30
0710 90	054.69	0809 20	057.93	1003 00	043.00	1207 30	223.50
0711 10	054.70	0809 30	057.93	1004 00	045.20	1207 40	222.50
0711 20	054.70	0809 40	057.93	1005 10	044.10	1207 50	222.62
0711 30	054.70	0810 10	057.94	1005 90	044.90	1207 60	222.70
0711 40	054.70	0810 20	057.94	1006 10	042.10	1207 91	223.70
0711 90	054.70	0810 30	057.94	1006 20	042.20	1207 92	223.70
0712 20	056.12	0810 40	057.94	1006 30	042.31	1207 99	223.70
0712 30	056.13	0810 50	057.98	1006 40	042.32	1208 10	223.90
0712 90	056.19	0810 90	057.98	1007 00	045.30	1208 90	223.90
0712 90	056.11	0811 10	058.31	1008 10	045.92	1209 11	292.51
0713 10	054.21	0811 20	058.32	1008 20	045.91	1209 19	292.54
0713 20	054.22	0811 90	058.39	1008 30	045.93	1209 21	292.52
0713 31	054.23	0812 10	058.21	1008 90	045.99	1209 22	292.52
0713 32	054.23	0812 20	058.21	1101 00	046.10	1209 23	292.52
0713 33	054.23	0812 90	058.21	1102 10	047.19	1209 24	292.52
0713 39	054.23	0813 10	057.99	1102 20	047.11	1209 25	292.52
0713 40	054.24	0813 20	057.99	1102 30	047.19	1209 26	292.52
0713 50	054.25	0813 30	057.99	1102 90	047.19	1209 29	292.52
0713 90	054.29	0813 40	057.99	1103 11	046.20	1209 30	292.53
0714 10	054.81	0813 50	057.99	1103 12	047.22	1209 91	292.54
0714 20	054.83	0814 00	058.22	1103 13	047.21	1209 99	292.59
0714 90	054.83	0901 11	071.11	1103 14	047.22	1210 10	054.84
0801 11	057.71	0901 12	071.12	1103 19	047.22	1210 20	054.84
0801 19	057.71	0901 21	071.20	1103 21	046.20	1211 10	292.41
0801 21	057.72	0901 22	071.20	1103 29	047.29	1211 20	292.42
0801 22	057.72	0901 90	071.32	1104 11	048.13	1211 90	292.49
0801 31	057.73	0902 10	074.11	1104 12	048.13	1212 10	054.89
0801 32	057.73	0902 20	074.12	1104 19	048.13	1212 20	292.97
0802 11	057.74	0902 30	074.13	1104 21	048.14	1212 30	054.85
0802 12	057.74	0902 40	074.14	1104 22	048.14	1212 91	054.87

HS	SITC(R3)	HS	SITC(R3)	HS	SITC(R3)	HS	SITC(R3)
1212 92	054.88	1514 90	421.79	1702 60	061.96	2007 99	058.10
1212 99	054.89	1515 11	422.11	1702 90	061.99	2008 11	058.92
1213 00	081.11	1515 19	422.19	1703 10	061.51	2008 19	058.92
1214 10	081.12	1515 21	421.61	1703 90	061.59	2008 20	058.93
1214 90	081.12	1515 29	421.69	1704 10	062.21	2008 30	058.94
1301 10	292.21	1515 30	422.50	1704 90	062.29	2008 40	058.96
1301 20	292.22	1515 40	422.91	1801 00	072.10	2008 50	058.95
1301 90	292.29	1515 50	421.80	1802 00	072.50	2008 60	058.95
1302 11	292.94	1515 60	422.99	1803 10	072.31	2008 70	058.95
1302 12	292.94	1515 90	422.99	1803 20	072.32	2008 80	058.96
1302 13	292.94	1516 10	431.21	1804 00	072.40	2008 91	058.96
1302 14	292.94	1516 20	431.22	1805 00	072.20	2008 92	058.97
1302 19	292.94	1517 10	091.01	1806 10	073.10	2008 99	058.96
1302 19	551.35	1517 90	091.09	1806 20	073.20	2009 11	059.10
1302 20	292.95	1518 00	431.10	1806 31	073.30	2009 19	059.10
1302 31	292.96	1520 00	512.22	1806 32	073.30	2009 20	059.20
1302 32	292.96	1521 10	431.41	1806 90	073.90	2009 30	059.30
1302 39	292.96	1521 90	431.42	1901 10	098.93	2009 40	059.91
1401 10	292.31	1522 00	431.33	1901 20	048.50	2009 50	059.92
1401 20	292.32	1599 00	499.99	1901 90	098.94	2009 60	059.93
1401 90	292.39	1601 00	017.20	1902 11	048.30	2009 70	059.94
1402 10	292.92	1602 10	098.11	1902 19	048.30	2009 80	059.95
1402 90	292.92	1602 20	017.30	1902 20	098.91	2009 90	059.96
1403 10	292.93	1602 31	017.40	1902 30	098.91	2101 11	071.31
1403 90	292.93	1602 32	017.40	1902 40	098.91	2101 12	071.31
1404 10	292.99	1602 39	017.40	1903 00	056.45	2101 20	074.32
1404 20	263.20	1602 41	017.50	1904 10	048.11	2101 30	071.33
1404 90	292.99	1602 42	017.50	1904 20	048.11	2102 10	098.60
1501 00	411.20	1602 49	017.50	1904 90	048.12	2102 20	098.60
1502 00	411.32	1602 50	017.60	1905 10	048.41	2102 30	098.60
1503 00	411.33	1602 90	017.90	1905 20	048.42	2103 10	098.41
1504 10	411.11	1603 00	017.10	1905 30	048.42	2103 20	098.42
1504 20	411.12	1604 11	037.11	1905 40	048.41	2103 30	098.43
1504 30	411.13	1604 12	037.12	1905 90	048.49	2103 90	112.43
1505 10	411.34	1604 13	037.12	2001 10	056.71	2103 90	098.49
1505 90	411.35	1604 14	037.13	2001 20	056.71	2104 10	098.50
1506 00	411.39	1604 15	037.14	2001 90	056.71	2104 20	098.14
1507 10	421.11	1604 16	037.15	2002 10	056.72	2105 00	022.33
1507 90	421.19	1604 19	037.15	2002 90	056.73	2106 10	098.99
1508 10	421.31	1604 20	037.16	2003 10	056.74	2106 90	098.99
1508 90	421.39	1604 30	037.17	2003 20	056.74	2201 10	111.01
1509 10	421.41	1605 10	037.21	2004 10	056.61	2201 90	111.01
1509 90	421.42	1605 20	037.21	2004 90	056.69	2202 10	111.02
1510 00	421.49	1605 30	037.21	2005 10	098.12	2202 90	111.02
1511 10	422.21	1605 40	037.21	2005 20	056.76	2203 00	112.30
1511 90	422.29	1605 90	037.22	2005 40	056.79	2204 10	112.15
1512 11	421.51	1701 11	061.11	2005 51	056.79	2204 21	112.17
1512 19	421.59	1701 12	061.12	2005 59	056.79	2204 29	112.17
1512 21	421.29	1701 91	061.21	2005 60	056.79	2204 30	112.11
1512 21	421.21	1701 99	061.29	2005 70	056.79	2205 10	112.13
1512 29	421.29	1702 11	061.91	2005 80	056.77	2205 90	112.13
1513 11	422.31	1702 19	061.91	2005 90	056.75	2206 00	112.20
1513 19	422.39	1702 20	061.92	2005 90	056.79	2207 10	512.15
1513 21	422.41	1702 30	061.93	2006 00	062.10	2207 20	512.16
1513 29	422.49	1702 40	061.94	2007 10	098.13	2208 20	112.42
1514 10	421.71	1702 50	061.95	2007 91	058.10	2208 30	112.41

HS	SITC(R3)	HS	SITC(R3)	HS	SITC(R3)	HS	SITC(R3)
2208 40	112.44	2508 50	278.29	2530 20	278.99	2708 20	335.32
2208 50	112.45	2508 60	278.29	2530 40	278.99	2709 00	333.00
2208 60	112.49	2508 70	278.29	2530 90	278.99	2710 00	334.11
2208 70	112.49	2509 00	278.91	2601 11	281.50	2710 00	334.12
2208 90	112.49	2510 10	272.31	2601 12	281.60	2710 00	334.21
2209 00	098.44	2510 20	272.32	2601 20	281.40	2710 00	334.29
2301 10	081.41	2511 10	278.92	2602 00	287.70	2710 00	334.30
2301 20	081.42	2511 20	278.92	2603 00	283.10	2710 00	334.40
2302 10	081.24	2512 00	278.95	2604 00	284.10	2710 00	334.50
2302 20	081.25	2513 11	277.22	2605 00	287.93	2710 00	334.19
2302 30	081.26	2513 19	277.29	2606 00	285.10	2711 11	343.10
2302 40	081.29	2513 20	277.22	2607 00	287.40	2711 12	342.10
2302 50	081.23	2514 00	273.11	2608 00	287.50	2711 13	342.50
2303 10	081.51	2515 11	273.12	2609 00	287.60	2711 14	344.10
2303 20	081.52	2515 12	273.12	2610 00	287.91	2711 19	344.20
2303 30	081.53	2515 20	273.12	2611 00	287.92	2711 21	343.20
2304 00	081.31	2516 11	273.13	2612 10	286.10	2711 29	344.90
2305 00	081.32	2516 12	273.13	2612 20	286.20	2712 10	335.11
2306 10	081.33	2516 21	273.13	2613 10	287.81	2712 20	335.12
2306 20	081.34	2516 22	273.13	2613 90	287.82	2712 90	335.12
2306 30	081.35	2516 90	273.13	2614 00	287.83	2713 11	335.42
2306 40	081.36	2517 10	273.40	2615 10	287.84	2713 12	335.42
2306 50	081.37	2517 20	273.40	2615 90	287.85	2713 20	335.41
2306 60	081.38	2517 30	273.40	2616 10	289.11	2713 90	335.41
2306 70	081.39	2517 41	273.40	2616 90	289.19	2714 10	278.96
2306 90	081.39	2517 49	273.40	2617 10	287.99	2714 90	278.97
2307 00	081.94	2518 10	278.23	2617 90	287.99	2715 00	335.43
2308 10	081.19	2518 20	278.23	2618 00	278.61	2716 00	351.00
2308 90	081.19	2518 30	278.23	2619 00	278.62	2801 10	522.24
2309 10	081.95	2519 10	278.24	2620 11	288.10	2801 20	522.25
2309 90	081.99	2519 90	278.25	2620 19	288.10	2801 30	522.25
2401 10	121.10	2520 10	273.23	2620 20	288.10	2802 00	522.26
2401 20	121.20	2520 20	273.24	2620 30	288.10	2803 00	522.10
2401 30	121.30	2521 00	273.22	2620 40	288.10	2804 10	522.21
2402 10	122.10	2522 10	661.11	2620 50	288.10	2804 21	522.21
2402 20	122.20	2522 20	661.12	2620 90	288.10	2804 29	522.21
2402 90	122.31	2522 30	661.13	2621 00	278.69	2804 30	522.21
2403 10	122.32	2523 10	661.21	2701 11	321.10	2804 40	522.21
2403 91	122.39	2523 21	661.22	2701 12	321.21	2804 50	522.22
2403 99	122.39	2523 29	661.22	2701 19	321.22	2804 61	522.23
2501 00	278.30	2523 30	661.23	2701 20	322.10	2804 69	522.23
2502 00	274.20	2523 90	661.29	2702 10	322.21	2804 70	522.22
2503 00	274.19	2524 00	278.40	2702 20	322.22	2804 80	522.22
2503 00	274.11	2525 10	278.52	2703 00	322.30	2804 90	522.22
2504 10	278.22	2525 20	278.52	2704 00	325.00	2805 11	522.28
2504 90	278.22	2525 30	278.52	2705 00	345.00	2805 19	522.28
2505 10	273.31	2526 10	278.93	2706 00	335.21	2805 21	522.29
2505 90	273.39	2526 20	278.93	2707 10	335.22	2805 22	522.29
2506 10	278.51	2527 00	278.55	2707 20	335.23	2805 30	522.29
2506 21	278.51	2528 10	278.94	2707 30	335.24	2805 40	522.27
2506 29	278.51	2528 90	278.94	2707 40	335.25	2806 10	522.31
2507 00	278.26	2529 10	278.53	2707 50	335.25	2806 20	522.31
2508 10	278.27	2529 21	278.54	2707 60	335.25	2807 00	522.32
2508 20	278.29	2529 22	278.54	2707 91	335.25	2808 00	522.33
2508 30	278.29	2529 30	278.53	2707 99	335.25	2809 10	522.34
2508 40	278.29	2530 10	278.98	2708 10	335.31	2809 20	522.34

HS	SITC(R3)	HS	SITC(R3)	HS	SITC(R3)	HS	SITC(R3)
2810 00	522.35	2827 35	523.29	2836 92	523.75	2902 30	511.23
2811 11	522.36	2827 36	523.29	2836 99	523.75	2902 41	511.24
2811 19	522.36	2827 38	523.29	2837 11	523.81	2902 42	511.24
2811 21	522.39	2827 39	523.29	2837 19	523.81	2902 43	511.24
2811 22	522.37	2827 41	523.29	2837 20	523.81	2902 44	511.24
2811 23	522.38	2827 49	523.29	2838 00	523.82	2902 50	511.25
2811 29	522.39	2827 51	523.29	2839 11	523.83	2902 60	511.26
2812 10	522.41	2827 59	523.29	2839 19	523.83	2902 70	511.27
2812 90	522.41	2827 60	523.29	2839 20	523.83	2902 90	511.29
2813 10	522.42	2828 10	523.31	2839 90	523.83	2903 11	511.36
2813 90	522.42	2828 90	523.31	2840 11	523.84	2903 12	511.36
2814 10	522.61	2829 11	523.32	2840 19	523.84	2903 13	511.36
2814 20	522.61	2829 19	523.39	2840 20	523.84	2903 14	511.36
2815 11	522.62	2829 90	523.39	2840 30	523.84	2903 15	511.35
2815 12	522.63	2830 10	523.41	2841 10	524.31	2903 16	511.36
2815 20	522.64	2830 20	523.42	2841 20	524.31	2903 19	511.36
2815 30	522.64	2830 30	523.42	2841 30	524.31	2903 21	511.31
2816 10	522.65	2830 90	523.42	2841 40	524.31	2903 22	511.32
2816 20	522.65	2831 10	523.43	2841 50	524.31	2903 23	511.33
2816 30	522.65	2831 90	523.43	2841 61	524.31	2903 29	511.34
2817 00	522.51	2832 10	523.44	2841 69	524.31	2903 30	511.37
2818 10	522.67	2832 20	523.44	2841 70	524.31	2903 41	511.38
2818 20	285.20	2832 30	523.44	2841 80	524.31	2903 42	511.38
2818 30	522.66	2833 11	523.45	2841 90	524.31	2903 43	511.38
2819 10	522.52	2833 19	523.45	2842 10	523.89	2903 44	511.38
2819 90	522.52	2833 21	523.49	2842 90	523.89	2903 45	511.38
2820 10	522.53	2833 22	523.49	2843 10	524.32	2903 46	511.38
2820 90	522.53	2833 23	523.49	2843 21	524.32	2903 47	511.38
2821 10	522.54	2833 24	523.49	2843 29	524.32	2903 49	511.38
2821 20	522.54	2833 25	523.49	2843 30	524.32	2903 51	511.39
2822 00	522.55	2833 26	523.49	2843 90	524.32	2903 59	511.39
2823 00	522.56	2833 27	523.49	2844 10	525.11	2903 61	511.39
2824 10	522.57	2833 29	523.49	2844 20	525.13	2903 62	511.39
2824 20	522.57	2833 30	523.49	2844 30	525.15	2903 69	511.39
2824 90	522.57	2833 40	523.49	2844 40	525.19	2904 10	511.40
2825 10	522.68	2834 10	523.51	2844 50	525.17	2904 20	511.40
2825 20	522.69	2834 21	523.52	2845 10	525.91	2904 90	511.40
2825 30	522.69	2834 22	523.59	2845 90	525.91	2905 11	512.11
2825 40	522.69	2834 29	523.59	2846 10	525.95	2905 12	512.12
2825 50	522.69	2835 10	523.61	2846 90	525.95	2905 13	512.13
2825 60	522.69	2835 22	523.63	2847 00	524.91	2905 14	512.13
2825 70	522.69	2835 23	523.63	2848 00	524.92	2905 15	512.19
2825 80	522.69	2835 24	523.63	2849 10	524.93	2905 16	512.14
2825 90	522.69	2835 25	523.63	2849 20	524.94	2905 17	512.19
2826 11	523.10	2835 26	523.63	2849 90	524.94	2905 19	512.19
2826 12	523.10	2835 29	523.63	2850 00	524.95	2905 22	512.19
2826 19	523.10	2835 31	523.64	2851 00	524.99	2905 29	512.19
2826 20	523.10	2835 39	523.64	2901 10	511.14	2905 31	512.21
2826 30	523.10	2836 10	523.71	2901 21	511.11	2905 32	512.29
2826 90	523.10	2836 20	523.72	2901 22	511.12	2905 39	512.29
2827 10	523.21	2836 30	523.73	2901 23	511.13	2905 41	512.29
2827 20	523.22	2836 40	523.74	2901 24	511.13	2905 42	512.23
2827 31	523.29	2836 50	523.75	2901 29	511.19	2905 43	512.24
2827 32	523.29	2836 60	523.75	2902 11	511.21	2905 44	512.25
2827 33	523.29	2836 70	523.75	2902 19	511.29	2905 45	512.22
2827 34	523.29	2836 91	523.75	2902 20	511.22	2905 49	512.29

HS	SITC(R3)	HS	SITC(R3)	HS	SITC(R3)	HS	SITC(R3)
2905 50	512.29	2914 22	516.28	2918 12	513.91	2926 90	514.84
2906 11	512.31	2914 23	516.28	2918 13	513.91	2927 00	514.85
2906 12	512.31	2914 29	516.28	2918 14	513.91	2928 00	514.86
2906 13	512.31	2914 31	516.29	2918 15	513.91	2929 10	514.89
2906 14	512.31	2914 39	516.29	2918 16	513.92	2929 90	514.89
2906 19	512.31	2914 40	516.29	2918 17	513.92	2930 10	515.41
2906 21	512.35	2914 50	516.29	2918 19	513.92	2930 20	515.42
2906 29	512.35	2914 61	516.29	2918 21	513.93	2930 30	515.43
2907 11	512.41	2914 69	516.29	2918 22	513.93	2930 40	515.44
2907 12	512.42	2914 70	516.29	2918 23	513.93	2930 90	515.49
2907 13	512.43	2915 11	513.74	2918 29	513.94	2931 00	515.50
2907 14	512.43	2915 12	513.74	2918 30	513.95	2932 11	515.69
2907 15	512.43	2915 13	513.74	2918 90	513.96	2932 12	515.69
2907 19	512.43	2915 21	513.71	2919 00	516.31	2932 13	515.69
2907 21	512.43	2915 22	513.71	2920 10	516.39	2932 19	515.69
2907 22	512.43	2915 23	513.71	2920 90	516.39	2932 21	515.62
2907 23	512.43	2915 24	513.77	2921 11	514.51	2932 29	515.63
2907 29	512.43	2915 29	513.71	2921 12	514.51	2932 91	515.69
2907 30	512.43	2915 31	513.72	2921 19	514.51	2932 92	515.69
2908 10	512.44	2915 32	513.72	2921 21	514.52	2932 93	515.69
2908 20	512.44	2915 33	513.72	2921 22	514.52	2932 94	515.69
2908 90	512.44	2915 34	513.72	2921 29	514.52	2932 99	515.69
2909 11	516.16	2915 35	513.72	2921 30	514.53	2933 11	515.71
2909 19	516.16	2915 39	513.72	2921 41	514.54	2933 19	515.71
2909 20	516.16	2915 40	513.77	2921 42	514.54	2933 21	515.72
2909 30	516.16	2915 50	513.77	2921 43	514.54	2933 29	515.73
2909 41	516.17	2915 60	513.75	2921 44	514.54	2933 31	515.74
2909 42	516.17	2915 70	513.76	2921 45	514.54	2933 32	515.74
2909 43	516.17	2915 90	513.77	2921 49	514.54	2933 39	515.74
2909 44	516.17	2916 11	513.79	2921 51	514.55	2933 40	515.77
2909 49	516.17	2916 12	513.79	2921 59	514.55	2933 40	515.75
2909 50	516.17	2916 13	513.73	2922 11	514.61	2933 51	515.76
2909 60	516.17	2916 14	513.73	2922 12	514.61	2933 59	515.76
2910 10	516.13	2916 15	513.78	2922 13	514.61	2933 61	515.76
2910 20	516.14	2916 19	513.79	2922 19	514.61	2933 69	515.77
2910 30	516.15	2916 20	513.79	2922 21	514.62	2933 69	515.76
2910 90	516.15	2916 31	513.79	2922 22	514.62	2933 71	515.61
2911 00	516.12	2916 32	513.79	2922 29	514.62	2933 79	515.61
2912 11	516.21	2916 34	513.79	2922 30	514.63	2933 90	515.77
2912 12	516.21	2916 35	513.79	2922 41	514.64	2934 10	515.79
2912 13	516.21	2916 39	513.79	2922 42	514.64	2934 20	515.79
2912 19	516.21	2917 11	513.89	2922 43	514.65	2934 30	515.78
2912 21	516.22	2917 12	513.89	2922 49	514.65	2934 90	515.79
2912 29	516.22	2917 13	513.89	2922 50	514.67	2935 00	515.80
2912 30	516.22	2917 14	513.81	2923 10	514.81	2936 10	541.11
2912 41	516.22	2917 19	513.89	2923 20	514.81	2936 21	541.12
2912 42	516.22	2917 20	513.85	2923 90	514.81	2936 22	541.13
2912 49	516.22	2917 31	513.89	2924 10	514.71	2936 23	541.13
2912 50	516.22	2917 32	513.83	2924 21	514.73	2936 24	541.13
2912 60	516.22	2917 33	513.89	2924 22	514.79	2936 25	541.13
2913 00	516.26	2917 34	513.89	2924 29	514.79	2936 26	541.13
2914 11	516.23	2917 35	513.82	2925 11	514.82	2936 27	541.14
2914 12	516.24	2917 36	513.89	2925 19	514.82	2936 28	541.15
2914 13	516.25	2917 37	513.84	2925 20	514.82	2936 29	541.16
2914 19	516.25	2917 39	513.89	2926 10	514.83	2936 90	541.17
2914 21	516.27	2918 11	513.91	2926 20	514.84	2937 10	541.52

HS	SITC(R3)	HS	SITC(R3)	HS	SITC(R3)	HS	SITC(R3)
2937 21	541.53	3004 90	542.93	3206 42	533.15	3307 41	553.54
2937 22	541.53	3005 10	541.91	3206 43	533.16	3307 49	553.54
2937 29	541.53	3005 90	541.91	3206 49	533.17	3307 90	553.59
2937 91	541.51	3006 10	541.99	3206 50	533.18	3401 11	554.11
2937 92	541.59	3006 20	541.92	3207 10	533.51	3401 19	554.15
2937 99	541.59	3006 30	541.93	3207 20	533.51	3401 20	554.19
2938 10	541.61	3006 40	541.99	3207 30	533.51	3402 11	554.21
2938 90	541.61	3006 50	541.99	3207 40	533.51	3402 12	554.21
2939 10	541.41	3006 60	541.99	3208 10	533.42	3402 13	554.21
2939 21	541.42	3101 00	272.10	3208 20	533.42	3402 19	554.21
2939 29	541.42	3102 10	562.16	3208 90	533.42	3402 20	554.22
2939 30	541.43	3102 21	562.13	3209 10	533.41	3402 90	554.23
2939 41	541.44	3102 29	562.12	3209 90	533.41	3403 11	597.71
2939 42	541.44	3102 30	562.11	3210 00	533.43	3403 19	597.72
2939 49	541.44	3102 40	562.19	3211 00	533.53	3403 91	597.73
2939 50	541.45	3102 50	272.20	3212 10	533.44	3403 99	597.74
2939 61	541.46	3102 60	562.14	3212 90	533.44	3404 10	598.31
2939 62	541.46	3102 70	562.15	3213 10	533.52	3404 20	598.35
2939 63	541.46	3102 80	562.17	3213 90	533.52	3404 90	598.39
2939 69	541.46	3102 90	562.19	3214 10	533.54	3405 10	554.31
2939 70	541.47	3103 10	562.22	3214 90	533.54	3405 20	554.32
2939 90	541.49	3103 20	562.21	3215 11	533.21	3405 30	554.33
2940 00	516.92	3103 90	562.29	3215 19	533.29	3405 40	554.34
2941 10	541.31	3104 10	272.40	3215 90	895.91	3405 90	554.35
2941 20	541.32	3104 20	562.31	3301 11	551.31	3406 00	899.31
2941 30	541.33	3104 30	562.32	3301 12	551.31	3407 00	598.95
2941 40	541.39	3104 90	562.39	3301 13	551.31	3501 10	592.21
2941 50	541.39	3105 10	562.96	3301 14	551.31	3501 90	592.22
2941 90	541.39	3105 20	562.91	3301 19	551.31	3502 11	025.30
2942 00	516.99	3105 30	562.93	3301 21	551.32	3502 19	025.30
3001 10	541.62	3105 40	562.94	3301 22	551.32	3502 20	592.23
3001 20	541.62	3105 51	562.95	3301 23	551.32	3502 90	592.23
3001 90	541.62	3105 60	562.92	3301 24	551.32	3503 00	592.24
3002 10	541.63	3105 90	562.99	3301 25	551.32	3504 00	592.25
3002 20	541.63	3201 10	532.21	3301 26	551.32	3505 10	592.26
3002 30	541.63	3201 20	532.21	3301 29	551.32	3505 20	592.27
3002 90	541.64	3201 90	532.21	3301 30	551.33	3506 10	592.29
3003 10	542.11	3202 10	532.31	3301 90	551.35	3506 91	592.29
3003 20	542.12	3202 90	532.32	3302 10	551.41	3506 99	592.29
3003 31	542.21	3203 00	532.22	3302 90	551.49	3507 10	516.91
3003 39	542.22	3204 11	531.11	3303 00	553.10	3507 90	516.91
3003 40	542.31	3204 12	531.12	3304 10	553.20	3601 00	593.11
3003 90	542.91	3204 13	531.13	3304 20	553.20	3602 00	593.12
3004 10	542.13	3204 14	531.14	3304 30	553.20	3603 00	593.20
3004 20	542.19	3204 15	531.15	3304 91	553.20	3604 10	593.31
3004 31	542.23	3204 16	531.16	3304 99	553.20	3604 90	593.33
3004 32	542.24	3204 17	531.17	3305 10	553.30	3605 00	899.32
3004 39	542.29	3204 19	531.19	3305 20	553.30	3606 10	899.34
3004 40	542.32	3204 20	531.21	3305 30	553.30	3606 90	899.39
3004 50	542.92	3204 90	531.21	3305 90	553.30	3701 10	882.20
3004 50	542.92	3205 00	531.22	3306 10	553.40	3701 20	882.20
3004 50	542.92	3206 11	533.11	3306 20	553.40	3701 30	882.20
3004 90	542.93	3206 19	533.11	3306 90	553.40	3701 91	882.20
3004 90	542.93	3206 20	533.12	3307 10	553.51	3701 99	882.20
3004 90	542.93	3206 30	533.13	3307 20	553.52	3702 10	882.30
3004 90	542.93	3206 41	533.14	3307 30	553.53	3702 20	882.30

HS	SITC(R3)	HS	SITC(R3)	HS	SITC(R3)	HS	SITC(R3)
3702 31	882.30	3810 90	598.96	3904 50	573.93	3918 10	893.31
3702 32	882.30	3810 90	598.96	3904 61	573.94	3918 90	893.31
3702 39	882.30	3811 11	597.21	3904 69	573.94	3919 10	582.11
3702 41	882.30	3811 19	597.21	3904 90	573.99	3919 90	582.19
3702 42	882.30	3811 21	597.25	3905 12	575.91	3920 10	582.21
3702 43	882.30	3811 29	597.25	3905 19	575.91	3920 20	582.22
3702 44	882.30	3811 90	597.29	3905 21	575.91	3920 30	582.23
3702 51	882.30	3812 10	598.63	3905 29	575.91	3920 41	582.24
3702 52	882.30	3812 20	598.93	3905 30	575.92	3920 42	582.24
3702 53	882.30	3812 30	598.93	3905 91	575.92	3920 51	582.25
3702 54	882.30	3813 00	598.94	3905 99	575.92	3920 59	582.25
3702 55	882.30	3814 00	533.55	3906 10	575.21	3920 61	582.26
3702 56	882.30	3815 11	598.81	3906 90	575.29	3920 62	582.26
3702 91	882.30	3815 12	598.83	3907 10	574.11	3920 63	582.26
3702 92	882.30	3815 19	598.85	3907 20	574.19	3920 69	582.26
3702 93	882.30	3815 90	598.89	3907 30	574.20	3920 71	582.28
3702 94	882.30	3816 00	662.33	3907 40	574.31	3920 72	582.27
3702 95	882.30	3817 10	598.41	3907 50	574.32	3920 73	582.28
3703 10	882.40	3817 20	598.45	3907 60	574.33	3920 79	582.28
3703 20	882.40	3818 00	598.50	3907 91	574.34	3920 91	582.29
3703 90	882.40	3819 00	597.31	3907 99	574.39	3920 92	582.29
3704 00	882.50	3820 00	597.33	3908 10	575.31	3920 93	582.29
3705 10	882.60	3821 00	598.67	3908 90	575.39	3920 94	582.29
3705 20	882.60	3822 00	598.69	3909 10	575.41	3920 99	582.29
3705 90	882.60	3823 11	431.31	3909 20	575.42	3921 11	582.91
3706 10	883.10	3823 12	431.31	3909 30	575.43	3921 12	582.91
3706 90	883.90	3823 13	431.31	3909 40	575.44	3921 13	582.91
3707 10	882.10	3823 19	431.31	3909 50	575.45	3921 14	582.91
3707 90	882.10	3823 70	512.17	3910 00	575.93	3921 19	582.91
3801 10	598.61	3824 10	598.99	3911 10	575.96	3921 90	582.99
3801 20	598.61	3824 20	598.99	3911 90	575.96	3922 10	893.21
3801 30	598.61	3824 30	598.99	3912 11	575.51	3922 20	893.21
3801 90	598.61	3824 40	598.97	3912 12	575.52	3922 90	893.21
3802 10	598.64	3824 50	598.98	3912 20	575.53	3923 10	893.19
3802 90	598.65	3824 60	598.99	3912 31	575.54	3923 21	893.11
3803 00	598.11	3824 71	598.99	3912 39	575.54	3923 29	893.11
3804 00	598.12	3824 79	598.99	3912 90	575.59	3923 30	893.19
3805 10	598.13	3824 90	598.99	3913 10	575.94	3923 40	893.19
3805 20	598.13	3901 10	571.11	3913 90	575.95	3923 50	893.19
3805 90	598.13	3901 20	571.12	3914 00	575.97	3923 90	893.19
3806 10	598.14	3901 30	571.20	3915 10	579.10	3924 10	893.32
3806 20	598.14	3901 90	571.90	3915 20	579.20	3924 90	893.32
3806 30	598.14	3902 10	575.11	3915 90	579.90	3925 10	893.29
3806 90	598.14	3902 20	575.12	3916 10	583.10	3925 20	893.29
3807 00	598.18	3902 30	575.13	3916 20	583.20	3925 30	893.29
3808 10	591.10	3902 90	575.19	3916 90	583.20	3925 90	893.29
3808 20	591.20	3903 11	572.11	3917 10	581.10	3926 10	893.94
3808 30	591.30	3903 19	572.19	3917 21	581.20	3926 20	848.21
3808 40	591.41	3903 20	572.91	3917 22	581.20	3926 30	893.95
3808 90	591.49	3903 30	572.92	3917 23	581.20	3926 40	893.99
3809 10	598.91	3903 90	572.99	3917 29	581.20	3926 90	893.99
3809 91	598.91	3904 10	573.11	3917 31	581.30	4001 10	231.10
3809 92	598.91	3904 21	573.12	3917 32	581.40	4001 21	231.21
3809 93	598.91	3904 22	573.13	3917 33	581.50	4001 22	231.25
3810 10	598.96	3904 30	573.91	3917 39	581.60	4001 29	231.29
3810 90	598.96	3904 40	573.92	3917 40	581.70	4001 30	231.30

HS	SITC(R3)	HS	SITC(R3)	HS	SITC(R3)	HS	SITC(R3)
4002 11	232.11	4014 90	629.19	4202 92	831.99	4408 31	634.12
4002 19	232.11	4015 11	848.22	4202 99	831.99	4408 39	634.12
4002 20	232.12	4015 19	848.22	4203 10	848.11	4408 90	634.12
4002 31	232.13	4015 90	848.29	4203 21	894.77	4409 10	248.30
4002 39	232.13	4016 10	629.92	4203 29	848.12	4409 20	248.50
4002 41	232.14	4016 91	629.99	4203 30	848.13	4410 11	634.22
4002 49	232.14	4016 92	629.99	4203 40	848.19	4410 19	634.22
4002 51	232.15	4016 93	629.99	4204 00	612.10	4410 90	634.23
4002 59	232.15	4016 94	629.99	4205 00	612.90	4411 11	634.51
4002 60	232.16	4016 95	629.99	4206 10	899.91	4411 19	634.51
4002 70	232.17	4016 99	629.99	4206 90	899.91	4411 21	634.52
4002 80	232.18	4017 00	629.91	4301 10	212.10	4411 29	634.52
4002 91	232.19	4101 10	211.20	4301 20	212.21	4411 31	634.53
4002 99	232.19	4101 21	211.11	4301 30	212.22	4411 39	634.53
4003 00	232.21	4101 22	211.11	4301 40	212.23	4411 91	634.59
4004 00	232.22	4101 29	211.11	4301 50	212.24	4411 99	634.59
4005 10	621.11	4101 30	211.12	4301 60	212.25	4412 13	634.31
4005 20	621.12	4101 40	211.13	4301 70	212.26	4412 14	634.31
4005 91	621.19	4102 10	211.60	4301 80	212.29	4412 19	634.39
4005 99	621.19	4102 21	211.70	4301 90	212.30	4412 22	634.41
4006 10	621.21	4102 29	211.70	4302 11	613.11	4412 23	634.41
4006 90	621.29	4103 10	211.40	4302 12	613.12	4412 29	634.41
4007 00	621.31	4103 20	211.99	4302 13	613.13	4412 92	634.49
4008 11	621.32	4103 90	211.99	4302 19	613.19	4412 93	634.49
4008 19	621.32	4104 10	611.30	4302 20	613.20	4412 99	634.49
4008 21	621.33	4104 21	611.41	4302 30	613.30	4413 00	634.12
4008 29	621.33	4104 22	611.41	4303 10	848.31	4414 00	635.41
4009 10	621.41	4104 29	611.41	4303 90	848.31	4415 10	635.11
4009 20	621.42	4104 31	611.42	4304 00	848.32	4415 20	635.12
4009 30	621.43	4104 39	611.42	4401 10	245.00	4416 00	635.20
4009 40	621.44	4105 11	611.51	4401 21	246.11	4417 00	635.91
4009 50	621.45	4105 12	611.51	4401 22	246.15	4418 10	635.31
4010 11	629.29	4105 19	611.51	4401 30	246.20	4418 20	635.32
4010 12	629.29	4105 20	611.52	4402 00	245.02	4418 30	635.33
4010 13	629.29	4106 11	611.61	4403 10	247.30	4418 30	635.39
4010 19	629.29	4106 12	611.61	4403 20	247.40	4418 40	635.33
4010 21	629.21	4106 19	611.61	4403 41	247.51	4418 50	635.33
4010 22	629.21	4106 20	611.62	4403 49	247.52	4418 90	635.39
4010 23	629.29	4107 10	611.71	4403 49	247.51	4419 00	635.42
4010 24	629.29	4107 21	611.72	4403 91	247.52	4420 10	635.49
4010 29	629.29	4107 29	611.72	4403 92	247.52	4420 90	635.49
4011 10	625.10	4107 90	611.79	4403 99	247.52	4421 10	635.99
4011 20	625.20	4108 00	611.81	4404 10	634.91	4421 90	635.99
4011 20	625.10	4109 00	611.83	4404 20	634.91	4501 10	244.03
4011 30	625.30	4110 00	211.91	4405 00	634.93	4501 90	244.04
4011 40	625.41	4111 00	611.20	4406 10	248.11	4502 00	244.02
4011 50	625.42	4201 00	612.20	4406 90	248.19	4503 10	633.19
4011 91	625.51	4202 11	831.21	4407 10	248.20	4503 10	633.11
4011 99	625.59	4202 12	831.22	4407 24	248.40	4503 90	633.19
4012 10	625.92	4202 19	831.29	4407 25	248.40	4504 10	633.29
4012 20	625.93	4202 21	831.11	4407 26	248.40	4504 10	633.29
4012 90	625.94	4202 22	831.12	4407 29	248.40	4504 10	633.21
4013 10	625.91	4202 29	831.19	4407 91	248.40	4504 90	633.29
4013 20	625.91	4202 31	831.91	4407 92	248.40	4601 10	899.73
4013 90	625.91	4202 32	831.91	4407 99	248.40	4601 20	899.74
4014 10	629.11	4202 91	831.99	4408 10	634.11	4601 20	899.74

HS	SITC(R3)	HS	SITC(R3)	HS	SITC(R3)	HS	SITC(R3)
4601 20	899.74	4805 70	641.58	4819 40	642.14	5101 29	268.29
4601 91	899.79	4805 80	641.59	4819 50	642.15	5101 30	268.29
4601 99	899.79	4806 10	641.53	4819 60	642.16	5102 10	268.30
4602 10	899.71	4806 20	641.53	4820 10	642.31	5102 20	268.59
4602 90	899.71	4806 30	641.53	4820 20	642.32	5103 10	268.63
4701 00	251.20	4806 40	641.53	4820 30	642.33	5103 20	268.69
4702 00	251.30	4807 10	641.91	4820 40	642.34	5103 30	268.69
4703 11	251.41	4807 90	641.92	4820 40	642.34	5104 00	268.62
4703 19	251.42	4808 10	641.64	4820 40	642.34	5105 10	268.71
4703 21	251.51	4808 20	641.61	4820 50	642.35	5105 21	268.71
4703 29	251.52	4808 30	641.62	4820 90	642.39	5105 29	268.73
4704 11	251.61	4808 90	641.69	4821 10	892.81	5105 30	268.77
4704 19	251.61	4809 10	641.31	4822 10	642.91	5105 40	268.77
4704 21	251.62	4809 20	641.31	4822 90	642.91	5106 10	651.12
4704 29	251.62	4809 90	641.31	4823 11	642.44	5106 20	651.17
4705 00	251.91	4810 11	641.32	4823 19	642.44	5106 20	651.12
4706 10	251.92	4810 12	641.33	4823 20	642.45	5107 10	651.13
4706 20	251.92	4810 21	641.34	4823 40	642.99	5107 20	651.18
4706 91	251.92	4810 29	641.34	4823 51	642.48	5108 10	651.14
4706 92	251.92	4810 31	641.74	4823 59	642.48	5108 20	651.14
4706 93	251.92	4810 32	641.75	4823 60	642.93	5109 10	651.16
4707 10	251.11	4810 39	641.76	4823 70	642.99	5109 90	651.19
4707 20	251.12	4810 91	641.77	4823 90	642.92	5110 00	651.15
4707 30	251.13	4810 99	641.77	4823 90	642.99	5111 11	654.21
4707 90	251.19	4811 10	641.73	4901 10	892.15	5111 19	654.21
4801 00	641.10	4811 21	641.78	4901 91	892.16	5111 20	654.31
4802 10	641.21	4811 29	641.78	4901 99	892.19	5111 30	654.31
4802 20	641.22	4811 31	641.71	4902 10	892.21	5111 90	654.33
4802 30	641.23	4811 39	641.72	4902 90	892.29	5112 11	654.22
4802 40	641.24	4811 40	641.79	4903 00	892.12	5112 19	654.22
4802 51	641.25	4811 90	641.79	4904 00	892.85	5112 20	654.32
4802 52	641.26	4812 00	641.93	4905 10	892.14	5112 30	654.32
4802 53	641.27	4813 10	642.41	4905 91	892.13	5112 90	654.34
4802 60	641.29	4813 20	642.41	4905 99	892.14	5113 00	654.92
4803 00	641.63	4813 90	641.55	4906 00	892.82	5201 00	263.10
4804 11	641.41	4814 10	641.94	4907 00	892.83	5202 10	263.31
4804 19	641.41	4814 20	641.94	4908 90	892.41	5202 91	263.32
4804 21	641.42	4814 30	641.94	4909 00	892.42	5202 99	263.39
4804 29	641.42	4814 90	641.94	4909 10	892.41	5203 00	263.40
4804 31	641.46	4815 00	659.11	4910 00	892.86	5204 11	651.21
4804 39	641.46	4816 10	642.42	4911 10	892.86	5204 19	651.21
4804 41	641.47	4816 20	642.42	4911 91	892.87	5204 20	651.22
4804 42	641.47	4816 30	642.42	4911 99	892.89	5205 11	651.33
4804 49	641.47	4816 90	642.42	5001 00	261.41	5205 12	651.33
4804 51	641.48	4817 10	642.21	5002 00	261.30	5205 13	651.33
4804 52	641.48	4817 20	642.22	5003 10	261.42	5205 14	651.33
4804 59	641.48	4817 30	642.23	5003 90	261.49	5205 15	651.33
4805 10	641.51	4818 10	642.43	5004 00	651.92	5205 21	651.33
4805 21	641.54	4818 20	642.94	5005 00	651.93	5205 22	651.33
4805 22	641.54	4818 30	642.94	5006 00	651.94	5205 23	651.33
4805 23	641.54	4818 40	642.95	5007 10	654.11	5205 24	651.33
4805 29	641.54	4818 50	642.94	5007 20	654.13	5205 26	651.33
4805 30	641.52	4818 90	642.94	5007 90	654.19	5205 27	651.33
4805 40	641.56	4819 10	642.11	5101 11	268.11	5205 28	651.33
4805 50	641.56	4819 20	642.12	5101 19	268.19	5205 31	651.33
4805 60	641.57	4819 30	642.13	5101 21	268.21	5205 32	651.33

HS	SITC(R3)	HS	SITC(R3)	HS	SITC(R3)	HS	SITC(R3)
5205 33	651.33	5209 22	652.41	5302 90	265.21	5406 20	651.71
5205 34	651.33	5209 29	652.41	5303 10	264.10	5407 10	653.11
5205 35	651.33	5209 31	652.42	5303 90	264.90	5407 20	653.12
5205 41	651.33	5209 32	652.42	5304 10	265.41	5407 30	653.13
5205 42	651.33	5209 39	652.42	5304 90	265.49	5407 41	653.14
5205 43	651.33	5209 41	652.44	5305 11	265.71	5407 42	653.14
5205 44	651.33	5209 42	652.43	5305 19	265.79	5407 43	653.14
5205 46	651.33	5209 43	652.44	5305 21	265.51	5407 44	653.14
5205 47	651.33	5209 49	652.44	5305 29	265.59	5407 51	653.15
5205 48	651.33	5209 51	652.45	5305 91	265.81	5407 52	653.15
5206 11	651.34	5209 52	652.45	5305 99	265.89	5407 53	653.15
5206 12	651.34	5209 59	652.45	5306 10	651.96	5407 54	653.15
5206 13	651.34	5210 11	652.23	5306 20	651.96	5407 61	653.16
5206 14	651.34	5210 12	652.23	5307 10	651.97	5407 69	653.17
5206 15	651.34	5210 19	652.23	5307 20	651.97	5407 71	653.17
5206 21	651.34	5210 21	652.51	5308 10	651.99	5407 72	653.17
5206 22	651.34	5210 31	652.52	5308 20	651.99	5407 73	653.17
5206 23	651.34	5210 32	652.52	5308 30	651.99	5407 74	653.17
5206 24	651.34	5210 39	652.52	5308 90	651.99	5407 81	653.18
5206 25	651.34	5210 41	652.53	5309 11	654.41	5407 82	653.18
5206 31	651.34	5210 42	652.53	5309 19	654.41	5407 83	653.18
5206 32	651.34	5210 49	652.53	5309 21	654.42	5407 84	653.18
5206 33	651.34	5210 51	652.54	5309 29	654.42	5407 91	653.19
5206 34	651.34	5210 52	652.54	5310 10	654.50	5407 92	653.19
5206 35	651.34	5210 59	652.54	5310 90	654.50	5407 93	653.19
5206 41	651.34	5211 11	652.24	5311 00	654.93	5407 94	653.19
5206 42	651.34	5211 12	652.24	5401 10	651.41	5408 10	653.51
5206 43	651.34	5211 19	652.24	5401 20	651.42	5408 21	653.52
5206 44	651.34	5211 21	652.61	5402 10	651.62	5408 22	653.52
5206 45	651.34	5211 22	652.61	5402 20	651.62	5408 23	653.52
5207 10	651.31	5211 29	652.61	5402 31	651.51	5408 24	653.52
5207 90	651.32	5211 31	652.62	5402 32	651.51	5408 31	653.59
5208 11	652.21	5211 32	652.62	5402 33	651.52	5408 32	653.59
5208 12	652.21	5211 39	652.62	5402 39	651.59	5408 33	653.59
5208 13	652.21	5211 41	652.64	5402 41	651.63	5408 34	653.59
5208 19	652.21	5211 42	652.63	5402 42	651.63	5501 10	266.61
5208 21	652.31	5211 43	652.64	5402 43	651.63	5501 20	266.62
5208 22	652.31	5211 49	652.64	5402 49	651.63	5501 30	266.63
5208 23	652.31	5211 51	652.65	5402 51	651.64	5501 90	266.69
5208 29	652.31	5211 52	652.65	5402 52	651.64	5502 00	267.12
5208 31	652.32	5211 59	652.65	5402 59	651.64	5503 10	266.51
5208 32	652.32	5212 11	652.25	5402 61	651.69	5503 20	266.52
5208 33	652.32	5212 12	652.91	5402 62	651.69	5503 30	266.53
5208 39	652.32	5212 13	652.92	5402 69	651.69	5503 40	266.59
5208 41	652.33	5212 14	652.93	5403 10	651.73	5503 90	266.59
5208 42	652.33	5212 15	652.94	5403 20	651.72	5504 10	267.11
5208 43	652.33	5212 21	652.26	5403 31	651.74	5504 90	267.11
5208 49	652.33	5212 22	652.95	5403 32	651.75	5505 10	267.21
5208 51	652.34	5212 23	652.96	5403 33	651.75	5505 20	267.22
5208 52	652.34	5212 24	652.97	5403 41	651.76	5506 10	266.71
5208 53	652.34	5212 25	652.98	5403 42	651.76	5506 20	266.72
5208 59	652.34	5301 10	265.11	5403 49	651.76	5506 30	266.73
5209 11	652.22	5301 21	265.12	5404 10	651.88	5506 90	266.79
5209 12	652.22	5301 29	265.12	5404 90	651.88	5507 00	267.13
5209 19	652.22	5301 30	265.13	5405 00	651.77	5508 10	651.43
5209 21	652.41	5302 10	265.21	5406 10	651.61	5508 20	651.44

HS	SITC(R3)	HS	SITC(R3)	HS	SITC(R3)	HS	SITC(R3)
5509 11	651.82	5514 32	653.33	5603 92	657.20	5801 90	654.95
5509 12	651.82	5514 33	653.33	5603 93	657.20	5802 11	652.12
5509 21	651.82	5514 39	653.34	5603 94	657.20	5802 19	652.13
5509 22	651.82	5514 41	653.33	5604 10	657.81	5802 20	654.96
5509 31	651.82	5514 42	653.33	5604 20	657.85	5802 30	654.97
5509 32	651.82	5514 43	653.33	5604 90	657.89	5803 10	652.11
5509 41	651.82	5514 49	653.34	5605 00	651.91	5803 90	654.94
5509 42	651.82	5515 11	653.43	5606 00	656.31	5804 10	656.41
5509 51	651.84	5515 12	653.42	5607 10	657.51	5804 21	656.42
5509 52	651.84	5515 13	653.41	5607 21	657.51	5804 29	656.42
5509 53	651.84	5515 19	653.43	5607 29	657.51	5804 30	656.43
5509 59	651.84	5515 21	653.42	5607 30	657.51	5805 00	658.91
5509 61	651.84	5515 21	653.42	5607 41	657.51	5806 10	656.11
5509 62	651.84	5515 21	653.42	5607 49	657.51	5806 20	656.12
5509 69	651.84	5515 21	653.42	5607 50	657.51	5806 31	656.13
5509 91	651.84	5515 22	653.41	5607 90	657.51	5806 32	656.13
5509 92	651.84	5515 29	653.43	5608 11	657.52	5806 39	656.13
5509 99	651.84	5515 29	653.43	5608 19	657.52	5806 40	656.14
5510 11	651.86	5515 91	653.42	5608 90	657.52	5807 10	656.21
5510 12	651.86	5515 92	653.41	5609 00	657.59	5807 90	656.29
5510 20	651.87	5515 99	653.43	5701 10	659.21	5808 10	656.32
5510 30	651.87	5515 99	653.43	5701 90	659.29	5808 90	656.32
5510 90	651.87	5516 11	653.60	5702 10	659.30	5809 00	654.91
5511 10	651.81	5516 12	653.60	5702 20	659.59	5810 10	656.51
5511 20	651.83	5516 13	653.60	5702 31	659.51	5810 91	656.59
5511 30	651.85	5516 14	653.60	5702 32	659.52	5810 92	656.59
5512 11	653.21	5516 21	653.83	5702 39	659.59	5810 99	656.59
5512 19	653.21	5516 22	653.83	5702 41	659.51	5811 00	657.40
5512 21	653.25	5516 23	653.83	5702 42	659.52	5901 10	657.31
5512 29	653.25	5516 24	653.83	5702 49	659.59	5901 90	657.31
5512 91	653.29	5516 31	653.82	5702 51	659.51	5902 10	657.93
5512 99	653.29	5516 32	653.82	5702 52	659.52	5902 20	657.93
5513 11	653.31	5516 33	653.82	5702 59	659.59	5902 90	657.93
5513 12	653.31	5516 34	653.82	5702 91	659.51	5903 10	657.32
5513 13	653.31	5516 41	653.81	5702 92	659.52	5903 20	657.32
5513 19	653.32	5516 42	653.81	5702 99	659.59	5903 90	657.32
5513 21	653.31	5516 43	653.81	5703 10	659.41	5904 10	659.12
5513 22	653.31	5516 44	653.81	5703 20	659.42	5904 91	659.12
5513 23	653.31	5516 91	653.89	5703 30	659.43	5904 92	659.12
5513 29	653.32	5516 92	653.89	5703 90	659.49	5905 00	657.35
5513 31	653.31	5516 93	653.89	5704 10	659.61	5906 10	657.33
5513 32	653.31	5516 94	653.89	5704 90	659.61	5906 91	657.33
5513 33	653.31	5601 10	657.71	5705 00	659.69	5906 99	657.33
5513 39	653.32	5601 21	657.71	5801 10	654.35	5907 00	657.34
5513 41	653.31	5601 22	657.71	5801 21	652.14	5908 00	657.72
5513 42	653.31	5601 29	657.71	5801 22	652.15	5909 00	657.91
5513 43	653.31	5601 30	657.71	5801 23	652.15	5910 00	657.92
5513 49	653.32	5602 10	657.11	5801 24	652.14	5911 10	657.73
5514 11	653.33	5602 21	657.12	5801 25	652.15	5911 20	657.73
5514 12	653.33	5602 29	657.12	5801 26	652.15	5911 31	657.73
5514 13	653.33	5602 90	657.19	5801 31	653.91	5911 32	657.73
5514 19	653.34	5603 11	657.20	5801 32	653.93	5911 40	657.73
5514 21	653.33	5603 12	657.20	5801 33	653.93	5911 90	657.73
5514 23	653.33	5603 13	657.20	5801 34	653.91	6001 10	655.11
5514 29	653.34	5603 14	657.20	5801 35	653.93	6001 21	655.12
5514 31	653.33	5603 91	657.20	5801 36	653.93	6001 22	655.12

HS	SITC(R3)	HS	SITC(R3)	HS	SITC(R3)	HS	SITC(R3)
6001 29	655.12	6104 52	844.25	6115 11	846.21	6204 31	842.30
6001 91	655.19	6104 53	844.25	6115 12	846.21	6204 32	842.30
6001 92	655.19	6104 59	844.25	6115 19	846.21	6204 32	842.30
6001 99	655.19	6104 61	844.26	6115 20	846.22	6204 32	842.30
6002 10	655.21	6104 62	844.26	6115 91	846.29	6204 33	842.30
6002 20	655.21	6104 63	844.26	6115 92	846.29	6204 39	842.30
6002 30	655.22	6104 69	844.26	6115 93	846.29	6204 41	842.40
6002 41	655.23	6105 10	843.71	6115 99	846.29	6204 42	842.40
6002 42	655.23	6105 20	843.79	6116 10	846.91	6204 43	842.40
6002 43	655.23	6105 90	843.79	6116 91	846.92	6204 44	842.40
6002 49	655.23	6106 10	844.70	6116 92	846.92	6204 49	842.40
6002 91	655.29	6106 20	844.70	6116 93	846.92	6204 51	842.50
6002 92	655.29	6106 90	844.70	6116 99	846.92	6204 52	842.50
6002 93	655.29	6107 11	843.81	6117 10	846.93	6204 53	842.50
6002 99	655.29	6107 12	843.81	6117 20	846.94	6204 59	842.50
6101 10	843.10	6107 19	843.81	6117 80	846.99	6204 61	842.60
6101 20	843.10	6107 21	843.82	6117 90	846.99	6204 62	842.60
6101 30	843.10	6107 22	843.82	6201 11	841.11	6204 63	842.60
6101 90	843.10	6107 29	843.82	6201 12	841.12	6204 69	842.60
6102 10	844.10	6107 91	843.89	6201 13	841.12	6205 10	841.59
6102 20	844.10	6107 92	843.89	6201 19	841.12	6205 20	841.51
6102 30	844.10	6107 99	843.89	6201 91	841.19	6205 30	841.59
6102 90	844.10	6108 11	844.81	6201 92	841.19	6205 90	841.59
6103 11	843.21	6108 19	844.81	6201 93	841.19	6206 10	842.70
6103 12	843.21	6108 21	844.82	6201 99	841.19	6206 20	842.70
6103 19	843.21	6108 22	844.82	6202 11	842.11	6206 30	842.70
6103 21	843.22	6108 29	844.82	6202 12	842.11	6206 40	842.70
6103 22	843.22	6108 31	844.83	6202 13	842.11	6206 90	842.70
6103 23	843.22	6108 32	844.83	6202 19	842.11	6207 11	841.61
6103 29	843.22	6108 39	844.83	6202 91	842.19	6207 19	841.61
6103 31	843.23	6108 91	844.89	6202 92	842.19	6207 21	841.62
6103 32	843.23	6108 92	844.89	6202 93	842.19	6207 22	841.62
6103 33	843.23	6108 99	844.89	6202 99	842.19	6207 29	841.62
6103 39	843.23	6109 10	845.40	6203 11	841.21	6207 91	841.69
6103 41	843.24	6109 90	845.40	6203 12	841.22	6207 92	841.69
6103 42	843.24	6110 10	845.30	6203 19	841.22	6207 99	841.69
6103 43	843.24	6110 20	845.30	6203 21	841.23	6208 11	842.81
6103 49	843.24	6110 30	845.30	6203 22	841.23	6208 19	842.81
6104 11	844.21	6110 90	845.30	6203 23	841.23	6208 21	842.82
6104 12	844.21	6111 10	845.12	6203 29	841.23	6208 22	842.82
6104 13	844.21	6111 20	845.12	6203 31	841.30	6208 29	842.82
6104 19	844.21	6111 30	845.12	6203 32	841.30	6208 91	842.89
6104 21	844.22	6111 90	845.12	6203 33	841.30	6208 92	842.89
6104 22	844.22	6112 11	845.91	6203 39	841.30	6209 10	845.11
6104 23	844.22	6112 12	845.91	6203 41	841.40	6209 20	845.11
6104 29	844.22	6112 19	845.91	6203 42	841.40	6209 30	845.11
6104 31	844.23	6112 20	845.92	6203 43	841.40	6209 90	845.11
6104 32	844.23	6112 31	845.62	6203 49	841.40	6210 10	845.21
6104 33	844.23	6112 39	845.62	6204 11	842.21	6210 20	845.22
6104 39	844.23	6112 41	845.64	6204 12	842.21	6210 30	845.23
6104 41	844.24	6112 49	845.64	6204 13	842.21	6210 40	845.22
6104 42	844.24	6113 00	845.24	6204 19	842.21	6210 50	845.23
6104 43	844.24	6114 10	845.99	6204 21	842.22	6211 11	845.61
6104 44	844.24	6114 20	845.99	6204 22	842.22	6211 12	845.63
6104 49	844.24	6114 30	845.99	6204 23	842.22	6211 20	845.81
6104 51	844.25	6114 90	845.99	6204 29	842.22	6211 31	845.87

HS	SITC(R3)	HS	SITC(R3)	HS	SITC(R3)	HS	SITC(R3)
6211 32	841.19	6304 93	658.59	6501 00	657.61	6810 91	663.33
6211 33	841.19	6304 99	658.59	6502 00	657.62	6810 99	663.34
6211 39	845.87	6305 10	658.11	6503 00	848.41	6811 10	661.83
6211 41	845.89	6305 20	658.12	6504 00	848.42	6811 20	661.83
6211 42	842.19	6305 32	658.13	6505 10	848.43	6811 30	661.83
6211 43	842.19	6305 33	658.13	6505 90	848.43	6811 90	661.83
6211 49	845.89	6305 39	658.13	6506 10	848.44	6812 10	663.81
6212 10	845.51	6305 90	658.19	6506 91	848.45	6812 20	663.81
6212 20	845.52	6306 11	658.21	6506 92	848.49	6812 30	663.81
6212 30	845.52	6306 12	658.21	6506 99	848.49	6812 40	663.81
6212 90	845.52	6306 19	658.21	6507 00	848.48	6812 50	663.81
6213 10	846.11	6306 21	658.22	6601 10	899.41	6812 60	663.81
6213 20	846.11	6306 22	658.22	6601 91	899.41	6812 70	663.81
6213 90	846.11	6306 29	658.22	6601 99	899.41	6812 90	663.81
6214 10	846.12	6306 31	658.23	6602 00	899.42	6813 10	663.82
6214 20	846.12	6306 39	658.23	6603 10	899.49	6813 90	663.82
6214 30	846.12	6306 41	658.24	6603 20	899.49	6814 10	663.35
6214 40	846.12	6306 49	658.24	6603 90	899.49	6814 90	663.35
6214 90	846.12	6306 91	658.29	6701 00	899.92	6815 10	663.36
6215 10	846.13	6306 99	658.29	6702 10	899.21	6815 20	663.37
6215 20	846.13	6307 10	658.92	6702 90	899.29	6815 91	663.38
6215 90	846.13	6307 20	658.93	6703 00	899.94	6815 99	663.39
6216 00	846.14	6307 90	658.93	6704 11	899.95	6901 00	662.31
6217 10	846.19	6308 00	658.99	6704 19	899.95	6902 10	662.32
6217 90	846.19	6309 00	269.01	6704 20	899.95	6902 20	662.32
6301 10	775.85	6310 10	269.02	6704 90	899.95	6902 90	662.32
6301 20	658.31	6310 90	269.02	6801 00	661.31	6903 10	663.70
6301 30	658.32	6401 10	851.11	6802 10	661.33	6903 20	663.70
6301 40	658.33	6401 91	851.31	6802 21	661.34	6903 90	663.70
6301 90	658.39	6401 92	851.31	6802 22	661.35	6904 10	662.41
6302 10	658.41	6401 99	851.31	6802 23	661.35	6904 90	662.41
6302 21	658.42	6402 12	851.21	6802 29	661.35	6905 10	662.42
6302 22	658.43	6402 19	851.23	6802 91	661.36	6905 90	662.42
6302 29	658.43	6402 20	851.32	6802 92	661.39	6906 00	662.43
6302 31	658.42	6402 30	851.13	6802 93	661.39	6907 10	662.44
6302 32	658.43	6402 91	851.32	6802 99	661.39	6907 90	662.44
6302 39	658.43	6402 99	851.32	6803 00	661.32	6908 10	662.45
6302 40	658.44	6403 12	851.22	6804 10	663.11	6908 90	662.45
6302 51	658.45	6403 19	851.24	6804 21	663.12	6909 11	663.91
6302 52	65846	6403 20	851.41	6804 22	663.12	6909 12	663.91
6302 53	65846	6403 30	851.42	6804 23	663.12	6909 19	663.91
6302 59	65846	6403 40	851.15	6804 30	663.13	6909 90	663.91
6302 60	658.47	6403 51	851.48	6805 10	663.21	6910 10	812.21
6302 91	658.47	6403 59	851.48	6805 20	663.22	6910 90	812.29
6302 92	658.48	6403 91	851.48	6805 30	663.29	6911 10	666.11
6302 93	658.48	6403 99	851.48	6806 10	663.51	6911 90	666.12
6302 99	658.48	6404 11	851.25	6806 20	663.52	6912 00	666.13
6303 11	658.51	6404 19	851.51	6806 90	663.53	6913 10	666.21
6303 12	658.51	6404 20	851.52	6807 10	661.81	6913 90	666.29
6303 19	658.51	6405 10	851.49	6807 90	661.81	6914 10	666.29
6303 91	658.51	6405 20	851.59	6808 00	661.82	6914 90	663.99
6303 92	658.51	6405 90	851.70	6809 11	663.31	7001 00	664.11
6303 99	658.51	6406 10	851.90	6809 19	663.31	7002 10	664.12
6304 11	658.52	6406 20	851.90	6809 90	663.31	7002 20	664.12
6304 91	658.59	6406 91	851.90	6810 11	663.32	7002 31	664.12
6304 92	658.59	6406 99	851.90	6810 19	663.32	7002 32	664.12

HS	SITC(R3)	HS	SITC(R3)	HS	SITC(R3)	HS	SITC(R3)
7002 39	664.12	7019 40	654.60	7118 10	961.00	7209 15	673.41
7003 12	664.51	7019 51	654.60	7118 90	974.00	7209 16	673.42
7003 19	664.51	7019 52	654.60	7201 10	671.21	7209 17	673.43
7003 20	664.52	7019 59	654.60	7201 20	671.22	7209 18	673.44
7003 30	664.53	7019 90	664.95	7201 50	671.23	7209 25	673.45
7004 20	664.31	7020 00	665.99	7202 11	671.41	7209 26	673.46
7004 90	664.39	7101 10	667.11	7202 19	671.49	7209 27	673.47
7005 10	664.41	7101 21	667.12	7202 21	671.51	7209 28	673.48
7005 10	664.91	7101 22	667.13	7202 29	671.51	7209 90	673.52
7005 21	664.41	7102 10	667.21	7202 30	671.52	7210 11	672.41
7005 29	664.41	7102 21	277.11	7202 41	671.53	7210 12	672.41
7005 30	664.42	7102 29	277.19	7202 49	671.53	7210 20	674.41
7006 00	664.91	7102 31	667.22	7202 50	671.54	7210 30	674.41
7007 11	664.71	7102 39	667.29	7202 60	671.55	7210 41	674.13
7007 19	664.71	7103 10	667.31	7202 70	671.59	7210 49	674.13
7007 21	664.72	7103 91	667.39	7202 80	671.59	7210 50	674.42
7007 29	664.72	7103 99	667.39	7202 91	671.59	7210 61	674.43
7008 00	664.92	7104 10	667.41	7202 92	671.59	7210 69	674.43
7009 10	664.81	7104 20	667.42	7202 93	671.59	7210 70	674.31
7009 91	664.89	7104 90	667.49	7202 99	671.59	7210 90	674.44
7009 92	664.89	7105 10	277.21	7203 10	671.33	7211 13	673.26
7010 10	665.92	7105 90	277.21	7203 90	671.33	7211 14	673.27
7010 20	665.11	7106 10	681.14	7204 10	282.10	7211 19	673.29
7010 91	665.11	7106 91	681.13	7204 21	282.21	7211 19	673.29
7010 92	665.11	7106 92	681.14	7204 29	282.29	7211 19	673.27
7010 93	665.11	7107 00	681.12	7204 30	283.21	7211 23	673.49
7010 94	665.11	7108 11	971.01	7204 41	282.32	7211 29	673.49
7011 10	664.93	7108 12	971.01	7204 49	282.39	7211 90	673.53
7011 20	664.93	7108 13	971.01	7204 50	282.33	7212 10	674.22
7011 90	664.93	7108 20	974.00	7205 10	671.31	7212 20	674.12
7012 00	665.12	7109 00	971.02	7205 21	671.32	7212 30	674.14
7013 10	665.21	7110 11	681.23	7205 29	671.32	7212 40	674.32
7013 21	665.22	7110 19	681.25	7206 10	674.21	7212 50	674.51
7013 29	665.22	7110 21	681.24	7206 90	672.45	7212 60	674.52
7013 31	665.23	7110 29	681.25	7207 11	672.61	7213 10	676.11
7013 32	665.23	7110 31	681.24	7207 12	672.62	7213 20	676.11
7013 39	665.23	7110 39	681.25	7207 19	672.69	7213 91	676.13
7013 91	665.29	7110 41	681.24	7207 20	672.70	7213 91	676.14
7013 99	665.29	7110 49	681.25	7208 10	673.10	7213 91	676.14
7014 00	665.95	7111 00	681.22	7208 25	673.21	7213 91	676.12
7015 10	664.94	7112 10	971.03	7208 26	673.22	7213 99	676.14
7015 90	664.94	7112 20	282.91	7208 27	673.22	7213 99	676.13
7016 10	664.94	7112 90	282.92	7208 36	673.21	7214 10	676.43
7016 90	664.96	7113 11	897.31	7208 37	673.21	7214 20	676.21
7017 10	665.91	7113 19	897.31	7208 38	673.22	7214 30	676.22
7017 20	665.91	7113 20	897.31	7208 39	673.22	7214 91	676.24
7017 90	665.91	7114 11	897.32	7208 40	673.25	7214 91	676.23
7018 10	665.93	7114 19	897.32	7208 40	673.24	7214 99	676.24
7018 20	665.93	7114 20	897.32	7208 51	673.24	7214 99	676.23
7018 90	665.93	7115 10	897.41	7208 51	673.23	7215 10	676.31
7019 11	651.95	7115 90	897.49	7208 52	673.24	7215 50	676.33
7019 12	651.95	7116 10	897.33	7208 52	673.23	7215 90	676.44
7019 19	651.95	7116 20	897.33	7208 53	673.25	7216 10	676.81
7019 31	664.95	7117 11	897.21	7208 53	673.23	7216 21	676.81
7019 32	664.95	7117 19	897.21	7208 54	673.25	7216 22	676.81
7019 39	664.95	7117 90	897.29	7208 90	673.51	7216 31	676.82

HS	SITC(R3)	HS	SITC(R3)	HS	SITC(R3)	HS	SITC(R3)
7216 32	676.82	7225 91	675.73	7306 90	679.49	7318 29	694.22
7216 33	676.82	7225 92	675.73	7307 11	679.51	7319 10	699.31
7216 40	676.82	7225 99	675.73	7307 19	679.52	7319 20	699.32
7216 50	676.83	7226 11	675.12	7307 21	679.53	7319 30	699.32
7216 61	676.84	7226 19	675.12	7307 22	679.54	7319 90	699.31
7216 69	676.84	7226 20	675.22	7307 23	679.55	7320 10	699.41
7216 91	676.85	7226 91	675.43	7307 29	679.56	7320 20	699.41
7216 99	676.85	7226 92	675.62	7307 91	679.59	7320 90	699.41
7217 10	678.12	7226 93	675.74	7307 92	679.59	7321 11	697.31
7217 10	678.13	7226 94	675.74	7307 93	679.59	7321 12	697.31
7217 10	678.11	7226 99	675.74	7307 99	679.59	7321 13	697.31
7217 20	678.12	7227 10	676.17	7308 10	691.11	7321 81	697.32
7217 20	678.13	7227 20	676.19	7308 20	691.12	7321 82	697.32
7217 20	678.11	7227 90	676.17	7308 30	691.13	7321 83	697.32
7217 30	678.12	7228 10	676.41	7308 40	691.14	7321 90	697.33
7217 30	678.13	7228 20	676.42	7308 90	691.19	7322 11	812.11
7217 30	678.11	7228 30	676.29	7309 00	692.11	7322 19	812.11
7217 90	678.12	7228 40	676.46	7310 10	692.41	7322 90	812.15
7217 90	678.13	7228 50	676.39	7310 21	692.41	7323 10	697.44
7217 90	678.11	7228 60	676.47	7310 29	692.41	7323 91	697.41
7218 10	672.47	7228 70	676.88	7311 00	692.43	7323 92	697.41
7218 91	672.81	7228 80	676.48	7312 10	693.11	7323 93	697.41
7218 99	672.81	7229 10	678.29	7312 90	693.11	7323 94	697.41
7219 11	675.31	7229 20	678.29	7313 00	693.2	7323 99	697.41
7219 12	675.31	7229 90	678.29	7314 12	693.51	7324 10	697.51
7219 13	675.32	7301 10	676.86	7314 13	693.51	7324 21	697.51
7219 14	675.33	7301 20	676.86	7314 14	693.51	7324 29	697.51
7219 21	675.34	7302 10	677.01	7314 19	693.51	7324 90	697.51
7219 22	675.34	7302 20	677.09	7314 20	693.51	7325 10	699.62
7219 23	675.35	7302 30	677.09	7314 31	693.51	7325 91	699.63
7219 24	675.36	7302 40	677.09	7314 39	693.51	7325 99	699.63
7219 31	675.51	7302 90	677.09	7314 41	693.51	7326 11	699.65
7219 32	675.52	7303 00	679.11	7314 42	693.51	7326 19	699.65
7219 33	675.53	7304 10	679.12	7314 49	693.51	7326 20	699.67
7219 34	675.54	7304 21	679.13	7314 50	693.51	7326 90	699.69
7219 35	675.55	7304 29	679.13	7315 11	748.31	7401 10	283.21
7219 90	675.71	7304 31	679.14	7315 12	748.32	7401 20	283.22
7220 11	675.37	7304 39	679.14	7315 19	748.39	7402 00	682.11
7220 12	673.58	7304 41	679.15	7315 20	699.21	7403 11	682.12
7220 20	675.56	7304 49	679.15	7315 81	699.22	7403 12	682.12
7220 90	675.72	7304 51	679.16	7315 82	699.22	7403 13	682.12
7221 00	676.15	7304 59	679.16	7315 89	699.22	7403 19	682.12
7222 11	676.25	7304 90	679.16	7315 90	699.22	7403 21	682.14
7222 19	676.25	7305 11	679.17	7316 00	699.61	7403 22	682.14
7222 20	676.34	7305 12	679.31	7317 00	694.1	7403 23	682.14
7222 30	676.45	7305 19	679.31	7318 11	694.21	7403 29	682.14
7222 40	676.87	7305 20	679.32	7318 12	694.21	7404 00	288.21
7223 00	678.21	7305 31	679.33	7318 13	694.21	7405 00	682.13
7224 10	672.49	7305 39	679.33	7318 14	694.21	7406 10	682.62
7224 90	672.82	7305 90	679.39	7318 15	694.21	7406 20	682.62
7225 11	675.11	7306 10	679.41	7318 16	694.21	7407 10	682.31
7225 19	675.11	7306 20	679.42	7318 19	694.21	7407 21	682.32
7225 20	675.21	7306 30	679.43	7318 21	694.22	7407 22	682.32
7225 30	675.41	7306 40	679.43	7318 22	694.22	7407 29	682.32
7225 40	675.42	7306 50	679.43	7318 23	694.22	7408 11	682.41
7225 50	675.61	7306 60	679.44	7318 24	694.22	7408 19	682.41

HS	SITC(R3)	HS	SITC(R3)	HS	SITC(R3)	HS	SITC(R3)
7408 21	682.42	7602 00	288.23	8002 00	288.26	8203 10	695.22
7408 22	682.42	7603 10	684.25	8003 00	687.21	8203 20	695.23
7408 29	682.42	7603 20	684.25	8004 00	687.22	8203 30	695.23
7409 11	682.51	7604 10	684.21	8005 00	687.23	8203 40	695.23
7409 19	682.51	7604 21	684.21	8006 00	687.23	8204 11	695.30
7409 21	682.52	7604 29	684.21	8007 00	699.78	8204 12	695.30
7409 29	682.52	7605 11	684.22	8101 10	687.24	8204 20	695.30
7409 31	682.52	7605 19	684.22	8101 91	689.11	8205 10	695.41
7409 39	682.52	7605 21	684.22	8101 92	699.91	8205 20	695.42
7409 40	682.52	7605 29	684.22	8101 93	699.91	8205 30	695.43
7409 90	682.52	7606 11	684.23	8101 99	699.91	8205 40	695.44
7410 11	682.61	7606 12	684.23	8102 10	689.12	8205 51	695.45
7410 12	682.61	7606 91	684.23	8102 91	689.12	8205 59	695.46
7410 21	682.61	7606 92	684.23	8102 92	699.92	8205 70	695.47
7410 22	682.61	7607 11	684.24	8102 93	699.92	8205 80	695.48
7411 10	682.71	7607 19	684.24	8102 99	699.92	8205 90	695.49
7411 21	682.71	7607 20	684.24	8103 10	689.13	8206 00	695.70
7411 29	682.71	7608 10	684.26	8103 90	699.93	8207 13	695.63
7412 10	682.72	7608 20	684.26	8104 11	689.15	8207 19	695.63
7412 20	682.72	7609 00	684.27	8104 19	689.15	8207 20	695.64
7413 00	693.12	7610 10	691.21	8104 20	689.14	8207 30	695.64
7414 20	693.52	7610 90	691.29	8104 30	699.94	8207 40	695.64
7414 90	693.52	7611 00	692.12	8104 90	699.94	8207 50	695.64
7415 10	694.31	7612 10	692.42	8105 10	689.81	8207 60	695.64
7415 21	694.32	7612 90	692.42	8105 90	689.81	8207 70	695.64
7415 29	694.32	7613 00	692.44	8106 00	689.92	8207 80	695.64
7415 31	694.33	7614 10	693.13	8107 10	689.82	8207 90	695.64
7415 32	694.33	7614 90	693.13	8107 90	699.83	8208 10	695.61
7415 39	694.33	7615 11	697.43	8108 10	699.83	8208 20	695.61
7416 00	699.42	7615 19	697.43	8108 90	699.85	8208 30	695.61
7417 00	697.34	7615 20	697.53	8109 10	689.84	8208 40	695.61
7418 11	697.42	7616 10	694.40	8109 90	699.87	8208 90	695.61
7418 19	697.42	7616 91	699.79	8110 00	689.44	8209 00	695.62
7418 20	697.52	7616 99	699.79	8111 00	689.94	8210 00	697.81
7419 10	699.71	7801 10	685.12	8112 11	689.91	8211 10	696.80
7419 91	699.73	7801 91	685.11	8112 19	699.95	8211 91	696.80
7419 99	699.73	7801 99	685.11	8112 20	699.95	8211 92	696.80
7501 10	284.21	7802 00	288.24	8112 30	689.96	8211 93	696.80
7501 20	284.22	7803 00	685.21	8112 40	689.97	8211 94	696.80
7502 10	683.11	7804 11	685.22	8112 91	689.98	8211 95	696.80
7502 20	683.12	7804 19	685.22	8112 99	699.99	8212 10	696.31
7503 00	288.22	7804 20	685.22	8113 00	689.99	8212 20	696.35
7504 00	683.23	7805 00	685.24	8201 10	695.10	8212 90	696.38
7505 11	683.21	7806 00	699.76	8201 20	695.10	8213 00	696.40
7505 12	683.21	7901 11	686.11	8201 30	695.10	8214 10	696.51
7505 21	683.21	7901 12	686.11	8201 40	695.10	8214 20	696.55
7505 22	683.21	7901 20	686.12	8201 50	695.10	8214 90	696.59
7506 10	683.24	7902 00	288.25	8201 60	695.10	8215 10	696.61
7506 20	683.24	7903 10	686.33	8201 90	695.10	8215 20	696.62
7507 11	683.22	7903 90	686.33	8202 10	695.21	8215 91	696.63
7507 12	683.22	7904 00	686.31	8202 20	695.51	8215 99	696.69
7507 20	683.22	7905 00	686.32	8202 31	695.52	8301 10	699.11
7508 10	699.75	7906 00	686.34	8202 39	695.53	8301 20	699.11
7508 90	699.75	7907 00	699.77	8202 40	695.54	8301 30	699.11
7601 10	684.11	8001 10	687.11	8202 91	695.55	8301 40	699.11
7601 20	684.12	8001 20	687.12	8202 99	695.59	8301 50	699.11

HS	SITC(R3)	HS	SITC(R3)	HS	SITC(R3)	HS	SITC(R3)
8301 60	699.11	8407 34	713.22	8416 30	741.25	8424 10	745.61
8301 70	699.11	8407 90	713.81	8416 90	741.28	8424 20	745.62
8302 10	699.13	8408 10	713.33	8417 10	741.36	8424 30	745.63
8302 20	699.14	8408 20	713.23	8417 20	741.37	8424 30	745.65
8302 30	699.15	8408 90	713.82	8417 80	741.38	8424 81	745.64
8302 41	699.16	8409 10	713.19	8417 90	741.39	8424 89	745.65
8302 42	699.17	8409 91	713.91	8418 10	775.21	8424 90	745.68
8302 49	699.19	8409 99	713.92	8418 21	775.21	8425 11	744.21
8302 50	699.19	8410 11	718.11	8418 22	775.21	8425 19	744.21
8302 60	699.19	8410 12	718.11	8418 29	775.21	8425 20	744.23
8303 00	699.12	8410 13	718.11	8418 30	775.22	8425 31	744.25
8304 00	699.12	8410 90	718.19	8418 40	775.22	8425 39	744.25
8305 10	895.12	8411 11	714.41	8418 50	741.43	8425 41	744.41
8305 20	895.12	8411 12	714.41	8418 61	741.45	8425 42	744.43
8305 90	895.12	8411 21	714.81	8418 69	741.45	8425 49	744.49
8306 10	699.52	8411 22	714.81	8418 91	741.49	8426 11	744.31
8306 21	697.82	8411 81	714.89	8418 99	741.49	8426 12	744.32
8306 29	697.82	8411 82	714.89	8419 11	741.81	8426 19	744.33
8307 10	699.51	8411 91	714.91	8419 19	741.82	8426 20	744.34
8307 90	699.51	8411 99	714.99	8419 20	741.83	8426 30	744.35
8308 10	699.33	8412 10	714.49	8419 31	741.84	8426 41	744.37
8308 20	699.33	8412 21	718.91	8419 32	741.85	8426 49	744.37
8308 90	699.33	8412 29	718.93	8419 39	741.86	8426 91	744.39
8309 10	699.53	8412 31	718.92	8419 40	741.73	8426 99	744.39
8309 90	699.53	8412 39	718.93	8419 50	741.74	8427 10	744.11
8310 00	699.54	8412 80	718.93	8419 60	741.75	8427 20	744.12
8311 10	699.55	8412 90	718.99	8419 81	741.87	8427 90	744.13
8311 20	699.55	8413 11	742.11	8419 89	741.89	8428 10	744.81
8311 30	699.55	8413 19	742.19	8419 90	741.90	8428 20	744.71
8311 90	699.55	8413 20	742.71	8420 10	745.91	8428 31	744.72
8401 10	718.71	8413 30	742.20	8420 91	745.93	8428 32	744.73
8401 20	728.47	8413 40	742.30	8420 99	745.93	8428 33	744.74
8401 30	718.77	8413 50	742.40	8421 11	743.51	8428 39	744.79
8401 40	718.78	8413 60	742.50	8421 12	743.55	8428 40	744.85
8402 11	711.11	8413 70	742.60	8421 19	743.59	8428 50	744.89
8402 12	711.11	8413 81	742.71	8421 21	743.61	8428 90	744.89
8402 19	711.11	8413 82	742.75	8421 22	743.62	8429 11	723.11
8402 20	711.12	8413 91	742.91	8421 23	743.63	8429 19	723.11
8402 90	711.91	8413 92	742.95	8421 29	743.67	8429 20	723.12
8403 10	812.17	8414 10	743.11	8421 31	743.64	8429 30	723.31
8403 90	812.19	8414 20	743.13	8421 39	743.69	8429 40	723.33
8404 10	711.21	8414 30	743.15	8421 91	743.91	8429 51	723.21
8404 20	711.22	8414 40	743.17	8421 99	743.95	8429 52	723.22
8404 90	711.92	8414 51	743.41	8422 11	775.30	8429 59	723.29
8405 10	741.47	8414 59	743.43	8422 19	745.21	8430 10	723.41
8405 90	741.72	8414 60	743.45	8422 20	745.23	8430 20	723.42
8406 10	712.11	8414 80	743.19	8422 30	745.27	8430 31	723.35
8406 81	712.19	8414 90	743.80	8422 40	745.27	8430 39	723.43
8406 82	712.19	8415 10	741.51	8422 90	745.29	8430 41	723.37
8406 90	712.8	8415 20	741.55	8423 10	745.32	8430 49	723.44
8407 10	713.11	8415 81	741.55	8423 20	745.31	8430 50	723.39
8407 21	713.31	8415 82	741.55	8423 30	745.31	8430 61	723.45
8407 29	713.32	8415 83	741.55	8423 81	745.31	8430 62	723.46
8407 31	713.21	8415 90	741.59	8423 82	745.31	8430 69	723.47
8407 32	713.21	8416 10	741.21	8423 89	745.31	8431 10	744.91
8407 33	713.21	8416 20	741.23	8423 90	745.39	8431 20	744.92

HS	SITC(R3)	HS	SITC(R3)	HS	SITC(R3)	HS	SITC(R3)
8431 31	744.93	8441 40	725.27	8451 30	724.74	8461 20	731.71
8431 39	744.94	8441 80	725.29	8451 40	724.74	8461 30	731.73
8431 41	723.91	8441 90	725.99	8451 50	724.74	8461 40	731.75
8431 42	723.92	8442 10	726.31	8451 80	724.74	8461 50	731.77
8431 43	723.93	8442 20	726.31	8451 90	724.92	8461 90	731.79
8431 49	723.99	8442 30	726.31	8452 10	724.33	8462 10	733.11
8432 10	721.11	8442 40	726.91	8452 21	724.35	8462 21	733.12
8432 21	721.13	8442 50	726.35	8452 29	724.35	8462 29	733.13
8432 29	721.13	8443 11	726.51	8452 30	724.39	8462 31	733.14
8432 30	721.12	8443 12	726.55	8452 40	724.39	8462 39	733.15
8432 40	721.12	8443 19	726.59	8452 90	724.39	8462 41	733.16
8432 80	721.18	8443 21	726.61	8453 10	724.81	8462 49	733.17
8432 90	721.19	8443 29	726.61	8453 20	724.83	8462 91	733.18
8433 11	721.21	8443 30	726.63	8453 80	724.85	8462 99	733.18
8433 19	721.21	8443 40	726.65	8453 90	724.88	8463 10	733.91
8433 20	721.23	8443 51	745.65	8454 10	737.11	8463 20	733.93
8433 30	721.23	8443 59	726.67	8454 20	737.11	8463 30	733.95
8433 40	721.23	8443 60	726.68	8454 30	737.12	8463 90	733.99
8433 51	721.22	8443 90	726.99	8454 90	737.19	8464 10	728.11
8433 52	721.23	8444 00	724.41	8455 10	737.21	8464 20	728.11
8433 53	721.23	8445 11	724.42	8455 21	737.21	8464 90	728.11
8433 59	721.23	8445 12	724.42	8455 22	737.21	8465 10	728.12
8433 60	721.26	8445 13	724.42	8455 30	737.21	8465 91	728.12
8433 90	721.29	8445 19	724.42	8455 90	737.21	8465 92	728.12
8434 10	721.31	8445 20	724.43	8456 10	731.11	8465 93	728.12
8434 20	721.38	8445 30	724.43	8456 20	731.12	8465 94	728.12
8434 90	721.39	8445 40	724.43	8456 30	731.13	8465 95	728.12
8435 10	721.91	8445 90	724.54	8456 91	731.14	8465 96	728.12
8435 90	721.96	8446 10	724.51	8456 99	731.14	8465 99	728.12
8436 10	721.96	8446 21	724.51	8457 10	731.21	8466 10	735.11
8436 21	721.95	8446 29	724.51	8457 20	731.22	8466 20	735.13
8436 29	721.95	8446 30	724.51	8457 30	731.23	8466 30	735.15
8436 80	721.96	8447 11	724.52	8458 11	731.31	8466 91	728.19
8436 91	721.99	8447 12	724.52	8458 19	731.37	8466 92	728.19
8436 99	721.99	8447 20	724.52	8458 91	731.35	8466 93	735.91
8437 10	721.27	8447 90	724.53	8458 99	731.39	8466 94	735.95
8437 80	727.11	8448 11	724.61	8459 10	731.41	8467 11	745.11
8437 90	727.19	8448 19	724.61	8459 21	731.42	8467 19	745.11
8438 10	727.22	8448 20	724.49	8459 29	731.43	8467 81	745.12
8438 20	727.22	8448 31	724.49	8459 31	731.44	8467 89	745.12
8438 30	727.22	8448 32	724.49	8459 39	731.45	8467 91	745.19
8438 40	727.22	8448 33	724.49	8459 40	731.46	8467 92	745.19
8438 50	727.22	8448 41	724.67	8459 51	731.51	8467 99	745.19
8438 60	727.22	8448 42	724.67	8459 59	731.52	8468 10	737.41
8438 80	727.22	8448 49	724.67	8459 61	731.53	8468 20	737.42
8438 90	727.29	8448 51	724.68	8459 69	731.54	8468 80	737.43
8439 10	725.11	8448 59	724.68	8459 70	731.57	8468 90	737.49
8439 20	725.12	8449 00	724.55	8460 11	731.61	8469 11	751.13
8439 30	725.12	8450 11	775.11	8460 19	731.62	8469 12	751.13
8439 91	725.91	8450 12	775.11	8460 21	731.63	8469 20	751.15
8439 99	725.91	8450 19	775.11	8460 29	731.64	8469 30	751.18
8440 10	726.81	8450 20	724.71	8460 31	731.65	8470 10	778.78
8440 90	726.89	8450 90	724.91	8460 39	731.66	8470 10	75121
8441 10	725.21	8451 10	724.72	8460 40	731.67	8470 21	751.22
8441 20	725.23	8451 21	775.12	8460 90	731.69	8470 29	751.22
8441 30	725.25	8451 29	724.73	8461 10	731.78	8470 30	751.22

HS	SITC(R3)	HS	SITC(R3)	HS	SITC(R3)	HS	SITC(R3)
8470 40	751.23	8479 81	728.46	8502 20	716.51	8512 10	778.34
8470 50	751.24	8479 82	728.49	8502 31	716.52	8512 20	778.34
8470 90	751.28	8479 89	728.49	8502 39	716.52	8512 30	778.34
8471 10	752.10	8479 90	728.55	8502 40	716.40	8512 40	778.34
8471 30	752.20	8480 10	749.11	8503 00	716.90	8512 90	778.35
8471 41	752.21	8480 20	749.12	8504 10	771.23	8513 10	813.12
8471 49	752.90	8480 30	749.13	8504 21	771.11	8513 90	813.12
8471 49	752.60	8480 41	749.14	8504 22	771.11	8514 10	741.31
8471 50	752.30	8480 49	749.15	8504 23	771.11	8514 20	741.32
8471 60	752.61	8480 50	749.16	8504 31	771.19	8514 30	741.33
8471 70	759.97	8480 60	749.17	8504 32	771.19	8514 40	741.34
8471 70	752.70	8480 71	749.18	8504 33	771.19	8514 90	741.35
8471 80	752.91	8480 79	749.19	8504 34	771.19	8515 11	737.31
8471 90	752.92	8481 10	747.10	8504 40	752.93	8515 19	737.32
8472 10	751.91	8481 20	747.20	8504 40	771.21	8515 21	737.33
8472 20	751.92	8481 30	747.30	8504 50	771.25	8515 29	737.34
8472 30	751.93	8481 40	747.40	8504 90	771.29	8515 31	737.35
8472 90	751.99	8481 80	747.80	8505 11	778.81	8515 39	737.36
8473 10	759.91	8481 90	747.90	8505 19	778.81	8515 80	737.37
8473 21	759.95	8482 10	746.10	8505 20	778.81	8515 90	737.39
8473 29	759.95	8482 20	746.20	8505 30	778.81	8516 10	775.81
8473 30	759.97	8482 30	746.30	8505 90	778.81	8516 21	775.82
8473 40	759.93	8482 40	746.40	8506 10	778.81	8516 29	775.82
8473 50	759.93	8482 50	746.50	8506 30	778.81	8516 31	775.83
8474 10	728.31	8482 80	746.80	8506 40	778.81	8516 32	775.83
8474 20	728.32	8482 91	746.91	8506 50	778.81	8516 33	775.83
8474 31	728.33	8482 99	746.99	8506 60	778.81	8516 40	775.83
8474 32	728.33	8483 10	748.10	8506 80	778.81	8516 50	775.86
8474 39	728.33	8483 20	748.21	8506 90	778.17	8516 60	775.86
8474 80	728.34	8483 30	748.22	8507 10	778.12	8516 71	775.87
8474 90	728.39	8483 40	748.40	8507 20	778.12	8516 72	775.87
8475 10	728.41	8483 50	748.50	8507 30	778.12	8516 79	775.87
8475 21	728.41	8483 60	748.60	8507 40	778.12	8516 80	775.88
8475 29	728.41	8483 90	748.90	8507 80	778.12	8516 90	775.89
8475 90	728.51	8484 10	749.20	8507 90	778.19	8517 11	764.11
8476 21	745.95	8484 20	749.99	8508 10	778.41	8517 19	764.11
8476 29	745.95	8484 90	749.20	8508 20	778.43	8517 19	764.32
8476 81	745.95	8485 10	749.91	8508 80	778.45	8517 21	764.19
8476 89	745.95	8485 90	749.99	8508 90	778.48	8517 22	764.13
8476 90	749.57	8501 10	716.10	8509 10	775.71	8517 30	764.15
8477 10	728.42	8501 20	716.13	8509 20	775.71	8517 50	764.19
8477 20	728.42	8501 31	716.20	8509 30	775.73	8517 50	764.17
8477 30	728.42	8501 32	716.20	8509 40	775.72	8517 80	764.19
8477 40	728.42	8501 33	716.20	8509 80	775.73	8517 90	764.91
8477 51	728.42	8501 34	716.20	8509 90	775.79	8518 10	764.21
8477 59	728.42	8501 40	716.31	8510 10	775.41	8518 21	764.22
8477 80	728.42	8501 51	716.31	8510 20	775.42	8518 22	764.22
8477 90	728.52	8501 52	716.31	8510 30	775.73	8518 29	764.23
8478 10	728.43	8501 53	716.31	8510 90	775.49	8518 30	764.24
8478 90	728.53	8501 61	716.32	8511 10	778.31	8518 40	764.25
8479 10	723.48	8501 62	716.32	8511 20	778.31	8518 50	764.26
8479 20	727.21	8501 63	716.32	8511 30	778.31	8519 10	763.31
8479 30	728.84	8501 64	716.32	8511 40	778.31	8519 21	763.33
8479 40	728.49	8502 11	716.51	8511 50	778.31	8519 29	763.33
8479 50	728.49	8502 12	716.51	8511 80	778.31	8519 31	763.35
8479 60	728.49	8502 13	716.51	8511 90	778.33	8519 39	763.35

HS	SITC(R3)	HS	SITC(R3)	HS	SITC(R3)	HS	SITC(R3)
8519 40	763.82	8530 80	778.82	8540 60	776.23	8601 10	791.11
8519 92	763.83	8530 90	778.83	8540 71	776.25	8601 20	791.15
8519 93	763.83	8531 10	778.84	8540 72	776.25	8602 10	791.21
8519 99	763.83	8531 20	778.84	8540 79	776.25	8602 90	791.29
8520 10	763.84	8531 80	778.84	8540 81	776.27	8603 10	791.60
8520 20	763.84	8531 90	778.85	8540 89	776.27	8603 90	791.61
8520 32	763.84	8532 10	778.61	8540 91	776.27	8604 00	791.81
8520 33	763.84	8532 21	778.62	8540 99	776.27	8605 00	791.70
8520 39	763.84	8532 22	778.63	8541 10	776.31	8606 10	791.82
8520 90	763.84	8532 23	778.64	8541 21	776.32	8606 20	791.82
8521 10	763.81	8532 24	778.65	8541 29	776.33	8606 30	791.82
8521 90	763.81	8532 25	778.66	8541 30	776.35	8606 91	791.82
8522 10	764.99	8532 29	778.67	8541 40	776.37	8606 92	791.82
8522 90	764.99	8532 30	778.68	8541 50	776.39	8606 99	791.82
8523 11	898.41	8532 90	778.69	8541 60	776.81	8607 11	791.99
8523 13	898.45	8533 10	772.31	8541 90	776.88	8607 12	791.99
8523 20	898.51	8533 21	772.32	8542 12	776.41	8607 19	791.99
8523 30	898.59	8533 29	772.32	8542 13	776.41	8607 19	791.99
8523 90	898.59	8533 31	772.33	8542 14	776.41	8607 21	791.99
8524 10	898.71	8533 39	772.33	8542 19	776.41	8607 29	791.99
8524 31	898.79	8533 40	772.35	8542 30	776.43	8607 30	791.99
8524 32	898.79	8533 90	772.38	8542 40	776.45	8607 91	791.99
8524 39	898.79	8534 00	772.20	8542 50	776.49	8607 99	791.99
8524 40	898.60	8535 10	772.41	8542 90	776.89	8608 00	791.91
8524 51	898.60	8535 21	772.42	8543 11	778.71	8609 00	786.30
8524 52	898.60	8535 29	772.43	8543 19	778.71	8701 10	722.41
8524 53	898.60	8535 30	772.44	8543 20	778.78	8701 20	783.20
8524 60	898.79	8535 40	772.45	8543 30	778.78	8701 30	722.30
8524 91	898.79	8535 90	772.49	8543 40	778.78	8701 90	722.49
8524 99	898.79	8536 10	772.51	8543 81	778.78	8702 10	783.11
8525 10	764.31	8536 20	772.52	8543 89	778.78	8702 90	783.19
8525 20	764.32	8536 30	772.53	8543 90	778.79	8703 10	781.10
8525 30	764.82	8536 41	772.54	8544 11	773.11	8703 21	781.20
8525 40	763.81	8536 50	772.55	8544 19	773.11	8703 22	781.21
8525 40	764.82	8536 61	772.57	8544 20	773.12	8703 23	781.22
8526 10	764.83	8536 69	772.58	8544 30	773.13	8703 24	781.23
8526 91	764.83	8536 90	772.59	8544 41	773.14	8703 31	781.24
8526 92	764.83	8537 10	772.61	8544 49	773.14	8703 32	781.25
8527 12	762.21	8537 20	772.62	8544 51	773.15	8703 33	781.26
8527 13	762.21	8538 10	772.81	8544 59	773.15	8703 90	781.27
8527 19	762.22	8538 90	772.82	8544 60	773.17	8704 10	782.11
8527 21	762.11	8539 10	778.23	8544 70	773.18	8704 21	782.19
8527 29	762.12	8539 21	778.21	8545 11	778.86	8704 22	782.19
8527 31	762.81	8539 22	778.21	8545 19	778.86	8704 23	782.19
8527 32	762.82	8539 29	778.21	8545 20	778.86	8704 31	782.19
8527 39	762.89	8539 31	778.22	8545 90	778.86	8704 32	782.19
8527 90	764.81	8539 32	778.22	8546 10	773.22	8704 90	782.19
8528 12	761.10	8539 39	778.22	8546 20	773.23	8705 10	782.21
8528 13	761.20	8539 41	778.24	8546 90	773.24	8705 20	782.23
8528 21	761.10	8539 49	778.24	8547 10	773.26	8705 30	782.25
8528 22	761.20	8539 90	778.29	8547 20	773.28	8705 40	782.27
8528 30	761.22	8540 11	776.11	8547 90	773.29	8705 90	782.29
8528 30	761.12	8540 12	776.12	8548 10	282.39	8706 00	784.10
8529 10	764.93	8540 20	776.21	8548 10	778.12	8707 10	784.21
8529 90	764.93	8540 40	776.23	8548 10	778.11	8707 90	784.25
8530 10	778.82	8540 50	776.23	8548 90	778.89	8708 10	784.31

HS	SITC(R3)	HS	SITC(R3)	HS	SITC(R3)	HS	SITC(R3)
8708 21	784.32	8803 90	792.97	9008 10	881.32	9018 90	872.29
8708 29	784.32	8804 00	899.96	9008 20	881.31	9019 10	872.31
8708 31	784.33	8805 10	792.83	9008 30	881.32	9020 00	872.35
8708 39	784.33	8805 20	792.83	9008 40	881.33	9021 11	899.63
8708 40	784.34	8901 10	793.28	9008 90	881.34	9021 19	899.63
8708 50	784.35	8901 20	793.22	9009 11	751.31	9021 21	899.65
8708 60	784.36	8901 30	793.26	9009 12	751.32	9021 29	899.65
8708 70	784.39	8901 90	793.27	9009 21	751.33	9021 30	899.66
8708 80	784.39	8902 00	793.24	9009 22	751.34	9021 40	899.61
8708 91	784.39	8903 10	793.11	9009 30	751.35	9021 50	899.67
8708 92	784.39	8903 91	793.12	9009 90	759.10	9021 90	899.69
8708 93	784.39	8903 92	793.19	9010 10	881.35	9022 12	774.21
8708 94	784.39	8903 99	793.19	9010 41	881.35	9022 13	774.21
8708 99	784.39	8904 00	793.70	9010 42	881.35	9022 14	774.21
8709 11	744.14	8905 10	793.51	9010 49	881.35	9022 19	774.21
8709 19	744.15	8905 20	793.55	9010 50	881.35	9022 21	774.22
8709 90	744.19	8905 90	793.59	9010 60	881.35	9022 29	774.22
8710 00	891.11	8906 00	793.29	9010 90	881.36	9022 30	774.23
8711 10	785.11	8907 10	793.91	9011 10	871.41	9022 90	774.29
8711 20	785.13	8907 90	793.99	9011 20	871.43	9023 00	874.52
8711 30	785.15	8908 00	793.30	9011 80	871.45	9024 10	874.53
8711 40	785.16	9001 10	884.19	9011 90	871.49	9024 80	874.53
8711 50	785.17	9001 20	884.19	9012 10	871.31	9024 90	874.54
8711 90	785.19	9001 30	884.11	9012 90	871.39	9025 11	874.55
8712 00	785.20	9001 40	884.15	9013 10	871.91	9025 19	874.55
8713 10	785.31	9001 50	884.17	9013 20	871.92	9025 80	874.55
8713 90	785.31	9001 90	884.19	9013 80	871.93	9025 90	874.56
8714 11	785.35	9002 11	884.31	9013 90	871.99	9026 10	874.31
8714 19	785.35	9002 19	884.32	9014 10	874.11	9026 20	874.35
8714 20	785.35	9002 20	884.33	9014 20	874.11	9026 80	874.37
8714 91	785.37	9002 90	884.39	9014 80	874.11	9026 90	874.39
8714 92	785.37	9003 11	884.21	9014 90	874.12	9027 10	874.41
8714 93	785.37	9003 19	884.21	9015 10	874.12	9027 20	874.42
8714 94	785.37	9003 90	884.22	9015 20	874.12	9027 30	874.43
8714 95	785.37	9004 10	884.23	9015 30	874.12	9027 40	874.44
8714 96	785.37	9004 90	884.23	9015 40	874.12	9027 50	874.45
8714 99	785.37	9005 10	871.11	9015 80	874.12	9027 80	874.46
8715 00	894.10	9005 80	871.15	9015 90	874.14	9027 90	874.49
8716 10	894.10	9005 90	871.19	9016 00	874.51	9028 10	873.11
8716 20	786.21	9006 10	881.11	9017 10	874.22	9028 20	873.13
8716 31	786.22	9006 20	881.11	9017 20	874.22	9028 30	873.15
8716 39	786.29	9006 30	881.11	9017 30	874.23	9028 90	873.19
8716 40	786.83	9006 40	881.11	9017 80	874.23	9029 10	873.21
8716 80	786.85	9006 51	881.11	9017 90	874.24	9029 20	873.25
8716 90	786.89	9006 52	881.11	9018 11	774.11	9029 90	873.29
8801 10	792.81	9006 53	881.11	9018 12	774.12	9030 10	874.71
8801 90	792.82	9006 61	881.13	9018 13	774.12	9030 20	874.73
8802 11	792.11	9006 62	881.12	9018 14	774.12	9030 31	874.75
8802 12	792.15	9006 69	881.13	9018 19	774.12	9030 39	874.75
8802 20	792.20	9006 91	881.14	9018 20	774.13	9030 40	874.77
8802 30	792.30	9006 99	881.15	9018 31	872.21	9030 82	874.78
8802 40	792.40	9007 11	881.21	9018 32	872.21	9030 83	874.78
8802 60	792.50	9007 19	881.21	9018 39	872.21	9030 89	874.78
8803 10	792.91	9007 20	881.22	9018 41	872.11	9030 90	874.79
8803 20	792.93	9007 91	881.23	9018 49	872.19	9031 10	874.25
8803 30	792.95	9007 92	881.24	9018 50	872.25	9031 20	874.25

HS	SITC(R3)	HS	SITC(R3)	HS	SITC(R3)	HS	SITC(R3)
9031 30	874.25	9112 80	885.97	9401 20	821.12	9505 90	894.49
9031 41	874.25	9112 90	885.97	9401 30	821.14	9506 11	894.73
9031 49	874.25	9113 10	885.92	9401 40	821.15	9506 12	894.73
9031 80	874.25	9113 20	885.92	9401 50	821.13	9506 19	894.73
9031 90	874.26	9113 90	885.93	9401 61	821.16	9506 21	894.74
9032 10	874.61	9114 10	885.99	9401 69	821.16	9506 29	894.74
9032 20	874.63	9114 20	885.99	9401 71	821.17	9506 31	894.75
9032 81	874.65	9114 30	885.99	9401 79	821.17	9506 32	894.75
9032 89	874.65	9114 40	885.99	9401 80	821.18	9506 39	894.75
9032 90	874.69	9114 90	885.99	9401 90	821.19	9506 40	894.79
9033 00	874.90	9201 10	898.13	9402 10	872.40	9506 51	894.76
9101 11	885.31	9201 20	898.13	9402 90	872.40	9506 59	894.76
9101 12	885.31	9201 90	898.13	9403 10	821.31	9506 61	894.79
9101 19	885.31	9202 10	898.15	9403 20	821.39	9506 62	894.79
9101 21	885.32	9202 90	898.15	9403 30	821.51	9506 69	894.79
9101 29	885.32	9203 00	898.21	9403 40	821.53	9506 70	894.72
9101 91	885.39	9204 10	898.22	9403 50	821.55	9506 91	894.78
9101 99	885.39	9204 20	898.22	9403 60	821.59	9506 99	894.79
9102 11	885.41	9205 10	898.23	9403 70	821.71	9507 10	894.71
9102 12	885.41	9205 90	898.23	9403 80	821.79	9507 20	894.71
9102 19	885.41	9206 00	898.24	9403 90	821.80	9507 30	894.71
9102 21	885.42	9207 10	898.25	9404 10	821.21	9507 90	894.71
9102 29	885.42	9207 90	898.26	9404 21	821.23	9508 00	894.60
9102 91	885.49	9208 10	898.29	9404 29	821.25	9601 10	899.11
9102 99	885.49	9208 90	898.29	9404 30	821.27	9601 90	899.11
9103 10	885.72	9209 10	898.90	9404 90	821.29	9602 00	899.19
9103 90	885.73	9209 20	898.90	9405 10	813.11	9603 10	899.72
9104 00	885.71	9209 30	898.90	9405 20	813.13	9603 21	899.72
9105 11	885.74	9209 91	898.90	9405 30	894.41	9603 29	899.72
9105 19	885.75	9209 92	898.90	9405 40	813.15	9603 30	899.72
9105 21	885.76	9209 93	898.90	9405 50	813.17	9603 40	899.72
9105 29	885.77	9209 94	898.90	9405 60	813.20	9603 50	899.72
9105 91	885.78	9209 99	898.90	9405 91	813.91	9603 90	899.72
9105 99	885.79	9301 00	891.12	9405 92	813.92	9604 00	899.81
9106 10	885.94	9302 00	891.14	9405 99	813.99	9605 00	831.30
9106 20	885.94	9303 10	891.31	9406 00	811.00	9606 10	899.83
9106 90	885.94	9303 20	891.31	9501 00	894.21	9606 21	899.83
9107 00	885.95	9303 30	891.31	9502 10	894.22	9606 22	899.83
9108 11	885.51	9303 90	891.31	9502 91	894.23	9606 29	899.83
9108 12	885.51	9304 00	891.39	9502 99	894.23	9606 30	899.84
9108 19	885.51	9305 10	891.91	9503 10	894.24	9607 11	899.85
9108 20	885.52	9305 21	891.93	9503 20	894.24	9607 19	899.85
9108 91	885.52	9305 29	891.95	9503 30	894.24	9607 20	899.86
9108 99	885.52	9305 90	891.99	9503 41	894.25	9608 10	895.21
9109 11	885.96	9305 90	981.99	9503 49	894.25	9608 20	895.21
9109 19	885.96	9306 10	891.21	9503 50	894.26	9608 31	895.21
9109 90	885.96	9306 21	891.22	9503 60	894.27	9608 39	895.21
9110 11	885.98	9306 29	891.23	9503 70	894.29	9608 40	895.21
9110 12	885.98	9306 30	891.24	9503 80	894.29	9608 50	895.21
9110 19	885.98	9306 30	891.24	9503 90	894.29	9608 60	895.21
9110 90	885.98	9306 30	891.24	9504 10	894.31	9608 91	895.22
9111 10	885.91	9306 30	981.24	9504 20	894.33	9608 99	895.21
9111 20	885.91	9306 90	891.29	9504 30	894.35	9609 10	895.23
9111 80	885.91	9306 90	981.29	9504 40	894.37	9609 20	895.23
9111 90	885.91	9307 00	981.13	9504 90	894.39	9609 90	895.23
9112 10	885.97	9401 10	821.11	9505 10	894.45	9610 00	895.92

HS	SITC(R3)
9611 00	895.93
9612 10	895.94
9613 10	899.33
9613 20	899.33
9613 30	899.33
9613 80	899.33
9613 90	899.35
9614 20	899.36
9614 20	899.37
9614 20	899.36
9614 90	899.37
9615 11	899.89
9615 19	899.89
9615 90	899.89
9616 10	899.87
9616 20	899.82
9617 00	899.97
9617 00	899.97
9617 00	899.97
9617 00	899.97
9618 00	899.88
9701 10	896.11
9701 90	896.12
9702 00	896.20
9703 00	896.30
9704 00	896.40
9705 00	896.50
9706 00	896.60

A

A

Amplifiers, audio-frequency	764.25, 764.92
Ampoule files (saws)	695.22
Ampoules, glass	665.91,92
Amusement machines	894.35,39
Anchors, iron or steel	699.61
Anchovies	034.1,2; 034.12,13,4; 037.16
Andalusite	278.29
Angledozers	723.11

Angles (profiles) -

Aluminium	684.21
Copper	682.31,32
Iron or steel	676.8
Lead	685.21
Magnesium	699.94
Nickel	683.21
Tin	687.21
Zinc	686.31
Animal black	598.65
Animal feed preparations	081.95,99
Animal hair clippers (machinery)	721.96,99
Animal or vegetable fats and oil machinery	727.21
Animals, dead (unfit for human consumption)	291.94,96,99
Animals, live	Div.00
Anise seeds	075.26
Anodes, zinc	699.77
Anoraks	842.1; 843.1; 844.1
Anthracene	335.25, 511.29
Anthracene black	522.1
Anthracite	321.1
Anti-corrosive and anti-fouling compositions	533.41,42,43
Anti-freezing preparations	597.33
Anti-knock preparations	597.21
Anti-histamine medicaments	542.9
Anti-rust preparations	597.7, 598.99
Anti-sprouting products	591.3
Antibiotics	541.3, 542.1
Antimonates	524.31
Antimony	689.93, 699.99
Antimony ores and concentrates	287.99
Antiques	896.6
Antisera	541.63
Antlers	291.16
Anvils	695.48
Apparatus for games and sports	894

Apparel -

Asbestos	663.18
Fur, artificial (except headgear and footwear)	848.32
Furskin (except headgear and footwear)	848.31
Headgear	657.62, 848.4
Knitted or crocheted	843, 844, 845, 846
Leather	848.1
Plastics	848.21
Rubber	848.22,29
Worn, in bulk packings	269.01
Other textile	841, 842, 845, 846
Apple pomace, dried	081.11
Apples	see Fruit, edible
Appliance wires, electrical, insulated	773.1
Apricot kernels	054.85
Apricots	see Fruit, edible
Aprons	845.87,89,99
Aqueous distillates of essential oils	551.35
Aqueous solutions of essential oils	551.35
Arabic, gum	292.22
Arc-lamp carbons	778.86
Arc-lamps	778.24
Architectural plans and drawings	892.82
Areca and cola nuts	057.79
Argol	081.94
Armaments	891

A

Armoured fighting vehicles and parts	981.11
Arrowroot, fresh or dried	054.83
Arsenates	523.89
Arsenic	522.22
Arsenic sulphides, natural	278.99
Arsenites	523.89

Artificial -

Flowers, foliage or fruit	899.2
Graphite	598.61
Honey	061.99
Stone, articles of	663.32,34
Waxes	598.3
Artillery weapons	981.12
Artists' brushes	899.72
Artists' colours	533.52
Asbestos, articles of	663.81
Asbestos, crude and waste	278.4
Asbestos-cement, articles of	661.83
Asbestos-cement working machinery	728.11
Asparagus	see Vegetables, edible
Asphalt, articles of	661.81
Asphalt, natural	278.97
Asphaltic rock	278.97

Asprin (acetylsalicyclic acid) -

Tabletted or compounded	542.9
Other	513.94
Asses	001.52
Astronomical instruments	871.15,19
Athletic equipment	894.72-79
Atlases	892.13
Auger bits	695.63,64
Automata (animated shop window displays)	899.88

Automatic data processing machines (including systems) and units thereof-

Machines, systems and units thereof	752
Parts	759.97
Automatic door closers, base metal	699.16
Automatic stop motions, textile	724.6
Automatic vending machines	745.95,97
Automatics, bar and chucking (lathes)	731.3
Auxiliary boiler plant	711.21
Aviation fuel (kerosene type)	334.21
Aviation fuel (spirit type)	334.12
Avocados, fresh or dried	057.97
Awnings, textile	658.21
Axes	695.1
Axles for motor vehicles	784.3
Axles, tyres and wheels for railway and tramway rolling stock	791.99
Azides	524.95

B

Baby carriages and parts	894.1
Backsaws	695.21,5
Backward wave oscillators and amplifiers	778.78,79
Bacon	016.1
Bacon, canned, prepared or preserved	017.5
Bacon, prepared or preserved	017.5
Badges, woven textile, not embroidered	656.21
Badian seeds	075.26
Bag and envelope making machinery	725.23,99
Bagasse	081.52
Bagasse pulp	251.92
Bagatelle tables	894.39
Bags, for packing of goods, of woven textile materials	658.1
Bags, paper	642.13,14
Bags, of plastic sheeting, for packing of goods (without handles)	893.11
Bags, of plastic sheeting,	

B

B

Billiard tables	894.33
Binoculars, refracting	871.11,19
Bins, storage (furniture)	821.3,5,7,8
Birds (other than poultry)	001.9
Birds' nests (edible)	098.92
Biscuits, chocolate coated	048.42
Biscuits	048.42,49
Bismuth, metal	689.92, 699.99
Bits, drilling	695.63,64
Bitumen, natural	278.97
Bitumen, petroleum	335.41

Bituminous -
Asphalts (manufactured) and emulsions	335.43
Mineral oils, crude	333.0
Mixtures and mastics	335.43
Paints	533.43
Shale	278.96
Black, animal	598.65

Blades -
Bandsaw	695.51
Cutting, for machines or mechanical appliances	695.61
Knife	696.8
Safety razor	696.35
Saw, for hand or machine saws	695.5
Scissor	696.4
Bladders, animal	291.93
Bladders, fish	291.96

Blankets -
Electric (textile)	775.85
Other textile	658.3
Blanks, record	898.71
Bleaching machines for textiles	724.74,92
Blister copper	682.11
Blockboard	634.4
Blocks, pulley	748.5
Blood, animal	291.99
Blood-grouping reagents	541.92
Blouses	842.7, 844.7
Blow lamps	695.46
Boards, with writing or drawing surfaces	895.92
Boats	793.1,2,7

Bobbins -
For spinning and weaving, of iron or steel	699.67,69
Of paper	642.91
Of wood	635.99
Bodies (including cabs) for motor vehicles	784.2
Bodkins, iron or steel	699.31
Boilers, central heating (other than steam generating boilers), iron or steel	812.17,19
steam and other vapour generating	711.11,19
Boilers, sugar	741.89,9
Bolduc	656.13
Bolster cases	658.41-43
Bolt croppers	695.23
Bolting cloth	657.73
Bolts, copper	694.33
Bolts (for the securing of doors, windows, etc) of base metal	699.16
Bolts, iron or steel	694.2
Bolts and nuts, of nickel	699.75
Bombs	981.29
Bonded fibre fabrics, and articles thereof, other than stitch bonded	657.2
Bond, share and stock certificates	892.83
Bone black	598.65
Bone, worked	899.11
Bone-working machinery	728.12,19
Bones and bone pieces, meal and powder	291.11
Bonito	034.14,23; 037.13
Book-binding and book-sewing machinery	726.81,89
Bookcases	821.3,5,7,8

Bookcloth	657.31

Books -
Childrens' picture, drawing or colouring	892.12
Other printed	892.15,16,19
Boot and shoe (leather) machinery	724.83,88
Boots	851.1-7
Borates and concentrates (crude, natural)	278.94
Borates and perborates	523.84
Borax (disodium tetraborate)	523.84

Boric acid -
Crude natural	278.94
Other	522.35
Boric oxide	522.35
Borides	524.95
Boring and sinking machines	723.35,37,44,93,99
Boring machines, metal working	731.41,44-46,91
Boron	522.22
Bottle caps, base metal	699.53
Bottle cleaning and drying machines	745.23,29

Bottles -
Plastic	893.11
Glass	665.11
Bovine animals	001.11,19
Boxes, aluminium	692.42
Boxes, iron or steel	692.41
Boxes, paper and paperboard	642.11,12
Boxes, wood	635.11
Braces, carpenters	695.41
Braces (clothing)	845.5
Braid making machines	724.53,61,68
Braid, textile, in the piece	656.23

Brake linings -
Mounted	784.33
Unmounted	663.82
Brandy	112.42

Brans, sharps and other residues -
Cereals	081.24,26,29
Leguminous vegetables	081.23
Rice	081.25
Brass (alloy of copper and zinc)	682.12
Brassières	845.5
Brazil nuts, fresh or dried	057.72
Brazing appliances, gas-operated	737.41,42,49
Brazing machines and apparatus, electric	737.31,32,39
Brazing powders and pastes	598.96
Bread and breadcrumbs	048.41
Breakdown lorries	782.29, 784
Breathing appliances	872.33,35
Breeches	841.4, 842.6, 843.2, 844.26
Brewers pitch	598.18
Brewery machinery	727.22,29
Bridges, iron or steel	691.11
Brickmaking machinery	728.34,39

Bricks and blocks -
Concrete, including refractory concrete	663.32
Non refractory, clay	662.41

Refractory -
Chemically bonded	663.38
Fired after shaping	662.32
Of siliceous fossil meals or earths	662.31
Fusion cast	663.39
Pitch bonded	663.39
Tar bonded	663.39
Bricks, glass	664.96
Briefcases	831.2
Briquettes (coal)	322.1
Brisling (sprats) prepared or preserved	037.12
Bristles, animal	291.92
Broaching machines	731.77, 735.91
Broaching tools	695.64
Broadcasters, fertiliser	721.12,19

B

Brocades -
Cotton 652
Man-made filaments 653.1,5
Man-made staple fibres 653.2,3,4,6,8
Broccoli, dried, dehydrated or evaporated 056.19
Brochures, booklets, etc printed -
Advertising material 892.86
Other 895.15
Bromates and perbromates 523.39
Bromides and oxybromides 523.39
Bromine 522.25
Bronze alloy of copper and tin 682.12
Brooders, poultry 721.95,99
Broomcorn tops 292.93
Broom handles, wood 635.91
Brooms 899.72
Broths 098.5
Brushes 899.72
Brushes, carbon, electrical 778.86
Brush handles, wood 635.91
Brush making hair 291.92
Buckets, wood 635.2
Buckles, base metal, for clothing,
travel goods, watches, etc 699.33
Buckram 657.31
Buckwheat 045.92
Buds, flower 292.71
Buds, for grafting and budding 292.69
Buffaloes 001.19
Building materials, of asbestos cement 661.83
Building stone, crude 273.12,13
Buildings, pre-fabricated 811.0
Bulbs, electric lamp 778.21
Bulbs, flower 292.61
Bullace .... See Fruit, edible
Bulldozers 723.11
Bullion, lead 685.11
Bullocks 001.19
Bulls 001.11,19
Bung covers, base metal 699.53
Buoys 793.99
Burglar alarms, electric 778.84,85
Burners, furnace, non-electric 741.21,23,28
Bushes 292.69
Butane 342.5
Butchers' cleavers 696.59
Butt welded lathe tools 695.64
Butter, butter fat and oil 023.0
Butter, cocoa 072.4
Butter-knives of base metal 696.6
Butterfly nets 894.71
Buttermilk -
Fresh 022.11,12
Preserved 022.32
Buttons, button moulds and button blanks 899.83,84

C

Cabinets, filing, of base metal 821.31, 895.11
Cabinets (furniture) 821.3,5,7,8
Cabinets (radio and television) 764.93
Cable -
Electric, insulated 773.1
General wiring, electric, insulated 773.1
Mains (power distribution), insulated 773.1
Optical fibre, image transmitting 773.18
Submarine telecommunications, insulated 773.1
Telecommunications, insulated 773.1
Wire, not electrically insulated, aluminium 693.13
Wire, not electrically insulated, copper 693.12
Cable-making machinery 728.46,49,55

C

Cables, iron or steel 693.11
Cables, textile 657.51
Cables, textile, scrap or worn out 269.02
Cachets, empty, for pharmaceutical use 048.49
Cadmium 689.82, 699.83
Cadmium pigment colours 533.13
Caffeine 541.43
Cages and aviaries, small, of iron or steel 699.67,69
Cake, oil-seed 081.3
Cakes 048.42,49
Calcined bauxite, refractory grade 598.99
Calcium ammonium nitrate 562.14
Calcium citrate (crude) 598.99
Calcium cyanamide 562.15
Calcium hypochlorite 523.31
Calcium nitrate 523.59
Calcium tartrate (crude) 598.99
Calculating instruments 874.22,24
Calculating machines 751.21,22; 759.95
Calendars of any kind, printed 892.84
Calendering machines, other than
metalworking and glass-working 745.91,93
Calorimeters 874.46,49
Calves 001.11,19
Camelback (tyre retreading) 621.21
Camera lenses (mounted) 884.3
Camera motors 718.93,99
Camera powerwinders 881.14
Cameras, cinematographic 881.21
Cameras, photographic 881.11,14
Cameras, television 764.82,93
Camphor 516.27
Can casing machines 745.27,29
Canary seed 045.93
Candelilla wax 431.41
Candles, sulphur 591.49
Candles, other 899.31
Canes, bamboo, rattan and tsinglee, garden 292.3
Canes, walking etc 899.42
Cannabis sativa (true hemp), not spun 265.2
Canned fruit and nuts 058.9
Canned vegetables 056.72-79
Cans, aluminium 692.42
Cans, iron or steel 692.41
Cantharides 291.98
Canvas, cotton 652.2,4
Canvas, flax 654.4
Canvas, prepared painting 657.31
Capacitors, electrical 778.6
Capers .... See Vegetables, edible
Capping machines 745.27,29
Caps, bathing 848.45
Capsicums, sweet .... See Vegetables, edible
Capstans 744.25,91
Capsules, base metal, for bottles etc 699.53
Capsuling machines 745.27,29
Caramel 062.2
Caramels, confectionery (not containing cocoa) 061.99
Caravans, motorised 781.0, 784.0
Caravans, not mechanically propelled, and parts 786.1,89
Caraway seeds 075.26
Carbides 524.93,94
Carbines -
Military 981.12,99
Sporting 891.31,93,95
Carbon, activated 598.64
Carbon blocks, plates or other
semi-manufactures 598.61
Carbon brushes and blanks 778.86
Carbon dioxide 522.38
Carbon electrodes 778.86

C

C

C

C

C

C

Currency notes	892.83
Curtains, textile	658.51
Cushions	821.29
Cut flowers	292.71
Cutlasses	981.13
Cutlery	696.5,6,8
Cutters, coal	723.35,43,9
Cutters, milling	695.64
Cutting appliances, gas operated	737.4
Cutting machines and apparatus, by application of direct electrical energy	737.3
Cutting wheels, discs, etc	663.1
Cuttings	292.69
Cuttle-fish	036.33,37
Cyanamides -	
Calcium	562.15
Other	524.99
Cyanates and thiocyanates	523.82
Cyanides and complex cyanides	523.81
Cycles, not motorised	785.2
Cycles, not motorised parts	785.37
Cyclotrons	778.71,79
Cylinders for compressed or liquefied gas -	
Aluminium	692.44
Iron or steel	692.43
Cymbals	898.24

D

Dairy machinery	721.3
Damasks -	
Cotton	652
Flax	654.4
Man-made filaments	653.1,5
Man-made staple fibres	653.2-4,6-9
Dari	045.3
Dasheens, fresh or dried	054.83
Data recorders	778.78,79
Date stamps, hand-operated	895.93
Dates, fresh or dried	057.96
Deaf aids	899.61
Decalcomanias	892.41
Decorations, Christmas tree (except lights)	894.45
Decoys, game	894.71
Deed boxes, base metal	699.12
Deep freezers	741.4, 775.2
Defrosters and demisters, electric, for motor vehicles	778.34,35
Degras	431.33
Demonstrational instruments, apparatus or models	874.52
Dental -	
Fillings and cements	541.99
Instruments and appliances	872.1
Plate brushes	899.72
Preparations based on plaster	598.95
Wax put up in sets or in plates, sticks etc	598.95
Dentists' chairs -	
Incorporating dental equipment	872.19
Not incorporating dental equipment	872.4
Denture brushes	899.72
Denture-cleansing preparations	553.4
Denture fixatives	553.4
Deodorants, anti-perspirants and room deodorisers	553.52,54
Deodorisers, room prepared	553.54
Depilatories	553.59
Desiccated coconut	057.71
Designs (printed matter)	892.89
Desk racks, base metal	895.11
Desks	821.3,5,7,8

D

Detergents	554.1,2
Detonators, detonating fuses	593.2
Dextrins and dextrin glues	592.26,27
Diamond dies for wire drawing	695.64
Diamonds	277.1, 667.2
Diatomite, activated	598.65
Diatomite, not activated	278.95
Diazon, azo-and azoxy-compounds	514.85
Dictating machines and parts and accessories	763.82, 764.99
Dictation transcription machines and parts and accessories	763.82, 764.99
Die casting machines	737.12,19
Dies of sintered metal carbide	695.64
Dies, threading	695.64
Diesel engines	713.3,82,92
Diesel oil	334.3
Diggers, shaker	721.23,29
Digital audio disc players (laser optical reading systems - compact disc players) -	
Combined with a radio receiver	762.11,21,81
Other	763.81
Dinas earth	278.29
Diodes, valve and semi-conductor	776.3
Dipentene	511.29, 598.13
Dips, sheep and cattle	591.49
Disc brake pad assemblies	784.33
Discharge lamps	778.22,29
Discs -	
Computer	898.51
For the manufacture of crown corks	633.29
Dishwashing machines	755.21,29; 775.3,79
Disinfectants	591.41
Dispersions, rubber	621.12
Display cabinets, refrigeration	741.43,49
Distempers	533.43
Distilled water	524.99
Distributors, asphalt, bitumen, tar and tarmacadam	728.49,5
Distributors, fertilizer and seed	721.12,19
Dithionites	523.43
Divan beds	821.3,5,7,8,
Divan seats, whether or not convertible into beds	821.1
Dividing heads for machine tools	735.15
Dobbies, textile	724.61,68
Document cases	831.2
Documents of title	892.83
Dogfish	034.11,18,28,4,5; 035.12,13,29; 037.15,16
Dogs	001.9
Dolls	894.22
Dolomite, crude	278.23
Dom nuts	292.99
Dom palm seeds	292.99
Domestic articles -	
Of copper	692.42
Of iron or steel	692.41
Domestic glassware	665.2
Doors and door frames, iron or steel, for buildings	691.13
Doors and door frames, aluminium	691.21
Doors, wood	635.32
Doubling machines, textile	724.43,49
Dover sole	034.11,13,22,4,5; 035.12,13,29;037.15,16
Down	291.95
Drain pipes, ceramic	662.43
Drained fruit, fruit peel and parts of plants	062.1
Drawers (furniture)	821.3,5,7,8
Drawing chalks and charcoals	895.23
Drawing instruments	874.22,24
Drawing knives	695.4

F

Fire alarms, electric	778.84,85
Fire extinguishers preparations and charges	598.94
Fire extinguishers	745.61,68
Fire extinguishing grenades, charged	598.94
Fire fighting vehicles	782.25, 784
Fire floats	793.59
Fire tube boilers	711.1,91
Firearms	981.1,9
Fireclay	278.29
Firelighters	899.39
Fires, non-electric, domestic, of iron or steel	697.32,33
Fireworks	593.31
First-aid outfits	541.99
Fish -	
Bladders and waste	291.96
Fillets	034.4,51
Fresh or chilled	034.1
Frozen	034.2
In airtight containers	037.1
Inedible dead fish, livers and roes	291.96
Live	034.11
Livers	034.19,29; 035.4
Meal and flour (animal foods)	081.42
Paste	037.1
Prepared or preserved	037.1
Roes	034.19,29; 035.4; 037.17
Salted, dried or smoked	035.1-4
Shell	036, 037.2
Solubles	081.99
Wet, salted, split	035.1,2
Fish-eaters, of base metal	696.6
Fish glues	592.24
Fish-hooks	894.71
Fishing nets, industrial	657.52
Fishing tackle	894.71
Fishing vessels	793.24
Fittings, base metal, for furniture,	
doors, windows, etc	699.13,14,16,17,19
Fittings, pipe or tube -	
Aluminium	684.27
Copper	682.72
Lead	685.24
Nickel	683.22
Plastics	581.7
Tin	687.24
Zinc	686.34
Flagons, plastic	893.19
Flags, pennants, banners and bunting	
of textile fabric	658.93
Flagstones, of natural stone (excluding slate)	661.31
Flakes -	
Aluminium	684.25
Copper	682.62
Lead	685.22
Magnesium	699.94
Nickel	683.23
Tin	687.23
Zinc	686.34
Flasks, vacuum	899.97
Flavouring materials, odoriferous	551.4
Flax -	
Fabric, woven (linen)	654.4
Raw or processed, but not spun	265.1
Rope, twine	657.51
Seed	223.4
Yarn and thread	651.96
Flaxboard	634.23
Flexible tubing and piping, base metal	699.51
Flint, crude	273.4
Flint, for lining grinders	661.33
Flints, lighter	899.39

F

Float glass	664.4
Floating cranes	793.59
Floating docks	793.59
Floating or submersible drilling or	
production platforms for oil or	
gas extraction	793.55
Floating structures	793.99
Flock, textile	657.71
Floor coverings, felt (not underlay)	659.61
Floor coverings, paper based	659.11
Floor coverings, plastics	893.31
Floor coverings, coated on a textile base	659.12
Floorpolishers and scrubbers, electric -	
Domestic	775.71,79
Industrial	728.49,55
Floor polishes and creams	554.32
Flooring, rubber, in the piece	621.3
Floppy disc drives	752.9
Floppy discs	898.5,7
Flour -	
Arrowroot	056.47
Fruit, edible	056.48
Gluten	592.17
Leguminous vegetable	056.46
Malt	048.2
Manioc	056.47
Of oil seeds and oleaginous fruit,	
non-defatted (excluding mustard flour)	223.9
Potato	056.41
Preparations	048.5
Sago	056.47
Salep	056.47
Wheat and other cereals -	
Wheat or meslin	046.1
Others	047.1
Wood	634.93
Flour and meals (animal foods)	081.4
Flow meters and controllers -	
Electrical	874.31
Non-electric	874.31
Parts	874.39
Flower buds	292.71
Flower bulbs	292.61
Flower seed	292.35
Flowers, artificial	899.2
Flowers, cut	292.71
Fluorescent lamps	778.22,29
Fluorides	523.1
Fluorine	522.25
Fluorine salts	523.1
Fluoroborates	523.1
Fluorosilicates	523.1
Fluorspar, o/t precious stones	278.54
Flux, soldering, etc	598.96
Fly papers	591.49
Fly-wheels	748.5,9
Flying machines	792.1-4,9
Foamed vinyls	See Expanded vinyls
Fodder presses	721.23,29
Foil -	
Aluminium	684.24
Copper	682.61
Gold	971.01
Lead	685.22
Magnesium	699.94
Nickel	683.24
Platinum	681.25
Silver	681.14
Tin	687.23
Zinc	686.32
Folders -	

F

F

G

G

Gas or smoke analysis apparatus, non-electric 874.41,49
Gauges -
  Electrical 873,874
  Non-electric 873,874
  Parts 873,874
Gauze -
  Bonded fibre 657.2
  Impregnated with pharmaceuticals 541.91
  In retail packs for medical use 541.91
  Iron or steel 693.51
  Textile 652.11,654.94
  Wire, aluminium 699.79
  Wire, copper 699.52
Gear making and finishing machines 731.75,735.91
Gearboxes for motor vehicles 784.34
Gear and gearing (including gearboxes),
  for machinery 748.4,9
Geese, dead 012.3
Geese, live 001.4
Gelatin and gelatin derivatives 592.24
Gelatin copying pastes 598.99
Gelatin, hardened, in primary form 575.95
Gelatin, unhardened, worked 592.24,899.19
Generating sets, electric 716.59
Generators, electric 716.2,3,9
Generators, gas 741.71,72
Geophysical instruments -
  Electrical 874.13
  Non-electric 874.13
  Parts 874.14
Germanium 689.96,699.99
Germanium and silicon rectifying apparatus 771.21,29
Germination plant, agricultural 721.96,99
Getters for vacuum tubes 598.99
Ghee, natural 023.0
Gimped yarn 656.31
Gimping machines, textile 724.53,68
Gin 112.45
Ginger, drained, glacé or crystallised 062.1
Ginger preserved in syrup 058.96
Ginger (spices) 075.27
Gingerbread 048.42
Girdles 845.52
Glacé fruit, fruit peel and part of plants 062.1
Glands, animal (unfit for human consumption) 291.98
Glands or other organs and extracts (medicinal) 541.62
Glass and glassware 664, 665
Glass -
  Balls, rods and tubes (unworked) 664.12
  Bottle-making machines 728.41,51
  Cast or rolled, unworked 664.5
  Clears, rigid and flexible plastics 582
  Pressed or moulded, of a kind used in
   building 664.96
  Drawn or blown, unworked 664.3
  Envelopes 664.93
  Fibre 664.95
  Float 664.4
  Frit 533.51
  In sheets, surface polished 664.4
  Microspheres 665.93
  Powder, granules or flakes 533.51
  Sheet, unworked 664.3-5
  Tiles 664.96, 665.94
Glass fibre reinforced plastics Div.57,58
Glass wool 664.95
Glass-working ((in the cold) machinery) 728.11,19
Glass-working machines (other than for
  working glass in the cold) 728.41,51
Glaziers' diamonds, mounted 695.46
Gliders 792.81,9

G

Globes, printed 892.14
Globes and shades, glass 813.1,9
Gloves 846.14,9; 848.12,22,3
Gluconic acid 513.92
Glucose 061.93,94
Glues and size 592.2
Glutamates 514.64
Gluten bread for diabetics 048.4
Gluten (Wheat) 592.17
Glycerol and glycerol lyes 512.22
Glycosides 541.61
Goat hair 268.3,59
Goat meat 012.13,55,56
Goat skins (Yemen, Mongolian & Tibetan raw) 212.29,3
Goats 001.22
Goggles 884.23
Gold and goldsmiths' wares 897.32
Gold coin II
Gold ore 289.19
Gold, unwrought or semi-manufactured 971.01
Gold, waste and scrap 971.03
Golf balls, clubs and requisites 894.75
Golf club head covers 658.93, 893.99
Gomuti (gumati) fibre 292.93
Gongs, non-electric, base metal 699.52
Gouges 695.43
Graders, motor 723.12,9
Grading machines for agricultural produce 721.26,29
Grain cleaning machines 721.27
Gramophone records 898.71
Gramophones, and parts 763.3, 764.99
Granite, crude 273.13
Granite, worked and articles thereof 661.3
Grape juice 059.93
Grape marc 081.19
Grape must 059.93, 112.11
Grapes .... See Fruit, edible
Graphite -
  Artificial 598.61
  Natural 278.22
  Non-electrical, non-ceramic, articles of 663.36
Grapnels, iron or steel 699.61
Grass mowers 721.21,29
Grass seed 292.52
Grasses for ornamental purposes 292.72
Grates, domestic, of iron or steel 697.32
Gravel 273.4
Grease guns, hand powered 695.46
Grease paints 553.2
Grease, wool 411.34,35; 431.1,21
Greaves 081.41
Greetings cards 892.42
Grenades (munitions) 981.29
Greyhounds 001.9
Grill, of iron or steel wire 693.51
Grinding machines, metal working, other than
  gear grinding machines 731.61-64; 735.91
Grinding machines, mineral 728.32,39
Grinding wheels, mounted on framework
  (hand or pedal operated) 695.48
Grindstones and grinding wheels, unmounted 663.11,12
Ground flying trainers 792.83,9
Groundnut cake and meal 081.32
Groundnut oil 421.3; 431.1,22
Groundnuts 222.1
Groundnuts, roasted 058.92
Groundsheets, textile 658.29
Guano 272.1
Guar seed flour and gum 292.94
Guavas, fresh or dried 057.97
Guided weapons launchers 981.12

H

I

I

J

K

M

M

M

Metal thread, woven fabrics of	654.91
Metal working machinery -	
Foundry machinery	737.1
Machine-tools	731; 733
Rolling mills and rolls therefor	737.2
Metallic ash and residues (non-ferrous)	288.1
Metallic salts & peroxysalts of inorganic acids	523
Metalliferous ores and concentrates	Div 28
Metallised textile yarn	651.91
Metallised textile yarn, woven fabrics of	654.91
Metaphosphoric acid	522.34
Meteorological instruments -	
Electrical	874.13
Non-electrical	874.13
Parts	874.14
Meters -	
Electrical quantities	874.75,78,79
Electricity supply or production	873.15,19
Frequency deviation and phase deviation	874.78,79
Gas supply or production	873.11,19
Liquid supply or production	873.13,19
Methanal (formaldehyde)	516.21
Methane	344.2
Methane black	522.1
Methanol (methyl alcohol)	512.11
Methylated spirits	512.16
Metronomes	898.9
Mexican fibre	292.93
Mica, crude and waste	278.52
Mica, worked, and articles thereof	663.35
Micro-organism cultures	541.64
Micro-crystalline wax	335.12
Microfilm-	
Exposed and developed	882.6
Sensitised and unexposed, in rolls	882.3
Microfilm readers	881.31,34
Microphones	764.21,92
Microscopes -	
Compound, optical	871.4
Electron and proton	871.3
Microspheres, glass	665.93
Microtomes	874.49
Micro-wave test equipment	874.7
Micro-wave test equipment, parts	874.7
Micro-wave tubes	776.25,29
Middlings	081.2
Mileometers, non-electric	873.21
Mileometers, non-electric, parts	873.29
Milk churns, aluminium	692.42
Milk churns, iron or steel	692.41
Milk, fresh -	
Natural	022.1
Flavoured	111.02
Milk, other than fresh	022.1-4
Milking machines	721.31,39
Milkweed	292.92
Mill nep	657.71
Millboard, asbestos	663.81
Millets	045.91
Milling cutters	695.64
Milling machinery for bread grain	727.11,19
Milling machines, metal working	731.51-54; 735.91
Millstones	663.11,12
Milo	045.3
Mincers, food, domestic, non-electric	697.81
Mine roof supports, hydraulic	728.49,55
Mineral products, crude	Div.27
Mineral waxes	335.12
Mineral wool	663.51
Minerals, activated	598.65
Mines (munitions)	981.29

M

Mining machinery	723.35,77,43,44,9; 744.23,72,9
Mink furskins, tanned or dressed	613.11,2,3
Mink skins, raw	212.1
Mirabelles	See Fruit,edible
Mirrors, base metal, not optically worked	697.82
Mirrors, glass	664.8
Mirrors, optical elements (unmounted)	884.19
Mirrors, optical elements (mounted)	884.39
Missiles (guided weapons)	981.29
Mitts and mittens	846.14,92
Mixing machines, mineral	728.33,39
Modelling pastes	598.95
Molasses	061.5
Molluscs	036.3; 037.22
Molybdates	524.31
Molybdenum	689.12; 699.92
Molybdenum ores and concentrates	287.81,82
Monofil, plastic	Div.57,58; 651.5-7,88
Mooring ropes	657.59
Mopeds	785.1
Mopeds, parts and accessories	785.35
Mops	899.72
Moquettes (woven pile fabrics)	652.14,15; 653.9; 654.35-95
Mordants, prepared	598.91
Morse re-perforators	764.1,91
Morse transmitters and receivers	764.1,91
Mortars (weapons)	981.12
Mosquito netting	656.41
Mosses for ornamental purposes	292.72
Mother-of-pearl, unworked	291.15
Mother-of-pearl, worked	899.11
Motor-cycles	785.1
Motor-cycle and side-car parts and accessories	785.35
Motor generator sets, electric	716.51,9
Motor graders (scrapers)	723.12,31,46,9
Motor lorries	782.1
Motor scooters	785.1
Motor scooters, parts and accessories	785.1
Motor spirit, including aviation spirit	334.11
Motor vehicles	781-784
Motor vehicle parts and accessories -	
Axles	784.35,36
Bearings	746.1,9; 748.2
Bodies (including cabs) -	
Complete	784.2
Parts	784.32
Brakes	784.33
Brake linings -	
Mounted	784.33
Unmounted	663.82
Chassis -	
Fitted with engines	784.1
Without engines	784.39
Coachwork fittings of plastics	893.95
Clutches	784.39
Crankshafts	748.1
Door handles and winders, base metal	699.15
Electrical	See Electrical apparatus, appliances and machinery
Engines and parts thereof -	
Internal combustion	713.2,8,9
Other	718.9
Fan belts, rubber	629.2
Filters	743.6,95
Fuel tanks	784.39
Gearboxes	784.34
Hand tools, base metal	695
Hoses, rubber	621.4
Instruments	See under type of instrument

P

P

Iron or steel	671.32
Lead	685.22
Magnesium	699.94
Nickel	683.23
Scouring	554.34
Tin	687.23
Zinc	686.33
Power supplies -	
For computers	752.6,9
Other	771.21,29
Prams, dolls	894.21
Prawns	036.11,2; 037.21
Precious metals	See under constituent metal
Precious metal chemical compounds, colloids and amalgams	524.32
Precious stones	667
Prefabricated buildings and parts thereof	See Buildings
Premier jus	411.32
Prepared waxes	431.4; 598.3
Press fasteners (for clothing, household linen etc)	899.83
Press tools	695.64
Presses -	
Cheese	721.38,39
Filter	743.6,95
Metal working	733.1; 735.95
Straw and fodder	721.23,29
Tableting and pelleting	728.49,55
Pressure gauges and recorders -	
Electrical	874.35
Non-electric	874.35
Parts	874.39
Primary cells and batteries	778.11,17
Printed circuits, bare or with printed passive components	772.2
Printed matter	892
Printers' blankets, rubber	621.32,33; 629.92,99
Printing blocks, plates or cylinders	726.35
Printing ink	533.2
Printing machinery for textiles	724.74,92
Printing machinery, other	726.31,5,6,9
Printing sets, hand	895.93
Printing type of all kinds	726.35
Prints, original	896.2
Prints, photographic and pictures	892.7
Prisms -	
Mounted	884.39
Unmounted	884.19
Process pressure vessels (incorporating thermal equipment)	741.89,9
Process timers	885.94
Producer gas generators	741.71,9
Production counters -	
Electric	873.21
Non-electric	873.21
Parts	873.29
Profile projectors	874.25,26
Profiles -	
Aluminium	684.21
Copper	682.3
Glass	664.5
Iron or steel, hollow	679.1,4
Lead	685.21
Magnesium	699.94
Nickel	683.21
Plastics	583
Tin	687.21
Zinc	686.31
Projectors (missiles)	981.12,99
Projectors -	
Cinematographic	881.22,24
Image, overhead or slide	881.32,34
Propane	342.1
Propellent powders	593.11
Propellers, ships'	749.91
Protein concentrates	098.99
Protein hydrolysates	098.99
Proteins -	
Hardened, in primary forms	575.95
Other	592.25
Proton microscopes	871.3
Provitamins and vitamins	541.1; 542.92
Pruning knives	696.8
Psychrometers	874.55
Psychrometers, parts	874.56
Puffed rice	048.12
Pulleys and pulley blocks	748.5,9
Pullovers	845.3
Pulp -	
Of cotton linter	251.92
Of esparto	251.92
Of straw	251.92
Of vegetable fibre	251.92
Of wood	251.2-6,91
Pulpwood, in the form of chips	246.1
Pulpwood, other	247.4,52
Pulverising machinery, mineral	728.32,39
Pumice stone, crude	277.22,29
Pumpkins	See Vegetables, edible
Pumps, air vacuum	743.1,8
Pumps for liquids, including petrol and oil measuring	742
Punched-card (accounting and statistical) machines	752.9
Punches, perforating	695.23
Punching machines (metal working)	733.16,17; 735.95
Purée, fruit	058.1
Purée, tomato	056.73
Purifying apparatus	743.6,95
Purses, leather, plastics or textile	831.91
Push chairs, baby	894.1
Puttees	851.9
Putty	533.54
Pyjamas	84.62; 842.82; 843.82; 844.83
Pyrethrum	292.49,94
Pyrolignites	598.99
Pyrometers	874.4
Pyrometers, parts	874.49
Pyrophoric alloys	899.39
Pyrophosphoric acid	522.34
Pyrotechnic articles	593.3

Q

Quartz and quartzite, crude o/t precious stones	278.51
Quartz crystals, piezo-electric, mounted	776.81,88
Quartz crystals, piezo-electric, unmounted	667.41
Quartz, fused	664; 665
Quaternary ammonium salts and hydroxides	514.81
Quebracho extract	532.21
Quicklime	661.11
Quillaia bark	292.99
Quills, raw	291.95
Quilt covers	658.42,43
Quilted textile products in the piece	657.4
Quilts (stuffed furnishings)	821.29
Quinces	See Fruit, edible
Quinine	541.42; 542.9

R

R

R

S

S

Iron or steel	697.51
Plastics	893.21
Sintered metal carbide tools	695.64
Sirens, electric	778.84,85
Sisal -	
Not spun	265.4
Rope, twine	657.51
Yarn	651.99
Skate boards	894.79
Skates	894.72
Skins -	
Bird	291.95; 899.92
Fur, raw	212
Other, raw	211.1-7,9
Waste	291.99
Skipping ropes	894.29
Skirts, textile	842.5; 844.25
Skis (snow)	894.73
Skylight frames, zinc	699.77
Slag (iron and steel)	278.61,62
Slag wool	663.51
Slate, crude	273.11
Slate, worked, and articles thereof	661.32
Slates, drawing	895.92
Sleepers, railway or tramway, of wood	248.1
Sleeping bags (filled)	821.27
Slide fasteners	899.85
Slide projectors	881.32,34
Slings, wire, iron or steel	693.11
Slippers	Div 85
Slips, plant	292.69
Slotting machines, metal working	731.71; 735.91
Smoothing irons, electric	775.84,89
Snails, other than sea snails	012.93
Snap fasteners (for clothing, household linen etc)	899.83
Snow-ploughs -	
Mechanically propelled	782.29; 784
Not mechanically propelled	723.42,9
Snuff	122.39
Snuff boxes, of iron or steel	699.69
Soap, soap flakes and powders	554.1
Soap substitutes	554.2
Soapstocks	431.33
Socket sets	695.3
Socks	846.19,29
Soda ash	523.7
Sodium bicarbonate (Bicarbonate of soda)	523.73; 542.93
Sodium chloride	278.3
Sodium, nitrate	272.2
Softboard	634.5
Soft soap	554.1
Soft toys	894.29
Soil heating apparatus, electric	775.82,89
Solder -	
Base metal, coated or cored with flux material	699.55
Predominately of lead	685.21
Predominately of tin -	
Cast sticks	687.1
Wire	687.21
Predominately of aluminium	684.21,22
Soldering machines and apparatus, electric	737.31,32,39
Solubles -	
Fish	081.99
Marine mammal	081.99
Solvents, composite, organic for varnish etc	533.55
Soot removers	711.21,92
Sorbitol -	
Chemically defined	512.25
Other	598.99
Sorghum tops	292.93

Sorghums, including grain sorghum	045.3
Sorting boxes, office, of base metal	895.11
Sorting machines -	
Coin	751.99; 759.93
Mineral	728.31,39
Punched-card	752.9; 759.97
Sound amplifiers sets	764.26,92
Sound recorders and reproducers -	
Photo-electric	763.84; 764.99
Laser optical reading systems (digital audio discs players - compact disc players) -	
Combined with a radio receiver	762.81; 764.93
Other	763.83; 764.99
Sound recording and reproducing apparatus -	
Combined with radio or television receivers	761; 762.81; 764.93
Other	763.84; 764.99
Sound track, exposed and developed, cinematographic	883
Soups	098.5
Soya bean cake and meal	081.31
Soya bean flour (non-defatted)	223.9
Soya bean oil	421.1; 431.1,22
Soya beans	222.2
Spa waters	111.01
Spa waters (flavoured)	111.02
Space heaters, electric	775.82,89
Spades	695.1
Spaghetti, uncooked	048.3
Spaghetti, cooked	098.91
Spangles, base metal	699.33
Spanners	695.3
Spark erosion machines, metal working	731.1
Spark ignition (petrol) engines	713.11,21,22,31,32,81,91
Sparking plugs for internal combustion engines	778.31,33
Spats	851.9
Spectacle and goggle frames, etc	884.21,22
Spectacle lenses, unmounted	884.15,17
Spectacles and goggles	884.23
Spectrometers -	
Electric	874.43
Non-electric	874.43
Parts	874.49
Spectrophotometers (photo-electric)	874.43
Spectrophotometers (photo-electric), parts	874.49
Spectrum analysers	874.7
Spectrum analysers, parts	874.79
Speed indicators	873.25
Speed indicators, parts	873.29
Speiss, nickel	284.22
Spent oxide	598.99
Sperm oil	411.13; 431.1,21
Spermaceti	431.42
Spices	075
Spiegeleisen	671.23
Spikes, iron or steel, for sports footwear	851.9
Spinach	See Vegetables, edible
Spin dryers	743.55,91
Spindles and spindle flyers, textile	724.49
Spinning machines, textile	724.43,49
Spirit, petroleum and white	334.19
Spirits -	
Beverages	112.4
Methylated and neutral	512.15,16
Of turpentine	598.13
Perfumed	553.1
Splints and other fracture appliances	899.63
Split peas	054.21
Spokeshaves	695.46
Sponge iron or steel -	
Not in powder form	671.33

S

S

T

T

V

W

W

Y

Z

Printed in the United Kingdom for The Stationery Office
Dd302964 12/96 G3397/7 10170